Houghton Mifflin English GRAMMAR AND COMPOSITION is a six-level, multi-component basal program designed for use in junior and senior high school English courses. Available at each level are a student's textbook, an annotated *Teacher's Edition*, a teacher's *Resource Book*, a *Practice Book* with accompanying teacher's edition, a *Tests* booklet with companion teacher's edition, and *Composition Workshops* in workbook format.

As you review *Houghton Mifflin English GRAMMAR AND COMPOSITION, Second Course*, be certain to check these features:

- **Unit Previews** to introduce the unit and demonstrate the importance of the topic *(page 94)*.
- **Color labels, arrows,** and bracketed **explanations** to highlight and clarify example sentences *(page 159)*.
- **Usage Notes** derived from the authoritative *American Heritage Dictionary (pages 179–189)*.
- Frequent **Exercises** and **Assignments** to practice important concepts and skills *(pages 154–157)*.
- Brief **Writer's Workshops** to link specific points of grammar, usage, and mechanics to the students' writing *(page 123)*.
- **Unit Practices** and **Unit Tests** to provide both specialized and comprehensive coverage of the concepts presented in a unit *(pages 190–195)*.
- The **writing process** — prewriting, writing, revising — taught systematically and applied extensively *(pages 236–237)*.
- Student-written **composition models** to illustrate the types of writing taught *(page 397)*.
- Detailed **Strategies** and **Procedures** for students to follow in handling any writing task *(pages 240, 252)*.
- **Continuing Assignments** to guide students through extended writing activities one step at a time *(page 424)*.
- **Assignment Checklists** to assist students in revising their writing assignments *(page 401)*.
- **Writer's Workshops** to simulate writing situations in the world beyond the classroom *(pages 354–355)*.
- **Unit Assignments** to expand the suggested topics for writing *(page 307)*.
- This **Teacher's Edition** — complete and convenient — containing Classroom Insights, full-size student pages with complete answers adjacent, unit objectives, related references — and more — to support your teaching efforts.

Houghton Mifflin English
Grammar and Composition

This is the grammar and composition program that's <u>more</u> than a handbook.

Let us show you what <u>more</u> means for you.

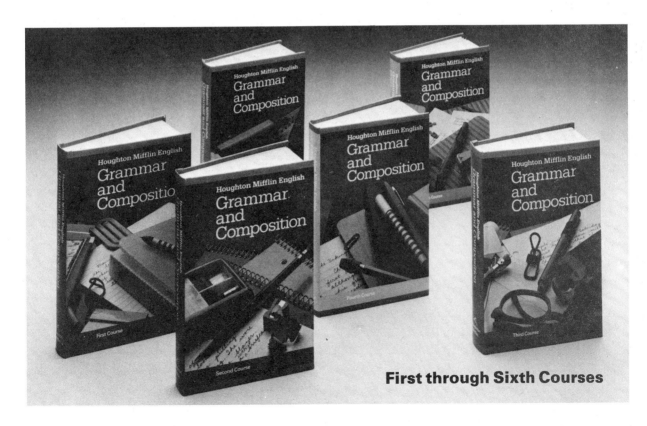

First through Sixth Courses

More means that it teaches traditional grammar — _and_ how to use it in writing.

Instruction follows a step-by-step sequence: simply stated explanation or rule, clear examples, immediate practice. Throughout Part One this reliable teaching pattern, divided into manageable sections, helps students learn with confidence and enjoy success.

A **Unit Preview** presents the central idea of each unit through examples and questions for analysis. Students learn the role of grammar in making their writing effective.

Key terms are always in bold type when they are defined.

Clear labels help you and your students find everything quickly and easily.

Elements of grammar are clearly identified; their functions are plainly illustrated.

Sample pages shown reduced.

Third Course (Grade 9)

Unit 1

Parts of Speech

Unit Preview

Words can be classified into parts of speech, all of which play an important role in helping people to communicate. To see just how important a particular part of speech is in helping you to express yourself, read the following paragraph. What do you think the paragraph is about? What makes it difficult to understand?

Few realize that there are more than one million. Most occur far beneath and do not threaten any. Unfortunately, some occur where there are many, and that which they cause can be ~~serious ones there, it was still~~ ~~them. Let's hope that they find~~

~~ph is that it does not contain~~ ~~s, things, and ideas. The first~~ ~~r one million, but it does not~~ ~~he second sentence says that~~ ~~what occurs.~~

~~ph that follows, and answer~~

~~are over one million earth-~~ ~~ur far beneath the surface of~~ ~~nger to people. Unfortunately,~~

Fourth Course (Grade 10)

Unit 4   Usage

4.3   Correct Use of Pronouns

4.3a   Pronoun Antecedents

An **antecedent** is the word that a pronoun refers to or replaces in a sentence. A pronoun must agree with its antecedent in number, gender, and person (_pages 8–9_).

Agreement in Number

Rule   Use a singular pronoun to refer to a singular antecedent. Use a plural pronoun to refer to a plural antecedent.

SINGULAR	PLURAL
I, me, my, mine	we, us, our, ours
you, your, yours	you, your, yours
he, him, his	they, them, their, theirs
she, her, hers	
it, its	

SINGULAR   After _David_ got up, **he** fixed **his** breakfast.

PLURAL   The _girls_ set **their** book bags under a tree.

Rule   Use a plural pronoun to refer to two or more singular antecedents joined by _and_.

Alan and Jean are washing **their** car. **They** have almost finished.

Rule   Use a singular pronoun to refer to two or more singular antecedents joined by _or_ or _nor_.

Neither _Wanda nor Ruth_ finished **her** book report on time.

Indefinite Pronouns as Antecedents.   The following indefinite pronouns are usually singular in meaning. Use singular pronouns to refer to them when they are antecedents.

148

B

Unit Practice

Practice 1

A. Phrases *(pages 77–90)* On your paper, write the following sentences, replacing each blank with the kind of phrase indicated in parentheses. Underline each phrase that you write.

1. The tree __?__ is a weeping willow. (prepositional phrase)
2. Arnie's dream __?__ is one of great ambition and courage. (infinitive phrase)
3. __?__, the Rich___ (infinitive phrase)
4. We asked Phyl___
5. Many of us fee___

B. Subordinat___ the subordinate subordinate clau___

6. The fishing po___ wonderful gift___
7. Robert seemed___
8. No one could___
9.
10.

C.
yo___
C___
11.
12.
13.
14.
15.

Fifth Course
(Grade 11)

Fourth Course
(Grade 10)

Third
Course
(Grade 9)

Unit Tests

Test 1

A. Correct Use of Verbs *(pages 145–157)* On your paper, write the verb form that correctly completes each of the following sentences.

1. Mary had darted away before the scooter (backs, backed) up.

3.1c

Infinitive Clauses

Exercise 5 Infinitives On your paper, combine each of the following sets of sentences by rewriting at least one sentence as an infinitive phrase or an infinitive clause. Underline the infinitive phrases and infinitive clauses in your rewritten sentences.

SAMPLE	Stan usually uses earphones. He listens to albums.
ANSWER	Stan usually uses earphones to listen to albums.

1. Nick and Pam___ will record th___
2. Did you lift t___ burning.
3. Rhonda, who___ England. She___
4. Harry should___ convince him___
5. Harriet took___ River. She ha___
6. I must apply___ that I have be___
7. The navigator___ would explore___
8. On their trip___ license plates___

Exercise 6 V___
your paper, and___
kind of verbal p___
the verbal phras___

SAMPLE

ANSWER

1. Certain birds___
2. __?__ is an acti___ for holidays. (___
3. A well-known___
4. In the autumn___

Unit 4 Usage

misplaced or dangling modifiers. Look for them in newspapers and magazines. Write down those that you hear on radio and television. Exchange examples with your classmates and correct the examples.

Writer's Workshop

Comparison and Contrast

Step 1: Find a photograph of a well-known person. Write a list of this person's physical features, such as age, height, weight, hair color, and other details. Include as many details as you can. Then write another list of physical features that describes a friend or a relative. *Step 2:* Using your lists, write a paragraph comparing and contrasting the well-known person to your friend or relative. Then check your paragraph to be sure that you have used comparisons correctly.

4.5 Usage Notes

The following pages contain an alphabetical list of words and phrases that often present usage problems. Each entry describes correct usage, and most entries include examples. Cross-references help you to locate related information.

a lot, alot *A lot* means "a great number or amount" and is always two words. Avoid using it except in informal usage. *Alot* is not a word.

a while, awhile *While* is a noun and can be preceded by *for a* or *in a* to make a prepositional phrase. *Awhile* is an adverb. Do not use *for* or *in* before *awhile*.

170

Fourth Course (Grade 10)

Intensive, consistent reinforcement and evaluation. Following each unit in Part One are highly focused practice exercises and unit tests that help profile your students' strengths and weaknesses. Both exercises and tests are organized to match the major blocks of instruction.

Frequent exercises give students practice in each new concept as soon as they study it.

Assignments and brief Writer's Workshops let students apply to their writing what they have learned.

Alphabetized Usage Notes present explanations based on the authoritative *American Heritage Dictionary.*

More means it teaches the complete writing process and develops competent writers.

The units in Part Two teach the **process of writing,** the **major modes of writing,** and the **writing products** that students will use now and in everyday life.

Writing models — often written by students — offer examples your students can emulate.

Unit 11   Descriptive Writing

exist in space. Present them as they would be seen—from left to right, from top to bottom, from foreground to background, and so on. The most natural way of viewing the scene is best. For example, in describing a room, the best way to organize the details often is to start at the entrance and proceed in whatever direction you would actually follow in viewing the room.

Notice how the writer of the following description makes the spatial order clear by using phrases that suggest direction. The phrases appear in italic type.

Model

Garden viewed from yard

Garden seen from nearer vantage point

Garden seen from path

A close-up view

Following the calls of the black starlings, Diana walked toward her garden. *From the yard* she appraised the neat rows that she had made in the rich soil. *Coming closer,* she could see the small healthy plants, a few inches high now, spread new leaves to the sun. She *walked along the path,* admiring the feathered green of her carrots and the broad purple cabbage leaves. She *squatted down* on her heels to watch the quiet progress of a spider as it built its fine web between the stalks of two milkweed plants.

Amanda Yskamp, Brookline High School
Brookline, Massachusetts

Exercise 2   Prewriting: Spatial Order   The sentences in the following description need to be arranged in spatial order. Determine a logical sequence for the sentences. On your paper, write the sentences (and their numbers) in the correct order. Save your paper.

(1) Fragile white cobweb strings wave at me from the ceiling before I reach the last step.   (2) In the right-hand corner, there are more stacks of cardboard boxes heaped with faded striped blankets.   (3) Coming down uneven and narrow basement steps, I find it difficult to see at first.   (4) Once

452

Unit 6

Prewriting

Unit Preview

To become proficient at writing, as at anything, you must learn the steps involved and practice the skills required at each step. Whatever you are writing, you follow a process that consists of three steps: prewriting, writing a draft, and revising.

Prewriting is the planning and preparation that you do before you write. In the prewriting stage, you gather ideas and information. You also determine topics, identify audiences, and assign purposes for writing assignments. Careful and thoughtful prewriting will simplify the remainder of the writing process.

The following are prewriting notes on the subject of horses.

Used for fun, exercise, work, transportation
Pony express, Royal Canadian Mounted Police
Polo, steeplechase, hunting, circus bareback riders
Kinds of saddles: Western, English
"Don't look a gift horse in the mouth."
Horse sense; horsing around
Horseshoes: good-luck symbol
Horse-drawn carriages
What is the history of horses? —Horse fossils have been found all over the world, except Australia; primitive people hunted them for food; used for sport and war for at least 3000 years; horses brought to Western Hemisphere by Spanish explorers and conquerors; cavalry important in military until 1917
Famous horses and books about horses: Pegasus, Trojan horse, *The Black Stallion, Black Beauty, National Velvet*
Examples of breeds: —Arabian, Thoroughbred, Percheron

236

In answering these questions, you observed part of the process of prewriting, which involves collecting ideas and determining how to use them. In this unit you will learn how to find and develop ideas for writing and how to sort your ideas for the topic in light of the purpose and audience that you select.

6.1   Finding Ideas for Writing

One important goal of prewriting is to find ideas for writing. With observation, thought, and practice you will become aware of many possible writing ideas from your own interests, your activities, and the world around you.

6.1a   Keeping a Writer's Notebook

It is important to record your ideas and sources of ideas so that, when you have a writing assignment, you will have material from which to start. A writer's notebook is a good place to store information and the ideas suggested by that information. You need not record your ideas in complete sentences. Your writer's notebook will become a source of possible writing ideas. Each idea is a subject that can be developed when you need it.

237

D

First Course
(Grade 7)

13.3 Describing Places and Persons

No two persons or places are the same. When you write a description of a person or a place, your purpose is to give your reader a clear and vivid impression of the particular person or location.

13.3a Describing a Place

A good description of a place will make your readers feel as though they are there. The following suggestions will help you to describe a place effectively.

Strategies

1. *Begin with a topic sentence.* Like any paragraph, a descriptive paragraph has a topic sentence in which

2.

3.

4.

Strategies — practical approaches to help students accomplish a writing task.

Procedures — the exact steps that students follow to plan and complete a composition.

Unit 12   Writing About Literature

Exercise 4   Revising: Point of View   The point of view in the following paragraph from a literary essay is inappropriate. Using an appropriate point of view, write a revised version.

> I have just finished reading "Bartleby the Scrivener," by Herman Melville. Something I noticed that was interesting about the story is the subtle change in the narrator, Bartleby's employer, who is an unnamed Wall Street lawyer. I think that watching Bartleby withdraw from society, and finally from life, makes the narrator change his own view of the world.

Assignment   Revising   The following passage fails to observe the conventions of a literary essay. Write a revised version that follows those conventions.

> Most of the characters in *Searching for Caleb*, by Anne Tyler, were members of the Peck family. The main characters were Justine, Duncan, Daniel, and Caleb Peck, the only Pecks who wanted to live away from their family in Baltimore. You won't believe it, but the rest of the Pecks looked alike, talked alike, thought alike, and associated only with one another. Whole chunks of the book explored why four members of the family wanted to move away from the rest. That exploration made the reader realize the importance of freedom and individuality. However, I noticed that the importance of family ties was emphasized too. It was apparent to me that the four Pecks who just took off on their own could relax and enjoy themselves only when they had the best of both worlds.

Continuing Assignment   Prewriting   Begin to read a literary work of your choice or one that is assigned by your teacher. You will use this work as the basis of a literary essay of three to five pages.

Assignment Checklist

Check your revising assignments for the following points:

☑ 1. Did you revise the passage to give it a more serious tone?
☑ 2. Did you rewrite the passage from the third-person point of view?
☑ 3. Did you use the present tense when it was appropriate to do so?

452

Exercises — practice that immediately follows the teaching to develop and fine-tune students' writing abilities.

Assignments — writing activities that combine and apply all the instruction from one section.

Continuing Assignments — cumulative writing projects that students develop in stages from prewriting to finished product.

Assignment Checklists — frequent revising tools to help students check their writing assignments point by point.

Fourth Course
(Grade 10)

Unit Assignme

Assignment 1   Decide wha your high school would be a goo persuasive paragraph for the p subject should be taught. Mak expresses your opinion clearly.

Assignment 2   Write a par someone who lives in the city offer, or write a paragraph in wh lives in the country that life in

Assignment 3   Write a pers that a particular athlete is the b audience to be fans of the sport. many facts as possible, especial accomplishments.

Assignment 4   Write a para friend to join a certain club or three or more reasons that justif from the least to the most impo

Assignment 5   Think of a worthwhile project that your class could sponsor. Write a persuasive paragraph in which you urge your classmates to support the project. Conclude your argument by recommending a specific action.

Assignment 6   Take a position on the question of which musical group in a certain category is the most likely to become or to remain popular. Write a persuasive paragraph in support of your view. Consider your audience to be people familiar with the music of the group about which you are writing.

452

Fifth Course
(Grade 11)

E

Writer's Workshops build writing versatility. Each Workshop in Part Two simulates an actual writing experience in everyday life. Students are asked to assume a role such as a reporter for a school newspaper, a set designer, a sports writer, and many others. All the necessary information is provided right on the Workshop pages. Your students will be eager to apply the writing process — and their individual ingenuity — to complete these engrossing assignments.

Fourth Course (Grade 10)

Writer's Workshop

Environmental Improvements: An Expository Essay

Situation: The Fulton River Action Corps, a group dedicated to improving the condition of the Fulton River area, is preparing to publish a pamphlet about its work. As an officer of the Fulton River Action Corps, you have volunteered to contribute an essay entitled "The Fulton River Area: Improvements During the Last Five Years." Your assistant has prepared a data sheet for you. Because the pamphlet will be small, you have decided to limit your essay to 350 words. As you write the essay, you will keep in mind the following information.

Writer: you as an officer of the Fulton River Action Corps

Audience: the general public

Topic: improvements in the Fulton River Area during the last five years

Purpose: to explain the improvements in an essay of no more than 350 words

Directions: To write your essay, follow these steps.

Step 1. Read the data sheet on the facing page and select the facts that you will use.

Step 2. Write a thesis statement.

Step 3. Prepare an outline. Allow for an introductory paragraph, body paragraphs, and a concluding paragraph.

Step 4. Write the essay; then revise it.

486

Data Sheet for Essay

FIVE YEARS AGO

Heavy pollution in part of river off Payne's Point: only two milligrams of oxygen per liter of water

Highest count of PCB (polychlorinated biphenyl, a toxic substance) found in striped bass: 26.35 parts per million

Few Canada geese found nesting along river

General Chemical, Major Dye Corporation, and Fowler Industries all dumping chemicals and other wastes into river

Three riverfront parks in existence, all in poor condition

TODAY

Moderate pollution in part of river off Payne's Point: five milligrams of oxygen per liter of water

Highest PCB count found in striped bass: 13.78 parts per million (still much too high!)

Slow increase in nesting population of Canada geese along river

General Chemical, Major Dye have paid fines and improved procedures for the disposal of wastes; lawsuit against Fowler pending

Three riverfront parks improved, one new one built, one more planned

487

F

More means that it teaches related skills to reinforce good writing and good scholarship.

Fourth Course (Grade 10)

20.3g Concluding Your Discussion

A successful discussion needs a definite conclusion. If time runs out before your group has finished working or if your discussion simply dwindles to a close, the value of your entire discussion may be lost.

It is the leader's responsibility to keep track of time during the discussion and to budget it to allow for an effective conclusion. If there is no stated time limit, the leader should determine when there has been enough discussion to make conclusions appropriate. As the leader, you should try not to interrupt valuable discussion, but you should also not allow the session to drag on any longer than necessary. Once participants begin to repeat ideas, an experienced leader senses that it is time to summarize and call for conclusions.

During the final phase of a group discussion, the following steps should be accomplished.

Procedure

1. *Reach a consensus or take a vote.* Throughout your discussion and during the conclusion, your group should arrive at decisions by consensus or by taking a vote. **Consensus** means general agreement among members of the group, although the opinion may not be unanimous. When your group takes a vote, a simple majority usually rules. Both voting and reaching consensus allow you to continue the discussion or to reach a conclusion in spite of some difference of opinion.

2. *Make note of differing views.* If there is a strong difference of opinion that is not resolved during the discussion, your concluding statement or report should acknowledge the point of view of those in the minority.

3. *Summarize the main points and the conclusions of your discussion.* If your goal is to solve a problem, your summary should restate the problem and outline the solutions considered and accepted.

598

4. *State your plan of action.* Once your group has made a decision or developed a solution, you need to decide what should happen next. The plan may involve the assigning of tasks to participants, further investigation of the topic, or additional discussion at a later time.

The conclusion of your discussion may include plans for reporting on the discussion either orally or in writing. The leader may take a moment to commend the group or to evaluate the discussion.

Assignment   **Symposium or Panel Discussion**   Your teacher will divide your class into groups of four to six students and appoint a leader for each group. With your group, select a book, movie, play, or television program to evaluate. Then plan a symposium or a panel discussion and present it to the rest of your class.

Continuing Assignment   **The Small-Group Discussion** Return to the group that you were in for the Continuing Assignment on page 593. Use your agenda and the information that you gathered, and hold a twenty-minute discussion with your group. After your discussion, spend an additional five minutes evaluating the discussion with your group. Note examples of the different techniques that were use

---

19.2 Note-Taking Skills

The ability to take good notes is important because it will enable you to study more efficiently. Because note taking is a selective process, you will learn to determine what is important. You will also find that writing something down will help you to remember it.

19.2a Taking Notes from Textbooks

You will do most of your note taking in school from textbooks. Before taking notes on a selection, read the entire selection through. Then use the following strategies to take notes.

Strategies

1. *Write your notes in your own words.*

2. *Use words and phrases, not complete sentences.* Use mostly nouns and verbs. Omit articles (a, an, the). Use adjectives and adverbs sparingly.

3. *Use abbreviations and symbols when possible.*

4. *Pay close attention to words in boldface and italic type, in quotation marks, or in another color in order to determine what is important.*

5. *Watch for words and phrases that signal main points.* Examples include *first, then, finally, in summary, in conclusion, most important, more important, the reason for, the causes of, the result was, for instance,* and *for example.*

6. *Separate your notes from different classes.*

7. *Review your notes shortly after you write them.*

8. *Write your notes in ink.* Notes in pencil will fade or blur.

500

In Part Three, **concise resource units teach the related skills students need in school and college** and, ultimately, in their careers. Varying with the course, these units treat such related skills as spelling, vocabulary, study skills, listening and speaking, library skills, and test-taking.

First Course
(Grade 7)

G

More means a complete program that gives you total support.

Your **Teacher's Edition** gives you more — one organized volume for each course with the special support you have always wanted.

Full-size student pages with all answers — including sample responses for questions with answers that vary.

Extra help — unit objectives, and references to related teaching resources in easy-to-read, adjacent columns.

▮Unit 10▮

Expository Writing

Objectives

After studying this unit, students should be able to do the following:

- Write an explanation of what something is.
- Write an explanation of how to get to a place.
- Write an explanation of how to make or do something.
- Write an explanation of how a process or a device works.
- Write an explanation of the ideas in a book by writing a book review.

Teaching Suggestions

See "Classroom Insights" for Unit 10 in the front of this Teacher's Edition.

Program Resources

Resource Book, Third Course: Bonus Activities, Unit 10 Composition Checklist, Unit 10
Practice Book, Third Course, Unit 10
Tests, Third Course, Unit 10
Composition Workshops, Third Course, Unit 10

Related Resources

The American Heritage Dictionary of the English Language
Roget's II: The New Thesaurus

Unit Preview

What you write in school is most often **expository**, or explanatory, writing. The purpose of expository writing is usually to explain something to your reader, or audience: How do you get to Shoppers' Plaza from here? How do you make corn muffins? How does a pulley work? What are algae? What is the main idea of *The Red Badge of Courage*? In the unit on developing paragraphs, you learned how to use facts, reasons, and examples to explain a topic sentence. In this unit you will learn the special requirements of various types of explanations.

Directions for getting to a place are one kind of explanation. To provide a framework for a set of directions, begin with a topic sentence and end, usually, with a concluding sentence that brings the paragraph to a definite close. In between, you should include every necessary step. On the other hand, you should *not* include any extra information. Good directions are concise.

Topic sentence   This is the easiest way for you to get a bus
Steps in   to Denver. First, walk from the apartment to the
order   corner of Moreno and Eighth. Then, from there
take a number 36 bus going east on Moreno, and
get off at Cresta, next to the Thrifty gas station.
Next, take a number 11 bus going south on
Cresta. The bus will be marked "City Terminal."
Stay on the bus till it reaches the end of the line,

402

402   Unit 10

Exercise 3 *(page 25)*

Sample answers:

1. Noun: They found silver in the abandoned mine.
   Adjective: A sleek silver car was parked in front of our house.
2. Noun: Please fill in each blank.
   Adjective: Mr. Ferris handed me a blank form.
3. Noun: Dan's mother works for the railroad.
   Adjective: Railroad trains go by every two hours.
4. Noun: A model of the new playground was on display in the school office.
   Adjective: Alan's hobby was building model airplanes.
5. Noun: Is spring or summer your favorite season?
   Adjective: The house was surrounded by bright spring flow-

---

Classroom Insights —

a section-by-section guide through each unit that includes perspectives on teaching the units, highly practical suggestions on introducing topics, proven ways to motivate students, and tips on adapting the lessons to students' needs.

Unit 6 Prewriting

To overcome the difficulty associated with getting started on a writing task, students need to develop a certain amount of confidence about what to do when asked to write. They can develop this confidence by understanding the writing process and by learning a set of skills at each stage of the process. You may emphasize the benefits of learning prewriting skills as a way to begin any writing task.

The Unit Preview shows some prewriting notes about horses. Consider having the students add their own thoughts to the list of notes. From looking at their notes, they should be able to suggest other topics to write about. This activity will help them to see that they can easily find something interesting to write about.

6.1 Finding Ideas for Writing
(pages 237–242)

What to Write About. Keeping a writer's notebook will help the students to overcome the problem of not knowing what to write about. To help the students to see that ideas for writing can come from any source, you might ask them to name their favorite weekly television programs. You can write a few of them on the board. Then ask the students to try to imagine where the writers of these programs find ideas for each week's script. After a brief discussion, you can point out that people who generate ideas have learned to be observant and inquisitive about events. Emphasize that finding ideas for writing is a skill that the students can learn. The exercises in this section will help them to start their writer's notebooks; urge them regularly to add to their notebooks.

Notebook Entries. Encourage the students to develop a questioning attitude toward things that seem familiar and to think about whatever they put in their writer's notebooks. Urge them to go beyond the obvious in writing their entries: their questions or thoughts about the entries, more than

the particular items themselves, may provide them with good ideas for writing. For example, you can ask them whether they know what a meteorologist is. Then ask them if they know how meteorologists learn to do their jobs. Point out that reflecting on what they know and what they do *not* know about familiar things will yield writing ideas.

Personal Issues. Some students may feel uncomfortable if they are urged to include personal thoughts in their writer's notebooks. Reassure them that their privacy will be respected. Stress that the writer's notebook is for the student's own use. However, students should feel free, even encouraged, to go beyond simply recording experiences and events. Urge them to reflect on their experiences and to give meaning to them. They should recognize that much good writing comes from a person's perception of an event and feelings about it. When using items from their notebooks, the students must decide which items they would be willing to develop in writing and share with others. By using loose-leaf paper, the students can remove and keep pages containing very personal items if notebooks are collected.

Outside Reading. Because some students read infrequently, they may think that they are unable to find writing ideas this way. You might point out that any written source can stimulate ideas. Noticing the back of a cereal box, for example, may provoke the question "What are artificial flavors?" Reading a billboard may inspire the question "How are such huge signs printed?" Consider providing a variety of books, newspapers, and magazines for the students to look through during one class period. In addition, you may encourage the students to bring their own reading materials to class for this activity.

6.2 Developing Your Ideas
(pages 242–246)

Generating Ideas. There are many effective ways for students to generate ideas about a subject. Point out to the students that they may

T22 Classroom Insights

Sample pages: Third Course (Grade 9)

H

Diagnostic Test

Name _____ **Date** _____

Unit 1 Parts of Speech (pages 2-55)

Directions: In the following sentences, the words in italic type are a certain part of speech. On the answer line, label the words *Nouns, Pronouns, Verbs, Adjectives, Adverbs, Prepositions, Conjunctions,* or

---

Unit 1 Parts of Speech   Unit Test

Name _____ **Date** _____

Test 1

Extra Practice   Unit 3 Phrases and Clauses

Name _____ **Date** _____

(Continued from page 35.)

Practice 2

Unit 8 Organizing Paragraphs   **Composition Checklist**

Name _____ **Date** _____

                                                    Comments

____ 1. Does your paragraph contain a topic
         sentence that states exactly what the rest of
         the paragraph is about?

____ 2. Did yo
         that is
         details

____ 3. If you
         chrono
         events

____ 4. Did yo
         chronol

____ 5. If you
         order,
         movem

____ 6. Did yo
         spatial

____ 7. If you
         importa
         order o
         most in

____ 8. Did th
         relative

____ 9. If you
         compar
         combin
         points
         AB AB

____ 10. Did yo
         compar

____ 11. Does th
         conclud

____ 12. Did yo
         spelling

____ 13. Did yo
         copy?

Copyright ©1984 by
Houghton Mifflin E

Unit 1 Parts of Speech   *Bonus*

Name _____ **Date** _____

1.4 An Adjective Crossword (pages 21–27)

Directions: Complete the crossword puzzle by writing the *first* adjective from each sentence in the appropriate space. Do not include the articles *a, an,* and *the.*

Across

 1. We put the kittens in a safe, warm spot.
 4. Marcos is an alert student.
 6. When you arrive, come to the rear door.
 7. You will need to buy lining material for the coat.
10. After being caught in a downpour, I changed into dry clothes.
13. A wan face is sometimes a sign of illness.
14. The brochures were free.
16. Hot July days are here again.
17. A low shelf was reserved for toys.
19. The skaters did toe raises to strengthen their ankle muscles.
21. She spent the idle time reading.
22. The old books were dusty and worn.
23. Wee people in Irish legends are called leprechauns.

Down

 1. The athletes are used to having sore muscles.
 2. We took the early train home.
 3. The jogger was lean and tall.
 5. The tan suitcase is mine.
 8. The innate goodness of the girl was obvious.
 9. She plans to enter graduate school next fall.
11. Rare gems are very expensive.
12. The affable man had many friends.
15. A jolly laugh makes everyone laugh.
18. Although the doorway was wide, the piano would not fit through it.
20. The brushes are oily and should be cleaned.

Copyright ©1984 by Houghton Mifflin Company.
Houghton Mifflin English, GRAMMAR AND COMPOSITION, Third Course, Resource Book

47

A **Resource Book** — your special bank of follow-up worksheets and extension activities on convenient, black-line masters. One for each course includes:

Diagnostic Test and Achievement Test — before-and-after assessment. Tests students' knowledge of grammar, usage, and mechanics at the beginning of the course; confirms their achievement at the end of the course.

Unit Tests — a convenient back-up whenever you want to check students' understanding of grammar, usage, and mechanics.

Extra Practice — all that you need. Intensive practice to reinforce the students' learning.

Composition Checklist — master lists of the elements of good writing, correlated to each composition unit in Part Two. Helps students check their own compositions, helps you grade papers. Plenty of space for teacher-student comments.

Bonus — intriguing skill building. Games, puzzles, and lively activities to extend and sharpen skills.

Sample pages: Third Course (Grade 9)

I

Practice Book — supple-mental practice in a consum-able workbook

✔ Practice in grammar, usage, mechanics, composition, and related skills

✔ Roomy format; quick con-tent review; clear direc-tions; simple to correct

✔ Teacher's Edition with com-plete answers

✔ One for each course

Tests — comprehensive assessment in individual booklets

✔ Broad coverage of gram-mar, usage, mechanics, and composition

✔ Easy-to-correct, multiple-choice questions

✔ Teacher's Edition with all test answers

✔ One for each course

Sample pages: Third Course (Grade 9)

J

Name   Date

Gerund Phrases *(pages 103–104)*

A **gerund phrase** consists of a gerund and its modifiers and

---

Unit 11   Descriptive Writing

Name   Date

Describing Objects and Places *(pages 446–454)*

When you describe a place, use a topic sentence and sensory details. The most effective organization to use is spatial order. Present the details the way an observer would see them—from left to right, from top to bottom, and so forth.

Practice 1: Describing an Object   Write one or two sentences to describe one of the following objects. Use as many sensory details as possible.

Describe: the desk or table where you are writing or your favorite pair

---

Unit Test   Unit 2   Sentence Structure

Name   Date

Unit Test   Unit 7   Developing Paragraphs

Name   Date

What is a Paragraph? *(pages 295–299)*   (7.1)
The following sentences are taken from one paragraph of a report. One supporting sentence disrupts the unity of the paragraph. In the answer box, write

    a. if a sentence is a topic sentence.
    b. if a sentence supports the main idea.
    c. if a sentence is not directly related to the main idea.

1. Professor Cassidy teaches English at the University of Wisconsin.
2. He and his researchers have unearthed 175 colorful names for a sudden, heavy rain-storm, including *sewer clogger* and *goose drownder.*
3. Professor F. G. Cassidy's forthcoming *Dictionary of American Regional English* will contain fascinating examples of words and phrases used in different parts of the country.
4. The time before sunrise has several names throughout the country, among them *fo-'day* and *peep-of-day.*
5. Even more colorful are *difflewuzz* and *collywobbles,* two of 176 terms for the clumps of dust that collect under chairs and beds.

Selecting and Limiting a Topic *(pages 299–303)*   (7.2)
In the answer box, write the letter of the most limited topic for each numbered topic idea.

6. Useful information sources
    a. Encyclopedias   **c.** *Guinness Book of World Records*
    b. Card catalogs

7. Origins of state names
    a. The Southern states   **c.** The history of the name *Ohio*
    b. States with French names

8. Weather in different parts of the world
    a. Hurricanes in the Southern   **c.** Types of wind storms
        United States
    b. Kinds of storms

9. Literature
    a. Biography and autobiography **c.** Robert Frost's "Mending Wall"
    b. Famous American authors

10. Useful tools
    a. Plumber's tools   **c.** Uses of the wrench
    b. Tools for home use

Writing a Topic Sentence *(pages 304–308)*   (7.3)
Each paragraph needs a topic sentence. Following each paragraph are three possible topic sentences. Only one states the common features of the details included in the sup-porting sentences. Each of the others is either too general or too narrow. In the answer box, write the letter of the topic sentence that should begin each paragraph.

Unit 7 Test
Page 25
ANSWERS

1. _____
2. _____
3. _____
4. _____
5. _____
6. _____
7. _____
8. _____
9. _____
10. _____

(Continue on page 26.)

Extended Workshop

Sharing an Experience

Situation: A new youth group is being formed in your community, and you have decided to join. As a getting-acquainted activity, the group has decided that each member should share an experience with the others. You can write about an experience in which something that you thought would be easy turned out to be difficult or about an experience in which something turned out to be easier than you expected.

The group members have posted on the bulletin board some questions that might be helpful in thinking about a topic.

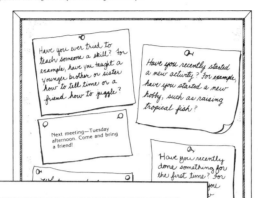

Have you ever tried to teach someone a skill? For example, have you taught a younger brother or sister how to tell time or a friend how to juggle?

Have you recently started a new activity? For example, have you started a new hobby, such as raising tropical fish?

Next meeting—Tuesday afternoon. Come and bring a friend!

Have you recently done something for the first time? For example...

(Continue on page 54.)

53

Extended Workshop

Sharing an Experience

(Continued from page 53.)

Directions: Use the following eleven steps to plan and write an essay that you can share with your youth group.

As a rule, the topic of an essay should be one to which you can bring knowledge of your own, rather than one that requires research.

Step 1.   *Prewriting: Choosing Your Topic*
Choose an experience to write about that would be suitable for this essay. Remember that you are asked to write about something that turned out to be either harder or easier than you expected it to be. The questions on the bulletin board on page 53 may help you to think about a topic.

When you have decided on a general topic for your essay, write the general topic on the following lines.

_____

_____

_____

_____

A limited topic usually suggests a purpose for writing about it and an audience that will be interested in reading about it.

Step 2.   *Prewriting: Limiting Your Topic*
Now that you have chosen a general topic for your essay, you have to make your topic more specific. Decide what you want to emphasize about the topic. Do you want to tell your audience what you learned from the experience? Do you want to tell them why it was easier or harder or more exciting or more satisfying than you expected? On the following lines, write a sentence that limits your topic by telling what specific aspect of it you plan to emphasize.

_____

_____

_____

_____

_____

_____

(Continue on page 55.)

54

Composition Workshops
— unique writing reinforcement in a consumable workbook

✔ Simulated true-to-life situations that broaden students' writing experiences

✔ Opportunities to apply the writing process in a clear, step-by-step sequence

✔ Ideal independent writing assignments

✔ One for each course

Sample pages: Third Course (Grade 9)

K

We offer you more than a handbook:
This program <u>teaches</u>!

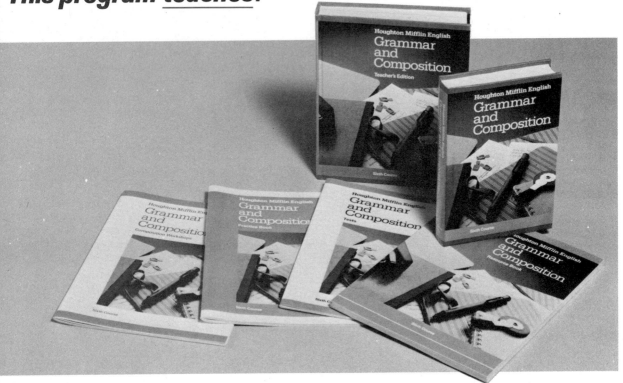

Houghton Mifflin English

Grammar
and
Composition

First through Sixth Courses

L

Houghton Mifflin English

Grammar and Composition

Teacher's Edition

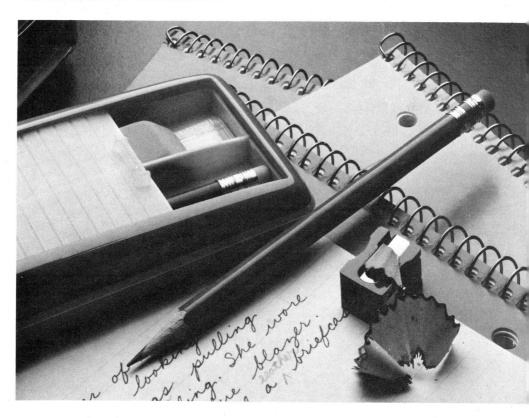

Second Course

Houghton Mifflin Company • **Boston**

Atlanta   Dallas   Geneva, Illinois
Hopewell, New Jersey   Palo Alto   Toronto

Authors

Ann Cole Brown   Lecturer in English composition and literature at Northern Virginia Community College in Alexandria, Virginia

Jeffrey Nilson   Former teacher of English at the Wixon Middle School, South Dennis, Massachusetts, and independent computer software designer

Fran Weber Shaw   Assistant Professor of English and Coordinator of the Writing Center at the University of Connecticut, Stamford

Richard A. Weldon   Vice Principal, Associate Dean of Studies, and teacher of English at the Christian Brothers High School in Sacramento, California

Editorial Advisers

Edwin Newman   Veteran broadcast journalist, author, and chairman of the Usage Panel of the *American Heritage Dictionary of the English Language*

Robert Cotton   Vice Principal, Curriculum Director, and former chairman of the English Department at Servite High School in Anaheim, California

Special Contributors

Ernestine Sewell, University of Texas at Arlington

Luella M. Wolff, Washburn University, Topeka, Kansas

Contents

Preface   T1

Classroom Insights   T3

    Part One   **Grammar, Usage, and Mechanics**   T3
      Unit 1   Parts of Speech   T5
      Unit 2   Sentence Structure   T8
      Unit 3   Phrases   T11
      Unit 4   Clauses   T13
      Unit 5   Compound and Complex Sentences   T15
      Unit 6   Usage   T17
      Unit 7   Mechanics   T20

    Part Two   **Composition**   T25
      Unit 8   Prewriting   T27
      Unit 9   Writing Sentences   T29
      Unit 10   Writing Paragraphs   T31
      Unit 11   Revising   T34
      Unit 12   Explaining   T37
      Unit 13   Describing   T40
      Unit 14   Narrating   T42
      Unit 15   Writing a Report   T45
      Unit 16   Writing Letters   T49

    Part Three   **Related Skills**   T52
      Unit 17   Spelling Skills   T53
      Unit 18   Vocabulary Skills   T55
      Unit 19   Study Skills   T56
      Unit 20   Listening Skills   T58
      Unit 21   Speaking Skills   T60
      Unit 22   Library Skills   T61
      Unit 23   Test-Taking Skills   T63

Answers (continued)   T65

Bibliography   T76

Student Text   Objectives, Complete Answers, and Related Resources   follows T80

Preface

Words for the Occasion

People in the news business sometimes make mistakes. For those to whom this comes as news itself, here is a bit of proof. In 1958, the College of Cardinals in Rome was choosing a Pope. I was one of the correspondents on the colonnades in St. Peter's Square at the Vatican waiting for the white smoke to go up to tell the world that a Pope had been elected. Up it went—or so it seemed to us—and the correspondent I was working with announced that it had. Everybody reported that it had—everyone, that is, except one man, who happened to be employed by a rival network. To him, the smoke looked gray. Perhaps it was his greater experience in Rome. Perhaps he had more acute eyesight. In any case, he turned out to be right.

My colleague and I were alternating on the air, so it fell to me to say that we had made a mistake and that a Pope had not been elected. I remember the words I used at the beginning of that report: "There is no Pope. There is no Pope." I am not criticizing my colleague; from his vantage point he reported what he believed he had seen. A Catholic priest was working with us as an adviser; the smoke looked white to him too. Nevertheless, the earlier report was incorrect, and the record had to be set straight.

As I said, I do remember the words I used, because later, as I thought about them, I was rather proud of myself. "There is no Pope. There is no Pope." Four words, four syllables, twice spoken, and they summed up the situation neatly. In retrospect, I don't say that those words were immortal. I don't even say that they were inspired, but they served the immediate purpose very well. They were appropriate to the occasion—no more, no less.

That, it seems to me, is what language ought to be. It need not be complicated. It need not be flowery (though every so often it will be one or both; there is, after all, a time and place for everything). Whatever kind of language it is, it ought to be the language we choose, that does what we want it to do, that works for us. To make it so, there is no alternative to studying English, to learning its rules, making ourselves as familiar as we can with its richness, its world of possibilities. Nobody can know it all, but the more of it we know, the more fortunate we are, and the more likely we are to get ahead. What if we don't want to get ahead? I think it would help even a hermit to know English well, for it would surely bring richness to his thoughts, if not to his surroundings.

That, finally, is what studying the language is all about. Depending on how well we use it, language helps to determine how interesting and rewarding our lives will be. It is a treasure of unmatched value that is available to each of us—without charge.

Edwin Newman

Classroom Insights

Part One   Grammar, Usage, and Mechanics

The units in Part One, taken together, constitute a complete handbook of English fundamentals. Units 1 through 5 present an authoritative and traditional treatment of parts of speech, sentence structure, phrases and clauses, and their related syntactic elements. Unit 6, "Usage," offers a thorough guide to traditionally accepted usage conventions, including an alphabetically organized glossary of recurring usage problems, such as *good* and *well*. Entries contained in the Usage Notes section have been researched and validated according to the recommendations of the Usage Panel of the *American Heritage Dictionary of the English Language*. Unit 7, "Mechanics," furnishes a comprehensive treatment of the major rules governing capitalization and punctuation and offers suggestions for manuscript preparation and proofreading.

These units are placed at the front of the textbook so that students can refer to them easily and frequently regardless of how the books may be used in classroom instruction. For example, to help students use the textbooks as reference books, the topics within these units are presented in a succinct, straightforward manner, supported by numerous illustrative examples. Important rules and definitions are highlighted typographically for emphasis and for convenient reference. The students can use the easy-to-follow tabs in the upper right corner of the pages for locating important topics quickly and conveniently.

These units are equally well suited to serve as the basis for regular classroom instruction in English. Abundant and varied exercises and assignments are furnished to complement the presentation of key points. The brief Writer's Workshop features, in particular, are designed to help the students see the widespread applicability of grammar, usage, and mechanics to their written work. Frequent cross-references to other units provide opportunities for the students to apply what they know about grammar, usage, and mechanics in other contexts. Further, the practice and testing materials at the end of each unit will allow you to assess student progress on a regular basis.

There are several basic tenets that characterize the content and organization of these units. Knowing them may help you to place this course in perspective for your students.

1. The study of grammar and composition should focus on their utility.

We treat grammar, usage, and mechanics not as ends in themselves, but as necessary conventions for the orderly and effective communication of ideas. Consequently, our objective in these units is not merely to familiarize the students with the differences between "proper" and "improper" English but also to equip them with the skills to apply this knowledge in order to write clearly, precisely, and effectively. In these units, therefore, we place the primary emphasis on those aspects of English that are "enabling" while still being attentive to those that are "ennobling." Seen in this light, we view the study of grammar, usage, and mechanics as subordinate to the task of writing. Thus, we have structured the material in these units to satisfy the students' need not only to *identify* various elements in the language but also to *apply* that understanding, principally in writing.

2. The study of language should treat both its descriptive and prescriptive aspects.

Whenever a language is studied, one naturally faces the question as to whether it should be viewed as it *is used* or as it *should be used*. In the units in Part One, we have chosen to embrace both points of view, according to the content of the unit. For example, our treatment of grammar in Units 1 through 5 is largely descriptive. We view grammar as the analysis of the various elements of syntax that allow us to communicate. Consequently, we treat the sentence as the central element in the study of grammar, for it is in the form of sentences—predications—that we express our thoughts. We deal with the parts of speech, phrases, and clauses in terms of their function within the sentence, and we treat sentences themselves in terms of their function in communicating ideas. Because every sentence consists of a *subject* about which something is said and a *predicate* that says something about the subject, the words of the language can be readily classified according to how they contribute to one or the other of these two essential sentence elements. These five grammar units, therefore, are principally *descriptive*, for they show how we express our thoughts in syntactically structured forms—sentences—that are understandable.

The material in the Usage and Mechanics units, on the other hand, serves a different function; the purpose of these units is to ensure that sentences—especially written sentences—contain the required precision in wording and the necessary safeguards in format to make clear their intended meaning. For this reason, these two units specify the conventional rules of subject-verb agreement, pronoun-antecedent agreement, punctuation, capitalization, and so forth. These units, therefore, are *prescriptive*, for they specify how we must express our thoughts in the required conventional forms in order to be understood.

It may be an oversimplification to say that the study of grammar promotes clear thinking, while the application of usage and mechanics ensures clear expression. It is generally agreed, however, that both aspects of language study are valuable and both warrant the students' attention. Consequently, in Part One we have sought to give a thorough, yet balanced, presentation of descriptive and prescriptive information about our language.

3. *Knowledge of grammar and facility with writing are interrelated, not interdependent.*

While it has been well documented that knowledge of grammar does not necessarily contribute to successful writing, writing is unlikely to be successful if it ignores grammar. To the degree, therefore, that common pedagogical devices bring together grammar and writing, the students will increase their competence with both syntax and composition. For this reason, we have included in Part One many assignments that require original writing on the part of the students. Likewise, in Part Two we have provided numerous exercises, notably in the areas of sentence generation, sentence expansion, and revision, that afford the students opportunities to draw on their understanding of sentence structure and the nature of phrases and clauses. We believe that fundamentally sound pedagogy dictates that we expose the students to this important interrelationship of grammar and writing.

Unit 1 Parts of Speech

In this unit, the focus is on the eight parts of speech and how they function in a sentence. The emphasis is on determining the part of speech of a word by examining that word's function in a particular sentence. Consequently, the unit shows how the same word can function as more than one part of speech. For example, the textbook introduces possessive pronouns on page 8. Some of these words are later discussed as adjectives on pages 20–26.

The Unit Preview shows students how to build a sentence by using the parts of speech. You might give the students a noun besides *branch* and ask them to build another sentence by going through the same process that is used in the Preview. When the students are finished doing so, explain that each part of speech gives a certain kind of information and that this unit will cover the differences among the parts of speech.

1.1 Nouns
(pages 3–6)

Compound Nouns. Some students may think of compound words only as two smaller words joined to form a longer word. You might point out to these students that compound nouns can also be two separate words, such as *safe deposit,* or hyphenated words, such as *son-in-law.* Ask the students to find and list other examples of two-word or hyphenated compounds. Suggest to the students that they look through a textbook or a library book for examples of each kind.

Collective Nouns and Plural Nouns. Students may confuse collective nouns such as *club, troop,* and *class* with plural nouns such as *persons, children,* and *women.* Explain that a collective noun refers to a group treated as a unit but that a plural noun refers to two or more individuals. To help the students distinguish between plural nouns and collective nouns, try giving them the following clues:

1. A collective noun can take an *s* or *es* ending, indicating that there is more than one of a group. *Club* is a singular collective noun; *clubs* is a plural collective noun.
2. A plural noun cannot take an *s* or *es* ending because it is already plural. *Women* cannot be made into *womens.*

You may also need to remind the students that a collective noun is replaced by a singular pronoun when its meaning is construed as singular. (Refer to page 160 in Unit 6, "Usage.") Have the students think of five collective nouns and five plural nouns and use each in a sentence.

1.2 Pronouns
(pages 7–11)

Pronoun Antecedents. In writing, students sometimes tend to use pronouns that do not have clear antecedents. Explain to the students how important it is that each personal pronoun refer clearly to a noun or another pronoun. Give the students an example like the following sentence: "Manuel and Sophie sent away for the concert tickets. They didn't arrive in time for the concert." Ask the students who or what did not arrive in time for the concert, and help them to see that the pronoun *they* does not have a clear antecedent. Ask the students to rewrite the second sentence so that it is clear.

Repetitive Nouns. To help the students see the important function that pronouns have, try the following activity. Use a one- or two-paragraph passage, but rewrite it so that there are no pronouns. The result will be a passage that the students should recognize as repetitive. Have them rewrite the paragraph, replacing nouns with pronouns where appropriate.

1.3 Verbs
(pages 11–16)

Action Verbs. Most students have no trouble understanding action verbs that refer to physical activities. However, you may have to explain why verbs that refer to mental activities are also action verbs. Point out that even though the action in a verb such as *think* may be invisible, there is still action. Ask the students to compile a list of verbs that refer to mental activities. Encourage the students to look through books or magazines and to list several examples of action verbs that describe mental activities. You might list these verbs on the board and have the students copy them in their writer's notebooks for future reference.

Linking Verbs. To help the students identify linking verbs, consider telling them that if the verb can be replaced by a form of the verb *be,* it is a linking verb. Point out that a sentence such as "Jake seemed sad this morning" means the same as "Jake was sad this morning." In addition, give examples of the less common linking verbs, such as *appear, feel, smell, sound, grow,* and *taste.* Caution the students that these words may also be action verbs.

Action and Linking Verbs. Some students may ask why they must learn to identify action verbs and linking verbs. Explain to these students that by knowing the difference, they can find sentences in their writing in which action verbs would be more effective than linking verbs. You might want to give the students an example such as the following one: "Bruce looked restless during the assembly program." Ask the students to contrast that sentence with the following: "Bruce squirmed restlessly during the assembly program." Help the students to see why the second sentence is more effective than the first. Encourage them to be aware of places in their writing where they can use action verbs instead of linking verbs.

1.4 Adjectives
(pages 17–22)

Adjectives in Writing. When students attempt to make their writing more colorful, they sometimes use too many adjectives in one sentence. Consider giving the students an example such as

the following: "The burly, aggressive, muscle-bound bully pushed the timid, fragile-looking, spindly-legged frightened fellow against the hard brick wall." Ask the students which adjectives seem unnecessary and why they seem so. They can then rewrite the sentence to eliminate the unnecessary adjectives.

Articles. Caution the students against misusing the article *the* in their writing. Remind them that *the* refers to specific persons, places, things, or ideas but *a* and *an* do not refer to specifics. You might ask the students to explain the difference in meaning between the two sentences that follow: "This path is *the* way to the cabin" and "This path is *a* way to the cabin."

Degrees of Comparison. Some students may need to be reminded that when they use the comparative or superlative form of an adjective, they should use either *-er, -est, more,* or *most* but should avoid double comparisons *(page 176 in Unit 6).* You could give the students the following examples of this common error: *more better, most prettiest, more happier.*

Pronouns Used as Adjectives. You might want to emphasize to the students that the demonstrative pronouns, *that, this, these,* and *those,* listed on page 21, frequently function as adjectives. Give them examples like those that follow: "This is Jenny's book" and "This book is Jenny's." Explain to the students that *this* functions as a pronoun in the first sentence and as an adjective in the second. Ask the students to write other sentences to illustrate how *that, these,* and *those* function as both pronouns and adjectives.

Usefulness of Adjectives. Select any paragraph from a textbook or a library book and write the paragraph on the board. Ask the students to read the paragraph. Then have volunteers identify all the adjectives. As they identify each adjective, erase it. When you have erased all the adjectives, ask the students to read the paragraph again. Lead a discussion of how dull the new paragraph is compared with the original version. Ask the students to suggest new adjectives to replace the erased ones, and insert the new adjectives in the paragraph. Have the students read the paragraph once again and compare this version with the other two.

1.5 Adverbs
(pages 22–28)

Adverbs After Linking Verbs. Sometimes students mistakenly use adverbs in such sentences as the following: "I feel *badly* about breaking the vase." Point out that *badly* is an adverb and that *bad* is an adjective. Then explain that the word *badly* is incorrect because the modifier must be a predicate adjective modifying *I,* not an adverb modifying the linking verb *feel.* The Usage Notes on pages 179–189 contain several other pairs of adjectives and adverbs, including *good—well, real—really,* and *slow—slowly.* Ask the students to write a paragraph, using each modifier correctly.

Adverbs in Writing. Explain to the students that when they write, they can use adverbs to tell how an action takes place. Point out that the sentence "The runner ran" is more descriptive if they add the adverb *effortlessly:* "The runner ran effortlessly." Ask the students to rewrite a sentence like the following one three times, adding an adverb each time to indicate fatigue, disappointment, and joy: "The runner crossed the finish line."

1.6 Prepositions
(pages 28–31)

Preposition or Adverb? Some students confuse prepositions with adverbs. You might tell the students that an adverb is used alone in a sentence but a preposition is always used with a noun or pronoun that is the object of the preposition. Ask the students to identify the part of speech of *out* in each of the following sentences: "Please put the cat out" and "The cat ran out the door." For more practice have the students choose some of the prepositions listed on pages 28–29 and use them as adverbs in sentences.

Function of Prepositions. Some students may not understand the importance of prepositions and prepositional phrases in their writing. Explain to them that prepositions are important tools for showing the relationships between people, places, things, events, or ideas. To make this point clear, have the students choose five sentences from Exercise 1 *(pages 29–30)* and five from Exercise 2 *(page 31),* and have them explain the relationship indicated by the preposition in each sentence.

In addition, ask the students to observe an object in the classroom and to write down details about it. They should write a one-paragraph description using prepositional phrases to show where one detail is in relation to another. Ask volunteers to read their paragraphs, and ask the other students to identify the prepositional phrases and explain the relationship that each phrase shows.

1.7 Conjunctions
(pages 32–36)

***Coordinate* and *Subordinate*.** Some students might have trouble distinguishing between coordinating conjunctions and subordinating conjunctions. You might define the words *coordinate* and *subordinate* for them and explain what the prefixes *co-* and *sub-* mean. In addition, ask them to look through a page from a textbook or a library book and list all the examples of coordinating conjunctions and subordinating conjunctions that they can find. Using the conjunctions that they have found, the students might also write their own sentences.

Revising Sentences. You may want to explain to the students how to revise sentences by using coordinating conjunctions and subordinating conjunctions. (For further explanation refer the students to pages 316–325 in Unit 11, "Revising.") Consider giving the students a passage made up of simple declarative sentences. Have them revise the passage by using subordinating conjunctions and coordinating conjunctions. As an example, give a pair of sentences such as "Tip ran home" and "He wanted to eat." Show how the two sentences can be combined: "Tip ran home, for he wanted to eat."

1.8 Interjections
(pages 36–37)

Dramatic Impact. Point out to the students the benefit of using interjections in narrative writing—particularly in dialogue—to add dramatic impact. Have the students look through short stories or plays and compile a list of interjections. They could copy their lists into their writer's notebook for future reference when they write. You may want to caution them against using interjections too much—particularly in formal writing.

Connotation of Interjections. Students should become aware of the various connotations of specific interjections. Ask them to tell what kind of emotional reaction is indicated when the interjection *gosh, hurray,* or *aw* is inserted in the following sentence: "__?__! It's almost dismissal time."

Reinforcement

Sentence Formation. A good way to review the parts of speech is to show the students how each part of speech contributes to the development of a sentence. You might want to consider the following group activity. Begin by asking the students who or what a sentence should be about. Select one of the suggestions, such as the Olympic games. Then build the sentence by asking questions like the following: "When did the first Olympic games take place? Where were they held? Who participated? How many events were there?" As the students build the sentence, ask them what kind of information each part of speech adds. You might want the students to create their own sentences.

Enrichment

Verbs to Describe Action. To give the students

practice both in identifying verbs and in using verbs in writing, try giving them the following assignment. Have them look through a passage of an action story, such as Jack London's "To Build a Fire," and write down at least ten verbs that describe the action in the story. Then they should use several of these same verbs in a short narrative of their own, in which the emphasis is on action.

Unit 2   Sentence Structure

The Unit Preview implies that a sentence has at least a noun and a verb. You might point out that even in a two-word sentence, the order of the words is important for conveying meaning. Have the students read the three headlines in the Preview, reversing the order of the words. They should see that "Rages hurricane" conveys little meaning because we are accustomed to hearing the noun before the verb.

To reinforce the Unit Preview, you might have the students bring in headlines from newspapers and revise the headlines so that they form complete sentences.

2.1   Sentences Classified by Purpose
(pages 45–47)

Meaning and Purpose. You may want to emphasize to the students the connection between purpose and meaning. Point out that two sentences may have almost the same words yet will have different meanings if one is a question and one is a statement. You might have the students select five of the sentences in the Exercise on pages 46–47 and rewrite them so that they have different purposes.

Spoken Language. Explain to the students that printed material may contain a majority of declarative sentences and not many of the other kinds of sentences. However, an exception is the printed interview, which usually contains a variety of sentence types. Ask the students to find interviews, or hand out an interview to them. They should look for several examples of each kind of sentence and write them down.

2.2 Simple Subjects and Simple Predicates
(pages 47–49)

Motivation.   You may want to explain the purpose of identifying subjects and predicates. Point out to the students that if they can identify subjects and predicates, they can decide whether a verb agrees with its subject *(see pages 144–146 in Unit 6, "Usage").* Have the students decide what is the correct verb in the two sentences that follow:
1. From inside the haunted house (comes, come) a symphony of horrible sounds.
2. Four containers of cleaning fluid (is, are) in the corner of the warehouse.

Auxiliary Verbs and Modifiers.   Some students may confuse auxiliary verbs with modifiers. You may wish to list all the auxiliary verbs so that the students can see that there are not too many to remember.

2.3 Compound Subjects and Compound Predicates
(pages 49–51)

Combining Sentences.   An effective preparation for the Writer's Workshop might be to provide the students with some practice in combining sentences by using compound subjects and compound predicates. Here are some groups of sentences that the students can use:
1. Kevin climbed the mountain. Karen climbed the mountain.
2. Maria found a silver dollar. She put it in her pocket.
3. Randy picked up the ringing phone. He was expecting a call.
4. Marty raced half a block to reach the shelter. So did Carl. They both waited there for the thunderstorm to stop.

2.4 Complete Subjects and Complete Predicates
(pages 51–55)

Placement.   On pages 53–54 the textbook gives several examples of sentences that do not follow the normal subject-predicate pattern. You might suggest that the students follow these three steps in identifying complete subjects and predicates:
1. Find the simple predicate first and then the simple subject.
2. Identify all the words that modify the simple predicate or complete its meaning. These words are part of the complete predicate.
3. Identify all the words that modify the simple subject. These words are part of the complete subject.

Before the students do the Workshop on page 55, you might have them identify the complete subjects and complete predicates in the following sentences:
1. Find the math book before the class begins.
2. Has Keith's math book been found yet?
3. Whose math book have you found?
4. There is the math book under the desk!

One-Word Subjects and Predicates.   Tell the students that if a subject consists of just one word, it forms both the simple subject and the complete subject of the sentence. If a predicate consists of just one word, it forms both the simple predicate and the complete predicate.

Using a Variety of Sentences.   Exercise 2 on page 54 can serve as good preparation for the Writer's Workshop on page 55. You may want to take some time to have volunteers read aloud their sentences for Exercise 2 so that the other students can identify subjects and predicates. Some students may get the idea that a sentence should never start with its predicate. Help them to understand that in order to have a variety of sentences, they should use some sentences in which the predicate comes before the subject.

2.5 Complements
(pages 55–60)

Complements as Completers. Students may grasp the concept of complements more readily if you point out that complements are *completers*— that is, they complete the thought of a sentence. In addition, you could show the students that without the complement, the sentence is incomplete.

Direct Objects and Indirect Objects. You may need to remind the students to mentally insert *for* or *to* in front of a word to decide whether that word is a direct object or an indirect object. In addition, point out that in a sentence with only one object, the object is a direct object. You might write several nouns and pronouns on the board and have the students use them as direct objects and indirect objects in sentences.

Pronoun Case. You may want to tell the students that pronouns should be in the objective case when they function as direct objects or indirect objects. The textbook explains pronoun case in Section 6.3b on pages 163–169.

If the students have trouble identifying the correct case for pronouns used as compound objects, suggest that they say the sentence to themselves with just one of the objects. You might give them an example like the following one: "Dad gave Bill and (I, me) the hammer." To see which pronoun is correct, the students should say the sentence without the other object, *Bill.*

Predicate Nominatives and Direct Objects. You may wish to remind the students that a predicate nominative renames the subject but a direct object receives the action of the predicate. If they have difficulty telling predicate nominatives from direct objects, suggest that they try the complement in the subject position in the sentence. If the complement is a predicate nominative, the meaning of the sentence will remain essentially the same. As an example, give them sentences like the following: "Kenneth is the captain of the chess team" and "The captain of the chess team is Kenneth."

On the other hand, if the complement is a direct object, it cannot be made the subject, as is obvious in the following two sentences: "Kelly put more cheese into the sandwich" and "The cheese put more Kelly into the sandwich."

2.6 Sentence Diagrams
(pages 61–67)

Reasons for Diagraming. If the students ask why we diagram sentences, you might compare the process with drawing a map. Explain that many people find it much easier to follow a visual representation of directions than to follow a verbal explanation. A map is a visual means of helping people see the relationships between places; similarly, a sentence diagram is a visual means of helping people see how different parts of a sentence relate to one another. A diagram allows people to view a sentence not as a string of separate words but as groups of words arranged in a logical pattern.

You may want to encourage the students to use diagraming for some of the awkward or unclear sentences in their own writing. By diagraming the sentence, the students should be able to see the source of confusion in it; they can then rewrite the sentence to change its structure and to clarify its meaning. You might have the students go through previously written compositions, select three confusing sentences from each, and diagram those sentences. Then the students should revise the sentences.

Diagraming Students' Sentences To provide motivation for learning to diagram, you might try the following activity. Have the students write sentences that can be diagramed. In class the students should exchange sentences with a partner and diagram that partner's sentences. Alternatively, you might have the students make diagrams that their partners should write out as sentences.

Wall Charts. Students may enjoy developing wall charts of the basic diagrams. They could either use sample sentences or write the names of the parts of speech in the appropriate places in the diagram.

New Elements in Red. You might point out to the students that in this textbook, the color red indicates new elements in a diagram. After the explanation of how to diagram a particular element, that element appears in red in the diagram that immediately follows and illustrates it.

Reinforcement

Labeling Sentence Elements. Some students may gain a better understanding of the sentence elements taught in this unit if they label those elements in their own sentences and in those of their fellow students. Ask them to go through their own writing or that of another student and identify the subjects, predicates, and complements.

Enrichment

Sentence Variety. The students could write paragraphs in which every sentence follows the subject-predicate pattern. Have each student trade papers with a partner. Then they should rewrite each other's paragraphs so that not all the sentences follow the subject-predicate pattern.

Diagraming Contest. To create interest in sentence diagraming, try conducting a contest throughout the year. Every week, write a challenging sentence or set of sentences on the board, and give the students a few days to submit their solutions. From among the correct diagramers, select one or two students to help you write the next set of sentences to be diagramed. You might give a point to each student for each sentence diagramed correctly and keep a record from week to week of the students' total points.

Unit 3   Phrases

After the students have added different prepositional phrases to the sentence on page 72 in the Unit Preview, discuss how such phrases help show relationships among people, places, things, ideas, and events. For example, point out that the phrase *in the park* tells where the man was; the phrase *on the handball court* tells where the teen-agers were; the phrase *for directions* tells what the man asked the teen-agers. Make sure that the students understand that different phrases show different relationships.

Conclude by explaining to the students that in this unit they will study three different kinds of phrases and will learn how to use these phrases to write clearly and precisely.

3.1   Prepositional Phrases
(pages 73–77)

Placement of Adjective Phrases. Explain to the students that for the purpose of clarity, they should put adjective phrases directly after the nouns or pronouns that they modify. (The textbook covers correct placement of modifiers on pages 177–179 in Unit 6, "Usage.") You might give the students the following examples to revise:

1. The boy threw the ball in the brown sweater.
2. The horse belonged to the man with the blond mane and tail.
3. The architect designed that building with wire-rimmed glasses.

Words Modified by Adverb Phrases. Sometimes the students may not be sure what word an adverb phrase modifies. Point out that in most sentences, the adverb phrase modifies a verb and tells how, when, where, or how often. Adverb phrases that modify adjectives or adverbs usually tell to what extent. In other words, they make the adjective or adverb more specific. You might have the students find the prepositional phrases in the following sentences and tell what they modify:

1. The rain is necessary for the flowers.
2. We arrived late at night.
3. Sara did not work at the fair.

3.2 Verbals and Verbal Phrases
(pages 77–85)

Verb or Verbal?   Explain to the students that while a verb and a verbal may appear to be the same part of speech, they serve different functions in a sentence. Emphasize that even though a verbal has the properties of a verb, it functions as another part of speech, not as a verb. Encourage the students to use verbals in their writing as an effective way to write precisely. Point out, for example, that *the pounding surf* may be more descriptive than *the rough surf.* You might ask the students to look through descriptions in short stories for examples of verbals.

Using *-ing* as a Clue.   After learning about participles, some students may assume that the suffix *-ing* is a clue that a word is a verbal. Remind these students that some participles have *-ed* endings or irregular endings for the past participle *(see pages 131–136 in Unit 6, "Usage.")* In addition, point out that verbs may end in *-ing* when they function as the predicate of a sentence or a clause. To make the point, you might ask the students how *talking* functions in each of the following sentences: "Al was talking to the group" and "Mrs. Jefferson looked at the talking children."

Complements in Infinitive Phrases.   Explain to the students that in an infinitive phrase, the infinitive is often followed by a complement that adds important information to the sentence. As an example point out that "I offered to help Dan" is clearer than "I offered to help." You might give the students several infinitives from which they should form infinitive phrases and write sentences. Each infinitive should be followed by a direct object, an indirect object, a predicate nominative, or a predicate adjective.

3.3 Diagraming Sentences with Phrases
(pages 85–88)

Words Within a Phrase.   Students sometimes have difficulty diagraming complements and modifiers in participial phrases and infinitive phrases. To help them, suggest that they go through these steps when diagraming verbal phrases:

1. Find the verbal.
2. Find the complement of the verbal. This could be a direct object, an indirect object, a predicate nominative, or a predicate adjective.
3. Find the modifiers and identify the words that they modify.

As an example, you might apply these steps to the infinitive phrase "to find the marbles in the basement" in the sentence "Jerry hoped to find the marbles in the basement." You might also have the students write several sentences with participial phrases and infinitive phrases and exchange them with partners for practice in diagraming.

Diagraming Infinitive Phrases.   You may need to emphasize to the students that they should diagram an infinitive phrase according to the function of that phrase in a sentence. Explain that in the diagram on page 88, the phrase *to train his dog* is diagramed as if it were an adverb because it modifies a verb. Then show the students how to diagram infinitive phrases that perform other functions, as in the following examples:

1. To visit the Taj Mahal is an exciting experience. (noun)
2. The path to take through the forest leads to your left. (adjective)

Reinforcement

Using Phrases in Sentences.   To help the students write effective descriptions, consider giving them a list of prepositional phrases, participial phrases, and infinitive phrases that they can use in sentences. You might want to have the students first use each phrase in a sentence describing a person and then in a sentence describing a place or an object. Remind them to put phrases close to the word or words that they modify.

Forming Verbals and Verbal Phrases. To reinforce the connection between verbs, verbals, and verbal phrases, you might have the students make a list of descriptive action verbs. Suggest such words as *whisper, glare,* and *attack* to help them get started. Have them make each word into a verbal and then into a verbal phrase that they use in sentences. They might even use their verbal phrases in a paragraph that they write.

Enrichment

Infinitives in Writing. Point out to the students that infinitives allow writers to write more clearly and concisely than would otherwise be possible. Ask them to write three sentences in which they use the same infinitive as a noun, an adjective, and an adverb. As examples, give them three sentences like the following ones:

1. To lose can be instructive.
2. The surest way to lose is by wasting time.
3. People should not be afraid to lose.

You might also have the students write three sentences in which they use the same infinitive phrase as a noun, an adjective, and an adverb.

Finally, ask the students to look in books or newspapers to find infinitives and infinitive phrases. Suggest that they make a list of examples, underlining each infinitive or infinitive phrase and identifying its part of speech. The students may find sentences with infinitive clauses, such as "I asked Fred to help me with the math homework." Because the textbook does not cover infinitive clauses, you may want to explain what they are to the students who find such sentences.

Diagraming Phrases. Ask the students to turn to Exercise 3 on page 65 in Unit 2. Have them select five of the exercise sentences and add a prepositional phrase, a participial phrase, or an infinitive phrase to each one. The students should write their new sentences and then diagram them. Remind them to follow the rules given in Unit 3 for diagraming phrases.

Participles. Ask the students to write the present and past participles of several irregular verbs.

(These forms are listed on pages 134–135 in Unit 6, "Usage.") Have the students form participial phrases from the irregular verbs and write sentences with those phrases.

Unit 4 Clauses

The Unit Preview contrasts simple and compound sentences in order to show that clauses clarify the relationships between ideas. To demonstrate the various uses of clauses, you might consider the following activity. Before the students turn to the unit, write the paragraph in the For Analysis section on the board so that it has only simple sentences. Ask the class to combine the sentences in ways that make sense to them. The students should then compare their own paragraphs with the one in the book. Help them to see that they can combine the sentences in the paragraph in a number of ways. Conclude by stating that this unit will help the students to identify clauses and to use them to combine sentences and to clarify relationships between ideas.

4.1 Independent Clauses
(pages 95–96)

Phrase or Clause? To help the students see the differences between clauses and phrases, you might put the following word groups on the board and ask which half of each pair is a complete sentence and which is not:

1. Those long-lasting radial tires. Those tires are good, but they are expensive.
2. We chose the eagle as our national symbol. That rare and inspiring bird.
3. Black and white and read all over. That definition of a newspaper is silly.

Independent Clauses. To give the class extra practice in forming independent clauses, consider giving a series of phrases and having the students use them to write independent clauses. Here are some phrases that you can use to help them start:

1. Raining now; will clear by tomorrow
2. Snowing now; more expected
3. Equaling the record; setting a new one

4.2 Subordinate Clauses
(pages 96–104)

Subjects and Predicates in Clauses. You may want to emphasize that a subordinate clause has a subject and a predicate but that the subject and predicate may be difficult to identify. As an example, give the students a sentence like the following: "The man whom we saw riding his bicycle is my uncle." Ask the students to identify the subordinate clause and the subject and predicate of that clause. For further practice, ask the students to identify the subjects and predicates of the subordinate clauses in the examples and exercises on pages 97–98.

Subordination. When discussing subordinate clauses, you might want to point out what the prefix *sub-* means. Explain that a subordinate clause is subordinate to the independent clause because it depends on the independent clause. In addition, point out that subordinate clauses add information, just as single-word modifiers do. For each sentence in Exercise 1 on pages 97–98, you might have the students write a paraphrase of the information contained in the subordinate clause. For example, for Sentence 1 the student might write, "The clause tells the reader that Robert Frost was forty-one when he became famous."

Function of Pronouns. Some students may assume that the word *that* always functions as a demonstrative pronoun and that the words *which, who, whose,* and *whom* always function as interrogative pronouns. Point out that all five words are relative pronouns when they introduce adjective clauses. To give the students practice in identifying how these pronouns are used, write sentences like the following on the board. Ask the students to identify the function of each pronoun in italics.

1. *Who* is that person?
2. *That* is the woman *who* teaches swimming.
3. *Which* woman teaches you swimming?
4. *Whom* should I call for lessons?
5. *Whose* schedule is *that*?
6. It is the schedule *that* I prepared.

Writing Adjective Clauses. To help the students become accustomed to using adjective clauses in their writing, you might use the following activity. Give the students the following simple sentences. Have them rewrite each sentence, adding an adjective clause to make the sentence more specific. For rules about punctuating essential and nonessential adjective clauses, refer the students to page 212 in Unit 7, "Mechanics."

1. The carnival was on River Road.
2. Aunt May is visiting our house for a week.
3. Ed started as a clerk in the company.
4. The Bensons are taking their vacation in the mountains.
5. Will the person please pick up these papers?

After the students have finished writing, they could compare their sentences to see the great variety in meaning that adjective clauses add to sentences.

Writing Adverb Clauses. To give the students practice in using adverb clauses in their writing, try this activity. Have the students rewrite the following sentences, adding adverb clauses that provide the kind of information indicated in parentheses. Before they start writing, you may want to tell them that an introductory adverb clause must be followed by a comma (see page 211 in Unit 7, "Mechanics").

1. Your line was busy. (adverb clause that tells when)
2. Melinda is happy. (adverb clause that tells why)
3. You act. (adverb clause that tells how)
4. Set up camp. (adverb clause that tells where)
5. That building seems taller. (adverb clause that tells to what degree)

In addition, you might have the students write simple sentences and exchange them with classmates, who should add adverb clauses to those simple sentences. The students could read their resulting sentences aloud in order to see how varied they are.

Identifying the Modified Word. Sometimes students have difficulty identifying the word or words that an adverb clause modifies. Suggest that they read each verb, adjective, and adverb in the independent clause and ask themselves these questions: "How? When? Where? How often? To what extent?" The modified word is the one for which the adverb clause answers one of the questions. You might have the students apply this procedure to the sample sentences on page 101.

4.3 Diagraming Sentences with Clauses
(pages 104–107)

Function of Relative Pronoun. When the students are diagraming adjective clauses, they may not be sure of the function of the relative pronoun in the clause. Suggest that they go through three steps before they diagram the clause:

1. Find the predicate of the clause.
2. Find the subject of the clause.
3. Find the complement in the clause if there is one.

Caution the students that adjective clauses do not always follow the normal subject-predicate pattern. As an example, you might give them the following sample sentence from page 99: "Here is a picture of my cousin, whom I have not seen in five years." Point out that *whom* is the direct object in the clause and, therefore, should be diagramed in the position of a direct object.

Reinforcement

Writing Clauses. To help the students practice using clauses in their writing, you might have them try this activity. Give them a list of ten pairs of nouns and verbs. For each noun-verb pair, they must write one subordinate clause. For each subordinate clause that they write, they should add an independent clause to make the sentence complete. Have the students underline the subject of each clause once and the predicate of each clause twice.

Enrichment

Completing a Story. Give the students a passage from a story or an article from which you have omitted several independent clauses and subordinate clauses. In place of each omitted clause, put a blank and, in parentheses, state the kind of clause that the students should write. The students must complete the passage by filling in each blank with a clause that is correct and that fits the meaning of the passage.

Unit 5 Compound and Complex Sentences

The Unit Preview contrasts one paragraph containing sentence fragments and run-on sentences with another paragraph containing complete sentences. The contrast between the paragraphs demonstrates how errors in sentence structure interfere with communication.

To help the students see the contrast, have them analyze one at a time the sentences in Paragraph A. The students should tell whether each sentence contains a complete thought, an incomplete thought, or too many thoughts for one sentence. Then discuss how each sentence aids or impedes the reader's comprehension. Conclude by pointing out that in a paragraph, good sentence structure is important for clear writing.

5.1 Sentences Classified by Structure
(pages 113–118)

Reasons for Classification. Students may ask why they need to be able to identify sentences by structure. To demonstrate one reason, you might present a paragraph that consists of all simple, all compound, or all complex sentences. Have the students analyze the paragraph by answering questions such as the following: "Is the paragraph interesting? What do you notice about the sentences? How could the paragraph be improved?" Help the students realize that a paragraph containing only one kind of sentence is usually dull and that identifying sentences by structure is the first step in writing paragraphs with a variety of sentences.

Using Commas. As the students learn about compound and compound-complex sentences, you may want to introduce basic rules for using commas in those kinds of sentences. (For the rules on using commas, see pages 209–215 in Unit 7, "Mechanics.") Using the sample sentences on page 114, explain that a comma must come before the coordinating conjunction in a compound sentence. Using the sample sentences on pages 116–117, point out that a comma sets off an introductory adverb clause from the independent clause.

You may also wish to introduce semicolons at this point. Tell the students that they can use a semicolon to separate two independent clauses, in place of a coordinating conjunction and a comma. (For the rule concerning the use of semicolons, refer the students to page 214 in Unit 7, "Mechanics.")

5.2 Writing Complete Sentences
(pages 118–123)

Fragments in Writing. Students may say that they have seen sentence fragments in many published works, especially in plays and novels. Explain that fragments are acceptable in dialogue because the writer's purpose is to imitate speech. Emphasize that in all formal writing, the students should use complete sentences to express their ideas clearly and completely. You might give them a passage of dialogue containing several fragments and ask them to rewrite the passage so that it has complete sentences.

Sentence Fragments in Notes. You might point out that when the students take notes for prewriting or during speeches, lectures, or discussions, they will have little time for writing complete sentences. When the time comes to transform their prewriting and research notes into compositions, they should write complete sentences from their notes. The Writer's Workshop on page 123 provides practice in taking notes and transforming them into complete sentences.

Correcting Run-on Sentences. Point out to the students that not every long sentence is a run-on sentence. Remind them that a run-on sentence consists of two or more complete sentences written as if it were one sentence. After discussing the four methods for correcting run-on sentences on pages 121–122, explain that the students should choose the method appropriate to the purpose of the sentence. For example, using a semicolon with the conjunctive adverb *however* can help to show contrast. You might have the students go through their own writing, identify run-on sentences, and correct those run-on sentences.

5.3 Diagraming Sentences
(pages 124–125)

Compound Sentences with Semicolons. Explain that when only a semicolon joins clauses of a compound sentence, the students should diagram the sentence by placing the semicolon on the step between the two clauses.

Compound-Complex Sentences. Point out that in diagraming compound-complex sentences, the students need only to follow the rules for diagraming compound sentences and those for complex sentences. For compound-complex sentences that are suitable for practice in diagraming, try Sentences 3, 5, and 6 in Exercise 3 on page 117.

Reinforcement

Identifying Sentence Structure. Ask the students to use a textbook from another subject area to find two examples of each of the four kinds of sentences. They should copy the sentences, identify the structure of each one, and then revise the sentences to form a sentence that has another structure.

Making Fragments into Sentences. Try giving the students a list of fragments and having them use the fragments to form complete sentences. In addition, you might indicate the kind of sentence—simple, compound, complex, or compound-complex—that the students should write from each fragment.

Enrichment

Compound and Complex Sentences. Ask the students to write a paragraph explaining what classes they would like to see offered at school. They should use at least two compound sentences and two complex sentences in the paragraph.

Sentence Variety. Ask the students to select a paragraph from their own writing and to examine it for sentence variety. Suggest that they count the number of simple, compound, complex, and compound-complex sentences in the paragraph. If the paragraph has a much greater number of one kind of sentence, have them rewrite the paragraph to improve the sentence variety. They should consider carefully which sentences most need revision. When they are finished writing, they should reread their paragraphs to check for smoothness and clarity.

Unit 6 Usage

The Unit Preview points out examples of five types of usage errors and asks the students to categorize these errors. After the students have answered the questions for analysis, you might ask them how the errors in each of the incorrect sentences cause confusion. Help the students to understand that following standard rules of usage will make their speaking and writing clear and precise.

6.1 Correct Use of Verbs
(pages 131–144)

Memorization. You may wish to remind students who have difficulty memorizing irregular verbs that memorizing the principal parts can actually save them time when they are writing. However, you can also reassure them that they can check the textbook or their dictionary if they are in doubt about certain principal parts.

Distinguishing the Tenses. Many students who can readily name verb tenses in sentences in the textbook have difficulty using verb tenses correctly. You may wish to reinforce correct usage by having the students periodically take ten minutes to conjugate verbs orally. Have the students use full sentences rather than the simple subject-simple predicate pattern; the full sentence will provide a context for using the correct tense.

You might also show the importance of using correct tenses by giving the students two similar sentences whose meanings are distinctly different because of tense differences. In sentences such as "Dad has wanted you to do the dishes for the past two nights" and "Dad wanted you to do the dishes for the past two nights," the students should be able to explain that the action described in the first sentence has taken place over a specified time and *for the past two nights* modifies *has wanted.* They should understand that in the second sentence, the action took place at one moment and that *for the past two nights* modifies *to do.* Encourage the students to give other examples of sentence pairs in which the verbs are in different tenses. Have them discuss the differences in the meanings of the two sentences.

Active and Passive Voice. One way to help the students determine whether to use active or passive voice in their writing is to give them two similar sentences such as "Mother planted these flowers" and "These flowers were planted by Mother." Ask the students whether *Mother* or *these flowers* is more important. If they wish to emphasize *Mother*, then they should use the active voice; if they wish to emphasize *these flowers*, then they should use the passive voice.

Caution the students that the passive voice can sound dull and wordy. Although it can be effective to emphasize the receiver of an action, to show that the doer of an action is unknown, or to create surprise and suspense, the students should revise sentences like "The game was won by us" to the stronger active voice: "We won the game."

6.2 Subject-Verb Agreement
(pages 144–157)

Doesn't and Don't. The students may use *doesn't* and *don't* incorrectly. Remind them that the correct contraction for *does not* is *doesn't* and the correct contraction for *do not* is *don't*. Explain to them that they should check themselves by using the form that is not contracted. It would not sound right to say "he do not" or "they does not." The students will therefore know that the incorrect contractions are just as wrong. The same guidelines apply to other contractions, such as *wasn't, weren't; isn't, aren't;* and *hasn't, haven't.*

Phrase Between Subject and Verb. If students make mistakes in agreement because a prepositional phrase separates the subject from the verb, you might suggest that they diagram Sentences 3, 6, 8, 9, 11, 13, and 15 in Exercise 2, pages 148–149. Visualizing the structure of these types of sentences should help to clarify subject-verb agreement for the students.

As an alternative to diagraming, consider having the students copy the sentences on a piece of paper. They can then cross out or bracket the prepositional phrases. Removing the intervening elements should help the students identify the subject and the verb.

You might have the students illustrate their understanding of subject-verb agreement with intervening phrases, with collective nouns, and with words of amount and time by completing sentences like the following:

My pay for these services. . . .

Have the parents of that child. . . .

A small heap of coins. . . .

One page of the exercises. . . .

The answer to your questions. . . .

The opinions of this author. . . .

One third of all tests. . . .

Nouns Ending in *s*. The students may have an easier time determining which nouns ending in *s* are singular and which are plural if they ask themselves, "Does this noun make sense without the *s*? Without the *s*, is this word still a noun?" Using these questions, students should realize that *measle* and *mump* would not make sense and that *economic* is not a noun.

6.3 Correct Use of Pronouns
(pages 157–171)

Relative Pronouns in Subordinate Clauses. Students sometimes have difficulty understanding that the correct case of the relative pronoun is determined by its use in the clause, not by the rest of the sentence. Suggest that the students use the following procedure to decide on the correct relative pronoun. You might use a sentence such as "Give the book to (whoever, whomever) you think will enjoy it" as an example.

1. Isolate the clause from the rest of the sentence: "(whoever, whomever) you think will enjoy it."
2. Eliminate any unnecessary expressions from the clause: "(whoever, whomever) . . . will enjoy it."
3. Try substituting the nominative case pronoun *he* and the objective case pronoun *him* for the relative pronoun: "*He* will enjoy it." *He* would be the correct pronoun; thus, *whoever* would be correct because it is also in the nominative case.

Pronouns and Writing. Remind the students that to communicate effectively they must make certain that their pronouns clearly reveal who or what they are talking about. You might have the students select several of their compositions and examine them for clear pronoun reference. Students could ask themselves questions like these: "Can I reword any sentences to keep pronoun antecedents from being ambiguous? Can I reword sentences in which the pronouns *which, this, that,* or *it* refer to vague ideas? Can I reword sentences in which the pronouns *it, they,* and *you* do not have clear antecedents?"

6.4 Correct Use of Modifiers
(pages 171–179)

Comparison of Adjectives. You may need to remind the students that the mere presence of words like *more, less, least,* and *most* does not automatically signal a comparison. These words sometimes act as pronouns or adjectives in their own right. For example, *more* is an adjective in "I would like more pizza, please" but a pronoun in "I couldn't possibly eat any more." Point out to the students that sentences containing comparisons always have answers to questions like "More than *what*?" and "Less than *what*?"

Illogical Comparisons. Remind the students not to compare certain adjectives that logically cannot be compared. *Round, full, square, dead, fatal, perfect, dominant, unique, equal, paramount,* and *exact* all refer to qualities that do not vary in degree. Suggest that the students ask themselves, "Does this adjective already imply the superlative degree?"

Placement of Modifiers. To help the students understand how sentence meaning relies on the correct and effective placement of modifiers, give them pairs of sentences such as these:

The restaurant *only* serves brunch on Sunday.

The restaurant serves brunch on Sunday *only.*

The senator announced that he would not run for re-election *in New York.*

The senator announced *in New York* that he would not run for re-election.

Ask the students to explain the difference in meaning between the sentences in each pair. Then ask them which sentence of each pair is more effective. They should be able to understand and explain that any of the sentences could be effective depending on the intended meaning.

Squinting Modifiers. You may want to tell the students about "squinting" modifiers. A modifier is said to "squint" if it is placed between two words so that it seems to modify either word. Use sentences like "The horse that was pawing viciously kicked its owner" and "The tug that was whistling noisily chugged up the river"; then help the students to see that *viciously* can modify either *pawing* or *kicked* and that *noisily* can modify either *whistling* or *chugged.* Have the students rewrite the sentences that you give them twice so that the modifier clearly describes each word.

6.5 Usage Notes
(pages 179–189)

The Usage Notes can be used in several ways. As you cover various issues in class, you might refer to specific notes as examples. For instance, when covering certain points of grammar, such as the difference between adjectives and adverbs, you might call attention to the *good, well* and *almost, most* distinctions. When covering verbs, you could point out the difference in meaning between the auxiliary verbs *can* and *may* or between the following verbs: *lie, lay; sit, sat;* and *leave, let.* When treating spelling and vocabulary *(Units 17 and 18),* you might use the notes on *accept, except, passed, past,* and *than, then.*

You might also have the students refer to the Usage Notes as a reference, consulting particular entries as needed in revising their compositions. Finally, you might encourage the students to reserve a section of their notebooks to record their own usage problems. Students could record any usage errors they make in the textbook exercises and in compositions and other writing. They could record each error, its correct form, the appropriate rule, and a sentence or example of the correct form. The students should review their own usage notes until they are sure that they are using the correct forms in their writing.

Reinforcement

Irregular Verbs.   Students having difficulty remembering the principal parts of irregular verbs may benefit from referring to verb conjugations as they write. Ask them to write a paragraph using some or all of the following verbs: *lie, rise, swim, bring, burst, sting, go, ride, know, drink, shrink,* and so forth. The students should reread their paragraph carefully, checking to see that they have used the correct forms and tenses of the verbs.

Comparative Degree.   Consider having the students extend the Writer's Workshop assignment on page 179. In addition to describing something in the positive and superlative degrees, the students could also write a comparison. Using the three kinds of modifiers should help the students to understand how modifiers change in the three degrees.

Enrichment

Pronouns and Point of View.   You may want the students to practice using pronouns and to extend their understanding of pronoun usage by writing a paragraph using the first-person point of view. The students should then rewrite the paragraph from the third-person point of view. The students should check their paragraphs carefully to see that they have maintained one point of view throughout each paragraph. You might have several volunteers read their two paragraphs aloud and have the other students

discuss how the paragraphs change when the point of view changes.

Sentence Combining.   Students can learn much about sentence variety in addition to correct placement of modifiers by combining two complete sentences or by incorporating a phrase or a clause into a sentence. Give the students sentences and phrases like the following:

1. I was speaking before a large audience for the first time. I was very nervous.
2. The guard stood at attention. His medals gleamed in the noonday sun.
3. The emerald gets its color from chromium. A distinctive bright green.

Encourage the students to combine or incorporate sentences creatively, but caution them to pay close attention to where they place the modifiers. In addition, remind them to check their sentences to make sure that they are grammatically correct. You may want to refer the students to Unit 11, "Revising," for additional guidelines for combining sentences.

Unit 7 Mechanics

The conventions of mechanics can be among the most confusing and frustrating elements of studying language. Try to guide students through this unit with the idea that although some of these conventions may seem arbitrary, all are necessary to communicate effectively in writing. If the students view these conventions as aids to a reader, then they may be encouraged to try to understand and follow the rules of mechanics.

After they have read the sample passage in the Unit Preview, the students should realize the kinds of problems that occur when the rules of mechanics are not observed. You might want to consider using the passage to identify the students' areas of strength and weakness. Have them devote extra study and practice to their weak areas as they study this unit.

You may wish to suggest to the students that they refer to this unit when they write and proofread their work.

7.1 Capitalization
(pages 197–205)

Misusing Capital Letters. Caution the students not to capitalize a word for emphasis or for some reason other than those presented in the rules. If students worry about trying to remember when to capitalize and when not to capitalize, point out that the rules in the text are contained in three general rules, as follows:

1. Capitalize the first word of every sentence.
2. Capitalize the pronoun *I*.
3. Capitalize proper nouns and most proper adjectives.

Learning Rules. Sometimes students may feel overwhelmed by the number of the rules governing capitalization. If they question the validity of learning rules to which there are so many exceptions, help them focus their attention on those rules that apply to the situations that will most often arise in their writing. Suggest that they refer to this unit when they have specific questions. When exceptions to these rules occur in students' work, take advantage of the opportunity to explain the reasons for those exceptions.

7.2 Punctuation
(pages 206–224)

Rules. Students may find it helpful to know the reasons for the use of punctuation. You might point out that punctuation in writing shows where pauses and inflection occur in speech; it also clarifies relationships among words in a sentence. Encourage the students to refer to this unit when they have questions about punctuation.

Run-on Sentences. Caution the students not to confuse compound and complex sentences *(Unit 5)* with run-on sentences. Show them how they can use punctuation to correct run-ons. You might wish to provide them with practice in identifying and correcting run-on sentences. Remind students of their options in correcting this problem:

1. Divide the sentence into two sentences. Be sure that each sentence has a subject and a predicate.
2. Add a comma and a coordinating conjunction between independent clauses.
3. For those sentences in which the ideas are closely related, use a semicolon between the independent clauses.

Suggest to the students that one way to detect run-on sentences is to read the sentence aloud to hear where the voice stops naturally. This point signals the end of the sentence and the need for an end mark or, in the case of two sentences whose ideas are closely related, the need for a semicolon. Consider having the students reread their sentences as written—without pausing and without inflection—to emphasize the need for end punctuation.

Quotation Marks with Other Punctuation. Emphasize to the students that quotation marks should enclose all quoted material, including its punctuation. Students may find it helpful to remember that quotation marks usually appear outside other punctuation marks. Emphasize that in interrupted quotations, only the quoted words and the punctuation related to them are enclosed in quotation marks.

Using Abbreviations. You may wish to make a point of reminding students not to use abbreviations in formal writing such as reports, tests, and compositions. Stress that in formal writing, the students should spell out words that are often abbreviated, such as the names of days of the week, months, and states. The exception is the use of abbreviations for people's titles and for the time of day.

Apostrophes. Consider having the students discuss the reasons for using apostrophes: to show where letters are left out in contractions; to indicate certain plurals, such as the plural of letters; and to show possession in nouns. Suggest that students refer to pages 219–220 if they are in doubt about whether or where to use an apostrophe.

At this point you may wish to point out that the number of the possessive noun and the number of the item that is possessed do not have to be the same. For example, the students can use the plural noun *books* with a singular possessive noun, such as *the boy's,* or with a plural possessive noun, such as *the boys'.*

Caution the students that they will very often see the apostrophe used incorrectly to form a plural in advertisements, signs, and so on. Point out that these are errors, not models to follow. Urge the students to think about why they are adding an *s* to a word and to use the apostrophe with the *s* only when they want to show possession.

Overusing the Dash. Stress that students should use the dash sparingly, if at all, and should not use the dash as a replacement for correct punctuation. Remind the students that they should use the dash only to show an unfinished or interrupted thought or speech. Emphasize that they should not use many unfinished or interrupted sentences in a selection, as the reader would find it difficult to understand what is being said. You may want to point out to the students that the dash is often overused in advertising copy and in other types of casual writing. Consider having the students discuss the reasons for the excessive use of dashes in advertising. Advise them not to use these types of writing as models for their formal writing.

7.3 Italics
(pages 224–225)

Underlining. Explain to the students that italic type appears only in printed material. They will not actually use italics in their writing. Remind the

students that they use underlining to indicate italics in their written work.

Punctuating Titles. Students are often uncertain whether to underline titles of works or to enclose them in quotation marks. Explain that they should put quotation marks around titles of shorter works and underline titles of longer works. Suggest that the students remember to use quotation marks for a title that is or could be part of a longer work. For example, they should use quotation marks around the title of a short story, but they would underline the name of a book of short stories.

Remind the students that when they write titles on their own compositions, they should use neither quotation marks nor underlining.

7.4 Using Numbers in Writing
(pages 226–227)

Taking Notes. You might want to point out to the students that when they take notes, they should use numerals rather than spell out the numbers. Explain that using numerals is a more efficient way to record information. Remind them to spell out numbers correctly when they incorporate their notes into compositions.

Compound Numbers. Caution the students to remember the hyphen when they spell out compound numbers from twenty-one through ninety-nine.

7.5 Proofreading Symbols
(pages 227–228)

Usefulness in Revising. Emphasize that proofreading symbols are a tool to use when revising written work. You may point out that these symbols are the same as those used by professional writers and editors. Emphasize that these symbols are intended to help make proofreading easier and faster. Remind the students that they are not to pass in papers with proofreading marks; they are only an aid in revising.

Revising. You may wish to emphasize to the students the importance of revising as well as proofreading their written work. Explain that most writers prepare several drafts before they are satisfied with what they have written. Emphasize that students *revise* a first draft *(Unit 11)* before they proofread it.

Proofreading. Suggest that the students prepare a checklist to use when they proofread their work. Urge them to include questions about the style and presentation of the work as well as questions about the correct use of mechanics.

7.6 Manuscript Form
(pages 228–229)

Standard Forms. Students can follow the text suggestions for preparing either a handwritten or a typewritten manuscript. Point out to the students that they can use these forms for most of their school assignments. You may wish to adapt these suggestions to suit your own requirements for manuscript form.

Reinforcement

Punctuation Errors. To help the students identify their most frequent errors in punctuation, suggest that they review their corrected written work. Help them to prepare a chart on which they record the types of errors. Next to the description of each error, they should put a check mark to indicate each time that they made that error. Suggest that they proofread their written work especially for those errors, perhaps concentrating on only one error at a time.

Examples for Rules. Consider having the students make up their own examples to illustrate each rule in this unit. Review their examples to make sure that they have applied each rule correctly.

Understanding Commas. Have the students use a textbook in another subject area to find ten sentences, each of which has at least one comma. Ask the students to copy the sentence and to give the rule that explains the use of each comma in each sentence.

Punctuating Dialogue. Encourage the students to work in pairs or in small groups to write a dialogue in which they are the speakers. The dialogue may be based on real or imaginary situations. Urge the students to include narrative sentences as needed. Remind them to enclose all dialogue in quotation marks and to begin a new paragraph when the speaker changes.

When the students have finished, have them proofread their dialogues to make sure that they have used capitalization and punctuation correctly. Remind them to pay special attention to quotation marks and to make sure that they have included the punctuation of the quoted material within the quotation marks.

An alternate approach to this activity is to have the students create dialogue for characters in pictures or photographs cut from magazines and pasted onto sheets of paper. Students should write the dialogue as direct quotations rather than as sentences within speech balloons.

Enrichment

Punctuation and Clarity. To illustrate the need for correct punctuation and capitalization in sentences, you might present the following sentences:
1. Why is James here?
2. Why? Is James here?

Ask the students to explain how the meanings are different. Then encourage them to write pairs of sentences in which the words are the same but the meanings are different as the result of punctuation. You might wish to duplicate and distribute copies of sentence pairs without punctuation. Have the students add punctuation to each sentence so that the meaning of the sentences within each pair is different. Remind the students to change only punctuation and capitalization, not the order of the words within a sentence.

Possessives. Invite the students to construct sentences in which they use both the singular possessive and the plural possessive of the same noun, as in the following example: "The *horse's* tail swished across the other *horses'* faces." Remind the students to use the apostrophe correctly when writing possessive nouns.

Explaining Mechanics. Have the students write brief stories or skits to explain or illustrate rules of mechanics. For example, they might personify a mark of punctuation and develop a plot based on a rule. The purpose of these stories or skits would be to explain the use of mechanics to elementary school students.

Part Two Composition

The units in Part Two focus on three major aspects of writing. Units 8 through 11 present a sequential treatment of the entire writing process from prewriting through revising. Units 12 through 14 introduce the students to three of the major modes, or purposes, of their writing—to explain, to describe, and to narrate. Units 15 and 16 cover frequently used forms of writing in which matters of format as well as content merit special consideration—the library report and social and business letters.

In each unit the usual instructional pattern consists of a preliminary discussion of the composition topic, one or several illustrative models, and a list of helpful Strategies or Procedures for students to follow while writing. The actual writing is achieved first through structured warm-up exercises designed to let the students practice aspects of the writing craft, followed by assignments that require the students to weave together several previously practiced skills in clearly described, yet open-ended, writing activities. An Assignment Checklist accompanies each set of assignments to encourage the students to become their own best critics.

Although each of the units in Part Two is self-contained and can be taught in any sequence, we recommend that Units 8 through 11, which present the complete writing process, be studied in order, in their entirety, and that the students refer to them frequently thereafter. The remaining units may be studied in whole or in part, in any order, as student interests and course requirements dictate.

In developing the material in these composition units, we have been guided by several principles that characterize the approach taken in Part Two.

1. *The study of writing entails study of both the products and the process.*

In general, English courses tend to accentuate one or the other of the twin aspects of writing: the process and the product. In some situations the importance of developing a writing technique, or process, receives primary stress. In numerous other situations, the focus is on writing with strict adherence to prescribed forms and formats. Most classroom instruction incorporates aspects of both points of view, with emphasis varying as circumstances and student needs dictate. In fact, both approaches are essential to the craft of writing, and both are worthy of study. Thus, in the opening units of Part Two, we present the writing process as a universal activity that has broad application beyond the realm of prose discourse. The students gain insight and confidence in units of instruction designed to teach and practice each phase of the writing process: (1) prewriting— brainstorming, selecting and limiting a topic, focusing ideas; (2) generating and expanding sentences—suiting the language to the audience and purpose; (3) drafting—developing and organizing the first draft; (4) revising—checking for unity and coherence, correcting run-on sentences and sentence fragments, achieving sentence variety, checking for details in content and form; (5) editing and proofreading—correcting errors in grammar, usage, spelling, and mechanics.

Within the rest of Part Two, we provide two different kinds of composition units, depending on the nature of the material covered: (1) *genre units* survey the various kinds of writing that fall under a generic mode; the focus is on the distinctive traits of writing within this genre, as shown by representative pieces of such writing or by distinctive features commonly found in such writing. In general, a genre unit approaches the subject primarily as a product. For example, Unit 13, "Describing," is a genre unit in that it presents, compares, and contrasts for the student several common features of descriptive prose. (2) *cumulative units* describe the stages of writing involved in any writing task; the focus is on the various sequenced activities that the writer must carry out in order to develop a finished piece of writing of a particular kind. In this sense, such a unit approaches the subject primarily as a process. Unit 15, "Writing a Report," is a cumulative unit in that it suggests a chronological sequence of steps for the student to follow in preparing any library report.

In the final analysis, we recognize that all writing entails attention to both product and process, and each unit in the program reflects this duality. What varies is the amount of emphasis placed on one aspect or the other.

2. *The writing process should be treated as a branch of rhetoric.*

In addition to focusing on the products and the process of writing, the units in Part Two place considerable emphasis on the four major *rhetorical variables*: (1) writer, (2) audience, (3) topic, and (4) purpose. Depending on the kind of writing being studied, one (or more) of these four variables receives greater attention, although each receives some. We chose this approach because we believe that it can help the students to see that writing is *not* a set of separate and isolated tasks, but rather a single activity with a varying focus on the writer, the audience, the topic, or the purpose, as the situation requires.

Although each composition unit refers frequently to these four variables, the full expression of this four-pronged approach is found in the Writer's Workshop feature that concludes each composition unit in the textbook. Each Writer's Workshop consists of a simulation; the four rhetorical conditions affecting the writing task are spelled out fully at the outset. For each writing assignment in the simulation, the writer's *persona* is described sufficiently to permit the student to assume a fictitious role, generally one related to a career. The designated *audience* is also identified in order to establish the tone and style of the subsequent writing. The *topic* to be treated in the simulation is described in sufficient detail—either through words, charts, or illustrations—to allow the writer to elaborate on it during the writing assignment. Finally, the intended *purpose* of the writing is set forth for the writer. Thus, with all four of the rhetorical conditions specified, the student undertakes an assignment that is uniquely structured yet permits creative opportunities for writing.

In the unit-by-unit Classroom Insights in this Teacher's Edition, you will find suggestions for ways to extend the Writer's Workshops, sometimes by changing one of the four rhetorical variables. In this way, the students will gain insight and experience in shaping and reshaping written language to reflect and accommodate a variety of writers, audiences, topics, and purposes.

3. *The goal of instruction in writing is to develop an objectively critical attitude.*

The thrust of the units in Part Two is to engage the students in a variety of exercises and assignments designed to cause writing (always), and to cause improved writing (continually). In this connection, we view the act of revision to be as significant as the act of writing itself. Throughout Part Two we stress the importance of revising by providing instruction in basic revision techniques and by furnishing frequent Assignment Checklists that encourage voluntary revising by the students. Similarly, the suggested adaptations of the Writer's Workshops provide the students with firsthand experience in making the necessary changes in word choice, organization, emphasis, extent of detail, level of generalization, and the other essential ingredients of purposeful writing. We believe that as students gain experience in revising, not only does their finished writing show greater polish, but their preliminary drafts display increased clarity. Writing and revising, therefore, are complementary activities that encourage the students to be independent writers.

Unit 8 Prewriting

The Unit Preview emphasizes that prewriting is the foundation of the writing process. Point out to the students that this stage includes all the thinking, exploring, planning, and organizing that they do before they actually write a first draft. Emphasize that prewriting includes a set of skills that they can learn, skills that will help them to proceed with any writing assignment.

The Preview shows a writer's notes on the subject of solar energy. After discussing the questions for analysis, consider allowing extra time for the students to share their responses to Question 3. Hearing the variety of questions will help the students to value their own responses as well as to recognize the possibilities for exploring the subject further.

8.1 Finding Ideas for Writing
(pages 239–244)

Keeping a Writer's Notebook. Point out that the notebook should include material from many sources—reading, observation, discussions, and even daydreams. When discussing the Strategies on page 240, you might suggest that the students try to keep their notebook entries open-ended enough to allow exploration. For example, you could ask the class which of the following notes allows more room for development.

1. The White Sox—Why do I always feel as though there isn't enough talent on the bench?
2. The White Sox, 25 players

Notebook Format. The students may find that a crowded notebook is difficult to use. To allow space for second thoughts and expansion of ideas, have the students leave either wide side margins or approximately one quarter of the page unfilled.

Notebook and Privacy. Frequent writing is essential in the development of fluent writing.

However, be aware that spontaneous writing may have drawbacks: students who pour out their feelings on paper increase the ease with which they write but may feel uneasy about sharing personal thoughts. Consider having the students set up a two-notebook or two-part-notebook system to solve the problem. If you favor a two-notebook system, suggest that the students keep a personal notebook and a writer's notebook; make clear to the students that the personal notebook is to be shared *only* if the student so wishes. In a one-notebook arrangement, the students can remove the personal section whenever it is time for you to review the other section.

Taking an Interest Inventory. To introduce or augment Section 8.1b, you might ask the students to suggest anything that interests them at the moment. Write responses on the board until you have about two dozen and then ask the students to vote on the five most popular topics. Invite them to expand these subjects by asking *how, which, what, when,* and *where* questions, as appropriate.

Using Experiences. Students might find it instructive to ask themselves such questions as the following: "What makes me smile? Am I especially touched by something? Have I seen someone or something familiar in a completely different way recently?" Their answers will help them to see that everyday experiences have potential as subjects for writing.

Alternatively, to make the point more forcefully, ask students to name the most uninteresting thing that they did in the past week. The discussion resulting from this topic will be surprisingly rich.

8.2 Gathering and Developing Ideas
(pages 244–248)

Making Lists. Brainstorming may be a more familiar term for this activity. Encourage the students to go beyond the obvious in listing ideas. As they let their minds wander over their subjects, they may come up with recollections, impressions, tangential thoughts, and perhaps inferences. Urge them to write down each new thought, no matter how distantly related to the starting idea. Point out that any thought may set off a new chain of ideas. If you do this activity in class, be sure to allow enough time for the students to be thorough.

Asking Questions.   After the students have made thorough lists, they may feel buried by detail and have a more difficult time asking questions about their own topics than about one another's topics. Consider having the students work in small groups to ask questions about the topics of the members of the group.

8.3 Focusing Your Ideas
(pages 249–255)

Sorting Notes.   Some students may need help in finding organizing principles in their prewriting notes. Suggest they skim the notes and circle all the related items with a colored pencil. They may use different colors for items that are related in different ways. The students may find it easier to work with their notes if they then transfer each group to a clean sheet of paper.

Identifying Purpose and Audience.   Point out to the students that they may treat ideas in different ways for the benefit of different audiences and that one topic may serve many purposes. Audiences may range from experts to mere beginners and from adults to children. Before studying the examples in Section 8.3a, try having the students describe various audiences and suggest appropriate topics for each. For example, have them think of a topic for an audience of young experts and one for an audience of adult beginners.

Emphasize that purpose, too, can vary. To demonstrate that there are variations within purposes, ask the students to describe the purpose and probable audience for each of these kinds of stories: horror story, fairy tale, news story, joke, myth, tall tale.

Choosing a Topic.   As a warm-up, explore how the subject of gem stones *(page 252)* has been narrowed, and discuss other topics that the writer

might have chosen. Ask the students what notes might have led to such topics as the use of diamonds in industry, the high human cost of diamond mining, or methods for making synthetic diamonds.

To emphasize the importance of choosing a *specific aspect* of a subject, remind the students to follow the Procedure on pages 252–253. At times the students might find that their notes are too scanty to justify writing about the chosen topic. Suggest that they shift to a second topic at this point; they will find it much less frustrating in the long run than stalling in the middle of writing a composition.

Focusing on Topics.   After the students have done a considerable amount of prewriting, they may want to use all of their notes in a composition. Point out that their notes contain many possible topics; remind them that a topic is a very specific or narrow way of looking at the subject. Therefore, after they have decided on a topic, they no longer need the information that is not closely related to the limited topic. If the students are reluctant to give up any information, suggest that they save their notes for another composition.

Reinforcement

Group Activities.   Students who are having difficulty generating ideas will benefit from a group or class brainstorming session. Working in a group can help the sudents to overcome "writer's block" and relieve some of the anxiety that they may feel about committing their thoughts to paper.

Choosing Appropriate Topics.   For this activity you may use index cards or strips of paper. Make a set of audience cards by writing a different audience on each card. You may specify people of different ages, occupations, interests, locales, and so on. Then make another set of cards on which you write different purposes for writing. (You may need duplicate cards in each set in order to have one for each student.) Then have the class suggest an interesting subject. Have each student draw a card from the audience group and one from the purpose group. Using this information and the suggested subject, the students should generate an appropriate topic. You may have the students, singly or in groups, generate the audiences and purposes to be put on the cards for this activity.

Enrichment

Generating Topics.   Have the members of the class imagine that they are the editors of a newspaper for teen-agers. Ask them to make a list of suggestions for articles that could be used in the paper.

Answer and Question.   To give the students practice in narrowing topics and in generalizing, play "Answer and Question." Team A draws up lists of five to ten related details, from which Team B deduces questions. Team C takes Team B's questions and lists four or five topics that each question suggests. The class then compares lists and discusses the lists generated by Teams A and C.

Writer's Workshop.   After the students have completed the Writer's Workshop, consider having them repeat the activity, this time focusing on "little wonders" that have not yet been invented. Suggest that they begin by listing needs for household gadgets. Then they can describe, and possibly name, mechanical objects to fill the needs.

Unit 9   Writing Sentences

After the students have completed the Unit Preview, you might write on the board a brief declarative sentence, such as "The storm began" or "Carlos swam." After noting that the sentence expresses a complete thought but provides only scant information, ask the students to expand the sentence as the writer of the sample sentence in the Unit Preview has done so that the sentence provides the reader with more information. Have

several students read their sentences aloud to the class.

The students should realize from this activity that expanding a sentence can make it more informative as well as more interesting. Discuss with students how their awareness of a particular audience and purpose influences how they compose the content and structure of a sentence.

9.1   Expressing Your Ideas in Sentences
(pages 261–265)

Selecting a Focus.   To give the students practice in selecting a focus for a sentence, consider having them look at the prewriting notes on solar energy *(page 238)* in the Unit Preview for Unit 8. Suggest that they compose two sentences for each note, with a different focus in each sentence. For example, for the first note, they might write the following sentences:

1. Solar energy is the energy that comes from the sun.
2. We are trying to use the energy that comes from the sun.
3. The energy that comes from the sun can replace conventional sources of energy in many instances.

This activity will give the students practice in composing sentences and will help them to realize their options for expressing an idea.

Word Choice.   Point out to the students that when writing sentences, they should make each word count. Encourage them to use vivid words to convey the precise meaning of their sentences. Suggest that they consult a thesaurus for specific nouns and verbs that could be used in place of more common ones. Point out that while synonyms share a general meaning, there are usually subtle distinctions among them. Suggest that the students take care when selecting a word, making sure that each chosen word brings clarity, expressiveness, and interest to the sentence. (See the Classroom Insights for Unit 18.)

9.2 Expanding Sentences with Modifiers
(pages 265–267)

Excessive Use of Modifiers. Suggest that the students use caution and judgment when they add modifiers to a sentence. Remind them to use only those words, phrases, and clauses that are essential to the meaning or the clarity of the sentence. Point out that just because they can think of a modifier, they should not necessarily use it. Caution them about writing wordy, rambling sentences. When they add a modifier to a sentence, have the students ask themselves the following questions: "Does this modifier add information that is essential to the sentence? Will this detail help the reader or confuse the reader?"

Modifiers and Meaning. To demonstrate how the modifiers affect the meaning of a sentence, have the students expand the sentence *The house burned* by adding modifiers different from those in the examples on page 266. After the students have written a number of different sentences, have them compare the differences in meaning and discuss the situations in which each sentence would be appropriate.

Placement of Modifiers. Explain to the students that one way to attain variety in sentences is by using certain modifiers, especially phrases and clauses, in different positions in the sentence. Point out that when the modifier does not affect the meaning of a sentence, its position is a question of preference and smoothness. For example, the phrase "except for the Hunters" might appear at the beginning, in the middle, or at the end of the sentence "Everyone attended the party." Remind the students to proofread their paragraphs to make sure that they have placed each modifier so that it enhances the meaning of the sentence.

Misplaced Modifiers. In their efforts to include modifiers in their sentences, students might misplace them. Such misplaced modifiers *(pages 177–179)* can produce sentences with distorted meanings. As an example, present the following sentence and discuss it with the students: "Streaming through the window, the driver had to shade her eyes from the sun." Have the students identify the word that the opening phrase is modifying *(driver)* and the word that it is supposed to modify *(sun)*. Then have the students restate the sentence so that it makes better sense.

9.3 Considering Your Audience and Your Purpose
(pages 268–271)

Audience. To help the students try to write for an audience other than the teacher, consider having them analyze their proposed audience by stating on their papers who the audience is and listing the characteristics of that audience. These characteristics may include age, concerns, level of education, interest or involvement in the subject, and so on. You may even suggest that the students consult this information as they write their sentences and review it as they proceed through the writing process.

Selecting a Purpose. Suggest that the students ask themselves these questions if they have trouble recognizing a purpose for their sentences: "Do I want to inform the audience? Do I want to describe my subject? Do I want to tell a story? Do I want to express an opinion?"

Provide the students with additional practice in identifying audience and choosing a purpose. After the students have completed Exercise 1 on pages 269–270, suggest that they choose an audience and identify a purpose for the sentence that they did not choose in each pair.

Reinforcement

Topic Treatment. Have the students form small groups. Direct each student, in turn, to name a topic and an audience. Each of the other students in the group should decide on a purpose for a sentence about the topic and then make up a sentence based on the topic, the audience, and the purpose. After each student reads a sentence, the listeners should identify its purpose. If the listeners disagree with the student's purpose, suggest that they provide reasons for their answer. Encourage the student, or a listener, to restate the sentence so that its purpose is clear to everyone.

Reaching an Audience.   To reinforce the relation between the treatment of a topic and the intended audience, have the students turn again to Assignment 4 on page 274. Using the same topic, have them repeat the assignment, this time directing their sentences to these audiences: classmates with limited interest in the topic; classmates with extensive interest in the topic.

Enrichment

Writing Sentences.   Suggest that the students pretend that they have a foreign pen pal. Have them write a postcard of three or four sentences in which they describe their city or town. Urge them to choose their words and their modifiers carefully so that they can include as much information as possible in the few sentences that they have.

Unit 10 Writing Paragraphs

Before the students begin this unit, you can show the importance of orderly thought in a paragraph. Present the model in the Unit Preview with the sentences in a jumbled order and ask the class questions such as the following: "What is the main idea of the paragraph? Why are the ideas hard to follow? How can the paragraph be improved?" Then have the students read the model in the Unit Preview.

After the students have completed the questions for analysis in the Unit Preview, consider having them discuss these additional questions: "Can any supporting detail be eliminated from the paragraph without affecting the conclusion? What would be the effect of moving the concluding sentence to the beginning of the paragraph?" The resulting discussion should demonstrate the importance of structure in a paragraph.

10.1   What Is a Paragraph?
(pages 277–280)

Topic and Concluding Sentences.   The students may benefit from analyzing the functions of topic sentences and concluding sentences. Point out that, as a rule, a topic sentence can stand alone, but a concluding sentence often sounds incomplete alone. In context, however, the concluding sentence ties together the main idea and all the information in the supporting sentences. You might write on the board Sentences 1 and 7 of the model in the Unit Preview, asking the class such questions as the following: "Which sentence seems self-contained? Which sentence contains a term that is not explained in the same sentence? Which sentence is directly related to all those that follow? Which sentence refers to information previously stated?"

Structure of a Paragraph.   The students might grasp paragraph structure more readily if they think of it as having three parts: a beginning, a middle, and an end. Point out that these parts usually correlate with topic sentence, supporting sentences, and concluding sentence.

Paragraph Unity.   To illustrate the negative effect of unrelated details, you might copy and distribute the model in the Unit Preview with the following sentences inserted:

"This is the King Arthur of *Camelot* fame." (between Sentences 1 and 2)

"One wonders whether it was granite or soapstone. Perhaps so many had tried before Arthur that the sword was loose." (between Sentences 3 and 4)

"Personally, I favor the first version. If you've ever read Sir Walter Scott's poem, this is the same lake and the same lady." (between Sentences 5 and 6)

"Some of these old legends are pretty far-fetched. I wonder whose arm it was anyway." (between Sentences 6 and 7)

Help the students to see that personal conjecture and even plausible sounding information have a negative effect if they interrupt the logic or the tone of the paragraph.

10.2 Planning a Paragraph
(pages 280–285)

Selecting and Limiting a Topic. If you are allowing the students to choose their own topics, suggest that they refer to their writer's notebooks for ideas. There, they may also have recorded notes that will help them to limit or support their topics.

Before assigning Exercises 1 and 2 on pages 281–282, consider having the class apply the Strategies on page 281 to the topics given here, contrasting those in Column A with those in Column B. Have them discuss which list contains items that are too broad and which contains items that are sufficiently narrow. They should give a reason for their choice.

Column A
Gardens
Trees
Dry weather
Flowers
Gardening in the United States

Column B
Longwood Gardens, Pennsylvania
Cultivating evergreen trees
Gardening in the desert
Growing tulips for profit
Trends in backyard gardening since 1975

Topics That Are Too Narrow. Caution the students about limiting a topic too much. Emphasize that a topic that is too limited has too few possibilities for development and encourages the writer to include unrelated information. Suggest that the students be sure that they can list at least three related details about their topic; if not, it is too limited and they should modify it.

Listing and Choosing Details. If the students find that after limiting their topics they have only a few closely related details, encourage them to augment their lists with additional facts from reference books or other sources. You may also suggest that they use the techniques presented in Section 8.2, "Gathering and Developing Ideas," to discover additional supporting details. Impress upon the students that if they have a strong set of details, they will find the actual writing of the paragraph much easier.

10.3 Writing a Topic Sentence
(pages 285–288)

Writing Topic Sentences. Consider giving the students paragraphs without topic sentences and having them compose suitable topic sentences. They may compose the sentences individually or in groups. Remind them that a topic sentence presents the writer's point of view at the same time that it entices the reader to continue.

To show the importance of writing topic sentences that have a clear focus, you might want to bring to class newspaper editorials and have students find and discuss the effectiveness of their topic sentences.

Evaluating Topic Sentences. Consider the following activity for additional work with topic sentences:

1. Write a group of related details on the board.
2. Elicit possible topic sentences.
3. Have the students evaluate each topic sentence according to the following criteria: too broad? too narrow? on target? interesting? appropriate?
4. Have them vote on the best sentence.
5. Have them discuss why the chosen sentence is best.

10.4 Writing Supporting Sentences
(pages 288–293)

Fact or Opinion? To help the students distinguish fact from opinion, point out that opinions are never verifiable in an objective way, even though they may seem to state truths. Suggest that the students examine the authority of those who hold a statement to be true. For example, probably no one would hold as fact the statement "The planet Pluto is made of cheese." Evidence against this statement is purely circumstantial but it is nonetheless compelling. The statement "The planet Jupiter is about 75 percent hydrogen and 23 percent helium" is also conjecture, but it is an opinion widely held by scientists and it is therefore safe to assume as fact *pending evidence to the contrary.* Encourage the students to ask these questions as "tests" of fact or opinion: "Is this 'fact' checkable? Is this 'fact' generally accepted as true by those who should know? Is there any reasonable body of evidence to the contrary?"

Facts and Examples. If some students have difficulty distinguishing between facts and examples or deciding when to use them, you might point out that the distinction is not always as clear as it is in the models. For clarity and instructional purposes, each of the paragraphs shows just one type of supporting detail. You may point out that facts can be used as examples, as they are in the model on pages 290–291. Urge the students to use the supporting details that make their point, without being overly concerned about whether the detail is a fact or an example.

10.5 Organizing Supporting Sentences
(pages 293–300)

Selecting an Order. Emphasize that an appropriate order is any order that helps the reader to follow the writer's train of thought without having to skip forward or backward. For general guidelines about sensible and effective arrangement of supporting details, refer the students to the Strategies on page 314.

To introduce the relationship between the type of order and the topic, you might ask students to discuss which type of order would probably be most appropriate for topics such as the following:

1. The history of the word *gerrymander*
2. The view from the top of a ski jump
3. Reasons for the Boston Tea Party

Chronological Order. For a drill on chronological order, consider having each student give a very brief oral report on a strictly chronological event, such as getting up in the morning or using a particular tool or instrument. Have them list the steps on paper before they give the report.

Time Span. Point out to the students that they may use chronological order for an event or a trend that spans many years—even centuries, or they may use it for events that happen very quickly—in minutes or even seconds. The same principles apply in either case. Try having the students suggest topics that demonstrate the variety of time spans that are suitable for chronological order.

The Topic Sentence. You may wish to emphasize that in the topic sentence of a chronologically arranged paragraph, the writer sets up the situation or mentions the event to be developed in the paragraph. You might have the students discuss how the writer of the model on page 294 creates a successful topic sentence. You might also point out that skill in writing topic sentences for chronologically arranged paragraphs will help the students when they write narratives *(Unit 14).*

Spatial Order. You might wish to draw a comparison between the writer's eye and the eye of a camera. Suggest to the students that spatial order is especially appropriate for anything that can be scanned visually, such as a landscape or a stamp. You might have the students name other subjects that they could describe spatially.

Encourage the class to differentiate between types of spatial order. Point out, for example, that the Empire State Building might best be described from bottom to top, whereas a family portrait might be described from side to side. Suggest that the students consider two factors in deciding on a particular spatial order: the object or the scene itself and the impression that they want their description to create. Consider having them discuss the best way to present spatial details about items such as the following: a luxury passenger train, a group of buildings, a hot-air balloon, pictures hanging on a wall, and so on. You may find it more effective with some students to show them pictures of such objects and scenes and have them discuss the best type of spatial order.

Order of Importance. To emphasize that both most-to-least important and least-to-most important orders are useful, you might ask the students to name topics that could be developed in order of importance and have them discuss which type of order of importance would be most appropriate for each topic. Point out, for example, that the topic "Why our town is a good place to live," would probably have more impact if they arranged their supporting details from least-to-most important.

The Concluding Sentence. You might want to introduce the concluding sentence by reading the class a paragraph that lacks a concluding sentence and, therefore, ends abruptly. Ask the students to identify what is lacking in the paragraph. After they have determined the need for a concluding sentence, have them suggest a sentence that would end the paragraph appropriately. Point out that a concluding sentence has two functions: to tie together the supporting details and to make a final statement about the topic. Consider showing examples of paragraphs whose concluding sentences serve a variety of functions: restatement of topic, logical conclusion, personal reaction, recommended course of action, and so on. For practice, have the students write their own concluding sentences to replace the existing one in a paragraph such as the one in the Unit Preview *(page 276)* or the model on page 278. Then suggest that they write new concluding sentences for one of their own paragraphs and evaluate the effect on the paragraph of each different concluding sentence.

Reinforcement

Selecting and Limiting Topics. Have each student write a general topic and exchange papers with someone else, who writes a more limited topic underneath. The students should then exchange their papers again, and the third person should limit the second person's topic. Consider reading some of the topic lists to the class, who can then decide the best order for developing a paragraph on the most limited topic.

Supporting Details. Have the students select two paragraphs from a history or science textbook and write the topic sentence of each paragraph on a piece of paper. Then have them list the details in each paragraph that support the topic sentence.

Enrichment

Concluding Sentences. Give the students a list of topic sentences such as the following:
1. Auto racing is one of America's most popular spectator sports.
2. Procrastination is a habit that can be changed.
3. Flea markets are good places to find bargains.

Ask the students to write a concluding sentence for a paragraph on each of the topics.

Transitional Words and Phrases. You might suggest that the students examine textbooks and other written materials to find examples of transitional words and phrases. Have them bring the examples to class and explain how these words and phrases act as "signposts" to guide the reader through the material. If they discover particularly effective transitional words and phrases, suggest that they try to use these in their writing.

Unit 11 Revising

You might point out to the students that *revising* means "seeing again"; urge them to view revising as an opportunity to look at their writing again to improve what they have written.

The example of a writer's revision in the Unit Preview demonstrates what is involved in revising. After the students have completed the Unit Preview, have them look again at the revised paragraph and discuss whether they would make any further changes in it. You might want to find other examples of writers' revisions, or you might complete an assignment yourself and share your revision with the students. Knowing that other writers revise because they want to improve their work will encourage the students to revise in the same spirit, not because they "didn't get it right" the first time.

Many students confuse revising with proofreading. The questions for analysis in the Unit Preview will help them to see some of the steps that a writer takes in revising. To be able to recognize problems in their own writing and to know how to solve them, the students need very specific instruction and practice in revising. This unit identifies the problems that students should address when they revise and gives them techniques for correcting them.

You might consider having the students revise a draft as a continuing assignment. After they have studied and practiced the method of revising discussed in each section, they can apply that method to their drafts. Alternatively, you may use the information in this unit selectively. After diagnosing the students' weaknesses in writing, you can refer them to specific sections of this unit.

Another approach to revising is to have the students revise each assignment for one point only, such as organization or sentence variety. To emphasize the importance of each point, you might consider grading the papers only for the particular point that the students have worked on.

No matter how the students revise, consider advising them to skip every other line when they write their first drafts. This method will give them the space they need to add information, to rewrite, and to move words and sections.

Time permitting, suggest that the students put their drafts aside for a day or two before they begin to revise. The interval will help them to see their work more objectively when they return to it.

11.1 Revising Paragraphs
(pages 311–316)

Content. Urge the students to evaluate the content of their paragraphs at the beginning of their revision. In addition to removing unrelated details, the students should ask themselves questions like the following: "Does this paragraph make a point? Does it say what I mean? If the audience knows nothing about this topic, would this paragraph make sense to them?"

Rearranging Sentences. To facilitate reorganizing, the students may find it helpful to write each sentence on a separate strip of paper. They can lay the sentence strips on their desk and shuffle the order until they determine the most effective organization.

Other students may prefer to cut their first drafts and tape them together again with the sentences in the desired order. If you suggest this method of reorganizing, be sure to have the students write their drafts on only one side of the paper.

11.2 Revising Sentences: Coordination
(pages 316–321)

Combining Sentences. You might point out to the students that learning to combine sentences gives them the ability to express their ideas in different ways. Emphasize that not all sentences should be combined. Suggest that after they have revised the content and the organization of their work, they read it again with the idea of "pulling everything together." If they are uncertain about whether to combine particular sentences, suggest that they try combining them and then judging the result, using questions such as these: "Does the revised sentence make sense? Does it say what I mean? Does it fit well in this paragraph?"

Run-on Sentences. Caution the students against creating run-on sentences when they revise their work. Run-on sentences are frequently compound sentences in which the clauses have not been joined properly. Try duplicating examples of run-on sentences and having the students correct them by writing them as compound sentences. They may use the examples on page 319 as models. To help them avoid writing run-ons when revising, suggest that they ask themselves questions such as the following: "Am I combining too many ideas? Have I used punctuation correctly between the clauses?"

Commas in Compound Sentences. Explain to the students that they should always use a comma *before* the conjunction that joins the two parts of a compound sentence. To help them remember this rule, suggest that they think of the comma as a replacement for the period in the first of the two sentences that they combined.

11.3 Revising Sentences: Subordination
(pages 321–325)

Sentence Fragments. One common kind of sentence fragment in student writing is a subordinate clause punctuated as if it were a sentence. Studying subordination will help the students to realize that subordinate clauses by themselves are fragments. Point out to the students that using the techniques for subordination in this section will not only help them to express their ideas more precisely but will also give them the means to change fragments into complete sentences.

Placement of Subordinate Clauses. Remind the students always to place adjective clauses next to the words that they modify. However, you may show them that they can place adverb clauses in different locations in a sentence. After the students have completed Exercise 2 on page 324, have them try putting each adverb clause in a different position. You may have them do this orally. As they do, point out that they may have to adjust other words in the sentence. Suggest that when the students are writing or revising their own

sentences, they can use their judgment about where to place an adverb clause. They should base their decision on the effectiveness of the revised sentence in its paragraph.

11.4 Revising Sentences: Prepositional Phrases
(pages 325–327)

Using Prepositional Phrases. Before the students begin to combine sentences by using prepositional phrases, they can practice writing prepositional phrases to add information. (You might wish to have the students review Section 3.1, "Prepositional Phrases," and Section 9.2, "Expanding Sentences with Modifiers.") Consider giving them groups of words to which they must add information in the form of prepositional phrases. You may use examples such as the following:
1. Cars sped (Which? Where?)
2. Puppies wobbled (How? Where?)
3. Racers ran (Which? How long?)

11.5 Revising Sentences: Conciseness
(pages 327–329)

Defining *Conciseness*. You can help the students arrive at a definition of *conciseness* by giving them two versions of the same sentence, one of which is concise and the other not. Consider using sentences like the following:
1. Most species of shark will not harm human beings, but some sharks will harm them, so divers should be careful and cautious when they are near white sharks.
2. Because some species of shark, like the white shark, may harm human beings, divers should use caution near them.

Have the students analyze the two sentences and draw a conclusion about what conciseness is.

11.6 Revising Sentences: Variety
(pages 330–332)

Reading Aloud. An effective way to emphasize the need for variety in a group of sentences is to read aloud a paragraph that lacks variety. You might use the monotonous paragraph on page 331, using a dull monotone to add to the effect. Have the students discuss the effect on the audience. For contrast, read aloud the revised version of the same paragraph. Encourage the students to read aloud their own work to develop an ear for variety and monotony.

Four Kinds of Sentences. Review with the students the four kinds of sentences *(Unit 2)* and the function of each kind. Consider having the students compose a sentence of each kind on a given topic. Explain to them that they can occasionally include an imperative sentence in a paragraph or use a question as the topic sentence or the concluding sentence.

11.7 Completing Your Revision
(pages 333–335)

The Final Review. When the students have reached this stage in revising, consider having them ask themselves questions such as the following: "Have I accomplished what I set out to do in this paragraph? If not, what can I do to accomplish that purpose? Are there any other changes that I can make to improve this paragraph?"

Proofreading. You might emphasize that proofreading is necessary because clear communication requires correctness. Encourage the students to use the proofreading symbols on page 228 to facilitate this step. Remind them also to proofread their finished papers to be sure that they have not made any errors in copying their revised drafts.

As the students are proofreading their first drafts, refer them as necessary to the appropriate units in Part One and Part Three of their textbook for information on grammar, usage, mechanics, and spelling.

Reinforcement

Writing Conferences. Consider scheduling time for individual conferences with the students. During these conferences, you can discuss and guide their revision efforts, using the opportunity to address individual issues, such as the need for reorganization, for more effective word choice, and so on. You can also use the opportunity to reinforce what the students do well.

Group Review. The students may benefit from working in groups to revise one another's papers. Before they begin, consider revising a sample with the class. In doing so, you can demonstrate what to do and how to do it. Then, in groups, the students can do the same with one another's papers. You might suggest that they revise for only one point at a time. As they gain proficiency and experience success in recognizing and correcting certain problems, they can proceed to additional revising issues.

Enrichment

"Publishing" Writing. To motivate the students to write and revise carefully, try "publishing" their writing in some way. You may have them write for a class magazine or a school newspaper, for instance, or you may have them write letters to an editor or to their representatives in Congress. What is important is that they write and revise for an audience other than their teacher.

Unit 12 Explaining

You might begin this unit by emphasizing to the students that explaining is a step-by-step process whose purpose is to answer a direct or an implied question. To illustrate, ask the students to reread the model paragraph in the Unit Preview and determine what implied question it answers. Suggest that as the students write the three types of explanations taught in this unit, they ask themselves, "What is the question that my explanation must answer?"

To emphasize the importance of clarity in explanations, ask the students whether they could follow the directions in the paragraph in the Preview. Trying to follow the directions mentally should help the students to see that an explanation is clear when a person not familiar with the content understands it.

12.1 Explaining What Something Is
(pages 341–344)

Parallelism in Definitions. To help the students write parallel definitions, suggest that they begin their definitions by using the following formula: "a __?__ is a __?__." Point out that if the word in the first blank is a noun, the word in the second blank must also be a noun. You might illustrate by writing on the board an example such as the following: "A kohlrabi is a vegetable." To double-check for parallelism, the students might reverse the words: "kohlrabi = vegetable; vegetable = kohlrabi."

Help the students to see that occasionally the first blank in the formula will not be preceded by *a* or *an,* as in "basketball is a game." At times, the students will fill the second blank with a phrase, rather than a word, as in "a bureau is a piece of furniture."

If the students make a habit of using this formula, they may no longer write definitions using "is when" or "is where."

Avoiding Personal References. Consider writing on the board a definition such as the following: "Thyme is an herb that I use for seasoning various foods." Then ask the students what is wrong with the definition. Help them to see that while a good definition is precise, it is also impersonal, making no reference to either the reader or the writer. Ask the students to rewrite the definition, omitting the personal reference.

Selecting Details. Before the students write a definition, suggest that they list on scratch paper the details that characterize the term being defined. Then have them select only those details that distinguish the term from other members of its class.

To illustrate, have the students look again at the definition of an eland on page 341. Then ask the students whether they would add any of the following words to that definition: "quadruped, cud-chewing, mammalian, swift-running, slender." Through discussion, help the students to see that although these details are specific, they do not distinguish the eland from any other antelope.

12.2 Explaining How to Get to a Place
(pages 344–348)

Using the Imperative. If the students have a tendency to use "you should" with the steps in an explanation, have them reread the model on page 346 and list the imperative verbs in each step. Ask the students to identify the subject in each sentence. They should see that the subject is the understood *you.* Help the students to see that the phrase "you should" is unnecessary.

Using Transitional Words and Phrases. You might want the class to discuss the importance of transitional words and phrases to make directions clear. Exercise 1 on pages 346–347 and the models on pages 340 and 346 provide opportunities for the students to examine transitional words and phrases.

If the students overuse *then* and *next,* you might suggest that they keep a list of transitional words and phrases in their writer's notebook. In addition to the ones found in the model paragraphs, suggest that the students list such phrases as *after you pass, just beyond,* and *when you have crossed.*

Suggest that the students also note the use of commas with transitional words and phrases. Looking again at the models on pages 340 and 346, the students should observe that commas are used with some transitional phrases and transitional words, but not with all. You might want to refer the students to pages 210–211 in Unit 7, "Mechanics." As reinforcement, suggest that students add commas to the appropriate words and phrases listed in their writer's notebook.

Omitting Unnecessary Information. To avoid including unnecessary information in their directions, the students might assume the role of the reader. When they revise, suggest that they ask themselves about each sentence, "Does the reader need to know this?" They should delete all information that is not necesssary to the reader.

12.3 Explaining How to Make or Do Something
(pages 348–353)

Limiting a Topic. You might begin this section by pointing out that when the students write directions or a definition, they are writing on topics that are already limited. You may need to remind them, however, that they will have to limit their topics when explaining how to make or do something. To provide additional practice, have the students limit those topics that are too broad in Exercise 1, page 350.

Specific Words. When the students prepare the assignments on page 352, encourage them to use specific words and phrases in their explanations. Before they begin, you might have them review the model on pages 349–350. Ask them why the writer included *four-by-six-inch index card* instead of *index card.* Have the students locate other examples of specific words and phrases in the model.

Complete Explanations. The students will write more confidently when explaining something that they know about. Caution them, however, that it is easy to overlook important steps in something that they know well. Assuming the role of the intended reader will help them to be alert for missing steps when they revise their explanations. You might also suggest that the

students exchange papers with a classmate to check for missing steps.

Transitional Words and Phrases. You may want to remind the students to refer to the list of transitional words and phrases that they are keeping in their writer's notebook. Discuss their lists with them to see that they have included *after, as soon as, before, late, meanwhile, second,* and *soon.* You may wish to add others to the list.

Reinforcement

Definitions. Have the students write definitions of terms that they have learned in other classes. Suggest that they think of terms from mathematics, social studies, science, art, or physical education. Remind them to include all three parts in their definitions. You might ask them to write some one-sentence definitions and some paragraph definitions.

Giving Directions. Have the students use a street map of a city or town and write an explanation of how to get from one building to another or from one area of the city to another. Encourage the students to include landmarks in their directions.

Enrichment

Extended Definition. Have the students write extended definitions of items belonging to the same class, such as *mouse, squirrel,* and *hamster.* Suggest that they list the characteristic details of each on scratch paper and then use only the most appropriate ones in their definitions.

Giving Directions. As a class activity, have the students prepare a booklet for students new to the school. In the booklet, the students could give directions on how to get from the main entrance to various parts of the school. You might want the students to work in teams or small groups, with each team or group responsible for a different set of directions.

Unit 13   Describing

Because many students associate only adjectives with descriptive writing, you might want to begin this unit by pointing out that all parts of speech can be effective in writing descriptions. Suggest that the students list and classify the descriptive words in the model in the Unit Preview. (If the students classify *slipping, sliding,* and *crashing* as verbs, you might refer them to page 77 in Unit 3, "Phrases," for a review of participles.)

You might also want the students to identify those details that appeal to more than one sense. *Smooth,* for example, is a detail of both sight and touch. As the students complete the exercises and assignments in this unit, encourage them to use precise, vivid descriptions that appeal to more than one sense.

13.1   Using Your Senses
(pages 361–364)

Becoming a Keen Observer.   In order to write effective descriptions, the students may need to develop their skills of observation. Point out that with practice they can become more aware of their surroundings. To get them started, consider writing on the board a setting, such as "at a baseball game." Then, with the students' participation, list sensory details for each of the five senses. Encourage them to list details that appeal to more than one sense, such as the taste and the smell of popcorn.

You might want to suggest that the students record their sensory observations in their writer's notebook. Remind them not to concentrate solely on special events, but to record the details of their daily activities, as well. Students can refer to these entries to add vivid details to their writing.

Using Effective Words.   Point out to the students that making their writing interesting is as important as making it clear. Encourage the students to keep the reader in mind when they choose descriptive details for their writing. You might write on the board the words *good, moved, noise, thing,* and *person* and ask the students to replace these nonspecific words with more descriptive ones.

At this point you might also want to caution the students against using redundant adjectives. Help them to see that one well-chosen adjective is better than two or three that say the same thing.

Suggest to the students that they make a habit of using a dictionary, a dictionary of synonyms, and a thesaurus as they write. You may wish to refer the students to Unit 18, "Vocabulary Skills," for a discussion of synonyms.

Identifying Descriptive Details.   As the students complete Assignment 2 on page 364, suggest that they label each of the sensory details on their lists.

13.2   Using Descriptive Words
(pages 365–368)

Vocabulary Enrichment.   Students may have difficulty choosing precise descriptive words if their vocabulary is limited. Suggest that the students refer to Unit 18, "Vocabulary Skills," for ways to expand their vocabulary.

Suggest also that the students keep a list in their writer's notebook of words encountered in their reading. Encourage them to learn both the definition and the pronunciation of each new word. Point out that they are more likely to use words that they know how to pronounce.

Using Phrases as Modifiers.   If necessary, refer the students to Unit 3, "Phrases," for a review of prepositional phrases and participial phrases as modifiers. Point out that in addition to using single words as modifiers, the students should use phrases to provide sensory details. Suggest that the students rewrite the sentences in Exercise 4 on pages 367–368, using either prepositional phrases or participial phrases. If the students have difficulty with the correct placement of phrases, refer them to pages 177–179 of "Usage."

13.3 Describing a Place
(pages 368–371)

Unity. You may wish to refer the students to Unit 10, "Writing Paragraphs," to review the techniques for writing an effective paragraph. Emphasize that the students should strive for unity in their descriptions. Urge them to keep their topic sentence in mind when choosing supporting details.

Listing Details. The students might find it helpful to list on separate paper all the descriptive details that they think of before they write a description of a place. Suggest that the students group the details according to the sense to which they appeal. This technique will give the students a chance to choose from each list only the most effective details.

Uniqueness. Stress the importance of the word *uniqueness* in the second Strategy on page 369. Suggest to the students that they try to think of the unique features of a place as they describe it. To help them choose details that show how a place is unique, the students should ask themselves questions such as these: "In what ways is this place different from others similar to it? What is there about this place that captures my attention?" Suggest that the students make sure that their descriptions answer these questions.

Vivid Words. Because the students will be concentrating on spatial order when writing descriptions of a place, you might remind them of the importance of using vivid words in their sensory details. Remind them also to use mixed sensory details when describing a place.

13.4 Describing People
(pages 372–375)

Purpose of Descriptions. Before the students write a description of a person, suggest that they first determine the purpose of their description. Only after they have established their purpose will they know whether to write objective or subjective description. Point out that objective description is an unbiased factual list of a person's physical characteristics and personality traits. Subjective description conveys the writer's feelings about the person described. To illustrate, have the students look at the list of characteristics in Exercise 2 on page 374 and help them to see that the list is objective. Then ask the students to rewrite several of the characteristics subjectively.

Sentence Variety. Point out to the students that one way to make their descriptions more interesting is to vary the types of sentences and to vary the word order within sentences. Encourage the students to include statements, questions, and exclamations in their descriptions, as well as simple, compound, and complex sentences. You may want to refer the students to Unit 5, "Compound and Complex Sentences," and to Unit 11, "Revising."

Reinforcement

Sensory Details. Ask the students to look for colorful descriptions of places in travel brochures or in advertisements. Have them copy the descriptive phrases and list them on their paper under the headings *Sight, Sound, Smell, Taste,* and *Touch.*

Descriptive Words. Provide the students with a sentence such as "The dog came down the street" and ask them to revise it four different ways, describing the dog, its movement, and the street differently in each sentence. Suggest that the students use prepositional phrases or participial phrases in some of their sentences.

Describing a Place. Have the students select a location such as a city park, the school yard, or the view from their bedroom window. Have them write four paragraphs, each one describing the scene at a different time of the year or at different times of the day.

Enrichment

Sensory Details. Ask the students to write the sensory details that they would use in a description of the following situations, using only the sense specified:

1. Preparing breakfast (sound)
2. Planting bulbs in spring (smell)
3. Making a clay bowl or a sculpture (touch)

Describing a Scene. Have the students write a paragraph describing a scene that involves movement, such as an airplane taking off, someone hauling a fish out of the water, or a young child eating spaghetti. Remind the students to include strong verbs and vivid words.

Unit 14 Narrating

Before the students read the Unit Preview, consider having them discuss how a writer goes about writing a story. You might ask them questions like these: "If I asked you to write a story now, what would it be about? Where would you get ideas for stories? How would you begin your story? How would you build suspense? What would your characters be like? How would you make sure your story is interesting? How would you end your story?"

After the students have read the narrative in the Preview and have answered the questions for analysis, you might have them discuss whether they think that the writer of the paragraph about the race followed the same procedures as the students themselves would follow to write an interesting story.

14.1 Planning Your Narrative
(pages 383–389)

Choosing a Topic. If students have difficulty deciding on a topic for their narrative, they might use the following kinds of questions to help them think of story ideas:

1. What is one of the most exciting or interesting situations that I have been in?

2. What is the first experience I can remember from my childhood?
3. What has been my greatest triumph or my biggest disappointment?
4. What is the funniest or the most embarrassing thing that has ever happened to me?

These questions should help the students realize that just about any incident in their experience could be the basis of a narrative. In addition, remind them to consider imaginary situations or historical events as starting points for writing.

Problem and High Point. To help the students understand how a story is built on a problem or conflict and how the action of a story builds to a high point, you might have them practice identifying these elements in fairy tales or in several familiar short stories in their literature textbook. Students can also use Exercise 2, page 387, for additional practice. After they have listed the actions in chronological order, they could write a one-sentence summary of the problem and could indicate the number or numbers of the actions that serve as the high point of the story. This preparation should help the students to create the problem and high point in their own narrative.

14.2 Writing Your Narrative
(pages 389–401)

Beginning the Story. Some students may use the beginning of their narrative to talk *about* the story instead of telling the story. Point out to the students that an introduction to a narrative differs from an introduction to other kinds of writing. Remind them that the first sentence of a report or an explanatory paragraph is the topic sentence, which explains what the rest of the paper is about. In writing a narrative, on the other hand, the first sentence can set a mood, introduce a character, establish the situation, describe the setting, or arouse the reader's interest.

Remind the students to avoid weak beginnings, such as "This story is about . . . ."

Suggest that the students try a variety of ways to plunge right into the story, such as starting with dialogue, a description, or the first incident in the action.

Describing Characters. You may want to review with the students the four ways in which writers reveal or suggest characters' personalities. In their literature textbook, students can locate examples of the revelation of personality through physical description, through actions, through the characters' own words, and through other characters' comments about them. Remind the students that it is not necessary to use a great many details to reveal personality. If the students provide several specific hints, the reader can mentally fill in the rest of the picture.

Have the students practice each of the four methods to suggest the following kinds of personality characteristics: a careless person, a loyal person, a frank person, and a friendly person. Students should be able to see that they can use any combination of the four methods to reveal personality.

Using Dialogue. To help the students incorporate dialogue into their narrative, you may wish to give them the following guidelines:

1. Make the dialogue natural to the situation and people involved. If appropriate, you may want to incorporate slang into the dialogue to portray realistic conversation.

2. Create an impression of conversational give and take between the speakers. Remember that people waver, pause, hesitate, and interrupt in conversation. Use punctuation to show pauses and hesitation. Use italics (underlining) sparingly for emphasis. Check Unit 7, "Mechanics," for guidelines for punctuation and italics.

3. Make word choice and sentence structure appropriate to the speaker's age, education, background, and personality.

4. Use, but do not overuse, explanatory details that identify the characters. The reader does not always need a label for who said what.

5. Use strong verbs and adverbs in explanatory

details that identify the characters. Vivid words can provide even more information about personality.

Amount of Details. Some students may have a tendency to use too many details, making the narrative unnecessarily long and repetitious. Remind the students to be selective in using their prewriting notes. Explain that not all steps in the action need to be described in equal detail. Give the students an example of a situation, such as walking from home to a neighborhood store. Show the students that they can summarize the walk in a single sentence or they can write a separate sentence for every tree, house, person, and street passed on the way. Remind the students that the writer should select only those actions and details that contribute to the point of the story. You may want to ask the students under what sorts of circumstances they would want to record all of the details of the walk from home to the store and under what circumstances they would summarize those details.

The Ending. Students often have difficulty knowing how and when to end their narrative. You might suggest that they consider these guidelines for writing an effective conclusion:

1. End the story quickly once the problem or situation has been resolved. In addition, the story should reach a conclusion quickly after the high point.

2. Include the reaction of the main character or the narrator to the final events or resolution.

3. In some cases indicate briefly what will happen in the future.

4. Make the ending natural to the situation you have narrated; avoid inappropriate happy endings or sudden twists of fate.

Titles. If students have difficulty selecting an effective title for their story, you might have them examine the table of contents of their literature book for titles that catch their eye. You might ask them questions like these: "Why do certain titles attract your attention? Do the most interesting titles hint clearly at what kind of story will follow?

Which titles are too indefinite? Which give away the plot?"

Consider giving the students these guidelines for writing effective titles:

1. The title should suggest what the story is about without telling the high point or ending.
2. The title should generally be short.
3. The title should arouse the reader's curiosity as to why it was chosen.
4. The title should fit the story; in other words, the story should not disappoint the reader by failing to live up to its title.

Before students compose the title for their narrative, you might have them work in small groups to brainstorm about titles for stories. Give them some general story ideas, such as animals, sports, family, childhood, and so forth. One student from each group could present the best title ideas, and the rest of the students could evaluate the titles on the basis of the guidelines given above.

Reinforcement

Choosing a Topic. Students who have difficulty choosing a topic for narration may get some creative ideas by working with sentence-completion items. Suggest that they complete several of the following sentences and then write down five or six details for each: "My greatest fear is __?__. At first, there seemed nothing unusual about __?__. For one unforgettable day, I was __?__. The tiniest things can be __?__."

Writing Dialogue. To help the students understand how to write dialogue that is natural to the people and situations the students create, suggest that they write a short dialogue between the same two characters in two different situations. For example, the students could first write a conversation between a salesclerk and a teen-ager who is buying a birthday gift. The second conversation could be between a teen-ager working in a store and an adult who comes in to buy a gift.

The difference between the two situations should lead the students to use different language and characterization appropriate to the people involved.

Creating Characters. To help the students understand how the physical description of a character can suggest personality, give the students several descriptions like the following: "He looked the same as always, with a frayed shirt collar, grimy sleeves, and wrinkled and patched work pants. She wore a stiff black suit and a matching frown." Ask the students to identify the character trait revealed in each description. Then ask the students to write several sentences of description that *show,* rather than tell about, the personalities of these people:

"Mr. Battles is a man full of business."

"Carey is a good person, always ready to do someone a favor."

Enrichment

Illustrative Stories. Students might enjoy writing a narrative to illustrate a familiar saying such as these:

"It's a nice place to visit, but I wouldn't want to live there."

"It's a wise hen who knows her own chickens."

"If you can't stand the heat, get out of the kitchen."

Point of View. Students might enjoy rewriting their narrative from a different point of view. For example, if they originally wrote the narrative from personal experience, suggest that they rewrite it from the point of view of a parent, of someone remembering the incident as it happened twenty–five years before, or even of an animal or an inanimate object.

Storytelling Bees. Consider combining some of the skills from Units 20 and 21, "Listening Skills" and "Speaking Skills," with narration by having the students tell their stories orally to the class.

You might first discuss with the students some of the similarities and differences between telling and writing a story. Students should be able to point out how the teller's personality, facial expression, voice, and body position can influence the audience's reaction. They should also be able to explain how and why the elements of narration that they learned in this unit are important regardless of whether the person writes the story or tells it aloud.

You might consider developing a checklist about narration so that the students in the audience can evaluate each story. In their evaluations, the listeners should make certain that they point out features that they liked and that they suggest specific ways to improve any weaknesses in a particular story.

Unit 15   Writing a Report

Consider approaching this unit by explaining to the students that a report based on research is a natural extension of the kinds of writing that they have already practiced. Writing a report requires the student to apply on a larger scale the steps of the writing process: prewriting, limiting a topic, outlining, using details to explain and support the main idea, and so forth.

Because writing a report involves more time than writing other forms of compositions, you may want to require the students to hand in their work for approval at certain stages. Deadlines based on major sections of the unit will help the students budget their time for research, writing, and revising.

15.1   Selecting and Limiting a Topic
(pages 409–413)

Selecting a Topic.   You may need to clarify for the students that even though a report should not

be based on their personal experience, it should be based on their own interests. Explain to them that it is enjoyable to investigate something that interests them. Furthermore, encourage them to use this assignment as an opportunity to learn something new.

To help the students generate ideas for report topics, suggest that they make a list of historical events, hobbies, professions, and people that particularly interest them. They might also get ideas from the exercises and examples throughout this unit. In addition, you might refer the students to the interest inventory in Unit 8, "Prewriting."

Limiting a Topic.   Many students have difficulty doing research because they attempt to investigate too broad a topic. Remind them that they should choose the single aspect that interests them most about a topic and that offers the best opportunity for gathering information. The students should use the questions on page 411 to help them choose one aspect of their topic to develop.

Explain to the students that doing research is also a way of limiting a topic. By investigating the *Readers' Guide,* encyclopedias, and other general reference works, students will not only be able to determine the amount of information available but also will get an overview of the subject, ideas on how to further limit the topic, terms, names, and dates that they may need in their research, and other sources of information. You may want to emphasize that while encyclopedias provide excellent background, the students will want to use other books and magazines for gathering specific facts.

15.2   Gathering Information
(pages 413–420)

Source Cards.   If students prefer investigating and recording one source at a time, encourage them to try the method suggested in the textbook. By recording all of the information about their references before they begin their research, they can save time and effort. Writing source cards will help them to locate all of their information without having to backtrack.

You may also want to emphasize the flexibility of individual source cards. Using separate three-by-five-inch index cards for each reference allows the students to arrange their references in alphabetical order for their source list at the end of the report, to add new references, and to discard any references not used in the report.

Taking Notes. You may want to explain to the students that taking notes is an active process and the best means of learning and organizing other people's ideas to use in their own report. Urge them to read small sections of their references, making sure that they understand each passage before they take notes on it. They should use their dictionary to define any unfamiliar words.

Remind the students not to copy the words of others without using quotation marks and citing the source. Consider explaining that using someone else's words as their own is plagiarism, a form of cheating or stealing. Refer the students to Unit 7, "Mechanics," for guidelines on using quotation marks. If the students do choose to quote a sentence or passage that is particularly suited to their report, they should do so sparingly. Remind the students that summarizing the material that they read helps them to grasp the meaning.

15.3 Organizing Your Information
(pages 420–424)

Topic Statement. To help the students write a topic statement that presents the main idea of the report, you might provide them with these guidelines:

1. State an idea, not a topic. You might start by making your specific topic the subject of the sentence and then adding one or more strong action verbs and complements. "The Braille system has allowed thousands of blind people to gain all the benefits and enjoyment of reading."
2. State your idea as exactly as you can. A sentence like "Teaching chimpanzees to use typewriters and sign language to communicate raised many questions about

the nature of intelligence and language" is more exact and specific than "Chimpanzees have learned to use the typewriter and sign language."
3. Try to indicate by your wording how you will develop the topic. The first sentence about the chimpanzees does this by suggesting that questions concerning intelligence and language will be answered.
4. Try to arouse the reader's interest by choosing specific words, an appropriate point of view, and a suitable method of development.

Outlining. Assuming that the paper will flow once they begin writing, many students are tempted to cut short or eliminate the outlining procedure. Remind them that in making their outline, they are making decisions that establish the order and relationship of the ideas as well as the way these ideas support the topic statement.

You may want to review logical order with the students or refer them to Unit 10, "Writing Paragraphs." Emphasize that as the students review and sort their note cards, they should decide on a pattern of organization most appropriate to their subject. Their outline headings should show the logical divisions of their report.

15.4 Writing Your Report
(pages 424–429)

First Draft. Many students have difficulty using their notes and their outline as the basis for the sentences and paragraphs of their report. Remind them that they should not attempt to write their report simply by transferring their information from the note cards. The purpose of the material gathered in their research is to support their judgments and to provide evidence for their topic statement. You may want to suggest the following procedures for writing the rough draft:

1. Write your introductory paragraph by following the guidelines on page 425 of the textbook.

2. Arrange all of your note cards relating to the second Roman numeral heading of your outline in an order that seems to make the best sense to you. Read all of the cards until you feel sure about the information in the notes. Then put the cards aside and write a good paragraph using your own words about what you have learned from your notes. Following this process with each heading of your outline will help you avoid copying your notes.

3. Be sure to use transitions to link the parts of your report. Check Unit 10, "Writing Paragraphs," for lists of appropriate transitions.

4. As you write each paragraph, ask yourself, "Does this paragraph support the topic statement?"

5. At this point, do not worry about sentence structure, spelling, punctuation, or the other mechanics of writing. You can concentrate on these areas when you revise.

6. Give special attention to your concluding paragraph. A good conclusion draws together all of the important ideas; it is the place where you try to make sense out of all you have discovered and reported.

Incorporating Quotations. Students who decide to use direct quotations in their report will need some suggestions about how to incorporate these quotations. First, you may want to remind them again that they should use quotations only when they think that the author has expressed an idea in a very original and effective way or when they think that the author's exact words are important.

Emphasize that in incorporating quotations into the text of their report, the students will need to do so in a way that allows their sentences to flow smoothly. You might give them suggestions such as these:

"According to William Breckon, the process of fingerprinting. . . ."

"As Breckon points out, fingerprints. . . ."

"Breckon's book indicates that crime. . . ."

"One source, Breckon's *Science Versus Crime,* suggests that. . . ."

15.5 Revising and Finishing Your Report
(pages 430–434)

Revising. Urge the students to complete their rough draft early enough to put it away for a day or two. Explain that time away from their report will enable them to be more objective about it than they can be when they are in the midst of writing.

In addition to the Strategies on page 430 of the textbook, you may want to provide the students with questions like these that they can ask themselves as they revise:

1. Is my report coherent? Does it move logically from one idea to the next? Are the ideas in the best possible order?

2. Does each idea begin with a new paragraph? Does each paragraph contain a strong topic sentence?

3. Have I supported my general statements with details and examples?

4. Have I used transitions effectively?

5. Do I need to check my dictionary for the spelling of any words? Do I need to refer to the "Mechanics" or "Usage" units in the textbook?

15.6 Writing a Book Report
(pages 435–445)

Verb Tense. You may want to discuss with the students the correct verb tense to be used in writing a book report. Many students will probably think that a book report should be written in the past tense since they will have read the book before writing about it. They should understand, however, that regardless of when they read the book, the action, characters, and so forth remain in the same time period. Tell the students to use the present tense when they write about literature.

Taking Notes. If the students are not familiar with taking notes as preparation for writing a report on a fiction book, you may need to discuss with them the reasons for note taking. Ask them why they need to take notes on references from the library in preparation for writing a report. The students should be able to see that they need to remember and include specific details in all types of reports.

You might provide the students with questions like these to help them take accurate and appropriate notes on a work of fiction:
1. What are the main events of the plot?
2. What is the time span of the action?
3. Where and when does the action take place? How important is the setting? Does the setting influence the action, or could the story have taken place anywhere? Does the setting have a particular effect on the characters?
4. Who are the most important major and minor characters? What are they like? Why do they act the way they do? How do they interact with and affect one another? Do they change in the course of the action?
5. What do you think of the book? Does it have the power to make a person laugh or cry? Did it cause you to think or feel more deeply about a particular situation or idea?

Mechanics. You may need to remind the students to underline the title of the book and to use quotation marks if they quote from the book. Refer them to the appropriate sections in Unit 7, "Mechanics."

Reinforcement

Selecting and Limiting a Topic. For additional practice in selecting and limiting a topic, students could choose an article from a newspaper or a magazine. Using the information in the article as a starting point, they could list as many topics as they can think of, including topics that are indirectly related to the subject of the article. For example, the student who reads a review of a jazz concert or a new jazz album might generate these possible topics: the history of jazz, jazz in New Orleans, early jazz musicians, improvisation, and so forth. The student might then do some preliminary library research on one of these topics to determine the amount of information available and the extent to which the topic would have to be limited.

Book Letters. Students who are unfamiliar with the process of writing a book report might find it helpful to write for a particular audience of their choice. Suggest that the students pretend that they are writing to a friend and that in part of the letter they recommend a book that the friend would really enjoy. In writing the letter, the students would follow the Procedure for reporting on a work of fiction *(pages 435–436)*, the Procedure for reporting on a biography or an autobiography *(pages 439–440)*, or the Procedure for reporting on general nonfiction *(pages 440–441)*.

Enrichment

Constructive Criticism. Students generally choose to do reports on books that they like. In order to help them begin to evaluate what they read and to help them support a negative judgment as effectively as they can support a positive one, you might encourage them to do a report on a book that they disliked. The students should follow the appropriate Procedure for reports on fiction, biography or autobiography, or general nonfiction, but they should also explain which aspects of the book they disagreed with or disliked. Remind the students that they should give enough details from the book to help the reader decide whether the writer's judgment is fair.

Comparison and Contrast. Students might enjoy and benefit from comparing the film version with a book that they have read. Again the students should follow the Procedure for writing a report on a fiction book; however, for each step they should include a second paragraph in which they compare or contrast the movie and book versions in terms of the action, characters, setting, and so forth. This same activity also can be done if students have the opportunity to see a production of a play they have read.

Unit 16   Writing Letters

To begin this unit, you might have the students discuss the differences between social letters and business letters. Through looking at the examples of both kinds of letters in this unit, the students should see that there are differences in purpose, form, content, and tone.

Continue the discussion by asking the students to name occasions on which they would need to write social letters and business letters. The students may see many reasons for writing business letters; they may mention requesting information and ordering merchandise through the mail. However, they may not as readily see reasons for writing social letters. They may feel that it is easier, faster, and more practical to telephone a friend or relative. You may then ask how they would keep in touch with a friend or a relative who has moved to another city or is a member of the military, stationed far from home. Some students may even have pen pals in other countries. Such a discussion should help the students to see the value of social letters. You might also point out that social letters can be saved and reread many times; they can be shared with family members and friends.

16.1   Writing Social Letters
(pages 453–460)

Social or Friendly?   If the students are unfamiliar with the term *social letters* and assume that they differ from friendly letters, point out that social letters include all personal correspondence that is not related to business. You might ask the students to name the various kinds of social letters, including thank-you notes, invitations, letters of condolence or sympathy, and announcements of births, weddings, and anniversaries.

Appropriate Stationery.   Students who write many social letters might want to have their own stationery. However, you should point out that the students do not need to buy special paper for writing social letters; they may use typing paper. Point out that using white or light-colored unlined paper and dark ink makes their letters easier to read and is a sign of consideration for their reader.

Getting Started.   If the students have a difficult time thinking of something to say when writing social letters, suggest that they follow these strategies:

1. Keep a journal in which you list information or questions to include in your letter. Make notes about ordinary events as well as extraordinary ones. If you keep a journal for a few days, you will find that you have many things to say when you actually write your letter.

2. If you are answering a letter, reread it before you start to write. Even if you are not answering specific questions, you should find that the letter gives you some ideas of things to write about.

3. Imagine that you are telephoning your friend or relative or that you are visiting the person. Include in your letter those things that you would say over the phone or in person.

You might also suggest that the students consider writing a "diary letter," in which they write a few lines or a few paragraphs each day over a period of several days.

Making Letters Interesting.   Ask the students to think of interesting letters that they have received and to describe what made the letters interesting. Their specific answers may vary, but most students will probably describe a sense that the writer enjoyed writing the letter. Point out that the students can convey this feeling in their own letters if they keep their reader in mind as they write.

Suggest that the students include newspaper clippings, snapshots, recipes, cartoons, and other items that they think the reader would find interesting. They should include information about mutual acquaintances, and news of personal or local events.

Also recommend that the students begin their letters with an interesting comment or question. Suggest that they avoid such clichés as "How are you? I am fine" and "While sitting here with nothing to do. . . ."

Asking Questions. A social letter should be more than a list of questions. You may need to remind the students that questions need not always be asked directly. Have the students think of other ways of eliciting information. To get them started, you might suggest "I was wondering whether . . ." "I'm not sure you'd agree, but . . .," or "Let me know how you feel about. . . ."

Writing Thank-You Notes. Because writing thank-you notes can be difficult, many people send printed notes instead of writing their own. Point out that while such cards are acceptable, most people appreciate more the thoughtfulness and effort that go into writing a personal note.

If the students indicate that they too have difficulty writing thank-you notes, ask them what part of writing the notes presents the most difficulty: Finding a way to begin? Thinking of enough to say? Concluding the note? Through discussion, the students should discover that thanking the person directly for the gift or favor is the best way to begin. Suggest that the students put themselves in the place of the reader and ask, "What would I like to hear about the gift?" Most people will want to hear how the gift will be used or enjoyed. The students might conclude their notes by once again expressing their appreciation for the gift or favor.

16.2 Writing Business Letters
(pages 460–471)

Form and Content. If the students understand the reasons for the format and content conventions in business letters, they may take greater care in following those conventions. You might begin a class discussion by asking the students why a heading is important in a business letter. Help them to understand that most businesses discard envelopes; without the envelope, the heading is the only source of the writer's return address. You might also point out that the heading is important because it contains the date. A letter without a date may be among the last to be answered.

Help the students to see that an illegible signature with no typed name against which to check it may mean that a letter goes unanswered. If the students then wonder why they might not include a typed signature only, point out that a typed signature is only for clarity. A handwritten signature is legal; it means that the writer is aware of and agrees to the contents of the letter.

Finally, you might want to be certain that the students understand the reason for keeping the body of their letters brief. Point out that businesses receive hundreds of letters a week and have neither the time nor the personnel to devote to answering long letters. A brief letter that is to the point is more likely to be answered quickly.

Appropriate Tone. You might begin a discussion of tone by asking the students how the tone of a business letter differs from that of a social letter and why. They should already be aware that the tone of a social letter is casual, informal, and personal. Help the students to see that because a business letter has a different purpose, its tone must be courteous, formal, and impersonal. Remind the students that not only should they avoid the casualness and personal references used in social letters, but they should also avoid impatience, sarcasm, excessive apologies, meekness, and irrelevant information. To help the students make sure that their business letters have the proper tone, suggest that they consider the reader and ask themselves the following questions: "Have I said everything that the reader needs to know? Have I said anything that the reader does not need to know? Is my tone courteous and businesslike? Have I said anything that will offend the reader?" Questions such as these should help the students to write effective business letters.

Folding Business Letters. You might want to have the students use blank or scrap paper to practice folding business letters for long and short envelopes until they are able to do it successfully on their first attempt. Point out that a business letter that has been folded and refolded several times does not create a favorable impression and may be difficult to read.

Reinforcement

Writing a Social Letter. Have the students turn again to the Writer's Workshop on pages 472–473 and begin preparing an answer to the letter that they expect from their pen pal. Suggest that they start writing the "diary letter" discussed earlier in the Classroom Insights for this unit, in which they include information that will give their pen pal a clearer idea of life in this country. Suggest that the students include answers to questions that they anticipate from their pen pal.

Writing a Request Letter. Ask the students to use their telephone directories or library resources to find the name of a state or federal agency from which they can get information on proper nutrition or on another subject that you suggest. Then have them write a request letter for the information.

Enrichment

Writing a Thank-You Note. Have the students assume that they have spent a holiday weekend at the home of a friend in another city. Ask them to write two thank-you notes, one to their friend and one to their friend's parents.

Part Three   Related Skills

Part Three consists of a number of independent, self-contained units devoted to topics that are either applications or enhancements of the writing process. These optional units are placed last so that they may be taught or omitted at your discretion. Because these units retain the popular handbook format, however, the students will find them to be convenient sources of information related to their studies.

Unit 17, "Spelling Skills," offers a review of the formation of plurals and other endings, the *ie / ei* pattern, homophones, words often confused, and spelling aids. A list of "spelling demons"— common words frequently misspelled—is included in the textbook for special concentration; an expanded list of difficult spelling words is also provided in this Teacher's Edition.

Unit 18, "Vocabulary Skills," contains sure-fire methods for expanding one's personal vocabulary through the use of dictionary aids, prefix-root-suffix manipulations, and contextual clues. Taken together, the Spelling and Vocabulary units provide a sound review of basic word skills that the students can use in their written and oral work.

Three units offer special help to the students in work outside their English course. Unit 19, "Study Skills," provides proven suggestions for developing successful study habits through the use of the SQRRR Method to improve critical reading skills and by practice in note taking. Unit 23, "Test-Taking Skills," furnishes insights and strategies to help students prepare for and take various kinds of examinations, including objective and essay-style tests.

Because of the increasing importance attached to locating and managing information, students will find Unit 22, "Library Skills," to be particularly valuable. It contains a concise orientation to the widely used Dewey decimal system and to standard library reference works such as encyclopedias, almanacs, the *Readers' Guide to Periodical Literature,* and so on.

Finally, we have included two units designed to help the students develop facility with spoken English. Unit 20, "Listening Skills," gives practical suggestions on how to become a better listener through active and critical listening techniques. Unit 21, "Speaking Skills," is a guide to public speaking, including instruction in planning and delivering formal and informal speeches to inform, to persuade, and to entertain.

These units are presented in a straightforward manner, with pertinent information clearly labeled to help the students locate and study appropriate sections, as needed. Although these units are briefer than those in Parts One and Two, they do contain frequent Assignments to allow students to apply what they are learning. Additional activities for enlarging the scope of these units to accommodate particular curriculum or student needs are given in these Classroom Insights.

Taken as a group, the units in Part Three offer the students a variety of ways to apply the writing techniques taught in Part Two to new, but related, situations. In answering essay questions, for example, the students will draw upon their knowledge of expository writing and their capacity to use facts and examples to develop and support their writing convincingly. Similarly, the students will see that their prewriting techniques and the methods of organizing their writing are as suitable for preparing a speech as for drafting a composition.

Because many related activities outside the strict scope of writing can bring clarity, insight, and vitality to the writing process, we illustrate many of these situations in Part Three of the textbook. For example, the students' attention to correct spelling and their greater awareness of vocabulary should bring fresh wording to their compositions and augment their efforts in revising. Their ability to use library reference materials can provide them with a rich source of ideas for writing, regardless of the mode of writing being called for. Their growing capacity to listen attentively and to speak effectively can help greatly, whether they are polishing their writing in groups or having an individual conference on their progress as writers. In all these ways, we believe that students can benefit from exposure to these units.

Unit 17   Spelling Skills

Students frequently believe that poor spelling habits are unbreakable. Instead of accepting incorrect spelling as a fact of life, the students need to see that with effort and concentration, they can reduce their errors. This unit will help them to recognize and solve their problems with spelling.

Spelling Lists.   You can use the lists of frequently misspelled and commonly confused words in the textbook and the list of additional spelling demons included in the Classroom Insights for this unit to diagnose individual spelling problems. Students could then work on their weak areas by using spelling lists and tests, oral drills, dictionary exercises, and crossword puzzles based on the spelling rules. Brainstorming about memory aids and homophones also helps to improve spelling.

Spelling and Writing.   You might use this unit as the basis for discussing spelling errors that are common in student writing. Demonstrate how spelling mistakes interfere with clear writing. For example, write a sentence such as the following one on the board: "The skis opened up and reign poored down." Ask the students to read the sentence and to tell whether it makes sense. Point out that this example shows how misspelled words can confuse readers or can cause readers to lose track of ideas. Urge the students to proofread their papers carefully and remind them that many of their errors probably stem from oversights rather than from an inability to spell. Suggest that the students try proofreading for spelling errors by beginning at the bottom of the page. They should read upward, focusing briefly on each individual word. Reading from the bottom can help the students to concentrate on individual words rather than meaning as a whole. Holding a ruler above the line they are reading will help them to concentrate. Whenever they find a word that may be misspelled, they could lightly circle it in pencil or place a check in the margin. Once they have

finished proofreading, they can use their dictionary to check the spelling. Remind the students that this is only one way to proofread; they can check Unit 11, "Revising," for additional methods.

Individual Methods.   Students can use this unit as a valuable reference. As they revise their compositions, they can check spelling rules and examples. They can follow a similar procedure when they record new vocabulary words in their notebook.

Suggest that students keep a record of their spelling errors in their notebook. They could record the word's correct spelling in the first column, underline the part of the word they have misspelled in the second column, divide the word into accented syllables in the third column, and write a memory device or the rule in the fourth column. Remind the students that recording this spelling information is the first step to changing spelling habits; they should follow the Procedure on page 480 to master the spelling of their problem words.

Urge the students to use all the senses they can when studying their words; they should see the word, hear it, say it, spell it aloud by syllables, and write it. Some people even find that tracing the letters with their finger helps. Explain to the students that if they use many of their senses, they are more likely to remember the spelling than if they use only one or two.

Spelling Rules and Exceptions.   Many students are frustrated by the need to memorize spelling rules and their exceptions. Remind the students that memorizing actually saves them time; if they know how to spell a word, they do not have to search through a dictionary. Reassure them that if they do forget how to spell a word, they can consult the textbook or their dictionary.

Additional Spelling Demons

accessories	aquarium
accurate	artificial
adolescent	attached
aerial	birch

blossom
butcher
catalogue
caterpillar
cereal
certificate
changing
civilization
closely
closing
companies
companion
complexion
consent
considerable
conversation
cough
cradle
curious
daintiness
debt
declaration
defense
deodorant
diameter
diary
document
doubt
earlier
entrance
errand
expedition
experiment
fault
fortunate
foundation
friendship
giraffe
glaciers
goal
graduate
gravy
guitar
happier
headache
ignorance
imagination

impatient
incident
influence
innocent
interior
inventor
investigate
iodine
jewelry
judicial
license
literature
marshmallows
medium
mentioned
meow
merely
monument
mosquito
motto
movement
multiplication
muscles
noisy
ordinary
organization
orphan
ouch
pageant
parachute
partly
passenger
patient
peaceful
peasant
physical
poisonous
porous
possession
poultry
practically
prairie
preamble
precious
preposition
primitive
propelled

proteins
quarrel
refugees
rescue
resources
roar
rosy
sample
shelves
shiny
shrubs
singular
skillful
source

startled
style
subscription
substance
thrift
thumb
tournament
travelers
trial
twelfth
vessel
weary
welfare
wharf

Reinforcement

Homophones. To help the students understand the impact that misspellings have on communication, have them make up sentences or phrases in which they use homophones. You might give them the following examples to get them started: "We went by plane to the Great Plains" and "It doesn't seem fair that we have to pay full fare on the bus." Remind the students that although these sentences can help them to remember the spelling of homophones, they would not be effective sentences in their compositions.

Word Search Games. To help the students practice their spelling and vocabulary, you might make up puzzles in which the students fill in the correct letters or whole words after hearing a clue from you. For example, you might give a clue like "This is the word for the fabric that a bride wears over her face as she walks down the aisle. Fill in the correct letters between the *v* and the *l* on your paper." Students can also improve their spelling by doing word searches from horizontally and vertically arranged letters.

Enrichment

Alternate Spellings. Students who are good spellers might enjoy using history of language books to investigate the origins of preferred and alternate spellings. They might do research on words like *theater, aesthetic, catalogue,* and so forth.

Irregular Spellings.   Students who are good spellers might also enjoy locating the plural forms of nouns or the principal parts of verbs that they do not use ordinarily in conversation and writing. Students could use their dictionary to find the plurals of the following nouns: *dormouse, alumnus, cranium, criterion,* and *species.* They might find the spelling of the principal parts of these and other verbs: *seek, cleave, strive, bear, beseech,* and *choose.* In addition to finding the spelling, which does not follow what the general rules would lead them to expect, students should also write the definitions of these nouns and verbs and include the spelling and definition in their notebook.

Unit 18 Vocabulary Skills

Students may be interested to know that they have two different vocabularies: one comprised of the words they use in speaking and writing, and the other comprised of words they recognize and understand somewhat but do not use. Point out to the students that they can expand their vocabulary and make their speaking and writing more precise by learning to use the words that they recognize.

Students can build their vocabulary in a variety of ways. Consider having them keep lists of words that they encounter in reading, in conversation, on television, and on radio. You might prefer to combine the study of spelling and vocabulary, providing the students with weekly lists and tests of words that you select. Regardless of your method of compiling lists of new words, urge the students to keep a vocabulary notebook, to use their dictionary, to pay attention to context clues, and to learn the definitions of new words.

Getting Meaning from Word Parts.   Students can expand their vocabulary rapidly and can increase their word-attack skills by studying the meanings of roots, prefixes, and suffixes. Consider giving them a weekly list of prefixes, suffixes, and roots, along with definitions of the word parts and several examples of words formed from those word parts. The students can use their dictionary to find their own examples. The ability to figure out the meanings of unfamiliar words should increase as the students learn more roots, prefixes, and suffixes.

Suggest that the students use the following strategies in using word parts to unlock the meanings of unfamiliar words:

1. Look for familiar word parts. Perhaps the only new thing to you about a word is a prefix or suffix. For example, in the word *inaudible,* you may recognize *audible.* If you know that the prefix *in-* means *not,* you will see quickly that *inaudible* means "not capable of being heard."

2. In applying the meanings of prefixes, roots, and suffixes, change the form of the root definition if necessary. For example, in the word *vision, -vis-* means "see" and *-ion* means "act of." Changing "act of see" to "act of seeing" helps you make more sense of the definition.

3. Remember that context clues will give you extra help in unlocking word meanings. For example, if you see the word *illegible* by itself, you would know from the prefix *il-* and the suffix *-ible* that the word means "not able to be" something, but without knowing the meaning of the root *-leg-,* you might be stumped. If the word were in a sentence, however, the context might give you a clue to that root: "Because the ink had smeared, her writing was *illegible.*" *Smeared* is the clue that you need to help you figure out that *illegible* means "not able to be read."

Synonyms and Connotation.   You can help students learn new words quickly if you present words in related groups. For example, provide a category such as "lacking in judgment" and words like *rash, imprudent, short-sighted, foolhardy,* and *reckless.* Have the students use their dictionary to find definitions for each word. After the students have used each word in a sentence, consider discussing the different shades of meaning of the words. Ask the students questions like these: "Which words have positive connotations? Which have negative connotations? Are any of the words neutral?"

Reinforcement

Vocabulary and Writing. If students tend to overuse certain verbs, such as *said* or *walked,* or certain adjectives, such as *nice* or *beautiful,* you might have them brainstorm to produce a list of synonyms. Students could record words like *mumbled, barked, stumbled, ambled,* and so forth in their vocabulary notebook or their writer's notebook along with a definition and a sentence for each word. These lists of synonyms could be used as a reference when the students are writing their paragraphs.

Vocabulary and Grammar. You might want to combine the study of grammar and vocabulary by having the students add suffixes to roots to create different parts of speech. With each change, the students would identify the part of speech. For example, the verb *serve* becomes the noun *servant* when the suffix *-ant* is added, the noun *servitude* when the *-tude* suffix is added, and the adjective *servile* when the suffix *-ile* is added. Once the students have added the suffixes and labeled the parts of speech, they should use each word in a sentence. You may want to refer the students to Unit 17 for the spelling rules that apply when adding suffixes to roots.

Another way to combine grammar study and vocabulary study might be to examine the additional meanings of common nouns or verbs. For example, the students could find all the meanings for such common nouns as *mouth, eye, boot, hand,* and *elbow.* The students should note the part of speech of each definition and should use each word in a sentence that shows the change of meaning. This exercise should help the students to realize that many words have more than one definition and grammatical use.

Enrichment

Vocabulary and Writing. Suggest that the students choose several sentences from their own compositions that could be improved by including more vivid words. Keeping the meaning the same, the students should rewrite each sentence by substituting more vivid nouns, verbs, and adjectives. For example, "The bread was good" might become "Sesame seeds on the crust of the aromatic bread added to its crunchy texture."

Word Origins. You can stimulate interest in words and help students to expand their vocabulary by having them do research on word origins. Small groups of students could use encyclopedias and books on the history of language to find out how various words have come into English. For example, one group of students could investigate words that came from the names of places, such as *cologne, turquoise, marathon, bedlam,* and *calico.* Another group of students might investigate words that came from the names of people, such as *macadam, boycott, platonic,* and *sandwich.* The groups might present their most interesting word stories accompanied by the spelling, pronunciation, definition, and part of speech of each word.

Unit 19   Study Skills

You might begin this unit by asking the students whether they know how to study. Encourage them to discuss their study habits by asking them questions such as the following: "Why should you listen carefully to all assignments as they are given? Should you review your notes from time to time, or wait until you need to study for a test? How do you locate specific information in your textbook?"

Suggest to the students that by following the Strategies and other suggestions in this unit, they should improve their reading skills and note-taking skills; through improving these skills, they will be able to use their study time more efficiently.

Choosing the Right Source.   Although the students may understand the parts of a book and the kinds of information that each part contains, they may still experience some uncertainty in deciding which part to use for locating a particular piece of information. Discuss fully with the students the parts of a book as they are detailed on pages 504–506. If the students are to study more efficiently, you will want to make sure that they know the difference between the table of contents and the index. You might follow the discussion with an activity in which the students use one of their textbooks to find specific information that you request.

Caution the students not to overlook the illustrations in a book—diagrams, charts, maps, tables, and photographs. Point out that illustrations often contain important, related information that amplifies the text. Illustrations can also help to clarify information presented in the text by showing it another way.

Using SQRRR Effectively.   You may wish to point out to the students that they should use the SQRRR (pronounced *S Q Three R*) reading method for information rather than for recreational reading. You may want to review each step carefully with the students, perhaps applying the steps to a particular selection as you review. Stress to the students that using the method effectively involves completing each of the five steps thoroughly and in order. Caution the students not to eliminate a step in order to save time. Emphasize that if they use the SQRRR reading method effectively, then they will read more efficiently and retain material better.

Taking Notes.   The students may already have had experience in taking notes. If so, you might want to discuss with them the occasions on which they have taken notes. Most will have taken notes in class, from a textbook or a reference book, or when interviewing someone.

Help the students to see that to be useful, notes should be succinct and specific. You might want to point out that taking notes is one time when writing incomplete sentences is not only acceptable, but desirable. Caution the students against making their notes so brief that they are later meaningless or so rough that they cannot be deciphered.

Selecting Information.   Deciding which information to include in their notes is perplexing to some students. To aid them, suggest that as they read, they ask themselves, *"Who?" "What?" "Where?" "When?" "Why?"* and *"How?"* Keeping these questions in mind as they read should help the students to focus on important information. The answers to these questions should be the basis of good study notes.

Remind the students that their knowledge of paragraph development will also help them to determine what is important as they read. You might want to take time to review Unit 10, "Writing Paragraphs." Encourage the students to be alert for topic sentences, supporting details, and concluding statements as they read.

If the students are accustomed to copying material verbatim from books, you might want to stress the importance of Strategy 1 on page 512. Explain that copying verbatim without crediting the source is plagiarism, and make sure that the students comprehend the seriousness of the issue. Also point out that putting information into their own words will help them to see whether they understand what they have read. If they cannot rephrase material, they need to reread the passage and look up all unfamiliar words.

Reinforcement

Improving Study Habits.   Have the class consider and discuss the best environment for studying as well as specific strategies for studying various subjects. For example, what is different in the way that they study social studies and Spanish?

They might also discuss how to fit study time into their daily schedule, where they study, and whether they use their study time efficiently.

When the students have completed their discussion, suggest that they make a classroom chart showing their collected ideas on good study habits. From time to time, they should review the chart and make revisions as they discover better ways to study.

Explaining the SQRRR. Consider having the students prepare a brief speech in which they describe the SQRRR reading method to members of an elementary school class. If you prefer, the students could do this as a group activity, with each member of the group addressing one step of the reading method. Encourage the students to include directions on how to follow each step by giving actual examples. Refer the students to Unit 21, "Speaking Skills," for help in preparing an oral presentation.

Enrichment

Reading and Taking Notes. Have the students apply the SQRRR reading method to a specific passage that you select. Then, using the Strategies for note taking, have the students take notes. You might want the students to compare their notes when everyone has finished. Encourage them to discuss why they did or did not include particular information in their notes.

Unit 20 Listening Skills

One way to introduce this unit is to have the students think of a person they know who is a good listener. The person could be a friend, a teacher, a counselor, or anyone else who shows attention and understanding when listening to the student. Have the students describe the characteristics of this good listener by answering

questions like the following: "How does the person show that he or she is paying attention to the speaker? How does he or she give feedback? How does he or she handle distractions?"

In addition, you might have the students discuss the consequences of not listening well. Ask them to describe the likely consequences of not listening carefully in the following situations:

1. A player does not listen when the coach changes defensive or offensive assignments for a particular game.
2. An owner of a car does not listen when a mechanic explains what is wrong with the car.
3. A traveler does not listen when someone gives directions.
4. A student does not listen when a counselor explains how to register for classes.

Before starting the unit, you might also suggest that the students think of times when they wished that they had listened more closely.

Sources of Speeches. Several of the suggestions for teaching this unit involve playing recordings of speeches for the students. Your school library or public library probably has records and cassettes of famous speeches that you can use. In addition, the audio-visual department of your school library may have videotapes of some speeches. Finally, you might try reading speeches aloud to the class. The library may have books with texts of speeches, and the students' literature anthology may have selections suitable for reading aloud. By using several of these sources, you should be able to present the students with a variety of speeches to listen to.

Eliminating Confusion. Explain to the students that from time to time, they will listen to lectures or participate in conversations in which they do not understand the speaker's statements. Confusion is particularly likely if the speaker is addressing a technical subject in which the listener has little expertise. Advise the students to respond to a lecture and a conversation in two different ways. Suggest that during a lecture, they write a brief question about the part of the speech that they do not understand. If they do not understand an entire section, they can leave a blank space in their notes to fill in later when they get clarification. Advise the students to continue listening and to resume taking notes when they understand the material. When the speaker has finished or asks for questions, the student can ask for clarification of the points causing confusion.

Suggest that during a conversation, the students wait for an appropriate break in the conversation and then ask the speaker for clarification of the ideas causing confusion. One way of asking for clarification is to ask for an example or other specific information that could make the idea more concrete. Finally, tell the students that most speakers prefer being asked questions to continuing to speak when their listeners do not understand.

Methods of Organization. The four methods of organizing a speech, described on pages 518–519, are similar to the organizational methods for writing, presented in Unit 10, "Writing Paragraphs." Before starting Section 20.3, you might ask the class to explain what is meant by each method of organization (topical, chronological, spatial, and problem-solution). Ask them what method of organization they would expect if they were listening to the following speakers:

1. A tour guide at the Great Wall of China
2. A geology professor lecturing on how granite is formed
3. A chef describing how to make gravy
4. An astronaut describing a flight into space

Deciding What Is Important. One perennial problem that students have in listening to a speech is deciding what is important and what is not. After the students have read pages 520–522, you might try the following activity. Select a recorded speech that you will play for the class. Listen to it beforehand, and write down ideas and details of varying importance. List these ideas and details on a sheet of paper that you duplicate and hand out

to the students. Play the speech for the students. After the speech is over, have them rank each idea and detail as follows: *1* for *Very important, 2* for *Fairly important,* and *3* for *Not important.* The students should write a short explanation of their reason for the rating that they give to each idea or detail. Then discuss the students' ratings in class and help them develop criteria for deciding what is and what is not important in a speech.

Signals and Transitions. To help the students become familiar with signals and transitions—both those listed on pages 519–520 and others that the students might add to the list—try the following activity. Play a speech for the students, and have them write every signal and transition that they hear. When the speech is finished, they should write one of the following purposes next to each word or phrase:

1. *Organization*—to indicate how the speech is organized
2. *Importance*—to tell the listener what is important
3. *Background*—to give the listener background information
4. *Transition*—to provide transition from one part of the speech to another

Reinforcement

Listening to an Editorial. Have the students listen to a radio or television editorial and write a summary of the position presented. The students should include both the speaker's main ideas and the important facts, reasons, and examples provided to support the ideas. The students can also evaluate how clearly stated and well supported the argument was.

Enrichment

Evaluating a Speech. Ask the students to evaluate a speech that they hear on a recording, on the radio, or on television. First they should write a short paragraph summarizing the main points in the speech. Then they should write a detailed evaluation of the speech, asking themselves questions such as the following:

1. Did the speaker completely develop the topic?
2. Was each key term defined adequately?
3. If the speech was about a problem, did the speaker present a realistic solution?
4. Was the speech unified? Were the main ideas and the supporting details logically connected?
5. Did the speaker provide signals and transitions to help the listener understand and take notes?

Unit 21 Speaking Skills

You might begin the unit by playing a recording of an impressive speech for the students. The speech might be on a record in the school library, or it could even be a videotape that the audio-visual department of your school can make available. Then ask the students to think of examples of ineffective speeches that they have heard on television or radio. Have the students compare and contrast effective and ineffective speeches. You might ask them questions like the following: "How did the effective speaker make you interested?" Why didn't the ineffective speech interest you? Which speech was easier to understand? Why? What made the delivery of one speaker effective and the delivery of the other speaker ineffective?" Conclude by pointing out to the students that giving an effective speech requires careful planning and a step-by-step process, just as writing an effective paragraph does.

Identifying the Purpose of a Speech.
Emphasize to the students the importance of establishing a purpose for a speech. They must first decide on their general purpose—to inform, to persuade, or to entertain. They should consider whether they are speaking to a small group, a class, or an assembly. They should gather information with the purpose and audience in mind. Then they should decide on the specific facts or points that they want the audience to understand from the speech. Students should keep the specific purpose in mind as they choose appropriate details and organize their speech.

You might wish to draw a parallel between writing a paragraph and giving a speech, for purpose is important in both forms of communication. The students may find it helpful to review Unit 10 for ways to write an effective paragraph. Students can use their skill at organizing and writing a paragraph as they organize and deliver a speech.

Deciding on Specific Purposes.   To help the students think of specific purposes for a speech, consider the following activity. Give them general subjects such as the following: animals, sports, transportation, magazines, television, video games, vacations, and clothes. For each subject, they should write three specific topics for a speech: one for a speech that informs, one for a speech that persuades, and one for a speech that entertains.

Outlining a Speech.   Make sure that the students understand that making an outline is helpful in preparing and delivering the speech. If they do not already know how to do so, help them organize their ideas into headings, subheadings, and related details. In fact, you may want to have them make and hand in an outline of their speeches before they deliver them. An explanation of how to outline is on pages 420–424 in Unit 15, "Writing a Report."

Writing Introductions.   To help the students learn to prepare different introductions for different subjects, audiences, and purposes, try the following activity. Prepare three buckets, one for general subjects, one for purposes, and one for audiences. Into each bucket put several folded slips of paper; those in the bucket for subjects should each name a subject, those in the bucket for purposes should specify one of the three purposes (to inform, to persuade, or to entertain), and those in the bucket for audiences should describe specific audiences. Have the students draw a slip from each bucket. Then they should write the introductory paragraph that would be appropriate for the subject, purpose, and audience that they have selected.

Least-to-Most-Important Idea.   Because most of the students are probably inexperienced in giving speeches, you might find it beneficial to have them use one method of organization at first. Moving from the least important to the most important idea is often effective. First, have them listen to a speech that is organized according to this method; the speech might be one that you prepare and deliver. Using the listening skills taught in Unit 20, the students should analyze the organization of the ideas in the speech, the placement of important details, and the use of transitional words and phrases. Then have the students make an outline for a short speech that will go from the least important idea to the most important idea. The outline should include transitions. Finally, have the students deliver the speech that they have prepared.

Overcoming Nervousness.   Some students will probably feel extremely nervous before giving a speech. You might be able to help them by reassuring them that thorough preparation of the speech will help them overcome their nervousness. Tell them not to memorize their speech word for word but to memorize the key ideas and the sequence of those ideas in the speech. They may also find it helpful to print important ideas, facts, and figures in large letters and numbers on the notes that they will use for delivering the speech. Stress also that they rehearse the speech in front of family members or in front of a mirror. Finally, recording the speech and playing it back may help them to remember the important parts of the speech and to improve their delivery of it.

Reinforcement

Student Interview.   Have the members of the class pair off and interview one another for information about their hobbies, career interests, accomplishments, places where they have lived, and so on. After interviews of twenty minutes, each student should prepare and deliver a five-minute speech introducing his or her partner to the class. Remind the students to use the speech strategies explained in the textbook.

Enrichment

Evaluating Speeches.   Consider working with the students to develop a list of guidelines for evaluating a speech. Then, as class members give their speech, have the rest of the class evaluate each speaker's performance, telling the speaker one or two areas in which he or she could improve speaking ability.

The students might also use these guidelines to chart their own progress as public speakers. Have them rate their own ability according to the criteria on the list. Then, at the end of the unit, they should evaluate themselves, taking note of areas in which they have improved and those in which they could still work for improvement.

Unit 22   Library Skills

Many students may equate using the library with looking up information in an encyclopedia or taking out books to read. To help them realize how varied a library's resources are, you might ask a series of questions like the following: "What country produces the most diamonds? What is the former name for Zimbabwe? What did the word *sincere* mean originally? Who was the famous woman who cautioned her husband to 'remember the ladies' when drafting the Constitution? How would you find a book by Rudyard Kipling?"

Explain that this unit will give the students the knowledge and strategies to enable them to use library resources with ease.

Using a Floor Plan. If the students have not already done so, suggest that they take the time to familiarize themselves with the floor plans of their school and local libraries. Point out that because libraries have separate sections for fiction, reference, nonfiction, and biography, knowing where these sections are will save the students time and effort. The floor plan is often clearly displayed for easy reference. Some larger libraries also provide maps for the visitors' convenience.

Fiction and Nonfiction. If the students confuse fiction and nonfiction, write both terms on the board and help the students to arrive at a definition of both. Then ask them to supply examples of both.

Point out to the students that some libraries have separate sections of books set aside for younger readers. Suggest that the students check their library to see if it has a separate section for Young Adult Literature.

Call Slips. You might want to remind the students that many large libraries have preprinted call slips for use in noting call numbers. Urge the students to use these forms. If possible, bring some samples to show the class. Encourage the students to take note cards or small slips of paper when they are doing research, in case call slips are not available.

Classification Systems. Although most school and small local libraries use the Dewey decimal system of classification, many larger libraries are converting to the Library of Congress system. You might remind the students to check which system a library uses before they begin their research on a specific topic.

Fictionalized Biographies. If the students do not know the term *fictionalized biography,* explain that in the fiction section of a library, they may find books that combine both factual and fictional information about well-known people. Students should know that these books are primarily for entertainment. If the students need to research the life of a famous person, suggest that they consult the biography section of the library.

Abbreviations. Some library catalog cards contain abbreviations that give additional information. Among these are *illus,* for "illustrated," *b/w* for "black and white photographs," *biblio.* for "bibliography," and *cont.* for "continued." Encourage the students to bring to class any additional abbreviations that they find while doing research and share them with the class.

General Reference Books. When the students are preparing the assignments in Section 22.3, help them to see that most general reference books are more appropriate for finding or verifying isolated facts than for in-depth study. The encyclopedia is the only general reference book that provides more than cursory information. Encourage the students to use resources other than general reference books when they are doing research for a report.

Using an Atlas. Some students may have difficulty locating specific places on a map in an atlas. If so, explain to the students how to use an index in an atlas and how to use the letter-number coordinates to each indexed city and town. Consider having the students locate several places for practice.

Non-Book Materials. Explain to the students that their library may have some non-book materials, such as films, filmstrips, and slides. In addition, have the students find out whether their library has sound recordings such as tapes, records, and cassettes. Finally, they should find out whether their library has videotapes that can be viewed on closed-circuit television.

The *Readers' Guide.* The students may be unaccustomed to using the *Readers' Guide.* To encourage them to use it, discuss in detail the excerpt on page 546 and make sure that they know how to read an entry. To help the students understand the importance of the *Readers' Guide,* point out that it is the source of the most up-to-date information on current topics.

Reinforcement

The Dewey Decimal System. As a class project, you might ask the students to prepare a classroom chart listing the categories of the Dewey decimal system with the subjects that belong under each category. The students could then refer to this chart before starting research on a topic for this or any other class.

General References. Have the students work in pairs, in which each member makes up fifteen questions based on information found in various general reference books. Then have the students exchange lists and find the answers to the questions.

General References. Have each student list one famous person and one topic of current interest. Then have the student find and list five sources of information about each. You might then suggest that the students use the sources to make notes for an oral or written report on one of their subjects.

The Card Catalog. If the students need additional work in using the card catalog, you might provide a list of topics and have the students use the card catalog to find books on those topics. As an alternative, you might list several names and have the students locate books by those authors.

Enrichment

Locating Reference Books. To help the students discover what reference books are available in their school library, divide the class into four teams. Have the first team list the titles and subjects of all dictionaries in the library. Have the second team investigate and record the types of encyclopedias. The third team could gather all information on atlases and gazetteers. The fourth team could research and list all biographical references. Have each team bring its findings to class; the students might want to consolidate the information in the form of a chart.

Unit 23   Test-Taking Skills

The focus of this unit is preparing for and taking tests. You might begin by having the students describe how they prepare for a test. You might also encourage them to discuss how they "attack" a test once they have received it. Explain to the students that in this unit they will learn useful techniques to follow when studying for and taking tests. Emphasize that these techniques will help them to develop a feeling of confidence that is based on being prepared. Being confident should help them to perform better on tests.

Early Preparation. Although the students might agree that cramming the night before a test is self-defeating, they might not recognize that cramming exists in situations that are less obvious but equally self-defeating. To illustrate, ask the students whether they have ever delayed reading previously assigned material until the teacher announces a test. If so, emphasize that reading and studying in manageable periods of time will increase their ability to retain what they read.

SQRRR Reading Method. You might suggest that the students apply the SQRRR reading method to the material that they must cover when studying for a test. Refer the students to pages 508–509 for a review of this method.

Studying with a Partner. Some students may find it helpful to study with a partner, but you might want to point out that this method does not work for everyone. If the students find that they are unable to concentrate, suggest that they study alone. For those students who can study efficiently with a partner, suggest that they choose a partner whose needs and methods of studying are similar to their own. Also remind them that studying with a partner should be only one part of their preparation for a test.

Mnemonic Devices. If the students have to learn formulas, rules, and other data that they think they might forget, suggest that they think of mnemonic devices to help them remember. For example, the word *Homes* should help the students to remember the Great Lakes: *H*uron, *O*ntario, *M*ichigan, *E*rie, and *S*uperior. Have the students suggest other devices for use in various classes.

Additional Test-Taking Hints. In addition to the Strategies presented in the unit, you might want to suggest that the students consider the following:

1. Arrive early or on time for a test. Lateness may increase tension as well as cause you to miss hearing valuable information or instructions.

2. After reading the directions, skim the contents of the test. Then estimate the time you think you will need to complete each part of the test. Pay attention to the time as you work.

3. Move on to the next question or part of a test if you have trouble. Return to the problem section later if you have time.

4. Leave time to review all your answers. Look for and correct careless mistakes in spelling and computation.

5. Review your paper to make sure that you answered all the questions and completed each part of the test.

6. Work at a comfortable pace. Do not be concerned about how fast the person next to you is working.

7. Ask the teacher to clarify any directions that confuse you.

8. Do not let yourself be overwhelmed by the appearance of a test. The information that you have learned should help to build your confidence.

If the students have any suggestions to add, discuss each suggestion with the class. The students should try to review these strategies before taking any test.

Changing Answers. Suggest that the students be careful about changing the answers to multiple-choice, true-false, and matching questions when they review their answers before handing in their papers. Caution them to make changes only if they are certain that they have made a mistake. Uncertainty causes many students to change correct answers to incorrect ones. Suggest that the students keep track of any changes that they make and see how often the change was really a correction.

Paragraph Tests. Some students may have difficulty answering questions that require a paragraph answer, or essay questions. To aid them, suggest that the students keep in mind what they learned about writing paragraphs. If necessary, refer them to Unit 10, "Writing Paragraphs." Suggest that if time permits, they should try to answer the question first on scratch paper. The main idea of the question should be their topic sentence; additional sentences should provide supporting details.

Reinforcement

Using the Strategies. A practical way for the students to apply the test-taking Strategies of this unit is in taking the Unit Tests in Part Two of the textbook. After taking the tests, the students might write a paragraph in which they tell how they used the Strategies and what effect the Strategies had on their performance.

Enrichment

Surveying Tests for Problems. In examining tests that they have taken in the past, the students should try to identify areas where using a particular Strategy might have helped them to improve their performance. Suggest that the students compile the results from their observations of past tests into a personal test-taking profile. Once the students have identified areas of weakness, they should review pertinent Strategies before taking a test.

Answers (continued)

Answers that do not fit conveniently next to the student page are presented here.

Unit 2

Exercise 1 *(page 62)*

1. Children | performed

2. they | Did sing

3. Everyone | applauded

4. (you) | Smile

5. you | Are leaving

Exercise 2 *(page 63)*

1.

2.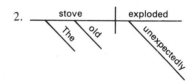

3. factory | will open — The, new, soon

4. sister | smiles — My, older, always, cheerfully

5.

6.

7.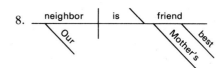

Exercise 3 *(page 65)*

1.

2.

3.

4.

5.

8.

9.

10.

Exercise 4 *(page 67)*

1.

2.

17.

3.

18.

4.

19.

5.

20.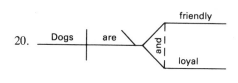

Test 1 *(pages 70–71)*

D.

16.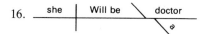

Practice 1 *(pages 68–69)*

D.

16.

17.

2.

18.

3.

19.

4.

20.

Unit 3

Exercise *(page 88)*

5.

6.

1.

7.

12.

Practice 1 *(pages 90–91)*

8.

D.

16.

9.

17.

10.

18.

11.

19.

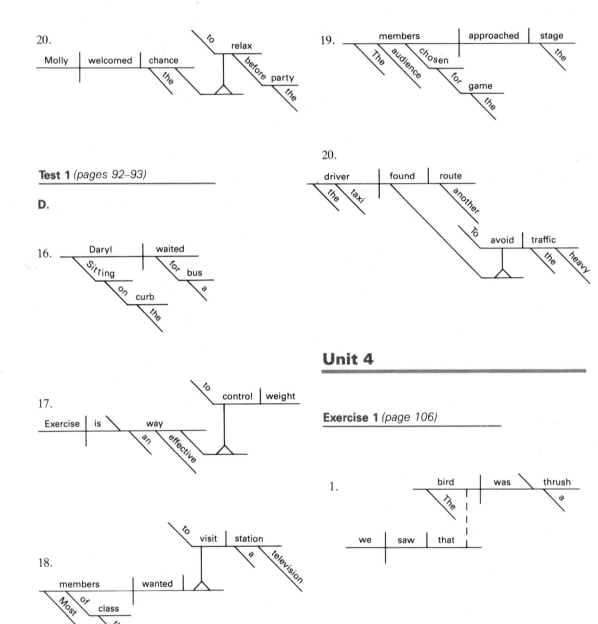

Test 1 *(pages 92–93)*

D.

Unit 4

Exercise 1 *(page 106)*

2.

3.

4.

5.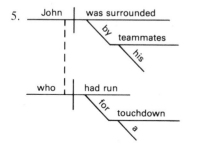

Exercise 2 *(page 107)*

1.

2.

3.

4.

Answers (continued) T**71**

5.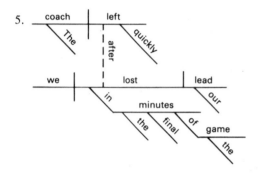

Practice 1 (page 108)

C.

11.

12.

13.

14.

15.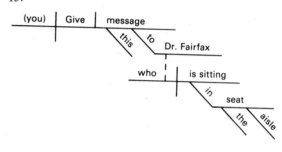

Test 1 (page 110)

C.

11.

12.

13.

14.

15.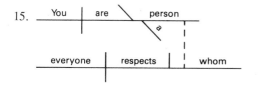

Unit 5

Exercise *(page 125)*

1.

2.

3.

4.

5.

Practice 1 *(pages 126–127)*

C.

11.

12.

13.

14.

15.

Test 1 *(pages 128–129)*

C.

11.

12.

13.

15.

14.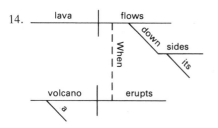

Unit 6

Exercise 2 *(pages 161–162)*

1. Each of the boys cooked his own supper.

2. Ann likes to play catch with her brothers.

3. The ant made its way along the edge of the table.

4. My aunt has her own business.

5. Anyone can attend the meeting if he or she is interested.

6. The kitten followed its mother from room to room.

7. Everyone did his or her best to guess the answer to the riddle.

8. Grandfather showed us his collection of scrimshaw.

9. The azalea bush has lost its blossoms.

10. Everyone fastened his or her seat belt.

Bibliography

Grammar, Usage, and Mechanics

Fowler, H.W. *A Dictionary of Modern English Usage.* 2d ed. Revised by Sir Ernest Gowers. Oxford: Clarendon Press, 1965.

Fraser, Ian S., and Lynda M. Hodson. "Twenty-One Kicks at the Grammar Horse: Close-Up: Grammar and Composition." *English Journal,* December 1978, pp. 49 – 54.

Jolly, Thomas. "ERIC/RCS Report: What If They Don't Speak Standard English?" *English Journal,* November 1979, pp. 87 – 89.

Knickerbocker, Joan L. "A Hidden Grammar Lesson." *Exercise Exchange,* Fall 1979, pp. 51 – 53.

Miller, Doris F. "Save Our Language: A Student Campaign." *Media and Methods,* November 1978, pp. 48 – 49.

Newman, Edwin. *A Civil Tongue.* New York: Warner Books, 1977.

----------. *Strictly Speaking.* New York: Warner Books, 1975.

Pearse, O. R. "Where After 'Process'? Further Points on Teaching the Passive." *English Language Teaching Journal,* January 1981, pp. 153 – 158.

Tchudi (Judy), Stephen N., and others. "Forms and Meaning: An Exercise in Punctuation." *Exercise Exchange,* Fall 1978, pp. 9 – 10.

Tritch, Maria. "Improving Vocabulary Problems in Co-Occurrence and Grammatical Marking." *English Teaching Forum,* April 1981, pp. 22 – 27

Weaver, Constance. *Grammar for Teachers: Perspectives and Definitions.* Urbana, Ill.: NCTE, 1979.

Wheeler, Rod. "Structure Interaction—Its 'Companions.' " *English Language Teaching Journal,* January 1981, pp. 106 – 109.

Teaching Composition

All About Letters. Rev. ed. Urbana, Ill.: United States Postal Service and NCTE, 1982.

Applebee, Arthur N. "Teaching High-Achieving Students: A Survey of the Winners of the 1977 NCTE Achievement Awards in Writing." *Research in the Teaching of English,* December 1978, pp. 339 ff.

Bramer, Mary. *The Desperation Day Book Two.* New York: Scholastic Book Services, 1980.

----------, and others. "Quick Takes." *Media and Methods,* May-June 1980, pp. 34 – 35.

Carlson, Ruth Kearney. *Sparkling Words: Three Hundred and Fifteen Practical and Creative Writing Ideas.* Rev. ed. Geneva, Ill.: Paladin House, 1979.

Coe, Richard. "Rhetoric and Composition: An Overview." *English Quarterly,* Fall 1978, pp. 67 – 73.

Cutter, Mary Low. "EJ Workshop: Journal Writing Is Only the Beginning." *English Journal,* October 1979, pp. 68 – 71.

D'Angelo, Frank. "Assumptions About the Teaching of Writing." *CEA Critic,* November 1978, pp. 11 – 16.

DeSalvo, Louise A. "Writers at Work." *Media and Methods,* December 1979, pp. 12 ff.

Donelson, Ken, and Beverly Haley. "One Way to the Short Story: Newspaper Clippings as Source Materials." *Exercise Exchange,* Spring 1982, pp. 9 – 14.

Fowles, Joy. "EJ Workshop: Ideas for Teaching Writing to Seventh and Eighth Grade Students." *English Journal,* September 1978, pp. 66 – 68.

Gnagy, Susan, and others. "EJ Workshop." *English Journal,* May 1980, pp. 64 – 68.

Hagemann, Meyly Chin. "Taking the 'Wrench' Out of Letter Writing." *English Journal,* March 1980, pp. 38 – 40.

Haley-James, Shirley M., ed. *Perspectives on Writing in Grades 1 – 8.* Urbana, Ill.: NCTE, 1981.

Hardy, A.W. "A Study of the Acquisition of the Skill of Creative Writing." *English in Education,* Fall 1978, pp. 46 ff.

Haymon, Theresa Drew. "Dialogue-Writing in the Teaching of Composition." *Reading Improvement,* Fall 1979, pp. 34 – 35.

Kirby, Dan R., and Tom Liner. "Revision: Yes, They Do It; Yes, You Can Teach It." *English Journal,* March 1980, pp. 41 – 45.

"Our Readers Write: I Tried It and Surprise, Surprise, It 'Really' Works." *English Journal,* February 1982, pp. 68 – 76.

Penfield, Elizabeth F. "Revision Revisited." *Exercise Exchange,* Spring 1978, pp. 19 – 22.

Petrosky, Anthony R., and James R. Brozick. "A Model for Teaching Writing Based upon Current Knowledge of the Composing Process." *English Journal,* January 1979, pp. 96 – 101.

Shaughnessy, Mina P. *Errors and expectations: A Guide for the Teacher of Basic Writing.* New York: Oxford University Press, 1977.

Shaw, Fran Weber. *30 Ways to Help You Write.* New York: Bantam Books, 1980.

Strunk, William, Jr., and E. B. White. *The Elements of Style.* 3d ed. New York: Macmillan, 1979.

Walling, Donovan R. "Sense Exploration and Descriptive Writing: A Practical Experience." *Exercise Exchange,* Fall 1978, pp. 30 – 34.

Woodward, Marcia Rollin. "A Tutorial Component in the ESL Writing Course." *English Language Teaching Journal,* January 1981, pp. 158 – 161.

Zinsser, William. *On Writing Well: An Informal Guide to Writing Nonfiction.* 2d ed. New York: Harper and Row, 1980.

Evaluating Composition

Fitzgibbon, Joseph. "Reducing the Drudgery of Correcting Compositions." *Media and Methods,* March 1980, pp. 27 – 29.

Myers, Miles. *A Procedure for Writing Assessment and Holistic Scoring.* Urbana, Ill.: NCTE and ERIC/RCS, 1980.

Najimy, Norman C., ed. *Measure for Measure: A Guidebook for Evaluating Students' Expository Writing*. Urbana, Ill.: NCTE, 1981.

Spelling and Vocabulary

The American Heritage School Dictionary. Boston: Houghton Mifflin, 1977.
The Right Word: A Concise Thesaurus. Boston, Houghton Mifflin, 1978.
Roget's II: The New Thesaurus. Boston: Houghton Mifflin, 1978.
The Word Book. Boston: Houghton Mifflin, 1976.
The Written Word. Boston: Houghton Mifflin, 1977.

Speaking and Listening Skills

Alder, Mortimer J. *How to Speak, How to Listen*. New York: Macmillan, 1983.
Devine, Thomas C. *Listening Skills Schoolwide: Activities and Programs*. Urbana, Ill.: ERIC/RCS and NCTE, 1982.
Gallo, Donald R. "The Heard Word." *Connecticut English Journal,* Fall 1979, pp. 1 – 144.
Kroll, Barry M., and Roberta J. Vann. *Exploring Speaking-Writing Relationships, Connections and Contrasts*. Urbana, Ill.: NCTE, 1981.

Study and Test-Taking Skills

Cooper, Charles R., ed. *The Nature and Measurement of Competency in English*. Urbana, Ill.: NCTE, 1981.
Tchudi (Judy), Stephen N. "Testing and Measuring Growth in English." In *The ABC's of Literacy: A Guide for Parents and Educators*. New York: Oxford University Press, 1980, pp. 138 – 165.
Zjawin, Dorothy. "Ways to Help Kids Take Tests." *Instructor,* October 1979, pp. 70 – 71.

Houghton Mifflin English

Grammar and Composition

Second Course

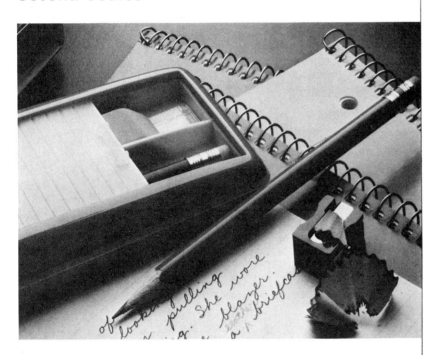

Houghton Mifflin Company • **Boston**

Atlanta   Dallas   Geneva, Illinois
Hopewell, New Jersey   Palo Alto   Toronto

Authors

Ann Cole Brown   Lecturer in English composition and literature at Northern Virginia Community College in Alexandria, Virginia

Jeffrey Nilson   Former teacher of English at the Wixon Middle School, South Dennis, Massachusetts, and independent computer software designer

Fran Weber Shaw   Assistant Professor of English and Coordinator of the Writing Center at the University of Connecticut, Stamford

Richard A. Weldon   Vice Principal, Associate Dean of Studies, and teacher of English at the Christian Brothers High School in Sacramento, California

Editorial Advisers

Edwin Newman   Veteran broadcast journalist, author, and chairman of the Usage Panel of the *American Heritage Dictionary of the English Language*

Robert Cotton   Vice Principal, Curriculum Director, and former chairman of the English Department at Servite High School in Anaheim, California

Special Contributors

Ernestine Sewell, University of Texas at Arlington

Luella M. Wolff, Washburn University, Topeka, Kansas

Acknowledgments

The Publisher gratefully acknowledges the cooperation of the National Council of Teachers of English for making available student writing from the Council's Achievement Awards in Writing Program.

The Publisher also wishes to thank all the students whose names appear in this textbook for granting permission to use their writing as models. The editors and the Publisher have been solely responsible for selecting the student writing used as models.

(Acknowledgments continue on page 567.)

Printed in U.S.A.

ISBN: 0-395-31402-X

Contents

Part One **Grammar, Usage, and Mechanics**   1

    Unit 1   Parts of Speech   2

       1.1   Nouns   3
       1.2   Pronouns   7
       1.3   Verbs   11
       1.4   Adjectives   17
       1.5   Adverbs   22
       1.6   Prepositions   28
       1.7   Conjunctions   32
       1.8   Interjections   36

    Unit 2   Sentence Structure   44

       2.1   Sentence Classified by Purpose   45
       2.2   Simple Subjects
           and Simple Predicates   47
       2.3   Compound Subjects
           and Compound Predicates   49
       2.4   Complete Subjects
           and Complete Predicates   51
       2.5   Complements   55
       2.6   Sentence Diagrams   61

    Unit 3   Phrases   72

       3.1   Prepositional Phrases   73
       3.2   Verbals and Verbal Phrases   77
       3.3   Diagraming Sentences with Phrases   85

    Unit 4   Clauses   94

       4.1   Independent Clauses   95
       4.2   Subordinate Clauses   96
       4.3   Diagraming Sentences with Clauses   104

iii

Unit 5 Compound Sentences
and Complex Sentences   112

    5.1 Sentences Classified by Structure   113
    5.2 Writing Complete Sentences   118
    5.3 Diagraming Sentences   124

Unit 6 Usage   130

    6.1 Correct Use of Verbs   131
    6.2 Subject-Verb Agreement   144
    6.3 Correct Use of Pronouns   157
    6.4 Correct Use of Modifiers   171
    6.5 Usage Notes   179

Unit 7 Mechanics   196

    7.1 Capitalization   197
    7.2 Punctuation   206
    7.3 Italics   224
    7.4 Using Numbers in Writing   226
    7.5 Proofreading Symbols   227
    7.6 Manuscript Form   228

Part Two Composition   236

Unit 8 Prewriting   238

    8.1 Finding Ideas for Writing   239
    8.2 Gathering and Developing Ideas   244
    8.3 Focusing Your Ideas   249

Unit 9 Writing Sentences   260

    9.1 Expressing Your Ideas
in Sentences   261
    9.2 Expanding Sentences
with Modifiers   265
    9.3 Considering Your Audience
and Your Purpose   268

iv

Unit 10 Writing Paragraphs   276

    10.1 What Is a Paragraph?   277
    10.2 Planning a Paragraph   280
    10.3 Writing a Topic Sentence   285
    10.4 Writing Supporting Sentences   288
    10.5 Organizing Supporting Sentences   293
    10.6 Writing a Concluding Sentence   300

Unit 11 Revising   310

    11.1 Revising Paragraphs   311
    11.2 Revising Sentences: Coordination   316
    11.3 Revising Sentences: Subordination   321
    11.4 Revising Sentences: Prepositional
          Phrases   325
    11.5 Revising Sentences: Conciseness   327
    11.6 Revising Sentences: Variety   330
    11.7 Completing Your Revision   333

Unit 12 Explaining   340

    12.1 Explaining What Something Is   341
    12.2 Explaining How to Get to a Place   344
    12.3 Explaining How to Make
          or Do Something   348

Unit 13 Describing   360

    13.1 Using Your Senses   361
    13.2 Using Descriptive Words   365
    13.3 Describing a Place   368
    13.4 Describing People   372

Unit 14 Narrating   382

    14.1 Planning Your Narrative   383
    14.2 Writing Your Narrative   389

v

Unit 15 Writing a Report   408

    15.1 Selecting and Limiting a Topic   409
    15.2 Gathering Information   413
    15.3 Organizing Your Information   420
    15.4 Writing Your Report   424
    15.5 Revising and Finishing Your Report   430
    15.6 Writing a Book Report   435

Unit 16 Writing Letters   452

    16.1 Writing Social Letters   453
    16.2 Writing Business Letters   460

Part Three Related Skills   478

Unit 17 Spelling Skills   480

    17.1 How to Study Spelling Words   480
    17.2 Spelling Rules   481
    17.3 The *ie/ei* Pattern   486
    17.4 Spelling What You Hear   487
    17.5 Spelling What You See   488
    17.6 Other Spelling Helps   490

Unit 18 Vocabulary Skills   492

    18.1 How to Learn New Words   492
    18.2 Using Context to Get Meaning   493
    18.3 How to Learn New Words
             from Word Parts   494
    18.4 How to Choose the Best Word   498
    18.5 Using the Dictionary   500

Unit 19 Study Skills   504

    19.1 Reading Skills   504
    19.2 Note-Taking Skills   512

Unit 20 Listening Skills   514

    20.1 Why Learn Listening Skills?   514
    20.2 Getting Ready to Listen   516
    20.3 What to Listen For   517
    20.4 Being a Responsive
           and Courteous Listener   522

Unit 21 Speaking Skills   524

    21.1 Speaking to a Group   524
    21.2 Planning Your Speech   526
    21.3 Organizing Your Speech   530
    21.4 Delivering Your Speech   533

Unit 22 Library Skills   536

    22.1 How to Locate Books   536
    22.2 The Card Catalog   539
    22.3 General Reference Books   542
    22.4 Biographical Reference Books   545
    22.5 The *Readers' Guide*
           to Periodical Literature   546

Unit 23 Test-Taking Skills   548

    23.1 Preparing for a Test   548
    23.2 Taking a Test   550

Index   558

Acknowledgments   567

Checklist for Revision   568

Part One

Grammar, Usage, and Mechanics

Unit 1	Parts of Speech	2
Unit 2	Sentence Structure	44
Unit 3	Phrases	72
Unit 4	Clauses	94
Unit 5	Compound Sentences and Complex Sentences	112
Unit 6	Usage	130
Unit 7	Mechanics	196

When you put your thoughts into writing, your goal is to present them clearly. These units on English grammar, usage, and mechanics provide rules and guidelines that will help you to express your thoughts in writing. For example, you can learn how to use conjunctions to reveal the connections between your ideas. You can also refer to the rules to find out what form of a modifier to use or where to place commas in your sentences.

As you study the units in Part One, you will see that they describe the English language today. By learning about our language and applying its rules, you will be better able to convey your thoughts in sentences that your readers will easily understand.

Unit 1

After studying this unit, students should be able to do the following:

- Identify proper, common, compound, and collective nouns.

- Identify personal pronouns and indefinite, interrogative, demonstrative, and relative pronouns.

- Identify action verbs, linking verbs, and auxiliary verbs.

- Identify adjectives, proper adjectives, and nouns and pronouns used as adjectives, and identify the words that they modify.

- Identify adverbs that modify verbs, adverbs that modify adjectives, and adverbs that modify adverbs, and distinguish between adjectives and adverbs.

- Identify prepositions and their objects.

- Identify coordinating, correlative, and subordinating conjunctions.

- Identify interjections.

Parts of Speech

Unit Preview

When you write or speak, you choose the words that you use from the eight parts of speech: nouns, pronouns, verbs, adjectives, adverbs, prepositions, conjunctions, and interjections. For example, in talking about an experience, you might begin with the noun *branch*. Then to show which branch, you might add descriptive words:

That heavy branch . . .

Now you need a word that shows what the branch did.

That heavy branch **hit** . . .

Did the branch actually hit someone or something? Or did it just miss? Now you need another descriptive word.

That heavy branch **nearly** hit . . .

Who or what was nearly hit by the branch? Suppose that you and a friend were nearly hit by the branch. You now need a noun and a pronoun joined by a conjunction:

That heavy branch nearly hit **Tim and me.**

Now you need an interjection to express your relief at not having been hit by the branch.

Whew! That heavy branch nearly hit Tim and me.

2

You have used several parts of speech to form this sentence. To communicate effectively, you must be familiar with all of the parts of speech and with the ways in which they fit together to make sentences.

For Analysis   Answer the questions about the following sentence: *The black cat quietly crossed the floor.*

1. Which word tells whom or what the sentence is about?
2. Which word describes the action in the sentence?
3. Which descriptive word tells which?
4. Which descriptive word tells how?
5. Which word identifies the receiver of the action in the sentence?

If you were able to answer the preceding questions, you already understand that different words serve different functions in sentences. In this unit you will learn more about the functions of the eight parts of speech.

1.1   Nouns

A **noun** is a word that names a person, a place, a thing, or an idea. The first words that you spoke were probably nouns. People use nouns to refer to the world around them and to the ideas that they have about the world.

PERSONS	PLACES	THINGS	IDEAS
pitcher	stadium	field	talent
Satchel Paige	Hall of Fame	baseball	skill
team	Cooperstown	bat	courage

There are several kinds of nouns. All nouns are either common or proper. Some nouns are collective nouns, and some are compound nouns.

Teaching Suggestions

See ''Classroom Insights'' for Unit 1 in the front of this Teacher's Edition.

Program Resources

Resource Book, Second Course:
    Diagnostic Test, Unit 1
    Achievement Test, Unit 1
    Bonus Activities, Unit 1
    Extra Practice, Unit 1
    Unit Test, Unit 1
Practice Book, Second Course,
    Unit 1
Tests, Second Course, Unit 1

Related Resources

Houghton Mifflin Microcourse:
    Language Arts, Levels 7, 8
*The American Heritage
    Dictionary of the English
    Language*

For Analysis *(page 3)*

1. The word cat tells what the sentence is about.
2. The word crossed tells the action.
3. The descriptive word black tells which.
4. The descriptive word quietly tells how.
5. The word floor identifies the receiver of the action.

Exercise 1 *(page 4)*

Answers may vary. Samples:

1. catcher—Common; Carlton Fisk
2. senator—Common; Edward M. Kennedy
3. Eiffel Tower—Proper; landmark
4. Mexico—Proper; country
5. company—Common; Brown Corporation
6. bank—Common; Metropolitan Bank of Ohio
7. entertainer—Common; Lena Horne
8. Mars—Proper; planet
9. University of Michigan —Proper; college
10. Los Angeles Dodgers—Proper; team
11. dancer—Common; Nureyev
12. O. J. Simpson—Proper; athlete
13. cousin—Common; Alice
14. Harlem Globetrotters —Proper; team
15. Katharine Hepburn—Proper; actress
16. Staten Island—Proper; place

1.1a   Proper and Common Nouns

A **proper noun** names a particular person, place, thing, or idea. A proper noun always begins with a capital letter. Some proper nouns consist of more than one word: *Empire State Building.*

A **common noun** refers to a class of persons, places, things, or ideas. Do not capitalize a common noun unless it begins a sentence.

COMMON NOUNS   In the **mountains** the **snows** lasted until **spring.**

PROPER NOUNS   In the **Rockies** the snows lasted until **May.**

Here are some examples of common and proper nouns:

	COMMON NOUNS	PROPER NOUNS
PERSONS	champion	Chris Evert Lloyd
PLACES	town	Huntington
THINGS	ship	the *Norway*
IDEAS	religion	Islam

Exercise 1   Proper and Common Nouns   On your paper, label the following nouns *Proper* or *Common.* For each common noun, write a related proper noun. For each proper noun, write a related common noun.

SAMPLE   pitcher

ANSWER   pitcher—common; Steve Carlton

1. catcher
2. senator
3. Eiffel Tower
4. Mexico
5. company
6. bank
7. entertainer
8. Mars
9. University of Michigan
10. Los Angeles Dodgers
11. dancer
12. O. J. Simpson
13. cousin
14. Harlem Globetrotters
15. Katharine Hepburn
16. Staten Island

4

1.1b Compound Nouns

A **compound noun** is a noun that consists of two or more words. Some compound nouns are written as single words; others as separate words, and others as words separated by hyphens.

SINGLE WORDS	football, clubhouse, heartbeat, sunburn
SEPARATE WORDS	high school, tiger lily, disk jockey
HYPHENS	hurdy-gurdy, standard-bearer, mother-of-pearl

A proper noun that consists of more than one word is a compound noun.

COMPOUND NOUNS	Dr. Formato, House of Representatives

Exercise 2 Compound Nouns *Step 1:* Read the following list of words: *line, plate, springs, houses, cakes. Step 2:* Combine each of the words from the list with the word *hot* to form a compound word. *Step 3:* On your paper, write the compound word next to the number of the sentence in which it makes sense. Use a dictionary to check the spelling and capitalization of each compound noun.

SAMPLE	A __?__ is someone who has a quick temper.
ANSWER	hothead

1. My grandmother uses a __?__ to keep food warm at the table.
2. For breakfast, Dad made __?__ with ground-wheat flour.
3. Many tropical plants are grown in __?__.
4. The __?__ to the President's office is always open.
5. We visited __?__, a popular resort in Arkansas.

Assignment Compound Nouns The word *house* is used to form many compound nouns. On your paper, write

Exercise 2 *(page 5)*

1. hot plate
2. hot cakes
3. hothouses
4. hot line
5. Hot Springs

5

Exercise 3 *(page 6)*

1. class—Collective; cave; magazine
2. colony—Collective; bats; cave
3. school—Collective; fish; stream; entrance; cave
4. flock—Collective; birds; cliff; cave
5. daybreak; troop—Collective; hike; cave
6. treasure; band—Collective; pirates
7. morning; group—Collective; cave
8. eyes; darkness
9. flashlights; drawings; walls
10. drawings; tribe—Collective

as many of those compound nouns as you can think of. Use the dictionary to check the spellings of your words. Then use each of the compound nouns in a sentence.

1.1c   Collective Nouns

A **collective noun** is a noun that refers to a group of people, places, or things but is singular in form.

Class is dismissed.
The **audience** remains seated during the intermission.

Exercise 3   Collective Nouns   On your paper, write the nouns in the following sentences. Write *Collective* next to the collective nouns. Two sentences do not contain collective nouns.

SAMPLE   By nightfall our party had reached the hills near the cave.

ANSWER   nightfall; party—Collective; hills; cave

1. Our class had read about the cave in a magazine.
2. A colony of bats lived in the cave.
3. A small school of fish swam in the stream that was near the entrance to the cave.
4. A flock of rare birds nested in the cliff above the cave.
5. At daybreak our troop began its hike to the cave.
6. Perhaps we would find a treasure left by a band of pirates.
7. In the morning our group entered the cave.
8. Our eyes soon adjusted to the darkness.
9. With our flashlights, we could see some drawings on the walls.
10. The drawings belonged to an ancient tribe that had once lived there.

6

1.2 Pronouns

A **pronoun** is a word that takes the place of a noun. You use pronouns to refer to persons, places, things, or ideas without renaming them.

Anita won the *marathon*. **She** ran **it** in record time. [The pronoun *She* takes the place of the noun *Anita*. The pronoun *it* takes the place of the noun *marathon*.]

The noun or pronoun that a pronoun replaces is called the **antecedent** of the pronoun. In the example above, the noun *Anita* is the antecedent of the pronoun *She*. The noun *marathon* is the antecedent of the pronoun *it*. Sometimes an antecedent is not stated within the sentence.

Let **me** help **you** with that package.

In this section, you will study five kinds of pronouns: personal pronouns, indefinite pronouns, interrogative pronouns, demonstrative pronouns, and relative pronouns.

1.2a   Personal Pronouns

Personal pronouns change their forms to show person, number, gender, and case.

Person.   Personal pronouns are in the first person, the second person, or the third person. You use a first-person pronoun to refer to yourself. You use a second-person pronoun to refer to the person whom you are speaking or writing to. You use a third-person pronoun to refer to the person, place, thing, or idea being spoken about.

FIRST PERSON   I think that **I** will go to bed now.

SECOND PERSON   Have **you** returned the book to the library?

THIRD PERSON   **She** chained the bikes to the rack.

7

Exercise 1 *(pages 8–9)*

See page 9 for the answers.

The chart that appears later on this page lists the first-person, second-person, and third-person pronouns.

Number.   Number means whether the pronoun is singular or plural. Personal pronouns have different forms depending on whether their antecedents are singular or plural.

SINGULAR   **He** blew the whistle.

PLURAL   **They** blew the whistles.

Gender.   The third-person-singular personal pronouns have different forms for the three genders: masculine, feminine, and neuter. Masculine pronouns (*he, him, his*) refer to nouns that name males. Feminine pronouns (*she, her, hers*) refer to nouns that name females. Neuter pronouns (*it, its*) refer to places, things, and ideas.

Possessive Pronouns.   Personal pronouns have possessive forms to show ownership or belonging. Such pronouns are possessive pronouns. The following chart shows the personal pronouns; the possessive forms are in parentheses. Some possessive forms can be used as adjectives *(pages 20–21)*.

	SINGULAR	PLURAL
FIRST PERSON	I, me (my, mine)	we, us (our, ours)
SECOND PERSON	you (your, yours)	you (your, yours)
THIRD PERSON	he, him (his)	them, they
	she, her (her, hers)	(their, theirs)
	it (its)	

Exercise 1 Personal Pronouns   On your paper, write the personal pronouns in the following sentences. Tell whether each pronoun is in the first person, the second person, or the third person. Also tell whether each personal pronoun (except *you*) is singular or plural.

SAMPLE   Did he give the check to Mother or to you?

ANSWER   He—third person, singular; you—second person

1. I told them to stop it.
2. They elected us co-captains.
3. Between you and me, the plans will never succeed.
4. Every Friday she tutors Amanda in math.
5. We cheered the team to victory.
6. He wrapped Jan's present and mailed it to her the next day.
7. I invited her to the concert.
8. She challenged me to a game of chess.
9. I painted the room pale yellow.
10. He studied thoroughly for the test.
11. Shall I send the record to him or to her?
12. Did you call me last night?

1.2b Other Kinds of Pronouns

Indefinite Pronouns

Indefinite pronouns refer to people, places, or things in general. You often use indefinite pronouns without antecedents.

I heard **someone** knock.

I opened the door, but **nobody** was there.

The following list contains some frequently used indefinite pronouns.

all	everyone	neither	others
anybody	everything	nobody	several
anyone	few	none	some
anything	many	no one	somebody
each	most	nothing	someone
either	much	one	something
everybody			

Exercise 1 *(pages 8–9)*

1. I—first person, singular; them—third person, plural; it—third person, singular
2. They—third person, plural; us—first person, plural
3. you—second person; me—first person, singular
4. she—third person, singular
5. We—first person, plural
6. He—third person, singular; it—third person, singular; her—third person, singular
7. I—first person, singular; her—third person, singular
8. She—third person, singular; me—first person, singular
9. I—first person, singular
10. He—third person, singular
11. I—first person, singular; him—third person, singular; her—third person, singular
12. you—second person; me—first person, singular

9

Interrogative Pronouns

Interrogative pronouns are pronouns that introduce questions. The most frequently used interrogative pronouns are *who, whom, which,* and *what.*

Who is that masked man?
With **whom** are you going?
Which is the better route to Midville?
What are you doing tomorrow?

Demonstrative Pronouns

Demonstrative pronouns tell which one or which group of persons, places, or things is referred to. A list of demonstrative pronouns follows:

that   this   these   those

That and *those* are used to point out something far away. *This* and *these* point out something nearby.

This is first base; **that** is home plate.
These are ripe; **those** are still green.

Relative Pronouns

Relative pronouns are pronouns that introduce adjective clauses *(Unit 4),* which are word groups that modify nouns or pronouns. A relative pronoun that introduces an adjective clause always has an antecedent. A list of the relative pronouns follows:

who   whose   that
whom   which

The *runner* **who** finished first is from Cuba.

The *runner* **whom** everyone cheered was Salazar.

Do you know the *runner* **whose** sponsor donated a prize?

10

The *race,* **which** is run every year, attracts thousands.

One *marathon* **that** many runners enter is the Boston Marathon.

Exercise 2 Pronouns in a Passage   Number your paper from 1 to 8. Next to each number, list the pronouns in that sentence. Label each pronoun *Personal, Indefinite, Interrogative, Demonstrative,* or *Relative.*

SAMPLE The bowerbird is one of the birds that are native to Australia and New Guinea.

ANSWER one—Indefinite; that—Relative

(1) Birds build nests that they use as homes for young birds. (2) Some, like the bowerbird, build nests that are attached to bowers, which are shaded areas created by tree boughs or vines. (3) Many build bowers by heaping twigs and grasses between two trees. (4) Others simply pile twigs around the base of a bush. (5) Some decorate the bowers with colored stones, bright shells, and shiny beads. (6) What accounts for the special display? (7) That is something no one really knows. (8) The bowerbird has dull feathers that people do not notice.

Assignment Nouns and Pronouns   From a newspaper or a magazine, cut out an article about a sports personality. Tape the article to a piece of notebook paper and underline each noun and pronoun that refers to the person that the article is about. Beneath the article, list each pronoun and label it *Personal, Interrogative, Indefinite, Demonstrative,* or *Relative.*

1.3   Verbs

A **verb** is a word that expresses an action or a state of being. There are three kinds of verbs: action verbs, linking verbs, and auxiliary verbs.

11

Exercise 2 *(page 11)*

1. that—Relative;
   they—Personal
2. Some—Indefinite;
   that—Relative;
   which—Relative
3. Many—Indefinite
4. Others—Indefinite
5. Some—Indefinite
6. What—Interrogative
7. That—Demonstrative;
   something—Indefinite;
   no one—Indefinite
8. that—Relative

Exercise 1 *(page 12)*

1. struggled, flapped
2. made
3. learned
4. killed
5. made
6. opposed
7. bred
8. freed
9. brought
10. walked, hopped
11. flung
12. soared, dived

1.3a Action Verbs

An **action verb** describes the behavior or action of someone or something. Some action verbs express physical actions. Other action verbs express mental activities.

PHYSICAL   The hikers **leaned** against the sun-warmed boulders.

MENTAL   They **hoped** for sunny skies and cool breezes.

Exercise 1 Action Verbs   On your paper, write the action verbs in the following sentences. Some sentences have more than one action verb.

SAMPLE   The scientists carried the cages to the top of the mountain.

ANSWER   carried

1. Inside their cages, four peregrine falcons struggled and flapped their wings.
2. Scientists at a nearby university made a study of falcons.
3. They learned a great deal about the behavior of peregrine falcons in captivity.
4. During the 1960s pesticides killed peregrine falcons by the thousands.
5. Scientists made a plan for the protection of the peregrine falcon.
6. They opposed the use of certain pesticides.
7. They bred the falcons in captivity.
8. Then they freed the birds.
9. One summer morning, the scientists brought the birds to the mountains.
10. One falcon walked to the edge of the cliff and hopped along the rocky ledge.
11. Then she flung herself into the air.
12. She soared and dived gracefully through the air.

12

1.3b Linking Verbs

A **linking verb** is a verb that connects a noun or a pronoun with words that identify or describe the noun or the pronoun.

> The sky **was** clear. [The verb, *was,* links the descriptive word, *clear,* to the noun, *sky.*]
>
> Our guides **were** veterans of the outdoors. [The verb, *were,* links the identifying word, *veterans,* to the noun, *guides.*]

The most frequently used linking verbs are the different forms of the verb *be.* Some of these forms appear in the following list:

am	can be	shall have been
are	could be	will have been
be	has been	may have been
being	have been	might have been
is	shall be	could have been
was	should be	should have been
were	will be	would have been
	would be	

The following verbs may also be used as linking verbs:

appear	grow	smell	remain
become	look	sound	stay
feel	seem	taste	

> The dog **appeared** friendly. [*Appeared* links the descriptive word, *friendly,* to the noun, *dog.*]
>
> He **became** my best friend. [*Became* links the identifying word, *friend,* to the pronoun, *He.*]

Some verbs can be either linking verbs or action verbs, depending on how they are used in a sentence.

13

Exercise 2 *(page 14)*

1. feel
2. appears
3. smelled
4. tasted
5. remained
6. is
7. are
8. stayed
9. seemed
10. became

ACTION VERB   I **tasted** the dandelion salad. [*Tasted* expresses an action.]

LINKING VERB   It **tasted** bitter. [*Tasted* links the descriptive word, *bitter,* to the pronoun, *it.*]

Exercise 2   Linking Verbs   On your paper, write the linking verbs in the following sentences.

SAMPLE   The infield looks wet.
ANSWER   looks

1. I still feel energetic, don't you?
2. The water appears unusually calm tonight.
3. The freshly baked bread smelled delicious.
4. It tasted even better.
5. Everyone remained quiet during the President's speech.
6. Dr. Peter White is our dentist.
7. Those passengers are immigrants from Greece.
8. The apples stayed crisp for several days.
9. The assignment seemed difficult at first.
10. We became restless during the long intermission.

1.3c   Auxiliary Verbs

Sometimes an action verb or a linking verb needs the help of one or more other verbs. This other verb is called an **auxiliary verb,** or a **helping verb.** The verb that it helps is called the **main verb.** Together, a main verb and one or more auxiliary verbs form a **verb phrase.** In the following sentences, the auxiliary verbs are in italic type, and the main verbs are in boldface type.

The boulder *had* **slipped** inch by inch.
Suddenly it *was* **hurtling** toward them.

14

The most common auxiliary verbs are forms of *be, have,* and *do.* Common auxiliary verbs are in the following list:

am, are, be, been, is, was, were   will, would
have, has, had   can, could
do, does, did   may, might
shall, should   must

Forms of *be, have,* and *do* can be either auxiliary verbs or main verbs.

MAIN VERB	AUXILIARY VERB
I **am** tired.	I *am* **leaving**.
I **have** a new book.	I *have* **read** most of it.
I **did** my best.	I *did* **try** my hardest.

A verb phrase may contain two or even three auxiliary verbs.

The geraniums *should have been* **transplanted** by now.

Sometimes, a verb phrase is interrupted by another word, such as *not* or *never.*

You *should* not **transplant** the flowers until late spring.

In questions, the verb phrase is usually interrupted by other words.

Do geraniums **grow** indoors?
Can they *be* **transplanted** again in the spring?

Exercise 3   Verb Phrases   On your paper, write the verb phrases in the following sentences. Underline the auxiliary verbs once and the main verbs twice.

SAMPLE   I have never visited Chicago before.
ANSWER   have visited

1. You are spoiling that dog.
2. Who could have drawn that clever cartoon?

Exercise 3 *(pages 15–16)*

1. are spoiling
2. could have drawn

(Continue on the next page.)

15

Exercise 3 *(pages 15–16),*
continued

3. has seen
4. had driven
5. must have loosened
6. Will be published
7. has worked
8. must have been daydreaming
9. should have been repaired
10. can play

3. The doctor has not seen the patient yet.
4. Dad had never driven a truck.
5. The storm must have loosened the shingles during the night.
6. Will your poem be published in the school paper?
7. Mother has worked as a volunteer at the hospital.
8. I must have been daydreaming during the last part of the program.
9. The car should have been repaired last week.
10. My sister can play the harmonica.

Using Vivid Nouns and Verbs

A noun and a verb usually carry the essential meaning of the sentence. To communicate effectively, you must choose your nouns and verbs with care. In the sentences that follow, for example, notice how the choice of nouns and verbs makes this dull sentence more interesting: *The rain came down.*

The rain **pounded** against the bulkhead.
Large drops of rain **splashed** on the sidewalk.
Sheets of water washed against the windowpanes.

Rewrite each of the following sentences in at least three different ways. In your sentences use vivid nouns and verbs.

1. The scenery was beautiful.
2. The sea was rough.
3. The day was pleasant.

16

1.4 Adjectives

An **adjective** is a word that modifies a noun or a pronoun. The word *modify* means "to change" or "to give more information about." An adjective modifies a noun by describing it or limiting it. Sometimes nouns and certain pronouns can be used as adjectives in sentences. In such cases consider them adjectives, not nouns or pronouns. An adjective answers one of these questions: *Which? What kind?* or *How many?*

Those *children* are becoming restless. [*Which* children? Those children.]

The **excited** *children* waited for the fireworks. [*What kind* of children? Excited children.]

Three *adults* sat in lawn chairs. [*How many* adults? Three adults.]

More than one adjective may modify the same noun or pronoun.

Two noisy *rockets* exploded in midair. [*How many* rockets? Two rockets. *What kind* of rockets? Noisy rockets.]

The **tired, impatient** *crowd* pressed forward. [*What kind* of crowd? A crowd that is tired and impatient.]

Articles. The most frequently used adjectives are the **articles,** *a, an,* and *the. A* and *an* are **indefinite articles** because they do not point out a particular person, place, thing, or idea. *The* is a **definite article** because it points out a particular person, place, thing, or idea.

INDEFINITE   I enjoy **a** cup of broth on **a** cold day.

DEFINITE   **The** cup of broth was steaming hot.

17

Placement of Adjectives

Many adjectives come before the nouns or pronouns that they modify.

The **warm** *sun* melted the **deep** *snow.*

Sometimes, however, adjectives appear in other places in a sentence. For example, an adjective may come after a linking verb. In this position, the adjective modifies a noun or a pronoun that comes before the verb.

The *snow* was **deep.**

It looked **frozen.**

Sometimes an adjective comes immediately after the noun or pronoun that it modifies. Adjectives in this position are set off by commas.

The *child,* **pale** and **solemn,** shook hands with the mayor.

An adjective may come before the noun or pronoun that it modifies and be set off by a comma.

Pale and **solemn,** the *child* shook hands with the mayor.

Exercise 1   Placement of Adjectives   On your paper, write the adjectives in the following sentences. Then write the noun or pronoun that each adjective modifies. Do not include articles.

SAMPLE	The potato is nutritious.
ANSWER	nutritious—potato

1. The potato, plentiful and hardy, is also inexpensive.
2. North Americans eat different kinds of potatoes.
3. These include new potatoes, mealy potatoes, and waxy potatoes.

Exercise 1 *(pages 18–19)*

1. plentiful—potato;
hardy—potato;
inexpensive—potato
2. different—kinds
3. new—potatoes;
mealy—potatoes;
waxy—potatoes
4. New—potatoes;
firm—potatoes;
thin—skin
5. best—They
6. Mealy—potatoes;
soft—potatoes
7. large—bags
8. Crisp—skins;
crunchy—skins;
delicious—snack
9. Waxy—potatoes;
solid—potatoes
10. Waxy—potatoes;
thin—slices;
small—cubes

4. New potatoes are firm and have a thin skin.
5. They are best for salads.
6. Mealy potatoes are soft.
7. People buy large bags of potatoes.
8. Crisp and crunchy, the skins of potatoes make a delicious snack.
9. Waxy potatoes are solid.
10. Waxy potatoes can be cut into thin slices and small cubes.

Exercise 2 Adjectives in a Passage Number your paper from 1 to 6. Next to each number, list the adjectives in that sentence. Do not include articles. Next to each adjective, write the noun or pronoun that it modifies. There are fourteen adjectives.

SAMPLE   Short yellow skis were standing against the rough, blackened chimney.

ANSWER   short—skis; yellow—skis; rough—chimney; blackened—chimney

(1) Someone was skiing down the treacherous path. (2) The skier raised a high white cloud of powdery snow. (3) The husky figure was almost invisible because of the blinding snow.   (4) The skier made two sharp turns and shot into an open field.   (5) He raced between two blazing fires.   (6) Loud shouts erupted from the dark figures who had gathered in the darkness.

Proper Adjectives

A **proper adjective** is a proper noun that modifies another noun or pronoun; it always begins with a capital letter.

My sister is planning a **June** *wedding*. [*What kind* of wedding? A June wedding. *June* is a proper adjective.]

To form many proper adjectives, you add a suffix such as *-n, -an, -ian, -ic,* or *-i* to the proper noun.

Exercise 2 *(page 19)*

1. treacherous—path
2. high—cloud;
   white—cloud;
   powdery—snow
3. husky—figure;
   invisible—figure;
   blinding—snow
4. two—turns;
   sharp—turns;
   open—field
5. two—fires;
   blazing—fires
6. Loud—shouts;
   dark—figures

19

PROPER NOUNS	PROPER ADJECTIVES
Hawaii	Hawaiian customs
Egypt	Egyptian art
Gael	Gaelic language
Israel	Israeli leader

Nouns Used as Adjectives

Some nouns may function as adjectives without changing form.

Ms. Baxter is a **history** *teacher.* [*What kind* of teacher? A history teacher.]

I can't find my **locker** *key.* [*Which* key? Locker key.]

Possessive Nouns

Nouns that show possession can be used as adjectives. **Possessive nouns** answer the questions *Whose?* or *Which?* To form the singular possessive of most nouns, add -'s.

The **jockey's** *shirt* was made of silk. [*Whose* shirt? The jockey's shirt.]

You form the plural possessive of most nouns by adding -s' or -es' to a singular form of the noun.

The **parents'** *committee* will meet on Tuesday. [*Which* committee? The parents' committee.]

Possessive Pronouns Used as Adjectives

Possessive pronouns* show ownership or belonging. Some possessive pronouns (*page 8*) modify nouns or pronouns and therefore function as adjectives.

* Possessive pronouns that modify nouns or pronouns are sometimes called pronominal adjectives.

The possessive pronouns that can be used as adjectives are in the following list.

Exercise 3 *(pages 21–22)*

See page 22 for the answers.

	SINGULAR	PLURAL
FIRST PERSON	my	our
SECOND PERSON	your	your
THIRD PERSON	his, her, its	their

My *books* must be in **your** *locker.* [Whose books? My books. *Whose* locker? Your locker.]

Other Pronouns Used as Adjectives

Indefinite pronouns, demonstrative pronouns, interrogative pronouns, and one of the relative pronouns may also modify nouns or pronouns. Here is a list of pronouns that are often used as adjectives.

INDEFINITE	some, many, several, few
DEMONSTRATIVE	this, that, these, those
INTERROGATIVE	which, what, whose
RELATIVE	whose

Several *players* have won trophies. [*How many* players? Several players.]

Why not take **this** *path* instead of **that** *one*? [*Which* path? This path. *Which* one? That one.]

Which *bus* do you take to school? [*Which* modifies *bus.*]

Exercise 3 Adjectives   On your paper, write the words used as adjectives in the following sentences. Then write the noun or pronoun modified by each word. Do not include articles.

21

Exercise 3 *(pages 21–22)*

1. that—leak;
   kitchen—sink
2. My—uncle
   uncle's—cat;
   porch—steps;
   morning—sun
3. Our—teacher
   French—teacher
4. Few—girls;
   spring—dance;
   this—year
5. popular—form;
   Japanese—poetry
6. Her—grandfather;
   evening—flight
7. Russian—novel
8. model—airplane;
   my—money
   birthday—money
9. which—direction;
   my—dog;
   this—way;
   that—way
10. Roman—ruins

SAMPLE   Should I sew these patches on my soccer jacket?

ANSWER   these—patches; my—jacket; soccer—jacket

1. Has someone repaired that leak in the kitchen sink?
2. My uncle's cat lies on the porch steps and soaks up the morning sun.
3. Our French teacher was born in Mexico.
4. Few girls favor a spring dance this year.
5. A popular form of Japanese poetry is haiku.
6. Her grandfather took an evening flight to Brazil.
7. *War and Peace* is a Russian novel.
8. I bought a model airplane with my birthday money.
9. In which direction did my dog run—this way or that way?
10. Tourists in Italy enjoy visiting the Roman ruins.

Assignment Words as Different Parts of Speech
On your paper, write two sentences for each word listed below. In the first sentence, use the word as a noun. In the second sentence, use the word as an adjective.

1. guest	3. bus	5. January	7. chief	9. television
2. baseball	4. birthday	6. school	8. health	10. record

1.5   Adverbs

An **adverb** is a word that modifies a verb, an adjective, or another adverb.

ADVERB MODIFYING A VERB

The dog *barked* **loudly.**

ADVERB MODIFYING AN ADJECTIVE

The dog has an **unusually** *loud* bark.

22

ADVERB MODIFYING AN ADVERB

The dog barked **quite** *loudly.*

An adverb answers one of five questions about the word that it modifies:

1. How or in what manner?
2. When?
3. Where?
4. How often?
5. To what degree or extent?

Don's car *runs* **well**. [*How* does Don's car run? It runs well.]

They *arrived* **late** for the concert. [*When* did they arrive? They arrived late.]

The troops *moved* **forward**. [*Where* did the troops move? They moved forward.]

Some birds **seldom** *leave* their nests. [*How often* do some birds leave? They seldom leave.]

Everyone seemed **completely** *satisfied* with the arrangements. [*To what degree* did everyone seem satisfied? They seemed completely satisfied.]

The words *not* and *never* are adverbs. They tell to what extent (not at all) and when (never).

We *did* **not** *win.* [*Not* modifies *did win.*]

We **never** *win.* [*Never* modifies *win.*]

1.5a   Adverbs Modifying Verbs

An adverb that modifies a verb modifies the entire verb phrase, which includes the main verb and any auxiliary verbs.

23

Exercise 1 *(page 24)*

1. slowly—were rolling—How?
2. occasionally—could hear—How often?
3. noisily—were flapping—How?
4. mysteriously—whispered—How?
5. violently—boomed—How? overhead—boomed—Where?
6. suddenly—lit—When?
7. wildly—shook—How?
8. thunderously—were breaking—How?
9. unexpectedly—stopped—How?
10. quickly—had passed—How?

A bell *was clanging* **loudly** in the distance. [The adverb, *loudly,* modifies the verb phrase, *was clanging.*]

An adverb sometimes interrupts a verb phrase, as in the following example.

Someone *was* **slowly** *opening* the door.

An adverb that modifies a verb does not have to appear next to that verb. The adverb may appear in any of several places in a sentence.

NEXT TO VERB   They **slowly** *opened* the door.

AT BEGINNING   **Slowly,** they *opened* the door.

AT END   They *opened* the door **slowly.**

Exercise 1   Adverbs Modifying Verbs   *Step 1:* On your paper, write the adverb in each of the following sentences. *Step 2:* Write the verb or verb phrase that each adverb modifies. *Step 3:* Write the question that each adverb answers: *How? When? Where? How often? To what extent?*

SAMPLE   The sky suddenly became dark.
ANSWER   suddenly—became—How?

1. Huge clouds were rolling slowly over the ocean.
2. We could occasionally hear thunder in the distance.
3. The shades were flapping noisily in the wind.
4. The trees whispered mysteriously.
5. The thunder boomed violently overhead.
6. Streaks of lightning suddenly lit the sky.
7. The tops of the trees shook wildly in the wind.
8. Waves were breaking thunderously on the shore.
9. The wind unexpectedly stopped.
10. The storm had passed quickly!

24

1.5b Adverbs Modifying Adjectives

Exercise 2 *(page 25)*

An adverb may also modify an adjective. An adverb usually comes just before the adjective that it modifies.

       adv.   adj.

The rhinoceros has an **extremely** *heavy* body. [The adverb, *extremely,* tells the degree of heaviness of the body.]

       adv.   adj.

The huge creature is **usually** *harmless* but can become

adv.   adj.

very *dangerous.* [The adverb *usually* tells how often the creature is harmless. The adverb *very* tells how dangerous.]

1. barely—legible
2. usually—visible
3. dangerously—tired
4. very—poor;
   remarkably—keen
5. surprisingly—curious
6. sufficiently—safe
7. delightfully—sunny
8. too—large;
   rather—small
9. extremely—funny
10. highly—valuable;
   very—dark

Exercise 2 Adverbs Modifying Adjectives On your paper, write the adverbs in the following sentences. Then, next to each adverb, write the adjective that the adverb modifies.

SAMPLE   That movie is unbelievably bad.

ANSWER   unbelievably—bad

1. The legend on the map was barely legible.
2. The stars are usually visible from our roof.
3. A runner who is out of shape can become dangerously tired during a race.
4. The elephant has very poor eyesight, but it has a remarkably keen sense of smell.
5. The hamster is a surprisingly curious creature.
6. The jewels are in a sufficiently safe place.
7. The day was delightfully sunny.
8. The desk was too large for the rather small room.
9. That joke is extremely funny.
10. The highly valuable painting hung in a very dark corner of the room.

25

Exercise 3 *(page 26)*

1. very—young (adjective);
   beautifully—plays (verb)
2. very—carefully (adverb);
   carefully—cleaned (verb);
   away—put (verb)
3. pretty—well (adverb);
   well—did (verb);
   rather—difficult (adjective)
4. unusually—early (adverb);
   early—were awakened (verb)
5. neatly—dressed (verb)
6. always—arrives (verb);
   early—arrives (verb);
   usually—late (adjective)
7. eagerly—seized (verb)
8. again—Will visit (verb);
   soon—Will visit (verb)
9. surprisingly—sensible
   (adjective)
10. very—hoarse (adjective);
   barely—audible (adjective)

1.5c   Adverbs Modifying Adverbs

Sometimes an adverb modifies another adverb. Such adverbs usually come before the adverbs that they modify.

adv.   adv.
She skates **quite** *skillfully.* [*Quite* tells to what degree she skated skillfully.]

adv. adv.
She performed **rather** *well* during the practice. [*Rather* tells to what extent she performed well.]

Exercise 3   Adverbs   *Step 1:* On your paper, write the adverbs in the following sentences. *Step 2:* Next to each adverb, write the word that it modifies. *Step 3:* In parentheses, write the part of speech of the word that the adverb modifies.

> **SAMPLE**   Selling can be a very challenging job.
> **ANSWER**   very—challenging (adjective)

1. Sandra is very young, but she plays the piano beautifully.
2. We cleaned the tools very carefully before we put them away.
3. I did pretty well on that rather difficult math test.
4. We were awakened unusually early by the sound of the wind.
5. The applicant dressed neatly for the interview.
6. Henry always arrives early, but I'm usually late.
7. The survivors eagerly seized the plates of hot food.
8. Will you visit us again soon?
9. Some ancient beliefs about health are surprisingly sensible.
10. My aunt was very hoarse, and her voice was barely audible.

1.5d   Adjective or Adverb?

It is sometimes difficult to decide whether a word is an adjective or an adverb. For example, a large number of adverbs end in *-ly,* but so do some adjectives.

26

ADVERB   He *tied* the knot **loosely.**

ADJECTIVE   The **kindly** *woman* gave us directions.

Sometimes the same word may be used as either an adjective or an adverb.

ADVERB   That magazine *is published* **monthly.**

ADJECTIVE   That is a **monthly** *magazine.*

To decide whether a word is an adjective or an adverb, decide which question the modifier answers.

ADJECTIVE	ADVERB
1. Which?	1. How or in what manner?
2. What kind?	2. When?
3. How many?	3. Where?
	4. How often?
	5. To what extent or degree?

ADJECTIVE   She is a **hard** *worker.* [**Think:** *Hard* tells what kind of worker. *Hard* modifies *worker,* which is a noun. *Hard* is therefore an adjective.]

ADVERB   She *works* **hard.** [**Think:** *Hard* tells how she works. *Hard* modifies *works,* which is a verb. *Hard* is therefore an adverb.]

Exercise 4   Adjective or Adverb?   *Step 1:* On your paper, list the words in italic type in the following sentences. Label each word *Adjective* or *Adverb. Step 2:* Write the word that is modified by the adjective or adverb. *Step 3:* In parentheses, write the part of speech of the modified word.

SAMPLE   The plane left *late.*

ANSWER   late—Adverb, left (verb)

1. The plane flew *low.*
2. The plane flew at a *low* altitude.

27

Exercise 4 *(pages 27–28)*

1. low—Adverb, flew (verb)
2. low—Adjective, altitude (noun)

(Continue on the next page.)

Exercise 4 *(pages 27–28),* continued

3. fast—Adjective, train (noun)
4. fast—Adverb, travel (verb)
5. early—Adjective, bird (noun)
6. early—Adverb, came (verb)
7. straight—Adverb, flew (verb)
8. straight—Adjective, line (noun)

3. The commuter express is a *fast* train.
4. Some trains travel *fast*.
5. Are you an *early* bird?
6. Everyone came *early* for a change.
7. The robin flew *straight* to its nest.
8. I drew a *straight* line connecting two points.

Assignment   Adjectives and Adverbs   On your paper, write two sentences for each word listed below. In the first sentence, use the word as an adverb. In the second sentence, use the word as an adjective.

1. close	3. late	5. early
2. next	4. kindly	6. daily

1.6   Prepositions

A **preposition** is a word that expresses a relation between a noun or a pronoun and another word in the sentence.

The lion tamer stood **inside** the *cage.* [The preposition, *inside,* tells where the lion tamer was in relation to the cage.]

The lions behaved **like** tame *kittens.* [The preposition, *like,* expresses the similarity between *lions* and *kittens.*]

The prepositions in italic type in the following list are used frequently in speaking and writing.

about thirty cents	*around* the table
above the clouds	*at* daybreak
across the hall	*before* the concert
after the storm	*behind* the chair
against the wall	*below* the bridge
along the fence	*beneath* the oak
among the teachers	*beside* the bandstand

28

besides the money	*onto* the trail
between Tom and Sarah	*out* the window
beyond the hangar	*outside* the shed
by tomorrow	*over* the chimney
despite the smiles	*past* the restaurant
down the other side	*since* the party
during the game	*through* the trees
except this class	*till* Monday
for the prince	*to* me
from the government	*toward* the museum
in her experiment	*under* the arch
inside the bus	*underneath* the window
into the water	*until* the end
like a bird	*up* the telephone pole
near the bus stop	*upon* her shoulders
of fruit	*with* the captain
off the path	*within* our group
on the roof	*without* an answer

Exercise 1 *(pages 29–30)*

1. inside
2. out of; under

(Continue on the next page.)

Some prepositions, called **compound prepositions,** are made up of more than one word. In the following list, the compound prepositions are in italic type.

according to the news	*in regard to* your objection
aside from his success	*in spite of* the score
as well as his keys	*instead of* television
because of the weather	*next to* the house
by means of questions	*on account of* the strike
in addition to history	*on top of* the bureau
in front of the barn	*out of* the question
in place of shortening	*prior to* your letter

Exercise 1 Prepositions   On your paper, write the prepositions in the following sentences.

SAMPLE   The scouts huddled around the campfire.
ANSWER   around

1. The contestants were waiting inside the auditorium.
2. The kitten jumped out of its box and hid under the couch.

29

Exercise 1 *(pages 29–30),*
continued

3. According to; for; on
4. Because of; for
5. with; for
6. into
7. in front of
8. up; through
9. in; to; of
10. near; by

3. According to this notice, school closes for the holidays on next Friday.
4. Because of several detours, we arrived late for the party.
5. The woman with the brown coat is running for office.
6. The diver touched her toes and dropped smoothly into the water.
7. A truck stopped in front of the house.
8. We walked up the driveway and through the front door.
9. A man in a ski parka pushed his way to the head of the line.
10. We sat near the fire and played checkers by the hour.

Prepositional Phrases

A preposition is usually followed by a noun or a pronoun, which is called the **object of the preposition.** The preposition, the object, and the modifiers of that object form a **prepositional phrase.**

> prep.   obj.
> There are deep cracks **in the moon's surface.** [The prepositional phrase consists of the preposition, *in,* the modifiers, *the* and *moon's,* and the object of the preposition, *surface.*]

In some sentences the preposition comes *after* the object. This arrangement often occurs in questions, as in the following example.

> obj.   prep.
> **Which state** are you **from?** [**Think:** From which state are you?]

A prepositional phrase may have more than one object, as in the following sentence.

> prep. obj.   obj.
> The moon's surface is covered **with rocks and dust.**

30

Prepositional phrases usually act as modifiers. A prepositional phrase functions as an adjective if it modifies a noun or a pronoun. A prepositional phrase functions as an adverb if it modifies a verb, an adjective, or an adverb.

USED AS AN ADJECTIVE

prep. phrase

I still have to paint the other *side* **of the house.** [*Of the house* tells which side.]

USED AS AN ADVERB

prep. phrase

Max *hit* the golf ball **into the pond.** [*Into the pond* tells where Max hit the ball.]

Exercise 2 Prepositional Phrases On your paper, write the prepositional phrases in the following sentences. Underline the prepositions once and the object(s) of the prepositions twice.

    SAMPLE   Astronomers have always made maps of the moon.

    ANSWER   of the moon

1. Lunar maps give the names of mountain ranges and craters.
2. There are ten great ranges on the moon.
3. These mountains have been named after mountains on the earth.
4. Are you familiar with the terrain of the moon?
5. A variety of craters covers the moon's surface.
6. Map makers named the craters for well-known astronomers.
7. The craters look like extinct volcanoes.
8. Some are filled with lava and dust.
9. Mountain peaks rise from other craters.
10. There are even craters within craters.

Exercise 2 *(page 31)*

1. of mountain <u>ranges</u> and <u>craters</u>
2. on the <u>moon</u>
3. after <u>mountains</u>; on the <u>earth</u>
4. with the <u>terrain</u>; of the <u>moon</u>
5. of <u>craters</u>
6. for well-known <u>astronomers</u>
7. like extinct <u>volcanoes</u>
8. with <u>lava</u> and <u>dust</u>
9. from other <u>craters</u>
10. within <u>craters</u>

31

1.7 Conjunctions

A **conjunction** is a word that connects individual words or groups of words. In fact, the word *conjunction* literally means "the act of joining" or "combination."

INDIVIDUAL WORDS

Antelopes are usually *tawny* **or** *reddish*. [The conjunction, *or*, connects the two words *tawny* and *reddish*.]

GROUPS OF WORDS

Many antelopes live on open plains, **but** *some live on cliffs.* [The conjunction, *but*, connects the two groups of words *Many antelopes live on open plains* and *some live on cliffs.*]

There are three kinds of conjunctions: coordinating conjunctions, correlative conjunctions, and subordinating conjunctions.

Coordinating Conjunctions

A **coordinating conjunction** connects words or groups of words that perform the same function in a sentence. The coordinating conjunctions are in the following list:

and   but   for   nor   or   yet

A coordinating conjunction can connect two or more nouns, pronouns, verbs, adjectives, adverbs, or prepositions.

Gazelles **and** *antelopes* belong to the cattle family. [*And* connects two subjects.]

She **and** *I* are interested in animals. [*And* connects two subjects.]

Most antelopes are *graceful* **and** *shy*. [*And* connects two adjectives.]

They move *swiftly* **but** *surely*. [*But* connects two adverbs.]

32

A coordinating conjunction can connect two or more independent clauses *(Unit 4)*, which are groups of words that can stand by themselves as sentences.

> *Wolves track slowly,* **but** *their pace is tireless.* [The coordinating conjunction, *but,* connects the two independent clauses, *Wolves track slowly* and *their pace is tireless.*]

A coordinating conjunction also can connect two or more sentence parts that are used in the same way.

> Eels *live in water* **and** *breathe through their gills.* [The coordinating conjunction, *and,* connects two verbs and their modifiers: *live in water* and *breathe through their gills.*]

> The platypus can be found *in eastern Australia* **and** *in Tasmania.* [The coordinating conjunction, *and,* connects two prepositional phrases: *in eastern Australia* and *in Tasmania.*]

Correlative Conjunctions

A **correlative conjunction** consists of two or more words that work together as a set. Correlative conjunctions function like coordinating conjunctions because they connect words that perform equal functions in a sentence. The correlative conjunctions are in the following list:

either . . . or	whether . . . or
neither . . . nor	not only . . . but (also)
both . . . and	

> I would like to be **either** a lifeguard **or** a tutor this summer. [*Either . . . or* connects *a lifeguard* and *a tutor.*]

> Janice couldn't decide **whether** to read a book **or** to watch a movie on television. [*Whether . . . or* connects *to read a book* and *to watch a movie on television.*]

Exercise 1 Conjunctions On your paper, write the coordinating conjunctions and correlative conjunctions in the following sentences.

Exercise 1 *(pages 33–34)*

See page 34 for the answers.

33

Exercise 1 *(pages 33–34)*

1. both . . . and
2. but
3. and
4. and
5. but
6. not only . . . but
7. for
8. and
9. Neither . . . nor
10. and

SAMPLE   The game was close, but we managed to win.
ANSWER   but

1. Write both your name and your address clearly.
2. The joke was long but funny.
3. We walked down several steps and through a long corridor.
4. The hammer, the anvil, and the stirrup are small bones in the inner ear.
5. A sweet potato is a root, but an Irish potato is a stem.
6. Ivy is not only delicate, but it is hardy.
7. We took a taxi, for we were already late.
8. Fruits and vegetables supply natural vitamins.
9. Neither Jan nor Sue will be able to come to the party.
10. The walrus, the sea lion, and the seal walk on flippers that resemble fins.

Subordinating Conjunctions

Subordinating conjunctions introduce subordinate clauses *(Unit 4)*, which are clauses that cannot stand by themselves as complete sentences. Subordinating conjunctions connect subordinate clauses to independent clauses, which can stand by themselves as complete sentences.

```
 ┌─indep. clause─┐ ┌──── sub. clause ────┐
 Everyone waited until the game ended.
```

In the preceding sentence, the subordinating conjunction is *until*. *Until* introduces the subordinate clause, *until the game ended*. *Until* also connects the subordinate clause to the independent clause, *Everyone waited*.

Subordinating conjunctions usually express relationships of time, manner, cause, condition, comparison, or purpose.

TIME   after, as, as long as, as soon as, before, since, until, when, whenever, while

MANNER   as, as if, as though

CAUSE   because

34

CONDITION	although, as long as, even if, even though, if, provided that, though, unless, while
COMPARISON	as, than
PURPOSE	in order that, so that, that

Exercise 2 *(pages 35–36)*

1. since
2. until

(Continue on the next page.)

Carl covered the plants **so that** they would not be harmed by the frost. [*So that* expresses purpose.]

The children ran for cover **when** the rain started to come down. [*When* expresses time.]

If you want to help our club, please buy a raffle ticket. [*If* expresses condition.]

Certain words, such as *after, before, since,* and *until,* may be either conjunctions or prepositions (*pages 28–29*). A subordinating conjunction always introduces a word group that includes a verb. On the other hand, a preposition introduces a word group that does not include a verb.

SUBORDINATING CONJUNCTION

┌────── sub. clause ──────┐

We played **until** the sun went down. [**Think:** *went* is a verb].

PREPOSITION

┌─ prep. phrase ─┐

We played **until** sundown.

Exercise 2 Subordinating Conjunctions On your paper, write the subordinating conjunctions in the following sentences.

SAMPLE	We always shop where they give double coupons.
ANSWER	where

1. We haven't heard from our neighbors since they moved to New Mexico.
2. The picnickers stayed in the park until the gates closed.

35

Exercise 2 *(pages 35–36)*, continued

3. unless
4. If
5. When
6. Before
7. because
8. after
9. Although
10. While

3. I won't make the team unless you coach me.
4. If you are not careful, that balloon will burst.
5. When you hold a genuine dollar bill up to the light, you can see some of its fibers.
6. Before you decide, listen carefully to both sides of the question.
7. My cousin didn't buy the car because it had too many defects.
8. We'll open the presents after the cake is served.
9. Although my sister is confined to a wheelchair, she never misses a game.
10. While you are mopping the floor, I'll vacuum the rug.

1.8 Interjections

An **interjection** is an exclamatory word that usually expresses an emotion. An interjection can stand by itself, or it may be followed by a related sentence.

Alas!
Whew! That was a close call.

An interjection that shows mild feeling is followed by a comma. The word after the comma begins with a lower-case letter unless it is a word that is always capitalized.

My, that's interesting.
Well, I have my mother's permission. [The pronoun *I* is always capitalized.]

Following is a list of commonly used interjections:

aha	great	my	tsk tsk
alas	heavens	oh	well
good grief	help	oops	whew
goodness	hey	ouch	wow
gosh	hurray	psst	yippee

You use interjections in speech, but you should use them only occasionally in writing. Interjections are most useful in writing dialogue that sounds natural.

Exercise Interjections On your paper, write the following sentences, using an appropriate interjection in place of each blank. In the completed sentences, underline the interjections. Use the preceding list of interjections.

SAMPLE   _?_! We just won the chess championship of the state!

ANSWER   Yippee! We just won the chess championship of the state!

1. _?_, have you finished your report?
2. _?_! That hurt!
3. _?_, that's an interesting poster.
4. _?_! I thought we'd never make it.
5. _?_! Is that all you have to say?

Assignment Interjections On your paper, write an interjection that expresses each feeling listed below. Then use each interjection in an original sentence.

1. surprise
2. pain
3. exhaustion
4. helplessness
5. joy

Exercise 1 *(page 37)*

Answers may vary. Samples:

1. Goodness, have you finished your report?
2. Ouch! That hurt!
3. My, that's an interesting poster.
4. Wow! I thought we'd never make it.
5. Good grief! Is that all you have to say?

37

Practice 1 *(pages 38–39)*

A.

1. secretary-general; United Nations; official
2. Monroe Doctrine; President Monroe
3. pride; lions; shade
4. payload; part; cargo; carrier
5. legend; Arthur; king; sword; Excalibur, anvil

B.

6. he
7. It; who; everything
8. Which; them
9. These; that
10. that; mine

C.

11. is—Linking verb; gives—Action verb
12. feed—Action verb; are—Linking verb
13. Should be wearing—Action verb
14. has played—Action verb; played—Action verb
15. cracked—Action verb; leaked—Action verb

(Continue on the next page.)

Practice 1

A. Nouns *(pages 3–6)* On your paper, list the nouns in the following sentences.

1. The secretary-general of the United Nations is an elected official.
2. The Monroe Doctrine was formulated by President Monroe.
3. A pride of lions dozed contentedly in the shade.
4. A payload was originally that part of a cargo that was paid to the carrier.
5. In medieval legend, young Arthur became king when he removed the sword named Excalibur from an iron anvil.

B. Pronouns *(pages 7–11)* On your paper, list the pronouns in the following sentences.

6. At family gatherings, Uncle Earl tends to exaggerate when he tells stories.
7. It is important for people who live near water to have enough insurance to protect everything.
8. Which of them is the better pitcher?
9. These are the best essays that the class has ever written!
10. The record that came through the mail is mine.

C. Verbs *(pages 11–16)* On your paper, list the verbs and verb phrases in the following sentences. Label each verb or verb phrase *Action verb* or *Linking verb*.

11. Carbon dioxide is a colorless, odorless gas that gives carbonated drinks their fizz.
12. Whales, the largest animals on earth, feed on plankton, which are among the smallest plants and animals on earth.
13. Should you be wearing your costume?
14. The team has never played as well as it played today.
15. The frozen pipes cracked and water leaked into the basement.

38

D. Adjectives and Adverbs *(pages 17–28)* On your paper, list the modifiers in the following sentences. Label each modifier *Adjective* or *Adverb*. Do not include articles.

16. The performers waited nervously for the start of the first act.
17. Our new team has never won a game, but we are still trying.
18. My little brother stubbornly refuses to try any new foods.
19. The workers were somewhat concerned about all the new regulations.
20. I certainly prefer this yellow shirt to that plaid one.

E. Prepositions *(pages 28–31)* On your paper, list the prepositional phrases in the following sentences. Underline each preposition.

21. Do you want to finish the poster on Saturday or wait until Monday?
22. Around the large table sat four generations of the Lang family.
23. Did you leave your watch on top of the bureau, in the drawer, or on the shelf in the bathroom?
24. There will be a run-off election between Holly and me.
25. Because of the blizzard, I wasn't able to go outside and play hockey with my friends.

F. Conjunctions and Interjections *(pages 32–37)* On your paper, list the conjunctions and interjections in the following sentences.

26. Well, I guess we'll be late, but our seats are reserved.
27. I don't have the tools or the skill to fix this.
28. After he had flown over the treetops, the stunt pilot circled the field and flew upside down.
29. Oh, no! I left my lunch on the kitchen table.
30. Because you have other work to do, finish this assignment whenever you can.

(Continue on the next page.)

39

Practice 1 *(pages 38–39)*, continued

D.
16. nervously—Adverb; first—Adjective
17. Our—Adjective; new—Adjective; never—Adverb; still—Adverb
18. My—Adjective; little—Adjective; stubbornly—Adverb; any—Adjective; new—Adjective
19. somewhat—Adverb; new—Adjective
20. certainly—Adverb; this—Adjective; yellow—Adjective; that—Adjective; plaid—Adjective

E.
21. on Saturday; until Monday
22. Around the large table; of the Lang family
23. on top of the bureau; in the drawer; on the shelf; in the bathroom
24. between Holly and me
25. Because of the blizzard; with my friends

F.
26. Well; but
27. or
28. After; and
29. Oh no!
30. Because; whenever

Practice 2 *(page 40)*

1. central—Adjective
2. are known—Verb
3. Finger Lakes—Noun
4. received—Verb
5. closely—Adverb
6. of—Preposition
7. should be included—Verb
8. most—Pronoun
9. generally—Adverb
10. Keuka—Noun
11. and—Conjunction
12. largest—Adjective
13. thirty-seven—Adjective
14. consists—Verb
15. and—Conjunction
16. of—Preposition
17. lake—Adjective
18. Oh—Interjection
19. it—Pronoun
20. in—Preposition

Practice 2

Number your paper from 1 to 20, and list the words and phrases in italic type in the following passage. Next to each word or phrase, write the label *Noun, Pronoun, Verb, Adjective, Adverb, Preposition, Conjunction,* or *Interjection.*

In (1) *central* New York, there is a group of long, narrow lakes that (2) *are known* as the (3) *Finger Lakes.* They (4) *received* their unusual name because their shapes (5) *closely* resemble the fingers (6) *of* a hand. Experts differ on how many lakes (7) *should be included* in the group, but (8) *most* of them (9) *generally* agree on eleven. Some of the lakes' names are Cayuga, Seneca, (10) *Keuka,* (11) *and* Canandaigua. Seneca is the (12) *largest* of the Finger Lakes. It is (13) *thirty-seven* miles long. Most of the Finger Lakes region (14) *consists* of rolling country (15) *and* thick woods covering most (16) *of* the (17) *lake* shores. (18) *Oh,* how marvelous (19) *it* is to observe the spectacular scenery (20) *in* this area!

Unit Tests

Test 1

A. Nouns *(pages 3–6)*   On your paper, list the nouns in the following sentences.

1. A warship used to be known as a man-of-war.
2. The Panama Canal was built to shorten the journey by sea from one coast of the United States to the other coast.
3. A troupe of pantomimists is scheduled to perform on Monday and again on Tuesday.
4. A truckload of hay capsized in the tiny square.
5. The Mediterranean Sea is the largest inland sea in the world and divides Africa from Europe.

B. Pronouns *(pages 7–11)*   On your paper, list the pronouns in the following sentences.

6. We put the house up for sale after you decided to sell yours.
7. Anyone who wants to act in the school play may try out for one of the parts that are still available.
8. Who is the person you want me to meet?
9. That is something she should consider when she makes the final decision.
10. The performer whom everyone had come to hear developed a bad case of laryngitis.

C. Verbs *(pages 11–16)*   On your paper, list the verbs and verb phrases in the following sentences. Label each verb or verb phrase *Action verb* or *Linking verb.*

11. Peeling onions is difficult for many people because their eyes become irritated and watery.
12. The bridge was raised so that the ship could continue upriver.
13. Will he remember the props for the play?

(Continue on the next page.)

41

A.
1. warship; man-of-war
2. Panama Canal; journey; sea; coast; United States; coast
3. troupe; pantomimists; Monday; Tuesday
4. truckload; hay; square
5. Mediterranean Sea; sea; world; Africa; Europe

B.
6. We; you; yours
7. Anyone; who; one; that
8. Who; you; me
9. That; something; she; she
10. whom; everyone

C.
11. is—Linking verb; become—Linking verb
12. was raised—Action verb; could continue—Action verb
13. Will remember—Action verb

(Continue on the next page.)

Test 1 *(pages 41–43)*, continued

14. did move—Action verb; licked—Action verb

15. pelted—Action verb; watered—Action verb

D.

16. new—Adjective; unsteadily—Adverb; spindly—Adjective

17. Their—Adjective; backward—Adverb; five—Adjective

18. absolutely—Adverb; certain—Adjective; your—Adjective

19. gigantic—Adjective; steadily—Adverb; upward—Adverb

20. Now—Adverb; freshman—Adjective; its—Adjective; winter—Adjective

E.

21. to an agreement; on the schedule; before noon; on Tuesday

22. Among the yellow daffodils

23. For hide-and-seek; between the porch and the forsythia bush

24. with the decision; except Bart and me

25. On account of the storm; until next week

F.

26. Alas; Although

27. and; before

(Continue on the next page.)

14. The cat did not move as the puppy licked her face.

15. The rain pelted the earth and watered the newly planted fields.

D. Adjectives and Adverbs *(pages 17–28)* On your paper, list the modifiers in the following sentences. Label each modifier *Adjective* or *Adverb*. Do not include articles.

16. The new foal walked unsteadily on spindly legs.

17. Their quarterback was knocked backward for a loss of five yards.

18. Are you absolutely certain of your answer?

19. The gigantic rocket moved steadily upward.

20. Now the freshman class can finish its plans for a winter carnival.

E. Prepositions *(pages 28–31)* On your paper, list the prepositional phrases in the following sentences. Underline each preposition.

21. Can we come to an agreement on the schedule before noon on Tuesday?

22. Among the yellow daffodils were two tulips.

23. For hide-and-seek, Samantha's favorite hiding place is between the porch and the forsythia bush.

24. Everyone went along with the decision except Bart and me.

25. On account of the storm, we are postponing our club meeting until next week.

F. Conjunctions and Interjections *(pages 32–37)* On your paper, list the conjunctions and interjections in the following sentences.

26. Alas! Although I have made my decision, I still have doubts.

27. You should measure the width and the length of the room before you buy a carpet.

42

28. While you are waiting, read these instructions and fill out this form.
29. Oh, I remember that old song.
30. Because you meet all the requirements, you can start to work on Monday.

Test 2

Number your paper from 1 to 20, and list the words and phrases in italic type in the following passage. Next to each word or phrase, write the label *Noun, Pronoun, Verb, Adjective, Adverb, Preposition, Conjunction,* or *Interjection.*

The sitar is a stringed instrument   (1) *that* is
(2) *popular* in   (3) *India.* It is used   (4) *primarily* to play
classical   (5) *Indian* compositions called *ragas.*   (6) *It* has
six or seven main strings,   (7) *which* are plucked   (8) *with*
the right hand. It also has between twelve and twenty
(9) *sympathetic* strings. The sympathetic strings are not
plucked,   (10) *but* they vibrate when the main
(11) *strings*   (12) *are played.* The sitar   (13) *has* a rounded
body that is   (14) *usually* made   (15) *of* wood   (16) *and* a
long, broad neck that   (17) *is made* of teak. The instrument   (18) *probably* originated during the 1200s. The
Indian musician   (19) *Ravi Shankar* ranks as the world's
best-known   (20) *sitarist.*

Test 1 *(pages 41–43),*
continued
28. While; and
29. Oh
30. Because

Test 2 *(page 43)*

1. that—Pronoun
2. popular—Adjective
3. India—Noun
4. primarily—Adverb
5. Indian—Adjective;
   ragas—Noun
6. It—Pronoun
7. which—Pronoun
8. with—Preposition
9. sympathetic—Adjective
10. but—Conjunction
11. strings—Noun
12. are played—Verb
13. has—Verb
14. usually—Adverb
15. of—Preposition
16. and—Conjunction
17. is made—Verb
18. probably—Adverb
19. Ravi Shankar—Noun
20. sitarist—Noun

43

Unit 2

Objectives

After studying this unit, students should be able to do the following:

- Classify sentences according to their purpose as declarative, interrogative, imperative, or exclamatory, and punctuate them correctly.

- Identify the simple subjects and simple predicates of sentences.

- Identify compound subjects and compound predicates in sentences.

- Identify the complete subjects and complete predicates of declarative, interrogative, imperative, and exclamatory sentences.

- Identify two kinds of complements: objects and subject complements.

- Diagram sentences with modifiers, with complements, and with compound elements.

Teaching Suggestions

See "Classroom Insights" for Unit 2 in the front of this Teacher's Edition.

Sentence Structure

Unit Preview

The world that you live in is a world of action. Often an event is important enough or unusual enough to make the newspaper headlines:

HURRICANE RAGES

MAYOR RESIGNS

CARDINALS WIN

Newspapers frequently carry two-word headlines. Although they are not written in sentence form, most headlines usually include the two parts of speech that appear in most English sentences: a noun and a verb.

Your first spoken sentences probably sounded something like headlines:

Car runs.
Dog barks.

Your sentences became longer as you began adding words that gave more meaning to what you were trying to communicate to your listener:

My uncle's new car runs smoothly and economically.

The dog that belongs to the people next door barks most of the night.

44

For Analysis   Refer to the newspaper headlines and the short and long sentences as you answer the following questions:

1. Rewrite the three headlines so that they are sentences.
2. In the spoken sentence *Car runs,* which word tells what the sentence is about? Which word tells something about *Car?* In what way is *Car runs* the same as *My uncle's new car runs smoothly and economically?* How are the sentences different?
3. How are the two sentences about the barking dog alike? How are they different?

In this unit you will become more aware of the similarities and differences in the sentences that you speak, write, and read. The more you know about sentences, the better able you will be to communicate your ideas clearly and effectively.

2.1   Sentences Classified by Purpose

A **sentence** is a group of words that has at least one subject *(page 47)* and one predicate *(page 48)* and that expresses a complete thought. To be a sentence, a group of words must make sense by itself. A group of words is not a sentence if it makes sense only when you use it with another group of words.

NOT A SENTENCE   The two main units of time

SENTENCE   The two main units of time are the day and the year.

There are four kinds of sentences, classified according to purpose: (1) sentences that make statements; (2) sentences that ask questions; (3) sentences that give commands; and (4) sentences that express strong or sudden feelings.

A **declarative sentence** makes a statement. It always ends with a period.

The dogwood tree has blossomed.
The air smells sweet.

45

Program Resources

Resource Book, Second Course:
   Diagnostic Test, Unit 2
   Achievement Test, Unit 2
   Bonus Activities, Unit 2
   Extra Practice, Unit 2
   Unit Test, Unit 2
Practice Book, Second Course,
   Unit 2
Tests, Second Course, Unit 2

Related Resources

Houghton Mifflin Microcourse:
   Language Arts, Levels 7, 8
*The American Heritage
   Dictionary of the English
   Language*

For Analysis *(page 45)*

Answers may vary. Samples:

1. A fierce hurricane is raging across southwestern Texas.

   The mayor resigned today after telling the city council that ill health was interfering with his job.

   The Cardinals won the fifth game of the World Series this afternoon.

2. The word Car tells what the sentence is about.

   The word runs tells something about Car.

   Both sentences tell that the car runs, but the longer sentence describes the car and tells how it runs.

3. Both sentences tell that the dog barks, but the longer sentence tells whose dog it is and when it barks.

1. Are you coming with us?
   —Interrogative
2. How happy you look!
   —Exclamatory
3. Put the clothes in the dryer.
   —Imperative
4. The music grew louder and
   louder.—Declarative
5. Answer every other question.
   —Imperative
6. Why is your mother going to
   Chicago?—Interrogative
7. What a party we had!
   —Exclamatory
8. A crate of eggs spilled all over
   the highway.
   —Declarative
9. This water is freezing!
   —Exclamatory (*or* .
   —Declarative)
10. Put everything away neatly.
    (*or* !)—Imperative

An **interrogative sentence** asks a question. It always ends with a question mark.

> Did the pollen make you sneeze?
> What is pollen?

An **imperative sentence** gives a command or makes a request. If the command or request is mild, the sentence ends with a period. If the command or request is strong, the sentence ends with an exclamation point.

> Please turn out the lights.
> Stop right there!

An **exclamatory sentence** expresses strong or sudden feeling. Exclamatory sentences often begin with the modifier *what* or *how*. An exclamatory sentence always ends with an exclamation point.

> What fun we had!
> Here comes the parade!

Exercise   Sentence Purpose   Write the following sentences on your paper. Label each one *Declarative, Interrogative, Imperative,* or *Exclamatory.* Put the correct punctuation mark at the end of each sentence.

> SAMPLE   Feed the cat, please
> ANSWER   Feed the cat, please.—Imperative

1. Are you coming with us
2. How happy you look
3. Put the clothes in the dryer
4. The music grew louder and louder
5. Answer every other question
6. Why is your mother going to Chicago
7. What a party we had
8. A crate of eggs spilled all over the highway

46

9. This water is freezing
10. Put everything away neatly

Assignment   Making a Sentence Chart   On your
paper, make three columns with the following headings: (1)
Purpose, (2) *Punctuation,* and (3) *Examples.* In Column 1 list
the four sentence purposes. Leave space below each purpose.
Then complete the chart with appropriate punctuation and
write at least three examples of each kind of sentence.

2.2   Simple Subjects
and Simple Predicates

Simple Subjects

Every sentence has a subject and a predicate. A **simple
subject** is the noun or the pronoun that tells whom or what
the sentence is about. The simple subject does not include
modifiers.

> The basic **feature** of jazz is its rhythm. [The simple subject
> is the noun *feature.*]
> **That** was a funny puppet show! [The pronoun, *that,* is the
> simple subject.]

The complete subject *(page 51)* consists of the simple
subject and all of its modifiers. In this book *subject* refers to
the simple subject.

Usually the simple subject is a single word. Sometimes,
however, the simple subject consists of more than one word.

NAME OF A PERSON   **Victor Herbert** wrote several famous
operettas.

TITLE   ***Babes in Toyland*** is a well-known
operetta.

47

Exercise *(pages 48–49)*

1. My brother is going to college in the fall.
2. Dr. Lopez mows the lawn with a hand mower.
3. My aunt is manager of the record department.
4. The President will soon be choosing a new cabinet.
5. A dictionary can help a writer with problems in spelling and usage.
6. Termites have been eating the beams in the basement.
7. The history class will not have a test on Friday.
8. Jackie Brown found several valuable coins in the old sugar bowl.
9. A big yellow bus rolled slowly down the hill.
10. Five police officers carefully lifted the box into the truck.

NAME OF A PLACE	**Venice, Italy,** was the site of the first public opera house.
COMPOUND WORD	An **opera house** must have excellent acoustics.

The simple subject of an imperative sentence is always *you. You* is usually understood rather than stated.

Be careful with these tapes.   [**Think:** *You* be careful.]

Simple Predicates

The **simple predicate** is the verb or verb phrase that describes the action or states the condition of the subject. The simple predicate does not include its modifiers or words that complete the meaning of the verb. *Not* and *never* are not part of the simple predicate.

Cacti **are** well-known desert plants. [The linking verb, *are,* is the simple predicate.]
Farmers **have been losing** money because of the drought. [The verb phrase, *have been losing,* is the simple predicate.]

The complete predicate *(page 51)* consists of the simple predicate along with its modifiers and the words that complete the meaning of the verb. The term *predicate* refers to the simple predicate.

Exercise   Subjects and Predicates   Copy the following sentences on your paper. Underline each simple subject once and each simple predicate twice.

SAMPLE	The repairs will cost ten dollars.
ANSWER	The repairs will cost ten dollars.

1. My brother is going to college in the fall.
2. Dr. Lopez mows the lawn with a hand mower.

48

3. My aunt is manager of the record department.
4. The President will soon be choosing a new cabinet.
5. A dictionary can help a writer with problems in spelling and usage.
6. Termites have been eating the beams in the basement.
7. The history class will not have a test on Friday.
8. Jackie Brown found several valuable coins in the old sugar bowl.
9. A big yellow bus rolled slowly down the hill.
10. Five police officers carefully lifted the box into the truck.

2.3 Compound Subjects and Compound Predicates

Compound Subjects

A **compound subject** is a simple subject that consists of two or more nouns or pronouns. The term *compound subject* refers to a compound *simple* subject.

> **Peanuts** and certain **grains** contain protein. [*Peanuts* and *grains* form the compound subject.]
>
> **Ann** or **Shep** will collect the money for the food fair. [*Ann* and *Shep* form the compound subject.]

Compound Predicates

A **compound predicate** is a simple predicate that consists of two or more verbs or verb phrases. The term *compound predicate* refers to a compound *simple* predicate.

> Dr. Li **cleaned** my teeth and **examined** them. [*Cleaned* and *examined* form the compound predicate.]
>
> We **hiked** or **swam** almost every day. [*Hiked* and *swam* form the compound predicate.]

49

A sentence may have both a compound subject and a compound predicate.

subj.   subj.   pred.   pred.
Sam and *Janet* **listened** carefully but **missed** the announcement. [*Sam* and *Janet* form the compound subject. *Listened* and *missed* form the compound predicate.]

Exercise Subjects and Predicates   On your paper, write the following sentences. Underline the simple subjects once and the simple predicates twice. Some subjects and predicates are compound.

> **SAMPLE**   Kara and I looked for shells but found nothing interesting.
>
> **ANSWER**   Kara and I looked for shells but found nothing interesting.

1. Striped umbrellas and straw hats blew in the hot breeze at the seashore.
2. Several bathers scurried along the shore and occasionally dipped their toes into the water.
3. A boy and a girl jumped up and threw a plastic saucer back and forth.
4. On the boardwalk, grownups and children strolled or played games.
5. The hot sun and the blue sky slowed time down and almost stopped it.
6. The calf and its mother lifted their heads and bellowed.
7. Rain and sleet have been predicted but have not arrived yet.
8. The pitcher and the infielders worked together all morning and perfected a pick-off play.
9. An empty canvas sack and a map were found in the trunk of the abandoned car.
10. The customs officer opened the package and carefully inspected the contents.

50

Exercise *(page 50)*

1. Striped umbrellas and straw hats blew in the hot breeze at the seashore.
2. Several bathers scurried along the shore and occasionally dipped their toes into the water.
3. A boy and a girl jumped up and threw a plastic saucer back and forth.
4. On the boardwalk, grownups and children strolled or played games.
5. The hot sun and the blue sky slowed time down and almost stopped it.
6. The calf and its mother lifted their heads and bellowed.
7. Rain and sleet have been predicted but have not arrived yet.
8. The pitcher and the infielders worked together all morning and perfected a pick-off play.
9. An empty canvas sack and a map were found in the trunk of the abandoned car.
10. The customs officer opened the package and carefully inspected the contents.

Comparing Two Items

Write a paragraph in which you compare two items. For example, you could compare two kinds of cars, two kinds of bicycles, or two kinds of sneakers. Tell how the items are alike and how they are different. Use sentences that have compound subjects and compound predicates.

2.4 Complete Subjects and Complete Predicates

Complete Subjects

The **complete subject** of a sentence consists of the simple subject along with its modifiers and other words that identify the simple subject.

⌐————— complete subject ————⌐
The saltiest *water* in the ocean is found in the tropics. [The noun *water* is the simple subject. *The, saltiest,* and *in the ocean* modify *water.*]

⌐————— complete subject ————⌐
Steep *hills* and deep *valleys* can be found on the ocean floor. [The complete subject includes a compound simple subject, *hills* and *valleys. Steep* and *deep* are modifiers.]

Complete Predicates

The **complete predicate** consists of the simple predicate along with its modifiers and the words that complete the meaning of the verb.

51

Exercise 1 *(page 52)*

subj.
1. The last storm of the year
pred.
   swept along the Atlantic coast.

subj.
2. That china teapot and those
   subj. pred.
   silver forks are family

   heirlooms.

subj.
3. A battered boat with a
   pred.
   patched sail set course for

   Gull Island.

subj.
4. The first telescope with a
   ┌─pred.─┐
   radio antenna was built after

   World War II.

subj.
5. A rescue party with walkie-
   pred.
   talkies tramped through the

   snow.
   ┌────subj.────┐
6. Alexander Fleming, a

   biologist, accidentally
   pred.
   discovered penicillin.

subj.
7. Beasts of burden and house-
   subj. ┌──pred.──┐
   hold pets were found in the

   ruins of Pompeii.
   ┌──────subj.──────┐
8. Dr. Daniel Hale Williams, the

   first successful heart surgeon,
   pred.
   practiced medicine in the

   nineteenth century.

(Continue on the next page.)

┌──────────── complete predicate ────────────┐
A battered car **slowly *pulled* a trailer along the dirt road.**
[The simple predicate is the verb, *pulled.* The noun *trailer*
completes the meaning of the verb. *Slowly* and *along the
dirt road* modify *pulled.*]

┌──────── complete predicate ────────┐
The prosecutor ***reached* under the desk and *pulled* out an
object wrapped in a newspaper.** [The complete predicate
includes a compound simple predicate, *reached* and *pulled.*
Under the desk modifies *reached. Object* completes the
meaning of *pulled. Out* modifies *pulled. Wrapped in a
newspaper* modifies *object.*]

Exercise 1   Subjects and Predicates   *Step 1:* On your
paper, write the following sentences. *Step 2:* Underline the
complete subjects once and the complete predicates twice.
Step 3: Write *subj.* above each simple subject and *pred.* above
each simple predicate.

SAMPLE	Visions of far-off islands flashed before our eyes.
ANSWER	Visions of far-off islands flashed before our eyes.

1. The last storm of the year swept along the Atlantic coast.
2. That china teapot and those silver forks are family heirlooms.
3. A battered boat with a patched sail set course for Gull Island.
4. The first telescope with a radio antenna was built after World War II.
5. A rescue party with walkie-talkies tramped through the snow.
6. Alexander Fleming, a biologist, accidentally discovered penicillin.
7. Beasts of burden and household pets were found in the ruins of Pompeii.
8. Dr. Daniel Hale Williams, the first successful heart surgeon, practiced medicine in the nineteenth century.
9. The borrowed overcoat was too tight across the shoulders.
10. The low chatter of voices drifted down from the ridge, which was covered with snow.

52

Placement of Subjects and Predicates

Subjects and predicates may be placed in many different positions in sentences. The placement of the subject and the predicate often depends on the purpose of the sentence.

Declarative Sentences

In a declarative sentence, the complete subject usually comes before the complete predicate. In the examples that follow, the complete subjects are underlined once and the complete predicates are underlined twice.

The pitcher walked the first two batters.

However, in some declarative sentences, the complete predicate comes before the complete subject.

Out of the dugout stormed the manager.
There will be a new pitcher.

In other declarative sentences, the complete subject appears between two parts of the complete predicate.

Slowly and methodically, the pitcher struck out the other side.

Interrogative Sentences

In an interrogative sentence, the complete subject usually appears between two parts of the complete predicate.

Will he complete the game?
Why is the umpire examining the ball?

To find the subject and the predicate of a question, turn the question into a statement.

QUESTION   Will he complete the game?

STATEMENT   He will complete the game.

53

Exercise 1 *(page 52),*
continued

               subj.   pred.

9. The borrowed overcoat was

   too tight across the shoulders.
                  subj.

10. The low chatter of voices
         pred.
    drifted down from the ridge,

    which was covered with snow.

Exercise 2 *(pages 54–55)*

1. A whale suddenly surfaced near our boat.
   - subj. *A whale*
   - pred. *suddenly surfaced*

2. From its blowhole spouted a column of water.
   - pred. *spouted*
   - subj. *a column of water*

3. (You) Please hand me the binoculars.
   - subj. *(You)*
   - pred. *Please hand me the*

4. What an incredible animal the whale is!
   - subj. *the whale*
   - pred. *is*

5. Under its skin is a layer of blubber.
   - pred. *is*
   - subj. *a layer of blubber*

6. For thousands of years, whales have lived in the water.
   - subj. *whales*
   - pred. *have lived in the water*

7. How does a whale breathe?
   - pred. *does*
   - subj. *a whale*
   - pred. *breathe*

8. It takes in air through two nostrils on the top of its head.
   - subj. *It*
   - pred. *takes*

9. A whale's flippers have bones similar to those in a hand.
   - subj. *A whale's flippers*
   - pred. *have*

10. How fascinating whales can be!
    - subj. *whales*
    - pred. *can*
    - pred. *be*

Imperative Sentences

In an imperative sentence, the subject *you* is usually understood but not stated. Therefore, the entire sentence is the complete predicate.

Please autograph my program. [**Think:** *You* please autograph my program.]

Exclamatory Sentences

In many exclamatory sentences, the complete subject comes before the complete predicate. Sometimes, however, the complete subject appears between two parts of the complete predicate.

You won!
What a great game he pitched!

Exercise 2   Subjects and Predicates   *Step 1:* On your paper, write the following sentences. *Step 2:* Underline the complete subjects once and the complete predicates twice. If the subject *you* is understood, write *You* in parentheses and underline it. *Step 3:* Write *subj.* above each simple subject and *pred.* above each simple predicate.

SAMPLE   What an adventure the visitors to the theme park will have!

ANSWER   What an adventure *the visitors* to the theme park *will have*!

1. A whale suddenly surfaced near our boat.
2. From its blowhole spouted a column of water.
3. Please hand me the binoculars.
4. What an incredible animal the whale is!
5. Under its skin is a layer of blubber.
6. For thousands of years, whales have lived in the water.
7. How does a whale breathe?

8. It takes in air through two nostrils on the top of its head.
9. A whale's flippers have bones similar to those in a hand.
10. How fascinating whales can be!

Varying Sentences

Do you begin every declarative sentence with the subject? You can add interest to your writing by beginning some of your sentences in the ways shown on pages 53–54. For each topic below, write a descriptive paragraph that contains at least five sentences. In each paragraph write two sentences in which the subject does not come first.

1. a cat or a squirrel leaping from a tree
2. someone washing a car
3. a traffic jam on a busy street

2.5 Complements

A **complement** is a word or a group of words that completes the meaning of the predicate. Complements are always part of the complete predicate.

My cousin is saving her **money.** [The noun *money* is a complement.]

Sometimes she can be very **thrifty.** [The adjective, *thrifty*, is a complement.]

The meaning of both sentences would be incomplete without complements.

55

Exercise 1 *(pages 56–57)*

1. corn
2. movie
3. package
4. fire
5. car
6. books
7. assignment
8. me
9. him
10. boots

In this section you will study two kinds of complements: objects and subject complements.

2.5a   Objects

Objects are nouns or pronouns that follow action verbs *(page 12)*. There are two kinds of objects: direct objects and indirect objects.

Direct Objects

A **direct object** is a noun or a pronoun that follows an action verb and answers the question *What?* or *Whom?* A direct object receives the action of the verb. The modifiers of a direct object and the words that identify it do not form part of the direct object.

D.O.
Rudyard Kipling *has written* many **stories** about India. [**Think:** has written *what*? Has written *stories*. The noun *stories* is the direct object.]

D.O.
Did you *ask* **him**? [**Think:** did ask *whom*? Did ask *him*. The pronoun *him* is the direct object.]

D.O.
I just *finished* a **book** about an orphan. [**Think:** finished *what*? Finished *book*. The noun *book* is the direct object.]

Exercise 1   Direct Objects   On your paper, write the direct objects in the following sentences.

SAMPLE   She is visiting her relatives in Willingboro.
ANSWER   relatives

1. The farmer planted corn.
2. Did you watch the special movie last night?
3. I received a package in the mail.

56

4. The careless campers started a fire in spite of the warning.
5. Mom and I pushed the car to the nearest service area.
6. Please put these books on the cart.
7. My brother explained the assignment to me.
8. Please take me to the ball game with you.
9. Someone helped him across the street.
10. Who put these muddy boots in the closet?

Indirect Objects

An **indirect object** is a noun or a pronoun that comes before the direct object and names the person or thing *to* whom or *for* whom an action is done.

The traffic officer gave **us** very clear *directions*. [**Think:** gave directions to whom? Gave directions to us. The indirect object, *us*, tells *to* whom the action is done.]

Dad bought **Bill** a *watch*. [**Think:** bought a watch for whom? Bought a watch for *Bill*. The indirect object, *Bill*, tells *for* whom the action is done.]

If the word *to* or *for* appears in the sentence, the noun or pronoun that follows it is not an indirect object. It is an object of the preposition *to* or *for*.

INDIRECT OBJECT   She handed **me** the mail.

OBJECT OF A PREPOSITION   She handed the mail *to* **me.**

Compound Objects. Like subjects and predicates, objects may be compound. A **compound object** consists of two or more objects that complete the same predicate.

COMPOUND DIRECT OBJECT
> We added **potatoes** and **onions** to the stew.

COMPOUND INDIRECT OBJECT
> We gave **Mother** and **Dad** a surprise party.

57

1. principal—I.O.; questions—D.O.
2. us—I.O.; stories—D.O.
3. plumber—I.O.; wrench—D.O.; pail—D.O.
4. us—I.O.; apples—D.O.; pears—D.O.
5. Hilda—I.O.; me—I.O.; assignment—D.O.
6. mother—I.O.; promise—D.O.
7. bus—D.O.
8. carrots—D.O.
9. friend—I.O.; me—I.O.; joke—D.O.
10. pots—D.O., pans—D.O.

Exercise 2   Direct and Indirect Objects   On your paper, write the direct objects and the indirect objects in the following sentences. Label the direct objects *D.O.* and the indirect objects *I.O.* Some sentences have compound objects.

SAMPLE   Please hand me the scissors.

ANSWER   me—I.O.; scissors—D.O.

1. Mr. Brown asked the principal several questions.
2. Our neighbor told us stories about her life in China.
3. The assistant handed the plumber a wrench and a pail.
4. They always send us apples and pears for the holidays.
5. Our teacher gave Hilda and me a special assignment.
6. He made his mother a solemn promise.
7. Everyone boarded the bus for the picnic grounds.
8. Please pass the carrots.
9. He told my friend and me a funny joke.
10. We stored the old pots and pans in a labeled carton.

2.5b   Subject Complements

A **subject complement** is a word that comes after a linking verb *(page 13)* and identifies or describes the subject of the sentence. Subject complements often follow forms of the linking verb *be*. Other commonly used linking verbs that take subject complements are listed below.

appear	grow	seem	stay
become	look	smell	taste
feel	remain	sound	turn

There are two kinds of subject complements: predicate nominatives and predicate adjectives.

Predicate Nominatives

A **predicate nominative** is a noun or a pronoun that follows a linking verb and identifies the subject of the sen-

58

tence. The root of the word *nominative* is nominate, which means "to name." You might say that the predicate nominative renames the subject.

> P.N.
> *Venice* is a very old **city.** [The predicate nominative, *city*, renames the subject, *Venice*.]
>
> P.N.
> In 1866 *Venice* became **part** of Italy. [The predicate nominative, *part*, renames the subject, *Venice*.]

A sentence may have a compound predicate nominative, which consists of two or more predicate nominatives that rename the same subject.

> P.N.   P.N.
> *Venice* is a famous artistic **center** and a busy **port.**
> [The compound predicate nominative, *center* and *port*, renames the subject, *Venice*.]

Exercise 3 **Predicate Nominatives** On your paper, write the predicate nominatives in the following sentences. Some sentences have compound predicate nominatives.

> **SAMPLE**   My friend is an expert on coins.
>
> **ANSWER**   expert

1. Snow is a poor conductor of heat.
2. My brother has become an excellent skier.
3. In Antarctica the most common birds are gulls and penguins.
4. Quicksand is a mixture of loose sand and water.
5. Two popular poets are Longfellow and Dickinson.
6. By unanimous vote Sal remained our treasurer.
7. The cabbage was once a useless plant.
8. The hand was first a symbol of friendship in ancient Greece.
9. Igor Sikorsky is the inventor of the first practical helicopter with one rotor.
10. Geology is a fascinating science.

59

Exercise 3 *(page 59)*

1. conductor
2. skier
3. gulls, penguins
4. mixture
5. Longfellow, Dickinson
6. treasurer
7. plant
8. symbol
9. inventor
10. science

Exercise 4 *(page 60)*

1. pharmacist—P.N.
2. yellow—P.A.
3. woodpecker—P.N.
4. valuable—P.A.
5. state—P.N.
6. members—P.N.
7. primrose—P.N.
8. happy—P.A.
9. steep—P.A.
10. symbol—P.N.

Predicate Adjectives

A **predicate adjective** is an adjective that follows a linking verb and modifies the subject of the sentence.

P.A.

Their *forecasts* are usually **accurate.** [The predicate adjective, *accurate*, follows the linking verb, *are*, and modifies the subject, *forecasts*.]

P.A.

Suddenly the *weather* turned **cold.** [The predicate adjective, *cold*, follows the linking verb, *turned*, and modifies the subject, *weather*.]

A sentence may have a compound predicate adjective, which consists of two or more predicate adjectives that modify the same subject.

P.A.   P.A.

The *night* was **clear** and **cold.**

Exercise 4   Subject Complements   On your paper, write the subject complements in the following sentences. Label each complement *P.N.* (predicate nominative) or *P.A.* (predicate adjective).

SAMPLE   Horned toads are desert animals.
ANSWER   animals—P.N.

1. My uncle is a pharmacist in the U.S. Navy.
2. The leaves on the beech tree are turning yellow.
3. The bird that we saw is a woodpecker.
4. Why is that stamp valuable?
5. Alaska became our forty-ninth state in 1959.
6. Sponges are members of the animal kingdom.
7. That flower is a primrose.
8. She seems happy with her new computer.
9. Halfway up the mountain, the trail became very steep.
10. The eagle has been a symbol of power for centuries.

60

2.6 Sentence Diagrams

It is frequently helpful to see how the parts of speech relate to one another in sentences. One way to show this relationship is to make a **sentence diagram**—a picture of the structure of a sentence. To diagram correctly, you must follow certain guidelines.

2.6a Diagraming Subjects and Predicates

Begin a sentence diagram by drawing a horizontal line with a ruler. This line is called the base line. Then divide the base with a vertical line called the bar. The bar should be the same length above and below the base line.

BASIC DIAGRAM DESIGN

Write the simple subject of a sentence on the base line to the left of the bar. Write the simple predicate on the base line to the right of the bar. The punctuation marks are not included in a diagram. The first word in a sentence should be capitalized in a diagram even when it is not a proper noun.

DECLARATIVE SENTENCE   Louis Pasteur experimented.

In the diagram on the following page notice that the words in a verb phrase go together in a diagram even when part of the verb phrase comes before the subject. Note also that *Did* is capitalized because it is the first word in the sentence.

61

Exercise 1 *(page 62)*

*See the Answers (Continued)
pages in the front section of this
Teacher's Edition.*

INTERROGATIVE SENTENCE   Did he succeed?

When you diagram an imperative sentence, write the understood subject, *you,* in the subject position in the diagram. Put the understood subject in parentheses.

IMPERATIVE SENTENCE   Persevere!

(you)	Persevere

Exercise 1 Diagraming Subjects and Predicates

On your paper, diagram the following sentences. Remember to use a ruler and to allow enough space for each diagram.

1. Children performed.
2. Did they sing?
3. Everyone applauded.
4. Smile!
5. Are you leaving?

2.6b   Diagraming Modifiers

To diagram an adjective or an adverb, draw a slanted line from the base line below the word that the adjective or adverb modifies.

The discouraged scientist finally succeeded.

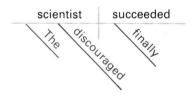

Some adverbs modify adjectives or other adverbs. Write this kind of adverb on an L-shaped line extending from the adjective or adverb that it modifies.

He worked very hard. [The adverb *very* modifies the adverb *hard*.]

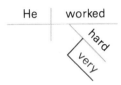

Exercise 2 *(page 63)*

See the Answers (Continued) pages in the front section of this Teacher's Edition.

Exercise 2 Diagraming Modifiers On your paper, diagram the following sentences. Remember to use a ruler.

1. The project is going very smoothly.
2. The old stove exploded unexpectedly.
3. The new factory will open soon.
4. My older sister always smiles cheerfully.
5. The extremely talented dancer performed brilliantly.

2.6c Diagraming Complements

Diagraming Direct Objects

To diagram a direct object, extend the base line to the right of the predicate. Separate the direct object from the predicate with a vertical line that extends above the base line but not below it. Write the direct object on the extended base line to the right of the predicate. Place the modifiers of the direct object on slanted lines below it.

Joseph Lister made a very important discovery.

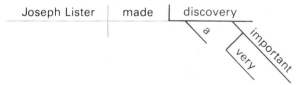

63

Diagraming Indirect Objects

To diagram an indirect object, draw a slanted line below the predicate. From the bottom of that line, draw a line parallel to the base line. Write the indirect object on the parallel line.

Other scientists gave Lister very little credit.

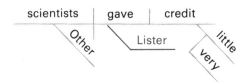

Diagraming Subject Complements

To diagram a predicate nominative or a predicate adjective, extend the base line to the right of the predicate. From the base line, draw a line that slants upward and toward the subject. Write the predicate nominative or the predicate adjective on the extended base line to the right of the predicate. Place any modifiers of the predicate nominative or the predicate adjective on slanted lines below it.

PREDICATE NOMINATIVE
She was a dedicated surgeon. [*Surgeon* is a predicate nominative.]

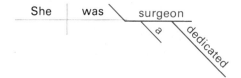

64

PREDICATE ADJECTIVE

His theories seemed very unusual. [*Unusual* is a predicate adjective.]

Exercise 3 *(page 65)*

See the Answers (Continued) pages in the front section of this Teacher's Edition.

Exercise 3 Diagraming Complements On your paper, diagram the following sentences. The sentences contain objects and subject complements.

1. Has anyone seen my book?
2. Our new house has an attached garage.
3. Will someone lend me a red pencil?
4. Your allowance seems quite generous.
5. Our motel room was surprisingly spacious.
6. The award was a gold statue.
7. The helpful clerk showed us several sweaters.
8. Our neighbor is Mother's best friend.
9. Can you sew an invisible seam?
10. Our new dog can be a terrible nuisance.

2.6d Diagraming Compound Elements

Write the parts of a compound subject or a compound predicate on parallel lines. Then connect the lines with a vertical line of dashes. On the line of dashes, write the conjunction that joins the compound elements. Connect the compound elements to the base of the diagram with a pair of solid diagonal lines. If a compound element has a modifier or a complement, diagram the modifier or the complement as you normally would.

65

COMPOUND SUBJECT

Lister and Pasteur were medical pioneers.

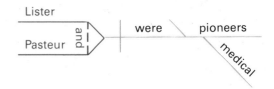

COMPOUND PREDICATE

They made important discoveries and willingly shared them.

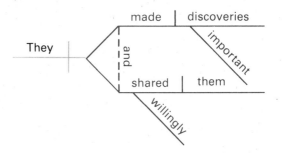

When two or more modifiers are connected by a conjunction, write the modifiers on slanted lines below the word that they modify. Then draw a line of dashes between the slanted lines. Write the conjunction on the line of dashes.

The young but experienced scientist worked skillfully and quickly.

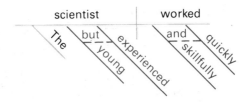

66

Diagram a compound complement by writing the complements on parallel lines and connecting the lines with a vertical line of dashes. Write the conjunction on the line of dashes.

COMPOUND DIRECT OBJECT

Jack will clean the porch and the front yard. [*Porch* and *yard* are direct objects.]

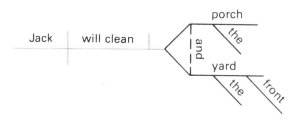

COMPOUND INDIRECT OBJECT

Frank showed Kate and me his science project. [*Kate* and *me* are indirect objects.]

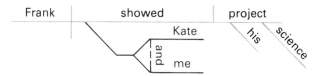

Exercise 4 Diagraming Compound Elements
On your paper, diagram the following sentences. The sentences contain compound subjects, compound predicates, compound modifiers, and compound complements.

1. Mail these packages and envelopes separately.
2. My grandmother sent my cousin and me some old lace.
3. The hikers looked tired but happy.
4. The helpful but inexperienced waiter smiled bravely.
5. We waxed the floors and polished the furniture.

Exercise 4 *(page 67)*

See the Answers (Continued) pages in the front section of this Teacher's Edition.

67

Unit Practice

Practice 1

Practice 1 (pages 68–69)

A.

1. Interrogative
2. Declarative
3. Imperative
4. Exclamatory
5. Imperative

B.

6. ┌─pred.─┐
   There has been one small
     subj.
   mistake.
                    subj.
7. In his carrier the puppy
     pred.
   yelped constantly.
       pred.subj. pred.
8. Where are you going?
   subj. pred.
9. (You) Pass the popcorn.
                     subj. pred.
10. What a difficult climb this is!

C.

11. call—Direct object
12. ill—Predicate adjective
13. me—Indirect object;
    schedule—Direct object
14. yellow, lifeless—Predicate
    adjectives
15. mushroom—Predicate
    nominative

(Continue on the next page.)

A. Sentence Purpose (pages 45–46)   On your paper, label each of the following sentences *Declarative*, *Interrogative*, *Imperative*, or *Exclamatory*.

1. Have you contributed to the scholarship fund?
2. The Common Market is an economic union of European nations.
3. Turn off the television right now!
4. How disappointed she was!
5. Please return this book to the library.

B. Subjects and Predicates (pages 47–55)   On your paper, write the following sentences. Underline each complete subject once and each complete predicate twice. Write *subj.* over each simple subject and *pred.* over each simple predicate. If the subject is the understood *you*, write *you* in parentheses and label it.

6. There has been one small mistake.
7. In his carrier the puppy yelped constantly.
8. Where are you going?
9. Pass the popcorn.
10. What a difficult climb this is!

C. Complements (pages 55–60)   On your paper, write the complements in the following sentences. Label each complement *Direct object*, *Indirect object*, *Predicate nominative*, or *Predicate adjective*.

11. The ship broadcast a call for help every ten minutes.
12. Have you been ill?
13. Give me the schedule.
14. Without light the plant turned yellow and lifeless.
15. The morel is a sponge-like mushroom.

68

D. Sentence Diagrams *(pages 61–67)* On your paper, diagram the following sentences. Remember to use a ruler.

16. Are you a lawyer?
17. The general awarded the lieutenant a medal.
18. The ceiling and one wall were yellow.
19. Max definitely wanted the red and white bike.
20. Dogs are friendly and loyal.

Practice 2

On your paper, write the numbered words and phrases that are in italic type in the following passage. Label each *Simple subject, Simple predicate, Complete subject, Complete predicate, Direct object, Indirect object, Predicate nominative,* or *Predicate adjective.*

(1) *My worst camping experience* occurred one winter. We had to lug our gear about a half mile from the road to the cabin. We made several (2) *trips* through knee-deep snow. Finally, after settling ourselves in the cabin, we (3) *tried* to build a fire in the fireplace. The old stone (4) *fireplace* wasn't working properly, and the room became (5) *smoky.* Our leader gave (6) *us* two choices. We (7) *could have* the fire with the smoke, or we could try to do without the fire. We chose the (8) *fire* and the *smoke.* That night it started to rain. Now our problem was a (9) *leak* in the roof! By the end of the weekend, I had red and watery eyes, a sore throat, and I smelled musty and smoky. Boy, (10) *was* I *glad to get home!*

Practice 1 *(pages 68–69),* continued

D.
See the Answers (Continued) pages in the front section of this Teacher's Edition.

Practice 2 *(page 69)*

1. My worst camping experience —Complete subject
2. trips—Direct object
3. tried—Simple predicate
4. fireplace—Simple subject
5. smoky—Predicate adjective
6. us—Indirect object
7. could have—Simple predicate
8. fire—Direct object; smoke—Direct object
9. leak—Predicate nominative
10. was glad to get home—Complete predicate

69

Test 1 *(pages 70–71)*

A.
1. Interrogative
2. Imperative
3. Declarative
4. Exclamatory
5. Imperative

B.
6. There will be a delay in the game.
   (pred. / subj.)
7. Slowly and cautiously, the rabbit emerged from its hiding place.
   (subj. / pred. / pred.)
8. Will you be home for dinner?
   (pred. subj. pred.)
9. (You) Set the table.
   (subj. pred.)
10. What a fast ball that pitcher throws!
    (subj. / pred.)

C.
11. message—Direct object
12. president—Predicate nominative
13. Colin—Indirect object; Simone—Indirect object; mention—Direct object
14. warm—Predicate adjective; salty—Predicate adjective
15. craftsperson—Predicate nominative

(Continue on the next page.)

Unit Tests

Test 1

A. Sentence Purpose *(pages 45–46)* On your paper, label each of the following sentences *Declarative, Interrogative, Imperative,* or *Exclamatory.*

1. Aren't you sorry that you didn't go to the game?
2. Please clean out the garage this Saturday.
3. The panther is a black leopard.
4. What a miserable day for a picnic!
5. Get that dog off the sofa!

B. Subjects and Predicates *(pages 47–55)* On your paper, write the following sentences. Underline each complete subject once and each complete predicate twice. Write *subj.* over each simple subject and *pred.* over each simple predicate. If the subject is the understood *you,* write *you* in parentheses and label it.

6. There will be a delay in the game.
7. Slowly and cautiously, the rabbit emerged from its hiding place.
8. Will you be home for dinner?
9. Set the table.
10. What a fastball that pitcher throws!

C. Complements *(pages 55–60)* On your paper, write the complements in the following sentences. Label each complement *Direct object, Indirect object, Predicate nominative,* or *Predicate adjective.*

11. An unknown informant sent a message to the police.
12. Will Jessica become president?
13. The judges gave Colin and Simone an honorable mention.
14. The sea water tasted warm and salty.
15. My sister is a skilled craftsperson.

70

D. Sentence Diagrams *(pages 61–67)* On your paper, diagram the following sentences. Remember to use a ruler.

16. Will she be a doctor?
17. The boy gave his grandmother a hug.
18. Sherry obviously preferred soccer and tennis.
19. Basketball is fast and exciting.
20. The broken chair was uncomfortable and dangerous.

Test 2

On your paper, write the numbered words and phrases that are in italic type in the following passage. Label each *Simple subject, Simple predicate, Complete subject, Complete predicate, Direct object, Indirect object, Predicate nominative,* or *Predicate adjective.*

All styles of bicycles (1) *have become* increasingly (2) *popular* in recent years. Basically, there are three (3) *types.* The lightweight bikes are the racing and touring (4) *models.* Most have gear systems of five, ten, or fifteen speeds. (5) *The middleweight bicycles* are more sturdy and especially suited for children. These may or may not have (6) *gears.* Specialty (7) *models* include the high-riser, the tandem, and the moped. The high-riser (8) *gets its name from its high-rise handlebars.* The tandem is built for two riders. The moped is the newest (9) *addition* to the bicycle family. It (10) *can attain* a speed of as much as thirty miles per hour.

Test 1 *(pages 70–71),* continued

D.
See the Answers (Continued) pages in the front section of this Teacher's Edition.

Test 2 *(page 71)*

1. have become—Simple predicate
2. popular—Predicate adjective
3. types—Simple subject
4. models—Predicate nominative
5. The middleweight bicycles —Complete subject
6. gears—Direct object
7. models—Simple subject
8. gets its name from its high-rise handlebars— Complete predicate
9. addition—Predicate nominative
10. can attain—Simple predicate

71

Objectives

After studying this unit, students should be able to do the following:

- Identify prepositional phrases and determine whether they are used as adjectives or adverbs.

- Identify and use participles and participial phrases and infinitives and infinitive phrases, and tell how they are used in sentences.

- Diagram sentences with phrases.

Teaching Suggestions

See "Classroom Insights" for Unit 3 in the front of this Teacher's Edition.

Program Resources

Resource Book, Second Course:
    Diagnostic Test, Unit 3
    Achievement Test, Unit 3
    Bonus Activities, Unit 3
    Extra Practice, Unit 3
    Unit Test, Unit 3
Practice Book, Second Course, Unit 3
Tests, Second Course, Unit 3

Related Resources

Houghton Mifflin Microcourse:
    Language Arts, Levels 7, 8
The American Heritage Dictionary of the English Language

Phrases

Unit Preview

Suppose that you wrote this sentence:

The man asked some teen-agers.

The sentence has a complete subject and a complete predicate. It communicates meaning, but it provides no information about the man or about the teen-agers. Someone reading the sentence might wonder: What did the man ask? Where was he? Where were the teen-agers? What were they doing?

In the following version, numbered blanks have been inserted in the sentence to show where more information might be added.

The man _1_ asked some teen-agers _2_   _3_ .

Study the word groups listed below. From each column, choose one of the four word groups and insert it in the blank with the corresponding number.

COLUMN 1	COLUMN 2	COLUMN 3
in the park	near the bandstand	for directions
eating his lunch	playing catch	to toss him the ball
sitting on a bench	on the handball court	about school
waiting for a bus	on the corner	to help him

Here is one example of the kinds of sentences that will result from this activity:

The man *in the park* asked some teen-agers *on the handball court for directions.*

Each group of words in the preceding columns is a phrase. By inserting different phrases in the blanks, you give different meanings to the sentences.

For Analysis Using the phrases in the preceding columns, write at least three different sentences about the man and the teen-agers. Then answer the following questions.

1. Which word in the original sentence do the phrases in Column 1 describe?
2. Which word in the original sentence do the phrases in Column 2 describe?
3. How do the phrases in Column 3 change the meaning of the original sentence?
4. Do all three of the sentences that you wrote make sense? Why or why not?

Using phrases in sentences can help you to express your ideas clearly and effectively. In this unit you will study three kinds of phrases: prepositional phrases, participial phrases, and infinitive phrases. Verb phrases are covered on pages 14–15.

3.1 Prepositional Phrases

A **phrase** is a group of related words used as a single part of speech. A **prepositional phrase** (*page 30*) consists of a preposition, its object, and any modifiers of that object. In the following sentences, the prepositional phrases are in boldface type.

The magazine article **about vitamins** was informative. *(prep. / obj.)*

Why don't you use it **in your science report?** *(prep. / obj.)*

73

For Analysis *(page 73)*

Answers may vary. Samples:

The man eating his lunch asked some teen-agers playing catch to toss him the ball.
The man sitting on a bench asked some teen-agers near the bandstand about school.
The man waiting for a bus asked some teen-agers on the corner for directions.

1. man
2. teen-agers
3. The phrases in Column 3 tell what the man asked the teen-agers.
4. Yes. The phrases in each column are all the same kind, and all can be used to describe the same word in the original sentence.

In some sentences, especially questions, the preposition comes after its object.

    Which topic are you writing **about?** [**Think**: *About which topic* are you writing?]

A prepositional phrase may have a compound object, which consists of more than one object.

    I have found up-to-date information **in newspapers and magazines.**

Prepositional Phrases Used as Adjectives

A prepositional phrase functions as an adjective when it modifies a noun or a pronoun. Such phrases are sometimes called **adjective phrases.** Adjective phrases answer the same questions answered by adjectives: *Which? What kind? How many?*

MODIFIES NOUN   The *sound* **of the trumpet** filled the hall. [*Which* sound? The sound of the trumpet.]

MODIFIES PRONOUN   *Someone* **with talent** was playing the trumpet. [*What kind* of someone? Someone with talent.]

A prepositional phrase can modify the object of another prepositional phrase.

    Will you play *one* of the *songs* in this book? [*Which one?* One of the songs. Which songs? Songs in this book.]

74

Prepositional Phrases Used as Adverbs

A prepositional phrase functions as an adverb when it modifies a verb, an adjective, or an adverb. Such phrases are sometimes called **adverb phrases.** Adverb phrases answer the same questions answered by adverbs: *How? When? Where? How often? To what extent or degree?*

MODIFIES VERB — The team *ran* **around the field.** [Ran *where*? Ran around the field. The prepositional phrase, *around the field,* modifies the verb *ran.*]

MODIFIES ADJECTIVE — Our team is *great* **at defense.** [Is great *how*? Is great at defense. The prepositional phrase, *at defense,* modifies the adjective *great.*]

MODIFIES ADVERB — They practice *early* **in the morning.** [They practice early *when*? Early in the morning. The prepositional phrase, *in the morning,* modifies the adverb *early.*]

Exercise 1   Prepositional Phrases   *Step 1:* On your paper, write the prepositional phrases in the following sentences. *Step 2:* Next to each phrase, write the word or words that it modifies. *Step 3:* Label each phrase *Adjective phrase* or *Adverb phrase.*

SAMPLE   After breakfast I will sweep the sidewalk.

ANSWER   After breakfast, will sweep—Adverb phrase

1. The commuters walked hurriedly toward their trains.
2. We all breathed a sigh of relief.
3. The plant on the windowsill is a geranium.
4. The tops of the trees disappeared into the fog.

75

Exercise 1 *(pages 75–76)*

1. toward their trains, walked —Adverb phrase
2. of relief, sigh—Adjective phrase
3. on the windowsill, plant —Adjective phrase
4. of the trees, tops—Adjective phrase;
   into the fog, disappeared—Adverb phrase

(Continue on the next page.)

Exercise 1 *(pages 75–76),*
continued

5. except you and me, everyone
   —Adjective phrase;
   on that book, report—
   Adjective phrase

6. over the gorge, bridge
   —Adjective phrase;
   of escape, means—Adjective
   phrase

7. during his saxophone solo,
   turned—Adverb phrase

8. at that game, skillful
   —Adverb phrase

9. of gold brocade, dress
   —Adjective phrase

10. By nightfall, had extinguished
    —Adverb phrase

11. on the table, put—Adverb
    phrase

12. by John Philip Sousa,
    marches —Adjective phrase

13. for you, job—Adjective
    phrase

14. in a circular theater, sat
    —Adverb phrase

15. with a long thin oar, propelled
    —Adverb phrase

Exercise 2 *(pages 76–77)*

1. in 1860—Adverb phrase;
   on a farm—Adverb phrase;
   in upstate New York
   —Adjective phrase

2. During her childhood
   —Adverb phrase;
   with the juice—Adverb
   phrase;
   from berries—Adjective
   phrase

(Continue on the next page.)

5. Everyone except you and me is writing a report on that book.
6. A rope bridge over the gorge was their only means of escape.
7. Bud's face turned beet-red during his saxophone solo.
8. You are quite skillful at that game.
9. The young princess wore a dress of gold brocade.
10. By nightfall the firefighters had extinguished the blaze.
11. I put the letter on the table.
12. The band played several marches by John Philip Sousa.
13. Here is a challenging job for you.
14. We sat in a circular theater and watched the artificial sky.
15. The gondolier propelled the boat with a long thin oar.

Exercise 2   Prepositional Phrases   Number your paper from 1 to 15. Next to the number of each sentence, write the prepositional phrase or phrases in that sentence. Then label each phrase *Adjective phrase* or *Adverb phrase.*

SAMPLE	Grandma Moses died in 1961 at the age of one hundred one.
ANSWER	in 1961—Adverb phrase at the age—Adverb phrase of one hundred one—Adjective phrase

(1) Anna Robertson was born in 1860 on a farm in upstate New York. (2) During her childhood Anna drew simple scenes and colored them with the juice from berries. (3) At thirteen she left home and earned her living as a hired girl. (4) After her marriage to Thomas Moses, she lived in Virginia. (5) Later, Anna and Thomas moved to a farm near Eagle Bridge in New York. (6) Anna lived on that farm for the rest of her life.

(7) Grandma Moses did not work with oil paints until her late seventies. (8) On fiberboard she painted scenes from her childhood. (9) Her earliest paintings were given away as gifts or sold for very small sums. (10) In 1939 several of her paintings were hung in the window of a

drugstore in Hoosick Falls.   (11) They attracted the attention of an art collector.   (12) He drove to her farm and bought her stock of fifteen paintings.   (13) Three of those paintings were exhibited at a museum in New York City. (14) Later a famous department store brought her to New York for the first day of an exhibition of her works. (15) Soon her paintings were exhibited throughout the United States and in Europe.

Assignment   Using Prepositional Phrases   On your paper, write six sentences in which you use the following prepositional phrases.

1. above the housetops
2. among the yellowed papers
3. on the surface
4. in the morning light
5. through the field
6. under the snow

3.2   Verbals and Verbal Phrases

A **verbal** is a word that is formed from a verb but is used in a sentence as another part of speech. Even when a verbal is used as another part of speech, it keeps some of the characteristics of a verb. For example, a verbal expresses an action or a state of being, it may have a complement *(page 55)*, and it may be modified by an adverb or an adverb phrase. In this unit you will study two kinds of verbals: participles and infinitives.

3.2a   Participles and Participial Phrases

Participles

A **participle** is a verbal that is used in a sentence as an adjective.

The **roaring** *wind* tore through the sails.

77

3. At thirteen—Adverb phrase;
   as a hired girl—Adverb phrase

4. After her marriage—Adverb phrase;
   to Thomas Moses—Adjective phrase;
   in Virginia—Adverb phrase

5. to a farm—Adverb phrase;
   near Eagle Bridge —Adjective phrase;
   in New York—Adjective phrase

6. on that farm—Adverb phrase;
   for the rest—Adverb phrase;
   of her life—Adjective phrase

7. with oil paints—Adverb phrase;
   until her late seventies —Adverb phrase

8. On fiberboard—Adverb phrase;
   from her childhood —Adjective phrase

9. as gifts—Adverb phrase;
   for very small sums —Adverb phrase

10. In 1939—Adverb phrase;
    of her paintings —Adjective phrase;
    in the window—Adverb phrase;
    of a drugstore— Adjective phrase;
    in Hoosick Falls—Adjective phrase

11. of an art collector —Adjective phrase

12. to her farm—Adverb phrase;
    of fifteen paintings —Adjective phrase

(Continue on the next page.)

Exercise 2 *(pages 76–77),*
continued

13. of those paintings
   —Adjective phrase;
   at a museum—Adverb phrase;
   in New York City—Adjective
   phrase
14. to New York—Adverb
   phrase;
   for the first day
   —Adverb phrase;
   of an exhibition
   —Adjective phrase;
   of her works—Adjective
   phrase
15. throughout the United States
   —Adverb phrase;
   in Europe—Adverb phrase

In the preceding sentence, the word *roaring* is a participle. *Roaring* has the properties of a verb because it expresses an action. *Roaring* functions as an adjective because it modifies the noun *wind*.

There are two kinds of participles: present participles and past participles. The present participle and the past participle are two of the four principal parts of a verb. See Section 6.1a of Unit 6 for a complete explanation of principal parts.

Present Participles.   The present participle is formed by adding the suffix *-ing* to the infinitive *(page 81).*

The **smiling** *principal* greeted the students. [The present participle *smiling* tells *what kind* of principal. It therefore modifies the noun *principal.*]

In the preceding sentence, the present participle *smiling* consists of the infinitive *smile* and the suffix *-ing*. Notice that you drop the final *e* before adding the suffix *-ing (Unit 17).*

Past Participles of Regular Verbs.   The past participle of regular verbs is formed by adding the suffix *-d* or *-ed* to the infinitive. Most verbs are regular.

The **honored** *students* took their places on the stage. [The past participle *honored* tells *which* students. It therefore modifies the noun *students.*]

In the preceding sentence, the past participle *honored* consists of the infinitive *honor* and the suffix *-ed*. See Unit 17 for spelling changes that may occur when *-ed* is added to the infinitive.

Past Participles of Irregular Verbs.   Because there are no rules for forming the past participle of irregular verbs, you should memorize those principal parts that you do not

78

know. See Section 6.1a of Unit 6 for the past participles of some frequently used irregular verbs.

The **chosen** *students* looked very happy. [*Chosen* is the past participle of the irregular verb *choose* and modifies the noun *students*.]

Present participles and past participles can also be part of a verb phrase *(page 14)*. When a participle is part of a verb phrase, it is not a verbal.

PART OF VERB PHRASE	The audience **was cheering** wildly.
	The committee **had** carefully **selected** the students.
VERBAL	The **cheering** *audience* applauded the students.
	The **selected** *students* are members of the Student Council.

Exercise 1 Participles   On your paper, write the participles that are used as adjectives in the following sentences. Next to each participle, write the word that it modifies.

SAMPLE   Ann made a running leap for the ball.

ANSWER   running—leap

1. Holmes finally solved the baffling mystery.
2. You are a valued customer.
3. The encouraged workers ended the strike.
4. Beth found a hidden passageway behind the shelves.
5. The yelping hounds woke us several times during the night.
6. The broken bat flew toward third base.
7. Grinning, Tom handed his mother a huge package.
8. The principal made a surprising announcement.
9. We covered the glowing coals with sand.
10. The crying child ran to his father for comfort.

79

Exercise 1 *(page 79)*

1. baffling—mystery
2. valued—customer
3. encouraged—workers
4. hidden—passageway
5. yelping—hounds
6. broken—bat
7. Grinning—Tom
8. surprising—announcement
9. glowing—coals
10. crying—child

Exercise 2 *(pages 80–81)*

1. Delayed by traffic—they
2. Banging excitedly on our door —neighbor
3. receiving the most votes —student
4. Still feeling hungry—we
5. Exhausted from too much activity—puppy
6. driving a bus—man
7. grazing in a meadow—herd
8. Giving Janet a play—coach
9. feeding peanuts to the monkeys—children
10. doing pushups—boys
11. Carefully removing the casserole from the oven—Larry
12. walking her dog—woman
13. soaking his feet in warm water—Dad
14. Alarmed by the noise—parakeet
15. excited by the championships —members

Participial Phrases

A **participial phrase** consists of a participle and any words that modify the participle or complete its meaning. The entire participial phrase functions as an adjective to modify a noun or a pronoun. Both present participles and past participles may be used in participial phrases. Participial phrases immediately precede or immediately follow the words that they modify.

Extending her hand, the *mayor* greeted me by name. [The participial phrase consists of the present participle, *extending,* and its direct object, *hand. Her* modifies *hand* and is part of the participial phrase.]

We drank *juice* **squeezed from oranges.** [The participial phrase consists of the past participle, *squeezed,* and the adverb phrase *from oranges.*]

Completely exhausted from my work in the yard, *I* showered and went to bed. [The participial phrase consists of the past participle, *exhausted,* the adverb *completely,* the adverb phrase *from my work,* and the adjective phrase *in the yard.*]

Exercise 2   Participial Phrases   On your paper, write the participial phrases in the following sentences. Next to each phrase, write the word that it modifies.

SAMPLE   Hurriedly sealing the letter, my aunt turned and left the room.

ANSWER   Hurriedly sealing the letter—aunt

1. Delayed by traffic, they arrived late for the concert.
2. Banging excitedly on our door, our neighbor told us the good news.
3. The student receiving the most votes will be nominated.
4. Still feeling hungry, we ate all the leftovers.
5. Exhausted from too much activity, the puppy fell asleep.

80

6. A man driving a bus pulled into the gas station.
7. We saw a herd of buffalo grazing in a meadow.
8. Giving Janet a play, the coach sent her into the game.
9. Look at those children feeding peanuts to the monkeys.
10. The boys doing pushups are trying out for the track team.
11. Carefully removing the casserole from the oven, Larry called us to the table.
12. A woman walking her dog gave us directions.
13. Dad, soaking his feet in warm water, gave a deep sigh of relief.
14. Alarmed by the noise, our parakeet ruffled its feathers.
15. The members of the chess club, excited by the championships, practiced far into the night.

3.2b   Infinitives and Infinitive Phrases

Infinitives

An **infinitive** consists of the first principal part (*Section 6.1a of Unit 6*), or basic form, of the verb. When used as a verbal, the infinitive is usually preceded by the word *to*. An infinitive may function as a noun, an adjective, or an adverb. Even when it is used as another part of speech, the infinitive keeps some of the characteristics of a verb. It expresses an action or a state of being, and it may be followed by a complement.

USED AS NOUN

To win is not everything. [*What* is not everything? To win. *To win* is the subject.]

We expect **to win**. [We expect *what?* We expect to win. *To win* is the direct object.]

USED AS ADJECTIVE

The hardest *game* **to play** is squash. [*Which* game? Game to play.]

81

Exercise 3 *(page 82)*

Labels in parentheses indicate exactly how the infinitives are used.

1. to do—adjective (modifies noun *work*)
2. To win—noun (subject)
3. to leave—adjective (modifies noun *time*)
4. To see—noun (subject); to believe—noun (predicate nominative)
5. to play—adverb (modifies adjective *ready*)
6. to remember—adverb (modifies adjective *painful*)
7. to study—noun (direct object of verb *Do like*)
8. to travel—noun (direct object of verb *likes*)
9. to testify—noun (direct object of verb *refused*)
10. to understand—adverb (modifies adjective *easy*)

USED AS ADVERB

I *turned* my head **to listen.** [I turned my head *why*? I turned to listen.]

This game is *hard* **to follow.** [*In what way* is this game hard? This game is hard to follow.]

Do not confuse infinitives with prepositional phrases that begin with the preposition *to*. Remember that *to* used with a verb is an infinitive, and *to* used with a noun or a pronoun is a prepositional phrase.

INFINITIVES	I came **to help.**
	To help is my intention.
PREPOSITIONAL PHRASES	The bus came **to a sudden halt.**
	To me your decision sounds wise.

Exercise 3   Infinitives   On your paper, write the infinitives in the following sentences. Tell whether each infinitive functions as a noun, an adjective, or an adverb.

SAMPLE   Is that the best route to take?
ANSWER   to take—adjective

1. I have plenty of work to do.
2. To win is always a pleasure.
3. Is it time to leave?
4. To see is to believe.
5. Are you ready to play?
6. Some things may be painful to remember.
7. Do you like to study?
8. During summer vacation, Dad likes to travel.
9. The witness suddenly refused to testify.
10. Some poems are easy to understand.

Infinitive Phrases

An **infinitive phrase** consists of an infinitive, its complements, and any modifiers of the infinitive or the complements.

MODIFIERS   I asked him **to come immediately.** [The adverb *immediately* modifies the infinitive, *come.*]

We decided **to paint with a roller.** [The adverb phrase *with a roller* modifies the infinitive, *paint.*]

COMPLEMENTS   My mother asked me **to wash the dirty windows.** [The noun *windows* is the direct object of the infinitive, *wash. The* and *dirty* modify *windows.*]

Have you ever tried **to look happy?** [*Happy* is a predicate adjective following the infinitive, *look.*]

An infinitive phrase can function as a noun, an adjective, or an adverb.

USED AS NOUN
To rent a machine is one possibility. [subject]
They tried **to sand the floors without a machine.** [direct object]
The best idea is **to rent a machine for the day.** [predicate nominative]

USED AS ADJECTIVE
We have discovered the best *way* **to sand floors.**
[*Which* way? Way to sand floors.]

USED AS ADVERB
We *rushed* **to return the machine by five o'clock.**
[Rushed *why?* Rushed to return the machine by five o'clock.]

83

Exercise 4 *(page 84)*

Labels in parentheses indicate exactly how the infinitives are used.

1. To play baseball in the major leagues—noun (subject)
2. to wash the car with a sponge—noun (direct object of verb *prefer*)
3. to protect it from the humidity—adverb (modifies verb *sealed*)
4. to adjourn the meeting —adjective (modifies noun *time*)
5. to send him flowers—noun (direct object of verb *decided*)
6. to swim in that pond—adverb (modifies adjective *dangerous*)
7. to sing before the assembly —adverb (modifies adjective *ready*)
8. To enter the marathon—noun (subject)
9. to leave the city—adjective (modifies noun *order*)
10. to stock shelves in his uncle's store—noun (direct object of verb *began*)

Exercise 5 *(pages 84–85)*

Answers may vary. Samples:

1. No one wants to feel left out.
2. The winners, excited about their achievement, claimed their prizes.
3. Spying the dog, the cat ran under the couch.
4. My intention is to write a winning essay.

(Continue on the next page.)

Exercise 4   Infinitive Phrases   On your paper, write the infinitive phrases in the following sentences. Tell whether each phrase functions as a noun, an adjective, or an adverb.

SAMPLE   My job is to remind Aunt Maureen about the game.

ANSWER   to remind Aunt Maureen about the game— noun

1. To play baseball in the major leagues is my dream.
2. Ralph prefers to wash the car with a sponge.
3. We sealed the document to protect it from the humidity.
4. It must be time to adjourn the meeting.
5. The class decided to send him flowers.
6. It is dangerous to swim in that pond.
7. The choir is ready to sing before the assembly.
8. To enter the marathon is her first goal.
9. The order to leave the city was quickly obeyed.
10. At thirteen he began to stock shelves in his uncle's store.

Exercise 5   Verbal Phrases   On your paper, write the following sentences, replacing each blank with the kind of verbal phrase indicated in parentheses. Underline the verbal phrase.

SAMPLE   __?__ is one of my ambitions. (infinitive phrase)

ANSWER   To play a musical instrument is one of my ambitions.

1. No one wants __?__. (infinitive phrase)
2. The winners, __?__, claimed their prizes. (participial phrase)
3. __?__, the cat ran under the couch. (participial phrase)
4. My intention is __?__. (infinitive phrase)
5. The jacket __?__ is mine. (participial phrase)
6. __?__ is an unforgettable experience. (infinitive phrase)
7. The officer set off in pursuit, __?__. (participial phrase)
8. __?__ would be exciting. (infinitive phrase)

84

9. The firefighters, __?__, entered the burning building. (participial phrase)

10. __?__, the clown went on his merry way. (participial phrase)

3.3 Diagraming Sentences with Phrases

This section will show you how to diagram the three kinds of phrases that you have studied. First, however, you may want to review "Sentence Diagrams" on pages 61–67.

Diagraming Prepositional Phrases

To diagram a prepositional phrase, draw a slanted line from the base line below the word that the phrase modifies. From the slanted line, draw a line parallel to the base line. Write the preposition on the slanted line. Write the object of the preposition on the parallel line. Write any words that modify the object of the preposition on slanted lines below the object.

The group of happy fans celebrated with a victory party.

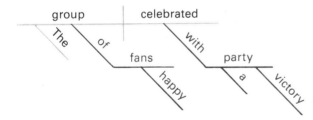

Diagraming Participial Phrases

To diagram a participial phrase, draw a slanted line from the base line below the word that the participle modifies. From the slanted line, draw a line parallel to the base line. Write the participle so that it starts on the slanted line and curves onto the parallel line. Write any words that modify the participle on slanted lines below it.

85

Exercise 5 *(pages 84–85)*, continued

5. The jacket <u>hanging on the hook in the hall</u> is mine.

6. <u>To canoe through rapids</u> is an unforgettable experience.

7. The officer set off in pursuit, <u>stepping firmly on the gas.</u>

8. <u>To climb Mount Everest</u> would be exciting.

9. The firefighters, <u>wearing masks and oxygen tanks,</u> entered the burning building.

10. <u>Teetering on his stilts and throwing confetti,</u> the clown went on his merry way.

Rowing steadily, we finally reached shore. [The adverb *steadily* modifies the participle, *rowing*. *Rowing* modifies the subject, *we*.]

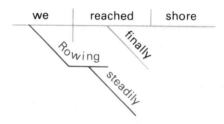

If a direct object follows the participle in a participial phrase, separate the two items with a vertical line that goes up from the base line. If a predicate adjective or a predicate nominative follows the participle, separate the participle and the subject complement with a slanted line.

Finding no one at home, our neighbor left a note. [The pronoun *no one* is the direct object of the participle, *finding*. The participial phrase modifies the subject, *neighbor*.]

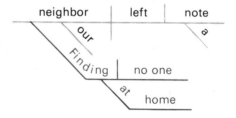

Looking happy, Dad raced up the path. [The predicate adjective *happy* follows the participle, *looking*. The participial phrase modifies the subject, *Dad*.]

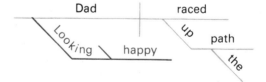

Diagraming Infinitives and
Infinitive Phrases

To diagram an infinitive phrase, draw a slanted line and a horizontal line and place them on a standard.

Write the word *to* on the slanted line and the verbal on the horizontal line, as shown above. Position modifiers and complements in an infinitive phrase as you would position them in a sentence. If the infinitive functions as a noun, place the standard with the infinitive in the appropriate position in the diagram.

The dog wants to play tag in the front yard. [The infinitive phrase, *to play tag in the front yard,* is the direct object of the verb, *wants. Tag* is the direct object of the infinitive, *play. In the front yard* is a prepositional phrase that modifies *play.*]

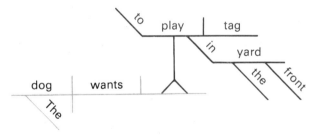

To diagram an infinitive phrase that is used as a modifier, place the standard with the infinitive phrase on a horizontal line below the modified word.

87

Exercise (page 88)

*See the Answers (Continued)
pages in the front section of this
Teacher's Edition.*

Andy worked hard to train his dog. [The infinitive phrase,
to train his dog, modifies the verb, *worked.*]

Exercise Diagraming Phrases   On your paper, diagram the following sentences. Be sure to use a ruler. The sentences contain prepositional phrases, participial phrases, and
infinitive phrases.

1. Lichens are plants without roots.
2. The tourists from Britain visited colonial houses preserved by
   the government.
3. We want to see that movie again.
4. Antarctica is the coldest part of the earth.
5. You were the second person to answer my invitation.
6. The players, encouraged by the fans, scored five runs in the
   first inning.
7. Find a good book to read.
8. I always walk to school with my little brother.
9. Laughing nervously, the young comedian began her routine
   for the Junior Show.
10. They came to this town to find work.
11. Hearing the distant thunder, we quickly closed the windows
    in the apartment.
12. The last train for Rahway leaves at midnight.

Phrases in Description

The phrases that you have studied in this unit contribute different kinds of meaning to sentences. Write a paragraph describing a person. Use prepositional phrases, participial phrases, and infinitive phrases in your paragraph. Describe the person's personality and appearance. Describe the person actually doing something.

A.

1. near Tucson, Arizona
   —Adjective phrase;
   of birds—Adjective phrase

2. Outside the farmer's market
   —Adverb phrase;
   for her mother—Adverb
   phrase

3. With a sheepish grin
   —Adverb phrase;
   of the sandwiches—Adjective
   phrase

4. despite the limited budget
   —Adverb phrase;
   for gymnastics—Adjective
   phrase

5. across the living room
   —Adverb phrase;
   through the window—Adverb
   phrase

B.

6. Zipping his jacket—Samuel

7. Surprised and delighted about
   the award—Ramón

8. Stomping angrily down the
   corridor—Mr. Levine

9. running toward the beach
   —children

10. Heartened by her father's
    encouragement—Sabrina

C.

*Labels in parentheses indicate
exactly how the infinitives are
used.*

11. to flee at the slightest sound—
    adverb (modifies adjective
    ready)

12. To remain optimistic—noun
    (subject)

(Continue on the next page.)

Unit Practice

Practice 1

A. Prepositional Phrases *(pages 73–77)*   On your paper, write the prepositional phrases in the following sentences. Next to each phrase, write the label *Adjective phrase* or *Adverb phrase*.

1. The Arizona-Sonora Desert Museum near Tucson, Arizona, features an unusual outdoor exhibition of birds.

2. Outside the farmer's market, Caroline waited patiently for her mother.

3. With a sheepish grin, Tom admitted that he had eaten both of the sandwiches.

4. Our girls' gymnastic team won the state championship despite the limited budget for gymnastics.

5. I paced nervously across the living room and peeked through the window.

B. Participial Phrases *(pages 77–81)*   On your paper, write the participial phrases in the following sentences. Next to each phrase, write the word that it modifies.

6. Zipping his jacket, Samuel stepped out into the chilly wind.

7. Surprised and delighted about the award, Ramón walked toward the stage.

8. Stomping angrily down the corridor, Mr. Levine ignored my cheerful greeting.

9. The children, running toward the beach, shouted happily over the noise of the crowd.

10. Heartened by her father's encouragement, Sabrina returned to the top of the trail.

C. Infinitive Phrases *(pages 81–84)*   On your paper, write the infinitive phrases in the following sentences. Next to each phrase, write whether that phrase functions as a noun, an adjective, or an adverb.

90

11. The mice were ready to flee at the slightest sound.

12. To remain optimistic was difficult as we watched the rain clouds rapidly building up.

13. During the Middle Ages, knights wore heavy armor to protect themselves from injuries in battle.

14. The scientists plan to use electron microscopes.

15. Robert's favorite author to reread is Robert Louis Stevenson.

D. Diagraming Sentences (pages 85–88) On your paper, diagram the following sentences. Be sure to use a ruler.

16. Mason decided to go to the barbershop after school.

17. Snapping the book shut, Ms. Binney looked out the window.

18. The guard, watching carefully for cars, led the children across the street.

19. Purring softly, Paul's cat started to drink its milk.

20. Molly welcomed the chance to relax before the party.

Practice 2

Number your paper from 1 to 10. List the phrases in italic type in the following passage. Label each phrase *Prepositional phrase, Participial phrase,* or *Infinitive phrase.*

When Leigh awoke   (1) *on Saturday morning* and saw the sun streaming   (2) *through her window*, she leaped out of bed excitedly. "Great!" she said to herself, "The weather is beautiful—a perfect day   (3) *to go hang gliding.*"   (4) *Hurrying down the stairs*, she tripped. She slowed down and went   (5) *into the kitchen*   (6) *to eat breakfast.* Just as she finished, her friend Patrice drove   (7) *up the driveway* and rang the doorbell.   (8) *Smiling with anticipation*, Leigh kissed her mother good-by and ran outside. Soon the two girls would be gliding   (9) *through the clear California skies.* They could hardly wait   (10) *to get started.*

Practice 1 *(pages 90–91),* continued

13. to protect themselves from injuries in battle—adverb (modifies verb *wore*)

14. to use electron microscopes —noun (direct object of verb *plan*)

15. to reread—adjective (modifies noun *author*)

D.

See the Answers (Continued) pages in the front section of this Teacher's Edition.

Practice 2 *(page 91)*

1. on Saturday morning —Prepositional phrase

2. through her window —Prepositional phrase

3. to go hang gliding—Infinitive phrase

4. Hurrying down the stairs —Participial phrase

5. into the kitchen —Prepositional phrase

6. to eat breakfast—Infinitive phrase

7. up the driveway— Prepositional phrase

8. Smiling with anticipation —Participial phrase

9. through the clear California skies—Prepositional phrase

10. to get started—Infinitive phrase

91

Test 1 *(pages 92–93)*

A.

1. on the lake—Adjective phrase
2. of the roof—Adjective phrase; near the peak—Adjective phrase
3. at the window—Adverb phrase
4. in the country—Adjective phrase; from a spring or a well—Adverb phrase
5. into dishes—Adverb phrase; in a special oven—Adverb phrase

B.

6. splashing in the bird bath —cardinal
7. Singing to herself—Anita
8. dressed in thick clothing —workers
9. Asking Jan not to hang up —Nancy
10. Startled by the hikers —deer

C.

Labels in parentheses indicate exactly how the infinitives are used.

11. To arrive late—noun (subject)
12. to make a salad for the dinner—noun (direct object of verb *Do want*)
13. to maintain control of your car—adverb (modifies adjective *difficult*)
14. to call for home delivery of the newspaper—adjective (modifies noun *person*)

(Continue on the next page.)

Test 1

A. Prepositional Phrases *(pages 73–77)* On your paper, write the prepositional phrases in the following sentences. Next to each phrase, write the label *Adjective phrase* or *Adverb phrase.*

1. The ice on the lake is finally melting.
2. The section of the roof near the peak has been repaired.
3. We stood at the window and watched the sudden downpour.
4. Many people in the country get their water from a spring or a well.
5. We molded the clay into dishes and baked them in a special oven.

B. Participial Phrases *(pages 77–81)* On your paper, write the participial phrases in the following sentences. Next to each phrase, write the word that it modifies.

6. Did you see the cardinal splashing in the bird bath?
7. Singing to herself, Anita walked toward the library.
8. The construction workers, dressed in thick clothing, worked in the cold weather.
9. Asking Jan not to hang up, Nancy ran to answer the doorbell.
10. Startled by the hikers, the deer disappeared into the forest.

C. Infinitive Phrases *(pages 81–84)* On your paper, write the infinitive phrases in the following sentences. Next to each phrase, write whether that phrase functions as a noun, an adjective, or an adverb.

11. To arrive late is an act of discourtesy.
12. Do you want to make a salad for the dinner?
13. On this bumpy road, it is difficult to maintain control of your car.
14. The person to call for home delivery of the newspaper is out to lunch.
15. The sun promises to break through the clouds this afternoon.

D. Diagraming Sentences *(pages 85–88)*   On your paper, diagram the following sentences. Be sure to use a ruler.

16. Sitting on the curb, Daryl waited for a bus.
17. Exercise is an effective way to control weight.
18. Most members of the class wanted to visit a television station.
19. The audience members chosen for the game approached the stage.
20. To avoid the heavy traffic, the taxi driver found another route.

Test 2

Number your paper from 1 to 10. List the phrases in italic type in the following passage. Label each phrase *Prepositional phrase*, *Participial phrase*, or *Infinitive phrase*.

(1) *Taking a deep breath,* Elizabeth walked   (2) *into the veterinarian's office.* "I'm here for an interview with Dr. Stoker," she said in response to the receptionist's inquiry, and she sat down   (3) *to wait for her appointment.* (4) *Despite her nervousness,* Elizabeth was looking forward to the interview.   (5) *To get this job as Dr. Stoker's assistant* would be an important step   (6) *toward her goal* of becoming a veterinarian.   (7) *According to the newspaper ad,* Dr. Stoker was seeking a hard-working, responsible person who loves animals, and Elizabeth knew she was well qualified. (8) *Determined to make a good impression,* Elizabeth rose immediately and introduced herself when the doctor appeared. Soon they were chatting like old friends. "Well, Elizabeth, it looks like you've gotten yourself a job," Dr. Stoker announced.   (9) *Grinning from ear to ear,* she thanked him and hurried home   (10) *to tell her family the good news.*

93

Test 1 *(pages 92–93),* continued

15. to break through the clouds this afternoon—noun (direct object of verb *promises*)

D.

See the Answers (Continued) pages in the front section of this Teacher's Edition.

Test 2 *(page 93)*

1. Taking a deep breath —Participial phrase
2. into the veterinarian's office—Prepositional phrase
3. to wait for her appointment —Infinitive phrase
4. Despite her nervousness —Prepositional phrase
5. To get this job as Dr. Stoker's assistant—Infinitive phrase
6. toward her goal—Prepositional phrase
7. According to the newspaper ad—Prepositional phrase
8. Determined to make a good impression—Participial phrase
9. Grinning from ear to ear —Participial phrase
10. to tell her family the good news—Infinitive phrase

Phrases   **93**

Unit 4

Objectives

After studying this unit, students should be able to do the following:

- Identify independent clauses.
- Identify subordinate clauses used as adjectives and subordinate clauses used as adverbs, and identify the words that they modify.
- Diagram sentences with adjective clauses and sentences with adverb clauses.

Teaching Suggestions

See "Classroom Insights" for Unit 4 in the front of this Teacher's Edition.

Program Resources

Resource Book, Second Course:
    Diagnostic Test, Unit 4
    Achievement Test, Unit 4
    Bonus Activities, Unit 4
    Extra Practice, Unit 4
    Unit Test, Unit 4
Practice Book, Second Course, Unit 4
Tests, Second Course, Unit 4

Related Resources

Houghton Mifflin Microcourse:
    Language Arts, Levels 7, 8
The American Heritage Dictionary of the English Language

Clauses

Unit Preview

The two sentences that follow express two ideas that are related to each other.

I would go with you.
I am working today.

However, the relationship between the two ideas is clearer if you join the two sentences.

I would go with you, but I am working today.

Both of the two sentences that have been joined are clauses. A clause is a group of related words that has a subject and a predicate. By learning about clauses, you learn how to write sentences that clearly show the relationships between your ideas.

For Analysis   Read the paragraph that follows. Then answer the questions about that paragraph.

(1) Because our theater club wanted to raise money for activities this year, we decided to present a talent show. (2) All the students in the club are talented, but we don't have much performing experience. (3) However, we have practiced very hard, and the show is sure to be a success.

1. What two ideas does Sentence 1 present? Why did the students put on the show?

94

2. What two ideas does Sentence 2 present? What problem does this sentence describe?
3. What two ideas does Sentence 3 present? How have the students solved their problem?

Each sentence in the paragraph presents two ideas, and each idea is presented in a different clause. In this unit you will learn how clauses function and how you can use them to make your writing clear.

4.1   Independent Clauses

A **clause** is a group of related words that contains both a subject and a predicate. There are two kinds of clauses: independent clauses and subordinate clauses.

An **independent clause** can stand by itself as a sentence. The following sentence contains two independent clauses.

```
      ┌──── indep. clause ────┐   ┌──── indep. clause ────┐
      Those tires will last longer, but they are more expensive.
```

Each independent clause can stand by itself as a sentence.

Those tires will last longer.
They are more expensive.

Like all clauses, an independent clause has a subject and a predicate. In the following example, the simple subject is underlined once, and the simple predicate is underlined twice.

```
   ┌─ indep. clause ─┐   ┌──────── indep. clause ────────┐
   Most birds fly, but turkeys cannot fly because of their
   weight.
```

95

For Analysis *(pages 94–95)*

Answers may vary. Samples:

1. Sentence 1 presents the ideas that the theater club wanted to raise money for activities and that the club decided to present a talent show. The students put on the show to raise the money.
2. Sentence 2 says that all the students in the club are talented and also that they don't have much performing experience. The problem is that talent without experience may not be enough to put on a really good performance.
3. Sentence 3 says that the students have practiced hard and that the show is sure to be a success. The students have solved their problem by working hard to compensate for their lack of experience.

Answers may vary. Samples:

1. The snow has finally stopped, but now we must shovel the walk.
2. Soil must be fertilized, or it will become depleted.
3. The doorbell rang loudly, and I dropped my book.
4. The rain beat against the windows, and the wind whistled through the eaves.
5. Will you wash the dishes, or shall I wash them?
6. Tim and I made the salad, and James cooked the spaghetti.
7. The senator campaigned tirelessly, but he lost the race.
8. Most people left after the meeting, but some people remained to chat about the discussion.
9. Suddenly a large crowd gathered, and then we heard the ambulance siren.
10. Speak more forcefully, or people will not accept your ideas.

Exercise   Independent Clauses   On your paper, rewrite each of the following sentences by replacing the blank with an independent clause that contains a related idea. In each independent clause that you supply, underline the simple subject once and the simple predicate twice.

SAMPLE   My grandfather was a sailor, and _?_.

ANSWER   My grandfather was a sailor, and he told fascinating stories about his adventures.

1. The snow has finally stopped, but _?_.
2. Soil must be fertilized, or _?_.
3. The doorbell rang loudly, and _?_.
4. The rain beat against the windows, and _?_.
5. Will you wash the dishes, or _?_?
6. Tim and I made the salad, and _?_.
7. The senator campaigned tirelessly, but _?_.
8. Most people left after the meeting, but _?_.
9. Suddenly a large crowd gathered, and _?_.
10. Speak more forcefully, or _?_.

4.2   Subordinate Clauses

A **subordinate clause** is a group of words that has a subject and a predicate but cannot stand alone as a sentence. Subordinate clauses are often called **dependent clauses.**

In the example that follows, the simple subject of the subordinate clause is underlined once and the simple predicate is underlined twice.

```
 ┌──── indep. clause ────┐┌─ sub. clause ─┐
 Everyone was happy when it snowed.
```

In the preceding example, the subordinate clause is combined with an independent clause. A subordinate clause by itself does not express a complete thought.

96

When he hears a siren [What happens?]

Which she had written [What had she written?]

Exercise 1 *(pages 97–98)*

See page 98 for the answers.

The subordinate clauses *when he hears a siren* and *which she had written* cannot stand by themselves as sentences because they do not express complete thoughts. To express complete thoughts, you must combine the subordinate clauses with independent clauses.

┌────── indep. clause ──────┬────── sub. clause ──────┐
My old sheepdog howls when he hears a siren.

┌────── indep. clause ──────┬────── sub. clause ──────┐
Tina read us the poem, which she had written herself.

┌── sub. clause ──┐ ┌────── indep. clause ──────┬──────
Before we left, we swept up the popcorn that had

────── sub. clause ──────┐
spilled on the floor. [The sentence has two subordinate clauses.]

To tell whether a clause is a subordinate clause or an independent clause, read each clause in the sentence to yourself. If the clause can stand alone as a sentence, it is an independent clause. If it cannot stand alone as a sentence, it is a subordinate clause.

SENTENCE   Before it goes to press, Ms. Barnes edits the newspaper.

SUBORDINATE CLAUSE Before it goes to press [The clause cannot stand by itself as a sentence because it does not express a complete thought.]

INDEPENDENT CLAUSE Ms. Barnes edits the newspaper. [The clause can stand by itself as a sentence because it expresses a complete thought.]

Exercise 1 Clauses On your paper, write each clause in the following sentences. Label each clause *Independent* or *Subordinate*.

97

Exercise 1 *(pages 97–98)*

1. Fame came to Robert Frost
   —Independent;
   when he was forty-one
   —Subordinate

2. This is the best movie
   —Independent;
   that I have ever seen
   —Subordinate

3. We will drop you off
   —Independent;
   wherever you want
   —Subordinate

4. They can't go—Independent;
   unless someone pays their
   fare—Subordinate

5. As soon as I come home
   —Subordinate;
   I take the meat out of the
   freezer—Independent

6. Whenever it rains—
   Subordinate;
   the flowers in the park take
   on a new fragrance
   —Independent

7. Although they lost the
   opening game—Subordinate;
   the team looked forward to a
   successful season
   —Independent

8. The great gray owl has a
   wing-spread of five feet
   —Independent;
   which is native to Canada and
   Alaska—Subordinate

9. Few architects design
   buildings—Independent;
   that please everyone
   —Subordinate

(Continue on the next page.)

SAMPLE	Thyme is an herb that belongs to the mint family.
ANSWER	Thyme is an herb—Independent that belongs to the mint family—Subordinate

1. Fame came to Robert Frost when he was forty-one.
2. This is the best movie that I have ever seen.
3. We will drop you off wherever you want.
4. They can't go unless someone pays their fare.
5. As soon as I come home, I take the meat out of the freezer.
6. Whenever it rains, the flowers in the park take on a new fragrance.
7. Although they lost the opening game, the team looked forward to a successful season.
8. The great gray owl, which is native to Canada and Alaska, has a wingspread of five feet.
9. Few architects design buildings that please everyone.
10. Mrs. Martinez, who is in Mexico, will be back next week.
11. Before the snow melted, we found the missing shovel.
12. We awakened earlier than we had planned.
13. My dog Rover comes when he is called.
14. This is the watch that my mother gave me.
15. If it rains, the volleyball game will be played indoors.

4.2a   Clauses Used as Adjectives

A subordinate clause functions as an adjective if it modifies a noun or a pronoun. Such clauses are sometimes called **adjective clauses.** Adjective clauses answer the same questions as adjectives: *Which? What kind? How many?*

The *man* who wrote the article about fitness is a retired coach. [*Which* man? The man who wrote the article about fitness. The adjective clause modifies the noun *man.*]

98

The *exercises* that he suggests are easy to do. [*What kind* of exercises? The exercises that he suggests. The adjective clause modifies the noun *exercises*.]

Most adjective clauses begin with a relative pronoun. There are five relative pronouns:

that   which   who   whom   whose

A relative pronoun relates an adjective clause to the word or words that it modifies. The relative pronoun is a subject or an object within the subordinate clause. In the following sentences, the relative pronoun is in boldface type.

My uncle owns a *dog* **that** walks on its hind legs. [The relative pronoun, *that,* is the subject of the adjective clause. The adjective clause modifies the noun *dog.*]

Here is a picture of my *cousin* **whom** I have not seen in five years. [The relative pronoun, *whom,* is the direct object of *have seen.* The adjective clause modifies the noun *cousin.*]

You may also begin an adjective clause with a relative adverb. The relative adverbs include *before, after, since, when,* and *where.*

This is the *spot* **where** Watson was last seen.

There was a *time* **when** I read nothing but mysteries.

The *weeks* **since** we returned from spring break have gone quickly.

Exercise 2 Adjective Clauses   *Step 1:* On your paper, write the adjective clauses in the following sentences. *Step 2:* Underline the relative pronoun or the relative adverb that

99

Exercise 1 *(pages 97–98),* continued

10. Mrs. Martinez will be back next week—Independent; who is in Mexico—Subordinate

11. Before the snow melted —Subordinate; we found the missing shovel —Independent

12. We awakened earlier —Independent; than we had planned —Subordinate

13. My dog Rover comes —Independent; when he is called —Subordinate

14. This is the watch —Independent; that my mother gave me —Subordinate

15. If it rains—Subordinate; the volleyball game will be played indoors—Independent

Exercise 2 *(pages 99–100)*

See page 100 for the answers.

Exercise 2 *(pages 99–100)*

1. who lives next door—man
2. whom you met last spring —cousin
3. whose future looks bright —pitcher
4. where Lincoln lived—house
5. who was directing traffic —officer
6. that belonged to my great-grandfather—hats
7. which had stood in the park for years—statue
8. that are known as yews —trees
9. whose father is a helicopter pilot—friend
10. when I become restless—time
11. that you made to go to summer camp—plans
12. where blueberries grow wild —spot
13. who wants to join the drama club—student
14. which was imported from Italy—table
15. that are accurate and easy to follow—directions

Exercise 3 *(pages 100–101)*

See page 101 for the answers.

begins each subordinate clause. *Step 3:* Write the word or words that the clause modifies.

SAMPLE	Last summer I caught a fish that weighed two pounds.
ANSWER	that weighed two pounds—fish

1. The man who lives next door is a firefighter.
2. This letter is from my cousin whom you met last spring.
3. He is a pitcher whose future looks bright.
4. In Springfield, Illinois, we visited the house where Lincoln lived.
5. The children waved to the police officer who was directing traffic.
6. In the attic we found some hats that belonged to my great-grandfather.
7. The statue, which had stood in the park for years, was taken down last week.
8. Trees that are known as yews remain green all year.
9. My sister has a friend whose father is a helicopter pilot.
10. This is the time of year when I become restless.
11. What happened to the plans that you made to go to summer camp?
12. The backpackers found a spot where blueberries grow wild.
13. Are you the student who wants to join the drama club?
14. This table, which was imported from Italy, is one of my uncle's prized possessions.
15. Always give directions that are accurate and easy to follow.

Exercise 3   Adjective Clauses   Number your paper from 1 to 5. Next to the number of each sentence, write the adjective clause in that sentence. Write the word modified by the adjective clause.

SAMPLE	Venice, which is a popular tourist resort, is known for its singing gondoliers.
ANSWER	which is a popular tourist resort—Venice

100

(1) Have you ever visited a city where most of the highways are canals? (2) In Venice, which is the capital city of Venetia in northeastern Italy, all traffic is either by boat or on foot. (3) Venice is built on mud banks that once formed more than one hundred small islands at the head of the Adriatic Sea. (4) All the buildings in Venice are erected on pilings that are driven into these banks. (5) In between the buildings are the canals that form the famous waterways of Venice.

4.2b Clauses Used as Adverbs

A subordinate clause functions as an adverb if it modifies a verb, an adjective, or an adverb. Such clauses are sometimes called **adverb clauses.**

MODIFIES VERB   We *arrived* before the concert began.

MODIFIES ADJECTIVE   We were *afraid* that we would be late.

MODIFIES ADVERB   We arrived *earlier* than we had before.

Like adverbs, adverb clauses tell *how, when, where,* and *to what extent or degree.* Adverb clauses may also explain *why.*

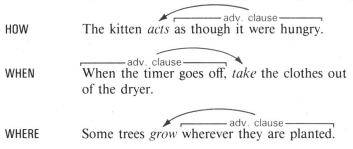

HOW   The kitten *acts* as though it were hungry.

WHEN   When the timer goes off, *take* the clothes out of the dryer.

WHERE   Some trees *grow* wherever they are planted.

101

Exercise 3 *(pages 100–101)*

1. where most of the highways are canals—city
2. which is the capital city of Venetia in northeastern Italy —Venice
3. that once formed more than one hundred small islands at the head of the Adriatic Sea —banks
4. that are driven into these banks—pilings
5. that form the famous waterways of Venice—canals

Exercise 4 *(pages 102–103)*

1. when she heard the good news
   —joyful

2. if I can—will help

3. When the climbers returned
   to the campsite—exhausted

4. If the rain stops before
   noon—will go

5. Whenever we drive to
   Manhattan—visit

6. until their skins were crisp
   —baked

7. because we planned to leave
   at six o'clock in the morning
   —early

8. as he approached the platform
   —waved

9. As soon as I can—will write

10. before the final scene was
    over—left

| TO WHAT DEGREE | My brother is *older* than I am. |
| WHY | School closed *early* so that we could get home before the blizzard. |

An adverb clause begins with a subordinating conjunction *(page 34)*. A **subordinating conjunction** shows the relationship between an adverb clause and an independent clause. The following list contains some frequently used subordinating conjunctions:

after	because	since	until
although	before	so that	when
as	even if	than	whenever
as if	even though	that	where
as soon as	if	though	wherever
as though	in order that	unless	while

Exercise 4 Adverb Clauses *Step 1:* On your paper, write the adverb clauses in the following sentences. *Step 2:* Underline the subordinating conjunction that introduces each adverb clause. *Step 3:* Next to each adverb clause, write the word or words that it modifies.

| SAMPLE | The new school will be built where you are standing. |
| ANSWER | where you are standing—will be built |

1. Mother was joyful when she heard the good news.
2. I will help you if I can.
3. When the climbers returned to the campsite, they were exhausted.
4. If the rain stops before noon, we will go to the beach.

102

5. Whenever we drive to Manhattan, we visit the Empire State Building.
6. We baked the potatoes until their skins were crisp.
7. We went to bed early because we planned to leave at six o'clock in the morning.
8. The speaker waved as he approached the platform.
9. I will write to you as soon as I can.
10. The critics left before the final scene was over.

Exercise 5 Subordinate Clauses Number your paper from 1 to 6. *Step 1:* Next to the number of the sentence, write the subordinate clause in that sentence. *Step 2:* Label each subordinate clause *Adjective clause* or *Adverb clause. Step 3:* Write the word or words modified by each subordinate clause.

SAMPLE	If you are not convinced of the importance of sleep, just try to do without it for a long period.
ANSWER	If you are not convinced of the importance of sleep—Adverb clause; try

(1) There is no living creature that does not need a period of rest every day. (2) Sleep is important because it helps to restore tired organs and tissues. (3) Sleep is also the time when our bodies build up energy for the next period of activity. (4) There are many people who can get along with eight hours of sleep. (5) There are some who may need more or less sleep. (6) A person usually needs less sleep as he or she grows older.

Assignment Clauses in Writing Write five sentences, each with a subordinate clause, about something that you have learned recently about current events, history, literature, mathematics, or science. Underline each clause that you write and tell whether it is an adjective clause or an adverb clause.

103

1. that does not need a period of rest every day—Adjective clause; creature
2. because it helps to restore tired organs and tissues —Adverb clause; important
3. when our bodies build up energy for the next period of activity—Adjective clause; time
4. who can get along with eight hours of sleep—Adjective clause; people
5. who may need more or less sleep—Adjective clause; some
6. as he or she grows older— Adverb clause; needs

Clauses in Writing

One way to learn about how to use clauses in writing is to observe how professional writers use them.

He was a brisk, waspish old gentleman, who had dried and wilted away. (Washington Irving)

Moths, when they rest, spread out their wings like grounded airplanes. (Donald Culross Peattie)

Look for examples of adjective clauses and adverb clauses in books, magazines, and newspapers. Copy five or more examples of each kind of clause. Then write a descriptive paragraph of your own in which you use adjective clauses and adverb clauses.

4.3   Diagraming Sentences with Clauses

This section will show you how to diagram the clauses that you studied in this unit. First, however, you may want to review "Sentence Diagrams" on pages 61–67 and "Diagraming Sentences with Phrases" on pages 85–88.

Diagraming Adjective Clauses

To diagram a sentence with an adjective clause, first diagram the independent clause as you would diagram a sentence. Then diagram the adjective clause as a separate sen-

104

tence on a horizontal line below the independent clause. Use a line of dashes to connect the relative pronoun in the adjective clause with the modified word in the independent clause. Position the adjective clause so that the relative pronoun and the modified word can be connected easily.

The girl who had the lead in the school play is my sister. [The adjective clause, *who had the lead in the school play,* modifies the noun *girl.* The relative pronoun, *who,* is the subject of the adjective clause and is diagramed in that position.]

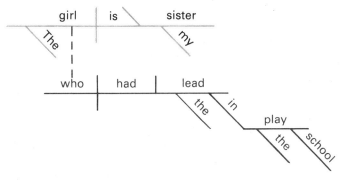

We are reading a script that my teacher wrote for his drama class. [The adjective clause, *that my teacher wrote for his drama class,* modifies the noun *script.* The relative pronoun, *that,* is the direct object in the adjective clause and is diagramed in that position.]

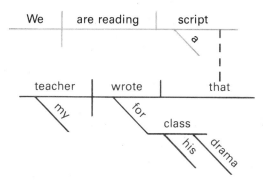

105

Exercise 1 *(page 106)*

See the Answers (Continued) pages in the front section of this Teacher's Edition.

Exercise 1 **Diagraming Adjective Clauses**   On your paper, diagram the following sentences. The sentences contain adjective clauses.

SAMPLE   Listen to the joke that Selma told me.

ANSWER

1. The bird that we saw was a thrush.
2. A boy whom I once knew is now a famous actor.
3. The visitors whom we are expecting have been delayed by traffic.
4. You are the only person who qualifies for that job on the school paper.
5. John, who had run for a touchdown, was surrounded by his teammates.

Diagraming Adverb Clauses

To diagram a sentence with an adverb clause, first diagram the independent clause as you would diagram a sentence. Then diagram the adverb clause as a separate sentence on a horizontal line below the independent clause. Use a line of dashes to connect the verb in the adverb clause with the modified word or words in the independent clause. Write the subordinating conjunction on the line of dashes. Position the adverb clause so that the verb and the modified word or words can be connected easily.

106

If I need help, I will call you. [The adverb clause, *If I need help,* modifies the verb phrase, *will call.*]

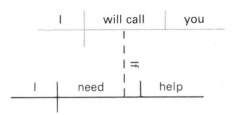

Exercise 2 *(page 107)*

See the Answers (Continued) pages in the front section of this Teacher's Edition.

Exercise 2 Diagraming Adverb Clauses On your paper, diagram the following sentences. The sentences contain adverb clauses.

SAMPLE   My family was happy when I finally made the team.

ANSWER

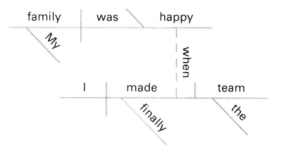

1. The car stopped because the gas tank was empty.
2. When the bell rang, everyone rushed for the doors.
3. The judge will dismiss the case unless more evidence is offered.
4. The movie was better than we had expected.
5. The coach left quickly after we lost our lead in the final minutes of the game.

107

Practice 1 *(page 108)*

A.

1. The equator is an imaginary line that divides the earth into the northern and southern hemispheres.

2. The gymnasts who were late for the meet, did not perform as well as expected.

3. Spring is a time when people celebrate the renewal of life.

4. The man whose lawnmower I borrowed let me use it all summer.

5. There have been many technological advances in the years since World War II ended.

B.

6. before we abandon it for the winter—lock

7. that her cat had four kittens —overjoyed

8. whenever he bicycled with his little brother—slower

9. as soon as you get here—will eat

10. even if it takes me all weekend—will complete

(Continue on the next page.)

Practice 1

A. Adjective Clauses *(pages 98–101)* On your paper, write the following sentences. Underline the adjective clauses and circle the relative pronoun or relative adverb that begins the clause.

1. The equator is an imaginary line that divides the earth into the northern and southern hemispheres.
2. The gymnasts, who were late for the meet, did not perform as well as expected.
3. Spring is a time when people celebrate the renewal of life.
4. The man whose lawnmower I borrowed let me use it all summer.
5. There have been many technological advances in the years since World War II ended.

B. Adverb Clauses *(pages 101–103)* On your paper, write the adverb clauses in the following sentences. Next to each clause, write the word or words that the clause modifies.

6. We lock up the cottage before we abandon it for the winter.
7. Phyllis was overjoyed that her cat had four kittens.
8. Buddy pedaled slower whenever he bicycled with his little brother.
9. We will eat as soon as you get here.
10. I will complete this project even if it takes me all weekend.

C. Diagraming Clauses *(pages 104–107)* On your paper, diagram the following sentences. Be sure to use a ruler.

11. I liked the shirt that Mark returned.
12. Olivia jumped slightly when we yelled "Surprise!"
13. I walk through the marsh unless it is very wet.
14. Take Samson when you go to the ball park.
15. Give this message to Dr. Fairfax, who is sitting in the aisle seat.

108

Practice 2

Number your paper from 1 to 8. Label each numbered clause in italic type in the following paragraph *Independent clause, Adjective clause,* or *Adverb clause.*

Braiding, (1) *which is a relatively simple technique,* has many uses. (2) *People braid their hair for decorative purposes.* Hats (3) *that are made out of straw* are manufactured by braiding. (4) *Strips of fabric are braided and then sewn together to form rugs.* Various types of cord are braided (5) *before they are used for such things as wicks and shoelaces.* Braided cords (6) *that are gold, black, or white* are used to decorate military uniforms. (7) *In addition, braided materials are used to make tires, wires, and cables.* (8) *When strength and flexibility are needed,* people often use braided materials.

109

Practice 1 *(page 108),* continued

C.
See the Answers (Continued) pages in the front section of this Teacher's Edition.

Practice 2 *(page 109)*

1. Adjective clause
2. Independent clause
3. Adjective clause
4. Independent clause
5. Adverb clause
6. Adjective clause
7. Independent clause
8. Adverb clause

Test 1 *(page 110)*

A.

1. We gazed at the moonlight, (which)was reflected in silver strands across the surface of the lake.

2. The trapeze artists, (who) worked without a net, had the audience gasping at each stunt.

3. The night(before)I take an exam, I relax and go to bed early.

4. I made a birthday present for Jackson,(who)is my best friend.

5. Over the weekend we drove to Phoenix,(where)we attended my cousin's college graduation.

B.

6. after the drum solo was over —heard

7. as he waited for the judges to announce the winners—calm

8. when she takes an early lead —best

(Continue on the next page.)

Test 1

A. Adjective Clauses *(pages 98–101)* On your paper, write the following sentences. Underline the adjective clause and circle the relative pronoun or relative adverb that begins the clause.

1. We gazed at the moonlight, which was reflected in silver strands across the surface of the lake.
2. The trapeze artists, who worked without a net, had the audience gasping at each stunt.
3. The night before I take an exam, I relax and go to bed early.
4. I made a birthday present for Jackson, who is my best friend.
5. Over the weekend we drove to Phoenix, where we attended my cousin's college graduation.

B. Adverb Clauses *(pages 101–103)* On your paper, write the adverb clauses in the following sentences. Next to each clause, write the word or words that the clause modifies.

6. We heard the cymbals after the drum solo was over.
7. Jonathan remained calm as he waited for the judges to announce the winners.
8. Anita runs best when she takes an early lead.
9. The bird acted as though it were hurt.
10. The hill was steeper than it looked from the bottom.

C. Diagraming Clauses *(pages 104–107)* On your paper, diagram the following sentences. Be sure to use a ruler.

11. Take the train that skips several stops.
12. Stop at the store after you visit Grandpa.
13. The puppy ate hungrily even though I had recently fed him.
14. I will paint the basement after you clean it.
15. You are a person whom everyone respects.

110

Test 2

Number your paper from 1 to 8. Label each numbered clause in italic type in the following paragraph *Independent clause, Adjective clause,* or *Adverb clause.*

Alexander Fleming discovered penicillin in 1928 (1) *while he was growing some cultures of common germs.* On one of the cultures, he found some mold (2) *that was dissolving the germs.* (3) *His discovery began the era of the "wonder drug."* (4) *Penicillin and similar drugs, called antibiotics, kill bacteria and other microorganisms.* However, they cannot do this (5) *unless they are applied directly to the infection or are conveyed to the infection through the blood stream.* Penicillin is usually injected (6) *because this has been the most effective method of treating the patient.* Recently, though, scientists have developed certain forms (7) *that can be taken orally.* (8) *Even though antibiotics kill germs in the body,* they do not affect healthy cells.

Test 1 *(page 110),* continued

9. as though it were hurt
—acted
10. than it looked from the bottom—steeper

C.

See the Answers (Continued) pages in the front section of this Teacher's Edition.

Test 2 *(page 111)*

1. Adverb clause
2. Adjective clause
3. Independent clause
4. Independent clause
5. Adverb clause
6. Adverb clause
7. Adjective clause
8. Adverb clause

111

Unit 5

Compound and Complex Sentences

Objectives

After studying this unit, students should be able to do the following:

- Classify sentences by structure as simple, compound, complex, or compound-complex.

- Write complete sentences, avoiding sentence fragments and run-on sentences.

- Diagram compound and complex sentences.

Teaching Suggestions

See "Classroom Insights" for Unit 5 in the front of this Teacher's Edition.

Program Resources

Resource Book, Second Course:
    Diagnostic Test, Unit 5
    Achievement Test, Unit 5
    Bonus Activities, Unit 5
    Extra Practice, Unit 5
    Unit Test, Unit 5
Practice Book, Second Course, Unit 5
Tests, Second Course, Unit 5

Related Resources

Houghton Mifflin Microcourse:
    Language Arts, Levels 7, 8
The American Heritage Dictionary of the English Language

Unit Preview

As you read the following paragraph, ask yourself why it is difficult to understand.

PARAGRAPH A

(1) On a cold winter day, a boy trudged through the snow, he was following some rabbit tracks. (2) To see where they went. (3) The tracks led into the woods. (4) Near the farm where he lived. (5) He climbed over a ridge. (6) And into a hollow that was sheltered from the wind and the cold. (7) All of a sudden, he forgot about the tracks, at the bottom of the hollow was a large area of green. (8) Small trees, berry bushes, lush moss, grass, and even some buttercups, they were growing around a warm spring. (9) The boy wondered how plants could thrive in the middle of winter, the boy was Luther Burbank. (10) From that moment in the hollow, Burbank was fascinated by plants he spent the rest of his life experimenting with them.

The paragraph is difficult to understand for two reasons. First, many of the ideas are not expressed in complete sentences. Second, sometimes the ideas that would normally be written in two sentences are included in one sentence.

For Analysis   Paragraph B is a rewritten version of Paragraph A. Read the paragraph and answer the questions that follow.

112

PARAGRAPH B

(1) On a cold winter day, a boy trudged through the snow. (2) He was following some rabbit tracks to see where they went. (3) The tracks led into the woods near the farm where he lived. (4) He climbed over a ridge and into a hollow that was sheltered from the wind and the cold. (5) All of a sudden, he forgot about the tracks. (6) At the bottom of the hollow was a large area of green. (7) Small trees, berry bushes, lush moss, grass, and even some buttercups were growing around a warm spring. (8) The boy wondered how plants could thrive in the middle of winter. (9) The boy was Luther Burbank. (10) From that moment in the hollow, Burbank was fascinated by plants. (11) He spent the rest of his life experimenting with them.

1. Reread Sentence 1 in Paragraph A. How has that sentence been rewritten in Paragraph B?
2. Reread Sentences 3 and 4 in Paragraph A. How have those sentences been rewritten in Paragraph B?
3. Reread Sentences 5 and 6 in Paragraph A. How have those sentences been rewritten in Paragraph B?
4. Why is Paragraph B easier to read?

In this unit you will learn to correct errors in sentence structure similar to those in the paragraph about Luther Burbank. You will also learn how compound, complex, and compound-complex sentences can lend variety and interest to your writing.

For Analysis *(page 113)*

1. The sentence has been rewritten as two sentences.
2. They have been combined to form one sentence.
3. They have been combined to form one sentence.
4. Paragraph B is easier to read because it is written in single, complete sentences. As a result, the reader can tell where each thought begins and ends.

5.1   Sentences Classified by Structure

Sentences may be classified according to the number and kinds of clauses that they contain. The four kinds of sentences are simple sentences, compound sentences, complex sentences, and compound-complex sentences.

113

Exercise 1 *(pages 114–115)*

See page 115 for the answers.

5.1a   Simple Sentences and Compound Sentences

A **simple sentence** is a sentence that contains one independent clause *(page 95)* and no subordinate clauses *(page 96)*. A simple sentence may have any number of phrases *(page 73)*. It may have a compound subject *(page 49)*, a compound predicate *(page 49)*, or both. However, it does not have more than one independent clause.

┌─────────────── indep. clause ───────────────┐
Tanya wrote me a long letter about life in Ohio.

┌─────────────── indep. clause ───────────────┐
She and her **brother** like their new school. [compound subject]

┌─────────────── indep. clause ───────────────┐
Her family **left** Arizona and **settled** in Ohio. [compound predicate]

A **compound sentence** is a sentence that contains two or more independent clauses that are joined. You usually join the independent clauses in a compound sentence with one of the coordinating conjunctions: *and, but, nor, or, for,* or *yet*. A comma usually precedes the coordinating conjunction.

┌──── indep. clause ────┐   ┌──── indep. clause ────┐
I would like to go, **but** I have to wash the car.

┌──── indep. clause ────┐   ┌──── indep. clause ────┐
She suffers from arthritis, **yet** she seldom complains.

You can also join the independent clauses in a compound sentence by using a semicolon.

┌──── indep. clause ────┐ ┌─indep. clause─┐
Some snails have shells; others do not.

Exercise 1   Simple and Compound Sentences

Write the following sentences on your paper. Underline the

simple subject of each clause once and the simple predicate twice. Label each sentence *Simple* or *Compound*.

SAMPLE   The flag is the symbol of our nation, and it should be treated with respect.

ANSWER   The <u>flag</u> <u>is</u> the symbol of our nation, and <u>it</u> <u>should be treated</u> with respect.—Compound

1. The happy boy walked along, whistling a merry tune.
2. Grandmother received a bouquet of roses and daisies for her birthday.
3. The sun was setting over the mountains, and the shadows were growing long.
4. Fog and drizzle have forced airport officials to close the runways.
5. The car ran off the road, but fortunately no one was hurt.
6. The traveler turned and walked off into the darkness.
7. Tires should be inflated properly, or they will wear out rapidly.
8. We just bought a new rake and a secondhand lawn mower.
9. The jonquils were already drooping, for the sun was very hot.
10. I rang the doorbell several times, but no one answered.

5.1b Complex Sentences

A **complex sentence** is a sentence that consists of one independent clause and one or more subordinate clauses. A subordinate clause may be an adjective clause *(page 98)* or an adverb clause *(page 101)*. It may interrupt an independent clause.

The candidate who is running for mayor is my uncle. [The adjective clause modifies *candidate*. It interrupts the independent clause, *The candidate is my uncle*.]

115

Exercise 1 *(pages 114–115)*

1. The happy <u>boy</u> <u>walked</u> along, whistling a merry tune. —Simple
2. <u>Grandmother</u> <u>received</u> a bouquet of roses and daisies for her birthday.—Simple
3. The <u>sun</u> <u>was setting</u> over the mountains, and the <u>shadows</u> <u>were growing</u> long.—Compound
4. <u>Fog</u> and <u>drizzle</u> <u>have forced</u> airport officials to close the runways.—Simple
5. The <u>car</u> <u>ran</u> off the road, but fortunately <u>no one</u> <u>was</u> hurt. —Compound
6. The <u>traveler</u> <u>turned</u> and <u>walked</u> off into the darkness. —Simple
7. <u>Tires</u> <u>should be inflated</u> properly, or <u>they</u> <u>will wear</u> out rapidly. —Compound
8. <u>We</u> just <u>bought</u> a new rake and a secondhand lawn mower.—Simple
9. The <u>jonquils</u> <u>were</u> already drooping, for the <u>sun</u> <u>was</u> very hot.—Compound
10. <u>I</u> <u>rang</u> the doorbell several times, but <u>no one</u> <u>answered</u>. —Compound

Exercise 2 *(page 116)*

1. My sister is a person who never betrays a confidence.—Complex

2. The storm left the city wet, but it covered the nearby suburbs with a blanket of snow.—Compound

3. Camels were once used in Texas as beasts of burden.—Simple

4. The typewriter that I want costs more than two hundred dollars.—Complex

5. We drove past the farm where my father was born.—Complex

6. After I fed the cat, I went to bed.—Complex

7. Dad has agreed to our plan, but Mother is thinking it over.—Compound

8. This is the book that the librarian recommended.—Complex

9. On the morning of his birthday, my brother was up at six o'clock.—Simple

10. Whenever my grandparents come to dinner, we have ravioli.—Complex

---

adv. clause

Although the fire department answered the alarm promptly,

indep. clause

adj. clause

the fire, which had smoldered in the store, had already burned itself out. [The adverb clause modifies *had burned*. The adjective clause modifies *fire*. The adjective clause interrupts the independent clause.]

Exercise 2   Classifying Sentences   Write the following sentences on your paper. Underline each independent clause once and each subordinate clause twice. Label each sentence *Simple, Compound,* or *Complex.*

> SAMPLE   We found the check in the letter that came in the mail today.
>
> ANSWER   We found the check in the letter that came in the mail today.—Complex

1. My sister is a person who never betrays a confidence.
2. The storm left the city wet, but it covered the nearby suburbs with a blanket of snow.
3. Camels were once used in Texas as beasts of burden.
4. The typewriter that I want costs more than two hundred dollars.
5. We drove past the farm where my father was born.
6. After I fed the cat, I went to bed.
7. Dad has agreed to our plan, but Mother is thinking it over.
8. This is the book that the librarian recommended.
9. On the morning of his birthday, my brother was up at six.
10. Whenever my grandparents come to dinner, we have ravioli.

5.1c   Compound-Complex Sentences

A **compound-complex sentence** is a sentence that consists of two or more independent clauses and one or more subordinate clauses.

116

```
  ┌────── sub. clause──────┐ ┌──────indep. clause──────┐
After the storm was over, we decided to go home, but
  ┌────────── indep. clause──────────┐
the snow had blocked the driveway.
```

A subordinate clause sometimes interrupts the independent clause.

```
        ┌────────────── indep. clause──────────────┐
        │         ┌──────────sub. clause──────────┐ │
The friend who recommended that car is a mechanic, and
  ┌──────indep. clause──────┐
I trust his judgment.
```
[The subordinate clause, *who recommended that car,* interrupts the independent clause *The friend is a mechanic.*]

Exercise 3 Classifying Sentences
Write the following sentences on your paper. Underline each independent clause once and each subordinate clause twice. Label each sentence *Complex* or *Compound-complex.*

SAMPLE   When the pinch hitter came to bat, he hit a home run, and the crowd went wild.

ANSWER   When the pinch hitter came to bat, he hit a home run, and the crowd went wild.— Compound-complex

1. I don't like oysters, but I will eat clams if they are baked.
2. The jury returned, and the spectators became very quiet when the judge asked for the verdict.
3. When the ice melted, heavy rains began to fall, and the mountain streams overflowed.
4. The bus stopped more quickly than we had expected, but no one was hurt.
5. Dad answered the phone, but the person who was calling had already hung up.
6. If the frosts are too severe, the citrus crops will be damaged, and fruit prices will rise.

117

Exercise 3 *(pages 117–118)*

1. I don't like oysters, but I will eat clams if they are baked.
—Compound-complex
2. The jury returned, and the spectators became very quiet when the judge asked for the verdict.
—Compound-complex
3. When the ice melted, heavy rains began to fall, and the mountain streams overflowed.
—Compound-complex
4. The bus stopped more quickly than we had expected, but no one was hurt.
—Compound complex
5. Dad answered the phone, but the person who was calling had already hung up.—Compound-complex
6. If the frosts are too severe, the citrus crops will be damaged, and fruit prices will rise.
—Compound-complex

(Continue on the next page.)

Exercise 3 *(pages 117–118)*, continued

7. Although his methods are not scientific, he usually gets results.—Complex

8. Dust clouds rose in the distance as the wind blew across the dry plains, and the settlers were forced to seek shelter.
   —Compound-complex

9. When we reached the clearing, the tiger was still in the bush, and we could see the fear on the faces of the villagers.
   —Compound-complex

10. As it swept inland, the storm, which had winds up to forty-five miles per hour, caused heavy seas along the coast.—Complex

7. Although his methods are not scientific, he usually gets results.

8. Dust clouds rose in the distance as the wind blew across the dry plains, and the settlers were forced to seek shelter.

9. When we reached the clearing, the tiger was still in the bush, and we could see the fear on the faces of the villagers.

10. As it swept inland, the storm, which had winds up to forty-five miles per hour, caused heavy seas along the coast.

5.2 Writing Complete Sentences

A **complete sentence** is a group of words that has at least one complete subject and one complete predicate and that expresses a complete thought. Many people make two common errors in writing: sentence fragments and run-on sentences. Neither sentence fragments nor run-on sentences are acceptable in most writing. In this section you will learn how to recognize these errors and how to correct them.

5.2a Avoiding Sentence Fragments

A **sentence fragment** is a word group that lacks a subject or a predicate or does not express a complete thought. In the examples that follow, the fragments are in boldface type.

LACKS SUBJECT	The artist sketched the tree. **And stepped back to admire his work.** [The second word group does not tell who stepped back.]
LACKS PREDICATE	**The artist sketching the tree.** [The word group does not tell what the artist did.]
COMPLETE SENTENCE	The artist sketching the tree stepped back to admire his work. [The word

118

group has a subject and a predicate, and it expresses a complete thought. Therefore, it is a sentence.]

A common kind of sentence fragment is a phrase. You can often correct this kind of fragment by including the phrase in a related sentence.

FRAGMENT   I bought Dad a can opener. **With six attachments.**

COMPLETE SENTENCE   I bought Dad a can opener **with six**
prepositional
-phrase——
attachments.

FRAGMENT   I saw two joggers. **Running along the river.**

COMPLETE SENTENCE   —participial phrase—
I saw two joggers **running along the river.**

FRAGMENT   **To own a bicycle with all the accessories.** That has always been my dream.

COMPLETE SENTENCE   ——— infinitive phrase ———
To own a bicycle with all the accessories has always been my dream.

Another common type of sentence fragment is the subordinate clause. You can often correct this type of fragment by combining the clause with a related sentence.

FRAGMENT   Several months had passed. **Before the news reached the outpost.**

COMPLETE SENTENCE   Several months had passed **before the**
—— subordinate clause ——
news reached the outpost.

119

Compound and Complex Sentences   **119**

Exercise 1 *(page 120)*

Answers may vary. Samples:

1. His classmates, who apparently came by bus, visited him at the hospital.
2. Julie was the best hitter on her team.
3. The band began to play some lively music, which everyone enjoyed.
4. The principal announced his decision to give us a day off.
5. The horses raced wildly through the mountain pass.
6. The painting was sold to Mrs. Clark, who lives in Revere Place.
7. Whenever I hear that song, I think of Uncle Charlie.
8. Not realizing the danger, we paddled our canoes close to the falls.
9. I usually meet friendly people wherever I go.
10. Jeremy was peering into the dimly lighted room.

FRAGMENT   The tiger lily is a tall garden flower. **That originally grew in Asia.**

COMPLETE SENTENCE   The tiger lily is a tall garden flower

┌── subordinate clause ──┐
that originally grew in Asia.

Exercise 1   Correcting Sentence Fragments   On your paper, rewrite the following word groups, correcting all the sentence fragments. Supply suitable subjects and predicates where they are needed.

SAMPLE   Two boys fishing from the bridge.

ANSWER   Two boys were fishing from the bridge.

1. His classmates visited him at the hospital. Who apparently came by bus.
2. The best hitter on her team.
3. The band began to play some lively music. Which everyone enjoyed.
4. The principal announced his decision. To give us a day off.
5. The horses raced wildly. Through the mountain pass.
6. The painting was sold to Mrs. Clark. Who lives in Revere Place.
7. Whenever I hear that song. I think of Uncle Charlie.
8. Not realizing the danger.
9. I usually meet friendly people. Wherever I go.
10. Peering into the dimly lighted room.

5.2b   Avoiding Run-On Sentences

A **run-on sentence** consists of two or more complete sentences that are written as though they were one sentence. In some run-on sentences, the two sentences are separated by a comma. In other run-on sentences, the sentences are not separated at all.

120

RUN-ON SENTENCE   There are four kinds of teeth, each type has a different function.

RUN-ON SENTENCE   There are four kinds of teeth each type has a different function.

CORRECT   There are four kinds of teeth, and each type has a different function.

There are several ways to correct run-on sentences.

1. Join the independent clauses with a comma and a coordinating conjunction. The coordinating conjunctions are *and, but, for, nor, or,* and *yet.*

   RUN-ON SENTENCE   The men stopped work, the factory became silent.

   CORRECT   The men stopped work, **and** the factory became silent.

2. Join the independent clauses with a semicolon.

   RUN-ON SENTENCE   Some animals migrate others hibernate.

   CORRECT   Some animals migrate; others hibernate.

3. Form two or more separate sentences from the run-on sentence.

   RUN-ON SENTENCE   My friend from Spokane visited me, we talked until midnight.

   CORRECT   My friend from Spokane visited me. **We** talked until midnight.

4. Change one of the independent clauses to a subordinate clause, adding a subordinating conjunction *(page 34)* or a relative pronoun *(page 10).*

   RUN-ON SENTENCE   The rain stopped, we went for a walk along the beach.

121

Exercise 2 *(page 122)*

Answers may vary. Samples:

1. Alec is our class president, and Jane is our treasurer.
2. Mercury thermometers are common, but alcohol can also be used in thermometers.
3. Have you ever driven a snowmobile? It can be a breathtaking experience.
4. There are different kinds of radio telescopes; all of them have antennas and receivers.
5. My brother is a talented musician who has won several awards.
6. Sleet fell all night, and in the morning the streets were covered with ice.
7. I will pay for the shoe that my dog ate. He meant no harm.
8. Although the price of wheat is down, there are few buyers.

CORRECT	**When** the rain stopped, we went for a walk along the beach. [The corrected sentence is a complex sentence that contains an adverb clause.]
RUN-ON SENTENCE	The lobby was crowded with teen-agers they wanted tickets for the concert.
CORRECT	The lobby was crowded with teen-agers **who** wanted tickets for the concert. [The corrected sentence is a complex sentence with an adjective clause.]

Exercise 2   Correcting Run-On Sentences   On your paper, rewrite and correct the following run-on sentences. You may rephrase the sentences.

SAMPLE	I got on the bus, it was unusually crowded.
ANSWER	I got on the bus, which was unusually crowded.

1. Alec is our class president, Jane is our treasurer.
2. Mercury thermometers are common, alcohol can also be used in thermometers.
3. Have you ever driven a snowmobile, it can be a breathtaking experience.
4. There are different kinds of radio telescopes, all of them have antennas and receivers.
5. My brother is a talented musician he has won several awards.
6. Sleet fell all night, in the morning the streets were covered with ice.
7. I will pay for the shoe that my dog ate he meant no harm.
8. The price of wheat is down, there are few buyers.

Assignment   Writing Sentences   Rewrite each of the following sentence pairs to form a compound, a complex, or a compound-complex sentence. Check each sentence that you write to make certain that it is not a sentence fragment or a run-on sentence.

122

SAMPLE   We often talk about Uncle Nick. He was one of the first airline pilots.

ANSWER   We often talk about Uncle Nick, who was one of the first airline pilots.

1. The evening light faded. The moon rose over the bay.
2. The tracks were coated with ice. The trains managed to run.
3. The weather was good. We decided to go for a ride.
4. The firefighters fought the blaze. It was finally brought under control.
5. The election was over. The senator had been elected for a fourth term.

Writing Complete Sentences from Notes

Taking notes is a useful skill. Reporters take notes during interviews. Students take notes during classes. In taking notes, most people do not write complete sentences. Instead, they write sentence fragments that contain key information. Then, when they write the composition or article, they use complete sentences.

On your paper, write notes containing the key information needed to give one of the following sets of directions. Then use your notes to write a paragraph explaining those directions to other students. Your paragraph should have complete sentences. You may explain one of the following:

1. how to do something, such as change a bicycle tire
2. how to make something, such as a ceramic bowl
3. how to get somewhere, such as from your house to a friend's house

5.3   Diagraming Sentences

In this section you will learn how to diagram compound sentences and complex sentences. First, however, you may want to review "Sentence Diagrams" *(pages 61–67),* "Diagraming Sentences with Phrases" *(pages 85–88),* and "Diagraming Sentences with Clauses" *(pages 104–107).*

Diagraming Compound Sentences

To diagram a compound sentence, place each independent clause on separate parallel base lines. Connect the verb or the verb phrase in one clause with the verb or the verb phrase in the other clause with a line of dashes that has a step. On the step write the conjunction that joins the two clauses.

Dale stepped into the batter's box, and the crowd roared.

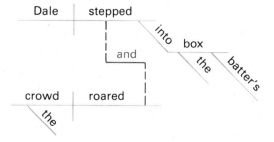

Diagraming Complex Sentences

To diagram a complex sentence, first decide whether the subordinate clause is an adjective clause or an adverb clause. Then follow the rules for diagraming adjective clauses *(pages 104–105)* and adverb clauses *(page 106–107).*

124

ADJECTIVE CLAUSE
The salesperson who found my wallet returned it immediately.

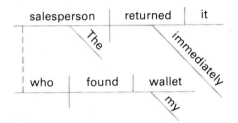

ADVERB CLAUSE
We will leave whenever you are ready.

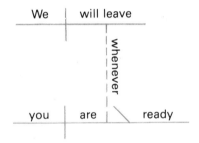

Exercise *(page 125)*

See the Answers (Continued) pages in the front section of this Teacher's Edition.

Exercise Diagraming Sentences On your paper, diagram the following compound and complex sentences. Be sure to use a ruler.

1. The family that lives next to us just bought a parrot.
2. Mother addressed the envelopes, and I stamped them.
3. Dad was upset because I lost the keys to the garage.
4. We fished for three hours, but nobody caught anything.
5. The city that we visited was Vancouver.

125

Compound and Complex Sentences **125**

A.

1. The downpour came without
   <u>warning</u>, and <u>and</u> <u>we all
   scrambled for shelter.</u>
   —Compound

2. <u>Susan,</u> <u>who has taken several
   art courses,</u> <u>designed our float
   for the parade.</u>—Complex

3. <u>The committee must choose a
   theme and decorate the gym.</u>
   —Simple

4. <u>Some fires can be fought with
   water,</u> but <u>an electrical fire,
   which is extremely dangerous,
   must be controlled with
   chemicals.</u>
   —Compound-complex

5. <u>Nitrogen is colorless,</u> and <u>it
   has no taste or odor.</u>
   —Compound

B.
Answers may vary. Samples:

6. To get away from the hurry of
   city life, we rented a small
   island in Canada.

7. Mammoths, who roamed the
   earth thousands of years ago,
   were huge creatures resembling
   elephants.

8. Many new products are tested
   in Kansas City, which is
   typical of the United States in
   many ways.

9. Robots in many factories are
   doing the work that people
   used to do.

10. Brenda got a new dirt bike for
    her birthday, and she spent all
    day riding it.

(Continue on the next page.)

Unit Practice

Practice 1

A. Classifying Sentences *(pages 113–118)* On your
paper, write the following sentences. Underline each independent clause once and each subordinate clause twice. Label
each sentence *Simple, Compound, Complex,* or *Compound-
complex.*

1. The downpour came without warning, and we all scrambled
   for shelter.
2. Susan, who has taken several art courses, designed our float
   for the parade.
3. The committee must choose a theme and decorate the gym.
4. Some fires can be fought with water, but an electrical fire,
   which is extremely dangerous, must be controlled with
   chemicals.
5. Nitrogen is colorless, and it has no taste or odor.

B. Fragments and Run-Ons *(pages 120–122)* On your
paper, rewrite the following sentences, correcting all fragments and run-on sentences.

6. To get away from the hurry of city life. That is why we
   rented a small island in Canada.
7. Mammoths were huge creatures resembling elephants, they
   roamed the earth thousands of years ago.
8. Many new products are tested in Kansas City. Which is
   typical of the United States in many ways.
9. Robots in many factories. They are doing the work that
   people used to do.
10. Brenda got a new dirt bike for her birthday she spent all day
    riding it.

C. Sentence Diagrams *(pages 124–125)* On your
paper, diagram the following sentences. Be sure to use a
ruler.

126

11. Whenever I eat strawberries, I get a rash.
12. One of the guides who accompanied our party was a descendant of Wyatt Earp.
13. Hand me your jacket, and I will mend it for you.
14. Dad will drive us to the station, or we may take the bus.
15. Although the show was a success, the profits disappointed us.

Practice 2

The following paragraph contains many sentence fragments and run-on sentences. Rewrite the paragraph by eliminating sentence fragments and correcting run-on sentences.

A new nation needs new heroes, this was just as true of the United States as it was of any other country. Davy Crockett. He was one of the legendary heroes of early American history. Born in eastern Tennessee in 1786. As a young man, he moved to western Tennessee. Where he built his reputation. At first he tried farming he found that he preferred hunting. He also had the ability. To tell interesting and amusing stories about the frontier. After he had been elected to the Tennessee state legislature. He ran for the United States Congress in 1826 and won. Using stories from the frontier. He became an effective speaker in Congress. Other people began to invent stories about Davy Crockett, in one story, Davy rode up Niagara Falls on an alligator. That was the kind of story that made a legend. Out of Davy Crockett.

Practice 1 *(pages 126–127),* continued

C.

See the Answers (Continued) pages in the front section of this Teacher's Edition.

Practice 2 *(page 127)*

Answers may vary. Sample:

That a new nation needs new heroes was just as true of the United States as it was of any other country. Davy Crockett was one of the legendary heroes of early American history. Born in eastern Tennessee in 1786, he moved as a young man to western Tennessee, where he built his reputation. At first he tried farming, but he found that he preferred hunting. He also had the ability to tell interesting and amusing stories about the frontier. After he had been elected to the Tennessee state legislature, he ran for the United States Congress in 1826 and won. Using stories from the frontier, he became an effective speaker in Congress. Other people began to invent stories about Davy Crockett. In one story, Davy rode up Niagara Falls on an alligator. That was the kind of story that made a legend out of Davy Crockett.

127

Unit Tests

Test 1

Test 1 (pages 128–129)

A.

1. The dog became excited when
   the children raced by him,
   and he jumped up and down
   on his hind legs.
   —Compound-complex

2. We visited a village whose
   main street leads down to the
   sea.—Complex

3. Rosa climbed slowly out of
   the pool; then she made her
   way back to the high board.
   —Compound

4. The catcher and the manager
   argued with the umpire over
   the call at home plate.—Simple

5. Tourists who seek excitement
   can find it on Tom Sawyer
   Island.—Complex

B.
Answers may vary. Samples:

6. Using rubber stamps to
   decorate letters is an old
   hobby; people in the early
   1900s did it.

7. There is our new windmill,
   which provides part of the
   electricity for the house.

8. The sombrero is a useful hat
   in Mexico and the
   southwestern United States.
   People wear it for protection
   from the sun and the rain.

(Continue on the next page.)

A. Classifying Sentences (pages 113–118) On your paper, write the following sentences. Underline each independent clause once and each subordinate clause twice. Label each sentence *Simple, Compound, Complex,* or *Compound-complex.*

1. The dog became excited when the children raced by him, and he jumped up and down on his hind legs.
2. We visited a village whose main street leads down to the sea.
3. Rosa climbed slowly out of the pool; then she made her way back to the high board.
4. The catcher and the manager argued with the umpire over the call at home plate.
5. Tourists who seek excitement can find it on Tom Sawyer Island.

B. Fragments and Run-Ons (pages 120–122) On your paper, rewrite the following sentences, correcting all fragments and run-on sentences.

6. Using rubber stamps to decorate letters is an old hobby, people in the early 1900s did it.
7. There is our new windmill. Which provides part of the electricity for the house.
8. The sombrero is a useful hat in Mexico and the southwestern United States people wear it for protection from the sun and the rain.
9. Outside the door. That is where the children's dirty boots belong.
10. Eddie often goes to the park. Just to be alone, to read, and to think.

C. Sentence Diagrams (pages 124–125) On your paper, diagram the following sentences. Be sure to use a ruler.

128

11. Our class is studying Greek mythology, which interests me very much.
12. The Huns were nomads from Mongolia who overran Europe around A.D. 450.
13. Kevin is an extremely serious person, but his sister has a good sense of humor.
14. When a volcano erupts, lava flows down its sides.
15. A lei, which is a necklace of flowers, is a Hawaiian sign of welcome.

Test 2

The following paragraph contains many sentence fragments and run-on sentences. Rewrite the paragraph by eliminating sentence fragments and correcting run-on sentences.

Probably no other tree in the world is more important for its timber. Than the pine tree. The pine yields lumber for furniture it also provides the material for pitch, tar, and turpentine. People in Germany and Sweden even use the pine needles to make "forest wool." Which can be used to stuff mattresses. And to weave warm clothing. Some varieties of pines have seeds that are good to eat these seeds provide nourishment for rabbits, squirrels, chipmunks, and other animals. Even the pine needles. They can be eaten by animals who cannot find other food. Finally, the pine tree is an evergreen it stays beautiful all through the year. The pine. Truly a tree for all seasons.

Test 1 *(pages 128–129),* continued

9. Outside the door is where the children's dirty boots belong.
10. Eddie often goes to the park just to be alone, to read, and to think.

C.

See the Answers (Continued) pages in the front section of this Teacher's Edition.

Test 2 *(page 129)*

Answers may vary. Sample:

Probably no other tree in the world is more important for its timber than the pine tree. The pine not only yields lumber for furniture, but it also provides the material for pitch, tar, and turpentine. People in Germany and Sweden even use the pine needles to make "forest wool," which can be used to stuff mattresses and to weave warm clothing. Some varieties of pines have seeds that are good to eat. These seeds provide nourishment for rabbits, squirrels, chipmunks, and other animals. Even the pine needles can be eaten by animals who cannot find other food. Finally, the pine tree is an evergreen that stays beautiful all through the year. The pine is truly a tree for all seasons.

129

Usage

Unit Preview

Some dictionaries use the label *nonstandard* to describe word usage that does not come up to the standards of educated speech. Suppose that, as an educated speaker, you were asked to make a list of nonstandard forms. Which of the word groups in italic type in the following sentences would you include in your list?

1. This information is strictly *between you and I*.
2. They must *have went* ahead without us.
3. My younger sister *reads good*.
4. The *dishes was* still in the sink.
5. My *mother doesn't* like noise.
6. A box of books *were* on the table.
7. The coach finally *sent Bill and he* into the game.
8. The wind *blew* all night.
9. *Ben and me went* fishing.
10. She *don't* live near us anymore.

Sentences 1–4, 6, 7, 9, and 10 contain mistakes in usage. The word groups in italic type in those sentences should have been included in your list of nonstandard forms.

For Analysis Answer the following questions about these ten sentences.

1. Which three sentences contain errors in pronoun usage?
2. In which sentence is the principal part of a verb used incorrectly?
3. In which sentence is an adjective used instead of an adverb?
4. In which sentence is a singular verb form used with a plural noun?

130

5. In which sentence is a plural verb form used with a singular noun?
6. How would you change the sentences? Rewrite the incorrect sentences, correcting as many mistakes as you can.

In this unit you will learn rules of usage that will help you to avoid these and other kinds of errors in your speaking and writing and to express yourself clearly.

6.1 Correct Use of Verbs

Verbs have different forms to show tense and voice and to reflect the person and number of the subject. Knowing how and when to make these changes in form will enable you to use verbs correctly in sentences.

6.1a Principal Parts of Verbs

Every verb has four basic forms called **principal parts.** The principal parts are (1) the infinitive, (2) the present participle, (3) the past, and (4) the past participle. All other verb forms are made from the four principal parts.

Here are the principal parts of the verb *laugh.*

INFINITIVE	PRESENT PARTICIPLE	PAST	PAST PARTICIPLE
laugh	(is) laughing	laughed	(has) laughed

The **infinitive** is the verb in its most basic form, the form given in the dictionary as the entry word.

The **present participle** consists of the infinitive plus *-ing*. A form of the auxiliary verb *be (page 15)* is used with the present participle. Sometimes a spelling change occurs when *-ing* is added to the infinitive *(Unit 17).*

race + -ing = racing [Final *e* is dropped.]
jog + -ing = jogging [Final *g* is doubled.]

131

Program Resources

Resource Book, Second Course:
Diagnostic Test, Unit 6
Achievement Test, Unit 6
Bonus Activities, Unit 6
Extra Practice, Unit 6
Unit Test, Unit 6
Practice Book, Second Course, Unit 6
Tests, Second Course, Unit 6

Related Resources

Houghton Mifflin Microcourse:
Language Arts, Levels 7, 8
The American Heritage Dictionary of the English Language

For Analysis *(pages 130–131)*

1. Sentences 1, 7, 9
2. Sentence 2
3. Sentence 3
4. Sentence 4
5. Sentences 6, 10
6. 1. This information is strictly between you and me.

   2. They must have gone ahead without us.

   3. My younger sister reads well.

   4. The dishes were still in the sink.

   6. A box of books was on the table.

   7. The coach finally sent Bill and him into the game.

   9. Ben and I went fishing.

   10. She doesn't live near us anymore.

A verb is either a regular verb or an irregular verb, depending on how its past and its past participle are formed.

Regular Verbs

Verbs that form the past and the past participle by adding -d or -ed to the infinitive are called **regular verbs.** A form of the auxiliary verb *have* is used with the past participle.

INFINITIVE			PAST	PAST PARTICIPLE
laugh	+ -ed	=	laughed	(has) laughed
race	+ -d	=	raced	(has) raced

Sometimes a spelling change occurs when -ed is added to the infinitive *(Unit 17).*

hurry + -ed = hurried [Final *y* is changed to *i.*]
trot + -ed = trotted [Final *t* is doubled.]

The following table lists the principal parts of three regular verbs. The auxiliary verbs in parentheses are there to remind you to use a form of *be* with the present participle and a form of *have* with the past participle.

INFINITIVE	PRESENT PARTICIPLE	PAST	PAST PARTICIPLE
work	(is) working	worked	(has) worked
try	(is) trying	tried	(has) tried
stop	(is) stopping	stopped	(has) stopped

The following sentences show the correct use of the principal parts of the regular verb *work.*

inf.
We **work** in that store.

pres.
aux.   part.
We **are working** to earn money for a class trip.

132

We **worked** [past] every night during the holiday season.

We **had** [aux.] not **worked** [past part.] that hard or that long before.

Exercise 1   Regular Verbs   On your paper, complete each of the following sentences. For each verb in parentheses, use the form listed at the end of the sentence.

SAMPLE	Alex *(practice)* every day without fail.—Past
ANSWER	practiced

1. Alex *(play)* the game in a daze.—Past
2. His heart was *(pound)* like a jackhammer.—Present participle
3. His breath *(rasp)* in painful gasps.—Past
4. Every muscle *(ache)* unbearably.—Past
5. Then the winning shot *(skim)* across the net.—Past
6. Alex *(walk)* off the court with his opponent.—Past
7. Everyone had *(rush)* down from the stands.—Past participle
8. Alex's coach was *(grin)* from ear to ear.—Present participle
9. The unbelievable had *(happen)*.—Past participle
10. Alex had *(defeat)* the county tennis champ.—Past participle

Irregular Verbs

Verbs that do not form the past and the past participle by adding *-d* or *-ed* to the infinitive are called **irregular verbs.** Here are the principal parts of the irregular verb *drive.*

INFINITIVE	PRESENT PARTICIPLE	PAST	PAST PARTICIPLE
drive	(is) driving	drove	(has) driven

As with regular verbs, a form of the auxiliary verb *be* is used with the present participle, and a form of the auxiliary

Exercise 1 *(page 133)*

1. played
2. pounding
3. rasped
4. ached
5. skimmed
6. walked
7. rushed
8. grinning
9. happened
10. defeated

133

verb *have* is used with the past participle. The following sentences show the correct use of the principal parts of the irregular verb *drive*.

         inf.
They usually **drive** into town once a week.

            pres.
      aux. part.
Mother **is driving** into town today.

       past
Dad **drove** into town on Monday.

            past
      aux. part.
They **have driven** into town twice this week.

Because there are no rules for forming the past and the past participle of irregular verbs, you should memorize those principal parts that you do not already know. The principal parts of many common irregular verbs are listed below. Study the list and refer to it while doing the exercises that follow.

INFINITIVE	PRESENT PARTICIPLE	PAST	PAST PARTICIPLE
be	(is) being	was, were	(has) been
begin	(is) beginning	began	(has) begun
blow	(is) blowing	blew	(has) blown
break	(is) breaking	broke	(has) broken
bring	(is) bringing	brought	(has) brought
burst	(is) bursting	burst	(has) burst
catch	(is) catching	caught	(has) caught
choose	(is) choosing	chose	(has) chosen
come	(is) coming	came	(has) come
do	(is) doing	did	(has) done
drink	(is) drinking	drank	(has) drunk
drive	(is) driving	drove	(has) driven
eat	(is) eating	ate	(has) eaten
fall	(is) falling	fell	(has) fallen
fly	(is) flying	flew	(has) flown
freeze	(is) freezing	froze	(has) frozen

134

get	(is) getting	got	(has) gotten
give	(is) giving	gave	(has) given
go	(is) going	went	(has) gone
grow	(is) growing	grew	(has) grown
have	(is) having	had	(has) had
know	(is) knowing	knew	(has) known
lay	(is) laying	laid	(has) laid
lead	(is) leading	led	(has) led
leave	(is) leaving	left	(has) left
lie	(is) lying	lay	(has) lain
make	(is) making	made	(has) made
put	(is) putting	put	(has) put
ride	(is) riding	rode	(has) ridden
ring	(is) ringing	rang	(has) rung
rise	(is) rising	rose	(has) risen
run	(is) running	ran	(has) run
see	(is) seeing	saw	(has) seen
set	(is) setting	set	(has) set
shrink	(is) shrinking	shrank	(has) shrunk
sing	(is) singing	sang	(has) sung
sit	(is) sitting	sat	(has) sat
speak	(is) speaking	spoke	(has) spoken
spring	(is) springing	sprang	(has) sprung
steal	(is) stealing	stole	(has) stolen
strike	(is) striking	struck	(has) struck, (has) stricken
swim	(is) swimming	swam	(has) swum
take	(is) taking	took	(has) taken
teach	(is) teaching	taught	(has) taught
throw	(is) throwing	threw	(has) thrown
wear	(is) wearing	wore	(has) worn
write	(is) writing	wrote	(has) written

Exercise 2 *(pages 135–136)*

See page 136 for the answers.

Exercise 2 Irregular Verbs On your paper, write the past or the past participle of each of the verbs in parentheses in the following sentences. Remember that a form of the auxiliary verb *have* is used with the past participle. Indicate which form you used to complete the sentence.

135

Exercise 2 *(pages 135–136)*

1. known—Past participle
2. eaten—Past participle
3. saw—Past
4. written—Past participle
5. set—Past
6. struck—Past
7. grew—Past
8. burst—Past
9. ran—Past
10. rode—Past
11. did—Past
12. came—Past
13. given—Past participle
14. rung—Past participle
15. gone—Past participle;
    began—Past

Exercise 3 *(pages 136–137)*

See page 138 for the answers.

SAMPLE	Just before dawn, two fishing boats *(steal)* out of the harbor.
ANSWER	stole—Past

1. If I had *(know)* about the delay, I would have called you.
2. Termites have *(eat)* away most of the beams.
3. For days he *(see)* no one.
4. She has *(write)* to me every day since she moved to Phoenix.
5. The waiter *(set)* a candle in the center of each table.
6. On the thirty-fifth day, they *(strike)* oil.
7. Last year we *(grow)* soybeans in that field.
8. Suddenly everyone *(burst)* into song.
9. The electrician *(run)* a cable from the roof to the cellar.
10. We *(ride)* on the roller coaster six times.
11. They *(do)* the dishes in a hurry.
12. Billy *(come)* to the door and asked for a drink of water.
13. Someone has *(give)* the dog a bath.
14. The bells have *(ring)* all morning.
15. When everyone had *(go)*, we *(begin)* to clean up.

Exercise 3 **Irregular Verbs** On your paper, answer each of the following questions by completing the statement with the past or the past participle of the verb in italic type. Write the whole statement.

SAMPLE	Did your socks *shrink*? Yes, they __?__ two sizes.
ANSWER	Yes, they shrank two sizes.

1. Did you *lay* the coats on the bed?
   Yes, I have __?__ them there.
2. Did you *put* the dishes away?
   Yes, I __?__ them in the cupboard.
3. Did the librarian *choose* these books?
   Yes, she __?__ two biographies and an autobiography.

136

4. Did he *catch* that fly ball?

   Yes, he __?__ it up against the outfield fence.

5. Did she *drive* all the way to California?

   Yes, she __?__ there in five days.

6. Did someone *drink* all the juice?

   Yes, the children have __?__ it.

7. Did you *bring* the salad?

   Yes, I __?__ a vegetable salad.

8. Did your bicycle tires *wear* well?

   No, they have already __?__ thin.

9. Did the instructor *teach* you to park?

   Yes, he has __?__ us parallel parking.

10. Did he *throw* the discus far?

    Yes, he __?__ it farther than anyone else.

11. Did you *swim* today?

    Yes, I have __?__ the length of the pool five times.

12. Did you *lie* in the new hammock?

    No, I have not __?__ in it yet.

13. Did you *leave* your boots in the hall?

    Yes, I __?__ them on the mat.

14. Did you *freeze* the surplus green beans?

    Yes, we have __?__ at least two quarts.

15. Did someone *blow* up the balloons?

    Yes, someone has __?__ them up.

Assignment **Irregular Verbs** On your paper, write five questions and answers similar to those in Exercise 3. Use irregular verbs from the list on pages 134–135.

6.1b   Verb Tense

A verb expresses time through tense. The **tense** of a verb makes clear whether something is happening now, has happened in the past, or will happen in the future.

Exercise 3 *(pages 136–137)*

1. Yes, I have laid them there.
2. Yes, I put them in the cupboard.
3. Yes, she chose two biographies and an autobiography.
4. Yes, he caught it up against the outfield fence.
5. Yes, she drove there in five days.
6. Yes, the children have drunk it.
7. Yes, I brought a vegetable salad.
8. No, they have already worn thin.
9. Yes, he has taught us parallel parking.
10. Yes, he threw it farther than anyone else.
11. Yes, I have swum the length of the pool five times.
12. No, I have not lain in it yet.
13. Yes, I left them on the mat.
14. Yes, we have frozen at least two quarts.
15. Yes, someone has blown them up.

137

Verbs in English have six tenses: (1) the present, (2) the past, (3) the future, (4) the present perfect, (5) the past perfect, and (6) the future perfect. You form the six tenses by using the principal parts of a verb and the auxiliary verbs *will* and *have*.

A **conjugation of a verb** lists all the forms of the six tenses of that verb. A conjugation also allows you to see how the verb changes its form in the present tense for the third-person singular *(page 8)*.

Conjugation of the Regular Verb *Talk*

Principal Parts

Infinitive	Present Participle	Past	Past Participle
talk	(is) talking	talked	(has) talked

	Singular	**Plural**

Present Tense

	Singular	Plural
	I talk	we talk
	you talk	you talk
	he/she/it talks	they talk

Past Tense

	Singular	Plural
	I talked	we talked
	you talked	you talked
	he/she/it talked	they talked

Future Tense

	Singular	Plural
	I will (shall) talk	we will (shall) talk
	you will talk	you will talk
	he/she/it will talk	they will talk

Present Perfect Tense

	Singular	Plural
	I have talked	we have talked
	you have talked	you have talked
	he/she/it has talked	they have talked

138

Past Perfect Tense

I had talked	we had talked
you had talked	you had talked
he/she/it had talked	they had talked

Future Perfect Tense

I will (shall) have talked	we will (shall) have talked
you will have talked	you will have talked
he/she/it will have talked	they will have talked

Present and Present Perfect Tenses

Rule Use verbs in the present tense to show (1) an action that takes place in the present, (2) an action that is repeated regularly, and (3) a condition that is true at any time.

I **need** help. [The action takes place in the present.]

We **visit** my grandmother every week. [The action is repeated.]

This book **contains** three parts. [The condition is true at any time.]

To form the present tense of regular and irregular verbs, use the infinitive or add -*s* or -*es* to the infinitive.

PRESENT   They **play** softball every Sunday. [infinitive]

Kathy **plays** first base. [infinitive plus -*s*]

Dad never **misses** a game. [infinitive plus -*es*]

Rule Use verbs in the present perfect tense to describe an action that began sometime in the past and either is still going on or has just been completed.

The show **has** finally **started.** [The action is still going on.]

Someone **has dimmed** the lights. [The action has just been completed.]

139

To form the present perfect tense of a verb, use *has* or *have* as an auxiliary verb with the past participle.

PRESENT PERFECT   That cartoon **has won** several awards.

We **have seen** it twice.

Past and Past Perfect Tenses

Rule   Use the past tense to describe an action that was completed entirely in the past.

Yesterday Dave **paved** the front path and the sidewalk.

When you need the past tense of a verb, use the past form of the verb. Regular verbs form the past by adding *-d* or *-ed* to the infinitive. Most irregular verbs have a special past form. Many appear in the list on pages 134–135.

PAST   The Glee Club **practiced** for the concert. [*Practiced* is the past form of the regular verb *practice*.]

The soloist **sang** several ballads. [*Sang* is the past form of the irregular verb *sing*.]

Rule   Use the past perfect tense to describe an action that was completed (1) by a certain time in the past or (2) before some other action was completed.

The Coast Guard **had cleared** the beaches by noon. [The action was finished by a certain time.]

We **had driven** as far as Tucson when the car broke down. [The action of driving to Tucson was completed before the car broke down.]

To form the past perfect tense, use *had* as an auxiliary verb with the past participle.

140

PAST PERFECT   They **had fished** for several hours before
they caught anything.

Future and Future Perfect Tenses

Rule Use the future tense to describe an action that will take
place in the future.

My sister **will leave** for college next week. [The action will
take place in the future.]

To form the future tense, use the auxiliary verb *will* or
shall with the infinitive form of the main verb.

FUTURE   She **will** probably **fly** to Rochester.

We **shall miss** her.

Rule Use the future perfect tense to describe an action that
will end at a specific time in the future.

The bus **will have left** by four o'clock. [The action will end
at a specific time in the future.]

To form the future perfect tense, use the auxiliary verbs
will have or *shall have* with the past participle.

FUTURE PERFECT By the end of the summer, we **will have
picked** thousands of berries.

Exercise 4 Verb Tense On your paper, list the verbs
and the verb phrases in the following sentences. Then write
whether the tense of each is *Present, Present perfect, Past, Past
perfect, Future,* or *Future perfect.*

SAMPLE   The parade route will begin at Eisenhower Park.

ANSWER   will begin—Future

Exercise 4 *(pages 141–142)*

See page 142 for the answers.

141

Exercise 4 *(pages 141–142)*

1. have visited—Present perfect
2. had driven—Past perfect
3. will have found—Future perfect
4. comes—Present
5. fed—Past
6. will buy—Future
7. have flown—Present perfect
8. swam—Past
9. drank—Past
10. Has rung—Present perfect
11. had begun—Past perfect
12. will write—Future
13. catches—Present
14. carry—Present
15. will have graduated—Future perfect

1. So far I have visited thirty of the fifty states.
2. By noon we had driven more than two hundred miles.
3. He surely will have found a job by now.
4. Cinnamon comes from the bark of a tree.
5. Bill fed the chickens before breakfast.
6. Next time Dad will buy a larger car.
7. Some birds have already flown south for the winter.
8. Yesterday we swam out to the float and back.
9. After the meet, Chip drank two glasses of lemonade.
10. Has the warning bell rung yet?
11. At eight o'clock, I had just begun my report.
12. Tomorrow I will write a thank-you note to Granddad.
13. Every year Harvey catches several bluefish.
14. Please carry the groceries into the kitchen.
15. By this time next year, we will have graduated.

Assignment   Verb Tense   Choose three verbs from the list of irregular verbs on pages 134–135. Use each verb in three related sentences. In the first sentence, use the past tense. In the second sentence, use the present perfect tense. In the third sentence, use the past perfect tense.

SAMPLE   give

ANSWER   The bank gave a large donation to the flood relief fund.
The bank has given to such causes for years.
The previous board had given to charities as well.

6.1c   Active Voice and Passive Voice

Verbs have an active voice and a passive voice. The **active voice** is the form used when the subject is the performer of the action expressed by the verb. The **passive**

142

voice is the form used when the subject is the receiver of the action expressed by the verb.

Exercise 5 *(pages 143–144)*

See page 144 for the answers.

ACTIVE VOICE   The *secretary* **typed** the letter. [The subject, *secretary*, is the performer of the action of typing.]

PASSIVE VOICE   The *letter* **was typed** by the secretary. [The subject, *letter*, is the receiver of the action of typing.]

To show the passive voice, use a form of the auxiliary verb *be* with the past participle.

PASSIVE VOICE   The village **was abandoned** by the settlers.

(aux. was = auxiliary, abandoned = past participle)

In the model sentences about the secretary and the letter, the passive voice is just as effective as the active voice. However, the active voice is usually more direct; it requires fewer words, and it highlights the person (in this case the secretary) who is performing the action. In your own writing, use the active voice unless there is a good reason for using the passive voice. For example, when the doer of the action is unknown or unimportant, the passive voice is appropriate.

The priceless diamonds **were stolen** from the vault. [The doer of the action is unknown.]

Our house **was built** in 1907 by a distant relative. [The doer of the action is unimportant.]

Exercise 5   **Active Voice and Passive Voice**   *Step 1:* On your paper, list the verb phrases in the following sentences. *Step 2:* Indicate whether each verb phrase is in the active voice or the passive voice. *Step 3:* If a verb phrase is in the passive voice, rewrite the sentence, changing the verb to the active voice.

143

Exercise 5 *(pages 143–144)*

1. was delivered—Passive voice
   A messenger delivered the
   mysterious package.
2. does like—Active voice
3. was appointed—Passive voice
   The mayor appointed a new
   commissioner.
4. will leave—Active voice
5. was damaged—Passive voice
   An unexpected shower
   damaged the book.
6. was built—Passive voice
   My little brother built this
   bookcase.
7. was designed—Passive voice
   A city architect designed the
   courthouse.
8. was carried—Passive voice
   The players carried the coach
   off the field.
9. has played—Active voice
10. was called—Passive voice
    The principal called the
    matter to our attention.

SAMPLE	The ball was caught by the shortstop.
ANSWER	was caught—Passive voice
	The shortstop caught the ball.

1. The mysterious package was delivered by a messenger.
2. My father does not like turnips.
3. A new commissioner was appointed by the mayor.
4. The senator will leave for Washington tomorrow.
5. The book was damaged by an unexpected shower.
6. This bookcase was built by my little brother.
7. The courthouse was designed by a city architect.
8. The coach was carried off the field by the players.
9. My mother has played the piano since early childhood.
10. The matter was called to our attention by the principal.

6.2   Subject-Verb Agreement

In order to write correct and effective sentences, you need to make your subjects and verbs agree in number. Either they must both be singular or they must both be plural.

6.2a   Number

Number means singular (one) or plural (more than one). Most nouns *(page 3)* and personal pronouns *(page 7)* have different forms for the singular and the plural. Many auxiliary verbs and all verbs in the present tense have different forms for the singular and the plural.

Singular and Plural Nouns and Pronouns

If a noun or a personal pronoun refers to one person, place, thing, or idea, it is **singular** in number.

144

SINGULAR NOUNS   person, river, poem, memory

SINGULAR PRONOUNS   he, she, it

If a noun or a personal pronoun refers to more than one person, place, thing, or idea, it is **plural** in number.

PLURAL NOUNS   persons, rivers, poems, memories

PLURAL PRONOUNS   we, they

Singular and Plural Verbs

In the present tense, a verb has a singular and a plural form. The third-person singular form of the verb ends in *s*.

SINGULAR PRESENT FORM   chooses, pushes, goes, helps

PLURAL PRESENT FORM   choose, push, go, help

Some auxiliary verbs also have singular and plural forms in the present tense. *Be* has singular and plural forms in the past tense as well as in the present tense.

AUXILIARY VERB	SINGULAR FORM(S)	PLURAL FORM(S)
be	is (present)	are (present)
	was (past)	were (past)
do	does	do
have	has	have

When *be, do,* and *have* are used as main verbs, they have the same singular and plural forms that they have as auxiliary verbs.

Singular and Plural Subjects and Verbs

Rule A subject and its verb must agree in number.

Singular Subject. Use a singular verb with a singular subject.

145

Exercise 1 *(pages 146–147)*

See page 147 for the answers.

That *guitar* **belongs** to my uncle. [The singular noun *guitar* and the singular verb *belongs* agree in number.]

He **teaches** at the music school. [The singular pronoun *He* and the singular verb *teaches* agree in number.]

Plural Subject.   Use a plural verb with a plural subject.

My *cousins* **sing** in the choir. [The plural noun *cousins* and the plural verb *sing* agree in number.]

They also **play** the ukelele. [The plural pronoun *They* and the plural verb *play* agree in number.]

Verb Phrases.   In a verb phrase, use an auxiliary verb that agrees in number with the subject.

SINGULAR   The *wind* **is blowing** from the north.

It **has howled** all night.

PLURAL   The *forecasters* **were discussing** the storm.

They **have revised** the forecast.

The Pronouns *I* and *You*.   The pronoun *I* is used with *am* and *was* and with the plural form of other verbs. The pronoun *you* is always used with the plural form.

I **am** uncertain.	*You* **are hoping** for the best.
I **was chosen.**	*You* **were** hopeful.
I **plan** carefully.	*You* **seem** confident.

Exercise 1   Subject-Verb Agreement   On your paper, write the verb or the verb phrase that agrees in number with the subject of each of the following sentences. Then indicate whether the subject is singular or plural.

146

SAMPLE   This glue (dries, dry) in five seconds.

ANSWER   dries—Singular

1. We (has worked, have worked) for days on our science project.
2. The new pitcher (throw, throws) a mean slider.
3. Babies usually (cries, cry) when they (are, is) hungry.
4. I (am playing, is playing) shortstop this year.
5. The students (was discussing, were discussing) the new schedule.
6. We usually (go, goes) to bed reasonably early.
7. The Smith twins (was, were) absent today.
8. Jan and Tino, you (was, were) early again this morning.
9. Every day she (sit, sits) and (wait, waits) for the mail.
10. I (wax, waxes) the furniture and then I (polish, polishes) it with a soft cloth.

6.2b   Locating the Subject

In some sentences a phrase comes between the subject and the verb. In other sentences the subject comes after the verb. To choose the correct verb form, you must first locate the subject.

Phrase Between the Subject and the Verb

A prepositional phrase that modifies the subject usually comes between the subject and the predicate.

The *bowl* of raw vegetables **looks** appetizing. [The singular noun, *bowl*, is the subject. The plural noun, *vegetables*, is the object of the preposition, *of*. The verb, *looks*, agrees with the subject of the sentence, not with the object of the preposition.]

Exercise 1 *(pages 146–147)*

1. have worked—Plural
2. throws—Singular
3. cry—Plural; are—Plural
4. am playing—Singular
5. were discussing—Plural
6. go—Plural
7. were—Plural
8. were—Plural
9. sits—Singular; waits—Singular
10. wax—Singular; polish—Singular

147

Exercise 2 *(pages 148–149)*

See page 149 for the answers.

Now study these examples carefully:

SINGULAR   That *basket* of tomatoes **is** for you. [**Think:** That basket is for you.]

PLURAL   The *tomatoes* in that basket **are** from our garden. [**Think:** The tomatoes are from our garden.]

Subject After the Verb

In questions and in sentences that begin with *Here* or *There,* the subject comes after the verb. Saying the sentence to yourself in subject-verb order can help you to find the subject and make the verb agree with it.

Where **are** my *shoes*? [**Think:** My shoes are where.]
Have *you* **seen** them? [**Think:** You have seen them.]
Here **are** your *books.* [**Think:** Your books are here.]
There **are** three *letters* in your box. [**Think:** Three letters are in your box.]

In sentences in which the subject comes after the verb, first find the subject. Then decide whether the subject is singular or plural, and make the verb agree with it in number.

In the box **were** three abandoned *kittens.* [**Think:** Three abandoned kittens were in the box.]

Exercise 2   Subject-Verb Agreement   *Step 1:* On your paper, write the subject of each of the following sentences. *Step 2:* Write the verb or the auxiliary verb that agrees in number with each subject. *Step 3:* Label each verb *Singular* or *Plural.*

SAMPLE   That can of peas (is, are) too small.
ANSWER   can—is—Singular

1. On the opposite wall (was, were) several copper pots that shone in the lamplight.

148

2. There (is, are) bookcases on both sides of the doorway.

3. A pile of logs always (stands, stand) on the hearth.

4. Here (comes, come) two hungry-looking bears!

5. (Was, Were) they able to find your sister in the crowd?

6. Heavy rains in early spring (causes, cause) flooding in the valley.

7. (Is, Are) two pounds of meat enough for twelve people?

8. The location of the islands (is, are) clearly marked on the old map.

9. The seats in the car (is, are) covered with plastic.

10. In the basket (was, were) some freshly picked cucumbers.

11. The morale of the workers (is, are) at an all-time high.

12. (Doesn't, Don't) he look handsome in his new suit?

13. Acres of farmland (was, were) ruined by erosion.

14. (Was, Were) they at the game last week?

15. The list of candidates (is, are) posted on the bulletin board.

6.2c Determining the Number of the Subject

Certain kinds of subjects require special attention as you choose verbs that agree with them in number.

Compound Subjects

A **compound subject** is made up of two or more subjects connected by a coordinating conjunction *(page 32)*. Both subjects have the same verb. The conjunctions *and, or,* and *nor* are frequently used to join compound subjects.

Rule Use a plural verb with most compound subjects connected by *and*.

PLURAL   The *begonia* and the *geranium* **are** popular flowering houseplants.

My *mother* and my *aunt* **prefer** African violets.

Exercise 2 *(pages 148–149)*

1. pots—were—Plural
2. bookcases—are—Plural
3. pile—stands—Singular
4. bears—come—Plural
5. they—Were—Plural
6. rains—cause—Plural
7. pounds—Are—Plural
8. location—is—Singular
9. seats—are—Plural
10. cucumbers—were—Plural
11. morale—is—Singular
12. he—Doesn't—Singular
13. Acres—were—Plural
14. they—Were—Plural
15. list—is—Singular

149

Rule   Use a singular verb with a compound subject that refers to one person or thing or to something that is generally considered as a unit.

SINGULAR   My *teammate and* worthy *rival* **is** Joe Margolies. [One person is both teammate and rival.]

Ham and beans **is** a popular dish in America. [one dish]

Weeping and wailing **doesn't** help to solve the problem. [one condition]

Rule   Use a singular verb with a compound subject that is made up of singular nouns or pronouns connected by *or* or *nor*. Use a plural verb with a compound subject that is made up of plural nouns or pronouns connected by *or* or *nor*.

SINGULAR   A *calculator* or an *adding machine* **is needed** for this job.
Neither *Ann* nor *Terese* **was** at practice today.

PLURAL   No *sweets* or *snacks* **are allowed** on this diet.
Neither the *manufacturers* nor the *consumers* **were pleased** with the ruling.

Rule   When *or* or *nor* connects a compound subject made up of a singular subject and a plural subject, use a verb form that agrees in number with the subject that is closer to the verb in the sentence.

Neither the *students* nor their *teacher* **was represented** at the assembly. [The singular noun *teacher* is closer to the verb.]
Either *Helen* or her *sisters* **are making** the decorations. [The plural noun *sisters* is closer to the verb.]

Although correct, these sentences sound awkward. Whenever possible, you should rewrite such sentences to eliminate the awkwardness.

150

The students were not represented at the assembly, nor was their teacher.

Either Helen is making the decorations, or her sisters are.

Exercise 3 Agreement with Compound Subjects

On your paper, write the compound subject of each of the following sentences. Include the conjunction. Then write the verb or the auxiliary verb in parentheses that agrees in number with the compound subject.

> **SAMPLE**   Neither Dick nor Pete (has, have) pitched a complete game.
>
> **ANSWER**   Dick nor Pete—has

1. My uncle and aunt (is, are) touring the Middle East.
2. Bacon and eggs (is, are) a satisfying supper.
3. The hillside and the valley (was, were) flooded with a golden light.
4. Neither breakfast nor lunch (was, were) served on time.
5. A starling and a jay (was, were) singing in the oak tree.
6. A casserole or salads (is, are) to be featured at the luncheon.
7. Neither the losers nor the winner (was, were) happy with the outcome.
8. Math and science (is, are) my best subjects.
9. Either Debbie or her brothers (cleans, clean) the car every Saturday.
10. Milk or juice (was, were) offered as a beverage.

Indefinite Pronouns as Subjects

Rule Use a singular verb with a singular indefinite pronoun. Use a plural verb with a plural indefinite pronoun.

Indefinite pronouns *(page 9)* are pronouns that refer to people or things in general. Some indefinite pronouns are always singular and therefore always take singular verbs. The following are examples of singular indefinite pronouns:

Exercise 3 *(page 151)*

1. uncle and aunt—are
2. Bacon and eggs—is
3. hillside and valley—were
4. breakfast nor lunch—was
5. starling and jay—were
6. casserole or salads—are
7. losers nor winner—was
8. math and science—are
9. Debbie or brothers—clean
10. milk or juice—was

151

anybody	everybody	nobody	somebody
anyone	everyone	no one	someone
anything	everything	nothing	something
each	much	one	
either	neither	other	

SINGULAR   *Either* **is** an appropriate answer.

                    Everybody **was hoping** for a victory.

Some indefinite pronouns are always plural and therefore always take plural verbs. The most common plural indefinite pronouns are *several, both, few,* and *many.*

PLURAL   *Few* **are expected** to stay for refreshments.

               Both **were** good choices.

The following indefinite pronouns can be either singular or plural, depending on how they are used in a sentence.

all	enough	most	plenty
any	more	none	some

The preceding indefinite pronouns are singular when they refer to one person or thing or to a portion of something.

SINGULAR   *Some* of the meat **is overcooked.** [*Some* refers to a portion of the meat.]

               Most of the program **was** a collection of film clips. [*Most* refers to a part of the program.]

The indefinite pronouns on the preceding list are plural when they refer to a number of individual persons, places, or things. Sometimes an indefinite pronoun refers to a word that is not in the sentence but is understood.

PLURAL   *Some* of my relatives **are coming** from California. [*Some* refers to several relatives.]

               Several **are taking** a night flight. [*Several* refers to *relatives,* which is understood.]

152

Exercise 4 Agreement with Indefinite Pronouns

Step 1: On your paper, write the subject of each of the following sentences. *Step 2:* Label each indefinite pronoun *Singular* or *Plural*. *Step 3:* Write the form of the verb or auxiliary verb that agrees in number with the indefinite pronoun.

SAMPLE   None of the players (has, have) boarded the bus.

ANSWER   None—Plural; have

1. Everybody (was, were) given a bus pass.
2. Either (is, are) an appropriate dress for the dance.
3. All of the money (has, have) been counted.
4. All of the quarters (has, have) been rolled.
5. Each (is, are) an acceptable choice.
6. Few of these cucumbers (is, are) ripe enough to pick.
7. Some of the hay (has, have) been cut.
8. Some of the workers (has, have) gone home.
9. Everyone (was, were) wearing a green carnation.
10. Neither (was, were) willing to settle for a tie.

Collective Nouns as Subjects

A collective noun is a noun that names a group of people or objects. *Team, class, band,* and *club* are examples of collective nouns. These nouns look singular, but they may take either a singular or a plural verb, depending on how they are used in a sentence.

Rule If a collective noun refers to a group as a single unit, use a singular verb. If a collective noun refers to the individual members or parts of a group, use a plural verb.

SINGULAR   The *family* **is going** on vacation. [The family is going as a single unit.]

PLURAL   The *family* **were seated** around the table. [The family members were seated as individuals.]

153

Exercise 4 *(page 153)*

1. Everybody—Singular; was
2. Either—Singular; is
3. All—Singular; has
4. All—Plural; have
5. Each—Singular; is
6. Few—Plural; are
7. Some—Singular; has
8. Some—Plural; have
9. Everyone—Singular; was
10. Neither—Singular; was

Exercise 5 *(pages 154–155)*

See page 155 for the answers.

| SINGULAR | The *herd* **is grazing** in the south pasture. [The herd is grazing as a unit.] |
| PLURAL | The *herd* **are scattered** in the south and north pastures. [The animals in the herd are scattered as individuals.] |

Nouns Ending in *s* as Subjects

Most nouns that end in *s* are plural. However, some nouns that end in *s* are plural in form but singular in meaning because they refer to a single thing. Examples of such nouns are *news, measles, mathematics,* and *economics.* These nouns take a singular verb.

SINGULAR	The *news* **grows** more and more encouraging.
	Measles **is** a contagious disease.
	Economics **continues** to be a controversial topic.

Other nouns ending in *s* take a plural verb, even though they refer to one thing or one pair. Examples of such nouns are *scissors, trousers, pants, glasses, spectacles, clothes,* and *thanks.*

PLURAL	Your *trousers* **go** well with your new jacket.
	The *scissors* **are** on the kitchen table.
	These *spectacles* **were invented** by Benjamin Franklin.

Exercise 5   Subject-Verb Agreement

On your paper, write the verb in parentheses that agrees in number with the subject of each of the following sentences.

| SAMPLE | (Is, Are) my blue trousers still in the laundry? |
| ANSWER | Are |

1. Physics (is, are) a science that covers a wide range of ideas.
2. The pliers (has, have) been misplaced.
3. The team (has, have) purchased a new bus.

154

4. The team (is, are) wearing their new uniforms.

5. Civics (studies, study) the rights and duties of citizens.

6. The crowd (was, were) waving signs and holding up banners.

7. Mumps (is, are) caused by a virus.

8. The orchestra (is, are) playing "The Anniversary Waltz."

9. The squadron (was, were) standing at attention.

10. Mathematics (employs, employ) a variety of symbols.

Titles and Names as Subjects

The title of a book, story, play, movie, television program, musical composition, or magazine refers to one work. A title is therefore singular, even though it may include plural words. The name of a country or of an organization is also singular when it refers to an entire group.

Rule Use a singular verb with a subject that is a title or the name of a country or group.

> *Problematical Recreations* **is** a collection of mathematical puzzlers.
> *Rocks and Minerals* **is published** every other month.
> The *United States* **is** a country of people with varied origins.

Words of Amount and Time as Subjects

Rule Use a singular verb with words and phrases that express a fraction, a measurement, an amount of money, a distance, or specific intervals of time whenever those words and phrases refer to a single unit.

SINGULAR   *Two thirds* of the money **was recovered.**
              Thirty-six inches **is** the equivalent of a yard.
              Fifty dollars **is** more than enough for that jacket.
              Two miles **is** the farthest that I've ever jogged.
              Three hours sometimes **seems** like three years.

155

Exercise 5 *(pages 154–155)*

1. is
2. have
3. has
4. are
5. studies
6. were
7. is
8. is
9. was
10. employs

Exercise 6 *(page 156)*

1. is
2. retells
3. is
4. is
5. are
6. is
7. is
8. have
9. has
10. is

Rule   Use a plural verb when a measurement, an amount of money, a distance, or an amount of time is considered as a number of separate units.

> PLURAL   *Three quarts* of milk **are** in the refrigerator.
> *Two dimes* **are needed** for that phone call.

Exercise 6   Titles, Names, Amounts, and Time   On your paper, write the form of the verb that agrees in number with the subject of each of the following sentences.

> SAMPLE   *Gulliver's Travels* (is, are) a political and social satire.
>
> ANSWER   is

1. Ten miles (is, are) a day's hike for our troop.
2. *The Heroes* (retells, retell) the stories of the ancient Greek warriors.
3. Two fifths of the mountain (is, are) always covered with snow.
4. Two dollars (is, are) the registration fee for the course.
5. Three quarters (is, are) all that I have.
6. The Philippines (is, are) a group of islands in the Pacific.
7. Four dollars (is, are) too much for that movie.
8. Several months (has, have) flown by since I last wrote to you.
9. Two thirds of the jewelry (has, have) been identified.
10. Eight ounces (is, are) the capacity of this jar.

Assignment   Subject-Verb Agreement   On your paper, make the indicated changes in the following sentences. Revise each new sentence for subject-verb agreement if necessary.

> SAMPLE   Rewrite with a compound subject.
> Here comes Sally.
>
> ANSWER   Here come Sally and her sister.

156

1. Rewrite with a compound subject.

   Mother is leaving for Denver tomorrow.

2. Rewrite with a compound subject and change *flower* to *flowers.*

   The daisy is Fran's favorite flower.

3. Add the phrase *in the hamper* after *shirts.*

   The shirts are to be laundered.

4. Substitute *his friends* for *his friend.*

   Neither James nor his friend is going to the party.

5. Change *meat* to *chops.*

   None of the meat looks appetizing.

Spoken and Written Usage

People often make mistakes in subject-verb agreement when they are speaking. Many times they transfer these mistakes to their writing. *Step 1:* Write a dialogue that contains an example of five of the mistakes in subject-verb agreement that you studied in this section. *Step 2:* Rewrite the dialogue, correcting each of the mistakes in subject-verb agreement. *Step 3:* In a sentence or two, tell which of the mistakes you think people would be most likely to transfer to their writing and why.

6.3   Correct Use of Pronouns

Pronouns have different forms to show person, number, gender, and case. To write clear sentences, you need to learn the correct use of each form.

157

6.3a Pronoun Antecedents

The **antecedent** of a pronoun is the word that the pronoun refers to or replaces in a sentence. A pronoun must agree with its antecedent in number, gender, and person *(pages 7–8)*. In the following examples, the two sentences are related.

> Before *Mrs. Spry* went away, **she** asked Dad to watch **her** house. [The pronouns, *she* and *her*, refer to the antecedent, *Mrs. Spry*.]
>
> Every night **he** checked the front and back doors and collected **her** mail. [The pronoun *he* replaces the antecedent *Dad*. The pronoun *her* replaces the antecedent *Mrs. Spry*.]

Agreement in Number

Rule Use a singular pronoun to refer to a singular antecedent. Use a plural pronoun to refer to a plural antecedent.

Here is a list of singular and plural pronouns.

SINGULAR	PLURAL
I, me, my, mine	we, us, our, ours
you, your, yours	you, your, yours
he, him, his	they, them, their, theirs
she, her, hers	
it, its	

SINGULAR   When *Anne* finished **her** *report,* **she** gave **it** to **her** grandmother to read.

PLURAL   The *members* of the class copied over **their** *reports* and handed **them** in.

Rule Use a plural pronoun to refer to two or more singular antecedents joined by *and*.

Bud and Tom looked everywhere for **their** dog.

158

Rule Use a singular pronoun to refer to two or more singular antecedents joined by *or* or *nor*.

Will *Jack or Dick* lend us **his** turntable?

Indefinite Pronouns as Antecedents. The indefinite pronouns listed here are usually singular in meaning. When they are antecedents, use singular pronouns to refer to them.

anybody	everybody	nobody	somebody
anyone	everyone	no one	someone
anything	everything	nothing	something
each	much	one	
either	neither	other	

SINGULAR   *Someone* left **her** jacket on the bus.

Put *everything* in **its** place, please.

Some indefinite pronouns, such as *several, many, both,* and *few,* are plural in meaning. When they are antecedents, use plural pronouns to refer to them.

PLURAL   *Many* have mailed **their** dues to the treasurer.

Some indefinite pronouns can be either singular or plural in meaning. Use singular or plural pronouns to refer to these indefinite pronouns, depending on the meaning of the sentence.

all	enough	most	plenty
any	more	none	some

SINGULAR   *Some* of this bread has lost **its** flavor. [The indefinite pronoun *Some* refers to the singular noun *bread*. The pronoun *its* refers to the singular antecedent *Some*.]

159

Exercise 1 *(page 160)*

1. Everyone—Singular; her
2. Mr. Brown or uncle—Singular; his
3. team—Singular; its
4. Some—Plural; their
5. dogs—Plural; them
6. Each—Singular; her
7. Jane or Lucy—Singular; her
8. mother and aunt—Plural; their
9. Neither—Singular; his
10. One—Singular; his

PLURAL   *Some* of the farmers have sold **their** crops. [The indefinite pronoun *Some* refers to the plural noun *farmers*. The pronoun *their* refers to the plural antecedent *Some*.]

Collective Nouns as Antecedents.   When an antecedent is a collective noun, the pronouns that refer to it can be singular or plural, depending on its number *(page 8)*.

SINGULAR   The *team* is electing **its** first captain. [The team is acting as a single unit.]

PLURAL   The *team* are casting **their** ballots for captain. [The team members are acting as individuals.]

Exercise 1   Agreement in Number   *Step 1:* On your paper, write the antecedent of the pronouns given in parentheses. *Step 2:* Label each antecedent *Singular* or *Plural. Step 3:* Write the pronoun that agrees in number with the antecedent.

SAMPLE   Either Nancy or Susan will show us (her, their) snapshots.

ANSWER   Nancy or Susan—Singular; her

1. Everyone on the team is responsible for (her, their) own uniform.
2. Mr. Brown or my uncle will lend us (his, their) lawnmower.
3. The team will play (its, their) first intercity game on Friday.
4. Some of the students have not turned in (his, their) uniforms.
5. I own two dogs, and I groom (it, them) every week.
6. Each of the women drove (her, their) car in the parade.
7. Jane or Lucy has requested that (her, their) membership dues be refunded immediately.
8. My mother and my aunt will volunteer (her, their) services.
9. Neither of my brothers has earned (his, their) merit badge.
10. One of the runners has lost (his, their) shoe.

160

Agreement in Gender

Rule Use a pronoun that agrees with its antecedent in gender.

The **gender** of a noun or pronoun can be masculine, feminine, or neuter *(page 8)*. When the gender of a singular antecedent is masculine, use *he, him,* or *his* to refer to the antecedent. When the gender of a singular antecedent is feminine, use *she, her,* or *hers* to refer to the antecedent. When the gender of a singular antecedent is neuter, use *it* or *its* to refer to the antecedent.

MASCULINE   My cousin *Ed* has **his** own room.

FEMININE   My *aunt* makes most of **her** clothes.

NEUTER   The *boat* lost **its** sail in the storm.

Sometimes the gender of the antecedent could be either masculine or feminine. You can often use *his or her* to refer to an antecedent that could be either gender.

Everyone on the bowling team owns **his or her** ball.

Using *his or her* to refer to the same antecedent sometimes sounds awkward. It is usually better to rephrase the sentence so that both the antecedent and the pronoun are plural.

AWKWARD   *Each* of the delegates had a badge on **his or her** coat.

BETTER   The *delegates* had badges on **their** coats.

Exercise 2 Agreement in Gender   On your paper, complete each of the following sentences with a pronoun that agrees in gender with its antecedent. Draw an arrow from each pronoun to its antecedent.

Exercise 2 *(pages 161–162)*

See the Answers (Continued) pages in the front section of this Teacher's Edition.

161

Exercise 2 *(pages 161–162)*

See the Answers (Continued) pages in the front section of this Teacher's Edition.

SAMPLE   Someone left __?__ lunch on the bus.

ANSWER   Someone left his or her lunch on the bus.

1. Each of the boys cooked __?__ own supper.
2. Ann likes to play catch with __?__ brothers.
3. The ant made __?__ way along the edge of the table.
4. My aunt has __?__ own business.
5. Anyone can attend the meeting if __?__ is interested.
6. The kitten followed __?__ mother from room to room.
7. Everyone did __?__ best to guess the answer to the riddle.
8. Grandfather showed us __?__ collection of scrimshaw.
9. The azalea bush has lost __?__ blossoms.
10. Everyone fastened __?__ seat belt.

Agreement in Person

Rule   Use a pronoun that agrees in person with its antecedent.

Pronouns are in either the first person, the second person, or the third person *(page 7)*. A first-person pronoun refers to the speaker(s). A second-person pronoun refers to the person(s) being spoken to. A third-person pronoun refers to person(s) or thing(s) being spoken about.

FIRST PERSON   *I* hope to visit **my** cousins this summer.

SECOND PERSON   Sam, is that **your** uncle?

THIRD PERSON   *Joe* is helping out at **his** father's store.

Do not use *you* or *your* when you are referring to someone other than the person to whom you are speaking.

Anyone can apply for membership if **he or she** is interested. [not *if you are interested*]

162

The indefinite pronoun *one* is in the third person. When *one* is an antecedent, use a third-person singular pronoun to refer to it.

If *one* values democracy, **he or she** will vote in every election. [not *you will vote*]

Exercise 3 Pronoun Agreement On your paper, complete each of the following sentences with a pronoun that agrees in person with its antecedent. Indicate whether you used a first-person, second-person, or third-person pronoun. In your sentences, be sure that the pronouns also agree in number and gender with their antecedents.

SAMPLE   My brother and I plan to ride __?__ bicycles to Joan's house.

ANSWER   our—First person

1. Did you remember to bring __?__ lunch?
2. I have already paid __?__ dues for the coming year.
3. The speaker asked the delegates for __?__ attention.
4. Helen's sneakers are too large for __?__ feet.
5. Someone left __?__ parking lights on.
6. One should hand in __?__ assignments on time.
7. They capsized __?__ canoe in the middle of the lake.
8. Has anyone given the dog __?__ dinner?
9. We always pay __?__ bills on time.
10. Have you found __?__ books?

6.3b   Pronoun Case

Personal pronouns have three different forms, or **cases,** to show how they are used in a sentence.

NOMINATIVE CASE   **We** painted the house. [The pronoun, *We*, is the subject.]

163

OBJECTIVE CASE	Nothing stopped **us**. [The pronoun, *us*, is the direct object.]
POSSESSIVE CASE	**Our** pride in the outcome is obvious. [The possessive pronoun, *Our*, shows ownership.]

Here are the forms for the three cases of the personal pronouns:

NOMINATIVE	I, you, he, she, it, we, they
OBJECTIVE	me, you, him, her, it, us, them
POSSESSIVE	my, mine, your, yours, his, her, hers, its, our, ours, their, theirs

Notice that the pronouns *you* and *it* are the same in the nominative and objective cases.

Pronouns in the Nominative Case

Rule   When a pronoun is a subject or a predicate nominative, use the nominative case.

SUBJECT	**They** have been to Ireland several times. Will **they** go again this year?
PREDICATE NOMINATIVE	The winners of the trip were **they**.

In informal usage, such as in a conversation among friends, people often say "It is me" instead of "It is I." In formal usage—that is, in most serious conversations and in writing—you should use the correct form, "It is I."

Pronouns in the Objective Case

Rule   When a pronoun is a direct object, an indirect object, or an object of a preposition, use the objective case.

DIRECT OBJECT	The lawyer invited **us** into the office.

164

INDIRECT OBJECT   A reporter asked **them** several questions.

OBJECT OF A
PREPOSITION   Someone handed the microphone to **me.**

Pronouns in Compound Constructions

Pronouns are sometimes used in a compound subject, in a compound direct or indirect object, or in a compound object of a preposition. A pronoun joined to a noun or another pronoun by *and, or,* or *nor* may pose a problem in pronoun usage. To decide which case to use, say the sentence to yourself without the noun or other pronoun and the conjunction.

Claudia and **she** made a bookcase for their bedroom.
[**Think:** **she** made]

Everyone complimented Claudia and **her** on their handiwork. [**Think:** complimented **her**]

That is a good project for you and **me.** [**Think:** for **me**]

Exercise 4 Nominative or Objective Case?
On your paper, write the pronoun that is correct in each of the following sentences.

    SAMPLE   Jane and (I, me) won the doubles match.
    ANSWER   I

1. The runners-up were Chet and (he, him).
2. Dad read Mother's letter to my sister and (I, me).
3. Our neighbor helped Tim and (I, me) with our paper route.
4. The finalists in the speech contest are Ted and (she, her).
5. Here are postcards for you and (I, me).
6. May (he and I, him and me) leave now?
7. They unanimously elected Jim and (she, her).
8. (She, Her) and Arthur promised to decorate the booth.
9. My cousin sat between Sharon and (she, her) at the game.

(Continue on the next page.)

165

1. he
2. me
3. me
4. she
5. me
6. he and I
7. her
8. She
9. her

(Continue on the next page.)

Exercise 4 *(pages 165–166)*,
continued

10. him
11. I
12. he
13. she
14. he
15. me

10. The lifeguard warned Rosa and (he, him) about the under-tow.
11. You and (I, me) should write a TV script.
12. Is that really (he, him)?
13. The only contestants left are Chris and (she, her).
14. The best speakers on the panel were Ms. Edison and (he, him).
15. The coach gave Dick and (I, me) two passes to the game.

Pronouns in the Possessive Case

Possessive pronouns show to whom or to what something belongs.

Rule   Use these possessive pronouns to replace or refer to nouns that show ownership: *mine, yours, his, hers, its, ours,* and *theirs*.

The possessive pronouns listed in the rule can replace nouns as subjects, as predicate nominatives, and as objects.

SUBJECT	**Mine** is the green sweater.
PREDICATE NOMINATIVE	The victory soon became **hers.**
DIRECT OBJECT	I saw your pictures; let me see **his.**
OBJECT OF A PREPOSITION	Everybody's basement except **ours** was flooded.

Note: A possessive pronoun is written without an apostrophe *(page 220)*.

Rule   Use these possessive pronouns to modify nouns: *my, your, his, her, its, our,* and *their.**

Where is **your** umbrella?
Here comes **their** bus.
Have you ever watched a spider spin **its** web?

* The words *my, your, his, her, its, our,* and *their* are sometimes called pronominal adjectives.

166

Exercise 5 Possessive Pronouns On your paper, complete each sentence with a possessive pronoun. Indicate whether each pronoun that you write is used as a subject, a predicate nominative, a direct object, an indirect object, or an object of a preposition.

SAMPLE   This is my pen; that is __?__.

ANSWER   This is my pen; that is yours.—Predicate nominative

1. Is this your book, or is it __?__?
2. This umbrella must be __?__.
3. I may buy a calculator, or I may borrow __?__.
4. Joe gave his mother a pair of earrings, and Debbie gave __?__ a book of poems.
5. __?__ is the house with green shingles; __?__ is the house with aluminum siding.
6. Sid's sweater is in the closet next to __?__.
7. Your trip sounds interesting, but wait until you hear about __?__.
8. If this is your jacket, that one must be __?__.
9. Everyone's bike is red except __?__.
10. My hobby is photography; __?__ is wood working.

Who and Whom

You can use *who* and *whom* either as interrogative pronouns or as relative pronouns *(page 10)*. As with other pronouns, your choice of form depends on how you use the pronoun in a sentence. *Who* is in the nominative case. *Whom* is in the objective case. Choosing between *who* and *whom* sometimes requires special attention.

Who and Whom as Interrogative Pronouns. When *who* and *whom* introduce questions, they are interrogative pronouns.

Rule If an interrogative pronoun is a subject or a predicate nominative, use *who*. If it is an object, use *whom*.

167

Exercise 5 *(page 167)*

Answers may vary. Samples:

1. Is this your book, or is it mine?—Predicate nominative
2. This umbrella must be hers. —Predicate nominative
3. I may buy a calculator, or I may borrow his.—Direct object
4. Joe gave his mother a pair of earrings, and Debbie gave hers a book of poems.—Indirect object
5. Ours is the house with green shingles; theirs is the house with aluminum siding.— Subjects
6. Sid's sweater is in the closet next to yours.—Object of a preposition
7. Your trip sounds interesting, but wait until you hear about mine.—Object of a preposition
8. If this is your jacket, that one must be mine.—Predicate nominative
9. Everyone's bike is red except hers.—Object of a preposition
10. My hobby is photography; his is wood working.—Subject

To decide whether to use the nominative form (*who*) or the objective form (*whom*), change the question to a statement.

SUBJECT

Who rang the bell? [*Who* is clearly the subject.]

PREDICATE NOMINATIVE

Who can that be at this time of night? [**Think:** That can be **who.** *Who* is the predicate nominative after the linking verb *can be.*]

DIRECT OBJECT

Whom did you call? [**Think:** You did call **whom.** *Whom* is the direct object of *did call.*]

OBJECT OF A PREPOSITION

To **whom** am I speaking? [**Think:** I am speaking to **whom.** *Whom* is the object of the preposition, *to.*]

In informal usage, such as in everyday conversations, people often use *who* to ask a question without considering whether it is a subject or an object. In formal usage, such as in a serious conversation or in writing, you should follow the preceding rules for using *who* and *whom.*

Who and Whom as Relative Pronouns. When *who* and *whom* introduce subordinate clauses *(page 96)*, they are relative pronouns.

Rule When a relative pronoun is the subject of the subordinate clause, use *who*. When it is an object within a subordinate clause, use *whom*.

To determine which form to use, first find the subordinate clause. Then decide how the relative pronoun is used in the clause.

She is the student **who** *will represent* us at the convention.

She is the student **whom** *we are sending* to the convention. [**Think:** We are sending whom.]

168

Exercise 6 *Who or Whom?* On your paper, use *who* or *whom* to complete each of the following sentences correctly.

SAMPLE   The quarterback is the player _?_ the writers nominated for the award.

ANSWER   whom

1. Mr. Bates is a candidate _?_ we can trust.
2. That is the senior _?_ my sister will debate.
3. _?_ can that mysterious stranger be?
4. To _?_ should I address this letter?
5. Marina is the girl _?_ my father recommended for a scholarship.
6. _?_ can we go to for more information?
7. _?_ should be nominated for class treasurer?
8. _?_ should we nominate for class treasurer?
9. The student _?_ Ms. Berry selected for the lead has never acted before.
10. We made a list of guests _?_ we are inviting to the special assembly.

6.3c Pronoun Reference

A pronoun must refer clearly to an antecedent. If the antecedent is missing or unclear, your readers or listeners may misunderstand what you are trying to communicate.

Rule Avoid using a pronoun that could refer to more than one antecedent.

Your readers should not have to guess which word in the sentence is the antecedent. You can usually avoid an unclear reference by rephrasing the sentence.

UNCLEAR   Sophie wanted to see her aunt before she left. [Before who left—Sophie or her aunt? The antecedent of *she* is unclear.]

CLEAR   Before *Sophie* left, **she** wanted to see her aunt.

169

Exercise 6 *(page 169)*

1. whom
2. whom
3. Who
4. whom
5. whom
6. Whom
7. Who
8. Whom
9. whom
10. whom

Exercise 7 *(pages 170–171)*

See page 171 for sample answers.

| UNCLEAR | After I decided to put the money in my bank, I couldn't find it. [Couldn't find what—the money or the bank?] |
| CLEAR | I couldn't find my *bank* after I decided to put the money in **it**. |

Rule In formal speaking and writing, avoid using *it, they, you,* or *your* without a definite antecedent.

You can avoid an indefinite reference by rephrasing the sentence or by replacing the pronoun with a noun.

INDEFINITE	In the *Guinness Book of World Records,* it claims that the first piano was built in 1720. [What claims? The pronoun *it* has no antecedent.]
CLEAR	The *Guinness Book of World Records* claims that the first piano was built in 1720.
CLEAR	According to the *Guinness Book of World Records,* the first piano was built in 1720.
INDEFINITE	We pointed out the rusty tire rims, but they insisted on a hundred dollars for it. [Who insisted? A hundred dollars for what? The pronouns *they* and *it* have no antecedents.]
CLEAR	We pointed out the rusty tire rims, but the dealer insisted on a hundred dollars for the used bicycle.
INDEFINITE	Yesterday they demolished that old building on Ely Avenue. [Who are *they*? The pronoun has no antecedent.]
CLEAR	Yesterday that old building on Ely Avenue was demolished.

Exercise 7 Pronoun Reference On your paper, rewrite the following sentences so that the pronoun references are clear and definite.

170

SAMPLE   It says in the paper that property taxes are being reduced.

ANSWER   According to the paper, property taxes are being reduced.

1. When Dad spoke to Mr. Ames, he was ill at ease.
2. In *Liberty's Women* it gives the biographies of more than a thousand remarkable Americans.
3. When we put the cloth on the table, we discovered that it was too long.
4. Two weeks after Mother's aunt moved to Florida, she sold her car.
5. When I waved a towel at the pigeon, it flew away.
6. Bill asked Tom where his baseball mitt was.
7. They converted the theater into an indoor flea market.
8. My cousin Tim saw Joe driving his car down Main Street.
9. I put a glass in the dishwasher and it broke.
10. They change the time so often that you never know whether to arrive at eight or at eight-thirty.

6.4 Correct Use of Modifiers

Misuse of adjectives and adverbs can make your sentences hard to understand. In this section, you will practice avoiding some common errors in the use of modifiers.

6.4a Comparison of Adjectives

Most adjectives have three degrees of comparison: the positive, the comparative, and the superlative.

In the **positive degree,** an adjective assigns a quality to a person, a place, a thing, or an idea. No comparison is made by a positive form itself.

POSITIVE   Marcie is **tall.**

171

Exercise 7 *(pages 170–171)*

Answers may vary. Samples:

1. Dad was ill at ease when he spoke to Mr. Ames.
2. Liberty's Women gives the biographies of more than a thousand remarkable Americans.
3. When we put the cloth on the table, we discovered that the cloth was too long.
4. Mother sold her aunt's car two weeks after her aunt moved to Florida.
5. The pigeon flew away when I waved a towel at it.
6. Bill asked Tom where Tom's baseball mitt was.
7. The theater was converted into an indoor flea market.
8. When Joe was driving his car down Main Street, my cousin Tim saw him.
9. The glass broke when I put it in the dishwasher.
10. The time has been changed so often that you never know whether to arrive at eight or at eight-thirty.

In the **comparative degree,** an adjective compares one person, thing, place, or idea with another one.

COMPARATIVE   She is **taller** than I.

In the **superlative degree,** an adjective compares one person, thing, place, or idea with at least two others.

SUPERLATIVE   She is the **tallest** girl on the team.

One-Syllable Adjectives.   If an adjective has only one syllable, add *-er* to form the comparative and *-est* to form the superlative. In some cases you must drop a final *e* or double a final consonant before adding the suffix *(Unit 17)*.

kind, kinder, kindest   pure, purer, purest
rich, richer, richest   slim, slimmer, slimmest

Two-Syllable Adjectives.   For most two-syllable adjectives, add *-er* to form the comparative and *-est* to form the superlative. In some cases, you must change a final *y* to *i* before adding the suffix *(Unit 17)*.

able, abler, ablest   sturdy, sturdier, sturdiest

If a two-syllable adjective is awkward or difficult to pronounce when *-er* and *-est* are added, form the comparative and the superlative by using *more* and *most* instead.

childish, more childish, most childish
grateful, more grateful, most grateful

Adjectives of Three or More Syllables.   If a modifier has three or more syllables, always form the comparative and superlative degrees by using *more* and *most* before the positive form.

beautiful, more beautiful, most beautiful
intelligent, more intelligent, most intelligent

172

Comparisons Using *Less* and *Least*. For comparisons showing less of a quality, form the comparative and superlative degrees by using *less* and *least* before the positive form.

> expensive, less expensive, least expensive
> forceful, less forceful, least forceful

Irregular Comparisons. Some adjectives do not form comparisons according to the preceding rules. The best way to learn the correct forms of irregular comparisons is to memorize them.

good, better, best	bad, worse, worst
many, more, most	ill, worse, worst
much, more, most	far, farther, farthest
little, less, least	far, further, furthest

Exercise 1 Comparative and Superlative Forms

On your paper, write the comparative and superlative forms of each of the following adjectives.

> **SAMPLE** unusual
>
> **ANSWER** more unusual, most unusual

1. big
2. happy
3. hasty
4. ambitious
5. quick
6. ill
7. rapid
8. polite
9. many
10. colorful
11. foolish
12. bad
13. energetic
14. good
15. cute

Exercise 2 Degrees of Comparison

On your paper, list each adjective in italic type and write its degree of comparison.

> **SAMPLE** She is the *most intelligent* girl in the class.
>
> **ANSWER** most intelligent—Superlative

1. That is the *most logical* reason I have heard so far.
2. My *younger* sister is *taller* than I am.
3. Sue is the *more graceful* of the two skaters.

173

Exercise 1 *(page 173)*

1. bigger, biggest
2. happier, happiest
3. hastier, hastiest
4. more ambitious, most ambitious
5. quicker, quickest
6. worse, worst
7. more rapid, most rapid
8. politer, politest
9. more, most
10. more colorful, most colorful
11. more foolish, most foolish
12. worse, worst
13. more energetic, most energetic
14. better, best
15. cuter, cutest

Exercise 2 *(pages 173–174)*

1. most logical—Superlative
2. younger—Comparative; taller—Comparative
3. more graceful—Comparative

(Continue on the next page.)

Exercise 2 *(pages 173–174),* continued

4. least bashful—Superlative

5. best—Superlative;
   early—Positive

6. farthest—Superlative

7. recent—Positive;
   late—Positive

8. small—Positive;
   more economical—
   Comparative;
   large—Positive

9. smaller—Comparative

10. better—Comparative

11. worse—Comparative

12. most loyal—Superlative

13. best—Superlative

14. less—Comparative

15. more helpful—Comparative

Exercise 3 *(page 174)*

1. You need a stronger chain for your bicycle.

2. That is the funniest dog I have ever seen.

3. This is the more colorful of the two paintings.

4. The new schedule is more convenient than the old one.

5. Today the wind seems worse than it was yesterday.

6. This lock is better than that one.

7. This is the most exciting thing that ever happened to us.

8. I hope that you are feeling better today.

9. All of a sudden, I feel sleepy.

10. This sweater looks the warmest of the three.

4. He is the *least bashful* of the three brothers.

5. The *best* time to go bicycle riding is in the *early* evening.

6. What is the *farthest* distance that you have ever been from home?

7. The *recent* downpour is the most rain that we have had since *late* June.

8. A *small* car is often *more economical* than a *large* one.

9. A Yorkshire terrier is *smaller* than a pug.

10. I feel *better* than I did last night.

11. The manager feels *worse* about the mixup than we do.

12. Plucky is the *most loyal* dog that we have ever had.

13. That is the *best* book that I have read in the past year.

14. I spend *less* time in the gym than I used to.

15. Try to be *more helpful,* please.

Exercise 3   Comparisons with Adjectives   On your paper, write each sentence, using the specified form of the adjective in parentheses.

> **SAMPLE**   This is the (*good*—superlative) typewriter that I have ever used.
>
> **ANSWER**   This is the best typewriter that I have ever used.

1. You need a (*strong*—comparative) chain for your bicycle.

2. That is the (*funny*—superlative) dog I have ever seen.

3. This is the (*colorful*—comparative) of the two paintings.

4. The new schedule is (*convenient*—comparative) than the old one.

5. Today the wind seems (*bad*—comparative) than it was yesterday.

6. This lock is (*good*—comparative) than that one.

7. This is the (*exciting*—superlative) thing that ever happened to us.

8. I hope that you are feeling (*well*—comparative) today.

9. All of a sudden, I feel (*sleepy*—positive).

10. This sweater looks the (*warm*—superlative) of the three.

174

6.4b   Comparison of Adverbs

Exercise 4 *(pages 175–176)*

See page 176 for the answers.

You can use adverbs to compare two or more actions. Like adjectives, adverbs have three degrees of comparison.

POSITIVE   Alice works **hard.**

COMPARATIVE   She works **harder** than you.

SUPERLATIVE   I work **hardest** of all.

Use the comparative degree of an adverb when comparing the actions of two persons or things. Use the superlative degree when comparing the actions of one person or thing with the actions of more than one other person or thing.

Like adjectives, most one-syllable adverbs form the comparative and the superlative by adding *-er* and *-est* to the positive form.

late, later, latest   soon, sooner, soonest

Adverbs that end in *-ly* form the comparative and superlative by using *more* and *most* or *less* and *least* before the positive form.

quickly, more quickly, most quickly
efficiently, less efficiently, least efficiently

Like adjectives, some adverbs have irregular comparisons. Memorize these forms:

well, better, best   little, less, least
badly, worse, worst   much, more, most
far, farther, farthest
far, further, furthest

Exercise 4   Comparative and Superlative Forms

On your paper, write the comparative and superlative forms of each of the following adverbs.

175

Exercise 4 *(pages 175–176)*

1. more politely, most politely
2. less, least
3. more suddenly, most suddenly
4. more, most
5. better, best
6. nearer, nearest
7. more often, most often
8. more nervously, most nervously
9. sooner, soonest
10. worse, worst

Exercise 5 *(page 176)*

1. Everyone crossed the street more carefully after the accident.
2. They arrived later than usual.
3. She studies the most diligently of all the seniors.
4. Mother works hardest on weekends.
5. My sister does better on tests than I do.
6. Pete can run faster than his brother.
7. Of the three outfielders, Tessie can throw the ball farthest.
8. The sun shines more brightly in summer than in winter.
9. Can't you speak more loudly than that?
10. Of all the runners, Paul moves the most gracefully.

SAMPLE	hard
ANSWER	harder, hardest

1. politely
2. little
3. suddenly
4. much
5. well
6. near
7. often
8. nervously
9. soon
10. badly

Exercise 5   Comparisons with Adverbs   On your paper, write each sentence, using the specified form of the adverb in parentheses.

SAMPLE	I work (*slowly*—comparative) than you.
ANSWER	I work more slowly than you.

1. Everyone crossed the street (*carefully*—comparative) after the accident.
2. They arrived (*late*—comparative) than usual.
3. She studies the (*diligently*—superative) of all the seniors.
4. Mother works (*hard*—superlative) on weekends.
5. My sister does (*well*—comparative) on tests than I do.
6. Pete can run (*fast*—comparative) than his brother.
7. Of the three outfielders, Tessie can throw the ball (*far*—superlative).
8. The sun shines (*brightly*—comparative) in summer than in winter.
9. Can't you speak (*loudly*—comparative) than that?
10. Of all the runners, Paul moves the (*gracefully*—superlative).

6.4c   Using Comparisons Correctly

Rule   Avoid double comparisons.

Use either the suffixes *-er* and *-est* or the words *more* and *most* to form the comparative and the superlative degrees of adjectives and adverbs. Do not use *-er* or *-est* when you use *more* or *most*.

176

INCORRECT	My uncle is the **most handsomest** person that I know.
CORRECT	My uncle is the **handsomest** person that I know.
CORRECT	My uncle is the **most handsome** person that I know.

Exercise 6 **Correct Use of Comparisons**

On your paper, rewrite each sentence to make the comparisons correct. Errors include incorrect use of the comparative and superlative degrees, incorrect forms, and double comparisons.

SAMPLE	She practices more harder than you do.
ANSWER	She practices harder than you do.

1. Of the two musicals that I have seen, I enjoyed *Oklahoma!* most.
2. Nothing is worser than a rainy Saturday.
3. Which is most exhausting, a game of tennis or a game of racquetball?
4. The charts made his explanation more clearer.
5. Who is the oldest, you or your sister?
6. Our garden is beautifuler than theirs.
7. This is the most loveliest card of all.
8. Is a dog more smarter than a cat?
9. Which costs the most, gold or silver jewelry?
10. This is the most homiest room in the house.

6.4d **Placement of Modifiers**

Rule Place a modifier as close as possible to the word that it modifies.

A misplaced modifier can make your sentence unintentionally funny and can make the meaning unclear. To correct a sentence with a misplaced modifier, you must first find

177

Exercise 6 *(page 177)*

1. Of the two musicals that I have seen, I enjoyed Oklahoma! more.
2. Nothing is worse than a rainy Saturday.
3. Which is more exhausting, a game of tennis or a game of racquetball?
4. The charts made his explanation clearer.
5. Who is older, you or your sister?
6. Our garden is more beautiful than theirs.
7. This is the loveliest card of all.
8. Is a dog smarter than a cat?
9. Which costs more, gold or silver jewelry?
10. This is the homiest room in the house.

Exercise 7 *(pages 178–179)*

1. Looking through my binoculars, I saw a robin and a cardinal.

2. In my head I went over the chess game that we would play.

3. The dog hid under the porch when the storm began (*or* When the storm began, the dog hid under the porch).

4. The hikers could see the mountains rising in the distance.

5. The woman that lives across the hall has a new dishwasher.

6. We saw a family of swans skimming gracefully across the water.

7. This book, which is a best seller, has a complicated plot.

8. The bird with bright green feathers was lost by a classmate.

9. With your book closed, please repeat what you just read.

10. Peg writes a column, which is called "Peg's Pointers," for the school paper (*or* For the school paper, Peg writes a column, which is called "Peg's Pointers").

the word being modified. Then place the modifying word or phrase as close as possible to the word that it modifies. Be sure not to change the intended meaning of your sentence.

MISPLACED PREPOSITIONAL PHRASE
A passerby jumped into the lake and saved the kitten with all his clothes on. [Who or what was wearing clothes—the passerby or the kitten?]
CORRECT
A passerby with all his clothes on jumped into the lake and saved the kitten.

MISPLACED PARTICIPIAL PHRASE
Robbing the bird feeder, Mother saw a squirrel. [Who or what was robbing the bird feeder—Mother or the squirrel?]
CORRECT
Mother saw a squirrel robbing the bird feeder.

MISPLACED SUBORDINATE CLAUSE
I bought a horn for my bicycle that cost ten dollars. [What cost ten dollars—the horn or the bicycle?]
CORRECT
I bought a horn that cost ten dollars for my bicycle.

Exercise 7   Placement of Modifiers   On your paper, rewrite the following sentences to eliminate misplaced modifiers.

SAMPLE   Lying in the middle of the road, I rescued the deer.

ANSWER   I rescued the deer lying in the middle of the road.

1. I saw a robin and a cardinal looking through my binoculars.

2. I went over the chess game that we would play in my head.

3. The dog hid when the storm began under the porch.

4. Rising in the distance, the hikers could see the mountains.

178

5. The woman has a new dishwasher that lives across the hall.

6. Skimming gracefully across the water, we saw a family of swans.

7. This book has a complicated plot, which is a best seller.

8. The bird was lost by a classmate with bright green feathers.

9. Please repeat what you just read with your book closed.

10. Peg writes a column for the school paper, which is called "Peg's Pointers."

Modifiers

Modifiers are an important part of some kinds of description. *Step 1:* Write a description of something, using a variety of adjectives and adverbs in the positive degree. You might describe an outdoor scene, a favorite article of clothing, the decorations for a dance, or a favorite product. *Step 2:* Rewrite the description, changing most of the adjectives and adverbs to the superlative degree. Make any necessary changes in the sentences to make them read correctly and smoothly. How do the two paragraphs differ?

6.5   Usage Notes

The following pages contain an alphabetical list of words and phrases that often present usage problems. Each entry describes the correct formal usage, and most entries include examples. Cross-references help you to locate related information. Refer to these usage notes when you are in doubt about which form of a word or phrase to use.

179

a, an Use the article *a* before words beginning with a consonant sound. Use the article *an* before words beginning with a vowel sound. The article that you use depends on the beginning *sound* of the word, not on the first *letter*.

> **a** humorous story   **an** honest person
> **a** united front   **an** upper berth

a while, awhile *Awhile* is an adverb. *While* is a noun and can be used as the object of a preposition. Do not use *for* or *in* before the adverb *awhile*.

> We will leave in **a while**. [noun]
> Let's wait **awhile** before leaving. [adverb]

accept, except *Accept* is a verb meaning "to receive" or "to find satisfactory." *Except* is a preposition meaning "leaving out" or "but."

> He will probably **accept** the news calmly.
> Everyone has replied **except** you.

ain't Do not use *ain't*.

all ready, already *All ready* means "entirely ready" or "prepared." *Already* means "previously."

> They were **all ready** for the picnic.
> They have **already** left for the park.

all right, alright *All right* means "satisfactory," "unhurt," "correct," or "yes, very well." *Alright* is not a word. Do not use it.

> Don't worry; you'll be **all right**.

almost, most The adverb *almost* means "nearly." The adjective *most* is the superlative of *many*.

> We jog **almost** every morning. [not *most*]

180

among, between Use *among* when you are discussing three or more persons or things. Use *between* when you are discussing two persons or things.

> They distributed the prizes **among** the three contestants. [not *between*]
> They divided the prize **between** Charles and Selma.

any more, anymore The phrase *any more* describes quantity. The adverb *anymore* means "at present" or "from now on."

> Do we have **any more** cucumbers?
> I don't plant them **anymore**.

because, on account of Do not use *on account of* instead of *because* to introduce an adverb clause *(page 101)*. *On account of* means "because of" or "due to." It is a preposition and should be followed by an object.

> ┌────────adverb clause────────┐
> The bus was late **because** the traffic was heavy.
> [not *on account of*]

> ┌───prep.───┐
> The bus was late **on account of** the heavy traffic. [or *because of*]

beside, besides *Beside* means "next to." *Besides* means "in addition to."

> They sat **beside** us at the game.
> **Besides** basketball, I also enjoy soccer.

between you and me Do not use a pronoun in the nominative case *(I)* as the object of a preposition *(between)*.

> prep. ┌── obj.──┐
> Between you and **me**, I think we're gaining on them.

bring, take   Use *bring* when you mean "to carry to." Use *take* when you mean "to carry away."

> **Bring** your own lunch.
> **Take** the leftovers home with you.

bust, busted   Do not substitute these words for forms of the verbs *break* and *burst*.

> He **broke** his arm. [not *busted*]
> Be careful, or that balloon may **burst**. [not *bust*]

can, may   *Can* means "be able to." *May* means "have permission to." Do not confuse the two.

> I **can** do a back flip from the diving board.
> **May** I show you how? [not *Can*]

can't hardly, can't scarcely   *Hardly* and *scarcely* are negative words. Do not form double negatives by using *hardly* and *scarcely* with other negative words, such as *can't*. (See also *double negative*.)

> I **can hardly** wait for my garden to bloom. [not *can't hardly*]
> I **can scarcely** see the new growth on those plants. [not *can't scarcely*]

could of, might of, should of, would of   Do not use these phrases for *could have, might have, should have,* and *would have.*

different from, different than   Do not use *different than.* One thing differs *from* another.

> Your goals are **different from** mine. [not *than*]

double negative   A double negative is the use of two negative words when only one is called for. Do not use *not*

or -*n't* with words such as *no, none, never,* or *nothing.*
(See also *can't hardly, can't scarcely.*)

I have **no** time.
I do**n't** have **any** time.
The doctor could find **nothing** wrong with my tonsils.
The doctor could**n't** find **anything** wrong with my
tonsils.

double subject   A double subject is the incorrect use of a
noun and a pronoun together as a single subject. Use
one or the other, but not both.

INCORRECT   My cousin she is a medical student.

CORRECT   My cousin is a medical student.

CORRECT   She is a medical student.

every day, everyday   *Every day* (separate words) means
"each day." Do not confuse it with *everyday,* an adjective meaning "ordinary."

I take vitamins **every day.**
Wear your **everyday** clothes to the field day.

every one, everyone   *Every one* refers to each individual in
a group. It is usually followed by *of. Everyone* is an indefinite pronoun meaning "everybody" or "every person."

Every one of these cards must be filed.
Everyone helped us file the cards.

fewer, less   Use *fewer* to refer to things that you can count.
Use *less* to refer to quantities that you cannot count.
Also use *less* to refer to amounts of time, money, or
distance when the amount is a single quantity.

Fewer than twenty members attended the meeting.
The club has **less** than ten dollars in the treasury.

183

good, well   Always use *good* as an adjective. Use *well* as an adverb to mean "ably" or "capably" or as an adjective to mean "satisfactory" or "in good health."

> He looks **good** in a band uniform. [adjective]
> He plays the tuba **well**. [not *good*]
> The patient looks **well**. [adjective meaning "in good health"]

got, have   *Got* is the past tense of the verb *get*. It means "obtained." Avoid using *got* with *have* or in place of *have*.

> I **got** some help from my father. [obtained]
> I **have** the flu. [not *have got* or *got*]

in, into   Use *in* to mean "within" or "inside." Use *into* to suggest movement toward the inside from the outside.

> The fish is **in** the pond.
> Dick fell **into** the pond. [not *in*]

its, it's   *Its* is a possessive pronoun. *It's* is the contraction for "it is." Do not confuse the two.

> A sparrow was feeding **its** young. [possessive pronoun]
> **It's** never too late. [contraction]

kind of, sort of   Do not use these phrases to mean "somewhat" or "rather."

> Everyone was feeling **somewhat** discouraged. [not *kind of*]

lay, lie   *Lay* is a verb meaning "to put or place something somewhere." It always takes a direct object. *Lie* is a verb meaning "to rest" or "to recline." It does not take a direct object. See page 135 for the principal parts of these irregular verbs. The following examples use forms of the verb *lay*.

184

I always **lay** out my clothes the night before. [*Clothes* is the direct object of *lay*.]
Some people **are** always **laying** the blame on someone else. [*Blame* is the direct object of *are laying*.]
Dad **has laid** a new kitchen floor. [*Floor* is the direct object of *laid*.]

The verbs in the following sentences are all forms of the verb *lie*. They do not have direct objects.

The cat **lies** on the windowsill.
Snow **is** still **lying** on the hillside.
I **lay** down for a long nap.
Sue **has lain** in the sun too long.

learn, teach *Learn* means "to gain knowledge." *Teach* means "to give knowledge." Do not use *learn* when you mean "to give knowledge."

My sister is **learning** to drive.
Dad **taught** her how to park. [not *learned*]

leave, let *Leave* means "to go away from" or "to abandon." *Let* means "to allow."

They will **leave** soon.
The bus **left** a half hour late.
My father **let** us watch a late movie. [not *left*]
Let us proceed. [not *Leave*]

less, fewer See *fewer, less*.

lie, lay See *lay, lie*.

loose, lose *Loose* is an adjective meaning "not tight," "not bound," or "free." *Lose* is a verb that means "to fail to find," "to misplace," or "not to win."

This screw is **loose**.
Please don't **lose** my keys.

185

many, much   Use the adjective *many* to describe things that you count (*toys, persons*). Use the adjective *much* to describe things that you cannot count (*water, justice*). When used as indefinite pronouns, *much* is singular and *many* is plural.

> We don't have **much** time.
> **Many** players arrived early.
> *Much* of the credit **is** his. [singular]
> *Many* **are** thanking him. [plural]

may, can   See *can, may.*

may be, maybe   In the verb phrase *may be, may* is an auxiliary. The adverb *maybe* means "perhaps."

> I **may be** at the party.
> **Maybe** I'll be there.

might of   See *could of.*

most, almost   See *almost, most.*

much, many   See *many, much.*

nohow, noway   *Nohow* and *noway* are not standard English. Do not use them. You can, however, use *no way* correctly as two words.

> INCORRECT   **Noway** can I leave now.
>
> CORRECT   There is **no way** that I can leave now.

off, off of   After *off*, the word *of* is not necessary. Do not use *off* in place of *from.*

> My notebook fell **off** the desk. [not *off of*]
> I got this book **from** my cousin. [not *off*]

on account of, because   See *because, on account of.*

186

passed, past *Passed* is the past tense of the verb *pass*. *Past* can be a noun, an adjective, an adverb, or a preposition depending on its use in a sentence.

> Jeff **passed** the baton to the runner. [verb]
> In the **past**, few people went to college. [noun]
> The **past** few days have been hectic. [adjective]
> A flock of geese flew **past**. [adverb]
> The park is two blocks **past** the school. [preposition]

raise, rise *Raise* is a verb that means "to lift something" or "to make something go upward." *Raise* always takes a direct object. *Rise* is a verb that means "to move upward." It does not take a direct object. *Raise* is a regular verb. See page 135 for the principal parts of the irregular verb *rise*.

> The custodian **raises** the flag every morning. [*Flag* is the direct object of *raises*.]
> The orchestra **rose** and bowed to the audience. [*Rose* does not have a direct object.]

real, really *Real* is an adjective; *really* is an adverb.

> This handbag is made of **real** leather. [adjective]
> It looks **really** smooth. [not *real*]

said, says *Said* is the past tense of the verb *say*. *Says* is the third person singular of the present tense. Do not substitute *says* for *said*.

> The mayor grabbed the microphone and **said,** "There will be no increase in the fare!" [not *says*]

set, sit *Set* is a verb meaning "to place." It always takes a direct object. *Sit* is a verb meaning "to rest in an upright position." It does not take a direct object.

> We **set** the bowl of flowers in the center of the table. [*Bowl* is the direct object of *set*.]
> Please **sit** at the head of the table. [*Sit* does not have a direct object.]

187

should of   See *could of.*

slow, slowly   *Slow* is an adjective. *Slowly* is an adverb. You may use *slow* as an adverb in informal speech, especially in commands or for emphasis. In writing, however, use *slowly* when an adverb is needed.

> Go **slow**. [adverb, informal]
> The procession moved **slowly**. [adverb]

sort of, kind of   See *kind of, sort of.*

supposed to, used to   Remember to spell *supposed* and *used* with a final *d*. Both are past forms and must have the *-d* ending.

> We were **supposed** to go swimming. [not *suppose to*]
> I'm still not **used** to my new schedule. [not *use to*]

take, bring   See *bring, take.*

teach, learn   See *learn, teach.*

than, then   Use *than* in comparisons. Use *then* as an adverb to show a sequence of events.

> This year's snow accumulation is less **than** last year's.
> First, we had warm weather; **then** temperatures dropped sharply.

that, which, who   Use the relative pronoun *(page 10) who* to refer to persons, real or imagined. Use *which* to refer to things and to animals. Use *that* to refer to persons, animals, and things.

> That is the student **who** belongs to the Audubon Society. [not *which*]
> The nuthatch feeds on acorns, **which** it carefully stores for future use.
> Nuthatches are birds **that** inhabit forests and woods, especially pine woods. [not *who*]

188

Do not use *what* to introduce an adjective clause.

> The nuthatch builds a nest **that** is made of grass, twigs, hair, and feathers. [not *what*]

their, there, they're *Their* is the possessive form of the pronoun *they. There* points out a place or introduces a sentence. *They're* is the contraction of *they* and *are.*

> **Their** house was sold yesterday.
> Wait in the lobby, and I'll meet you **there**.
> **There** are some lemons in the refrigerator.
> **They're** meeting us at eight o'clock.

this here, that there Simply say *this* or *that. Here* or *there* is unnecessary.

> **This** is my sister Justine. [not *This here*]
> **That** girl near the backstop is our cousin. [not *That there*]

used to, supposed to See *supposed to, used to.*

well, good See *good, well.*

which, who, that See *that, which, who.*

who, whom See page 167.

who's, whose *Who's* is the contraction of *who is* or of *who has. Whose* is the possessive form of *who.* Do not confuse the two.

> **Who's** helping to clean up? [contraction]
> **Whose** job is it to clean up? [possessive]

would of See *could of.*

189

Unit Practice

Practice 1

Practice 1 *(pages 190–191)*

A.

1. I saw a beautiful sunrise this morning.
2. At this time a decision has not been made.
3. Our closest rival has stolen our mascot every year!
4. Every Thursday I have an early class, so I get up at six o'clock.
5. One washing in hot water had shrunk the sweater.
6. Bill began the test before the instructions had been explained.
7. We will have run the five miles before our time is up.
8. The ship has gone on over two hundred cruises.
9. By next Wednesday I will (*or* shall) have finished the research for my project.
10. Thea was wishing that she had taken her coach's advice more seriously.

B.
11. is
12. seem
13. comes
14. celebrate
15. appeal
16. contains
17. plays
18. is
19. move
20. Do

(Continue on the next page.)

Practice 1

A. Correct Use of Verbs *(pages 131–144)* On your paper, rewrite the following sentences, correcting all errors in the use of verbs.

1. I seen a beautiful sunrise this morning.
2. At this time a decision had not been made.
3. Our closest rival has stole our mascot every year!
4. Every Thursday I have an early class, so I got up at six o'clock.
5. One washing in hot water had shrinked the sweater.
6. Bill began the test before the instructions has been explained.
7. We will have ran the five miles before our time is up.
8. The ship has went on over two hundred cruises.
9. By next Wednesday I have finished the research for my project.
10. Thea was wishing she had took her coach's advice more seriously.

B. Subject-Verb Agreement *(pages 144–157)* On your paper, write the verb form that correctly completes each sentence.

11. The mop (is, are) leaning against the door.
12. The reasons for his decision (seems, seem) clear.
13. Here (comes, come) a foul ball!
14. Lynda and Barbara (celebrates, celebrate) their birthdays together.
15. Neither the salad nor the soups (appeals, appeal) to me.
16. Each of the skits (contains, contain) a twist in the plot.
17. At the museum a quartet (plays, play) classical music every afternoon.
18. News (is, are) a highly competitive area in network television.
19. Three fourths of the zoo animals (moves, move) to new quarters this weekend.
20. (Does, Do) morning-glories close in the afternoon?

190

C. Correct Use of Pronouns (pages 157–171) On your paper, write the pronoun that correctly completes each sentence. Be sure that the pronoun you use makes sense and that it agrees with the antecedent, if there is one.

21. Everyone on the girls soccer team should turn in __?__ equipment by Friday.
22. Submit your entries to __?__ so that she can proofread them.
23. This is our assignment; it's up to you and __?__ to complete it on time.
24. To __?__ should I send these photographs?
25. Ms. Margolis or Ms. Pacini will volunteer __?__ time to sponsor the class trip.
26. The snake shed __?__ skin.
27. A few of the puppies were too small to leave __?__ mother.
28. Do you need some help with __?__ homework?
29. You and __?__ need to discuss our plans for Saturday.
30. If you forgot your science book, I can lend you __?__.

D. Correct Use of Modifiers (pages 171–179) On your paper, rewrite the following sentences, correcting all errors in the use of modifiers.

31. Sunning herself on the window sill, Maxine startled the cat.
32. Who is the oldest of the two brothers?
33. He is the most friendliest puppy in the litter.
34. Of all my friends, Noriko is the less critical.
35. That is the sentimentalist story I've read in years.
36. I scored more badly on the obstacle course than Paul did.
37. Is Molly feeling iller today?
38. I did more better than I had expected!
39. His lawn is more green than theirs.
40. Langston ran out of the house, but he still missed the bus without his jacket.

(Continue on the next page.)

191

C.

21. her	26. its
22. her	27. their
23. me	28. your
24. whom	29. I
25. her	30. mine

D.

31. Maxine startled the cat sunning herself on the window sill.
32. Who is the older of the two brothers?
33. He is the friendliest puppy in the litter.
34. Of all my friends, Noriko is the least critical.
35. That is the most sentimental story I've read in years.
36. I scored worse on the obstacle course than Paul did.
37. Is Molly feeling worse today?
38. I did better than I had expected!
39. His lawn is greener than theirs.
40. Langston ran out of the house without his jacket, but he still missed the bus.

Practice 2 *(page 192)*

Corrections are underlined in red.

Bees communicate with one
another through dances. Forager
bees search for sources of pollen
and nectar. When one discovers a
food source, it flies to the hive to
tell the others what it has found.
The bees pick up the scent on the
dancer and fly out to search for
plants with that particular scent.
The round dance means that the
flowers are close to the hive. The
wagging dance shows that the
food source is farther away. Both
direction and distance are
indicated. Part of the bee's dance
tells where the food is. The speed
of its dance shows the distance.
The more slowly the bee moves,
the greater the distance between
the hive and the food source.

Practice 2

On your paper, rewrite the following passage, correcting
all errors in the use of verbs, pronouns, and modifiers.

Bees communicates with one another through dances.
Forager bees searches for sources of pollen and nectar.
When one discovers a food source, it fly to the hive to tell
the others what she has found. On the dancer the bees pick
up the scent and fly out to search for plants with that
particular scent. The round dance means that the flowers is
close to the hive. The wagging dance show that the food
source is more far away. Both direction and distance is
indicated. Part of the bee's dance tells where the food are.
The speed of their dance shows the distance. The slowlier the
bee move, the greater the distance between the hive and the
food source.

Unit Tests

Test 1

A. Correct Use of Verbs *(pages 131–144)* On your paper, rewrite the following sentences, correcting all errors in the use of verbs.

1. As part of an assignment, Lois teached a lesson to a sixth-grade class.
2. As of today, both senators had received a limited number of complaints.
3. Bruce has wrote a prize-winning essay.
4. Every year when daylight-saving time begins, it took me two weeks to get adjusted.
5. He had sang the song only once in rehearsal.
6. Paul unscrewed the faucet before the water been turned off.
7. I will have saw all the sights before my vacation is over.
8. Amy has grew prize-winning vegetables for the last three state fairs.
9. By noon tomorrow we have completed the first leg of the trip.
10. By the end of the seventh inning, Dean had threw ninety-five pitches.

B. Subject-Verb Agreement *(pages 144–157)* On your paper, write the verb form that correctly completes each sentence.

11. The recipes (was, were) filed neatly.
12. The listeners in this experiment (follows, follow) every direction.
13. There (goes, go) the last band in the parade.
14. Velma and Nicolas (spends, spend) several hours a week as volunteers at the nursing home.
15. Either Ken or his son (is, are) bringing the chairs.
16. Neither (suspects, suspect) a surprise party.

(Continue on the next page.)

193

Test 1 *(pages 193–195)*

A.

1. As part of an assignment, Lois taught a lesson to a sixth-grade class.
2. As of today, both senators have received a limited number of complaints.
3. Bruce has written a prize-winning essay.
4. Every year when daylight-saving time begins, it takes me two weeks to get adjusted.
5. He had sung the song only once in rehearsal.
6. Paul unscrewed the faucet before the water was turned off.
7. I will have seen all the sights before my vacation is over.
8. Amy has grown prize-winning vegetables for the last three state fairs.
9. By noon tomorrow we will have completed the first leg of the trip.
10. By the end of the seventh inning, Dean had thrown ninety-five pitches.

B.

11. were
12. follow
13. goes
14. spend
15. is
16. suspects

(Continue on the next page.)

Test 1 *(pages 193–195),* continued

17. performs
18. are
19. have
20. Does

C.

21. its	26. her
22. him	27. their
23. me	28. their
24. Whom	29. I
25. their	30. yours

D.

31. I think I feel worse than you do.
32. Alex is the less outgoing of the twins.
33. This is the lightest backpack I could find.
34. Dudley is the most talented person I know.
35. We had worse weather than was predicted.
36. This is my least favorite painting in the entire exhibit.

(Continue on the next page.)

17. The touring dance troupe (performs, perform) in small cities all over the United States.
18. Tweezers (is, are) useful for removing splinters.
19. Two months (has, have) passed since I sent in my magazine subscription.
20. (Does, Do) she know how to play cat's cradle?

C. Correct Use of Pronouns *(pages 157–171)* On your paper, write the pronouns that correctly complete each sentence. Be sure that the pronoun you use makes sense and that it agrees with the antecedent, if there is one.

21. Nothing seems to be in __?__ proper place.
22. Andrew is in charge of the wardrobe, so return your costumes to __?__.
23. Between you and __?__ we should be able to decipher the code.
24. __?__ did you choose to perform the solo?
25. The carpenter and the electrician will donate __?__ services.
26. Emmie practiced daily to prepare for __?__ audition.
27. Several regular programs lost __?__ sponsors.
28. They decided where to go on __?__ vacation.
29. My brothers and __?__ made some extra money shoveling snow.
30. I will share my lunch with you if you share __?__ with me.

D. Correct Use of Modifiers *(pages 171–179)* On your paper, rewrite the following sentences, correcting all errors in the use of modifiers.

31. I think I feel worser than you do.
32. Alex is the least outgoing of the twins.
33. This is the most lightest backpack I could find.
34. Dudley is the talentedest person I know.
35. We had badder weather than was predicted.
36. This is my less favorite painting in the entire exhibit.

194

37. Who can throw a softball the most far?

38. Our lease was renewed by the company, which expired on Tuesday.

39. This puzzle is more hard than that one.

40. Curled up in her knitting bag, Mother found the cat.

Test 2

On your paper, rewrite the following passage, correcting all errors in the use of verbs, pronouns, and modifiers.

In 1800 France were at war, and their economy is lagging. Therefore, Napoleon sets up the Society for the Encouragement of Industry to get France's economy back on their feet. One of the society's first prizes were given to Nicolas Appert. In return Appert publishes his secret. Him had developed a method for preserving food, and he given the world one of their beneficialist processes. He putted food in bottles and sealed it with corks and wires. Then he boiled the bottles depending on the type of food for different amounts of time. Appert has discovered that heat sterilized food.

Test 1 *(pages 193–195)*, continued

37. Who can throw a softball the farthest?

38. Our lease, which expired on Tuesday, was renewed by the company.

39. This puzzle is harder than that one.

40. Mother found the cat curled up in her knitting bag.

Test 2 *(page 195)*

Corrections are underlined in red.

In 1800 France was at war, and its economy was lagging. Therefore, Napoleon set up the Society for the Encouragement of Industry to get France's economy back on its feet. One of the society's first prizes was given to Nicolas Appert. In return Appert published his secret. He had developed a method for preserving food, and he gave the world one of its most beneficial processes. He put food in bottles and sealed them with corks and wires. Then he boiled the bottles for different amounts of time, depending on the type of food. Appert had discovered that heat sterilizes food.

195

Unit 7

Objectives

After studying this unit, students should be able to do the following:

- Use capitalization correctly in sentences, with proper nouns, and with proper adjectives, *I*, and certain abbreviations.

- Use periods, question marks, exclamation points, commas, semicolons, colons, quotation marks, apostrophes, hyphens, dashes, and italics correctly.

- Use written numbers correctly.

- Use common proofreading symbols when revising and proofreading their work.

- Use correct manuscript form for their writing.

Teaching Suggestions

See "Classroom Insights" for Unit 7 in the front of this Teacher's Edition.

Program Resources

Resource Book, Second Course:
    Diagnostic Test, Unit 7
    Achievement Test, Unit 7
    Bonus Activities, Unit 7
    Extra Practice, Unit 7
    Unit Test, Unit 7
Practice Book, Second Course
    Unit 7
Tests, Second Course, Unit 7

Mechanics

Unit Preview

Capital letters and punctuation marks have been omitted from the following passage. As you read it, try to determine where one sentence ends and the next one begins.

i like adventure stories best of all they keep my interest and thats the key to reading as far as im concerned did you ever have a teacher who began a story in class and then stopped before the end i know that i have to get hold of that story to find out what happened some might say unfair it is a trick but it usually works dont you agree

Whenever you write, you must be sure that your readers understand what you mean. For example, only the writer of the preceding unpunctuated passage really knows whether the phrase *best of all* belongs to the first or the second sentence. One way to make your writing clear is to apply the rules of **mechanics,** which include capitalization and punctuation.

For Analysis On your paper, rewrite the passage about adventure stories, using capital letters and punctuation marks where you think they belong. Then answer the following questions about the passage.

1. How many sentences does the rewritten passage contain?
2. How did you signal the beginning of each sentence?
3. Did you use the same kind of punctuation mark to signal the end of each sentence?
4. What mark or marks did you use to separate the various parts of each sentence?

196

5. What mark did you use to signal contractions?
6. What marks did you use to signal that someone was being quoted directly?

In this unit you will learn about the rules of mechanics. These rules can help to clarify your writing so that it is understandable to anyone who reads it.

7.1 Capitalization

In English, capital letters are used for two main purposes: (1) to signal the beginning of a sentence and (2) to show that a noun is a proper noun *(page 4).*

7.1a Capitalization in Sentences

Rule Capitalize the first word of a sentence.

The new zoo does not have barred cages.

Rule Capitalize the first word of a direct quotation that is a complete sentence. A **direct quotation** contains the exact words that someone has said, written, or thought.

John exclaimed, **"Look** at that sunset!"

Interrupted Quotation. When a quoted sentence is interrupted by an expression such as *I said* or *Paul asked,* begin the second part of the quotation with a lower-case letter.

"My favorite subject," said Joanne, **"is** geometry."

New Sentence in a Quotation. When the second part of a quotation is a new sentence, put a period after the interrupting expression, and begin the second part of the quotation with a capital letter.

"I'm hungry," said Paul. **"Let's** eat lunch."

197

Related Resources

Houghton Mifflin Microcourse: Language Arts, Levels 7, 8
The American Heritage Dictionary of the English Language

For Analysis *(pages 196–197)*

Answers vary. Samples:

I like adventure stories best of all. They keep my attention, and that's the key to reading, as far as I'm concerned. Did you ever have a teacher who began a story in class and then stopped before the end? I know that I have to get hold of that story to find out what happened. Some might say, "Unfair! It is a trick"; but it usually works. Don't you agree?

1. The rewritten passage contains six sentences.
2. A capital letter was used to signal the beginning of each sentence.
3. Different marks were used to signal the end of each sentence.
4. Commas and semicolons were used to separate the various parts of sentences.
5. Apostrophes were used to signal contractions.
6. Quotation marks were used to signal that someone was being quoted directly.

Exercise 1 *(page 198)*

1. "When I was little, I always looked forward to weekends," said Ben.

2. "Sometimes my father would take my sister and me fishing," he continued. "Once we caught twenty fish."

3. Tim said with a chuckle, "We raised goats, and guess who had to feed them."

4. "Feeding them wasn't too hard," Tim explained, "but you had to be careful not to leave any clothes around."

5. Marcia asked, "What do you mean by that?"

6. "Oh, once a goat ate my shirt," Tim said with a laugh.

7. "Was Mom upset!" said Tim. "It was my best shirt."

8. "My family usually watches baseball or football," Marcia said with a sigh, "but I never cared much for spectator sports."

9. Ellen said, "On rainy weekends my brother and I sometimes explore the attic."

10. The world is too much with us; late and soon,
Getting and spending, we lay waste our powers:
Little we see in Nature that is ours;
We have given our hearts away, a sordid boon!

Rule Capitalize the first word of each line in a poem unless the word is not capitalized in the original.

> **Of** all the causes which conspire to blind
> **Man's** erring judgment, and misguide the mind,
> **What** the weak head with the strongest bias rules,
> **Is** pride, the never-failing vice of fools.

> Alexander Pope, *An Essay on Criticism*

Exercise 1 Capitalization in Sentences On your paper, write the following sentences, adding capital letters where needed.

SAMPLE   Marcia asked, "what do you do on weekends?"

ANSWER   Marcia asked, "What do you do on weekends?"

1. "when I was little, I always looked forward to weekends," said Ben.

2. "sometimes my father would take my sister and me fishing," he continued. "once we caught twenty fish."

3. Tim said with a chuckle, "we raised goats, and guess who had to feed them."

4. "feeding them wasn't too hard," Tim explained, "but you had to be careful not to leave any clothes around."

5. Marcia asked, "what do you mean by that?"

6. "oh, once a goat ate my shirt," Tim said with a laugh.

7. "was Mom upset!" said Tim. "it was my best shirt."

8. "my family usually watches baseball or football," Marcia said with a sigh, "but I never cared much for spectator sports."

9. Ellen said, "on rainy weekends my brother and I sometimes explore the attic."

10. the world is too much with us; late and soon,
getting and spending, we lay waste our powers:
little we see in Nature that is ours;
we have given our hearts away, a sordid boon!

> William Wordsworth, "The World Is Too Much with Us"

198

7.1b Capitalization of Proper Nouns

Rule Capitalize the names of people and the initials that go with the names of people. If a person's last name begins with *Mc* or *O,* capitalize the next letter as well.

> Lynne Kaufman   Dan **McAuliffe**   Walter **O'Shea**

Family-Relationship Words. Capitalize words that show family relationships when they are part of a person's name or when they take the place of a person's name.

> Last week **Aunt Alberta** called us from Australia.
> We're going to visit **Grandfather** for the holidays.

Do not capitalize family-relationship words when they are used as common nouns or when they are preceded by a possessive noun or a possessive pronoun.

> My **cousin** Fran is like a **sister** to me.
> Sylvia's **mother** and my **father** offered to drive us to the bowling alley.

BUT We were relieved when **Mother** said that she would drive us to the bowling alley.

Personal and Official Titles. Capitalize a personal or an official title and its abbreviation when it comes before a person's name or when it is used in direct address *(page 212)*. Do not capitalize a preposition, a conjunction, or an article that is part of a title unless it begins a sentence.

BEFORE NAME Yesterday **Governor Brown** signed the budget into law.

DIRECT ADDRESS Someone asked, "What are your thoughts on the budget, **Governor?**"

BUT We asked the governor if he had signed the budget into law.

199

President Harding	**Mayor** Unita Blackwell
Secretary of State Seward	**Dr.** Jonas Salk
Superintendent Grey	**Mr.** Medeiros

Do not capitalize the title that follows or is a substitute for a person's name unless it is a title of a head of a national government.

TITLE BEFORE NAME	TITLE AFTER NAME
Captain Helen McAfee	Helen McAfee, **captain**
President Ulysses S. Grant	Ulysses S. Grant, **President**

The **senator** greeted the **Prime Minister** at the airport.

Capitalize the names and abbreviations of academic degrees or honors that follow a person's name. Capitalize the abbreviations *Sr.* and *Jr.*

Vito Pagano, **Doctor of Medicine**	Virginia Lutz, **M.D.**
Martin Luther King, **Jr.**	Peter Stone, **D.D.S.**

Gods of Mythology. Capitalize the names of gods of mythology. Do not capitalize the word *god* when it refers to the gods of mythology.

Angry **Zeus,** the **god** of the sky, hurled thunderbolts.

Rule Capitalize the names of particular places. Place names include the names of countries, cities, states, mountains, streets, oceans, lakes, rivers, and so forth.

the Falkland Islands	Sierra Leone	Prospect Park

Compass Points. Capitalize a compass point that refers to a specific geographic area or that forms part of a place name. Do not capitalize a compass point that shows direction or a general region.

200

My father's family is from the **South.**
He was born in **South Carolina.**

BUT   My sister lives **south** of Greenville.

Heavenly Bodies. Capitalize the names of planets, stars, and constellations. Do not capitalize *sun* and *moon.*

the Little Dipper   Mars   Polaris

Capitalize *Earth* when you mean the planet and when the word does not have *the* before it.

The satellite photographs of **Earth** were breathtaking.
The moon revolves around **the earth.**

Rule Capitalize the names of peoples, races, tribes, nationalities, and languages.

Korean   Samoan   Mexican   Mongolian

Rule Capitalize the names of days, months, holidays, special days, and special events. Do not capitalize the name of a season unless it is part of a proper noun.

Friday   Autumn Festival   a day in **autumn**

Rule Capitalize the names of historical events and historical periods and the names of awards and documents.

the Civil War   the Medal of Honor   the Constitution

Rule Capitalize the first word, the last word, and all other important words in the titles of books, movies, songs, works of art, and so forth.

BOOK	*Profiles in Black and White*
MOVIE	*Singing in the Rain*
SONG	"We Gather Together"
PAINTING	*The Twittering Machine*

201

Exercise 2 *(pages 202–203)*

1. the Fourth of July
2. the last Thursday in November
3. the Apaches
4. Andrew Jackson, President
5. Senator Amelia Santos
6. twenty miles north of North Dakota
7. the god Poseidon and his brother Hades
8. a course in French
9. the Century Club
10. the University of Utah
11. the Tropic Rover
12. All Along the Way by John T. Moore
13. the Medal of Honor
14. Stickum glue
15. Conchas Lake in New Mexico
16. the Montreal Limited
17. Tina F. O'Rourke, M.D.
18. the Minneapolis Institute of Arts
19. the Crusades
20. Election Day

Conjunctions, Articles, and Prepositions in Titles. Capitalize a conjunction, an article, or a preposition when it is the first word or the last word in a title. Capitalize any preposition or conjunction that has five or more letters.

The Pearl   "**Through** the Tunnel"

Rule Capitalize the name of a school subject if it is a language or if it is followed by a course number.

English   biology   Bookkeeping 2

Rule Capitalize the names of structures (buildings, bridges, monuments) and the names of organizations (religions, businesses, government bodies, clubs, schools) and their members. Do not capitalize the articles *a* and *the* in such names.

the Leaning Tower of Pisa   an Anglican
the House of Representatives   Indiana University

Capitalize a word such as *college, university, high school, club, society,* or *store* only when it is part of a proper noun.

Adams High School   BUT   a high school in Brooklyn
the Bicycle Club   BUT   a club for bicyclists

Rule Capitalize trade names. Do not capitalize a common noun that follows a trade name.

Smoothee hand lotion   **Skid-Prufe** tires

Rule Capitalize the names of ships, trains, rockets, planes, and spacecraft. (See also pages 224–225.)

the *Half Moon*   the *Broadway Limited*
the *Columbia*   *Skylab 4*

Exercise 2 Capitalization of Proper Nouns   On your paper, write each of the following phrases, using capital letters where needed. Include underlining (italicizing) in your answers.

SAMPLE *in the company of clowns* by martha bacon

ANSWER In the Company of Clowns by Martha Bacon

1. the fourth of july
2. the last thursday in november
3. the apaches
4. andrew jackson, president
5. senator amelia santos
6. twenty miles north of north dakota
7. the god poseidon and his brother hades
8. a course in french
9. the century club
10. the university of utah
11. the *tropic rover*
12. *all along the way* by john t. moore
13. the medal of honor
14. stickum glue
15. conchas lake in new mexico
16. the *montreal limited*
17. tina f. o'rourke, m.d.
18. the minneapolis institute of arts
19. the crusades
20. election day

Exercise 3 Capitalization of Proper Nouns On your paper, write each sentence, using capital letters where needed. Include underlining (italicizing) in your answers.

SAMPLE Have you read *let me fall before i fly*?

ANSWER Have you read Let Me Fall Before I Fly?

1. The amon carter museum on camp bowie boulevard in fort worth, texas, displays paintings and bronzes by frederic remington and charles russell.
2. You can see plenty of wildlife in florida on the juniper river in the ocala national forest.
3. The wayside inn in sudbury, massachusetts, was the setting of longfellow's *tales of a wayside inn*.
4. The hero hercules ascended mount olympus after completing twelve tasks assigned by king eurystheus.
5. The *delta queen* makes many trips on the ohio river, the tennessee river, and the mississippi river—from st. paul in the north to new orleans in the south.

203

Exercise 3 *(pages 203–204)*

1. The Amon Carter Museum on Camp Bowie Boulevard in Fort Worth, Texas, displays paintings and bronzes by Frederic Remington and Charles Russell.
2. You can see plenty of wildlife in Florida on the Juniper River in the Ocala National Forest.
3. The Wayside Inn in Sudbury, Massachusetts, was the setting of Longfellow's Tales of a Wayside Inn.
4. The hero Hercules ascended Mount Olympus after completing twelve tasks assigned by King Eurystheus.
5. The Delta Queen makes many trips on the Ohio River, the Tennessee River, and the Mississippi River—from St. Paul in the North to New Orleans in the South.

(Continue on the next page.)

Exercise 3 *(pages 203–204)*, continued

6. The world's tallest flagpole was erected in 1915 outside the Oregon Building at the Panama–Pacific International Exposition in San Francisco.

7. In 1976 Dr. Suzanne Kennedy became the first woman veterinarian at the National Zoological Park in Washington, D.C.

8. I bought a jar of Sun Orchard apple butter and a bag of Crunchee sunflower seeds at the general store.

9. My cousin from Korea is taking night courses in English, general mathematics, and business accounting.

10. The planet with the most satellites is Jupiter; the earth is the only planet with a single satellite.

---

6. The world's tallest flagpole was erected in 1915 outside the oregon building at the panama-pacific international exposition in san francisco.

7. In 1976 dr. suzanne kennedy became the first woman veterinarian at the national zoological park in washington, d.c.

8. I bought a jar of sun orchard apple butter and a bag of crunchee sunflower seeds at the general store.

9. My cousin from korea is taking night courses in english, general mathematics, and business accounting.

10. The planet with the most satellites is jupiter; the earth is the only planet with a single satellite.

7.1c Other Uses of Capitalization

Rule Capitalize most proper adjectives *(pages 19–20)*.

CAPITALIZE THESE	DO NOT CAPITALIZE THESE
Roman numerals	**madras** cloth
Turkish bath	a **jersey** sweater
Irish lace	**pasteurized** cheese

If you are not sure whether a proper adjective should be capitalized, consult your dictionary.

Rule Capitalize the pronoun *I*.

Yesterday **I** wrote to my pen pal in Japan.

Rule Capitalize both letters in the abbreviations *A.D.*, *B.C.*, *A.M.*, and *P.M.* and in Postal Service ZIP code abbreviations. *B.C.* follows the date; *A.D.* precedes the date.

8:30 **P.M.**   Fresno, **CA** 93704   50 **B.C.**   **A.D.** 17

Note: Use Postal Service abbreviations only with ZIP codes in addresses.

Tucson, **AZ 85799**   Mount Vernon, **OH 43050**

204

Exercise 4 Other Uses of Capitalization On your paper, write each sentence, using capital letters where needed. Use your dictionary if you need help.

> SAMPLE The parisian gown was trimmed with chantilly lace.
>
> ANSWER The Parisian gown was trimmed with Chantilly lace.

1. These turkish towels are the softest that i could find.
2. Father started cleaning the basement at 7:00 a.m.
3. Every woman at the reception was dressed in a beautiful indian sari.
4. The game will begin at 3:00 p.m. and will end by 5:30 p.m.
5. My address is 9 villa drive, stevens, wi 54481.
6. Cornelius Nepos, the roman biographer, lived from 100 b.c. to 25 b.c.
7. One booth at the fair displayed irish linen, french tapestry, and italian embroidery.
8. King Robert I of Scotland was crowned in a.d. 1306.
9. The australian crawl is a basic swimming stroke that is fairly easy to learn.
10. William Shakespeare, probably the most renowned author in english literature, was a poet and dramatist of the elizabethan and early jacobean years.

Assignment Capitalization Number your paper from 1 to 10. Then for each item listed, write the name of someone you know or the name of something with which you are familiar. Use capital letters correctly.

1. A foreign food
2. A relative
3. A pet
4. A tall building
5. A school subject
6. A nearby city
7. A town
8. A body of water
9. An object and its trade name
10. A popular song

205

Exercise 4 *(page 205)*

1. These Turkish towels are the softest that I could find.
2. Father started cleaning the basement at 7:00 A.M.
3. Every woman at the reception was dresed in a beautiful Indian sari.
4. The game will begin at 3:00 P.M. and will end by 5:30 P.M.
5. My address is 9 Villa Drive, Stevens, WI 54481.
6. Cornelius Nepos, the Roman biographer, lived from 100 B.C. to 25 B.C.
7. One booth at the fair displayed Irish linen, French tapestry, and Italian embroidery.
8. King Robert I of Scotland was crowned in A.D. 1306.
9. The Australian crawl is a basic swimming stroke that is fairly easy to learn.
10. William Shakespeare, probably the most renowned author in English literature, was a poet and dramatist of the Elizabethan and early Jacobean years.

Using Capital Letters

Imagine that the editor of your class paper has asked you to write a brief autobiographical sketch for the "Classroom Profiles" feature. Write a paragraph in which you tell where and when you were born. Give the names of family members and pets. Tell about your interests: places you have seen or would like to see, songs you like or dislike, favorite entertainers, books you have read, and so forth. Use proper nouns and remember to use capitalization correctly.

7.2   Punctuation

Punctuation marks help others to read what you have written. As a writer, you use punctuation marks for a variety of reasons: (1) to show your readers when to slow down or to stop, (2) to show how ideas are related within a sentence, and (3) to indicate the purpose of a sentence.

7.2a   The Period

Rule Use a period at the end of a declarative sentence *(page 45)*.

The earth has a very thick crust.

Rule Use a period at the end of a sentence that asks a polite question or gives a mild command.

Will you please help me with this package.
Put the canned goods in the cupboard.

206

Rule Use a period after an initial that is part of a person's name or title.

E. B. White   Margaret McGovern, **Ph.D.**
Jay Hill, **Jr.**   **Dr.** Matthew Ludemann

Rule Use a period after most standard abbreviations. Do not use a period after abbreviations of the units of time and measurement. Use a period, however, after *in.* to show that you are writing the abbreviation of *inch,* not the word *in.*

USE PERIODS		DO NOT USE PERIODS	
Mr.	Mister	**l**	liter
P.M.	post meridiem	**oz**	ounce
A.M.	ante meridiem	**hr**	hour

Do not use periods when the abbreviation of a company or an organization is in all capital letters or when you are writing the Postal Service abbreviations of state names used with ZIP codes.

AFC   American Football Conference
AL   Alabama

Use periods, however, with the traditional state abbreviations, including the two-letter traditional state abbreviations used without the ZIP code.

S.C.   BUT   **SC** 29601

Note: Avoid using abbreviations in your written work. Spell out words instead.

7.2b The Question Mark

Rule Use a question mark at the end of an interrogative sentence *(page 46)*.

When will you return the books to the library?

207

Exercise 1 *(page 208)*

1. What a beautiful rose!
2. Did you see J. R. Smith, Sr., on the six o'clock news?
3. Will you please hand me the paper.
4. Hope Valley, R. I., is my home town.
5. Watch your step!
6. Whew! That was a close call. (*or* !)
7. NASA was established in 1958.
8. Springtime arrives early in the Southwest.
9. What exactly is float fishing?
10. Will you please close the window.
11. When are you going to the city?
12. Oops! I must have lost my key. (*or* !)
13. Tapioca is made from the roots of the manioc plant.
14. Mt. Vesuvius erupted in A.D. 79.
15. Is there any life in the Dead Sea?

7.2c   The Exclamation Point

Rule   Use an exclamation point at the end of an exclamatory sentence *(page 46)* or after a forceful command, an exclamatory expression, or a strong interjection *(page 36)*.

> What a spectacular sunset that was!
> Grab that rope!
> Wow! What a great shot!

Exercise 1   End Punctuation and Abbreviations

The following sentences are written without periods, question marks, and exclamation points. On your paper, write the sentences correctly, adding punctuation marks where needed.

SAMPLE   In 202 B C, the Han Dynasty took control of China

ANSWER   In 202 B.C., the Han Dynasty took control of China.

1. What a beautiful rose
2. Did you see J R Smith, Sr, on the six o'clock news
3. Will you please hand me the paper
4. Hope Valley, R I, is my home town
5. Watch your step
6. Whew That was a close call
7. NASA was established in 1958
8. Springtime arrives early in the Southwest
9. What exactly is float fishing
10. Will you please close the window
11. When are you going to the city
12. Oops I must have lost my key
13. Tapioca is made from the roots of the manioc plant
14. Mt Vesuvius erupted in A D 79
15. Is there any life in the Dead Sea

208

7.2d   The Comma

Commas in a Series

Rule   Use commas to separate three or more items in a series. Put a comma after each item except the last. Do not use commas to separate pairs of nouns that are thought of as a single unit.

Saturn, Uranus, and Neptune are similar to Jupiter.

We served fruit, ⌐——— unit ———⌐ **soup and crackers,** and sandwiches to our unexpected guests.   [**Think:** *Soup and crackers* is thought of as a single unit.]

Modifiers. Use commas to separate three or more modifiers in a series.

The horse that jumped easily over the hurdles was young, healthy, and strong.

The rainy, damp, oppressive weather was not what the vacationers had expected.

Phrases. Use commas to separate three or more phrases in a series.

Fans came to the show by bus, by car, and on foot.

Independent Clauses. Use commas to separate three or more short independent clauses *(page 95)* in a series.

He jogs, he works out, and he lifts weights.

Do not use commas to separate items, phrases, or clauses in a series when all of them are joined by coordinating conjunctions *(pages 32–33).*

Use glue or paste or tape.

209

Exercise 2 *(page 210)*

1. Greg went shopping, prepared dinner, and washed the dishes before he went out for the evening.
2. The movie was long, uninspired, and miscast.
3. We washed the dishes, we mopped the floor, and we put out the garbage.
4. The berths and cabins are simple, small, and adequate.
5. Correct
6. We were offered a choice of fresh peaches, baked apples, or cheese and crackers.
7. You can come by bus, by subway, or by taxi.
8. I came home, I did my homework, and I went to bed.
9. My aunt crochets matching mittens, scarves, and hats.
10. Correct

Exercise 2 Commas On your paper, write the following sentences, using commas where necessary. If no commas are needed, write *Correct* on your paper.

> SAMPLE   Our dog is friendly playful and energetic.
> ANSWER   Our dog is friendly, playful, and energetic.

1. Greg went shopping prepared dinner and washed the dishes before he went out for the evening.
2. The movie was long uninspired and miscast.
3. We washed the dishes we mopped the floor and we put out the garbage.
4. The berths and cabins are simple small and adequate.
5. I visited the zoo and the museum and the aquarium.
6. We were offered a choice of fresh peaches baked apples or cheese and crackers.
7. You can come by bus by subway or by taxi.
8. I came home I did my homework and I went to bed.
9. My aunt crochets matching mittens scarves and hats.
10. His little sister collects insects and frogs and butterflies.

Commas After Introductory Expressions

Rule Use a comma to show a pause after introductory words or phrases.

Prepositional Phrases. Use a comma after a prepositional phrase *(pages 73–75)* of four or more words at the beginning of a sentence.

Under a pile of old paper, we found the letter.

Participial Phrases. Use a comma after a participial phrase *(page 80)* at the beginning of a sentence.

Picking up speed, the rocket continued on course.

210

Adverb Clause. Use a comma after an adverb clause *(page 101)* at the beginning of a sentence.

Whenever there is a space launch, I remain glued to the television set.

Yes, No, and Interjections. Use a comma to separate *yes, no,* and interjections, such as *oh* and *well,* from the rest of the sentence.

Yes, I finished my report on time.

Confusing Sentence Parts. Use a comma to separate sentence parts that might otherwise run together in a confusing way.

Instead of **five, ten** guests showed up.

Exercise 3 Commas On your paper, write the following sentences, using commas where necessary.

SAMPLE   Because they destroy harmful rodents certain snakes should be protected.

ANSWER   Because they destroy harmful rodents, certain snakes should be protected.

1. When we were in Charleston we visited Magnolia Gardens.
2. Half-blinded by the rainstorm the hikers took shelter.
3. Although a comet may look solid it is made up of very thin gases and fine particles.
4. Well why didn't you call me?
5. Leaping out of the grass the toad disappeared into the bushes.
6. Above the jets flew in perfect formation.
7. Since we had plenty of time we walked to the theater.
8. Using anchovies for bait Tim hooked a huge salmon.
9. When Rome was founded in 753 B.C. Latin was an unwieldy language.
10. No I haven't seen that movie.

Exercise 3 *(page 211)*

1. When we were in Charleston, we visited Magnolia Gardens.
2. Half-blinded by the rainstorm, the hikers took shelter.
3. Although a comet may look solid, it is made up of very thin gases and fine particles.
4. Well, why didn't you call me?
5. Leaping out of the grass, the toad disappeared into the bushes.
6. Above, the jets flew in perfect formation.
7. Since we had plenty of time, we walked to the theater.
8. Using anchovies for bait, Tim hooked a huge salmon.
9. When Rome was founded in 753 B.C., Latin was an unwieldy language.
10. No, I haven't seen that movie.

211

Mechanics **211**

Commas to Separate Sentence Parts

Rule Use a comma before a coordinating conjunction *(pages 32–33)* that joins the independent clauses *(page 95)* of a compound sentence.

> Most sunspots last only a few days, **but** some last two months or more.

Rule Use commas to set off certain words or phrases within a sentence.

> *Direct Address.* Use a comma or a pair of commas to set off words that identify the person or persons being spoken to in a direct address.

> **John,** have you fed the fish?

> *Abbreviated Title or Degree.* Use a comma or a pair of commas to set off an abbreviated title or degree following a name.

> I just read a book about worms by Edna Root, **Ph.D.**

> *Nonessential Phrases.* Use a comma or a pair of commas to set off a **nonessential phrase,** a phrase that is not necessary to the meaning of the sentence.

> The game, **much to our surprise,** was canceled.

> Do not use commas to set off an essential phrase. An **essential phrase** is one that is necessary to the meaning of the sentence.

> The old chestnut tree **by the barn** measures three feet in diameter. [The phrase specifies which chestnut tree and is essential to the meaning of the sentence.]

212

Dates and Addresses. Use commas before and after the year when it is used with both the month and the day. Do not use a comma if only the month and the year are given.

> The first baseball game was played on **June 19, 1846,** in New Jersey.
>
> Joe Nuxhall started his baseball career in **June 1914.**

Use commas before and after the name of a state, province, or country when it is used with the name of a city. Do not use a comma after the state if it is used with a ZIP code.

> Ed plans to drive from **Atlanta, Georgia,** to **Huntsville, Alabama,** to visit his brother.
>
> Address the envelope as follows: 3 Sioux Court, Longview, **TX 75601.**

Rule Use a comma after the salutation and the closing of a friendly letter.

> Dear Ben,   Sincerely,   Your friend,

Exercise 4 Commas On your paper, write the following sentences, using commas where necessary. If no commas are needed, write *Correct* on your paper.

> **SAMPLE**   The referee blew the whistle and the players took their positions.
>
> **ANSWER**   The referee blew the whistle, and the players took their positions.

1. Our team having won three games in a row looked forward to a successful season.
2. Some sponges are less than an inch long but others measure two or three feet in height or width.
3. Dad on the other hand was worried.
4. Maureen have you checked the bus schedule?
5. The telephone rang and I raced to answer it.

Exercise 4 *(pages 213–214)*

1. Our team, having won three games in a row, looked forward to a successful season.
2. Some sponges are less than an inch long, but others measure two or three feet in height or width.
3. Dad, on the other hand, was worried.
4. Maureen, have you checked the bus schedule?
5. The telephone rang, and I raced to answer it.

(Continue on the next page.)

213

Exercise 4 *(pages 213–214)*,
continued

6. Correct
7. The song sounds familiar, but I can't think of the title.
8. For a copy of The New Day Almanac, write to the Free Press, 12 West 3rd Street, Philadelphia, PA 19103.
9. Enrico Fermi, Ph.D., was born on September 29, 1901.
10. Correct

Exercise 5 *(pages 214–215)*

See page 215 for the answers.

6. Ben Franklin flew his famous kite in June 1752.
7. The song sounds familiar but I can't think of the title.
8. For a copy of *The New-Day Almanac* write to the Free Press 12 West 3rd Street Philadelphia PA 19103.
9. Enrico Fermi Ph.D. was born on September 29 1901.
10. The girl standing next to the red car is my sister.

7.2e   The Semicolon

Rule   Use a semicolon in a compound sentence to connect independent clauses *(page 95)* that are not joined by a coordinating conjunction *(pages 32–33)*.

> My watch stopped**;** the battery must be dead.

BUT   I shook it**, but** nothing happened.

Exercise 5   Semicolons   In some of the following sentences, commas have been incorrectly used in place of semicolons. On your paper, write the sentences, substituting semicolons where necessary. If a sentence is already correct, write *Correct* on your paper.

SAMPLE   Our bus broke down, we had to walk the rest of the way in the rain.

ANSWER   Our bus broke down; we had to walk the rest of the way in the rain.

1. Computers are classified according to size, the smallest are called microcomputers.
2. The Indian rhinoceros has one horn, the African rhinoceros has two.
3. Giant pandas are popular zoo animals, but they are becoming increasingly scarce.
4. Poison ivy is a dangerous plant, fortunately it is easily recognized.

214

5. Birds have feathers, mammals have hair.
6. You probably use the abbreviations A.M. and P.M., but do you know their meanings?
7. My brother collects stamps as a hobby, my sister collects unusual stones.
8. I began with the math problems, after I had solved them, I started writing my English report.
9. Some people are not afraid of anything, at least, they act that way.
10. Please open the windows, this room is too hot.

7.2f   The Colon

Rule   Use a colon to introduce a list of items that ends a sentence. A statement before the list often contains a demonstrative word like *these* or *those* or an expression such as *the following* or *as follows*.

> So far, I have read these books for my report: *Beyond Two Rivers, A Jar of Dreams,* and *Japan in the Twentieth Century.*

Do not use a colon between a verb and its complements *(pages 55–56)* or between a preposition and its objects *(pages 28–31).*

> Last Saturday we saw a meadowlark, a nuthatch, and a scarlet tanager. [not *saw:*]
>
> Dad paints with a brush, a roller, and a sponge. [not *with:*]

Rule   Use a colon to separate the hour and the minutes in an expression of time, and to separate the chapter and the verse in a Biblical reference.

> My brother catches the train at **5:07** A.M.
>
> We discussed the meaning of I Kings **17: 10–16.**

Rule   Use a colon after the salutation of a business letter.

> Dear Sir or Madam: Dear Ms. Katz:

215

Exercise 5 *(pages 214–215)*

1. Computers are classified according to size; the smallest are called microcomputers.
2. The Indian rhinoceros has one horn; the African rhinoceros has two.
3. Correct
4. Poison ivy is a dangerous plant; fortunately, it is easily recognized.
5. Birds have feathers; mammals have hair.
6. Correct
7. My brother collects stamps as a hobby; my sister collects unusual stones.
8. I began with the math problems; after I had solved them, I started writing my English report.
9. Some people are not afraid of anything; at least, they act that way.
10. Please open the windows; this room is too hot.

Exercise 6 *(page 216)*

1. For the ceremony my sister chose readings from Proverbs 31:10–13 and Sirach 26:1–4.

2. The following highways have been closed because of flooding: Route 28, Route 6, and Route 6A.

3. At 12:45 P.M. the following players will report to Coach Weed's office: Joan Suarez, Terry Washington, and Marina Blake.

4. Correct

5. Dear Senator Payne:

6. You will need these ingredients for the casserole: chives, fresh mushrooms, fish, and tomato sauce.

7. The bus will leave at 7:30 A.M.; please be on time.

8. Three for Revolution includes the biographies of the following prominent Americans: Patrick Henry, George Washington, and Thomas Jefferson.

9. Correct

10. Correct

Exercise 6 Colons   Some of the following sentences need colons. On your paper, write the sentences, using colons where needed. If a sentence does not need a colon, write *Correct* on your paper.

SAMPLE   The play-offs will begin at 4 30 P.M.

ANSWER   The play-offs will begin at 4:30 P.M.

1. For the ceremony my sister chose readings from Proverbs 31 10–13 and Sirach 26 1–4.

2. The following highways have been closed because of flooding Route 28, Route 6, and Route 6A.

3. At 12 45 P.M. the following players will report to Coach Weed's office Joan Suarez, Terry Washington, and Marina Blake.

4. This section of our textbook includes semicolons, colons, and dashes.

5. Dear Senator Payne

6. You will need these ingredients for the casserole chives, fresh mushrooms, fish, and tomato sauce.

7. The bus will leave at 7 30 A.M.; please be on time.

8. *Three for Revolution* includes the biographies of the following prominent Americans Patrick Henry, George Washington, and Thomas Jefferson.

9. In her English notebook, Mona keeps lists of worthwhile books, movies, and television shows.

10. That cookbook has a table of weights and measures, a roasting table, an oven chart, and a useful index.

7.2g   Quotation Marks

Rule   Use quotation marks to show that you are quoting what someone else has said *(page 197)* or that you are copying words that someone else has written. Put quotation marks at the beginning and at the end of the quotation.

216

The stranger asked, **"Where is Elm Street?"**

The poem ends with this thought: **"We love the things we love for what they are."**

Do not use quotation marks with an indirect quotation. An **indirect quotation** is a retelling in the writer's words of what someone else has said, written, or thought.

INDIRECT QUOTATION   Mother said that **she would go with us.**

DIRECT QUOTATION   Mother said, **"I will go with you."**

Rule Each time the speaker changes in a dialogue, begin a new paragraph and use a separate set of quotation marks.

"I'll mail the letter for you tomorrow morning on my way to school," said Toby.

"I hoped you would," said Pete.

Rule Use quotation marks to set off titles of short works. Short works include stories, short poems, songs, articles in newspapers and magazines, and the chapters or units in a book.

SHORT STORY   I just finished reading **"To Build a Fire"** by Jack London.

MAGAZINE ARTICLE   I like to read **"Life in These United States"** in the *Reader's Digest.*

Rule Use single quotation marks to set off quoted material or a title within a longer quoted passage.

"I heard him shout, **'That's the winning spirit!'** " said the assistant coach.

Other Punctuation with Quotation Marks. The following rules will help you remember where to put other punctuation marks when you write a passage that includes quotation marks.

217

Exercise 7 *(pages 218–219)*

See page 219 for the answers.

Rule   Use a comma or commas to separate an explanatory phrase, such as *I asked* or *Dad replied,* from the quotation itself. Place the comma outside opening quotation marks but inside closing quotation marks.

> The coach said, "You'd better take another practice dive." [The comma is outside the opening quotation marks.]
> "This time I'll keep my feet together," I promised. [The comma is inside the closing quotation marks.]

Rule   Place a period inside closing quotation marks.

> Today I read Robert Frost's "After Apple-Picking."

Rule   Place a question mark or an exclamation point inside the quotation marks when it is part of the quotation. Place a question mark or an exclamation point outside the quotation marks when it is part of the entire sentence but not part of the quotation. If both the quotation and the sentence require a question mark or an exclamation point, put the punctuation mark inside the quotation marks.

INSIDE THE QUOTATION MARKS

> Someone shouted, "Clear the field!"
> I just read "Who Is Sylvia?"
> Did someone ask, "What time is it?"

OUTSIDE THE QUOTATION MARKS

> Will you sing "America, the Beautiful"?
> Did he say, "Not now"?

Exercise 7   Quotation Marks   Some of the following sentences need quotation marks. On your paper, write the sentences, using quotation marks where they are needed. If a sentence needs no quotation marks, write *Correct* on your paper. Remember to use other punctuation marks correctly in relation to the quotation marks.

218

SAMPLE	Shirley said, I feel confident about this test.
ANSWER	Shirley said, "I feel confident about this test."

1. Did someone say, Let's go fishing?
2. Two popular nonsense songs are I Went to the Movies Tomorrow and Midnight on the Ocean.
3. Have you read the poem Which Shall It Be?
4. I asked him what grade he had received in the course.
5. Tomorrow, said Mrs. James, we will discuss the short story The Blue Cup by B. J. Chute.
6. Aunt Mary asked, What time will dinner be ready?
7. Can anyone play Down by the Old Millstream?
8. Did your mother really ask, Have you enough money?
9. Wait for us! we shouted, but the bus pulled out without us.
10. Does one of the novels by Dickens begin with the sentence It was the best of times, it was the worst of times?

7.2h   The Apostrophe

Rule   Use an apostrophe to show possession.

Singular Nouns. Use an apostrophe and an *s* (*'s*) to form the possessive of singular nouns, including nouns ending in *s*, *x*, or *z*.

the book that belongs to Barbara	**Barbara's** book
the report that Les wrote	**Les's** report
the voice of Rex	**Rex's** voice

Plural Nouns. Use an apostrophe and an *s* (*'s*) to form the possessive of a plural noun that does not end in *s*.

the achievements of women	**women's** achievements

219

Exercise 7 *(pages 218–219)*

1. Did someone say, "Let's go fishing"?
2. Two popular nonsense songs are "I Went to the Movies Tomorrow" and "Midnight on the Ocean."
3. Have you read the poem "Which Shall It Be?"
4. Correct
5. "Tomorrow," said Mrs. James, "we will discuss the short story 'The Blue Cup' by B. J. Chute."
6. Aunt Mary asked, "What time will dinner be ready?"
7. Can anyone play "Down by the Old Millstream"?
8. Did your mother really ask, "Have you enough money?"
9. "Wait for us!" we shouted, but the bus pulled out without us.
10. Does one of the novels by Dickens begin with the sentence "It was the best of times, it was the worst of times"?

Exercise 8 *(pages 220–221)*

1. The new store sells men's, women's, and children's shoes.
2. The Smiths' tour of Scotland included a visit to Burns's cottage.
3. Don't overuse <u>and</u>'s, <u>but</u>'s, and <u>for</u>'s in your writing.
4. My dog wags her tail when she's happy.
5. Uncrossed <u>t</u>'s look like <u>l</u>'s; undotted <u>i</u>'s look like <u>e</u>'s.
6. Isn't ours one of the newer schools in this district?
7. Since he's not eighteen yet, he doesn't vote.
8. My sister baby-sits for Mrs. Brown's niece.
9. Isn't that music a bit loud?
10. Isn't the teachers' lounge available to students?

Plural Nouns Ending in s. Use an apostrophe alone to form the possessive of a plural noun that ends in s.

the car owned by the Browns	the **Browns'** car
the team on which the girls play	the **girls'** team

Possessive Pronouns. Do not add an apostrophe to a possessive pronoun: *yours, ours, his, hers, its,* and *theirs.* These words already show possession.

Here is our coach; where is **theirs**?

Rule Use an apostrophe to replace letters or numbers that have been omitted in a contraction.

it is   **it's**   Class of 1984   Class of **'84**

Rule Use an apostrophe and an s ('s) to form the plural of letters, numbers, signs, symbols, and words referred to as such *(page 225)*. Be sure to use underlining (italicizing) correctly; do not underline the 's.

My sister dots her ***i*'s** with a circle.
The speech was full of ***however*'s.**

Exercise 8   Apostrophes In the following sentences, plurals, possessives, and contractions have been written incorrectly. On your paper, rewrite the sentences, using the correct forms. Use underlining (italicizing) where necessary.

SAMPLE   His lecture was full of *should*s.
ANSWER   His lecture was full of <u>*should*'s.</u>

1. The new store sells mens, womens, and childrens shoes.
2. The Smiths tour of Scotland included a visit to Burnss cottage.
3. Dont overuse *and*s, *but*s, and *for*s in your writing.
4. My dog wags her tail when shes happy.

220

5. Uncrossed *t*s look like *l*s; undotted *i*s look like *e*s.
6. Isnt ours one of the newer schools in this district?
7. Since hes not eighteen yet, he doesnt vote.
8. My sister baby-sits for Mrs. Browns niece.
9. Isnt that music a bit loud?
10. Isnt the teachers lounge available to students?

Assignment Punctuation   On your paper, write a sentence for each item listed below. Punctuate and capitalize your sentences correctly, using the rules on pages 197–220.

1. A declarative sentence that includes a singular possessive noun
2. An interrogative sentence that includes a contraction
3. An exclamatory sentence preceded by an interjection
4. A sentence that includes a series of three or more items
5. A direct quotation that ends with a question mark

7.2i   The Hyphen

Rule   Use a hyphen to show the division of a word at the end of a line. Always divide a word between its syllables.

She wrote that her latest interest is **collecting** old glassware. [not *coll-ecting*]

Do not divide a word of one syllable.

INCORRECT	bre-ak	fri-ght	groan-ed
CORRECT	break	fright	groaned

Do not divide a word so that one letter stands by itself.

INCORRECT	a-greeable
CORRECT	agree-able

221

Prefixes and Suffixes. Divide a word with a prefix *(page 495)* after the prefix. Divide a word with a suffix *(page 495)* before the suffix.

AFTER PREFIX   BEFORE SUFFIX
non-fiction [for nonfiction]   **neat-ness** [for neatness]

Compound Words. Divide a compound word *(page 483)* that is written as one word between the words that form the compound. Divide a hyphenated compound word at the hyphen.

BETWEEN WORDS   AT HYPHEN
note-book [for notebook]   **light-year** [for light-year]

Rule   Use a hyphen after the prefixes *all-, ex-,* and *self-.* Use a hyphen to separate any prefix from a word that begins with a capital letter.

all-knowing   **pre-**Revolutionary   BUT   prepay

Rule   Hyphenate a compound modifier when it precedes the word that it modifies.

            They have a **well-kept** lawn.

BUT   The lawn was **well kept.**

Do not hyphenate a compound modifier that begins with an adverb ending in *-ly.*

The **dimly lighted** room looked uninviting.

Fractions. Use a hyphen in a fraction that is used as a modifier. Do not use a hyphen in a fraction that is used as a noun.

As a settlement, he received **two-thirds** pay. [The fraction *two-thirds* modifies *pay.*]
Two thirds of my free time is spent on homework. [The fraction *two thirds* is the subject of the sentence.]

222

Rule Use a hyphen in compound numbers from *twenty-one* through *ninety-nine.*

forty-four   eighty-nine

Exercise 9 Hyphens   On your paper, write each of the following words, using a hyphen to show how the word may be divided at the end of a line. If a word may be divided at more than one place, show each acceptable division. If you need help, use your dictionary.

SAMPLE   arrangement   arrange-ment   ar-rangement

1. ginger
2. swimmer
3. raincoat
4. mother-in-law
5. electric
6. passage
7. doorknob
8. nonprofit
9. four-fifths
10. uncertain

Exercise 10 Hyphens   On your paper, write the following sentences, using hyphens where needed. If no hyphens are needed, write *Correct* on your paper.

SAMPLE   He regretted his too hasty remark.
ANSWER   He regretted his too-hasty remark.

1. Lorna collects pre Columbian pottery for the museum.
2. We've already eaten one half of the apples.
3. That is a first rate suggestion.
4. A well planned vacation is certainly worth the effort.
5. Everyone says that my father is a self made man.
6. A two thirds vote is needed to change that rule.
7. In twenty two days we traveled a comfortable four thousand miles in our well packed car.
8. Our dog is well behaved now that we've trained him.
9. The ex mayor is self confident enough to run for governor.
10. Father cut the meat loaf into one eighth portions.

Exercise 9 *(page 223)*

1. gin-ger
2. swim-mer
3. rain-coat
4. mother-in-law
5. elec-tric
6. pas-sage
7. door-knob
8. non-profit
9. four-fifths
10. un-certain

Exercise 10 *(page 223)*

1. Lorna collects pre-Columbian pottery for the museum.
2. Correct
3. That is a first-rate suggestion.
4. A well-planned vacation is certainly worth the effort.
5. Everyone says that my father is a self-made man.
6. A two-thirds vote is needed to change that rule.
7. In twenty-two days we traveled a comfortable four thousand miles in our well-packed car.
8. Correct
9. The ex-mayor is self-confident enough to run for governor.
10. Father cut the meat loaf into one-eighth portions.

223

Mechanics **223**

Exercise 11 *(page 224)*

1. When Sharon arrives—oh, here she is now.
2. Can we—should we—ask for more free time?
3. Someone—I think it was John—said that the bus had arrived.
4. Our next problem—and it's a big one—is raising the money.
5. After a long wait—it seemed like a long wait to me at least—the show began.

7.2j   The Dash

Rule   Use a dash to show that a thought or a speech was unfinished or interrupted. If the sentence continues, use a second dash to mark the end of the interruption.

"Will you **help—oh,** you're busy," said Mother.

We serve this **dessert—at least I think we do—at** every family get-together.

Note: Avoid the overuse of dashes in your written work.

Exercise 11   **Dashes**   On your paper, write the following sentences, using dashes where needed.

> SAMPLE   Please come here no, not you and help me with these packages.
>
> ANSWER   Please come here—no, not you—and help me with these packages.

1. When Sharon arrives oh, here she is now.
2. Can we should we ask for more free time?
3. Someone I think it was John said that the bus had arrived.
4. Our next problem and it's a big one is raising the money.
5. After a long wait it seemed like a long wait to me at least the show began.

7.3   Italics

Italic type (*slanted letters such as these*) is used for a variety of reasons. When you are writing or typing something that should be in italic type, use underlining to stand for italicizing.

Rule   Italicize (underline) the titles of books, lengthy poems, newspapers, magazines, television series, paintings, ships, and

224

so forth. Do not capitalize or underline an article (*a, an,* or *the*) before a title unless it is part of the title.

Rime of the Ancient Mariner   *Real People*
the *Cleveland Daily Banner*   the *Bounty*

Rule Italicize (underline) letters, numbers, symbols, and words when you are writing about them as words or symbols.

There are two *m*'s and one *c* in *recommend.*

In your report, use the word *percent,* not the symbol %.

Exercise Italics In the following sentences, words that should be underlined to indicate italic type are not. On your paper, write the sentences, underlining all the words that should be italicized.

SAMPLE   The words merit and demerit were once synonyms.

ANSWER   The words <u>merit</u> and <u>demerit</u> were once synonyms.

1. Natty Bumppo is the hero of James Fenimore Cooper's novels The Deerslayer and The Pioneers.
2. Yes, Bumppo is spelled with two p's.
3. Four frequently misused word pairs are to and two, its and it's, their and there, and your and you're.
4. One of the first streamlined trains was the City of Denver.
5. In my bibliography I included an article from the September issue of Sky and Telescope.
6. We read the Savannah Morning News during our two-week stay in Georgia.
7. In Fur Traders on the Missouri, the artist pictures two trappers gliding downstream in a dugout canoe.
8. I mistakenly wrote rode for road.
9. The movie 2001: A Space Odyssey is based on a novel by Arthur C. Clarke.
10. Charles Lindbergh, who flew nonstop across the Atlantic in the Spirit of St. Louis, observed the launching of Apollo 11.

225

Exercise *(page 225)*

Corrections are underlined in red.

1. Natty Bumppo is the hero of James Fenimore Cooper's novels <u>The Deerslayer</u> and <u>The Pioneers.</u>
2. Yes, Bumppo is spelled with two <u>p</u>'s.
3. Four frequently misused word pairs are <u>to</u> and <u>two, its</u> and <u>it's, their</u> and <u>there,</u> and <u>your</u> and <u>you're.</u>
4. One of the first streamlined trains was the <u>City of Denver.</u>
5. In my bibliography I included an article from the September issue of <u>Sky and Telescope.</u>
6. We read the <u>Savannah Morning News</u> during our two-week stay in Georgia.
7. In <u>Fur Traders on the Missouri,</u> the artist pictures two trappers gliding downstream in a dugout canoe.
8. I mistakenly wrote <u>rode</u> for <u>road.</u>
9. The movie <u>2001: A Space Odyssey</u> is based on a novel by Arthur C. Clarke.
10. Charles Lindbergh, who flew nonstop across the Atlantic in the <u>Spirit of St. Louis,</u> observed the launching of the <u>Apollo 11.</u>

7.4   Using Numbers in Writing

Rule   Spell out numbers of *one hundred* or less and all numbers rounded to hundreds.

My mother and father were married **twenty-five** years ago.

Rule   Use numerals for numbers greater than *one hundred* that are not round numbers.

About **180** people came to their anniversary party.

Rule   If a number appears at the beginning of a sentence, spell out the number or rewrite the sentence.

INCORRECT   **115** people signed up for the bus trip.

CORRECT   **One hundred fifteen** people signed up for the bus trip.

Rule   The word *and* is unnecessary in writing out numbers except those between *one hundred* and *one hundred and ten, two hundred* and *two hundred and ten,* and so forth.

One hundred and two people attended the game.

Rule   Use words to express the time unless you are writing the exact time with the abbreviation *A.M.* or *P.M.*

We left for the airport at **four o'clock.**
We left the house at **4:30** P.M.

Rule   Use numerals to express dates, house and street numbers, apartment numbers, telephone numbers, page numbers, and percentages. Spell out the word *percent*.

May 22, 1964	Apartment 5E	page 26
Room 46	555-9097	50 percent

Rule   Do not add *-st, -nd, -rd,* or *-th* to a numeral naming the day of the month.

226

INCORRECT	May **2nd**, 1787	June **1st**
CORRECT	May **2**, 1787	June **1** or the **first** of June

Exercise Numbers in Writing On your paper, write the following sentences, using the correct forms for numbers in writing. If no corrections are needed, write *Correct.*

SAMPLE The *Monitor* fought the *Merrimack* on March 9th, 1862.

ANSWER The Monitor fought the Merrimack on March 9, 1862.

1. Our class picture can be found on page forty-two.
2. 1513 passengers went down with the *Titanic.*
3. On April 30, 1962, Joseph A. Walker flew the X-15 to an altitude of 246,700 feet.
4. The average person in the United States makes more than 300 phone calls a year.
5. My cousins live in Apartment twenty-two in a high rise on West 92nd Street.
6. The interest rate dropped from twelve % to ten %.
7. My brother will be 21 on December 7th.
8. 2 of my aunts live in Cedar Crossings, along with five hundred forty-two other inhabitants.
9. The first professional football game was played on August 31st, 1895, with 200 fans in attendance.
10. The October 17th, 1965, edition of *The New York Times* weighed 7 pounds and had nine hundred forty-six pages.

7.5 Proofreading Symbols

Proofreading symbols are sometimes used to identify and correct errors in composition. You may use the symbols on the following page when you proofread and revise your writing.

227

Exercise *(page 227)*

1. Our class picture can be found on page 42.
2. Fifteen hundred thirteen passengers went down with the Titanic.
3. Correct
4. The average person in the United States makes more than three hundred phone calls a year.
5. My cousins live in Apartment 22 in a high rise on West 92nd Street.
6. The interest rate dropped from 12 percent to 10 percent.
7. My brother will be twenty-one on December 7.
8. Two of my aunts live in Cedar Crossings, along with 542 other inhabitants.
9. The first professional football game was played on August 31, 1895, with two hundred fans in attendance.
10. The October 17, 1965, edition of The New York Times weighed seven pounds and had 946 pages.

Practice 1 *(pages 230–232)*

A.

1. Doreen explained, "The Swedish ivy will grow better near this window, where it will face south."

2. In November most Canadians celebrate Remembrance Day.

3. The slide show included satellite photographs of Earth in which the continents were visible.

4. Yesterday I received a long letter from my cousin who lives in the capital city of Ethiopia.

5. Monica addressed the package to 15 Burgess Street, Bridgeport, CT 06602.

6. The spacecraft <u>Pioneer 10</u> passed close enough to Jupiter to give us new and valuable information.

7. The first woman to swim the English Channel was an American swimmer named Gertrude Ederle.

8. A complicated genetic theory will be described by Lloyd S. Warren, M.D.

9. The Sherman Antitrust Act was passed in the 1800s to prevent the growth of business monopolies.

(Continue on the next page.)

∧	insert something	on her way the market
#	space	was the first person to
¶	begin new paragraph	of one another. There is a time
∿	transpose letter or words	our goal clearly is
ℓ	delete	studied the the history of
⌒	close up letters	do g
....	let it stand (under something crossed out)	He was obviously unaware of the time.
≡	capitalize	an ancient persian carpet
/	make lower case	She wrote to her Mother.

7.6   Manuscript Form

Unless your teacher gives you other instructions, follow the guidelines below for preparing a manuscript.

Suggestions for Handwritten Manuscripts

Paper. Write on standard-size ruled paper (8½ by 10 inches or 8½ by 11 inches). Write on one side only.

Ink. Use black or blue ink.

228

Margins. Leave margins of 1½ inches at the left side and 1 inch at the right side. The left margin must be even. The right margin should be as even as possible.

Title. Write the title, if any, in the center of the top line. Skip at least one line between the title and the first paragraph. Do not put quotation marks around the title.

Indentation. Indent the first line of every paragraph about 1 inch.

Suggestions for Typewritten Manuscripts

Paper. Use standard-size white typewriter paper (8½ by 11 inches). Double-space and use only one side of the paper.

Ribbon. Use a black ribbon.

Margins. Leave margins of 1½ inches at the left side and 1 inch at the right side. The left margin must be even. The right margin should be as even as possible. On all pages except the page with the title, place the first line at least 1 inch below the top of the page. Leave a margin of 1 inch at the bottom of every page.

Title. Center the title at least 2 inches from the top of the page. Do not put quotation marks around the title. Begin the first paragraph four lines below the title.

Indentation. Indent the first line of every paragraph five spaces.

Labeling and Numbering Pages

Write your name, the school subject, and the date (in that order) in the upper-right corner of the first page. On every page except the first page, put the page number in the upper-right corner unless your teacher gives you other instructions. Use Arabic numerals.

If your paper consists of more than one page, attach the pages at the upper-left corner with a staple or a paper clip.

229

Practice 1 *(pages 230–232), continued*

10. There is a definite rhythm in these lines by Longfellow:

     The tide rises, the tide falls,
     The twilight darkens, the curlew calls;
     Along the sea sands damp and brown
     The traveler hastens toward the town
     And the tide rises, the tide falls.

B.

11. Well, today's weather was sunny, warm, and humid.

12. Tricia asked, "Was it Will Rogers, the humorist and social critic, who said, 'I never met a man I didn't like'?"

13. The recipe gives the following directions: boil one min, stir constantly, and then remove from heat.

14. Approaching the podium nervously, Rosalyn gradually gained her self-confidence and began her speech.

15. The largest hailstone in the United States fell September 3, 1970, in Coffreyville, Kansas; it measured 17 in. around.

16. Oh! My sister just had her first child.

(Continue on the next page.)

Unit Practice

Practice 1 *(pages 230–232)*, continued

17. After a short warm-up session, I headed for the soccer field; I began practice, *(or;)* and then I played an informal game with my teammates.

18. You must read—if your local library has it—the short story "Dr. Heidegger's Experiment" by Nathaniel Hawthorne.

19. Bob, your sister Lea has qualified for the swim team.

20. The Rodriguezes' house is the yellow and white one on the corner; it's about two blocks from ours.

C.

Corrections are underlined in red.

21. Printed in 1784, the <u>Pennsylvania Packet & General Advertiser</u> was the first successful daily newspaper in the United States.

22. Hal hopes to receive a subscription to <u>Stereo Review</u> for his birthday.

23. Mr. Stein explained that the word <u>lark</u> can mean either a bird or an adventure.

24. Please remember to write a ! after the title of the musical <u>Oklahoma!</u> when you make the posters.

25. <u>The Clockmaker</u>, a painting by Paul Cézanne, has primarily dark brown and dark green hues.

(Continue on the next page.)

Practice 1

A. Capitalization *(pages 197–206)* On your paper, write each of the following sentences, correcting all errors in capitalization.

1. doreen explained, "the swedish ivy will grow better near this window, where it will face south."

2. in november most canadians celebrate remembrance day.

3. the slide show included satellite photographs of earth in which the continents were visible.

4. yesterday i received a long letter from my cousin who lives in the capital city of ethiopia.

5. Monica addressed the package to 15 burgess street, bridgeport, ct 06602.

6. the spacecraft *pioneer 10* passed close enough to jupiter to give us new and valuable information.

7. the first woman to swim the english channel was an american swimmer named gertrude ederle.

8. a complicated genetic theory will be described by lloyd s. warren, m.d.

9. the sherman antitrust act was passed in the 1800s to prevent the growth of business monopolies.

10. there is a definite rhythm in these lines by longfellow:

   the tide rises, the tide falls,

   the twilight darkens, the curlew calls;

   along the sea sands damp and brown

   the traveler hastens toward the town

       and the tide rises, the tide falls.

B. Punctuation *(pages 206–224)* On your paper, write the following sentences, correcting all errors in punctuation.

11. Well today's weather was sunny warm and humid.

12. Tricia asked Was it Will Rogers the humorist and social critic who said I never met a man I didn't like

13. The recipe gives the following directions boil one min stir constantly and then remove from heat
14. Approaching the podium nervously Rosalyn gradually gained her self confidence and began her speech
15. The largest hailstone in the United States fell September 3 1970 in Coffreyville Kansas it measured 17 in around
16. Oh My sister just had her first child
17. After a short warm up session I headed for the soccer field I began practice and then I played an informal game with my teammates
18. You must read if your local library has it the short story Dr Heideggers Experiment by Nathaniel Hawthorne
19. Bob your sister Lea has qualified for the swim team
20. The Rodriguezes house is the yellow and white one on the corner its about two blocks from ours

C. Italics *(pages 224–225)* On your paper, copy each of the following sentences. Underline the words that should be italicized.

21. Printed in 1784, the Pennsylvania Packet & General Advertiser was the first successful daily newspaper in the United States.
22. Hal hopes to receive a subscription to Stereo Review for his birthday.
23. Mr. Stein explained that the word lark can mean either a bird or an adventure.
24. Please remember to write a ! after the title of the musical Oklahoma! when you make the posters.
25. The Clockmaker, a painting by Paul Cézanne, has primarily dark brown and dark green hues.

D. Using Numbers in Writing *(pages 226–227)* On your paper, copy each of the following sentences, using the correct number form from the choices in parentheses.

(Continue on the next page.)

231

Practice 1 *(pages 230–232),* continued

D.

26. Fay located the photograph of the lyrebird on page 34 of her guide to exotic birds.
27. Be at the box office at 6:45 P.M.
28. Gary has collected almost 125 signatures for the petition.
29. Six helicopters circled in the sky during the special outdoor ceremony for the visiting royalty.
30. An American beech tree in Michigan has grown to the height of 161 feet.

Practice 2 *(page 232)*

Corrections are underlined in red.

My cousin and I visited Trailside Park in August 1984. One of the park volunteers was holding a baby opossum. She said that an opossum is a marsupial, an animal that lives inside its mother's pouch after it is born. She explained that the word marsupial comes from a Latin word that means "pouch." She also told us that when an opossum is frightened, its limbs stiffen, its breathing rate decreases, and it appears lifeless; (*or.*) this (*or* This) act often saves the opossum from danger. The volunteer said that we could read more about opossums in a book called Facts About North American Marsupials.

Test 1 *(pages 233–235)*

A.

1. In 1855 the Statue of Liberty arrived from France aboard the ship Isère, after the statue had been taken apart and packed into 214 crates.

2. "Have you ever walked on the trails of Cascade State Park?" asked Mike. "The view is remarkable."

3. In Greek myths Hermes is the messenger of the gods.

4. While she was visiting, Grandmother Tate gave me an illustrated book of Japanese poetry.

(Continue on the next page.)

26. Fay located the photograph of the lyrebird on page (thirty-four, 34) of her guide to exotic birds.

27. Be at the box office at (six forty-five, 6:45) P.M.

28. Gary has collected almost (125, one hundred twenty-five) signatures for the petition.

29. (6, Six) helicopters circled in the sky during the special outdoor ceremony for the visiting royalty.

30. An American beech tree in Michigan has grown to the height of (one hundred sixty-one, 161) feet.

Practice 2

Rewrite the following passage. Make the necessary corrections in capitalization, punctuation, italicizing (underlining), and the use of numbers.

My cousin and i visited trailside park in august 1984 one of the park volunteers was holding a baby opossum she said that an opossum is a marsupial an animal that lives inside its mothers pouch after it is born she explained that the word marsupial comes from a latin word that means "pouch" she also told us that when an opossum is frightened its limbs stiffen its breathing rate decreases and it appears lifeless this act often saves the opossum from danger the volunteer said that we could read more about opossums in a book called facts about north american marsupials

Unit Tests

Test 1

A. Capitalization *(pages 197–206)* On your paper, write each of the following sentences, correcting all errors in capitalization.

1. in 1855 the statue of liberty arrived from france aboard the ship *isère,* after the statue had been taken apart and packed into 214 crates.
2. "have you ever walked on the trails of cascade state park?" asked Mike. "the view is remarkable."
3. in greek myths hermes is the messenger of the gods.
4. while she was visiting, grandmother tate gave me an illustrated book of japanese poetry.
5. in poetry class martha recited "upon what base?" by edward taylor.
6. do you have an extra box of write-away ballpoint pens?
7. according to the newspaper, colonel j. thompson burke will arrive at the civic center at 2:00 p.m.
8. ken found the room where the mathematics II students were meeting for a seminar about computers.
9. the summer jamboree will be held at riverside community park on july 14.
10. next april dr. bruce erhard will be the featured speaker at a medical convention in st. louis.

B. Punctuation *(pages 206–224)* On your paper, write each of the following sentences, correcting all errors in punctuation.

11. There are twenty two engineers in Mrs Amess department
12. After we reached the campground we chose a spot unloaded our gear and pitched our tents immediately sunset was only an hour away

(Continue on the next page.)

233

Test 1 *(pages 233–235),* continued

5. In poetry class Martha recited "Upon What Base?" by Edward Taylor.
6. Do you have an extra box of Write-Away ballpoint pens?
7. According to the newspaper, Colonel J. Thompson Burke will arrive at the civic center at 2:00 P.M.
8. Ken found the room where the Mathematics II students were meeting for a seminar about computers.
9. The Summer Jamboree will be held at Riverside Community Park on July 14.
10. Next April Dr. Bruce Erhard will be the featured speaker at a medical convention in St. Louis.

B.

11. There are twenty-two engineers in Mrs. Ames's department.
12. After we reached the campground, we chose a spot, unloaded our gear, and pitched our tents immediately; sunset was only an hour away.
13. "Please buy the one with all natural ingredients," they told me, "if it's still available when you are at the store."
14. Coach Manfredi said, "Well, the first three meets of the season are against tough teams. However, we've got some excellent runners and the city's champion high jumper on our team."

(Continue on the next page.)

Test 1 *(pages 233–235)*, continued

15. Underneath a dusty brass-hinged trunk, Sheila found some magazines dated August 1915.

16. What is the origin of this phrase: "Don't forget to mind your p's and q's"?

17. I always read the column "What Happened Ten Years Ago This Week (*or*?)" in our local newspaper.

18. Be at the lobby desk at 9:30 A.M. for the tour of the television studios; we will begin promptly.

19. Charlie, will you please bring scissors, paint, and paper for the poster-making contest tomorrow. (*or*?)

20. At ten, twenty fans already stood in line with their tickets, their programs, and their cameras.

C.

21. I just noticed that there is a u in the British spelling of the word honor.

22. While sailing on the Endeavour, James Cook became the first European explorer to reach New Zealand.

23. Toby never misses an episode of the informative television series called New Horizons.

24. This month's issue of Heirlooms Magazine has a picture of an interesting clock.

(Continue on the next page.)

13. Please buy the one with all natural ingredients they told me if its still available when you are at the store

14. Coach Manfredi said Well the first three meets of the season are against tough teams however weve got some excellent runners and the citys champion high jumper on our team

15. Underneath a dusty brass hinged trunk Sheila found some magazines dated August 1915

16. What is the origin of this phrase Don't forget to mind your *p*s and *q*s

17. I always read the column What Happened Ten Years Ago This Week in our local newspaper

18. Be at the lobby desk at 9 30 A.M. for the tour of the television studios we will begin promptly

19. Charlie will you please bring scissors paints and paper for the poster making contest tomorrow

20. At ten twenty fans already stood in line with their tickets their programs and their cameras

C. Italics *(pages 224–225)* On your paper, copy each of the following sentences. Underline the words that should be italicized.

21. I just noticed that there is a u in the British spelling of the word honor.

22. While sailing on the Endeavour, James Cook became the first European explorer to reach New Zealand.

23. Toby never misses an episode of the informative television series called New Horizons.

24. This month's issue of Heirlooms Magazine has a picture of an interesting clock.

25. Last summer Katy thoroughly enjoyed reading Treasure Island by Robert Louis Stevenson.

D. Using Numbers in Writing *(pages 226–227)* On your paper, copy each of the following sentences, using the correct number form from the choices in parentheses.

26. Frank's experiment was completed at (two thirty, 2:30) P.M.
27. Does Melissa need instructions in order to get to the museum located at (fifteen, 15) Boyd Canyon Drive?
28. Brite's department store will have a sale offering (ten percent, 10 percent) off all sports equipment.
29. There were nearly (150, one hundred fifty) exhibits at this year's state fair.
30. When the Brooklyn Bridge opened on May (24, 24th), 1883, it was the largest suspension bridge in the world.

Test 2

Rewrite the following passage. Make the necessary corrections in capitalization, punctuation, italicizing (underlining), and the use of numbers.

what are cats eyes rainbows and moonstones these are the names of different marbles playing with marbles is an ancient practice egyptian children once enjoyed the game however todays game has very specific rules first a circle 10 feet across is marked on the ground 13 marbles are placed inside the ring the players use a large marble to knock the other marbles out of the ring this is the object of the game to be the first player to knock 7 marbles out of the ring

Test 1 *(pages 233–235)*, continued

25. Last summer Katy thoroughly enjoyed reading Treasure Island by Robert Louis Stevenson.

D.

26. Frank's experiment was completed at 2:30 P.M.
27. Does Melissa need instructions in order to get to the museum located at 15 Boyd Canyon Drive?
28. Brite's department store will have a sale offering 10 percent off all sports equipment.
29. There were nearly 150 exhibits at this year's state fair.
30. When the Brooklyn Bridge opened on May 24, 1883, it was the largest suspension bridge in the world.

Test 2 *(page 235)*

Corrections are underlined in red. Answers may vary. Samples:

What are cat's eyes, rainbows, and moonstones? These are the names of different marbles. Playing with marbles is an ancient practice; Egyptian children once enjoyed the game. However, today's game has very specific rules. First a circle ten feet across is marked on the ground; thirteen marbles are placed inside the ring. The players use a large marble to knock the other marbles out of the ring. This is the object of the game: to be the first player to knock seven marbles out of the ring.

Part Two

Composition

Unit	8	Prewriting	238
Unit	9	Writing Sentences	260
Unit	10	Writing Paragraphs	276
Unit	11	Revising	310
Unit	12	Explaining	340
Unit	13	Describing	360
Unit	14	Narrating	382
Unit	15	Writing a Report	408
Unit	16	Writing Letters	452

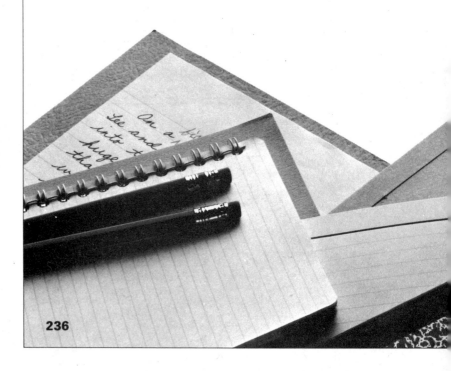

236

The writing process involves more than just arranging words into sentences and paragraphs. You must choose a topic, develop ideas on that topic, and then organize and present those ideas. You can carry out this process easily and effectively if you divide it into a series of steps. In Part Two, you will learn and practice those steps.

In Units 8 through 11, you will learn the three basic steps of writing: prewriting, writing, and revising. In Units 12 through 14, you will learn how to write for a specific purpose: to explain, to describe, or to narrate. In Units 15 and 16, you will learn the special forms of writing that you will use for reports and letters.

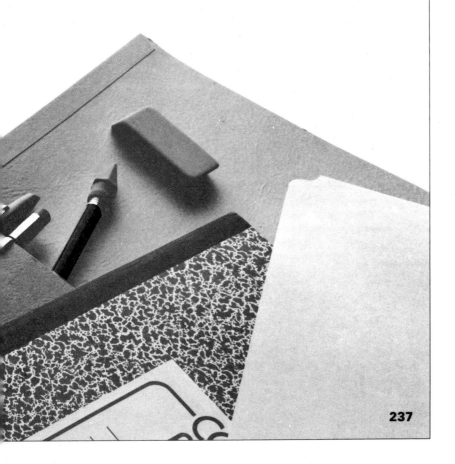

237

Objectives

After studying this unit, students should be able to do the following:

- Find ideas for their writing by keeping a writer's notebook, taking an interest inventory, and drawing upon their experiences.

- Gather and develop ideas for their writing by making lists and asking questions.

- Identify a purpose and audience for their writing and choose a topic accordingly.

Teaching Suggestions

See "Classroom Insights" for Unit 8 in the front of this Teacher's Edition.

Program Resources

Resource Book, Second Course:
  Bonus Activities, Unit 8
  Composition Checklist,
  Unit 8
Practice Book, Second Course,
  Unit 8
Tests, Second Course, Unit 8
Composition Workshops,
  Second Course, Unit 8

Related Resources

The American Heritage Dictionary of the English Language

Prewriting

Unit Preview

Prewriting. Writing. Revising. These are the three steps in the writing process. Approaching your writing one step at a time will make the process more manageable. **Prewriting,** the first step, is the planning and preparation that you do before you write. This is the foundation on which you will base your writing. During prewriting, you gather ideas, develop them, and decide what to write about. You also consider what your purpose is and whom you are writing for.

The following notes are part of one writer's prewriting material on the subject of solar energy.

Energy that comes from the sun
Many uses: stoves, furnaces, heaters, batteries
Can be used immediately or stored (batteries)
No waste products to pollute air, water
Free, but equipment is expensive

Who can use solar energy? —People who live in sunny climates and can afford the equipment
What are the advantages of solar energy? —An alternative to less available sources of energy such as oil and gas; a nonpollutant

For Analysis   On your paper, answer the following questions about the prewriting notes.

1. What are two methods that the writer used to collect ideas about the subject?
   a. Made a list of ideas about solar energy
   b. Made an outline
   c. Asked and answered questions about solar energy

238

2. Which of the following writing topics do the notes suggest?
   a. The shortage of fuel
   b. How to make a solar battery
   c. The benefits of solar energy
3. What additional questions would you ask if you wanted to learn more about solar energy?

In answering these questions, you observed part of what writers do in prewriting. In this unit you will learn effective ways to do your prewriting. You will discover that many of the ideas that you already have can serve as topics for writing. You will learn how to gather and develop ideas and how to focus your prewriting notes for specific writing assignments.

For Analysis *(pages 238–239)*

Answers to 3 may vary.

1. a, c
2. c
3a. Is there a consumer agency that provides information about equipment?
  b. Are there any disadvantages associated with solar energy?

8.1 Finding Ideas for Writing

Perhaps you have had the experience of sitting down to write and finding that you have nothing to say. Prewriting will help you to discover that you have more ideas to write about than you realize. Keeping a writer's notebook is one way to identify your ideas and to have them at your fingertips. In your notebook you can keep an inventory of your interests and a list of your experiences, which can supply you with ideas to develop for writing. The purpose of the notebook is to identify and record your ideas in a convenient place for later development.

8.1a Keeping a Writer's Notebook

A **writer's notebook** can be a folder or a binder in which you keep notes and clippings that might give you ideas for writing assignments. Use the following strategies to collect ideas for your writer's notebook.

239

Answers will vary.

Strategies

1. *Take notes on anything that you see, hear, think, or do that you want to remember.* You need not record your notes in complete sentences. For example:

   Finished reading *Oliver Twist*—Could I have survived in Oliver's world?

   A beautiful sunset over the river

   Cousin a paramedic; ask about requirements

2. *Record interesting comments that you hear people make and your reactions to their comments.* The following comment is an example:

   Coach Brown said, "Don't burn your bridges behind you." Does that mean that I shouldn't give up basketball because I didn't make the first team?

3. *Include articles, advertisements, pictures, and cartoons.* Read newspapers and magazines regularly, and clip and save those items that interest you. For example, you might include a magazine article about solar energy, a news photo that shows the first solar house, or a cartoon that humorously points out the results of a fuel shortage.

Exercise 1 Prewriting: Writer's Notebook From newspapers and magazines, clip examples of three or more of the following items that could suggest an idea for writing. Put your clippings in your writer's notebook.

1. A political cartoon or comic strip that makes an interesting point
2. An article on a subject about which you have an opinion
3. A photograph that makes a strong or controversial statement
4. An advertisement that catches your interest
5. A news story about an interesting or unusual person, idea, or event

240

8.1b   Taking an Interest Inventory

Exercise 2 *(pages 241–242)*

One way to collect ideas for your writer's notebook is to take an interest inventory. An **interest inventory** is an itemized list of your interests. It can include subjects in which you are now interested and subjects about which you would like to know more. Part of an interest inventory might look like this:

Sample answer:

Subjects I know about
model rocketry
science fiction
folk music
car engines
trampolines

WHAT I KNOW ABOUT
dogs
television trivia
gardening

WHAT I WANT TO KNOW ABOUT
careers in television
organic gardening
coin collecting

GROUPS I BELONG TO
chorus
scouts
softball team

SKILLS I WOULD LIKE TO HAVE
typing
playing the piano
speed reading

Keep a special section in your writer's notebook for your inventory so that you can add to it as you develop new interests.

Exercise 2   Prewriting: Interest Inventory   Make an interest inventory in your writer's notebook. Use five or more of the following questions to help you get started. For each question that you use, make a heading and list your answers under it. Add other interests of your own that these questions do not cover.

1. What subjects do I know about?
2. What are my hobbies?
3. What are my favorite sports?
4. Which subjects do I enjoy most in school?
5. What do I enjoy doing in my spare time?
6. What clubs or organizations do I belong to?

241

Sample answer:

1. Automobiles: solar- and electric-powered city cars, how to tune an engine

7. What kinds of books do I like to read?
8. What would I like to learn more about?
9. What cities or countries would I like to visit?
10. What careers interest me?

Exercise 3   Prewriting: Interest Inventory   In your writer's notebook, list five of the following subjects that interest you. Next to each subject that you list, write two related items that you would like to know more about.

SAMPLE	Weather
ANSWER	Weather: tornadoes, forecasting as a career

1. Automobiles
2. Bicycle safety
3. Endangered animals
4. Fashion
5. Health
6. History
7. Home computers
8. Law enforcement
9. Movies
10. Museums
11. Nutrition
12. Politics
13. Satellites
14. Veterinarians
15. Water sports

8.1c   Drawing Upon Your Experiences

Your experiences are another valuable source of ideas for writing. You may be surprised to discover how many possible writing subjects can come from a single experience. Suppose, for example, that you accompanied the school team on a bus ride to a neighboring town for a play-off game. You could draw on that experience to write about the following subjects:

Songs teen-agers sing on bus rides
Effective cheerleading
How athletes prepare themselves mentally

Keep a record of your experiences in a special section of your writer's notebook.

242

Exercise 4 Prewriting: Experiences In your writer's notebook, complete five or more of the following sentences with examples from your own experiences.

> SAMPLE   I learned about patience when __?__.
>
> ANSWER   I learned about patience when I baby-sat for two sets of twins.

1. The longest day of my life was __?__.
2. The bravest thing that I ever did was __?__.
3. One lesson that I learned that was worth learning was __?__.
4. The time I felt most like an adult was __?__.
5. I really earned my allowance the day that I __?__.
6. The happiest holiday that I ever spent was __?__.
7. I found out that "haste makes waste" when __?__.
8. The most interesting place that I have visited is __?__.
9. I learned the meaning of cooperation when __?__.
10. The problem that I solved most successfully was __?__.

Exercise 5 Prewriting: Experiences In your writer's notebook, list at least two examples of three of the following experiences.

> SAMPLE   Learning something new
>
> ANSWER   I learned how to make a crystal radio set.
>   I prepared my first omelet and cleaned up afterward.

1. Never making the same mistake twice
2. Humorous family incidents
3. Meeting interesting people
4. Losing something
5. Summertime adventures

Assignment 1 Prewriting Read a newspaper every day for a week. Put clippings of items that interest you into your writer's notebook. Write comments about each item.

243

Exercise 4 *(page 243)*

Sample answer:

1. The longest day of my life was when I waited for the results of the softball team tryouts.

Exercise 5 *(page 243)*

Sample answer:

1. I will never again try to pitch a tent without reading the instructions first.
   I will never again try to ski an expert slope while I am still a beginner.

Assignment 2   Prewriting   Keep your writer's notebook up to date for three consecutive days. At the end of each day, record under the date three or more ideas and one experience. Include comments on what you did, heard, and observed.

Continuing Assignment   Prewriting   From your writer's notebook, select three subjects that you would like to develop. Select one from your interest inventory, one from your list of experiences, and one from other items in your notebook. Write each subject at the head of a separate sheet of paper. Save your papers.

Assignment Checklist

Check your assignments for the following points:

✔ 1. Did you put into your writer's notebook news stories, articles, advertisements, pictures, and cartoons that interest you?

✔ 2. In Assignment 2, did you record three ideas and one experience for each day?

✔ 3. In the Continuing Assignment, did you select one subject from your interest inventory, one from your list of experiences, and one from other items in your writer's notebook?

8.2   Gathering and Developing Ideas

Each idea in your writer's notebook is a possible subject for development as a writing assignment. You can develop any idea by making lists of information related to it and by asking and answering questions about it.

8.2a Making Lists

Exercise 1 *(pages 245–246)*

See page 246 for a sample answer.

When you have chosen a subject to write about, begin developing it by writing down all the ideas and information about it that come to your mind. Then expand your list by writing down any related ideas that your imagination connects with the subject. Do not discard any ideas or try to organize the list. At this point, your purpose is to let your ideas flow freely and to get them down on paper.

Suppose that for a writing assignment you plan to write about an unusual sport. In your writer's notebook, you find hot-air ballooning listed in your interest inventory as one of the things that you would like to know more about. You also find a clipping about hot-air ballooning. Your list might look like this:

Propane burner heats air inside balloon.

Hot air makes balloon rise.

Should learn from qualified instructor.

Ground crew needed for liftoffs, landings.

Balloon is huge—carries two to four people.

Basket or gondola holds passengers.

Two-way radio strongly recommended.

Thrill of floating through sky without an engine.

Direction influenced by wind currents.

Sand bags carried as ballast; released to help ascend.

Safety helmets, flares, fire extinguisher, first-aid kit required in gondola.

Approximate cost of a three-hour expedition.

Exercise 1 Prewriting: Making Lists Choose three of the following subjects. On your paper, list eight or more ideas that come to mind for each subject.

245

Exercise 1 *(pages 245–246)*

Sample answer:

1. Always have heroes and villains
   Many have fantastic creatures
   A treasure hunt
   Some adventures humorous
   Some have deeper meaning
   A love interest usually present
   Science fiction
   Terrific entertainment

SAMPLE	Beachcombing
ANSWER	Best time—after a storm or at low tide
	Ordinary items: shells, driftwood, seaweeds
	Unusual items: bottle glass, polished stones, net buoys
	No equipment or skill needed
	Can become a hobby
	Can do it in any season
	Peaceful and relaxing

1. Adventure movies
2. Comic strips
3. Farming
4. Gold
5. Holidays
6. House plants
7. The human heart
8. Kites
9. Musical instruments
10. Pets

8.2b Asking Questions

Asking and answering questions about your subject will help you to develop it further. With your list of ideas in front of you, write questions that begin with *Who, What, When, Where, Why,* and *How.* If you do not have the answers to your questions, ask someone who might know, or look for the answers in a book, a magazine, or another source.

Here is a list of questions and answers related to hot-air ballooning.

1. *Who* goes up in hot-air balloons? —People who have been trained in ballooning safety and techniques.
2. *What* are the basic parts of a hot-air balloon? —A thousand yards of nylon fabric, called the envelope; a basket for passengers; a propane burner to heat the air inside the balloon.
3. *When* did ballooning begin? —Check encyclopedia.
4. *Where* do balloonists travel? —Anywhere, sometimes across entire continents or oceans.

246

5. *Why* has hot-air ballooning become so popular? —People like the sensation of floating and the silence of flight without an engine.
6. *How* is the hot-air balloon controlled? —To go up, turn on the propane burner; to go down, open vent in top of envelope; to steer, try to catch an air current moving in the direction that you want to go.

You can now explore the subject even further by devising follow-up questions. Some examples follow. Not all of the questions listed will apply to every subject, but you can use those that do. You can also ask others that are appropriate for your subject.

1. What are the special characteristics of the subject?
2. What is the history of the subject?
3. What are examples of the subject?
4. What terms need to be explained or defined?
5. What processes require explanation?
6. What important people or books are connected with the subject?
7. Can the subject be compared with anything?
8. Can any contrasts (advantages and disadvantages, safety and danger, and so on) be developed for the subject?
9. What are my experiences with the subject?
10. What problems are connected with the subject?

The following notes are the result of asking follow-up questions about hot-air ballooning:

Terms to be explained: Envelope, gondola, propane burner
Processes to be explained: How to operate the burner, how to open the vent
Comparisons: Skydiving, floating on a cloud
My experiences: None, but older cousins who are balloonists have allowed me in the gondola before lift-off.

247

Exercise 2 *(page 248)*

Sample answer:

1. Who does aerobic dancing?
   Usually teen-aged girls and
   women
   What kind of steps are
   involved? Various exercise
   movements set to music
   When is the best time to do
   aerobic dancing? At least an
   hour after eating and when
   you are well rested
   Where can aerobic dancing be
   done? Gyms, health clubs—
   anywhere there is a place to
   spread out and move
   Why is aerobic dancing good
   for you? Promotes good
   circulation and strengthens
   the heart
   How does aerobic dancing
   help overweight people? By
   consuming energy and
   calories

Exercise 3 *(page 248)*

Sample answer:

1. What kind of outfit should be
   worn for aerobic dancing?
   T-shirt and shorts, leotard, or
   any loose, comfortable outfit
   that lets you move easily but
   does not get in your way.

Exercise 2   Prewriting: Asking Questions   Choose
two of the following subjects. On separate sheets of paper,
write the subjects. Then write questions that ask *who, what,
when, where, why* and *how* about each subject. Answer the
questions. If necessary, use an encyclopedia or other reference books.

1. Aerobic dancing
2. Canoeing
3. Circuses
4. Digital watches
5. Folk songs

6. Guide dogs
7. Holiday customs
8. Swimming
9. Talking birds
10. Volleyball

Exercise 3   Prewriting: Asking Questions   On your
paper, write three follow-up questions and answers for each
subject that you chose in Exercise 2. If necessary, use an encyclopedia or other references.

Assignment   Prewriting   Choose a subject from your
writer's notebook. Develop it by making lists and by asking
and answering questions.

Continuing Assignment   By making lists and by asking
and answering questions, develop each of the three subjects
that you selected for the Continuing Assignment on page
244. Save your papers.

Assignment Checklist

Check your assignments for the following points:

✔ 1. Did you write down all the ideas and information about
     the subject that came to mind as you made your lists?
✔ 2. Did you ask and answer questions to develop your
     subject further?

248

8.3 Focusing Your Ideas

Up to this point, you have been using prewriting techniques to collect as many ideas as you can so that you will be prepared to write. You have made a lot of notes, not all of which are closely related. Your task now is to sort your prewriting notes for a specific writing assignment. To focus the ideas that you have collected, you must identify your purpose and your audience and choose a suitable topic.

8.3a Identifying Your Purpose and Audience

Your **purpose** is what you plan to accomplish with your writing. Your **audience** is the reader or the group of readers for whom your writing is intended. How you focus your ideas will depend on what your purpose is and who your audience is.

Purpose

The most common purposes for writing are to inform or explain, to tell a story, to describe, and to express an opinion. When you focus your ideas, your purpose helps to determine the details that you include and the ideas that you emphasize.

For example, suppose that you are planning to write about baseball. As you think about the subject, you have several purposes to choose from. You could *explain* what a double play is. You could *tell a story* about your first Little League game. You could *describe* the excitement of the World Series. You could *express your opinion* on the need for a youth baseball team.

The following notes show how the details that you would choose for explaining a double play are different from

249

Exercise 1 *(page 251)*

Answers may vary. Samples:

1. Why people should not litter
   To express an opinion
   To inform or explain

2. The poor condition of certain
   roads in our community
   To describe
   To inform or explain

3. How to perform CPR
   To inform or explain

4. The need for summer
   recreation programs
   To express an opinion

5. How to avoid sunstroke
   To inform or explain

6. How money earns interest in
   a savings account
   To inform or explain

7. The best way to save energy
   in your home
   To express an opinion
   To inform and explain

8. How I earned money mowing
   lawns
   To tell a story

9. Ways to build a campfire
   To inform or explain

10. How my muscles feel after the
    first workout of the soccer
    season
    To describe

those that you would choose for describing the excitement of the World Series.

EXPLAINING A DOUBLE PLAY

Runner is on first base.

Batter hits ground ball to shortstop.

Shortstop throws ball to second.

Second baseman touches second base before runner arrives from first base. Runner is out.

Second baseman throws ball to first.

First baseman touches first base before batter arrives. Batter is out.

DESCRIBING WORLD SERIES GAME

Long lines of people waiting to buy tickets

Jammed parking lots

Packed stands

Roar of crowd

Loyal fans waving pennants, wearing team jackets and hats

Vendors calling out wares

Teams introduced over loud-speakers

Quiet for national anthem

Governor throws first ball

Audience

As the writer, you decide to whom your writing is directed. If you write about baseball, for example, your audience could be readers who have never seen a baseball game or readers who play on a team. In either case, you should consider what would interest them and how much or how little they may know about your subject. In explaining a double play to a nonplayer, for instance, you might include the basic information listed in the example. In writing for an experienced player, on the other hand, you might emphasize the fine points of making a double play.

250

Exercise 1 Prewriting: Purpose   On your paper, list the following topics. For each one, write the appropriate purpose or purposes from those given below. Be prepared to explain your answers.

To inform or explain   To describe
To tell a story   To express an opinion

SAMPLE   How Lincoln wrote the Gettysburg Address
ANSWER   To tell a story
           To inform or explain

1. Why people should not litter
2. The poor condition of certain roads in our community
3. How to perform CPR (cardiopulmonary resuscitation)
4. The need for summer recreation programs
5. How to avoid sunstroke
6. How money earns interest in a savings account
7. The best way to save energy in your home
8. How I earned money mowing lawns
9. Ways to build a campfire
10. How my muscles feel after the first workout of the soccer season

Exercise 2 Prewriting: Audience   Select from the following list the audience or audiences that would probably be interested in reading about each topic in Exercise 1. Write your answer on your paper next to the number of the topic.

SAMPLE   How Lincoln wrote the Gettysburg Address
ANSWER   Teachers and students

An athlete   Someone who likes the outdoors
Parents   Members of the community
Teachers and students

Exercise 1 *(page 251)*

See page 250 for sample answers.

Exercise 2 *(page 251)*

Answers may vary. Samples:

1. Someone who likes the outdoors; Members of the community
2. Members of the community
3. An athlete; Parents; Teachers and students; Members of the community
4. Parents; Teachers and students; Members of the community; An athlete
5. An athlete; Parents; Teachers and students; Someone who likes the outdoors
6. Teachers and students; Members of the community
7. Parents; Teachers and students; Members of the community
8. Teachers and students
9. Someone who likes the outdoors
10. An athlete; Teachers and students

251

8.3b   Choosing a Topic

With your purpose and your audience in mind, you can choose your topic. A **topic** is a specific aspect of your subject. Your topic should indicate what you will say about your subject. For example:

SUBJECT	Gem stones
WHAT YOU WILL SAY	Cutting diamonds into gems
TOPIC	How diamonds are given sparkle

In this example, the purpose is to inform, and the audience is composed of people who do not know what makes diamonds sparkle.

The following suggestions will help you to focus your ideas and to choose a suitable topic.

Procedure

1. *Review your prewriting notes on your subject.* Write down ideas for topics that appear in your notes or are suggested by them. You may find a topic idea in a note on a list *(page 245)* or in the answer to a question that you asked about the subject *(pages 246–247).*

2. *Look in your notes for other information that supports an idea for a topic.* You may find details in the form of examples, descriptions, reasons, and so forth.

3. *Check the topic against your intended purpose and audience.* Make certain that the topic is appropriate to both.

4. *Choose the topic that interests you most and that suits a specific assignment.*

5. *Write a phase that clearly identifies your topic and what you will say about it.*

6. *Ask and answer additional questions about your topic.* By asking questions, perhaps for the second time, you will have the information that you need to plan your writing.

Once you have identified your purpose, your audience, and your topic, you may need to repeat some of the prewriting techniques described in this unit. You may need to make new lists, ask further questions, or obtain additional information for your topic. Each composition unit in this book will give you further instruction and practice in prewriting for specific kinds of writing.

Exercise 3   Prewriting: Choosing Topics   Each of the following items includes a subject, a purpose, and an audience, followed by three topics. On your paper, write the topic that is most appropriate for the indicated purpose and audience.

> SAMPLE   To explain a procedure to applicants for the Fire Department
> a. How to enter a burning building
> b. Using computers to fight fires
> c. How to meet the basic requirements for acceptance by the department
>
> ANSWER   How to meet the basic requirements for acceptance by the department

1. To express an opinion about traffic to the editor of your local newspaper
   a. Why commercial traffic should be banned from School Street
   b. How downtown traffic today compares with downtown traffic in the early 1920s
   c. How traffic is controlled in other countries

2. To explain sports safety to joggers
   a. How contour shoes were developed
   b. How to protect the feet during a race
   c. How a foot injury can damage the knee and hip

253

Exercise 3 *(pages 253–254)*

1a. Why commercial traffic should be banned from School Street
2b. How to protect the feet during a race

(Continue on the next page.)

Exercise 3 *(pages 253–254),*
continued

3b. How I almost missed the last
bus home

4b. How to set up a schedule of
indoor exercises

Exercise 4 *(pages 254–255)*

Answers may vary. Samples:

1. Three chimps that learned to
"talk"
The language of dolphins

2. Details about chimps Washoe,
Sarah, and Lana

3. To inform or explain

4. Students of language or
psychology

3. To tell a story about a trip to the city to your classmates
   a. How to plan a family trip
   b. How I almost missed the last bus home
   c. How the city has changed its profile

4. To explain how to keep fit in cold weather to a group of high
   school athletes
   a. How to dress for cold-weather activities
   b. How to set up a schedule of indoor exercises
   c. Why I enjoy cross-country skiing

Exercise 4   Prewriting: Focusing Ideas   Read the
following prewriting notes on the subject "Talking animals."
On your paper, answer Questions 1 to 4.

> Alexander Graham Bell taught his terrier to growl "How are
> you, Grandma?"
>
> Dolphins are known to beep and squeak in patterns.
>
> Chimpanzees—intelligent, but can they be trained to talk?
>
> In 1930s Dr. Winthrop Kellogg raised an infant chimp in
> home environment; chimp had no interest in forming
> words. Later, chimps found to have vocal equipment that
> made formation of words difficult.
>
> A chimp (Washoe) trained to read thirty-four signs in the
> language used by the hearing impaired; could put signs
> together to make sentences.
>
> Another chimp (Sarah) trained to use plastic shapes repre-
> senting words to "form sentences."
>
> A third chimp (Lana) trained to work computer panel with
> buttons representing words.

1. What are two possible topics for the general subject "Talking
   animals"?

2. Which details would you use if you were writing about
   "Chimps that have been trained to communicate"?

3. What would be an appropriate purpose for the topic "Chimps
   that have been trained to communicate"?

254

4. Who would be a likely audience for the topic "Chimps that have been trained to communicate"?

Assignment 1 Prewriting   *Step 1:* From your writer's notebook, select a subject that you would like to develop for a writing assignment. *Step 2:* Develop the subject by making lists and asking questions. *Step 3:* From your notes, identify two possible purposes and two suitable audiences for the subject.

Assignment 2 Prewriting   Use the prewriting notes that you developed in Assignment 1. *Step 1:* Write two different topics, one for the first purpose and audience and one for the second purpose and audience. *Step 2:* Under each topic, write the notes that relate to that topic. Some details will apply to both topics; others will apply to only one topic.

Continuing Assignment Prewriting   In the Continuing Assignment on page 248, you developed three subjects. For each of those subjects, write a purpose, an audience, and a topic. Then list the prewriting notes that you would use to write about each topic.

Assignment Checklist

Check your assignments for the following points:

1. Did you identify two possible purposes and audiences for your subject?
2. Did you write a topic to fit each purpose and audience?
3. In the Continuing Assignment, did you select prewriting notes related to each topic?

255

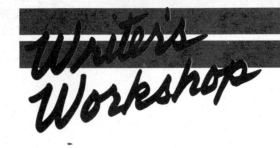

Little Wonders of the Modern World: Column Ideas

Situation: You are planning a newspaper feature article about little wonders of the modern world, familiar objects that would amaze a person who lived two hundred years ago. You want to develop a list of possible items to discuss in the article. As you do your prewriting, keep in mind the following information:

Writer: you as newspaper columnist
Audience: readers of the newspaper
Topic: little wonders of the modern world
Purpose: to develop ideas for your article

Directions: To develop your subject, follow these steps.

Step 1. Read the editor's memorandum on the facing page. You will first prepare a list of suitable objects and then ask questions about them.

Step 2. At the top of a piece of paper, write "Little wonders of the modern world." Begin your list with the items mentioned in the editor's memorandum. Then add to this list; think about an average house, room by room, to come up with ideas for your list. For example, what items would you find in a kitchen? In a living room? In a closet?

Step 3. On another sheet of paper, write seven or more questions that will help you to think about these objects as little wonders of the modern world. For example: What is the purpose of this item? Who uses it? What can I compare it to?

Step 4. In a sentence, state your purpose and your topic.

256

MEMORANDUM

From: Editor

To: Staff Writer

Subject: Feature article on little wonders of the modern
        world

    This is a great idea for an article. As you plan it,
focus on small, household items that we take for granted.
Imagine that you are a person from the 1700s. You walk
into a modern home. What would surprise you the most?
Coat hangers? Ball point pens? Tin cans? Toasters?
Think of objects that serve a familiar purpose but in a
modern way.

    Once you have a list of objects, think of questions
that you could use to make these marvels stand out.
Perhaps you could even use a question—answer format. Give
it a try. Then, let's discuss your list and your
questions. Remember that you're playing the role of
someone from the 1700s.

Good Luck!

257

Unit Assignments

Assignment 1   Choose a humorous experience that you recorded in your writer's notebook. Develop a writing idea suggested by that experience. On your paper, state a purpose and an audience and write a topic.

Assignment 2   You have been given a writing assignment with "to describe an unusual person" as its purpose. *Step 1:* Look in your writer's notebook for a suitable subject. *Step 2:* Develop the subject by listing ideas and asking questions. *Step 3:* Focus your ideas on a topic. On your paper, write the purpose, the audience, and the topic.

Assignment 3   Imagine that you have been asked to submit a plan for a time capsule that will be enclosed in the cornerstone of a new building in your community. You have been told to include in your plan a list of items that you would put in the capsule and a reason for choosing each item. Using your prewriting skills, develop your plan and write your notes.

Assignment 4   Do the prewriting for a letter to the editor of your school newspaper. Your subject can be any issue about which you would like to express an opinion. On your paper, list the details that you want to include in the letter. Then, with your audience and purpose in mind, state your topic.

Assignment 5   From your writer's notebook, choose a subject for an explanation of how to do something. On your paper, list the details that you would write about for someone who knows nothing about your subject. Then list the details that you would write about for someone who knows almost as much as you do about your subject.

Unit Tests

Test 1

A. Number your paper from 1 to 5. Next to each number, write *True* if the sentence is true or *False* if it is false.

1. During prewriting you decide what to write about and whom you are writing for.
2. In your interest inventory, list only subjects that you know well.
3. You can draw on your experiences to find writing subjects.
4. You can develop a subject by listing ideas and asking questions about it.
5. When you focus your prewriting notes, you should outline them by topics.

B. Number your paper from 6 to 10. Next to each number, write the letter of the term that correctly completes the sentence. You will use all but one of the terms.

a. idea d. writer's notebook
b. audience e. topic
c. prewriting f. purpose

6. __?__ is the planning and preparation that you do before you write.
7. In your __?__ you write comments on things that you see, hear, think, or do that you want to remember.
8. One __?__ for writing is to explain something.
9. The readers to whom your writing is directed are your __?__.
10. A(n) __?__ is a specific aspect of a subject.

Test 2

Choose one of the Unit Assignments or an assignment that your teacher suggests. Complete the assignment as directed and hand it in to your teacher.

259

Objectives

After studying this unit, students should be able to do the following:

- Express their ideas in written sentences.
- Expand their written sentences by adding modifiers.
- Consider their audience and purpose when writing sentences.

Teaching Suggestions

See "Classroom Insights" for Unit 9 in the front of this Teacher's Edition.

Program Resources

Resource Book, Second Course:
  Bonus Activities, Unit 9
  Composition Checklist,
  Unit 9
Practice Book, Second Course,
  Unit 9
Tests, Second Course, Unit 9
Composition Workshop, Second
  Course, Unit 9

Related Resources

Houghton Mifflin Microcourse:
  Language Arts, Levels 7,8
*The American Heritage.
  Dictionary of the English
  Language*
Roget's II: The New Thesaurus

Writing Sentences

Unit Preview

As you read the following statement, what picture comes to your mind?

Larry sat.

The statement meets the two requirements of a sentence: it has a complete subject and a complete predicate, and it expresses a complete thought. However, the statement does not give you much information.
Now read this sentence.

In the third quarter, while his team fought to keep the ball, Larry sat on the bench with his hands clenched, hoping for a nod from Coach Riggs.

The writer of the second sentence has included details to make the sentence clear and informative.

For Analysis   Follow these instructions about the second sentence in the Unit Preview.

1. Write the prepositional phrases that tell when and where Larry sat.
2. Write the subordinate clause. What does it add to the sentence?
3. Write the phrases that tell how Larry was feeling. What kind of phrases are they?

260

In this unit, you will practice expressing your ideas in interesting, informative sentences. You will also learn how to expand sentences with a variety of modifiers and how to suit your sentences to a particular audience and purpose.

9.1 Expressing Your Ideas in Sentences

Most sentences make a statement or ask a question (the predicate) about someone or something (the subject). In Unit 2, "Sentence Structure," you studied subjects and predicates. Now you will study effective ways to express your ideas in subjects and predicates in the sentences that you write for your composition assignments.

In your prewriting notes for a topic, you probably already have lists of ideas about that topic. Now you need to express your ideas in subject-predicate form. Suppose that you have listed several ideas about the topic "Halley's Comet." There are many ways that you can express those ideas in sentences. If you want to focus on the comet itself, then make *Halley's Comet* the subject of your sentence. What you want to say about Halley's Comet will be the predicate.

SUBJECT   Halley's Comet
PREDICATES reappears every seventy-six years
            is the object of irresistible attention

You may change your focus by making something else the subject. In the following example, the focus shifts to the astronomers who are tracking Halley's Comet.

SUBJECT   Astronomers
PREDICATES are preparing for detailed observations of Halley's Comet
            will observe Halley's Comet through a radio telescope

261

For Analysis *(page 260)*

1. In the third quarter; on the bench

2. while his team fought to keep the ball
   The subordinate clause helps to explain the reason for Larry's intense feeling.

3. with his hands clenched— participial phrase
   hoping for a nod from Coach Riggs—participial phrase

Exercise 1 *(page 263)*

Answers may vary. Samples:

1. Electric cars may become the cars of the future.
   Cars powered by the sun may become the cars of the future.

2. Helicopters are among our most useful aircraft.
   Wide-bodied planes are among our most useful aircraft.

3. Most fires can be prevented.
   Most accidents in the home can be prevented.

4. Being a parent is a tremendous responsibility.
   Fighting fires is a tremendous responsibility.

5. A cure for cancer may well be the scientific discovery of the future.
   A way to neutralize air pollution may well be the scientific discovery of the future.

6. The boy on the skateboard raced down the street.
   The motorcycle raced down the street.

7. The town cleanup usually occurs at this time each year.
   The science fair at school usually occurs at this time each year.

8. Those twins are rarely seen apart from each other.
   Michael and Lynn are rarely seen apart from each other.

9. That avalanche created an impassable barrier.
   The collapsed bridge created an impassable barrier.

10. There were only four people left in line.
    There were only two runners.

The sentences that result are clear and informative:

Halley's Comet reappears every seventy-six years.
Halley's Comet is the object of irresistible attention.
Astronomers are preparing for detailed observations of Halley's Comet.
Astronomers will observe Halley's Comet through a radio telescope.

The following strategies will help you to write clear and informative sentences.

Strategies

1. *Focus on an idea and make that idea the subject of your sentence.* If your focus is bees, for example, make *bees* your subject. If your focus is another aspect of bees, make that aspect your subject.

   SUBJECTS   Bees
              Fears about bees
              Bee stings

2. *Write a predicate in which you make a statement about the subject.* Use complements *(pages 55–56)* and other words in the predicate to help you express your ideas about the subject.

   Bees *depend on their stingers for self-defense.*
   Fears about bees *center on their aggressive behavior.*
   Bee stings *cause sudden pain and swelling.*

3. *Choose the words that best express your ideas.* Use specific nouns and vivid verbs.

   Killer bees may *invade* North America in the next decade.

262

Exercise 1 Writing: Subjects and Predicates On your paper, complete each of the following sentences with two different subjects. Write the two complete sentences.

SAMPLE   ___?___ can be an unforgettable experience.
ANSWERS   Bus rides can be an unforgettable experience.
                   Tryouts for the Drama Club can be an
                   unforgettable experience.

1. ___?___ may become the cars of the future.
2. ___?___ are among our most useful aircraft.
3. ___?___ can be prevented.
4. ___?___ is a tremendous responsibility.
5. ___?___ may well be the scientific discovery of the future.
6. ___?___ raced down the street.
7. ___?___ usually occurs at this time each year.
8. ___?___ are rarely seen apart from each other.
9. ___?___ created an impassable barrier.
10. There were only ___?___.

Exercise 2 Writing: Subjects and Predicates On your paper, complete each of the following sentences with two different predicates. Write the two complete sentences.

SAMPLE   Competitive sports ___?___
ANSWERS   Competitive sports can be one of the most
                   satisfying ways to keep fit.
                   Competitive sports are sometimes a source of
                   anxiety to the beginner.

1. Vitamins ___?___
2. High winds ___?___
3. Family reunions ___?___
4. Literature ___?___
5. Weekend chores ___?___
6. Weather ___?___
7. Word histories ___?___
8. Cooperation ___?___
9. Caring for pets ___?___
10. Teen-age fads ___?___

263

Exercise 1 *(page 263)*

See page 262 for sample answers.

Exercise 2 *(page 263)*

Answers may vary. Samples:

1. Vitamins are in all the foods that we eat.
   Vitamins help to keep us healthy.
2. High winds felled several trees in our town last night.
   High winds accompanied the snow.
3. Family reunions are times to reminisce with relatives.
   Family reunions bring my cousins and me together twice a year.
4. Literature is my favorite subject in school.
   Literature can tell us a great deal about people.
5. Weekend chores must be done before anything else.
   Weekend chores sometimes keep me busy for hours.
6. Weather can be the cause of much misery.
   Weather depends on such variables as temperature, moisture, wind, and pressure.
7. Word histories are called etymologies.
   Word histories can be fascinating.
8. Cooperation can help people accomplish tasks more efficiently.
   Cooperation allowed us to complete the project quickly.

(Continue on the next page.)

Exercise 2 *(page 263)*, continued

9. Caring for pets can be very rewarding.
   Caring for pets is an excellent way for children to learn responsibility.
10. Teen-age fads were very different in my parents' time.
    Teen-age fads often pass quickly.

Exercises 3 *(page 264)*

Answers may vary. Samples:

1. A panther growled in the jungle near the village.
2. A scorpion stung the prospector.
3. A firehouse stands on Vine Street.
4. This sweater was imported from Ireland.
5. My cousin knits sweaters.
6. Mrs. Brewer strode past the police officers.
7. Most of the picketers stormed out of town hall.
8. Those actors performed the play poorly.
9. Elaine owned a new bicycle.
10. Certain debates interest the student body.

Exercise 4 *(page 264)*

Answers may vary. Samples:

1. Tropical birds often have brilliant plumage.
   Our local pet store carried few tropical birds.

(Continue on the next page.)

Exercise 3   Writing: Specific Nouns and Verbs

On your paper, rewrite each of the following sentences, substituting specific nouns or verbs for the words in italic type.

SAMPLE	*People went* into the *place.*
ANSWER	Firefighters rushed into the factory.

1. An *animal cried* in the *area* near the *place.*
2. An *insect bit the person.*
3. A *building is* on the *street.*
4. This *item comes* from *another country.*
5. My *relative makes articles of clothing.*
6. Mrs. Brewer *walked* past the *people.*
7. Most of *them went* out of the town hall.
8. Those *people did* the *performance* poorly.
9. Elaine *had* a new *one.*
10. Certain *things stir up* the student body.

Exercise 4   Writing: Subjects and Predicates

On your paper, write two sentences for each of the following topic ideas. In your first sentence, use the idea as the subject of your sentence. In your second sentence, use the idea in the predicate.

SAMPLE	Contact lenses
ANSWERS	Contact lenses were invented shortly after World War II.
	Today, millions of Americans wear contact lenses.

1. Tropical birds
2. The school gymnasium
3. National flags
4. My favorite season
5. The sky at night
6. The common cold
7. Self-confidence
8. Exercise
9. Achievements by women
10. Sports for the physically disabled

264

Assignment Writing   Use the strategies on page 262 to write two sentences about each of the following topics.

1. Nutritious meals
2. Headphones
3. Home computers
4. Almanacs
5. Weather forecasts
6. Friendships

Assignment Checklist

Check your assignment for the following points:

✔ 1. Did you focus on an idea in order to write a clear subject for each sentence?

✔ 2. Did you make a statement about the subject in the predicate of each sentence?

✔ 3. Did you use specific nouns and vivid verbs?

9.2   Expanding Sentences with Modifiers

To make your sentences more informative and more interesting, you can add details in the form of modifiers. Modifiers can be single words, such as adjectives *(page 17)* and adverbs *(pages 22–23)*. They can also be word groups, such as phrases *(page 73)* and clauses *(page 95)*.

Modifiers make your ideas clearer and more specific by answering the following questions:

1. Which?
2. What kind?
3. How many?
4. How?
5. When?
6. Where?
7. To what degree or extent?
8. Why?

The following examples show how you can use modifiers to expand the sentence *The house burned.* As you read the expanded sentences, pay special attention to the modifiers in italic type.

265

Exercise 4 *(page 264),* continued

2. The school gymnasium is used every hour of the school day.
   When it rains, we play volleyball in the school gymnasium.

3. National flags often have several different colors.
   I drew several national flags for my history project.

4. My favorite season is spring, when everything is new.
   Sometimes I think that fall is my favorite season.

5. The sky at night is flecked with stars.
   I use my telescope to view the sky at night.

6. The common cold is part of my life every winter.
   Will science ever develop a cure for the common cold?

7. Self-confidence will help you in difficult situations.
   Practicing your speech over and over will give you more self-confidence.

8. Exercise is essential to good health.
   I exercise by swimming.

9. Achievements by women were ignored in some history books.
   Now people recognize the many achievements by women in various fields.

10. Sports for the physically disabled are encouraged.
    Basketball and swimming can be sports for the physically disabled.

Exercise 1 *(page 266)*

Answers may vary. Samples:

1. An agressive speaker may antagonize an audience.
2. The camel is called "the ship of the desert" because it efficiently transports people and goods across the desert.
3. People have developed various devices that make housework easier.
4. After she heard her father's voice, she turned the key and opened the door.
5. The farm truck was filled with chickens.
6. The planets in our solar system move in orbits around the sun.
7. Valley glaciers creep downward very slowly.
8. No great rivers originate in the desert.
9. Planets shine steadily, while stars appear to twinkle.
10. Farmers fight weeds to increase crop production.

WHAT KIND?
The *frame* house burned.

WHICH ONE?
The frame house *on State Street* burned.

WHEN?
During the night, the frame house burned.

TO WHAT EXTENT?
The frame house burned *to the ground.*

WHY?
Because the flames spread quickly, the house burned to the ground.

You may add one or several modifiers to a sentence, depending on the idea that you wish to express. However, it is generally better not to load a sentence with modifiers.

Exercise 1 Writing: Modifiers On your paper, expand each of the following sentences by replacing the blank with a modifier that answers the question in parentheses. The modifiers may be single words, phrases, or clauses.

> **SAMPLE** The mayfly lives __?__. (To what extent?)
> **ANSWER** The mayfly lives for only a few hours.

1. A(n) __?__ speaker may antagonize an audience. (What kind?)
2. The camel is called "the ship of the desert" __?__. (Why?)
3. People have developed various devices __?__. (What kind?)
4. __?__, she turned the key and opened the door. (When?)
5. The __?__ truck was filled with chickens (What kind?)
6. The planets in our solar system move in orbits __?__. (Where?)
7. Valley glaciers creep downward __?__. (To what degree or extent?)
8. No great rivers originate __?__. (Where?)
9. Planets shine __?__, while stars appear to twinkle. (How?)
10. Farmers fight weeds __?__. (Why?)

266

Exercise 2 Writing: Modifiers On your paper, expand each of the following sentences by adding at least two modifiers. The modifiers may be single words, phrases, or clauses.

SAMPLE	The tiger pawed.
ANSWER	The disturbed tiger pawed at its cage.

1. The driver looked at the officer.
2. They whitewashed the fence.
3. Rain began to fall.
4. Everyone dashed for shelter.
5. Fire broke out.
6. Animals protect their young.
7. The guard found a package.
8. A rainbow stretched.
9. The truck skidded.
10. The breeze blew the leaves.

Assignment Writing *Step 1:* Choose three of the following topics. For each topic, write an informative sentence in which you include two or more modifiers. *Step 2:* Write a second sentence for each topic using different modifiers.

1. How it feels to win (or lose)
2. How it feels to be outside during a storm
3. How it feels to be the center of unwanted attention
4. How it feels to be given responsibility
5. How it feels to make a new friend

Assignment Checklist

Check your assignment for the following points:

✔ 1. Did you include two or more modifiers in each sentence?
✔ 2. Did you use a variety of modifiers: single words, phrases, and clauses?

267

Exercise 2 *(page 267)*

Answers may vary. Samples:

1. The embarrassed driver looked meekly at the officer who had stopped him.
2. They quickly whitewashed the wooden fence around our yard.
3. A light rain began to fall just as the marathon began.
4. Everyone without a raincoat or umbrella dashed for shelter inside doorways.
5. A flash fire broke out in the abandoned warehouse.
6. Animals fiercely protect their young from predators.
7. The guard on duty last night found a suspicious-looking package in a trash can.
8. A shimmering rainbow stretched from mountain to valley.
9. The tractor-trailer truck skidded sideways into the railing.
10. The brisk breeze blew the last leaves from the tree.

9.3   Considering Your Audience and Your Purpose

By keeping your audience *(page 250)* and your purpose *(pages 249–250)* in mind, you can more easily focus on an idea for the subject of your sentence, write a predicate about that subject, and choose appropriate modifiers.

Suppose, for example, that you are explaining to a first-grader what a tundra is. You might write (or say) the following sentence:

A tundra is a cold, flat place without any trees.

If, on the other hand, your audience is teen-agers or adults, your explanation would include different words and more details.

A tundra is a continuously cold, treeless plain of the arctic regions, characterized by mosses, lichens, and small shrubs.

In your written and spoken sentences, use words and details that are appropriate for your audience. To make your sentences appropriate, consider the age and the interests of your audience and the extent of their knowledge about a particular topic.

You should also consider the purpose of your sentence. For example, is your purpose to inform, to describe, to tell a story, or to express an opinion? Notice how each of the following sentences accomplishes a different purpose.

TO INFORM OR EXPLAIN
> Turkeys were taken to Europe from Mexico by the Spanish.

TO DESCRIBE
> The crisp skin of the freshly roasted turkey gave off a delicious aroma.

268

TO TELL A STORY

> Every year at this time, we begin our search for the perfect Thanksgiving turkey.

TO EXPRESS AN OPINION

> There is nothing better than turkey at Thanksgiving.

Exercise 1 Prewriting: Audience and Purpose On your paper, list the audience and the purpose given for each of the following pairs of sentences. Then choose the sentence in each pair that best suits both the audience and the purpose.

SAMPLE *Audience:* Teacher, class
Purpose: To inform
a. The hummingbird builds a cute little nest.
b. The hummingbird builds a cup-shaped nest that is only an inch and a half wide.

ANSWER *Audience:* Teacher, class
Purpose: To inform
The hummingbird builds a cup-shaped nest that is only an inch and a half wide.

1. *Audience:* A group of nonsingers
   Purpose: To express an opinion
   a. The only people who don't sing are people who can't.
   b. Singing can lift your spirits, whether you have a good voice or not.
2. *Audience:* Parents   *Purpose:* To inform
   a. Parents are invited to attend the Tenth Annual Choral Recital to be presented by the school chorus in the auditorium on Tuesday, October 5, at 7:30 P.M.
   b. Everyone is invited to come to the auditorium for the show.
3. *Audience:* Classmates   *Purpose:* To tell a story
   a. So many things happened to me on my way to a career in music.
   b. It would be difficult for anyone to imagine the unusual events that occurred as I pursued my musical studies.

269

Exercise 1 *(pages 269–270)*

1. Audience: A group of nonsingers
   Purpose: To express an opinion
   Singing can lift your spirits, whether you have a good voice or not.
2. Audience: Parents
   Purpose: To inform
   Parents are invited to attend the Tenth Annual Choral Recital to be presented by the school chorus in the auditorium on Tuesday, October 5, at 7:30 P.M.
3. Audience: Classmates
   Purpose: To tell a story
   So many things happened to me on my way to a career in music.

(Continue on the next page.)

Exercise 1 *(pages 269–270),*
continued

4. Audience: Manufacturer
   Purpose: To inform
   One day after I purchased the
   enclosed marking pen, it ran
   out of ink.
5. Audience: A child
   Purpose: To describe
   An eagle looks as though it is
   floating in air.

Exercise 2 *(page 270)*

Answers may vary. Samples:

1. Rush-hour traffic could be
   significantly reduced if more
   people formed carpools.
2. Hydrofoils have been
   extremely useful in situations
   requiring air-sea rescue.
3. My tomatoes this year were
   ruined by the drought.
4. Birds have wings so that they
   can escape my cat Dandelion.
5. I want to buy leather sneakers
   because they are durable.

4. *Audience:* Manufacturer   *Purpose:* To inform
   a. I am returning this marking pen because it isn't any good.
   b. One day after I purchased the enclosed marking pen, it
      ran out of ink.
5. *Audience:* A child   *Purpose:* To describe
   a. An eagle looks as though it is floating in air.
   b. An eagle is a majestic flier, especially when it soars or
      swoops.

Exercise 2   Writing: Audience and Purpose   For
each of the topics below, write a sentence that suits the audience and the purpose given.

SAMPLE	*Audience:* Adults
	Purpose: To inform
	Topic: Leonardo da Vinci
ANSWER	Leonardo da Vinci's genius is revealed in his
	ideas for such modern inventions as the
	helicopter, the steam engine, and the glider.

1. *Audience:*   Adults
   Purpose: To express an opinion
   Topic: Rush-hour traffic
2. *Audience:*   Classmates
   Purpose: To inform
   Topic: Hydrofoils
3. *Audience:*   A neighbor
   Purpose: To describe
   Topic: The tomatoes in your vegetable garden
4. *Audience:*   A child
   Purpose: To tell a story
   Topic: Why birds have wings
5. *Audience:*   Parent or guardian
   Purpose: To express an opinion
   Topic: Sneakers

270

Assignment 1 Writing   Choose a topic about which you would like to write. For each combination of purpose and audience, write a sentence about your topic.

1. To tell a story to preschool children
2. To explain to your ten-year-old brother
3. To express an opinion to your best friend

Assignment 2 Writing   *Step 1:* Select three of the following topics, and write them on your paper. *Step 2:* Choose an audience and a purpose for each topic, and write them down. *Step 3:* Write one sentence for each of your topics. Include interesting and appropriate details.

1. Traffic control in the United States
2. Taking music lessons
3. Learning to assemble a model
4. How to settle an argument
5. Entertainment in your community

Assignment Checklist

Check your assignments for the following points:

1. Did you focus your ideas clearly in your subjects and predicates?
2. Did you use specific nouns and vivid verbs?
3. Did you use appropriate details for your audience and your purpose?

The Youth Club Catalogue: Writing Course Descriptions

Situation: You are the publicity director of the Brookside Youth Club. The activities director has given you notes on the courses to be offered in the coming season. You will write the course descriptions for the catalogue, which is sent to members. As you prepare the catalogue entries, keep in mind the following information.

Writer: you as publicity director of the youth club

Audience: members of the club

Topic: courses offered during the coming season

Purpose: to describe each course

Directions: To write the descriptions, follow these steps.

Step 1. Read the notes (on the facing page) about the courses.

Step 2. On your paper, write the name of the first course, "Bicycle Repair for Beginners." Then write three sentences using the following plan.

Sentence 1
Subject: the course
Predicate: when and where held (use "will be held")

Sentence 2
Subject: the instructor
Predicate: what the instructor will emphasize

Sentence 3
Subject: "This course"
Predicate: what the course will do or explain

Step 3. Follow the same plan for the other courses.

Step 4. Make sure that all your sentences are complete.

272

Notes on new courses at youth club

Bicycle Repair for Beginners
- taught by expert mechanic Edwina Shepherd
- will emphasize basic repairs for one-,
  three-, five-, and ten-speed bikes
- will show how to fix brakes, adjust
  steering, and check for safety
- youth club parking lot, Saturday mornings
  at 10:00 A.M., six sessions beginning
  September 15

Making Your Own Terrarium
- Room 318, one session, Saturday afternoon,
  October 12, 2:00 P.M.
- will show you how to design, plant,
  and care for a mini-garden under glass
- biology teacher Sal Olson will teach the
  session
- emphasis on selecting plants that will
  thrive in a terrarium

Fun with Magic
- professional magician Dr. Quarto will
  teach six Saturday sessions, beginning
  October 5 at 4:00 P.M. in Room A1
- will emphasize how to entertain
- will include the secrets of card tricks,
  sleight of hand, and other illusions

Unit Assignments

Assignment 1   Write two related sentences about each of the following topics. Use a different subject in the second sentence.

1. A sports celebrity
2. A television personality
3. A popular puppet
4. A well-known place

Assignment 2   Write a sentence in which you describe a group or a club to which you belong or would like to belong. Write another sentence that could be used as the motto of the group or the club.

Assignment 3   Select three topics from the following list and write one sentence about each. Use single-word modifiers, phrases, and clauses in your sentences.

1. A squirrel walking
2. Your favorite restaurant
3. An all-day shopping trip
4. A greenhouse
5. A herd of pigs
6. An international airport

Assignment 4   On your paper, write two sets of three sentences each about a topic that interests you. In the first set, write sentences that explain the topic to an audience of adults. In the second set, write sentences that explain the topic to an audience of children.

Assignment 5   On your paper, list two of your pet peeves—things that you especially dislike and would like to see changed. For each one identify an audience that you would like to address, and then write one sentence explaining why that particular thing bothers you. Write another sentence telling how you would like to see it changed. You may wish to include details that make your sentences humorous.

274

Unit Tests

Test 1

A. Number your paper from 1 to 4. Next to each number, write the letter of the term that correctly completes the sentence. You will not use two of the items.

a. modifiers   d. nouns
b. focus   e. predicate
c. audience   f. purpose

1. You express your ideas on a subject in the __?__ of a sentence.

2. Specific __?__ and verbs make your sentences clearer.

3. You add information to your sentences with __?__, which answer questions such as "Which one?" and "How?"

4. Use words and details that are appropriate for the age and the interests of your __?__.

B. Number your paper from 5 to 8. Read the following sentences. Next to each number, write the letter of the item that correctly answers the question about the sentences.

SENTENCE 1   The Rocky Mountain range is more than three thousand miles long.

SENTENCE 2   As we approached the Rockies, I could see jagged peaks topped with patches of snow.

5. Which sentence focuses on the mountains as the subject?
a. Sentence 1   b. Sentence 2

6. Which sentence contains a detail telling which peaks?
a. Sentence 1   b. Sentence 2

7. What is the purpose of Sentence 1?
a. To inform   b. To describe   c. To tell a story

8. Which sentence describes the appearance of the mountains?
a. Sentence 1   b. Sentence 2

Test 2

Choose one of the Unit Assignments. Write the assignment as directed and hand it in to your teacher.

Test 1 *(page 275)*

A.
1. e
2. d
3. a
4. c

B.
5. a
6. b
7. a
8. b

Test 2 *(page 275)*

Answers will vary.

275

Unit 10

Objectives

Objectives

After studying this unit, students should be able to do the following:

- Recognize a unified paragraph and its parts.

- Plan a paragraph, selecting and limiting a topic and listing and choosing details.

- Write a topic sentence for a paragraph.

- Write supporting sentences for a paragraph, using facts and examples.

- Organize the supporting sentences of a paragraph in chronological order, spatial order, or order of importance.

- Write a concluding sentence for a paragraph.

Teaching Suggestions

See "Classroom Insights" for Unit 10 in the front of this Teacher's Edition.

Program Resources

Resource Book, Second Course: Bonus Activities, Unit 10 Composition Checklist, Unit 10
Practice Book, Second Course, Unit 10
Tests, Second Course, Unit 10
Composition Workshops, Second Course, Unit 10

Writing Paragraphs

Unit Preview

A paragraph is a group of sentences that work together as a team to discuss a single main idea. In the following paragraph, notice how each sentence, or player on the team, helps to develop the idea stated in the first sentence.

(1) Main idea: Excalibur—popular English legend
(2) (3) Arthur pulls Excalibur from a stone

(4) (5) (6)Arthur receives sword from Lady of the Lake

(7) Symbol of power and greatness

(1) One of the most popular subjects of English legend is Excalibur, the sword that belonged to the sixth-century hero King Arthur. (2) According to one version, young Arthur earned his right to the sword by pulling it out of a stone in which it had been fixed. (3) His feat, which no older man had been able to perform, established Arthur as the rightful king of all Britain. (4) In another version, Arthur is said to have received Excalibur from the Lady of the Lake, who lived in an inaccessible castle in the middle of a lake. (5) Many years later, in response to Arthur's dying wish, Sir Bedevere threw Excalibur back into the lake. (6) An arm clad in white reached up from the water to receive the sword. (7) In both versions, Excalibur is a symbol of power and greatness.

Notice that the first line of the paragraph is indented, or set in. A paragraph indentation is a signal to your readers that all the sentences that follow will be about the same idea.

276

For Analysis On your paper, follow these instructions about the paragraph on Excalibur.

1. Write the sentence that states the main idea of the paragraph. Label this sentence *Topic sentence*.
2. Write the numbers of the sentences that provide details about the main idea.
3. Write the conclusion that the writer made about Excalibur. Label this sentence *Concluding sentence*.

In this unit, you will practice writing paragraphs. In the prewriting stage, you will select and limit a topic to develop in a paragraph. You will also list supporting details for that topic. Then you will write sentences that make up a paragraph: a topic sentence, supporting sentences, and a concluding sentence.

10.1 What Is a Paragraph?

A **paragraph** is a series of sentences that develops a single idea or topic. You can write a paragraph for any of several purposes *(pages 249–250),* but all paragraphs have one thing in common: each sentence relates to the same topic. A group of unrelated sentences is not a paragraph.

Most paragraphs are made up of a topic sentence, a series of supporting sentences, and a concluding sentence.

A **topic sentence** states the main idea of a paragraph. It is usually best to place it at the beginning of a paragraph so that your readers will know immediately what the paragraph is about.

The **supporting sentences** explain or develop what is stated in the topic sentence. Each supporting sentence should provide information that is related to the main idea.

A **concluding sentence** usually summarizes the supporting sentences, states a conclusion related to the main idea or otherwise brings the paragraph to a close. In some paragraphs a concluding sentence is not needed.

277

Related Resources

The American Heritage Dictionary of the English Language
Roget's II: The New Thesaurus

For Analysis *(page 277)*

1. Topic sentence: One of the most popular subjects of English legend is Excalibur, the sword that belonged to the sixth-century hero King Arthur.
2. 2, 3, 4, 5, 6
3. Concluding sentence: In both versions, Excalibur is a symbol of power and greatness.

Paragraph Unity.   A paragraph has **unity** when all of the supporting sentences relate to the main idea. Notice how the supporting sentences in the following unified paragraph develop the main idea.

Model

Topic sentence

In 1974, peasants living near Mount Li in China stumbled onto what may be the most astonishing archeological find of the century.

Supporting sentences

Three quarters of a mile from the tomb of the Ch'in emperor Shih Huang Ti, an enormous army of life-size clay soldiers and horses was discovered in an underground vault. According to archeologists, the emperor had the pottery army created twenty-two hundred years ago to guard his tomb. More than six thousand soldiers and horses, no two identical, were painstakingly sculpted from terra cotta. The soldiers, each wearing painted armor and carrying a real sword or crossbow, are lined up in battle formation. For twenty-two centuries the army has kept silent watch over the tomb

Concluding sentence

of Shih Huang Ti. Now archeologists hope to enlist the army in the search for more knowledge about a once magnificent empire.

In the model paragraph, all of the supporting sentences discuss the archeological discovery and thus form a unit of thought. The model paragraph would not have unity if the writer had included such statements as the following:

The tomb of the Ch'in emperor was invaded by robbers in 206 B.C.

Many of China's ancient tombs have not been excavated.

Thousands of laborers lost their lives while working on Shih Huang Ti's other monumental project, the Great Wall.

278

All three of these sentences relate to the subject of Chinese archeology. However, they do not relate to the specific topic of the model paragraph. In writing a paragraph, you must be sure that each sentence develops the idea presented in the topic sentence.

Exercise Prewriting: Paragraph Unity On your paper, write the topic sentence of the following paragraph. Then write the numbers of the two sentences that destroy the unity of the paragraph.

> (1) A career as a private investigator is not as exciting and glamorous as many people suppose. (2) Contrary to the way they are portrayed on the screen and in novels, very few private investigators solve unusual crimes, drive sports cars, or earn five hundred dollars a day plus expenses. (3) Most private investigators are hired for such routine jobs as locating someone who owes a client money, investigating an accident, or checking on a person's background. (4) Of course only a certain kind of person can succeed as a private investigator. (5) One has to be skillful at asking questions and uncovering facts. (6) On an average day, most private investigators can be found not behind the wheel of an expensive car but in an office, checking records or making phone calls. (7) Finally, while some private investigators earn large sums of money, many others barely earn a living.

Assignment Prewriting *Step 1:* On your paper, write the following pairs of sentences, leaving at least ten lines between each topic sentence and concluding sentence. *Step 2:* On those lines list six or more details that support each topic sentence. *Step 3:* Put a checkmark next to the four details on each list that would be most useful in writing a unified paragraph.

Exercise *(page 279)*

A career as a private investigator is not as exciting and glamorous as many people suppose.
4, 5

279

1. *Topic sentence:* School gives young people an opportunity to grow in a number of ways, not just academically.
   Concluding sentence: Clearly, there is more to school than reading, writing, and arithmetic.
2. *Topic sentence:* Many of the inventions that science-fiction writers once dreamed of are now part of our everyday lives.
   Concluding sentence: It is amazing how often an imagined device becomes a reality.

Assignment Checklist

Check your assignment for the following points:

✔ 1. Did you list six supporting details for each topic sentence?
✔ 2. Did you check the supporting details that most clearly relate to the topic sentence?

10.2 Planning a Paragraph

10.2a Selecting and Limiting a Topic

When selecting a topic, choose a subject that you know something about or that you are interested in studying. The topic that you select may be too general to develop in a few sentences. For example, if you choose a topic such as "Weather," you will find that you have too much to write about. On the other hand, if you limit the topic to "How to read a barometer," you will be able to cover your topic completely in a paragraph.

The following suggestions will help you to limit a general topic so that it is suitable for a paragraph.

280

Strategies

Exercise 1 *(pages 281–282)*

See page 282 for sample answers.

1. *Select an example of the general topic.*

   General topic: Nineteenth-century American authors
   Limited topic: Edgar Allan Poe

2. *Substitute a shorter time period for a longer one.*

   General topic: The history of American English
   Limited topic: Words that came into American English during the Space Age

3. *Divide your topic into parts and focus on one of the parts.*

   General topic: The White House
   Limited topic: The Oval Office

4. *Limit your topic to a specific condition, place, or purpose.*

   General topic: Shopping
   Limited topic: Shopping on a tight budget [condition]
   General topic: Touring the West Coast
   Limited topic: Touring San Francisco [place]
   General topic: Training a dog
   Limited topic: Training a dog to come on command [purpose]

Exercise 1 Limited Topics In each of the following lists, the topics become more limited as you move down the list. On your paper, write a topic that is even more limited than the last topic in each list.

SAMPLE	Timepieces
	Watches
	Pocket watches
ANSWER	My grandfather's gold watch

281

Exercise 1 *(pages 281–282)*

Answers may vary. Samples:

1. How greenbacks got their name
2. Pitching a pup tent
3. Stradivarius
4. The first United States flag
5. The world's most famous lion tamer
6. Fruit-bearing cacti

Exercise 2 *(page 282)*

Answers may vary. Samples:

1. TV movies in 1976
2. Lincoln Memorial
3. Bicycling to keep fit
4. How the lungs work
5. Historic sites in Boston

1. Money
   Paper money
   Greenbacks
2. Camping equipment
   Tents
   Pup tents
3. Orchestra
   String section
   The violin
4. Signs and symbols
   Flags
   The United States flag
5. Circus performers
   Animal trainers
   The lion tamer
6. Plants
   Succulents
   Cacti

Exercise 2   Prewriting: Limited Topics   The following topics are too general for developing in a paragraph. Limit each topic, using the method described on the right. On your paper, write the limited topic.

SAMPLE	GENERAL TOPIC	LIMIT TO
	Using tools	an example
ANSWER	How to use a carpenter's square	

GENERAL TOPIC	LIMIT TO
1. TV movies in the 1970s	a shorter time period
2. Historic shrines	an example
3. Bicycling	a specific purpose
4. The respiratory system	one part of that subject
5. Historic sites in New England	a specific place

10.2b Listing and Choosing Details

Listing details about your topic will often help you to limit it further. Begin by writing down your general topic and listing below it as many related details as you can. Some of the details may be ideas that you already have in your writer's notebook *(pages 239–240)*. Others may be ideas that you find by looking in reference books or by asking questions. The following is an example of this kind of list.

General topic: Rats

1. Have survived all attempts to wipe them out, including traps, fires, floods, poisons.
2. Destroy more than 20 percent of world's crops every year.
3. Adaptable to almost any climate.
4. Impossible to run down—can climb walls or leap from incredible heights.
5. Bite tens of thousands of people yearly, spreading twenty known types of diseases.
6. Caused epidemics that killed millions of people in Europe in Middle Ages.
7. Capable of swimming across rivers half a mile wide.
8. Can squeeze through hole one inch in diameter or crawl through extremely narrow pipe.
9. Can thrive on any diet.
10. Can gnaw through most food containers, even certain metal ones, with powerful chisel teeth.

Exercise 3 *(pages 283–284)*

See page 284 for the answers.

Each detail in the list that you just read relates to the general topic "Rats." Notice, however, that the details relate to the topic in different ways. For example, Items 2, 5, and 6 describe the damage caused by rats, while Items 1, 3, 4, 7, 8, 9, and 10 relate to the ability of rats to survive. Because the second group is the larger, you will probably choose those details and set aside the others. In this way the topic can be limited from "Rats" to "The ability of rats to survive."

Exercise 3   Prewriting: Choosing Details   Under the following general topic is a list of details related to it. *Step 1:* Group the details according to how they relate to the topic. *Step 2:* On your paper, write the numbers of those details that form the largest group. *Step 3:* Write a limited topic for the largest group of details.

283

Topics may vary.

1, 2, 5, 6, 8
How visitors damage the Grand
Canyon

General topic: The Grand Canyon

1. Overused for recreational purposes, causing disturbance to ecology.
2. Visited annually by nearly three million people; some, either intentionally or unintentionally, inflict damage on the canyon.
3. Regarded as one of Seven Wonders of the World.
4. Called "the most sublime spectacle on Earth" by Major John Wesley Powell, the geologist-explorer whose detailed reports in late 1800s first aroused public interest in the canyon.
5. Has suffered from fires caused by carelessly attended campfires or use of torches in caves.
6. Rafters bring noise, congestion, and debris to Colorado River, which winds through canyon.
7. Inhabited by Indians—4000 years ago.
8. Defaced by graffiti in many places—even on some Indian paintings.

Assignment   Prewriting   Select three of the following general topics and write them on your paper. For each general topic, write a limited topic. Then write a second topic that is even more limited.

SAMPLE	American frontier fighters
ANSWER	American frontier fighters
	Davy Crockett
	Davy Crockett at the Alamo

1. Sports played with a racket
2. Famous generals
3. Baking
4. Gymnastics
5. Astronauts
6. The year 2000

Continuing Assignment   Prewriting   *Step 1:* Select two topics that interest you and write each one on a separate sheet of paper. Under each topic, list eight or more details that are related to the topic. You may need to refer to an encyclopedia or another reference book to obtain information. *Step 2:* For each list, decide which of the details are related closely enough for use in developing a paragraph. Put checkmarks beside those details that form the largest group. *Step 3:* Write a limited topic for the group of details that you checked. Save your papers.

Assignment Checklist

Check your assignment for the following point:

> ✔ 1. Did you give a limited and a more limited topic for each general topic?

Check your Continuing Assignment for these points:

> ✔ 2. Did you list at least eight details for each topic?
> ✔ 3. Did you place a checkmark next to the details that form the largest group in each list?
> ✔ 4. Did you write a limited topic for each set of details that you checked?

10.3 Writing a Topic Sentence

To be effective, a topic sentence must state precisely the idea that unifies the other sentences in the paragraph. It should be neither too general nor too narrow.

A topic sentence is too general if it leads your readers to believe that the paragraph will discuss more than it actually does discuss. An example of a topic sentence that is too general is "Every season of the year has its special beauty," followed by sentences that describe the beauties of only two of the four seasons.

Your topic sentence also should not be too narrow. An example of a topic sentence that is too narrow is "Television networks do a fine job of covering sports," followed by sentences that discuss not only television sports coverage but also television news coverage.

285

Before writing a topic sentence, you should look over the list of details that you have chosen for your limited topic. This will give you a clearer picture of what you *are* and *are not* going to discuss in your paragraph and will help you to write an appropriate topic sentence.

Here are the limited topic and the list of details for the general topic "Rats." Study the details before reading the discussion that follows.

Limited topic: The ability of rats to survive

Have survived all attempts to wipe them out, including traps, fires, floods, poisons.

Adaptable to almost any climate.

Impossible to run down—can climb walls or leap from incredible heights.

Capable of swimming across rivers half a mile wide.

Can squeeze through hole one inch in diameter or crawl through extremely narrow pipe.

Can thrive on any diet.

Can gnaw through most food containers, even certain metal ones, with powerful chisel teeth.

Now consider the following statements as possible topic sentences for a paragraph written from the details on the preceding list.

A. Rats are among the many creatures with tremendous survival ability.
B. Rats are survivors because they are able to adapt to almost any climate.
C. Rats have a remarkable ability to survive.

Since the list does not include details on any other creatures, Statement A is too general and is not a good choice for a topic sentence. Statement B ignores all but one listed detail (Item 2) and is therefore too narrow to be an effective topic sentence for a paragraph based on the listed details.

Unlike Statements A and B, Statement C covers every detail on the list and does not suggest details that are not listed. Statement C expresses what common idea the details support: the remarkable ability of rats to survive. Statement C, then, is an effective topic sentence for a paragraph based on the listed details.

Exercise 1   Prewriting: Topic Sentences   Three possible topic sentences are given for the list of details that follows. On your paper, write the sentence that would be an effective topic sentence for a paragraph written from the listed details.

Human body is covered with approximately six pounds of skin: a highly durable, elastic wrapping ranging in thickness from one-fiftieth to one-sixth of an inch.

Difficult to realize from its appearance how complicated skin is.

One square inch of the palm contains thirteen hundred nerve endings, seventy feet of nerve fiber, five yards of blood vessels, and hundreds of sweat glands—all covered by skin.

Skin is as necessary for survival as heart or brain.

Aside from being a container for body fluids, skin makes possible sensations of touch, insulates body and keeps it from overheating, protects body from germs, injury, and other life-threatening situations.

Topic sentences:

a. The skin and the hair of the human body are both amazing materials.
b. Have you ever considered what an amazing substance the skin is?
c. The skin is the body's chief means of protection from the outside world.

287

Exercise 1 *(page 287)*

Have you ever considered what an amazing substance the skin is?

Exercise 2 *(page 288)*

Answers may vary. Samples:

1. Trapeze artists perform many daring and dangerous routines.
   Trapeze artists must work to stay in top physical condition.
2. Daydreaming can help a person gain self-confidence.
   Daydreaming can be an escape from real life.
3. Telephone courtesy is expected in an office.
   Telephone courtesy is a sign of maturity.
4. Movies about outer space have become popular.
   Movies about outer space use highly sophisticated techniques.

Exercise 2 Writing: Topic Sentences   On your paper, write two possible topic sentences for each of the following topics. Begin both sentences with the same subject, but in each sentence make a different statement about the topic.

SAMPLE	Comets
ANSWER	A comet is made up of a nucleus, a coma, and a tail.
	A comet has a long, curved tail.

1. Trapeze artists
2. Daydreaming
3. Telephone courtesy
4. Movies about outer space

Assignment Writing   *Step 1:* On your paper, list four general topics that you are familiar with or are interested in. Leave three or more lines between the topics. *Step 2:* Under each general topic, write a limited topic that can be developed in a paragraph. *Step 3:* Write a topic sentence for a paragraph on each limited topic.

Continuing Assignment Writing   In the Continuing Assignment on pages 284–285, you listed details and wrote a limited topic for your lists. Now write a topic sentence for each of the two limited topics. Save your paper.

Assignment Checklist

Check your assignments for the following points:

  ✔ 1. Did you write a limited topic for each general topic?
  ✔ 2. Does each topic sentence precisely express the idea to be developed in your paragraph?

10.4 Writing Supporting Sentences

While your topic sentence provides a brief look at your main idea, your supporting sentences provide a detailed picture of that idea. You create this picture by choosing supporting details according to your purpose. If your purpose is to describe a person or an object or to tell about an event, your supporting sentences will most likely contain facts, which could be descriptive details or a series of events. If your purpose is to explain, then your supporting sentences will probably give examples. You may develop a paragraph with facts or examples, or you may use a combination of the two.

Facts

A **fact** is information that you know with certainty or that can be checked for accuracy, such as dates, events, measurements, and physical characteristics. You will almost always use facts in paragraphs that explain or describe.

In the following paragraph, notice the number of facts that the writer uses to help you understand the idea expressed in the topic sentence.

Model

Topic sentence —| *A man named David Rice Atchison was President of the United States for one day and*

Fact ————|*didn't know it.* According to a nineteenth-century law, if neither the President nor the Vice President was in office, the president *pro tempore* of the Senate became the chief

Fact ————|executive. On March 4, 1849, President James Knox Polk's term had lapsed, and the newly elected Zachary Taylor could not yet be sworn

Fact ————|in (it was a Sunday). So for one day Atchison was president. It was not until several months later that Atchison learned of this, as the

Fact ————|law was then an obscure one. It has since been changed.

David Louis, Fascinating Facts

289

Exercise 1 *(page 290)*

1, 3, 4, 5, 6, 7

Exercise 1   Prewriting: Facts   Some of the sentences that support the following topic sentence state facts. Others state the opinion of the writer. On your paper, write the numbers of the supporting sentences that state facts.

Topic sentence: Although the whale lives in the water and has a body shaped like a fish, it is not considered a fish.

1. The whale is a mammal and is descended from ancestors that lived on land.
2. Whales are more interesting than sharks.
3. During its thousands and thousands of years in the water, the whale has grown to resemble fish.
4. Its flippers have the bones of a five-fingered hand.
5. The whale, like other mammals, is fed on its mother's milk.
6. Whales are born, not hatched from eggs.
7. The whale has lungs instead of gills.
8. Whales should not be hunted because they are members of an endangered species.

Examples

Another way to support your topic sentence is to give examples. An **example** is a member or a trait that is typical of a whole group. Examples help your readers to understand what a group is like without having to study every member of the group.

In the following paragraph, the topic sentence makes a general statement about bats as a group. The writer then provides seven examples that support the topic sentence.

Model

Topic sentence ⊣   *Bats hang themselves up in all kinds of*
Example ———⊣   *places.* Dark caves, old chimneys, or the attics
Example ———⊣   of houses are favorite spots. Some bats sleep in
Example ———⊣   hollow tree trunks. Others sleep in old bird

290

Example ———┤ nests. There is a kind of bat in India that likes the burrow of a crested porcupine as a bed-

Example ———┤ room. One of the tropical bats sleeps under a palm leaf, biting it until it breaks in half to

Example ———┤ form a tent. Another tropical bat sleeps in the hollow joint of a bamboo tree. This bat has suction pads so that it can cling to the smooth

Example ———┤ bamboo shoots. And many tropical bats hang themselves from the branches of trees.

Alec Dickinson, *The Real Book About Amazing Animals*

Exercise 2 Prewriting: Examples On your paper, write the topic sentence of the following paragraph. Then list the examples that support the topic sentence.

I had always thought that the people of England and of the United States spoke the same language, but when I traveled in England last year, I learned that the British have names different from those we use for many familiar items. For example, the English go to the "cinema," not to the movies, and they telephone from "call boxes" rather than from phone booths. In the United States, you might buy your newspaper at a newsstand, but in Britain you buy it at a "kiosk." The English do not ride elevators to their apartments; rather, they ride "lifts" to their "flats." Nowhere is the difference in language more confusing than when it comes to discussing cars. Try not to panic if someday you hear a Britisher say, "I filled up my motorcar with petrol from a can I always keep in the boot; then I checked under the bonnet and cleaned the windscreen." In American English it simply means, "I filled up my car with gas from a can I always keep in the trunk; then I checked under the hood and cleaned the windshield."

Exercise 3 Writing: Examples On your paper, write a paragraph using the topic sentence provided. Use the examples given to write a series of supporting sentences.

291

Exercise 2 *(page 291)*

I had always thought that the people of England and of the United States spoke the same language, but when I traveled in England last year, I learned that the British have names different from those we use for many familiar items.

"cinema" for movies
"call boxes" for phone booths
"kiosk" for newsstand
"lifts" for elevators
"flats" for apartments
"motorcar," "petrol," "boot," "bonnet," "windscreen" for car, gas, trunk, hood, windshield

Exercise 3 *(pages 291–292)*

See page 292 for a sample answer.

Exercise 3 *(pages 291–292)*

Answers may vary. Sample:

History records the courage of men and women. For example, Leonidas, a soldier-king of ancient Sparta, died with his small force while defending the pass at Thermopylae against a great Persian army. Then there was Joan of Arc, who restored the French dauphin to the throne and later died at the stake. In colonial times Paul Revere rode through the night to warn the colonists that the British were on their way. Later Frederick Douglass escaped from a life of slavery and became a respected leader in the anti-slavery movement. Another courageous person was Susan B. Anthony, who spent a lifetime fighting for the right of women to vote. More recently, Charles Lindbergh made the first solo nonstop transatlantic flight, and Amelia Earhart made the first flight from Hawaii to California.

Topic sentence: History records the courage of men and women.

1. Leonidas, a soldier-king of ancient Sparta, who died with his small force while defending the pass at Thermopylae against a great Persian army
2. Joan of Arc, who restored the French dauphin to the throne and later died at the stake
3. Paul Revere, who rode through the night to warn the colonists that the British were on their way
4. Frederick Douglass, who escaped from a life of slavery and became a respected leader in the anti-slavery movement
5. Susan B. Anthony, who spent a lifetime fighting for the right of women to vote
6. More recently, Charles Lindbergh, who made the first solo nonstop transatlantic flight; and Amelia Earhart, who made the first flight from Hawaii to California

Assignment 1 Writing Select one of the following topic sentences and copy it on your paper. Then list at least five facts that you might use to support the idea stated in the topic sentence. If necessary, use an encyclopedia or another reference book to find suitable facts.

1. The human heart does an astonishing amount of work.
2. The American frontierswoman Calamity Jane led an adventurous life.
3. The piranha is an extremely dangerous tropical fish.
4. A soccer match is easy to follow when you know the basic rules.

Assignment 2 Writing Select one of the following topic sentences and copy it on your paper. Then list three examples that you might use to support the idea stated in the topic sentence. If necessary, use a reference book to find suitable examples.

292

1. The mysteries of Agatha Christie are among the most widely read novels in the world.
2. Some spiders have intriguing names.
3. The capital cities of many states often are neither the largest nor the most famous cities in those states.
4. Judging from the *Guinness Book of World Records,* some people will do almost anything to get their names in print.
5. There is almost no limit to the number of interesting creatures that you can find in a pond.

Continuing Assignment Writing In the Continuing Assignment on page 288, you wrote topic sentences for your two lists of details. Now use your lists of details to write supporting sentences in which you state facts or give examples. Save your paper.

Assignment Checklist

Check your assignments for the following points:

✔1. Did you write supporting details that state facts such as measurements, events, and physical characteristics?
✔2. Did you write supporting details that give examples that are true of the whole group of items discussed in the topic sentence?

10.5 Organizing Supporting Sentences

The supporting details in a well-organized paragraph form a train of thought in which one idea closely follows another. You should arrange the details so that the reader knows immediately how each supporting sentence relates to the topic sentence and why one supporting sentence follows another. Three effective ways of arranging the details in a paragraph are chronological order, spatial order, and order of importance.

293

10.5a Chronological Order

Chronological order is a way of organizing events or steps in the time order in which they take place. When you use chronological order, you begin with what happens first and end with what happens last. Chronological order is useful for telling a story or explaining how to do something.

In the following paragraph, the writer arranges the events in the supporting sentences chronologically.

Model

> The expression "Your name is mud" came about as a result of the trial of Dr. Samuel Alexander Mudd for his alleged involvement in the assassination of President Abraham Lincoln. President Lincoln was shot by the actor John Wilkes Booth on the night of April 14, 1865, as the President watched a play at Ford's Theatre. While escaping from the theater, Booth broke his leg. Afterward, he showed up at the home of Dr. Mudd, asking for assistance. Dr. Mudd reportedly set Booth's leg, and Booth continued on his way. Later, Dr. Mudd was charged with being a conspirator in the assassination. Although he pleaded innocent, he was convicted and sentenced to life imprisonment in the military prison known as Shark Island. In time, his name became a badge of dishonor.

The supporting sentences in the paragraph begin with events leading to Dr. Mudd's alleged involvement in the assassination of President Lincoln and proceed, event by event, to his imprisonment as a conspirator. The resulting paragraph is easy to follow.

The chronological arrangement in the model paragraph is made clear by the use of such transitional words and phrases as *while, afterward, later,* and *in time* and a specific time-related phrase, *on the night of April 14, 1865.*

In your paragraphs, you should use transitional words and phrases to provide a bridge from one event to another or from one step to another. The following are among the most commonly used transitional words and phrases.

after	before	in the end
after a while	earlier	meanwhile
as soon as	first	next
at first	finally	then

Exercise 1 Prewriting: Chronological Order On your paper, write the topic sentence provided. Then write the supporting sentences in chronological order to form a well-organized paragraph. Underline all the transitional and time-related words and phrases.

Topic sentence: Just before the outbreak of the Revolutionary War, England's demands on the American colonists stirred up several acts of rebellion.

1. In 1773 a group of indignant colonists threw cargoes of tea from British ships into Boston harbor.
2. When a British ship ran aground in Naragansett Bay in 1772, several Rhode Islanders seized the crew and set fire to the ship.
3. Finally, in 1774, a group of Marylanders commandeered a British ship and destroyed its cargo.
4. First, to protest the Quartering Act of 1765, New Yorkers burned the vacant buildings to which British soldiers had been assigned.
5. Then, in 1770, Bostonians attacked a group of Redcoats as they patrolled the streets of Boston.

10.5b Spatial Order

Spatial order is a way of organizing details according to their location in space. To use spatial order, you choose a starting point, decide on a direction, and then move in that

295

Exercise 1 *(page 295)*

Original sentence numbers are shown in red.

Just before the outbreak of the Revolutionary War, England's demands on the American colonists stirred up several acts of rebellion. (4) First, to protest the Quartering Act of 1765, New Yorkers burned the vacant buildings to which British soldiers had been assigned. (5) Then, in 1770, Bostonians attacked a group of Redcoats as they patrolled the streets of Boston. (2) When a British ship ran aground in Narragansett Bay in 1772, several Rhode Islanders seized the crew and set fire to the ship. (1) In 1773 a group of indignant colonists threw cargoes of tea from British ships into Boston harbor. (3) Finally, in 1774, a group of Marylanders commandeered a British ship and destroyed its cargo.

direction from one detail to the next. The direction in which you move depends on your topic and on the effect that you want to create. For example, if you want to emphasize the height of an object, you can describe it from bottom to top. To stress its width, you can describe it from one side to the other. When you use spatial order, you can also present the details from near to far or from outside to inside.

In the following paragraph, the writer emphasizes the great height of a hot-air balloon by describing it from bottom to top.

Model

> Last week I went to a balloon race, where I had my first close look at a hot-air balloon. The giant balloon had just been inflated and was swaying softly in the air overhead, held fast by ropes tied to pegs in the ground. The gondola, a wicker basket attached to a tubular frame, couldn't have been more than five feet square and four feet tall. Strapped to the outside of the gondola were several bundles that served as ballast. About three feet above the pilot's head was a circular frame, in the center of which were two propane burners. The balloon itself rose upward above the gondola like an enormous scoop of ice cream in a cone. Vertical sections of yellow and green alternated halfway up the sides of the balloon where they merged with a field of dark blue. Near the top of the balloon's dome was a brilliant red sunburst. Next to this was the legend "Sun Searcher."

The use of words and phrases that indicate position helps to show spatial order. In the model paragraph, for example, you can easily follow the details of what the balloon looks like because the writer uses such words and phrases as *in the air overhead, outside, above, in the center, upward, halfway up, near,* and *next to.* Use words and phrases that show position to help your readers follow spatial order. The following are other words commonly used to show spatial order.

across	beneath	down	on
around	beside	in front of	toward
behind	between	inside	under

Exercise 2 Prewriting: Spatial Order   Read the following topic sentence. On your paper, write the numbers of the supporting details in near-to-far spatial order. Assume that you are outside the gate looking in.

Topic sentence: The abandoned house showed several signs of neglect.

1. In front, about thirty feet from the house, the remains of a picket fence, with gate hanging from single hinge
2. Several empty windows facing front yard, their shutters dangling
3. Enormous oak tree between fence and house, its sagging limbs shading yard
4. Overhang on front porch supported by two posts—one partly collapsed, causing overhang to sag
5. Traces of old brick walkway leading past oak tree to broken porch steps
6. On porch, two dilapidated rocking chairs, flanking boarded-over front door

Exercise 3 Writing: Spatial Order   Write a paragraph using the topic sentence and the list of details in Exercise 2. Use near-to-far spatial order in your supporting sentences. Include the words and phrases that show position. You may reword the details to use strong verbs.

10.5c Order of Importance

Order of importance is a way of organizing supporting details according to their importance. When you arrange details in this way, you may start with the most important idea

297

Exercise 2 *(page 297)*

1, 3, 5, 6, 4, 2

Exercise 3 *(page 297)*

Answers may vary. Sample:

   The abandoned house showed several signs of neglect. In front, about thirty feet from the house, leaned the remains of a picket fence, its gate hanging from a single hinge. An enormous oak tree, its sagging limbs shading the yard, stood between the fence and the house. Traces of an old brick walkway led past the tree to the broken porch steps. On the porch itself, two dilapidated rocking chairs flanked the boarded-over front door. Of the two posts that supported the overhang on the porch, one had partially collapsed, causing the overhang to sag. On either side of the porch, several empty windows faced the front yard, their shutters dangling.

and proceed to the least important idea, or you may start with the least important idea and proceed to the most important idea. You will probably find the order from least important to most important to be the more effective of the two. When you save the most important idea until last, you build interest in your paragraph.

In the paragraph that follows, the topic sentence is in italic type. The major ideas are in boldface type. The author begins with the least important idea and builds to the most important idea.

Model

Machu Picchu, the ancient Inca city discovered by archeologists in 1911, presents a number of puzzles to historians. **No one can figure out why the city was built where it is.** Machu Picchu is located on a peak high in the Peruvian Andes. The fortress city would have been extremely isolated and subjected to severe weather conditions. Moreover, farming the steep terrain must have proved both difficult and hazardous. Even more puzzling is **how the Incas were able to transport the huge granite blocks they used to construct the city.** Because the stone has been traced to quarries several miles from the city, the Incas must have moved it across the raging Urubamba River and then hauled it up over cliffs three thousand feet high—a seemingly impossible task. Most curious of all is **the tremendous skill with which the people of Machu Picchu erected their buildings and walls.** Although the Incas possessed only crude tools, the ruins of temples and palaces show that the townspeople were able to fit together massive stone blocks with incredible precision. Why and how Machu Picchu was built are two secrets that the ancient Incas took with them.

The writer of the model paragraph uses certain words and phrases to show the relative importance of the ideas: *even more puzzling, most curious of all*. The following are other expressions commonly used to show the relative importance of ideas.

better yet	first	more important
best of all	in the first place	worse yet
finally	least important	worst

Exercise 4 *(page 299)*

4. First of all
2. Better yet
1. Moreover
3. In addition to
5. Best of all

Exercise 4 Prewriting: Order of Importance   Read the following topic sentence. On your paper, write the numbers of the supporting details in the order of least to most important. Underline the words and phrases that show the relative importance of the ideas listed.

Topic sentence: Since I began using the local library regularly, I have really come to appreciate its value.

1. Moreover, offers every type of reading: mysteries, science fiction, plays, short stories, poetry
2. Better yet, always comfortable—warm in winter, cool in summer
3. In addition to providing a wide range of books, has helpful librarians (answer questions, show where to find things, and so forth)
4. First of all, has great smell—maybe it's all those old books
5. Best of all, the services are free.

Assignment 1 Prewriting   On your paper, indicate which method of organizing—chronological order, spatial order, or order of importance—you should use in writing an effective paragraph on each of the following topics. Explain your choice of order for each topic.

1. The design of the Eiffel Tower in Paris, France
2. The advantages of living in a large city
3. Steps to follow in wrapping a birthday gift
4. How I spent last New Year's Day
5. Stone Mountain, the country's largest sculpture
6. Factors contributing to school spirit

299

Assignment 2   Writing   Select two of the topics given in Assignment 1 and write a paragraph on each. Choose topics that call for different methods of organizing. If necessary, use an encyclopedia or other reference book to obtain information. In writing your supporting sentences, use the order that you indicated would be most suitable for each paragraph. In each paragraph include and underline at least three transitional words or phrases that will help your reader to follow the order.

Continuing Assignment   Writing   In the Continuing Assignment on page 293, you wrote supporting sentences for your two lists of details. Now arrange those supporting sentences in the order that will make the most sense to your readers. Use transitional words and phrases that help make clear the order of your ideas.

Assignment Checklist

Check your assignments for the following points:

   ✔ 1. Did you select the most effective method of organizing for each topic and did you explain your choice?
   ✔ 2. Did you choose two topics that call for different methods of organization?
   ✔ 3. Did you use words and phrases in the supporting sentences to help make clear the order of your ideas?

10.6 Writing a Concluding Sentence

You can sometimes end your paragraph with the final sentence in a series of supporting sentences. At other times, however, you may want to write a concluding sentence. A **concluding sentence** restates what you have said in the topic sentence or offers a final comment on the topic.

In the following paragraph, the concluding sentence restates what has been said in the topic sentence.

Model

Topic sentence

One of the greatest literary families of nineteenth-century England, the brothers Currer, Ellis, and Acton Bell, were actually sisters, not brothers, and their family name was Brontë, not Bell.

Supporting sentences

The middle of the nineteenth century did not offer favorable opportunities for female writers. Thus, when Charlotte, Emily, and Anne Brontë decided to submit their novels for publication, they did so using male names. Charlotte Brontë, the oldest sister and the creator of *Jane Eyre,* called herself Currer Bell. Emily Brontë, the middle sister and author of *Wuthering Heights*, used the name Ellis Bell. Anne Brontë, the youngest sister and author of *Agnes Grey,* became Acton Bell.

Concluding sentence

So it was that the Brontë sisters, three of the most talented novelists of the time, became the Bell brothers, three of the best-known novelists of the time.

The concluding sentence of a paragraph also may be used to draw a conclusion, to express a personal reaction, to recommend a course of action, and so on. You must, however, always relate your concluding sentence to what you have already said in the paragraph. Any one of the following sentences could be used to conclude the model paragraph on the Brontë sisters.

That they were willing to give up their names in order to have their novels published proves that the Brontë sisters loved writing more than they loved fame.

In many ways the lives of famous novelists are stranger than the stories that they write!

301

Exercise 1 *(page 302)*

2

This concluding sentence restates what has been said in the topic sentence. It mentions both the sending and receiving functions of the eyes, which the other two sentences do not.

Exercise 2 *(page 302)*

Answers may vary. Samples:

1. Your eyes are both receivers of information and silent communicators.
2. Not only can you see with your eyes, but you can also be seen in them.

People today who read the novels of the Brontë sisters should give some thought to the efforts they made to have their works published.

Exercise 1   Prewriting: Concluding Sentences   On your paper, write the number of the most suitable concluding sentence of the three given after the following paragraph. Explain your choice.

Your eyes are a window through which you see the world and in which the world sees you. The amount of information that you obtain through your eyes is simply staggering. In the time of a heartbeat, your eyes can take in more than half a billion impressions of the objects around you—their colors, shapes, sizes, distances, and locations. From the vast blueness of the sky to the slightest shading of a blade of grass, your eyes absorb the world in all its complexity. But human eyes are givers of information, too, not just receivers. All of your emotions are reflected in your eyes. Look into someone's eyes at any particular moment and you will see whether that person is feeling joy or sorrow, calmness or worry, interest or dullness, hope or despair.

1. Your eyes are receivers of information; thus, you should take good care of them.
2. This ability of your eyes to reveal as much as they perceive makes them your most versatile sense.
3. More than any other sense, your eyes open for you the beauty of the world.

Exercise 2   Writing: Concluding Sentences   On your paper, write two additional concluding sentences that could be used for the paragraph in Exercise 1.

Assignment   Writing   Find two well-developed paragraphs in a newspaper or magazine, clip them, and mount

302

them on opposite sides of a piece of paper. Choose paragraphs that do not have concluding sentences. Below each paragraph write two possible concluding sentences. In the first concluding sentence restate the topic sentence. In the second, draw a conclusion, express a personal reaction, or recommend a course of action. Make sure that each concluding sentence follows naturally from the paragraph.

Continuing Assignment **Writing** In the Continuing Assignments in this unit, you have written topic sentences and supporting sentences for two paragraphs. Now write a suitable concluding sentence for each paragraph.

Assignment Checklist

Check your assignments for the following points:

   ✔ 1. Did you write one concluding sentence that restates the topic sentence?

   ✔ 2. Did you write one concluding sentence that draws a conclusion, expresses a personal reaction, or recommends a course of action?

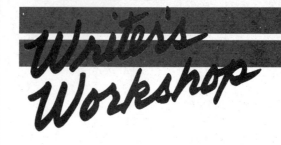

A Look at People and Pets: Writing a Paragraph

Situation: You are the owner of a new pet store, and you are preparing a Grand Opening celebration. To drum up business, you want to prepare an announcement flyer that will include a paragraph about the benefits of owning pets. You have made some prewriting notes for the paragraph, which appear on the opposite page. As you plan and develop your paragraph, keep the following information in mind.

Writer: you as pet store owner
Audience: potential customers
Topic: why people have pets
Purpose: to interest people in getting pets

Directions: To write your paragraph, follow these steps.

Step 1. On a sheet of paper, write the topic sentence "There are many good reasons why people have pets."

Step 2. From your prewriting notes, select the items that you consider to be the best supporting details.

Step 3. You have decided to organize the details from the least to the most important, as follows:

1. beauty and interest of pets
2. educational value
3. emotional benefits (company, protection, affection)

Number the items in your notes to correspond to the order of importance that you have decided on.

(Continue on page 306.)

304

Notes on pets

- Cats considered gods in ancient Egypt
- Dolphins are among most intelligent creatures on earth
- Benefits to human health: watching fish, stroking cat can lower blood pressure in humans, according to recent studies
- People have always kept pets
- Cats awaken owners when there is a fire
- Companionship, relief of loneliness
- Dogs as loyal guardians
- Greet you when you arrive
- Story of Romulus and Remus, brothers who were raised by a wolf and who grew up to found the ancient city of Rome
- Pets are interesting to watch
- Physically beautiful
- Move in unusual ways
- Make sounds that are pleasing and amusing
- Affection of pets as companions
- Can learn things from observing pets: how a bird eats, how a cat listens to sounds

305

Step 4. On a clean sheet of paper, write your paragraph. Begin with the topic sentence, and write a complete sentence for each supporting detail. Use the following transitional words and phrases to introduce your reasons:

first	*however, the main reason*
more important	*thus*

Step 5. Write a concluding sentence that summarizes the benefits of having a pet.

306

Unit Assignments

Assignment 1   For each of the following general topics, write a topic that is limited enough to be developed in a paragraph. Write a topic sentence for each limited topic.

1. Living on the moon
2. Colorful nicknames of athletes
3. Creatures that camouflage themselves

Assignment 2   *Step 1:* Select one of the topic sentences that you wrote in Assignment 1. List at least eight details that support it. *Step 2:* Make certain that your final topic sentence precisely states what the details in your list have in common. *Step 3:* Use your topic sentence and list of details to write a paragraph. Use transitional words and phrases.

Assignment 3   Write a paragraph about a strange incident in which you have been involved. Arrange your supporting sentences in chronological order. Include transitional words and phrases and time-related expressions. End your paragraph with a concluding sentence that expresses a personal thought about the incident.

Assignment 4   Write a paragraph describing a place where you once got lost. Arrange the supporting details in spatial order. Use your concluding sentence to draw a conclusion about why you got lost there.

Assignment 5   Write a paragraph about the qualities of a good leader. Arrange the qualities in order of least to most important, using words and phrases that make clear what the order is. In your concluding sentence recommend a course of action for people who want to be leaders.

Revising Your Assignments

For help in revising a paragraph, consult the Checklist for Revision on the last page of this book.

Unit Tests

Test 1

Test 1 (pages 308–309)

A. Number your paper from 1 to 5. Next to each number, write *True* if the sentence is true or *False* if it is false.

1. A paragraph is any group of sentences.
2. You may limit a topic by focusing on one time period, one place, or one example.
3. A paragraph requires at least six supporting sentences.
4. Transitional words and phrases make clear the order in your paragraph.
5. A concluding sentence may restate the topic sentence or offer a final comment on the topic.

B. Number your paper from 6 to 10. Next to each number, write the letter of the item that correctly completes the sentence. You will use all but one of the items.

a. unity
b. spatial order
c. order of importance
d. fact
e. example
f. topic sentence

6. A(n) _?_ states the main idea of a paragraph.
7. A paragraph has _?_ when all of the supporting sentences are related to the main idea.
8. A(n) _?_ is information that you know with certainty.
9. A(n) _?_ is a member or a trait that is typical of a group.
10. _?_ is a way of organizing details in order of importance.

C. Number your paper from 11 to 15. Read the following paragraph. Next to each number, write the letter of the item that correctly answers the question.

(1) When plans for the Golden Gate Bridge were suggested, many people thought that such a bridge could not be built. (2) In 1916 James Wilkins, who had studied engineering, suggested that the bridge be a suspension bridge. (3) The Brooklyn Bridge, which was completed in 1883, is also a suspension bridge. (4) Wilkins's plans called for the bridge span to be three thousand feet long, more than twice as long as any bridge that had been built to

308

Test 1 *(pages 308–309)*

A.
1. False
2. True
3. False
4. True
5. True

B.
6. f
7. a
8. d
9. e
10. c

(Continue on the next page.)

that time. (5) The city engineer liked the idea. (6) However, no plans were made for years because no bridge engineers could come up with a satisfactory design. (7) In 1921 Joseph Strauss presented a design for the bridge. (8) His first design was not accepted but his second design, a decade later, was approved. (9) Work began on the bridge in 1933, and it was completed in 1937. (10) As the bridge nears its fiftieth anniversary, it is clear that Strauss's design is successful.

11. Which of the following is the limited topic of the paragraph?
    a. Suspension bridges
    b. The work of Joseph Strauss
    c. Planning the Golden Gate Bridge
    d. Long bridges

12. Which of the following is the order used in the paragraph?
    a. Chronological order
    b. Spatial order
    c. Order of importance

13. Which sentence contains a phrase that helps make clear the order of the paragraph?
    a. Sentence 2   c. Sentence 5
    b. Sentence 4   d. Sentence 6

14. Which sentence destroys the unity of the pargaraph?
    a. Sentence 2   c. Sentence 8
    b. Sentence 3   d. Sentence 9

15. Which of the following is true of the concluding sentence?
    a. It is not related to the rest of the paragraph.
    b. It summarizes the supporting sentences.
    c. It presents a final comment on the topic sentence.

Test 2

Choose one of the Unit Assignments or a topic that your teacher suggests. Write the assignment as directed and hand it in to your teacher.

Test 1 *(pages 308–309),* continued

C.
11. c
12. a
13. a
14. b
15. c

Test 2 *(page 309)*

Answers will vary.

Unit 11

Objectives

After studying this unit, students should be able to do the following:

- Revise paragraphs for unity and organization.
- Revise sentences by coordination, using compound subjects, compound predicates, and compound sentences.
- Revise sentences by subordination, using adjective clauses and adverb clauses.
- Revise sentences by using prepositional phrases.
- Revise sentences for conciseness.
- Revise sentences for variety.
- Proofread their writing.

Teaching Suggestions

See "Classroom Insights" for Unit 11 in the front of this Teacher's Edition.

Program Resources

Resource Book, Second Course:
Bonus Activities, Unit 11
Composition Checklist,
Unit 11
Practice Book, Second Course,
Unit 11
Tests, Second Course, Unit 11
Composition Workshops,
Second Course, Unit 11

Revising

Unit Preview

As a writer you should express your ideas as clearly and as smoothly as possible. You can usually improve the first draft of a paragraph or other piece of writing by revising it. **Revising** is the reorganizing and rewriting of a first draft. As you revise, you will rearrange words and sentences, add or remove details, and combine or divide sentences to make your paragraph effective.

The following is the first draft of a paragraph. Next to it the writer has made some notes for revision. When you have studied the draft and the notes, compare the draft with the revised version that follows it. In the revised draft, the sentences have been numbered to help you answer the questions for analysis.

FIRST DRAFT

Make strong topic sentence.

Change order of sentences.

Add transition and combine sentences.

Separate sentences.

Vary sentence.

A mirage is an optical illusion. It is caused by the refraction of light rays by the earth's atmosphere. The density decreases at higher altitudes. The atmosphere is densest near the surface of the earth. The atmosphere acts like a giant prism. All prisms bend light downward. Light rays reflected by a distant object are bent downward toward the observer and thus an observer on an island can see a ship that is actually below the horizon. The observer sees a refracted image, or mirage.

310

REVISED DRAFT

(1) The optical illusion called a mirage is caused by refraction, which is the bending of light rays by the earth's atmosphere. (2) The atmosphere is densest near the surface of the earth. (3) It becomes less dense at higher altitudes. (4) As a result, the atmosphere acts like a giant prism that bends light downward. (5) Light rays reflected by a distant object are bent downward toward the observer. (6) Thus an observer on an island can see a ship that is actually below the horizon. (7) What the observer really sees is a refracted image of the ship, or a mirage.

For Analysis   On your paper, answer the following questions about the revised draft.

1. In Sentence 1 how did the writer make the topic sentence strong?
2. Which sentence did the writer move to improve the organization of the paragraph?
3. In Sentence 4 how did the writer combine the two original sentences?
4. Why, do you think, did the writer separate the original long sentence into Sentences 5 and 6?

Your answers to these questions will help you to understand the third step in the writing process: revising. In this unit, you will practice some techniques for revising your written work.

Related Resources

Houghton Mifflin Microcourse:
    Language Arts, Levels 7, 8
*The American Heritage
    Dictionary of the English
    Language*
Roget's II: The New Thesaurus

For Analysis *(page 311)*

Answers may vary. Samples:

1. In Sentence 1 the writer made the topic sentence strong by telling the cause of a mirage and explaining the meaning of the term refraction.
2. The writer moved Sentence 2.
3. In Sentence 4 the writer turned one of the two original sentences into an adjective clause.
4. The writer separated the original long sentence in order to separate the two thoughts and make them clearer.

11.1 Revising Paragraphs

A good paragraph makes a point clearly and effectively. To do so, it must have unity and good organization. Check for these two characteristics first as you revise a paragraph.

311

11.1a   Unity

A paragraph has unity *(page 278)* when all of the supporting sentences are directly related to the idea stated in your topic sentence. Use the following strategies to revise for unity.

Strategies

1. *Make sure that your paragraph has a main idea that you have stated in a topic sentence.*

   LACKS MAIN IDEA

   The movies began to talk around 1929. Some theater owners hired piano players. Others could afford to install an organ or to hire orchestras. The size of an orchestra ranged from twenty-five musicians to fifty.

   MAIN IDEA STATED IN TOPIC SENTENCE

   Until the movies began to talk, most theater owners hired a piano player to provide the audience with a soundtrack. The pianist was careful to match the notes with the action on the screen. When Laurel hit Hardy with a board, the piano player gave the keys a smart thump with one fist. If a doorbell rang, the piano player trilled two notes at the top of the keyboard. An on-screen fire was inevitably accompanied by a few bars from "A Hot Time in the Old Town Tonight."

2. *Make sure that your topic sentence states clearly what the paragraph is about.* If your topic sentence is vague, rewrite it to make it precise.

   VAGUE   Gettysburg is a good place to visit.

   PRECISE   The Gettysburg battlefield is a historic site that is well worth visiting.

312

Words such as *good* and *nice* are vague. If you explain what you mean by such words, you will make your topic sentence precise.

3. *Make sure that the remaining sentences support the topic sentence.* Take out any sentence that does not support or develop the idea stated in your topic sentence. Be sure that you have included enough supporting information to make your point.

Exercise 1   Revising: Unity   On your paper, revise the following paragraph to give it unity. *Step 1:* Make the topic sentence precise. *Step 2:* Remove the three sentences that do not provide supporting details for the revised topic sentence.

> The rules of etiquette vary. One example is the way people send invitations. Among some Native Americans, invitations were carried by runners to all of the prospective guests. Among the ancient warriors of Japan, dignity and honor were highly prized. In seventeenth-century England, invitations were written on large pieces of paper and decorated by hand. The invitations were sent by messenger, and the invited persons were expected to reply immediately. One symbol of hospitality in ancient Greece was a gift of salt. The ancient Greeks used their fingers, rather than silverware, for eating. Today it is considered polite to extend and to answer invitations by mail or by telephone.

11.1b Organization

To make sense to your readers, your paragraph must be well organized. Your readers must be able to see how the supporting sentences in your paragraph relate to one another. Use the following strategies to revise for organization.

313

Exercise 1 *(page 313)*

Topic sentences may vary.

The ways in which people send invitations to one another have varied over the centuries. Among some Native Americans, invitations were carried by runners to all of the prospective guests. In seventeenth-century England, invitations were written on large pieces of paper and decorated by hand. The invitations were sent by messenger, and the invited persons were expected to reply immediately. Today it is considered polite to extend and to answer invitations by mail or by telephone.

Exercise 2 *(pages 314–315)*

Answers to Paragraph 2 may vary.

1.   One of the loneliest and most mysterious places in the world is Easter Island. It is located far out in the South Pacific, more than two thousand miles west of Chile. The nearest inhabited island, Pitcairn Island, is some thirteen hundred miles away. Scattered over the forty-six square miles of Easter Island are huge statues carved of soft stone. Each figure contains a human upper torso and a large head. Some of the statues are over thirty feet high, and all have been carried or otherwise transported many miles from the quarry in which they were carved. These strange forms are arranged in small clusters in prominent places on the island. No one knows for sure how the statues were transported or even why they were produced at all.

2.   One method of removing salt from sea water is the direct-freezing process. This process can be understood by imagining two huge tanks, side by side. The sea water is pumped into the first tank, which contains a refrigerant that cools the water. In the process ice crystals are formed, which are free of salt. After the sea water is cooled to the freezing point, it is pumped into the second tank. Here the ice crystals are separated from the brine. Finally, when the ice crystals melt, fresh water is the result.

Strategies

1.   *Make sure that you have introduced your topic before you begin to discuss it.* It is usually best to place your topic sentence at the beginning of the paragraph.

2.   *Make sure that you have organized your supporting sentences in an order that makes sense to your readers.* If you are telling about a series of events, arrange the details in chronological order *(page 294)*. If you are presenting a series of examples, arrange the details in order of their importance *(page 297)*. If you are describing something, arrange the details in spatial order *(page 295)*.

3.   *Make sure that you have discussed a series of items in the same order in which you introduced them.* For example, if you have said in your topic sentence that you will discuss water, air, and noise pollution, do not discuss noise pollution first, then water pollution, and finally air pollution.

4.   *Make sure that you have used transitional words and phrases (pages 294–295)* to connect the ideas in your paragraph and to make your paragraph read more smoothly.

Exercise 2   Revising: Organization   On your paper, revise the following paragraphs to improve their organization. In Paragraph 1, identify the topic sentence and move it to the beginning. In Paragraph 2, arrange the supporting sentences in an appropriate order and add transitional words where necessary.

1.   It is located far out in the South Pacific, more than two thousand miles west of Chile. The nearest inhabited island, Pitcairn Island, is some thirteen hundred miles away. Scattered over the forty-six square miles of Easter Island are huge

314

statues carved of soft stone. Each figure contains a human upper torso and a large head. Some of the statues are over thirty feet high, and all have been carried or otherwise transported many miles from the quarry in which they were carved. These strange forms are arranged in small clusters in prominent places on the island. No one knows for sure how the statues were transported or even why they were produced at all. One of the loneliest and most mysterious places in the world is Easter Island.

2.   One method of removing salt from sea water is the direct-freezing process. This process can be understood by imagining two huge tanks, side by side. After the sea water is cooled to the freezing point, it is pumped into the second tank. Ice crystals are formed, which are free of salt. The sea water is pumped into the first tank, which contains a refrigerant that cools the water. Here the ice crystals are separated from the brine. When the ice crystals melt, fresh water is the result.

Assignment Revising   The following paragraph is a first draft. On your paper, revise the paragraph for unity, and organize the supporting details in order of importance.

    The annual All-American Soap Box Derby is a national event. Over fifty thousand young people compete in the trials. The race was begun in the mid–1930s. Several factors must be considered when building a racer, including wheel alignment, steering, and weight distribution. The vehicle must roll with as little friction as possible. The winning of the derby depends as much on the contestant's skill in building the vehicle as on his or her racing ability. A soapbox racer is a gravity-propelled vehicle with no engine or motor. The course is a steep hill about 950 feet long, along which the racers travel at speeds of up to thirty-five miles per hour. The winner of the final event receives a college scholarship. An automobile company began to sponsor the race in 1934.

315

Assignment Checklist

Check your assignment for the following points:

✔ 1. Did you make the topic sentence precise?
✔ 2. Did you eliminate sentences that do not support the main idea of the paragraph?
✔ 3. Did you arrange the supporting sentences in order of importance?

11.2 Revising Sentences: Coordination

One way to make your sentences smoother and more direct is to combine related ideas of equal importance into compound structures. Combining related ideas into compound structures is called **coordination.** The structures that you combine must be of equal grammatical rank, for example, compound subjects, compound predicates, and compound sentences. When you coordinate related ideas, you use coordinating conjunctions *(pages 32–33).*

Compound Subjects

A compound subject *(page 49)* is made up of two or more simple subjects that have the same predicate. Use the coordinating conjunction *and* or *or* to connect compound subjects. The following example shows how you can combine sentences by using a compound subject.

TWO SENTENCES
Ships follow invisible routes that have been planned for safety. Airplanes also follow invisible routes.

REVISED SENTENCE WITH COMPOUND SUBJECT
Ships and **airplanes** follow invisible routes that have been planned for safety.

316

Compound Predicates

A compound predicate *(pages 49–50)* is made up of two or more simple predicates that have the same subject. The following examples show how you can combine sentences by using compound predicates.

TWO SENTENCES
> The blue whale swims through the water with its mouth open. It can eat as much as ten tons of plankton a day.

REVISED SENTENCE WITH COMPOUND PREDICATE
> The blue whale **swims** through the water with its mouth open and **can eat** as much as ten tons of plankton a day.

TWO SENTENCES
> It usually rains on important days in my life. Sometimes it snows on these days.

REVISED SENTENCE WITH COMPOUND PREDICATE
> It usually **rains** or **snows** on important days in my life.

Exercise 1 Revising: Coordination On your paper, revise each pair of sentences by coordinating them in one sentence with either a compound subject or a compound predicate. Tell whether your revised sentence has a compound subject or a compound predicate.

SAMPLE   Washington Irving studied law. He never became a lawyer.

ANSWER   Washington Irving studied law but never became a lawyer. —compound predicate

1. Grass is an example of a renewable natural resource. Trees are another example.
2. At birth a baby elephant is three feet tall. It weighs about two hundred pounds.
3. Lewis Carroll wrote *Alice in Wonderland*. He did not draw the illustrations.

317

Exercise 1 *(pages 317–318)*

Answers may vary. Samples:

1. Grass and trees are examples of renewable natural resources.
   —compound subject
2. At birth a baby elephant is three feet tall and weighs about two hundred pounds.
   —compound predicate
3. Lewis Carroll wrote Alice in Wonderland but did not draw the illustrations.
   —compound predicate

(Continue on the next page.)

Exercise 1 *(pages 317–318),* continued

4. Today public schools and universities are available throughout the United States.—compound subject

5. Next year my grandfather may retire or stay on as a consultant.—compound predicate

6. Primroses and crocuses grew among the gnarled roots of the ancient oak.—compound subject

7. The Magna Charta was signed in 1215 and is considered the most important document in the history of England. —compound predicate

8. One major accident and sometimes several minor accidents occur at this corner every weekend. —compound subject

9. Rivers and canals were once widely depended on for transportation.—compound subject

10. Dad hung up his jacket, went into the living room, and sat down on the old couch. —compound predicate

4. Today public schools are available throughout the United States. Universities are available as well.

5. Next year my grandfather may retire. Instead, he may stay on as a consultant.

6. Primroses grew among the gnarled roots of the ancient oak. Crocuses grew there too.

7. The Magna Charta was signed in 1215. It is considered the most important document in the history of England.

8. One major accident occurs at this corner every weekend. Sometimes several minor accidents occur.

9. Rivers were once widely depended on for transportation. Canals also carried heavy traffic.

10. Dad hung up his jacket. He went into the living room. He sat down on the old couch.

Compound Sentences

You can eliminate choppy sentences from your writing by combining two or more simple sentences in a compound sentence *(page 114)*. However, the simple sentences that you combine must be related in meaning.

NOT RELATED The official name of the ship is the *Constitution,* and last week we visited the Boston Navy Yard.

RELATED The official name of the ship is the *Constitution,* but it was nicknamed "Old Ironsides" after a great sea battle.

When you write a compound sentence, you join two simple sentences with a comma and a coordinating conjunction—*and, but, or,* and *yet.* Each of these conjunctions expresses a specific relationship between ideas. The conjunction *and* expresses addition. The conjunctions *but* and *yet* express contrast. The conjunction *or* expresses a choice. As you read the following examples, pay special attention to the coordinating conjunctions.

318

TWO SENTENCES
>The plateau is Africa's major landform. Most of the interior is high, flat land.

COMPOUND SENTENCE
>The plateau is Africa's major landform, **and** most of the interior is high, flat land. [addition]

TWO SENTENCES
>Our country has many zoos. Most children have never seen a lion or an elephant.

COMPOUND SENTENCE
>Our country has many zoos, **yet** most children have never seen a lion or an elephant. [contrast]

TWO SENTENCES
>A country may contain only a few hundred people. It may include several million.

COMPOUND SENTENCE
>A country may contain only a few hundred people, **or** it may include several million. [choice]

Exercise 2 **Revising: Compound Sentences**   On your paper, revise each group of sentences by combining them in a compound sentence. Use a coordinating conjunction that expresses the relationship shown in parentheses. Remember to use a comma before the conjunction.

SAMPLE Air is an important natural resource. Water is equally precious. (Contrast)

ANSWER Air is an important natural resource, but water is equally precious.

1. Many Americans visit Mexico each year. The country depends on these visits as a major source of income. (Addition)
2. Central America covers a large area. It looks small on some maps. (Contrast)
3. The wing movements of most insects are similar. The size of their wings varies. (Contrast)

Exercise 2 *(pages 319–320)*

1. Many Americans visit Mexico each year, and the country depends on these visits as a major source of income.
2. Central America covers a large area, yet (*or* but) it looks small on some maps.
3. The wing movements of most insects are similar, but (*or* yet) the size of their wings varies.

(Continue on the next page.)

319

Exercise 2 *(pages 319–320),* continued

4. You can travel by car to Lima, or you can fly there in an airplane.

5. The wind whistled through the trees, and the air was bitterly cold.

6. The smallest galactic clusters contain only a few dozen stars, and the largest contain more than a thousand.

7. The sun is only an average-sized star, but *(or* yet) compared to the earth, its size is tremendous.

8. Air masses are usually very extensive, and they may take days to pass a given locality.

9. Many birds escape cold winter weather by migrating, but other animals hibernate.

10. Queen Elizabeth I's father was Henry VIII, and her mother was Anne Boleyn.

4. You can travel by car to Lima. You can fly there in an airplane. (Choice)

5. The wind whistled through the trees. The air was bitterly cold. (Addition)

6. The smallest galactic clusters contain only a few dozen stars. The largest contain more than a thousand. (Addition)

7. The sun is only an average-sized star. Compared to the earth, its size is tremendous. (Contrast)

8. Air masses are usually very extensive. They may take days to pass a given locality. (Addition)

9. Many birds escape cold winter weather by migrating. Other animals hibernate. (Contrast)

10. Queen Elizabeth I's father was Henry VIII. Her mother was Anne Boleyn. (Addition)

Assignment   Revising   On your paper, revise the following paragraph by coordinating related sentences. Use compound subjects, compound predicates, and compound sentences.

> In hot weather, most birds stop their singing. The air stays filled with music. At first the sound is low. The rhythm is weak. Then suddenly the music gets higher and stronger. Before long the insect orchestra is in full swing. Chirping crickets fill the air with the sounds of summer. Droning bees also sing in summer. Humming mosquitoes join in. A cricket occasionally invades the house. It chirps away in a dark corner. Grasshoppers rattle in the grass. Cicadas send out their loud trills from the treetops. Cold weather slows down the insect orchestra. The first frost ends the music.

Assignment Checklist

Check your assignment for the following points:

✔ 1. Did you combine some subjects that have the same predicate?

320

✔2. Did you combine some predicates that have the same subject?

✔3. Did you combine related simple sentences in compound sentences?

✔4. Did you use coordinating conjunctions that express the appropriate relationships between ideas?

✔5. Did you use a comma before the coordinating conjunction in a compound sentence?

11.3 Revising Sentences: Subordination

You can also improve sentences by **subordination,** which is the joining of ideas of unequal importance. When you use subordination to combine sentences, you place the most important idea in an independent clause *(page 95)* and the less important ideas in subordinate clauses *(pages 96–97).* The result is a complex sentence *(pages 115–116).* You can avoid the monotony of short, choppy sentences by using complex sentences to subordinate some of your ideas.

CHOPPY We climbed over a beam. It was bolted to the wall.

REVISED We climbed over a beam that was bolted to the wall.

11.3a Adjective Clauses

One way to subordinate a related idea is to put it in an adjective clause *(pages 98–99).* An adjective clause modifies a noun or a pronoun in an independent clause and is usually introduced by *that, which, who, whom,* or *whose.* In the following revised sentences, the adjective clauses are in italic type.

321

Exercise 1 *(pages 322–323)*

Answers may vary. Samples:

1. The train that leaves in an hour arrives in Houston at 2:00 P.M.
2. Susan, who has two dogs, wants to be a veterinarian.
3. The woman whose luggage we saw in the airport lost her claim ticket.
4. A mechanic replaced the muffler, which was completely rusted.
5. The students who were chosen for the play must be on time for rehearsal.
6. Diamonds, which are the hardest of all known substances, are valuable as cutting tools.
7. Errors that occur in printing stamps increase the value of the stamps.
8. Pythagorus, who was a Greek philosopher, had to leave Greece because of his beliefs.
9. Gilbert Stuart, whom we know best for his portraits of George Washington, painted the first five Presidents of the United States.
10. Animals like lions and tigers can thrive only in certain regions where meat must be plentiful.

TWO SENTENCES
People like to travel by train. They seldom fly.

REVISED SENTENCE WITH ADJECTIVE CLAUSE
People *who like to travel by train* seldom fly.

TWO SENTENCES
The driest desert in the world is the Atacama. It is located in northern Chile.

REVISED SENTENCE WITH ADJECTIVE CLAUSE
The driest desert in the world is the Atacama, *which is located in northern Chile.*

TWO SENTENCES
Cartographers use imaginary lines. These lines help you to find places on maps.

REVISED SENTENCE WITH ADJECTIVE CLAUSE
Cartographers use imaginary lines *that help you to find places on maps.*

Exercise 1 Revising: Subordination On your paper, revise each group of sentences by combining them in one complex sentence. Place the less important idea in an adjective clause. Introduce the adjective clause with the subordinating word given in parentheses. Make any other necessary changes in wording.

| SAMPLE | Crater Lake is surrounded by walls of lava. It has water of the deepest blue. *(which)* |
| ANSWER | Crater Lake, which is surrounded by walls of lava, has water of the deepest blue. |

1. The train leaves in an hour. It arrives in Houston at 2:00 P.M. *(that)*
2. Susan has two dogs. She wants to be a veterinarian. *(who)*
3. The woman in the airport lost her claim ticket. We saw her luggage. *(whose)*
4. A mechanic replaced the muffler. It was completely rusted. *(which)*

322

5. The students must be on time for rehearsal. They were chosen for the play. *(who)*
6. Diamonds are valuable as cutting tools. They are the hardest of all known substances. *(which)*
7. Errors occur in printing stamps. These errors increase the value of the stamps. *(that)*
8. Pythagorus was a Greek philosopher. He had to leave Greece because of his beliefs. *(who)*
9. Gilbert Stuart painted the first five Presidents of the United States. We know him best for his portraits of George Washington. *(whom)*
10. Animals like lions and tigers can thrive only in certain regions. Meat must be plentiful. *(where)*

11.3b Adverb Clauses

Another way to subordinate a related idea is to put it in an adverb clause *(pages 101–102)*. An adverb clause modifies a verb, an adjective, or an adverb in an independent clause and is introduced by a subordinating conjunction *(pages 34–35)*. In the following revised sentences, the adverb clauses are in italic type.

TWO SENTENCES
> The telescope was invented. Astronomers had already begun to classify the stars.

REVISED SENTENCE WITH ADVERB CLAUSE
> *Before the telescope was invented,* astronomers had already begun to classify the stars.

TWO SENTENCES
> I became a sky watcher. I was only six years old.

REVISED SENTENCE WITH ADVERB CLAUSE
> I became a sky watcher *when I was only six years old.*

When you begin a sentence with an adverb clause, separate it from the rest of the sentence with a comma.

323

Exercise 2 *(page 324)*

Answers may vary. Samples:

1. Although I am not unusually tall, my goal is to become a basketball star.

2. The pitcher plant is well named because its leaves are used to store water.

3. When a beam of light goes through a glass prism, we see all the colors of the rainbow.

4. Since I had never been on skis before, I was understandably nervous.

5. While the flag is being raised, all persons present should stand respectfully at attention.

6. Whenever they have enough time, they go mountain climbing.

7. The singer could not go on stage last night because his voice was hoarse.

8. After the book was published, it received an award.

9. The grass in the field was crushed as if it had been trampled by elephants.

10. If the sun is only a medium-sized star, why does it look so much larger than the other stars?

Exercise 2   Revising: Subordination   On your paper, revise each group of sentences by combining them in one complex sentence. Place the less important idea in an adverb clause. Introduce the adverb clause with the subordinating conjunction given in parentheses.

SAMPLE   They destroy harmful rodents. Nonpoisonous snakes should not be killed. *(because)*

ANSWER   Because they destroy harmful rodents, nonpoisonous snakes should not be killed.

1. I am not unusually tall. My goal is to become a basketball star. *(although)*

2. The pitcher plant is well named. Its leaves are used to store water. *(because)*

3. A beam of light goes through a glass prism. We see all the colors of the rainbow. *(when)*

4. I had never been on skis before. I was understandably nervous. *(since)*

5. The flag is being raised. All persons present should stand respectfully at attention. *(while)*

6. They go mountain climbing. They have enough time. *(whenever)*

7. The singer could not go on stage last night. His voice was hoarse. *(because)*

8. The book was published. It received an award. *(after)*

9. The grass in the field was crushed. It had been trampled by elephants. *(as if)*

10. The sun is only a medium-sized star. Why does it look so much larger than the other stars? *(if)*

Assignment   Revising   On your paper, revise the following paragraph. In your revision, use adjective clauses to combine Sentence 2 with Sentence 3, Sentence 6 with Sentence 7, and Sentence 8 with Sentence 9. Use an adverb clause to combine Sentence 4 with Sentence 5.

324

(1) The Nobel Prize for literature is given each year. (2) This prize was founded by Alfred Bernhard Nobel. (3) This prize was first awarded in 1901. (4) Many people would like to win it. (5) It is considered the most honorable prize for literature given in the world today. (6) The prize consists of a gold medal and several thousand dollars. (7) It is awarded by the Swedish Academy. (8) Each year on December 10, the winner is announced. (9) This is the anniversary of Nobel's death. (10) Eight writers from the United States have won this award. (11) Sinclair Lewis and Pearl Buck were among the prize winners.

Assignment Checklist

Check your assignment for the following points:

✔ 1. Did you make one sentence in each pair a subordinate clause?
✔ 2. Did you use a subordinating word to introduce the clause and combine it with the independent clause?

11.4 Revising Sentences: Prepositional Phrases

You can often improve your sentences by using prepositional phrases *(pages 73–75)*. The prepositional phrase may already appear in one of the sentences that you are combining, or you may have to write an original prepositional phrase. The prepositional phrases are in italic type in the following revised sentences.

TWO SENTENCES
> The mother whale carries her baby. She carries it on her flukes.

REVISED SENTENCE WITH PREPOSITIONAL PHRASE
> The mother whale carries her baby *on her flukes.* [The prepositional phrase is from the second sentence.]

325

Answers may vary. Samples:

1. Constant rain can leach the soil of nutrients.

2. I clipped this article about the new high school from our community newsletter.

3. When crops fail, many farmers move to the cities.

4. A transportation system moves people or things from one place to another.

5. Some people ride ostriches like horses for sport.

6. As the glaciers melted, they filled the basins with fresh water.

7. The pampas is a grassy South American plain with fertile soil and a long growing season.

8. People had been waiting in line for tickets since six o'clock.

9. The statue in front of the hotel was on a pedestal behind the fountain.

10. During a sheep-dog trial, each dog must herd a flock of sheep through a hedge and into a pen.

THREE SENTENCES
>   Regulations divide our town. They divide it into zones. The zones have restricted uses.

REVISED SENTENCE WITH PREPOSITIONAL PHRASES
>   Regulations divide our town *into zones with restricted uses.*

Exercise   Revising: Prepositional Phrases   On your paper, revise each group of sentences by writing a single sentence with a prepositional phrase or phrases.

SAMPLE   Some valleys were formed. They were formed by glaciers.

ANSWER   Some valleys were formed by glaciers.

1. Constant rain can leach the soil. It can leach it of nutrients.

2. I clipped this article. It is about the new high school. It is from our community newsletter.

3. When crops fail, many farmers move. They move to the cities.

4. A transportation system moves people or things. It moves them from one place to another.

5. Some people ride ostriches. The people ride them like horses. They ride them for sport.

6. As the glaciers melted, they filled the basins. The glaciers filled them with fresh water.

7. The pampas is a grassy South American plain. It has fertile soil and a long growing season.

8. People waited in line. They were waiting for tickets. They had been waiting since six o'clock.

9. The statue was in front of the hotel. It was on a pedestal. It was behind the fountain.

10. During a sheep-dog trial, each dog must herd a flock of sheep. It must herd the sheep through a hedge and into a pen.

326

Assignment Revising   On your paper, revise the following paragraph, using prepositional phrases to combine some of the sentences.

> A naturalist named Edward Forbes introduced the naturalist's dredge. He first used the dredge during the 1800s. The dredge is used to collect samples. The samples collected are of life on the sea floor. Forbes spent years studying sea life. He studied the sea life in the waters off the coast of England. He was also interested in sea life in the Mediterranean. Some of Forbes's theories were later disproved, but his name remains famous. It is a famous name in oceanography. Edward Forbes is regarded as the founder of marine biology.

Assignment Checklist

Check your assignment for the following point:

✔ Did you use prepositional phrases to combine some sentences?

11.5 Revising Sentences: Conciseness

Your writing has **conciseness** when you state your ideas directly and briefly. Do not try to overload your sentences with too many ideas or too many words. The following strategies will help you to revise for conciseness.

Strategies

1. *Make sure that you have not joined too many ideas in one sentence* by overusing coordinating words. Revise sentences with too many ideas by dividing them into two or more sentences, by using compound subjects and compound predicates, and by putting some ideas in subordinate clauses.

327

Answers may vary. Samples:

1. By the end of the story, the boy and his dog are together again.
2. We watched <u>High Noon</u>, a classic Western, on television last night.
3. I like mystery stories best.
4. The inspector had no clear idea of who the jewel thief was.
5. The restaurant was popular and inexpensive.
6. The coach scheduled a special practice.
7. It is important to make a good impression at the beginning of a school year.
8. Awakened by the sound of a siren at three o'clock on a winter morning, I rushed into the hallway, where the rest of my family was gathered.
9. I was convinced that the boiler could be repaired.
10. After the airplane was invented in 1903, air travel within North America became fast and convenient and soon connected the continent with the rest of the world.

WORDY	A river moves more slowly on level land, and so it spreads out over a wide area, and it traces a curve called a "meander."
CONCISE	A river moves more slowly on level land. It spreads out over a wide area and traces a curve called a "meander."

2. *Make sure that you have not used unnecessary words.* Eliminate words that do not add to the clarity of the sentence or that repeat an idea that has already been expressed.

UNNECESSARY WORDS
A solitary hawk soared aloft high in the air above the island. [The idea *aloft high in the air* has been expressed by the verb *soared*.]

REVISED FOR CONCISENESS
A solitary hawk soared above the island.

Exercise   Revising: Conciseness   On your paper, revise the following sentences. Use two or more sentences, if necessary, and eliminate unnecessary words.

SAMPLE	The water was warm in temperature, and so we swam all afternoon from noon until evening.
ANSWER	Since the water was warm, we swam all afternoon.

1. By the end of the story, the boy and his dog are once more together again.
2. *High Noon* was on television last night, and it is a classic Western movie, and so we watched it.
3. Above all things I like mystery stories best.
4. The inspector had no clear idea in his mind as to the identity of who the jewel thief was.

328

5. The restaurant was popular and the prices were inexpensive, and so many people in the neighborhood went there.

6. The coach scheduled a special practice in addition to our regular practice.

7. It is essential and important to make a good impression at the beginning of a new school year.

8. It was three o'clock on a winter morning, and I was awakened by the sound of a siren, and so I rushed out into the hallway, and the rest of my family was also gathered there.

9. In my opinion, I was convinced that the boiler could be repaired.

10. The airplane was invented in 1903, and so travel within North America became fast and convenient, and air travel soon connected the continent with the rest of the world.

Assignment **Revising** On your paper, revise the following paragraph to make the sentences more concise.

> Canada's population is small, and so it has only a few large cities, and Montreal is the largest, and it has over a million people in population. Toronto is Canada's second largest city in size. Banking and industry are important activities in Toronto, and the busy stock exchange there leads the whole world in buying and selling mining shares in mines. Ottawa, the capital of Canada, is the third largest city, and it is next in size after Montreal and Toronto. All three cities are close to the nearby United States. However, all three cities are far in distance from other parts of Canada, which are miles away.

Assignment Checklist

Check your assignment for the following points:

✔ 1. Did you rewrite sentences to avoid using *and* and *so* whenever possible?

✔ 2. Did you eliminate unnecessary words in your revised sentences?

329

11.6 Revising Sentences: Variety

When you revise sentences in a paragraph, check them for variety. Too many of the same kinds of sentences can be distracting or monotonous to your readers. Use the following strategies to revise for variety.

Strategies

1. *Make sure that every sentence does not begin the same way.* Vary your sentences by placing modifying words, phrases, and clauses before the subject.

ADVERB	*Slowly* the ice began to melt.
PREPOSITIONAL PHRASES	*Like a giant sheet of sandpaper,* a moving glacier grinds down the land.
ADVERB CLAUSE	*As it retreats,* a glacier leaves behind long lines of boulders.

   Be careful, however, to avoid any series of sentences with the same kind of beginning. Such a pattern can be as monotonous as beginning every sentence with the subject.

2. *Invert the normal order of the sentence (pages 53–54).* Instead of beginning with the subject, occasionally begin with the predicate or part of the predicate.

NORMAL ORDER	The remains of an extinct animal were in the glacier.
INVERTED ORDER	In the glacier were the remains of an extinct animal.

3. *Make sure that the length and the structure of your sentences are varied.* Use a mixture of simple sentences, sentences with compound subjects or compound predicates, compound sentences, and complex sentences.

330

MONOTONOUS

Suddenly the doorbell rang. I ran to answer it. My dog Tish came too. Carefully, I looked through the viewer. I unlocked the door. The dog tried to run out. I grabbed her by the collar. Tish had failed to escape. She barked a welcome to our guests.

REVISED FOR VARIETY

Suddenly the doorbell rang. My dog Tish and I ran to answer it. Carefully, I looked through the viewer and unlocked the door. The dog tried to run out, but I grabbed her by the collar. Since she had failed to escape, Tish barked a welcome to our guests.

Exercise 1 Revising: Variety On your paper, revise the following sentences by placing modifying words, phrases, or clauses before the subjects. Make any necessary changes in wording.

SAMPLE   The mountains lay to the east.

ANSWER   To the east lay the mountains.

1. Most people are willing to try almost anything in their pursuit of something different.
2. A house with seven gables stood halfway down the street.
3. The *Spoon River Anthology* became a best seller overnight.
4. The road ends beyond the fence.
5. The soil and the climate cannot support trees in some places.
6. Their tire tracks remain for years when heavy vehicles drive over the tundra.
7. The hurricane destroyed the house, although the house was firmly built.
8. We enjoyed walking over hills when the weather was cool.
9. The credit for starting miniature golf goes to a man from Tennessee.
10. He strode onto the stage without hesitating.

331

Exercise 1 *(page 331)*

Answers may vary. Samples:

1. In their pursuit of something different, most people are willing to try almost anything.
2. Halfway down the street stood a house with seven gables.
3. Overnight the Spoon River Anthology became a best seller.
4. Beyond the fence the road ends.
5. In some places the soil and the climate cannot support trees.
6. When heavy vehicles drive over the tundra, their tire tracks remain for years.
7. Although the house was firmly built, the hurricane destroyed it.
8. When the weather was cool, we enjoyed walking over hills.
9. To a man from Tennessee goes the credit for starting miniature golf.
10. Without hesitating he strode onto the stage.

Exercise 2 *(page 332)*

Answers may vary. Sample:

Back in 1893 Lord Stanley donated a hockey cup, which bears his name today. At the time he was Governor General of Canada, and he became interested in hockey as the sponsor of his sons' team. Soon afterwards Lord Stanley returned to England. He never saw a Stanley Cup game. A Montreal club and the Ottawa Capitals played the first Stanley Cup game. When Montreal defeated Ottawa, Montreal became the first team to win the now-coveted cup.

Exercise 2   Revising: Variety   On your paper, revise the following paragraph to vary the sentences. Use the notes to the left as a guide.

Combine: adjective clause

Combine: compound sentence
Move phrase to beginning

Combine: compound subject

Combine: adverb clause

Back in 1893 Lord Stanley donated a hockey cup. The cup bears his name today. He was governor general of Canada at the time. He became interested in hockey as the sponsor of his sons' team. Lord Stanley returned to England soon afterwards. He never saw a Stanley Cup game. A Montreal club played the first Stanley Cup game. The Ottawa Capitals also played. Montreal defeated Ottawa. Montreal became the first team to win the now-coveted cup.

Assignment   Revising   On your paper, revise the following paragraph for sentence variety. In your revision, vary some sentence beginnings and combine some sentences to provide varied structures. Change or omit words as necessary.

All living things need food to stay alive. Therefore, we eat. Food provides energy. It also builds our bodies. Hunger serves as a reminder. It reminds us of our need for food. We are children. We eat food that is put in front of us. We get older. We develop different tastes. Our parents influence us by enjoying certain foods. Our friends also influence us. We are constantly influenced by television advertising. We often buy a food product because of the packaging. Good food is essential to our health. We should choose only nutritional food.

Assignment Checklist

Check your assignment for the following points:

✔ 1. Did you vary some sentence beginnings?
✔ 2. Did you combine some sentences so that the paragraph contains a variety of structures?

332

11.7 Completing Your Revision

Proofreading

The final step in revising is proofreading. **Proofreading** is the careful checking of your written work for correct grammar, usage, spelling, capitalization, and punctuation. When you proofread your written work, examine each word and sentence individually. In this way you can be sure of identifying errors to be corrected. Use the following guide when you proofread.

1. Are all your sentences complete *(Unit 5)*?
2. Do all verbs agree with their subjects *(Unit 6)*?
3. Did you use pronouns correctly *(Unit 6)*?
4. Did you spell words correctly *(Unit 7)*?
5. Did you punctuate your sentences correctly *(Unit 7)*?
6. Did you use correct capitalization *(Unit 7)*?

Unless your teacher gives you other instructions, you may use the proofreading symbols shown on page 228.

After you have proofread your revised work, make a finished copy according to your teacher's instructions or the suggestions on pages 228–229.

An Example of Revising and Proofreading

The following is a first draft of a paragraph about ancient libraries. Some of the sentences need revision, and the paragraph must be proofread. To the left of the draft are notes for revisions and corrections. Read the first draft and the notes. Then compare the first draft with the revised version that follows it.

333

Exercise *(pages 334–335)*

Corrections are underlined in red.

Have you ever heard of a flying snake? Known as pterosaurs, flying reptiles were the second animals to learn how to fly. Pterosaurs were apparently an experiment that didn't quite work out. They became extinct millions of years ago and were replaced by the bird. Over one hundred years ago, an almost perfect fossil of this type of creature was discovered in Germany. Scientists renamed it archaeopteryx, a Greek word meaning "ancient wings."

FIRST DRAFT

Combine: adverb clause.

Correct spelling.

Correct fragment.

Combine: adjective clause.

Explain *papyrus*

Combine: prep. phrase.

Put phrase at beginning.

Add concluding sentence.

The libraries of today can trace their origins to the twenty-first century B.C. We would not reconize the "books" that filled the first libraries. Records of an early Chinese dynasty, for example. These were written on tortoise shells and on animal bones. The palace of King Ramses II of Egypt housed a library. It was filled with thousands of papyrus scrolls. A palace library in Nineveh preserved information on thirty thousand clay tablets. The purpose was to preserve the information for future use. Parchment made from animal skins was used as a writing surface in ancient Greece and Rome and eventually replaced papyrus and clay as a writing surface.

REVISED DRAFT

Although the libraries of today can trace their origins to the twenty-first century B.C., we would not recognize the "books" that filled the first libraries. Records of an early Chinese dynasty, for example, were written on tortoise shells and on animal bones. The palace of King Ramses II of Egypt housed a library, which was filled with thousands of papyrus scrolls made from the stems of the papyrus plant. A palace library in Nineveh preserved information for the future on thirty thousand clay tablets. In ancient Greece and Rome, parchment made from animal skins was used as writing material and eventually replaced papyrus and clay as a writing surface. When paper replaced parchment, books and libraries began to resemble those that we use today.

Exercise   Revising: Proofreading   The following paragraph needs to be proofread for correct spelling, capitalization, and punctuation. On your paper, rewrite the paragraph

334

with the needed corrections. *Pterosaur* and *archaeopteryx* are spelled correctly.

Have you ever heard of a flying snake. Known as pterosaurs flying reptiles were the second animals too learn how too fly. Pterosaurs were apparently an experment that didnt quiet work out. They became extinkt millions of years ago and were replaced by the bird. Over one hunred years ago an all most perfek fossil of this type of creature was discovered in germany. Scientists renamed it *archaeopteryx,* a greek word meaning "ancient wings."

Assignment **Revising**   On your paper, revise and proofread the following paragraph.

The koala is a tree-dweling animal It is native to australia. The kangaroo and the platypus can also be found in australia. The koala can most often be found at rest during the day. It rests in the fork of a tree. It eats more than two pounds of leafs a day. It almost never drinks water. It's name comes from an australian word. The word means "seldom drinks. Some toy bears resembels the koala. it is not a bear.

Assignment Checklist

Check your assignment for the following points:

1. Did you combine some sentences for variety?
2. Did you vary some sentence beginnings?
3. Did you omit the unrelated sentence?
4. Did you proofread for correct grammar, usage, spelling, capitalization, and punctuation?

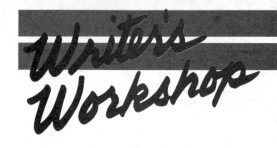

Twisters and Tempests: Revising a Paragraph

Situation: You are a meteorologist for the World Weather Bureau, which conducts research and prepares special weather information. The Bureau issues a monthly newsletter, the *World Weather Gazette.* Each issue offers informative articles about particular types of weather conditions and problems. You have drafted an article about tornadoes for the *Gazette.* The editor of the *Gazette* has reviewed your article and returned it to you with some suggestions for revising it before it is published. The article is well organized, but the sentences need some improvement. As you revise your article, keep in mind the following information.

Writer: you as a meteorologist
Audience: readers of the *World Weather Gazette*
Topic: tornadoes
Purpose: to revise an article to be clear and informative

Directions: To revise your article, follow these steps.

Step 1. Read the first draft on the facing page and the editor's notes for revision.
Step 2. On a clean sheet of paper, rewrite the paragraph, following the suggestions for each sentence in the notes for revision.
Step 3. Proofread the final paragraph for correct grammar, usage, spelling, capitalization, and punctuation.

336

(1) The tornado is a whirlwind of extreme violence. (2) It is the most powerful storm on earth. (3) A tornado forms under certain conditions. (4) Warm, moist air battling cold, dry air produces a whirling column. (5) The funnel first begins as a cloud of condensed water vapor. (6) The funnel gathers dirt and debris from the ground. (7) Then the cloud darkens. (8) Wind speeds at the center may reach five hundred miles per hour. (9) The tornado travels a comparatively short distance before dying out. (10) There is a partial vacuum at the center. (11) This accounts for the fact that tornadoes can cause houses and barns to explode. (12) A basement is the only safe place during a tornado. (13) A public shelter is the only other safe place. (14) People outside should lie face down in a ditch or ravine.

Notes for revising

Sentences 1 and 2: Combine to make a stronger topic sentence.

Sentences 3 and 4: Combine. Change Sentence 3 into an introductory prepositional phrase.

Sentence 5: Omit unnecessary word.

Sentences 6 and 7: Combine. Make Sentence 6 into an introductory adverb clause. Omit Then.

Sentences 8 and 9: Combine. Form a compound sentence using but.

Sentences 10 and 11: Combine. Change Sentence 10 into an introductory adverb clause. Omit unnecessary words.

Sentences 12 and 13: Combine. Form a compound subject.

337

Unit Assignments

Assignment 1 Select a paragraph that you have written for a previous assignment. Use the information in this unit to revise your first draft. Then proofread your revision and make a finished copy.

Assignment 2 Write a paragraph about a humorous incident. It may be one in which you were involved or one that you have heard about. Check the unity and organization of your first draft. Examine your sentences to see if you can improve any of them by combining them. Then review your paragraph for conciseness. Finally, proofread it and make a finished copy.

Assignment 3 Write a paragraph about an everyday occurrence in your life, such as riding a bus, eating lunch in the school cafeteria, or doing your homework. Revise and proofread your draft.

Assignment 4 Write a paragraph about a place that you have visited. Describe the place in such a way that your readers will know what it looks like and what you have found most interesting about it. Arrange the details in spatial order. Revise and proofread your draft.

Assignment 5 Write a paragraph about a famous person who lived in the eighteenth century. Use an encyclopedia or a book of biography to find information about that person. Then explain what the person did to make him or her noteworthy. Arrange the details in chronological order. Revise and proofread your draft.

Revising Your Assignments

For help in revising your writing, consult the Checklist for Revision on the last page of this book.

338

Unit Tests

Test 1

A. Number your paper from 1 to 5. Next to each number, write *True* if the sentence is true or *False* if the sentence is false.

1. When you revise a paragraph, you try to make all of the sentences have the same structure.
2. Combining many sentences with *and* improves a paragraph.
3. Using compound subjects and compound predicates can often be an effective way to combine related sentences.
4. Conciseness means repeating your ideas for effectiveness.
5. You can often use subordinate clauses to combine sentences.

B. Number your paper from 6 to 10. Next to each number, write the letter of the term that correctly completes the sentence. You will use all but one of the terms.

a. unity   d. compound sentence
b. proofreading   e. conciseness
c. topic sentence f. variety

6. When you revise a paragraph, you should be sure that it has a main idea stated in a __?__.
7. One of the first steps in revising is to see if your paragraph has __?__.
8. You can sometimes combine two related simple sentences in a __?__ to make them more effective.
9. The final step in revising, __?__, is correcting errors in grammar, usage, spelling, capitalization, and punctuation.
10. Using different beginnings gives __?__ to the sentences in a paragraph.

Test 2

Choose one of the Unit Assignments or a topic that your teacher suggests. Write and revise the assignment as directed and hand it in to your teacher.

339

Unit 12

After studying this unit, students should be able to do the following:

- Write an explanation of what something is.
- Write an explanation of how to get to a place.
- Write an explanation of how to make or do something.

Teaching Suggestions

See "Classroom Insights" for Unit 12 in the front of this Teacher's Edition.

Program Resources

Resource Book, Second Course:
 Bonus Activities, Unit 12
 Composition Checklist,
 Unit 12
Practice Book, Second Course,
 Unit 12
Tests, Second Course, Unit 12
Composition Workshops,
 Second Course, Unit 12

Related Resources

The American Heritage
 Dictionary of the English
 Language
Roget's II: The New Thesaurus

Explaining

Unit Preview

The type of writing that you do most often is explaining. The purpose of an explanation is to present information about a topic so that your reader will understand it completely. What is an acronymn? How do you go downtown by bus? How do you groom a pet? In this unit you will learn just what makes a good explanation of topics such as these.

A good explanation must be accurate and carefully organized. In the first sentence, you state what you will explain. Then, in the other sentences, you present the information in an order that your reader can easily follow. In the following explanation, the writer presents the information in steps.

Topic sentence —

Step 1 ——

Step 2 ——

Step 3 ——

Step 4 ——

You will need to know how to get to the Multi-Purpose Room of the Community Center for the Junior Red Cross meeting tonight. First, enter the Community Center on the Green Street side. Once you are in the lobby, pass the elevators on your right and continue down the hall until you see the door marked "Stairway." Then take the stairs up to the second floor. Finally, when you look to your left, you will see at the end of the hall a large set of double doors that are marked "Multi-Purpose Room."

For Analysis On your paper, answer the following questions about the explanation that you have just read.

1. What are the topic and purpose of the paragraph?
2. Into how many steps is the explanation divided?

340

3. Are all the necessary steps included? Would they be easy to follow?
4. Copy the first word in each step. How would these words help you to follow the steps?

As you answered the questions about the paragraph, you learned some of the requirements of a clear explanation. In this unit you will learn how to write three kinds of explanations, and you will practice writing each kind. As you write your explanations, you will follow the three steps of the writing process: prewriting, writing, and revising.

12.1 Explaining What Something Is

One basic kind of explanation is the definition of a word. You usually define a word by placing it in a general class and pointing out one or more of its characteristics. Study the following example.

WORD	*eland*
CLASS	African antelope
CHARACTERISTICS	light brown or gray coat, spirally twisted horns
DEFINITION	An eland is an African antelope with a light brown or gray coat and spirally twisted horns.

Although you can often define a word in a single sentence, some words require more explanation. You can expand a definition by presenting examples and details that may include information about the origin and history of the word.

The writer of the following model paragraph defines a word and then expands that definition.

341

For Analysis *(pages 340–341)*

1. The topic is how to get to the Multi-Purpose Room of the Community Center; the purpose is to inform or explain.
2. The explanation is divided into four steps.
3. All the necessary steps are included. They would be easy to follow.
4. First, Once, Then, Finally Each word signals the beginning of a new step and helps to show the order of the steps.

Exercise 1 *(pages 342–343)*

Answers may vary. Samples:

1. A myth is a traditional story that deals with gods or heroes and often explains a custom or a natural phenomenon.
2. A saxophone is a type of musical instrument known as a woodwind; it is made of brass and has a single reed.
3. A falcon is a bird of prey that is related to the hawk.

Model

One-sentence definition

Additional details and examples

Acronyms are words formed from the first letters of titles or series of words. An early acronym was *scuba*, which stands for "*s*elf-contained *u*nderwater *b*reathing *a*pparatus." Because acronyms are much easier to say than the series of words that they stand for, they are widely used. Other commonly used acronyms are NASA (National Aeronautics and Space Administration), UNICEF (United Nations International Children's Emergency Fund), and *laser* (*l*ight *a*mplification by *s*timulated *e*mission of *r*adiation). Acronyms make it possible to identify and say long titles quickly. Today some new organizations choose their official names so that they will become easily recognizable acronyms.

After defining the word *acronym,* the writer includes four examples of acronyms and explains their usefulness and importance.

Exercise 1   Writing: Definitions   On your paper, write one-sentence definitions of each of the following words. In each sentence include the word, the class, and one or more characteristics. Do not include examples.

1. *Myth.* Class: story. Characteristics: traditional, deals with gods and heroes, often explains a custom or a natural phenomenon. Examples: Persephone, Phaëthon, the labors of Hercules, Echo and Narcissus
2. *Saxophone.* Class: woodwind, musical instrument. Characteristics: made of brass, has a single reed, is played by pressing keys that control hole sockets, invented by Adolphe Sax, a Belgian, and named after him. Types: soprano, tenor, alto, baritone

342

3. *Falcon.* Class: bird. Characteristics: has wings that are long and pointed, has hooked beak and sharp talons, is related to the hawk, attacks prey, can be trained to hunt small game. Examples: gyrfalcon, peregrine falcon, sparrow hawk, prairie falcon

Exercise 2 Writing/Revising: The Definition Paragraph Select one of the one-sentence definitions that you wrote for Exercise 1. Using the information given in Exercise 1, expand the definition into a brief paragraph that includes examples.

Assignment 1 Prewriting Divide your paper into three columns: *Word, Class, Details.* Then choose three of the nine words that follow and list information about them under the proper headings. In the Details column, list characteristics, examples (if any), information about the origin and history of each word, and any other facts that you could use in a paragraph defining the word. Use a dictionary and an encyclopedia as needed.

1. Cobra
2. Rose
3. Lute
4. Morgan (horse)
5. Antibiotic
6. Retina
7. Dandelion
8. Shibboleth
9. Chaps

Assignment 2 Writing/Revising Using the information that you recorded for Assignment 1, write a paragraph in which you define one of the words that you selected. Begin with a topic sentence that gives a basic definition. Use the other information in your supporting sentences. Revise your paragraph, using as a guide the Assignment Checklist that follows Assignment 3.

Assignment 3 Writing/Revising Choose another word from the list that you prepared in Assignment 1. Then

343

Exercise 2 *(page 343)*

Sample answer:

    A falcon is a bird that has long and pointed wings, a hooked beak, and sharp talons. Related to the hawk, it attacks its prey and can be trained to hunt small game. Examples of the falcon include the gyrfalcon, the peregrine falcon, the sparrow hawk, and the prairie falcon.

write a paragraph in which you define the word. Revise your paragraph.

Assignment Checklist

Check your writing assignments for the following points:

   ✔ 1. Did you write a topic sentence that places the word in a general class and points out one or more of its identifying characteristics?

   ✔ 2. Did you expand the definition by presenting examples and additional details?

   ✔ 3. Did you proofread your paragraph for correct grammar, usage, spelling, and punctuation?

12.2 Explaining How to Get to a Place

Another type of explanation tells how to get from one place to another. Writing directions for someone else to follow requires care and attention to detail. If you follow these five guidelines, you will write directions that are clear to your reader.

Strategies

1. *Begin with a topic sentence.* In your first sentence, you should state what you are going to explain. For example, you might write, "Here is the best way to get from your house to McKinley Park by taking public transportation." Such a sentence tells your reader immediately what the purpose of the paragraph is.

2. *Divide the explanation into steps, and present them in chronological order.* On a sheet of scratch paper, list the steps in the order in which they are to be

344

followed. Use your list as you write the supporting sentences that explain the steps.

3. *Use transitional words to make clear the order of the steps.* Transitional words, such as *first, then, next, now,* and *finally,* signal your reader that a new step is beginning.

4. *Give complete and accurate information.* Include the details that will make it possible for your reader to follow each step. Name specific streets, and make it clear whether the reader should turn right or left, north or south, east or west. It is helpful to mention landmarks, as in "Turn right on La Piedra Road, just beyond Dyer Memorial Hospital."

5. *Include only the essential details.* Unnecessary information makes directions difficult to follow. If you are explaining how to get to a stadium, for example, there is no need to mention the year in which the stadium was built.

A model paragraph of directions appears on page 346. The writer of the paragraph made the following list as a guide for writing.

Topic: How to walk from the Washington Monument to the National Air and Space Museum in Washington, D.C.

1. Face east toward Capitol, at other end of Mall.
2. Walk east along Mall to 14th Street.
3. At 14th Street turn right and walk to first intersection, Jefferson Drive.
4. Turn left and walk east on Jefferson.
5. Continue along Jefferson and enter the museum halfway down Mall side of building.

In the model paragraph of directions, the transitional words are printed in italic type for easy identification. You would not italicize such words in your own writing.

345

Exercise 1 *(pages 346–347)*

Sentences may vary.

1. 2
2. 4, 5

Take the elevator on the right to the third floor.

Model

Topic sentence ——| Here is the best way to walk from the Washington Monument to the National Air and
Step 1 ——| Space Museum in Washington, D.C. *First,* face east toward the Capitol, which is at the other
Step 2 ——| end of the grassy Mall. *Then* walk east along the Mall to 14th Street, which is the busy
Step 3 ——| street in front of you. *Next,* turn right on 14th Street and walk to the first intersection, Jeffer-
Step 4 ——| son Drive. *Now* turn left and walk east on Jefferson Drive. You will pass the Department of Agriculture, the old red-brick Smithsonian "castle," and the Hirshhorn Museum and
Step 5 ——| Sculpture Garden. *As* you cross Seventh Street, you will see the huge marble Air and Space Museum ahead on your right. Continue along Jefferson Drive and enter the museum halfway down the Mall side of the building.

The writer has given all of the needed steps in order, without saying anything extra that could confuse the reader. The writer has also named the streets and indicated turns and directions with the words *east, right,* and *left.* Finally, landmarks are included at a point in the directions where the reader might be uncertain.

Exercise 1   Prewriting: Essential Information   The following set of directions contains an unneeded sentence and also omits one step. *Step 1:* On your paper, write the number of the extra sentence. *Step 2:* Write the numbers of the sentences between which the missing step should be placed. Then write a sentence that provides the needed information.

(1) Now that you have become a dog owner, one of your first responsibilities will be to get a license at City

346

Hall. (2) City Hall is a large building. (3) At City Hall use the Madison Street entrance. (4) Once you are in the lobby, you will see two separate elevators: one on the left for freight and another on the right for passengers. (5) When you get out of the elevator, turn left and walk straight down the hall. (6) At the end of the hall, turn left. (7) Then go to the third door on your right, which is Room 311, the Office of Animal Control.

Exercise 2   Prewriting: Chronological Order   Choose two of the three topics that follow. Then, on your paper, list in chronological order the steps necessary to complete each explanation.

1. How to get from your home to the nearest playing field (for any sport)
2. How to drive from your community to another community
3. How to get from your homeroom to the outside of your school, in the event of fire

Assignment 1   Prewriting   Choose a topic for directions that explain how to go from one place to another in your community. List the steps in the directions in chronological order. Include only essential details, giving landmarks when possible.

Assignment 2   Writing/Revising   Using the list from Assignment 1, write a paragraph of directions for a new student in your school. *Step 1:* Write a topic sentence. *Step 2:* Write the sentences that explain the steps. Begin some sentences with transitional words. *Step 3:* Revise your paragraph, keeping in mind that your reader does not know your community well. Use the Assignment Checklist that follows Assignment 3 as a guide to revision.

347

Exercise 2 *(page 347)*

Sample answer:

1. —Turn left out of the house.
   —Walk three blocks to Vanderbilt Parkway.
   —Turn right and walk east on parkway.
   —Pass empty lot on right.
   —Pass Forest Park School on left and entrance to community park.
   —Next corner is Madison Street.
   —On Madison, cross to other side of Vanderbilt Parkway.
   —Keep walking east for a half block.
   —Enter gate.
   —Tennis court to left of gate

Assignment 3 **Prewriting/Writing/Revising** Plan and write a paragraph that explains how to get to a notable landmark in your community or in a nearby community. When you are finished, revise the paragraph.

Assignment Checklist

Check your writing assignments for the following points:

✔ 1. Did you begin with a topic sentence?
✔ 2. Did you present the steps in chronological order?
✔ 3. Did you use transitional words to make clear the order of the steps?
✔ 4. Did you give accurate and complete information?
✔ 5. Did you mention landmarks?
✔ 6. Did you give only essential information?
✔ 7. Did you proofread your paragraph for correct grammar, usage, spelling, and punctuation?

12.3 Explaining How to Make or Do Something

A third kind of explanation tells how to make or do something. When you write this sort of explanation, you should follow the guidelines that you use when you write directions for getting from one place to another *(pages 344–345)*. You need to keep in mind three additional guidelines, however.

Strategies

1. *Limit your topic.* Choose a topic that you can explain completely in one paragraph. A paragraph is probably too long if it includes more than eight steps. By making a list of steps, you will be able to

tell whether your topic is limited enough. If it is not, see whether you can limit it to one part of the broader subject. The following example shows how to limit a topic.

BROAD TOPIC
>How to play basketball

LIMITED TOPIC
>How to make a free throw in basketball

2. *Mention any tools and supplies that will be needed.* Give this information early in the paragraph so that your reader can have all the necessary equipment at hand. If any of the items are unusual, you should explain them.

3. *End with a concluding sentence if possible.* As a rule, a concluding sentence is not absolutely necessary in a paragraph of instructions. It can make the end of a paragraph seem more definite, however. A concluding sentence tells the reader that he or she has come to the end of the directions.

The following paragraph explains a limited topic. Notice that the needed equipment is listed in the second sentence. One of the items—an index card—is explained.

Model

Topic sentence ⊣   This is the way to entertain your friends with a simple trick. To do the trick, all you need is a four-by-six-inch index card (the kind of card on which you might take notes for a

Step 1 ⊣ report) and a pair of scissors. *First,* show your friends the index card and challenge them to cut it in such a way that they can pass their bodies through it. Of course, they will say that

349

Exercise 1 *(pages 350–351)*

1, 2, 3, 6, 7, 10

Step 2 ———— such a thing is impossible. *Now* take the card
Step 3 ———— and fold it in half, lengthwise. *Then* carefully
make eleven cuts from the fold to a quarter
inch from the open edges. The cuts should be
a half inch apart and at right angles to the
Step 4 ———— fold. *Next,* turn the card around and make ten
cuts from the open edges to a quarter inch
from the fold. These cuts should be positioned
Step 5 ———— between the first eleven cuts. *Now,* without
cutting the first and last sections of the fold,
Step 6 ———— cut along the rest of it. *Finally,* unfold the card
gently into a big loop that you can climb
Concluding ———— through. Your friends will be amazed at this
sentence accomplishment.

The writer of the paragraph followed the guidelines for
writing explanations. The paragraph begins with a topic sentence, which introduces the topic and at the same time
arouses the reader's interest. The rest of the paragraph is
divided into steps in chronological order. Transitional words,
printed here in italic type, signal the beginnings of the steps.
A concluding sentence brings the paragraph to a definite
close.

Exercise 1   Prewriting: Limited Topics   Not all of
the topics that follow are limited enough to be explained in a
single paragraph. On your paper, write the numbers of the
limited topics.

1. How to make a greeting card
2. How to take a picture with a simple camera
3. How to do a cartwheel
4. How to operate a computer
5. How to play chess

6. How to serve a tennis ball
7. How to make a poster
8. How to build a robot
9. How to do maintenance on a car
10. How to clean an aquarium

Exercise 2 Prewriting: Limiting Topics   Each of the following topics is too broad to be explained completely in one paragraph. Limit each topic to one that can be explained in a single paragraph. Write the limited topic on your paper and save it.

1. How to cook
2. How to swim
3. How to make useful objects from wood
4. How to play baseball
5. How to camp

Exercise 3 Writing: Topic Sentences   Review your list of limited writing topics for Exercise 2. Choose three of the topics and for each write a topic sentence that could begin an explanatory paragraph.

Exercise 4 Prewriting: Chronological Order   The following paragraph explains how to plant grass seed in bare spots in a lawn. The sentences are out of order, however. On your paper, rewrite the paragraph so that the steps are in chronological order and the topic sentence and the concluding sentence are in the right places. Include the original numbers of the sentences.

(1) First, rake the bare areas so that they are free of leaves and stones.   (2) You can repair bare spots in a lawn if you follow these steps.   (3) Now sprinkle the soil with a

351

Exercise 2 *(page 351)*

Answers may vary. Samples:

1. How to fry an egg
2. How to do the scissors kick
3. How to build a simple bookshelf
4. How to bunt
5. How to build a campfire

Exercise 3 *(page 351)*

Sample answer:

1. Frying an egg is simple if you follow these steps carefully.

Exercise 4 *(pages 351–352)*

See page 352 for the answers.

Exercise 4 *(pages 351–352)*

(2) You can repair bare spots in a lawn if you follow these steps. (1) First, rake the bare areas so that they are free of leaves and stones. (5) Then hoe the soil, adding more topsoil if it is needed to make the patches level with the rest of the lawn. (7) Next, moisten the soil before seeding it. (3) Now sprinkle the soil with a thin layer of grass seed. (6) Then water once again, to moisten the layer of seed, but do not flood the area. (4) Finally, if you choose, you can cover the seeded spots with straw to protect them from wind, weather, and birds. (8) In about four weeks, the new lawn should be fully grown.

thin layer of grass seed.   (4) Finally, if you choose, you can cover the seeded spots with straw to protect them from wind, weather, and birds.   (5) Then hoe the soil, adding more topsoil if it is needed to make the patches level with the rest of the lawn.   (6) Then water once again, to moisten the layer of seed, but do not flood the area.   (7) Next, moisten the soil before seeding it.   (8) In about four weeks, the new lawn should be fully grown.

Assignment 1   Prewriting/Writing   *Step 1:* Select a topic from the following list. *Step 2:* Write a topic sentence for a paragraph about it. *Step 3:* List, in chronological order, all the steps that explain the topic. *Step 4:* Review your list and cross out any steps that are not needed.

1. How to find a town in an atlas
2. How to wrap a package for mailing
3. How to make a lettuce and tomato sandwich
4. How to wash a car
5. How to make a birdhouse

Assignment 2   Writing/Revising   Write the paragraph that you planned in Assignment 1. Include transitional words to emphasize the order of the steps. Then revise the paragraph, using as a guide the Assignment Checklist that follows Assignment 3.

Assignment 3   Prewriting/Writing/Revising
Step 1: Choose a "how to" topic of your own. Limit the topic, if necessary, to one that can be explained in one paragraph. *Step 2:* List the steps in chronological order. *Step 3:* Write the paragraph, beginning with a topic sentence and ending with a concluding sentence. *Step 4:* Revise the paragraph.

352

Assignment Checklist

Check your writing assignments for the following points:

✔ 1. Did you limit your topic to one that can be fully explained in one paragraph?

✔ 2. Did you begin your paragraph with a topic sentence?

✔ 3. Did you mention any needed tools and supplies?

✔ 4. Did you present the steps in chronological order?

✔ 5. Did you use transitional words to make clear the order of the steps?

✔ 6. Did you include only essential information?

✔ 7. Did you end with a concluding sentence when possible?

✔ 8. Did you proofread your paragraph for correct grammar, usage, spelling, and punctuation?

353

Making an Electromagnet: An Explanation

Situation: You are a staff writer for *Young Science Reader,* a newsletter for pupils in grades four to six. This week you plan to write a one-paragraph explanation of how to make an electromagnet. You have already typed some notes on your topic. Because the page on which your paragraph will appear has no room for pictures, you must make your explanation clear to your readers with words alone. As you write your paragraph, you will keep in mind the following information.

Writer: you as a writer for a junior science newsletter
Audience: readers of *Young Science Reader*
Topic: how to make an electromagnet
Purpose: to explain your topic in a single paragraph

Directions: To write your explanation, follow these steps.

Step 1. Read the notes on the facing page. You will not use all of them in writing your explanation.
Step 2. Write a topic sentence in which you tell your readers what you are going to explain. Then define the term *electromagnet*. As you write, keep in mind the age of your readers.
Step 3. Write a sentence in which you tell what equipment is needed. Explain terms as needed.
Step 4. Using chronological order, explain each step in one sentence. Use imperative verbs, such as *take* and *connect*, and such transitional words as *next*.
Step 5. Conclude your paragraph with a sentence making it clear that your explanation has come to an end.
Step 6. Read over your paragraph and revise it.

354

Notes on Electromagnets

—Permanent magnets are those that work all the time.

—Electromagnets are those that work only when an electric current is passing through them. (Sometimes called off—and—on magnets)

—Dry cell supplies power for the electromagnet.

—Dry cell: battery cell in which a chemical reaction generates electricity. Called "dry" because its contents are not spillable; actually, contents are in the form of a moist paste.

—Supplies needed for making electromagnet: dry cell; piece of long, thin coated wire with coating removed at both ends; a long iron nail; paper clips

Steps in making an electromagnet:

1. Middle section of wire must be wound around nail about fifteen times.

2. One bare end of wire must be connected to one screw fastener on top of dry cell.

3. As experiment, try to get nail to pick up paper clips (it won't yet).

4. Other bare end of wire must be connected to other screw fastener on top of dry cell.

5. Paper clips can be picked up by touching them with nail.

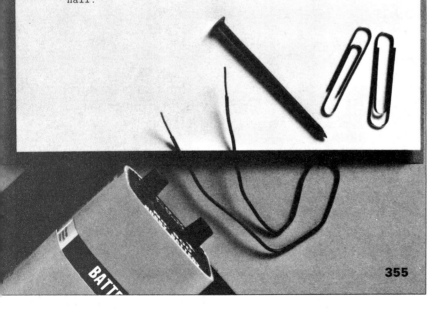

355

Unit Assignments

Assignment 1 Choose one of the words listed here. Read about that word in a dictionary and in an encyclopedia. Then write a paragraph in which you define the word and give additional information about it. If you wish, include information about the origin and history of the word.

1. Leopard
2. Carbohydrate
3. Granite
4. Sapphire
5. Alfalfa
6. Valhalla

Assignment 2 Choose one of the words listed here. Follow the directions given in Assignment 1.

1. Quinine
2. Mackinaw
3. Mussel
4. Coyote
5. Hominy
6. Muskrat

Assignment 3 Write a paragraph that gives directions for getting from your home to one of the following places. Write the directions for a relative who is visiting you. Make your directions clear by including street names, directions for turns, and landmarks.

1. How to get to your favorite restaurant
2. How to get to your favorite store
3. How to get to your favorite place for recreation

Assignment 4 Write a paragraph that gives directions for one of the following topics. Write the directions for a new classmate. Make the steps complete but concise.

1. How to get from your homeroom at school to the principal's office
2. How to get from your locker to the school library
3. How to get from your last class to a playing field

356

Assignment 5 Write a paragraph of directions in which you explain to a classmate how to get from his or her home to your home in one of the following ways.

1. By walking
2. By public transportation
3. By car

Assignment 6 Write a paragraph that explains one of the following topics.

1. How to use chopsticks
2. How to wash and wax a floor
3. How to pack a frame pack for overnight camping

Assignment 7 Write a paragraph that explains one of the following topics.

1. How to do a swan dive
2. How to do a gymnastics exercise
3. How to do a magic trick

Assignment 8 Write a paragraph that explains one of the following topics to an eight-year-old. Keep the age of your reader in mind as you write.

1. How to make an airplane from folded paper
2. How to make a toy space vehicle out of modeling clay
3. How to make a bird feeder

Revising Your Assignments

For help in revising an explanation, consult the Checklist for Revision on the last page of this book.

Test 1 *(pages 358–359)*

A.
1. False
2. True
3. False
4. True
5. True

B.
6. d
7. c
8. b
9. f
10. a

(Continue on the next page.)

Test 1

A. Number your paper from 1 to 5. Next to each number, write *True* if the sentence is true or *False* if it is false.

1. A limited topic for an explanation is one that you can cover in more than one paragraph.
2. You should arrange the steps of an explanation in chronological order.
3. Mentioning specific streets, landmarks, and directions for turns makes directions hard to follow.
4. You can expand a definition by presenting examples and additional details.
5. Before you write a paragraph of directions, you should make a complete list of the steps.

B. Number your paper from 6 to 10. Next to each number, write the letter of the term that correctly completes the sentence. You will use all but one of the items.

a. transitional words	d. concluding sentence
b. explanation	e. chronological order
c. topic sentence	f. definition

6. A(n) __?__ at the end of an explanatory paragraph signals the reader that the directions are complete.
7. The purpose of a paragraph is stated in the __?__.
8. A(n) __?__ may tell what something is, how to get to a place, or how to do or make something.
9. A(n) __?__ places a word in a general class and points out one or more of its characteristics.
10. __?__, such as *first, next,* and *finally,* link the steps in an explanatory paragraph.

C. Read the following paragraph. Number your paper from 11 to 15. Next to each number, write the letter of the item that correctly answers the question about the paragraph.

358

(1) The high jump is a track-and-field feat that you can learn to perform under the supervision of your coach. (2) To do a high jump, you need a bar supported by two posts, and you also need a foam-rubber mat to land on. (3) Before you actually make the jump, you run slowly towards the bar. (4) The Fosbury flop was invented by Dick Fosbury. (5) First, you set the foot nearest to the bar firmly in place while your outside leg and arm swing up towards the bar. (6) You spring up and begin to go over the bar. (7) Your inside leg goes over last. (8) Then, as you glide over the bar, your outside leg goes over first. (9) Finally, you roll onto the padded mat below. (10) You have cleared the bar, and you may now try the high jump again at another height.

11. Which of the following is the topic sentence?
   a. Sentence 1   c. Sentence 3
   b. Sentence 2   d. Sentence 4

12. Which of the following are *not* in chronological order and should be reversed?
   a. Sentences 5 and 6   c. Sentences 7 and 8
   b. Sentences 6 and 7   d. Sentences 8 and 9

13. Which of the following gives unnecessary information?
   a. Sentence 3   c. Sentence 5
   b. Sentence 4   d. Sentence 6

14. Which of the following mentions the equipment that you need to perform the high jump?
   a. Sentence 2   c. Sentence 4
   b. Sentence 3   d. Sentence 5

15. Which of the following begins with a transitional word?
   a. Sentence 2   c. Sentence 6
   b. Sentence 4   d. Sentence 8

Test 2

Choose one of the Unit Assignments. Write the assignment as directed and hand it in to your teacher.

Test 1 *(pages 358–359)*, continued

C.
11. a
12. c
13. b
14. a
15. d

Test 2 *(page 359)*

Answers will vary.

Objectives

After studying this unit, students should be able to do the following:

- Use their senses to note descriptive details for their writing.

- Use descriptive nouns, verbs, and modifiers in their writing.

- Write a description of a place.

- Write a description of a person.

Teaching Suggestions

See "Classroom Insights" for Unit 13 in the front of this Teacher's Edition.

Program Resources

Resource Book, Second Course:
   Bonus Activities, Unit 12
   Composition Checklist,
   Unit 12
Practice Book, Second Course,
   Unit 12
Tests, Second Course, Unit 12
Composition Workshop, Second
   Course, Unit 12

Related Resources

*The American Heritage
   Dictionary of the English
   Language*
Roget's II: The New Thesaurus

Describing

Unit Preview

When you write a description that is clear and vivid, the person, place, or object that you describe will seem to come alive for your reader. A vivid description is based on careful observation. If you use all of your senses—sight, hearing, touch, smell, and taste—you will observe your subject thoroughly.

Notice that the following description contains details that appeal to several senses, making it possible for you to imagine that you were there. Notice, too, that the writer uses precise words to describe objects and actions.

Slipping and sliding, the young boy scurried up the sand dunes. At last, clambering over a smooth, round boulder and around a patch of poison ivy, he emerged at the summit of the bluffs. He raced down a path through the brush and suddenly found himself looking out over the edge. In front of him, the blue, crashing waves of the Atlantic Ocean seemed to stretch out forever.

Matthew Jordan, Glastonbury High School
Glastonbury, Connecticut

For Analysis   On your paper, answer the following questions about the description that you have just read.

1. What subject does the writer describe?
2. To what senses does the description appeal?
3. Which words describe the waves? To which sense does each one appeal?
4. Which words describe the actions of the boy?

360

In answering the questions, you saw how words that are precise and details that appeal to several senses make a description effective. In this unit, you will learn about using your senses to make your descriptions come alive for your reader. You also will learn how to choose precise words to present your observations. As you practice writing descriptions, you will follow the three steps in the writing process: prewriting, writing, and revising.

13.1 Using Your Senses

To be a good observer, you must use all of your senses, not just your sense of sight. When you walk into an office, for example, you can *see* the glaring fluorescent lights and the large metal desks. You also can *hear* the tapping and the ringing bells of typewriters and the quiet voice of someone using the telephone. You can *feel* the hard, metal surface of the typewriter and the sponginess of the rug under your feet. You can *smell* the sharp fumes of typewriter correction fluid and the tempting aroma of the tunafish sandwich on someone's desk. These details are **sensory details,** details that appeal to your reader's senses.

In each of the following descriptions, the writer uses details that appeal to one of the five senses. As you read each description, identify the sensory details.

Model: Details of Sight

Patches of summer snow were sprinkled about the mountain sides. Yellow snow lilies nodded their heads in the breeze, and from beneath them peeked sapphire alpine forget-me-nots and yellow buttercups.

Heidi Tinsman, Pleasant Valley High School
Pleasant Valley, Iowa

361

For Analysis *(page 360)*

1. The writer describes a young boy's climb up the cliffs overlooking the ocean.
2. The description appeals to the senses of sight, touch, and hearing.
3. Blue appeals to the sense of sight; crashing appeals to the sense of hearing.
4. Slipping, sliding, scurried, clambering, emerged, raced, found, looking

Model: Details of Sound

With each footstep on the wooden floor, a dull echo reverberated off the walls, yet even the echo was destined to be lost in the hollow whiteness.

Kathy Beall, Walnut Ridge High School
Columbus, Ohio

Model: Details of Touch

He placed a box of oats under the horse's nose, and she ate while he stood beside her, his hands smoothing the satin-soft skin undermane. It had a nap as deep as plush.

Mary O'Hara, *My Friend Flicka*

Model: Details of Smell

These stables were well cleaned and freshly limed each day. They had an odor that will always be nostalgic to me—faintly acrid of course, but mingled too with the fragrance of clover hay, the sour tang of silage, and the warm, good smell of the cows themselves.

Sterling North, *Rascal*

Model: Details of Taste

I spied one of the berry bushes Grandfather had told us about. "You're lucky," he had said. "The berries are ripe in the spring, and they are delicious and nourishing." ... I popped one into my mouth. *Argh!* I spat it out. It was awful and bitter, and even grasshoppers were probably better tasting, although I never intended to find out.

Mary Whitebird, "Ta-Na-E-Ka"

Usually, the persons, places, and things that you describe have qualities that appeal to more than one sense. Therefore, your reader can imagine them most clearly if you

362

include sensory details from more than one sense in your description. The writer of the following passage presents details that appeal to three senses.

Model

      The day broke bright and gay. The air was crisp, and the sky was blue. From the cluster of vermilion clouds that hung on the horizon, the sun shone its rays in a direction nearly parallel to the ground. Little birds chirped and whistled, and a waterfowl floated effortlessly along the horizon. Dew covered everything that had been exposed to the air during the night and spurted into minute bursts when the tall grass swayed in the breeze.

Mauricio Gonzalez, Belmont High School
Los Angeles, California

Most of the details in the paragraph appeal to the sense of sight. Notice the details about the colors of the sky and clouds, the path of the sun's rays, the flight of the waterfowl, and the motion of the dew. In addition, the detail about the crispness of the air appeals to the sense of touch, and the details about the calls of the little birds appeal to the sense of hearing.

Exercise 1 Prewriting: Sensory Details On your paper, write the sense or senses—sight, hearing, touch, taste, or smell—to which each of the following items appeals.

SAMPLE A helicopter
ANSWER Sight, hearing

1. A bulldozer
2. A book
3. A roasted chicken
4. A calculator
5. A fruit tree
6. A guitar
7. A pair of shoes
8. A piece of aluminum foil
9. A starfish
10. A postage stamp

363

Exercise 1 *(page 363)*

Answers may vary. Samples:

1. Sight, hearing, touch
2. Sight, touch
3. Sight, taste, smell
4. Sight, touch, hearing
5. Sight, smell, touch
6. Sight, hearing, touch
7. Sight, touch, smell
8. Sight, touch, hearing
9. Sight, touch, smell
10. Sight, touch, taste

Sample answer:

1. A newspaper
   The smell of the newsprint
   The rustling of pages
   The black rubbing off on your hands
   The weight of the Sunday paper

Exercise 2 Prewriting: Sensory Details   On your paper, list five of the following objects or places, skipping three lines after each item. Then, after each item, list three sensory details. Use all of your senses to help you think of vivid sensory details.

SAMPLE	A coin
ANSWER	The bright copper color of a penny
	The smooth edge of a penny
	The clink of a penny against other coins in your pocket

1. A newspaper
2. A pine cone
3. A glass of water
4. A bicycle
5. A frozen lake

6. A campfire
7. A mushroom
8. A restaurant
9. A boat
10. A clothing store

Assignment 1 Prewriting   For a week list in your writer's notebook *(pages 239–240)* sensory details of the persons, places, and things around you. Record details that appeal to all five senses.

Assignment 2 Prewriting   Choose a place that you know well: a classroom, your kitchen at home, or your local grocery store, for example. Sit or stand in that place for several minutes with your eyes closed. Then list on a piece of paper all of the details that you observed without using your sight.

Assignment Checklist

Check your assignments for the following points:

✔ 1. Did you list details that appeal to each of the senses?
✔ 2. Did you include sensory details that clearly describe the persons, places, and things that you observed?

364

13.2 Using Descriptive Words

In writing your description, use words and phrases that will make your sensory details clear and interesting to your reader. Using many words does not necessarily make a description good. In fact, using the single noun, verb, or adjective that expresses exactly what you mean usually makes your description more vivid.

You may use adjectives *(page 17)* and adverbs *(pages 22–23)* to describe persons, places, things, and actions. You will not need to use many of them, however, if you use specific nouns and strong verbs to create a sharp impression of your subject. The following suggestions will help you to choose descriptive words.

Strategies

1. *Use specific nouns.* A specific noun alone creates a clearer picture for your reader than does a general noun that is modified by several adjectives. For example, "a room or building in which large audiences gather to participate in meetings or to watch performances" is wordy and unclear. The specific noun *auditorium* conveys an exact meaning.

2. *Use strong verbs.* Strong verbs make your description lively because they capture the action. For example, *sneer* is more exact and more direct than *smile scornfully*, and *vault* is more vivid than *jump over*.

3. *Use adjectives and adverbs carefully.* Add modifiers only when you need to present more information about specific nouns and strong verbs. Make sure that your modifiers, like your nouns and verbs, are specific. For example, *famished* is stronger than the more general *very hungry*. As a rule, avoid overused modifiers such as *so, very,* and *really*.

365

The writer of the following paragraph uses descriptive words effectively.

Model

From the open Atlantic beyond Timbalier Head, a few scattered fog horns grunted, muffled and faint. That fog bank had been hanging offshore for days. We'd been watching the big draggers chug up to it, get dimmer and dimmer, and finally disappear in its grayness, leaving only the stifled sounds of their horns behind. It had been there so long that we got used to it and came to think of it as always being there, like another piece of land, maybe.

Shirley Ann Grau, *The Wind Shifting West*

This passage shows that the use of specific nouns and strong verbs can make a description clear and interesting. Specific nouns such as *draggers,* the name for fishing boats with large nets, and strong verbs such as *grunted* and *chug* create sharp impressions. Adjectives and adverbs such as *muffled* and *stifled* make the impressions more vivid.

Exercise 1 Prewriting: Specific Nouns For each noun listed, write at least two nouns that are more specific.

| SAMPLE | Clothing |
| ANSWER | Shirt, raincoat |

1. Land	5. Plant	9. Machine
2. Building	6. Fish	10. Dish
3. Bird	7. Furniture	11. Vehicle
4. Game	8. Noise	12. Chore

Exercise 2 Prewriting: Strong Verbs On your paper, write the stronger verb in each pair given below. Then use the stronger verb in a sentence.

| SAMPLE | Look, stare |
| ANSWER | Stare—The shoppers stared at the gaudy window display. |

366

Exercise 1 *(page 366)*

Answers may vary. Samples:

1. Meadow, desert
2. Apartment house, factory
3. Eagle, pigeon
4. Badminton, football
5. Cactus, ivy
6. Flounder, catfish
7. Desk, rocking chair
8. Screech, thud
9. Lawn mower, typewriter
10. Bowl, mug
11. Bus, van
12. Dusting, sweeping

Exercise 2 *(pages 366–367)*

Answers may vary. Samples:

1. Plead—The dog was pleading for some of our lunch.
2. Yell—Our neighbor yelled and waved from across the street.
3. Sprint—Once out of the car, we sprinted to the theater.
4. Sniff—My dog sniffed at my pockets for the biscuit.
5. Harmonize—I love to play the piano and harmonize with a few friends.
6. Doze—In the warm sun, I began to doze over my book.
7. Labor—We labored for two hours raking leaves.
8. Pause—When Sue came in late, the teacher paused.
9. Snack—I never snack in the evening.
10. Scribble—Beth quickly scribbled a note to me.

1. Ask, plead
2. Speak, yell
3. Sprint, run
4. Smell, sniff
5. Harmonize, sing
6. Sleep, doze
7. Labor, work
8. Pause, stop
9. Eat, snack
10. Scribble, write

Exercise 3 Revising: Nouns and Verbs On your paper, rewrite each of the following sentences. Substitute more specific nouns and stronger verbs for the nouns and verbs in italic type.

> SAMPLE   Mark *walked* into the *water.*
>
> ANSWER   Mark waded into the ocean.

1. Rachel *talked* to the *person.*
2. The workers *made* the *building.*
3. The swimmers *looked* for the *object.*
4. The *animal was* in the sunlight.
5. The *object broke* on the floor.
6. The *person moved* the huge box.
7. The *object* protected the mail carrier from the *weather.*
8. The *things* belong in the *container.*
9. The *person* tossed the *item* into the yard.
10. The *person* made the *clothing.*

Exercise 4 Revising: Modifiers On your paper, rewrite each of the following sentences, adding adjectives and adverbs that make the sentence more descriptive.

> SAMPLE   The faucet dripped.
>
> ANSWER   The leaky faucet dripped steadily.

1. The snow fell.
2. The friends fixed the car.
3. The student read the book.
4. Margo left the party.
5. The lights went on.

367

Exercise 3 *(page 367)*

Answers may vary. Samples:

1. Rachel whispered to the coach.
2. The workers built the barn.
3. The swimmers dived for the treasure chest.
4. The kitten dozed in the sunlight.
5. The vase shattered on the floor.
6. The mover hoisted the huge box.
7. The parka protected the mail carrier from the sleet.
8. The safety pins belong in the box.
9. The girl tossed the newspaper into the yard.
10. The tailor made the suit.

Exercise 4 *(pages 367–368)*

Answers may vary. Samples:

1. The light, dry snow fell softly.
2. The three friends fixed the sputtering old car.
3. The harried student read the book quickly.
4. Margo reluctantly left the party early.
5. The bright lights went on suddenly.

(Continue on the next page.)

Exercise 4 *(pages 367–368)*, continued

6. The excited fisherman proudly displayed the thirty-inch trout.

7. The tired campers sat contentedly by the leaping, crackling fire.

8. Martin and Larry played the brand new record repeatedly.

9. The attentive reporter quietly asked the man an unexpected question.

10. The tireless trombone player resolutely practiced scales.

6. The fisherman displayed the trout.

7. The campers sat by the fire.

8. Martin and Larry played the record.

9. The reporter asked the man a question.

10. The trombone player practiced scales.

Assignment Writing Choose three of the following topics. On your paper, write a sentence describing each topic. Use specific nouns and strong verbs. Add modifiers only if you need them to make your description more vivid.

SAMPLE   The actions of a bird

ANSWER   The robin swooped to the ground and tugged a worm out of the earth.

1. The view from a tall building
2. A farmer's field in the winter
3. A messy room
4. The sound of a bell
5. The sky in the evening
6. A person at work
7. A cafeteria during lunch
8. A busy department store

Assignment Checklist

Check your assignment for the following points:

✔ 1. Did you use specific nouns and strong verbs?
✔ 2. Did you use vivid modifiers?

13.3 Describing a Place

When you write a description of a place, your purpose is to make your readers feel as though they are there. The following suggestions will help you to describe a place effectively.

Strategies

1. *Begin with a topic sentence.* As you would do in any paragraph, introduce your subject in a topic sentence. You may also include your general impres-

368

sion of the place. For example, you might write that a place is crowded or messy.

2. *Select only the best details.* Although you may list many details when you are preparing to write, choose only the details that capture the uniqueness of the place. For example, in writing about a bookstore, you could describe the features that make it different from other bookstores: the chairs set out for customers and the cat sleeping on a pile of books.

3. *Arrange the details in an order that is easy to follow.* Usually the best order is spatial order, the order in which objects are positioned in space. When you use spatial order to describe a scene, you can progress from left to right, from top to bottom, or from front to back.

4. *Use words and phrases that emphasize the order in which the details are arranged.* Phrases such as *in the middle, near the top,* or *in the front* help your reader to see the place that you are describing.

The writer of the following description presents the details in spatial order. As noted to the left of the paragraph, the writer arranges the details as seen from top to bottom. The words and phrases that emphasize the order of the details are in italic type.

Model

Topic sentence — Located near the Prince William Sound in southeastern Alaska, Columbia Glacier is an

Top — impressive sight. *At its top, three hundred feet in the air,* are jagged peaks of ice and snow that seem to blend into the gray sky behind them. *Farther down,* the face of the glacier is

369

Exercise 1 *(page 370)*

Topic: description of a remembered old house
the front of
On its left side
across the front
In the middle of the front
To the right
Farther right

Exercise 2 *(pages 370–371)*

See page 371 for sample answers.

Middle ——————

Bottom ——————

marked with many horizontal and vertical lines, but it also contains large, flat, smooth areas. Shadows *on the middle of the face* make the snow there appear to be a bright blue. *At the bottom of the glacier,* the ice cliff meets the ocean. There the ice seems to be as deep blue as the ocean is. Often large chunks of ice break off the glacier. They crash *down* into the water, creating a great spray.

Notice, too, that the writer introduces the subject in the topic sentence and then presents details that create a vivid picture of the glacier.

Exercise 1 Prewriting: Order of Details The following paragraph describes a house. On your paper, list the topic of the description and the words and phrases that emphasize the order in which details are arranged.

When I approached the front of the old one-story house, I was thrilled that it looked the same as it did when I was a young child. On its left side, worn concrete steps led up to the screened-in porch that was filled with plants. The shingles across the front of the house were still pale yellow and still in good condition. In the middle of the front, three large windows looked out at the cedar bird-feeder. To the right was the front door. Still painted apple red, it was the brightest spot of the whole house. Farther right, the shiny silver oil tank was surrounded by the same kind of tall, pale green weeds that used to cut my hands when I had to pull them out.

Exercise 2 Prewriting: Sensory Details On your paper, list three vivid sensory details for each of the following places.

370

SAMPLE   A construction site

ANSWER   Sight of mounds of dirt and piles of lumber
Roaring noise of bulldozers
The feel of the ground shaking when the
bulldozers move

1. A city park
2. A waiting room in a doctor's office
3. A desert
4. An old house
5. A theater before a film starts
6. A post office

Assignment 1   Prewriting   *Step 1:* List sensory details that describe a busy street in your community, either during the day or at night. *Step 2:* Select the details that will give your reader a clear impression of the street. Arrange them in spatial order as if you were walking down the street.

Assignment 2   Writing/Revising   *Step 1:* Using the details from Assignment 1, write a paragraph that describes the busy street. Present the details in the order in which they appear on your list. *Step 2:* Revise the paragraph. Pay special attention to the order of the details and to the words that emphasize the order of the details.

Assignment Checklist

Check your writing assignments for the following points:

✔ 1. Did you use all of your senses to observe the scene?
✔ 2. Did you include details that would capture the uniqueness of the scene?
✔ 3. Did you arrange the details in spatial order?
✔ 4. Did you use words and phrases to emphasize the order of the details?
✔ 5. Did you proofread your description for correct grammar, usage, spelling, and punctuation?

371

Exercise 2 *(pages 370–371)*

Answers may vary. Samples:

1. A city park
The scratchy feel of splintery wooden benches
Shouts and screams of small children playing tag
Sight of gray, bushy-tailed squirrels scampering up and down trees

2. A waiting room in a doctor's office
Cries and whines of small children
Medicinal smell of alcohol and disinfectants
Piles of magazines on tables

3. A desert
The feel of the burning sand
The sight of the limitless expanse of sand in every direction
The almost painful glare of the sun lighting up the sand

4. An old house
The creaking sound of the rickety staircase
The musty smell of the attic
The smooth feel of the bannister worn down with time

5. A theater before a film starts
The buttery smell of popcorn
The low conversation
The sight of the blank, whitish screen

6. A post office
The clickety-clack of postage machines
Lines of people carrying packages and envelopes
The sight of huge, colorful posters showing the newest stamps for collectors

13.4 Describing People

When you write a description of a person, your purpose is to make your readers feel as though they have met that person. The following strategies will help you to describe a person effectively.

Strategies

1. *Introduce in your topic sentence the person whom you will describe.* In this sentence you may also explain where the person is or what the person is doing. Alternatively, you may present your general impression of that person. For example, you might write that someone seems cheerful, confident, or strong, or you may mention the most striking feature of the person.

2. *Choose the best details.* When you are preparing to write, you will list many details about a person. When you write your description, however, you should include only the details that capture the uniqueness of that person. Using details from several senses will help you to reveal a person's uniqueness. For example, you can describe the sound of the person's voice, the texture of the hair or skin, or the smell of soap or perfume.

3. *Include details that describe your subject's motions.* Movements are important because they can reveal how a person feels. Tell how the person stands, sits, walks, moves hands and head, and uses facial expressions.

4. *Arrange the details in a logical order.* You should arrange the details so that you create a sharp impression of your subject. First, group together related details. Then put the groups in a logical order.

372

For example, you can use spatial order, going from head to foot or from foot to head. Alternatively, you can present the person's most noticeable or unusual features first. For instance, if your subject is unusually large, you can begin by describing the person's size.

5. *Use specific words.* For example, instead of describing a person's eyes as *brown,* describe them as *hazel* or *chestnut.*

In the following description, the writer introduces the subject in the topic sentence and also explains where the subject is.

Model

John Cleaver enters his brilliantly lit barn. He pauses momentarily as his pupils contract and then strolls into a maze of sturdy wire enclosures. Beads of perspiration slowly work their way out on his forehead and start journeying down the wrinkles in his aged face. His clean white coveralls begin to stick to his dampened skin. The heat makes his face redder and shinier than usual, setting off his white hair and yellowish eyes.

Franklin Jelsma, Ballard High School
Louisville, Kentucky

Notice that the writer presents the details in a logical order, the order in which the light and the heat produce them. Notice, too, that the writer creates a vivid description of the man's appearance and actions with specific nouns such as *beads* and *coveralls,* strong verbs such as *contract* and *strolls,* and precise modifiers such as *sturdy* and *dampened.*

Exercise 1 Prewriting: Sensory Details For each person who is listed below, write at least three sensory details that help to describe that person. Use specific words.

Exercise 1 *(pages 373–374)*

See page 374 for sample answers.

373

Exercise 1 *(pages 373–374)*

Answers may vary. Samples:

1. Carries a gray cloth bag slung over shoulder
   Rides bicycle slowly, one hand on handlebars
   Tosses papers onto porches from street

2. Wears blue smock and name-plate pin
   Fingers fly over cash register buttons
   Looks expertly at each item

3. Smiles and winks a lot
   Wears fashionable clothes
   Leans toward person being interviewed

4. Wears white lab coat over street clothes
   Efficient but friendly manner
   Listens carefully to patient

5. Wears leotard and tights
   Holds head erect
   Stretches arms in arc over head

6. Wears very broad shoulder pads
   Crouches alertly at the line
   Has hard, muscular arms and legs

Exercise 2 *(page 374)*

Answers may vary. Sample:

9, 10; 4, 3, 1, 8; 6, 7, 2; 5

Exercise 3 *(page 374)*

See page 375 for a sample answer.

SAMPLE	A bus driver
ANSWER	Wears blue-gray uniform
	Grips wheel firmly
	Peers intently at traffic

1. A newspaper delivery person
2. A cashier at a grocery store
3. A talk-show host
4. A doctor
5. A dancer
6. A football player

Exercise 2   Prewriting: Logical Order   Read the following list of details that describe a person named Joan. On your paper, write the numbers of the details in an order that would be logical. Group together details that are related.

1. Small nose; glasses keep slipping down
2. Large hands with short nails
3. Rosy complexion
4. Mahogany-colored hair; wavy, not curly except when it's humid
5. As a veterinarian, usually wears white jacket and slacks
6. Five and a half feet tall
7. Muscular, compact body
8. One eyelid droops slightly when tired
9. Thirty-five-year-old woman
10. Attitude—pleasant but businesslike

Exercise 3 Writing/Revising: Describing a Person
Using the list that you organized for Exercise 2, write a description of Joan. Be sure to introduce her in the topic sentence. Write clear and interesting sentences, changing the wording of the details as needed.

Assignment 1   Prewriting   *Step 1:* Choose one of the following topics. *Step 2:* On your paper, list the sensory details that describe the person at the moment that is identified in the topic. Include the movements and sounds that reveal

374

the way that the person feels. *Step 3:* Place check marks before the five details that best show the uniqueness of the person. *Step 4:* Arrange the details in a logical order.

1. A person riding a bus, a train, or an airplane
2. A person listening to a concert
3. A person returning home from work

Assignment 2 Writing/Revising *Step 1:* Using the details that you arranged in Assignment 1, write a paragraph that describes the person. Make your readers feel that they have seen the person. *Step 2:* Revise your paragraph, making sure that you have used specific words.

Assignment Checklist

Check your writing assignments for the following points:

✔ 1. Did you introduce your subject in a topic sentence?
✔ 2. Did you use several senses to observe the person?
✔ 3. Did you include vivid details that reveal the person's uniqueness?
✔ 4. Did you arrange the details in a logical order?
✔ 5. Did you describe physical features and movements accurately?
✔ 6. Did you proofread your description for correct grammar, usage, spelling, and punctuation?

Exercise 3 *(page 374)*

Answers may vary. Sample:

My friend Joan is a thirty-five-year-old woman with a pleasant but businesslike attitude. She has mahogany-colored hair that is wavy but curls in humid weather. Her rosy complexion makes her look healthy and fresh, although the glasses that keep slipping off her small nose and a slightly drooping eyelid when she's tired give her a look of distraction sometimes. She is five and half feet tall, with a muscular, compact body and strong hands with short nails. For her job as a veterinarian, she usually wears a white jacket and slacks.

375

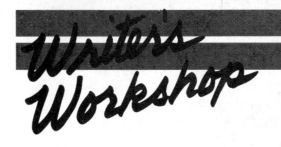

Quest for Nature: Describing a Place

Situation: The producer of the television series *Quest for Nature* has decided to devote one program to the animals of the redwood forests in northern California. As a writer for the series, you have been asked to write a descriptive paragraph to be read when photographs of the forests are shown at the beginning of the program. In your paragraph you will describe a typical spot in a redwood forest. In preparation for writing the paragraph, you have gathered facts about the forests. You have also acquired one of the photographs that will be shown. As you plan and write your description, keep in mind the following information.

Writer: you as a staff writer for *Quest for Nature*

Audience: viewers of *Quest for Nature*

Topic: a redwood forest in northern California

Purpose: to describe a typical spot in a redwood forest

Directions: To write your description, follow these steps.

Step 1. Study the photograph on the facing page and the fact sheet on page 378.

Step 2. Write a topic sentence that identifies the place and presents your general impression of it.

Step 3. Choose at least five details from the fact sheet and from the photograph. Select the details that best capture the uniqueness of the place. Choose details that appeal to at least three senses. Then, on your paper, list those details in spatial order, moving from the ground to the sky.

(Continue on page 378.)

376

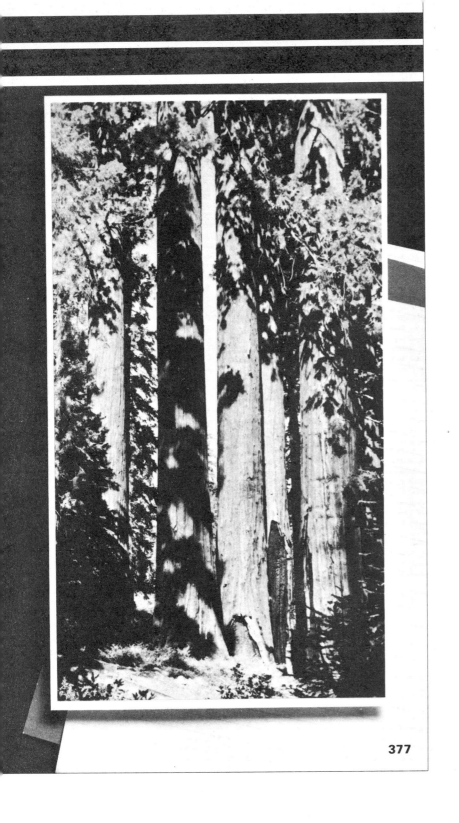

377

Step 4. Using vivid words, describe the spot in a redwood forest. Present the details in the order in which they appear on your list and use words and phrases that emphasize the spatial order.

Step 5. Review your paragraph. Check it for errors, and revise it if necessary.

Fact Sheet: A Redwood Forest

— Tall redwood trees
— Many branches at tops of trees; few on lower parts
— Soft, lime-green moss and ferns on ground
— Smell of trees in the cool, moist air
— Rough, reddish-brown bark on trees
— Sounds of brooks and streams in area
— Sticks and rocks on ground
— Warm sunlight coming through space between trees
— Sound of small animals on the ground
— Smell of fresh air

378

Unit Assignments

Assignment 1   Choose a room that is often noisy. For example, you might choose a typing room, a laundry room, or a cafeteria. Observe it carefully, using several senses, and write a paragraph describing it. Use specific nouns, strong verbs, and vivid modifiers in your description.

Assignment 2   Choose a large building. It might be your city hall, an office building, or your school. Observe as many sensory details about the building as you can. Then include the most effective details in a paragraph that describes the building.

Assignment 3   Recall the details about the way one scene in your community looks, sounds, and feels during a holiday or a celebration. For example, you might describe a park on the Fourth of July or how the school looks on graduation day. Use details from at least three senses to write a paragraph that describes the scene.

Assignment 4   Write a description of someone whom you see often. Mention a striking characteristic or feature. Include details from several senses, and use specific nouns, strong verbs, and vivid modifiers.

Assignment 5   Write a paragraph that describes one of your favorite characters from a film or a television program. Include details that contribute to the character's individuality: size, age, facial features, sound of voice, gestures, and so forth.

Revising Your Assignments

For help in revising a description, consult the Checklist for Revision on the last page of this book.

A.

1. a
2. c
3. b
4. d
5. a

(Continue on the next page.)

Unit Tests

Test 1

A. Number your paper from 1 to 5. Read the following paragraph. Next to each number on your paper, write the letter of the item that correctly answers the question.

(1) When I first walked in the door of the shop, it seemed to be an ordinary, small plant store. (2) In the front of the store, spider plants and ferns hung from hooks, and fragrant violets and geraniums filled the tops of several tables. (3) Then I looked farther back in the store. (4) Mixed with the cut flowers in the refrigerated glass case were a carton of milk, half a loaf of bread, and a stick of butter. (5) Near the humming refrigerator was a tattered green armchair with a gray cat perched silently on one arm. (6) In the back of the store, behind a beaded curtain, was a small cot with a neatly folded brown blanket. (7) Clearly, the shop was also a home for its owner. (8) The mixture of plants and simple belongings made the store the warmest and friendliest one that I have ever entered.

1. From which place does the person view the shop?
   a. Inside the front door c. By the refrigerated case
   b. The chair d. The back of the store

2. Which sentence contains a detail that appeals to the sense of hearing?
   a. Sentence 1 c. Sentence 5
   b. Sentence 2 d. Sentence 7

3. In Sentence 5, which word modifies *armchair*?
   a. Humming c. Gray
   b. Tattered d. Silently

4. In what order are the details of sight presented?
   a. Back to front c. Left to right
   b. Top to bottom d. Front to back

5. Which sentence contains a word that emphasizes the order of details of sight?
   a. Sentence 2 c. Sentence 7
   b. Sentence 4 d. Sentence 8

380

B. Number your paper from 6 to 10. Read the following paragraph. Next to each number on your paper, write the letter of the item that correctly completes the sentence. You will use all but three of the items.

(1) At daybreak Billy Buck emerged from the bunkhouse and stood for a moment on the porch looking up at the sky. (2) He was a broad, bandy-legged little man with a walrus mustache, with square hands, puffed and muscled on the palms. (3) His eyes were a contemplative, watery gray, and the hair that protruded from under his Stetson hat was spiky and weathered. (4) Billy was still stuffing his shirt into his blue jeans as he stood on the porch. (5) He unbuckled his belt and tightened it again. (6) The belt showed, by the worn shiny places opposite each hole, the gradual increase of Billy's middle over a period of years.

John Steinbeck, "The Gift"

a. was   c. concluding   e. hair   g. topic
b. size   d. hat   f. emerged   h. movements

6. The subject of a description is introduced in the __?__ sentence.
7. The paragraph describes not only Billy's appearance and clothing but also his __?__.
8. The adjective *spiky* in Sentence 3 describes Billy's __?__.
9. In the paragraph __?__ is a strong verb.
10. The details about Billy's belt in Sentence 6 tell the reader about Billy's __?__.

Test 2

Choose one of the Unit Assignments. Write the assignment as directed and hand it in to your teacher.

Test 1 *(pages 380–381),* continued

B.
6. g
7. h
8. e
9. f
10. b

Test 2 *(page 381)*

Answers will vary.

Unit 14

Objectives

After studying this unit, students should be able to do the following:

- Plan a written narrative, choosing the topic, characters, setting, and actions.

- Write a narrative, using an effective beginning, dialogue, actions in chronological order, and an effective ending.

Teaching Suggestions

See "Classroom Insights" for Unit 14 in the front of this Teacher's Edition.

Program Resources

Resource Book, Second Course:
Bonus Activities, Unit 14
Composition Checklist, Unit 14
Practice Book, Second Course, Unit 14
Tests, Second Course, Unit 14
Composition Workshops, Second Course, Unit 14

Related Resources

The American Heritage Dictionary of the English Language
Roget's II: The New Thesaurus

Narrating

Unit Preview

Narrating is another word for storytelling. A story can be about a true or fictional happening. It can have one paragraph, or it can have many paragraphs. The story that follows shows that even a brief incident can be the topic of a narrative.

> At our Friday afternoon meet in New Bern, I stepped up to the starting line in the two-mile, wanting to win very badly. The gun sounded, and my two opponents jumped off to a fast start. One dropped out after about a half mile, the quick pace having taken its toll. The other maintained a twenty-five-yard lead on me through the sixth lap and looked unbeatable. His coach, scenting victory, began shouting, "School record, go for it!" I began digging down a little harder, in an attempt to make the finish look respectable. Amazingly, the runner dropped back slightly, and the spectators started to cheer. On the next-to-the-last turn, I swept past him, fearing that he would catch me in the homestretch. I crossed the line first, scared to look back, to a storm of cheering.
>
> *(Adapted)*
> *Frederick Klutey, Kinston High School*
> *Kinston, North Carolina*

Like all narratives, this story tells what happened. It tells the actions in chronological order, the order in which they happen. The narrative has a definite beginning and a definite ending as well as a high point, where the suspense or excitement is greatest. Early in the narrative, the writer gives the setting—the time and place of the actions. The writer also introduces you to the characters who take part in the story.

382

For Analysis On your paper, answer the following questions about the brief narrative that you just read.

1. Who are the characters in the narrative?
2. What is the setting of the story?
3. What is the high point of the story?
4. Is the ending a good one? Why or why not?

In reading and reviewing one brief story, you have learned some of the important parts of any narrative. In this unit you will learn how to plan and to write your own narratives. As you do so, you will follow the three steps of the writing process: prewriting, writing, and revising.

14.1 Planning Your Narrative

Careful planning leads to a well-written story. After choosing a topic for your story, you should develop a plan that includes notes on who the characters are, where the story takes place, and what happens.

Choosing a Topic

Choosing a suitable topic, or story idea, is the first step in planning a narrative. You may decide to tell a story about something that happened to you or to someone whom you know. In either case, you will write about the real people who participated in the actions of the story.

On the other hand, you may decide to write a fictional narrative, for which you will make up the actions, the characters, or both. However, a fictional narrative does not have to come entirely from your imagination. It may come from one of your experiences, which you can narrate as fiction by changing the details. It could also come from the experiences of other people. For example, if you read a news story about someone who has invented a sharkproof suit for skin diving, you may imagine being inside such a suit and use your ideas as the basis of a fictional narrative.

383

Whether you are writing a true story or a fictional story, you must build it around a specific problem or situation. Otherwise, your narrative will wander aimlessly. For example, in the narrative about a track-meet incident *(page 382)*, the situation is the two-mile race. Details of the other events at the track meet are not included.

Listing the Characters

After you have chosen a topic, the next step is to make a list of the important characters in your story. If you write a story about something that happened to you, you will be one of the characters, along with the other people who were part of that experience. If you write a fictional story, the characters will come from your imagination, but you may model them on people whom you know.

Deciding on the Setting

The **setting** is the time and the place of the story. If it is important to the story, the time should include not only the time of day but the season and perhaps even the year. For example, in a story about a cross-country flight, it would be important to know that the story takes place before the invention of jet-propelled airplanes.

Planning the Actions

A good story answers the question "What happened?" In a one-paragraph story, you should write about a series of connected actions that occur within a few hours or on the same day. In a longer story, you should plan to place each group of related actions in a paragraph of its own.

Every story that you write—whether it has one paragraph or many paragraphs—must have a beginning, a middle, and an ending.

384

1. *The Beginning.* At the beginning of your story, you must introduce the characters and the setting. You should also present the situation or problem that must be settled by the end of the story.
2. *The Middle.* In the middle of your story, you must narrate the actions that include the **high point**—the action that creates the most excitement or suspense.
3. *The Ending.* At the end of your story, you must make clear how the situation or problem is settled. The ending should be definite. It should tell your reader how the action concludes and what happens to the characters.

In your prewriting notes, list the actions that you plan to include in all three parts of your story. List the actions in **chronological order,** the order in which they happen.

The prewriting notes that follow show how one story might have been planned.

BEGINNING

Situation: Catching the largest fish in Saffron Lake

Characters: Myself; my mother; a girl; and the fish, Largemouth

Setting: Place—my home and Saffron Lake. Time—afternoon

Actions: (1) At home I tell Mom I'm leaving, and she tells me to be back by 5:30. (2) I set off for Saffron Lake with my fishing gear. (3) Along the way, I think about Largemouth, the huge fish of my dreams, and my wish to catch him.

MIDDLE

Actions: (1) I arrive at the lake, snap my Lucky 13 lure onto my line, and make a cast. (2) I suddenly hook the fish of my dreams. (3) I battle with the fish for a long time, and he finally explodes into midair. (4) I reel him close to shore, grab him, and heave him onto the sand.

High point: As I stare at Largemouth, who is gasping for air, I suddenly become undecided about keeping him.

385

Exercise 1 *(pages 386–387)*

Answers may vary. Samples:

1. The narrator has reluctantly joined the girls' track team and is having difficulty keeping up with the others. Will she give up, or will she make it through the season? The setting is a school.

2. Smith and the narrator are trying to photograph a herd of baboons but have not been able to get close enough. The setting is a plateau in East Africa.

ENDING

Actions: (1) I remove the Lucky 13 from Largemouth's jaw and return him to the lake. (2) As I walk away, Largemouth makes a gesture of thanks. (3) I head home.
Conclusion: When a girl asks me about my luck at fishing, I decide to keep what happened a secret.

The prewriting notes for the beginning of the story list the situation, the characters, and the setting. In this instance, the characters include a fish that the writer has named Largemouth. The notes also list the actions that the writer plans to narrate at the beginning. In the notes for the middle of the story, the writer lists the actions in chronological order and identifies the high point of the story. The notes for the ending of the story list the actions that occur after the high point and show how the writer plans to bring the story to a conclusion.

Exercise 1 Prewriting: Narrative Situations For each of the following beginnings, write a sentence in which you explain the situation or problem that must be settled before the end of the narrative. In a second sentence, identify the setting of the story.

1. Last spring our school started a girls' track team. I would not have gone out for track if my friend Allison had not made me promise to go with her. At the first practice, on a Friday afternoon, Coach Tillman had us run endless laps around the field. When I felt that I could not run even one more step, the coach had us run up the hill next to the field. Allison seemed to run with ease, but my legs hurt and I could hardly breathe. I wondered how long the track season would last.

2. In East Africa, Smith and I were anxious to take motion pictures of a herd of baboons. We had tried and tried, with no success whatever, though we saw many of these creatures. Our camp was some miles from a little ravine through which a stream ran. Beyond the ravine was a plateau leading back

386

to thick woods. The baboons, scores of them, came out of these woods with their young to play on the plateau and to drink from the stream. Often Smith and I watched them and tried to photograph them, but we could never get close enough. The baboons enjoyed what we were doing. They thought it was a game of some sort.

Theodore J. Waldeck, *On Safari*

Exercise 2 Prewriting: Chronological Order   In the following prewriting notes, the actions are not listed in chronological order. On your paper, write the actions (with their original numbers) in the order in which they occur.

1. When we first entered the basement, everything seemed fine.
2. She handed each storage item to Dad, and he handed it to my sister, Michelle, who handed it to me—and I carried it to the stairs.
3. Three hours later heavy rain continued to fall.
4. Mom said that we could save our belongings if we worked quickly.
5. One night last winter, a rainstorm began just as my family sat down to dinner.
6. Worried about the things in our storage room, we went downstairs to check the basement.
7. In less than fifteen minutes, we had saved everything in the storage room.
8. At ten o'clock, when we turned on the radio for news of the weather, we heard an announcement about flooded basements in our area.
9. She kicked off her shoes and waded into the storage room.
10. When Dad opened the door to the storage room, however, we saw two inches of water on the floor.

Exercise 3 Prewriting: Parts of a Story   Divide your paper into three columns headed *Beginning, Middle,* and *Ending.* Using the chronological list that you wrote for Exer-

387

Exercise 2 *(page 387)*

5. One night last winter, a rainstorm began just as my family sat down to dinner.
3. Three hours later heavy rain continued to fall.
8. At ten o'clock, when we turned on the radio for news of the weather, we heard an announcement about flooded basements in our area.
6. Worried about the things in our storage room, we went downstairs to check the basement.
1. When we first entered the basement, everything seemed fine.
10. When Dad opened the door to the storage room, however, we saw two inches of water on the floor.
4. Mom said that we could save our belongings if we worked quickly.
9. She kicked off her shoes and waded into the storage room.
2. She handed each storage item to Dad, and he handed it to my sister, Michelle, who handed it to me—and I carried it to the stairs.
7. In less than fifteen minutes, we had saved everything in the storage room.

Exercise 3 *(pages 387–388)*

See page 388 for a sample answer.

Exercise 3 *(pages 387–388)*

Answers may vary. Sample:

Beginning

—Rainstorm at dinnertime
—Rain still falling after three hours
—Radio news about flooded basements

Middle

—Checked basement
—Looked fine at first
—Two inches of water on floor of storage room

Ending

—Mom said that we could save belongings
—She waded into storage room
—Mom, Dad, Michelle, and I handed down items from person to person
—Cleared storage room in less than fifteen minutes

cise 2, write each action in the column in which you think it belongs. In listing the actions, you do not need to use complete sentences.

Assignment 1 Prewriting On your paper, list five situations or events in your life that you think would be suitable topics for a narrative.

Assignment 2 Prewriting Choose two of the topics that you listed for Assignment 1. For each topic prepare prewriting notes like those on pages 385 and 386.

Assignment 3 Prewriting On your paper, list three story ideas for a fictional narrative. You may base your topic on happenings that come from your own experience or from something that you have heard or read about.

Assignment 4 Prewriting Prepare prewriting notes for one of the story ideas that you listed in Assignment 3. Be sure to divide your notes into *Beginning, Middle,* and *Ending.*

Continuing Assignment Prewriting *Step 1:* Choose a topic for which you prepared prewriting notes in either Assignment 2 or Assignment 4. Choose the topic in which you are most interested. *Step 2:* Review your prewriting notes for the selected topic, making any additions or changes that you think will help to improve your story. Save your paper.

Assignment Checklist

Check your assignments for the following points:

  ✔ 1. Did you choose a topic that is suitable for a narrative— one that has a beginning, a middle, and an ending?

  ✔ 2. Did you identify the situation or problem that must be settled before the end of the story?

388

✔ 3. Did you include only those characters who are involved in the actions of your story?

✔ 4. Did you make clear what the setting is?

✔ 5. Did you list the actions in chronological order?

✔ 6. Did you include a high point in the middle section of the story?

14.2 Writing Your Narrative

When possible, it is a good idea to write your story in one sitting—from the first word to the last. In that way, you can concentrate on the story and narrate its actions effectively. With the whole story in front of you, you can then revise and polish it into a finished narrative.

14.2a Writing the Beginning

The following suggestions will help you to write a story beginning that will make your readers want to read the rest of your story.

Strategies

1. *Begin your story in an interesting way.* Try to capture the attention of your readers at once. For example, you can begin your story with a question, an action-filled sentence, or a direct quotation.

   WEAK   When Robin and Martina saw the poster announcing the Spring Kite Competition at Great Field, they decided to enter it.

   BETTER   "Robin, let's try it," exclaimed Martina when the two girls saw the poster announcing the Spring Kite Competition at Great Field.

389

2. *Introduce the characters.* Mention the main characters and, as briefly as possible, tell who they are and how they are involved in your story.

> WEAK   This is a story about the time last summer when my family had a picnic.
>
> BETTER   When my parents, my grandmother, my brother Jon, and I arrived at Roosevelt Park for our annual May picnic, we scarcely noticed the Great Dane that eyed us as we spread the cloth on the grass.

3. *Briefly give the setting of the story.* Tell where and when the actions of your story occur. Provide any details that will help your reader to understand what happens, but do not give more information than is needed. For example, in the second example sentence in Strategy 2, the writer briefly gives the setting: Roosevelt Park in May. If time were important in the actions that follow, the writer could add a sentence like this: "It was late afternoon, and we expected to stay until sunset."

4. *Quickly identify the situation or problem.* Get to the point of the story as quickly as possible by clearly identifying the situation or the problem that must be settled before the end of the story.

In the second example in Strategy 2, the writer hints at the situation by mentioning the dog. Readers will expect the role of the Great Dane to be developed in the sentences that follow.

The following paragraphs begin the narrative that is outlined in the prewriting notes on pages 385 and 386. As you read it, notice how the writer follows the strategies for writing a good story beginning.

390

"Mom, I'm leaving," I called, as I picked up my fishing gear and headed for the door. "I'll be home around six."

"You'll be home at exactly five-thirty," Mom replied, with more than a hint of steel in her voice.

I have been known to miss a meal because of my fishing excursions. Not wanting to argue the point, I mumbled a hurried "Okay" and quickly closed the door behind me. It was early afternoon, and I was headed for Saffron Lake. Hidden in the depths of a pine forest, Saffron offers some of the best fishing in the country. The one fish it had not offered was Largemouth, an old bass, mean and huge, that swam through my dreams. He was the largest bass in the lake, and no one had ever hooked him. What chance did I have of catching him?

David Liebergall, Suffern High School
Suffern, New York

Exercise 1 *(pages 391–392)*

See page 392 for the answers.

The writer arouses the reader's interest by beginning the story with two brief paragraphs that present a conversation between the narrator—the "I" of the story—and his mother. In the third paragraph, the writer introduces another main character: Largemouth, the huge fish that no one has ever caught. The writer also describes the setting. The time is early afternoon, and the narrator is walking toward a lake hidden in a pine forest. Finally, the situation—the narrator's wish to catch the fish of his dreams—is identified.

Exercise 1   Prewriting: Story Beginnings   Decide which story beginning in each of the following numbered pairs is more interesting. After each number on your paper, write the letter of the better story beginning.

1. a.   When Mrs. Bartz started out, she did not realize that it would be an unusual day. She walked along her regular

391

Exercise 1 *(pages 391–392)*

1. a
2. a

Exercise 2 *(pages 392–394)*

Sample answer:

Rosa Lopez and her friend Amy Wallace enjoyed the summer at Cannon Beach, Oregon, not only because they could spend the long, hot days sunning and swimming, but also because they could watch the annual sand-sculpture contest.

"I wonder what kinds of things people are going to make this year," Amy said to Rosa as they walked past the registration line for the contest.

"They could be anything," Rosa said, her eyes sparkling. "Do you remember the Eiffel Tower last year? I thought that was the best one."

"I liked Rick Haley's statue of Bugs Bunny," said Amy.

"I'd like to see a sculpture of a pair of worn sneakers—like these." Rosa pointed to her own.

Amy stopped walking and stared at Rosa for a few seconds. "Why don't we enter and see if we can do it?" she asked finally.

"You're kidding!" Rosa looked at Amy with surprise. "We've never actually made any sculptures before. We've only watched. And there'll be over fifty other contestants to compete against. We won't have a chance."

(Continue on the next page.)

route to work. As usual, she greeted the grocer and the florist along her way. She arrived on time and opened the hardware store without any problems. Then her first customer—a short, white-haired man—arrived, and the day changed.

b.   Mrs. Bartz had a very unusual day, but it did not start out that way. It started out as usual, She did all of her usual morning activities. It was her first customer at the hardware store that made the day very unusual. Mrs. Bartz was surprised by what happened.

2. a.   Twenty-five dollars! That was the amount that I needed to buy a pair of secondhand cross-country skis at the ski exchange. To me, that amount was a fortune. Because I could not get a part-time job, I had no way of earning money. Suddenly, I thought of a way to earn those skis.

b.   I wanted very much to buy a pair of secondhand cross-country skis at the ski exchange. I had tried to get a part-time job to earn the money, but I had not been successful. Therefore, I had to find another solution. Suddenly, I thought of a way in which I could earn the skis that I wanted so much.

Exercise 2   Writing: Story Beginnings   Two sets of prewriting notes follow. Each is a plan for an entire narrative. You will develop one set of notes into a practice narrative that you will write as you study this section. Choose the story idea that you prefer, and write a beginning for it. The beginning should interest the reader, identify the situation, introduce the characters, and set the scene. Save your paper.

1. BEGINNING

Situation: Two girls enter a sand-sculpture contest, their first competition, along with fifty other contestants.
Characters: Rosa Lopez, fourteen, and her friend Amy Wallace.
Setting: Place—Cannon Beach, Oregon. Time—summer
Action: The girls decide to enter the contest.

392

MIDDLE

Actions: (1) Rosa and Amy arrive at the beach early in the morning with pails, shovels, rakes, and rulers. (2) The contest begins as the tide starts to go out, and each group of contestants is assigned a twenty-foot square of beach. (3) Rosa and Amy begin digging and piling sand as they had planned: in the shape of a pair of worn-out sneakers. (4) Onlookers stand behind a rope fence watching and making comments as the sculptures take shape. (5) At the halfway mark, Rosa and Amy stand up and, for the first time, see what the other contestants have made: recognizable cartoon characters, bigger-than-life automobiles, detailed buildings and bridges.

High point: Discouraged, Amy tells Rosa that they may as well pack up their gear and go home.

ENDING

Actions: (1) Rosa convinces Amy that they should complete their sculpture. (2) Half an hour later, as the winners are announced, the second prize for first-time competitors is awarded to Rosa and Amy.

Conclusion: Rosa and Amy sit holding their trophy as the tide comes in and washes away their sand sneakers.

2. BEGINNING

Situation: While sailing in familiar waters, two boys come upon a mysterious old ship.

Characters: Tom Farrell, fourteen, and his older cousin Stephen

Setting: Place—the waters off Beaufort, South Carolina. Time—a day in July

Action: Tom and Stephen set sail, as they often do, in a small boat owned by Tom's father.

MIDDLE

Actions: (1) Tom spies a large wooden sailing ship, anchored not far from shore, that he has never seen before. (2) The

393

Exercise 2 *(pages 392–394),* continued

"We can try, can't we?" Amy started to grin. "Come on," she said, "let's sign up."

"Well . . . " Rosa hesitated.

"You know you've always wanted to enter," Amy prodded.

"You're right. Let's go." The girls took their place in the registration line.

boys sail close to the ship, which is obviously very old and has no modern equipment. (3) Tom calls, but no one answers. (4) Their curiosity aroused, the boys secure a line to the ship and board it. (5) To the boys, the ship looks abandoned, as though it has been untouched since the Revolutionary War, which in part was fought in Beaufort.

High point: The boys suddenly hear the sounds of creaking wood and of the rigging moving in the breeze, and from below comes what could be the sound of a cabin door opening.

ENDING

Actions: (1) The boys leave to get Tom's father. (2) When they return, there is no sign of the ship.

Conclusion: The boys consult a retired sea captain, but he can offer no explanation.

14.2b Using Dialogue in Your Story

When you narrate a story, you tell not only what the characters do but also what they say. You can tell what a character says in one of two ways: (1) You can give the exact words spoken by the characters. (2) You can summarize, or tell in your own words, what the character says.

EXACT WORDS

"Our phone is dead," Beth announced as she put down the receiver. "How can we call the doctor?"

"Don't worry," her mother replied. "I'll drive toward town until I find a phone."

SUMMARY

As she put down the receiver, Beth announced that the phone was dead. She asked how they could call the doctor. Her mother said that she would drive toward town until she found a phone.

394

When you use the exact words that your characters say, you are using **dialogue**. The following guidelines explain when and how to write dialogue.

Strategies

1. *Use dialogue to make your characters come alive.* For example, instead of telling your readers that a character is worried about doing something, use the character's words to make clear that worry.

> "That diving board seems very high," Jo said. "I'm not sure that I want to climb all the way up there—and then jump off."

2. *Use explanatory details* to tell who is speaking and *how* he or she is speaking. In the following passage, the explanatory details are printed in italic type.

> "See what I found," *John said with a wide grin on his face.* "I discovered this old camera at a rummage sale," *he boasted.*

3. *Use dialogue to tell some of the actions of your story.* By using dialogue, you can narrate part of your story in a way that is likely to interest your reader. The following dialogue, for example, presents some of the actions of a story about friends who get lost in a city.

> "These stores don't look familiar to me," Sandy said uncertainly. "Let's walk for two more blocks and then ask for directions."
> "This has got to be the right way," claimed Hank, who started to walk more briskly.

There are three basic rules for punctuating and paragraphing dialogue in a story.

Rule Put the spoken words in quotation marks.

Rule Start each new sentence with a capital letter.

395

Exercise 3 *(page 396)*

Answers may vary. Sample:

One day the wind challenged the sun to a contest that would prove which one was stronger. "Do you see that man walking along the road beneath us?" asked the wind. "Whoever can make him take off his coat will be the winner."

"I accept your challenge," replied the sun quietly. "Why don't you go first?"

The wind blasted the man with cold, hard gusts as the sun watched with some amusement. "The man is holding his coat closed more tightly," teased the sun gently.

The wind kept huffing angrily but had no success. "Oh, I give up," sighed the wind at last. "Let's see if you can do any better."

"I would be happy to try." The sun began to shine, and the air grew quite hot.

"Hey," huffed the wind in surprise, "the man is loosening his coat. I don't believe this, but the man is actually taking off his coat and folding it over his arm!"

The sun chuckled and said, "I've won the contest, and I've also proved that gentleness is stronger than force."

Rule   Begin a new paragraph each time the speaker changes.

See pages 216–217 for more information on punctuating dialogue (direct quotations).

Exercise 3   Writing: Dialogue   The narrative that follows is a famous story. Rewrite it, using dialogue wherever it is appropriate. Include explanatory details and other information to make the story read smoothly and interestingly.

One day the wind challenged the sun to a contest that would prove which one was stronger. A man happened to be walking along a road beneath them. The wind said that the winner of the contest would be the one who could make the man take off his coat. The sun agreed and said that the wind should try first. The wind blasted the man with cold, hard gusts. The sun told the wind to notice that the man was holding his coat closed more tightly. The wind kept huffing angrily but had no success. Finally, the wind told the sun that he was giving up. He told the sun to take his turn. The sun said that he would be happy to try. The sun began to shine, and the air grew hot. The wind said in a surprised way that the man was loosening his coat. Then the wind said that he did not believe it but the man was actually taking off his coat and folding it over his arm. The sun said that he had won the contest and also had proved that gentleness is stronger than force.

14.2c   Telling the Actions in Chronological Order

Your prewriting notes should contain a chronological list of the actions that occur in your story. As you write your story, follow the list, making any changes that seem necessary. In a narrative of more than one paragraph, place each group of related actions in a paragraph of its own.

As you write your narrative, use transitional words, such as *first, soon, next,* and *later,* to link the actions within a par-

396

agraph or to link one paragraph to another. Think of transitional words as signposts that help your reader to follow the actions in your story.

The following model contains the middle paragraphs of the fishing story that is outlined in the prewriting notes on pages 385 and 386.

Model

Arriving at the lake, I opened the tackle box. The Lucky 13 lure that Dad had given me for my birthday was easy to spot as it shone in the sun. I snapped it on my line and cast the line far out into the motionless water. As I reeled it in, I thought of Largemouth. A tremendous splash interrupted my pleasant daydream. I scanned the water for my beloved Lucky 13. It was gone! I gave my line a powerful tug, and when the line began to move, I realized that I had hooked the fish of my dreams.

The battle began with the massive fish simply overpowering me. Despite my energetic efforts, the fish swam on. Then, after what seemed like hours, Largemouth began to tire. I was reeling in the line when it suddenly jerked upward and the fish slowly rose to the surface. He exploded into midair. I gasped at his size.

I reeled in faster, hoping that Largemouth would stay on my line. Perspiration poured down my forehead as I pulled with all my might. Finally, he was close to shore. I jumped into the lake, grabbed Largemouth by the gills, and heaved him onto the sand.

"He must weigh at least twelve pounds," I thought as I stood there, marveling at his size. "He could feed our family easily, and other families besides." I stared at the fish. Already Largemouth was gasping for air, his red gills protruding. I thought of the gallant battle that he had waged to survive. Did I really want to win that battle?

David Liebergall, Suffern High School
Suffern, New York

397

Exercise 4 *(page 398)*

Answers may vary. Samples:

1. At first
2. After a while
3. Finally
4. Then
5. As a result

Exercise 5 *(pages 398–399)*

Sample answer:

On the day of the contest, Amy and Rosa arrived at the beach early in the morning, carrying pails, shovels, rakes, and rulers. As the tide began to go out, each group of contestants was assigned a twenty-foot square of beach.

"Here we go," Amy said, starting to dig.

The two girls dug and piled sand and dug and piled sand, oblivious to the comments of the onlookers standing behind a rope fence. Gradually the worn-out sneakers began to take shape.

"Put a little more sand around this part," Amy directed. "It's coming out great."

"We're just about finished with the left sneaker. The other one shouldn't be too hard." Rosa wiped her forehead with her sandy hand.

(Continue on the next page.)

Notice that the writer tells the actions in the middle of the story in the order in which they happened, using the transitional words *then* and *finally* to emphasize chronological order. The writer begins with a paragraph in which the actions concern the start of the fishing and the hooking of Largemouth. In the next two paragraphs, the writer narrates the actions that concern the battle with Largemouth and, finally, landing him. In the final paragraph, the writer builds to a high point: the narrator's indecision about keeping Largemouth.

Exercise 4   Prewriting: Transitional Words   The following brief narrative lacks transitional words. Number your paper from 1 to 5. For each numbered blank in the paragraph, write a suitable transitional word or phrase from the following list. You will use all but one of the items.

then	after a while
as a result	at first
as soon as	finally

This year the sports banquet was held in the school cafeteria. __1__, the room was pleasant. __2__, however, it became hot and stuffy. The audience found it hard to sit through all of the long speeches. __3__, the basketball coach stood up to give the last speech. Members of the audience became restless when they saw a speech of several pages in the coach's hands, but the coach surprised them. "Friends," he said, "it is so late that I have decided to have my speech printed in the school paper instead of reading it to you." __4__ he smiled and sat down. __5__, the audience applauded loudly before leaving to find fresh air.

Exercise 5   Writing: The Middle of a Story   Take out the story beginning that you wrote for Exercise 2 on pages 392–394. Using the prewriting notes on those

398

pages, write the middle of your practice story, stopping with the high point. Include dialogue where it is appropriate. Save your paper.

14.2d Writing the Ending

To conclude your story, you must settle the problem or resolve the situation that you identified in the beginning. You must make clear to your reader what happens at the end to bring the story to a definite close. You may also tell your reader what happens to the characters afterward or how they feel about what has happened to them.

The following model contains the ending paragraphs of the fishing story that is outlined in the prewriting notes on pages 385 and 386.

Model

Suddenly I bent down, removed the Lucky 13 from Largemouth's jaw, and placed it in the tackle box. I took one more long look at this tremendous creature and then slowly slid him back into the lake. He was still for a moment and then slowly began swimming. I turned away, closed my tackle box, picked up my gear, and started walking away from the water, stunned at what I had done.

A sudden splash from the lake made me turn. Glancing back, I saw Largemouth somersault from the water, hang briefly in the air, and finally return to the lake. I accepted his gesture as one of thanks. "You're welcome," I said.

I smiled to myself and then headed home with my gear. As I reached my street, I met the girl who delivers our paper. Realizing that I had gone fishing, she asked me if I had caught anything.

I was going to tell her about the champion bass, but I suddenly changed my mind. "No, nothing was biting," I replied.

David Liebergall, Suffern High School
Suffern, New York

399

Exercise 5 *(pages 398–399),* continued

At the halfway mark, a whistle blew and one of the judges announced a ten-minute break. As Amy and Rosa stood up, they saw for the first time what the other contestants were making: figures of Mickey Mouse and Garfield, bigger-than-life automobiles, detailed castles and skyscrapers, and intricately constructed bridges.

"Oh no," Amy sighed heavily. "All this stuff looks so great. We're never going to win. We might as well pack up our gear now and leave."

Exercise 6 *(page 400)*

Sample answer:

"Wait a minute!" Rosa grabbed Amy's arm. "We can't leave now. I still think our idea is a good one. We've gone this far, and I say we should finish. Besides, I want to see what our sculpture's going to look like."

Amy looked at Rosa and saw the strong conviction in her friend's eyes. "O.K.," she said, "I got you into this, and we should finish together."

Half an hour later, after the finishing touches were put on the sculptures, the judges made their final decision. Amy and Rosa waited to hear which of the other sculptures had won.

"And the second prize for first-time competitors goes to Amy Wallace and Rosa Lopez for their pair of worn-out sneakers."

Stunned, the two girls walked up to accept their trophy. They shook the judges' hands and then turned to hug each other.

Later, as the girls sat on the sand holding their trophy, they watched the tide come in and wash away their sand sneakers.

"What should we make next year?" Amy asked with a smile.

In the ending of the story, the writer settles the situation that he introduces at the beginning. Having landed Largemouth, the narrator feels pity for the gasping creature and returns him to his home, the lake. The conclusion is interesting because it is not the ending expected of a fishing story.

Exercise 6   Writing: Story Endings   Take out the practice story that you wrote for Exercise 2 on pages 392–394 and for Exercise 5 on pages 398–399. Using the prewriting notes from Exercise 2, write the ending of your story. Be sure to bring the story to a definite close. Use dialogue where it is appropriate.

Assignment 1   Prewriting/Writing   *Step 1:* Think of an amusing or unusual incident that you or someone you know witnessed or took part in. Choose a brief incident that you can narrate in a single paragraph. *Step 2:* Plan your paragraph by listing the actions in chronological order. *Step 3:* Write a paragraph in which you narrate the incident. Use transitional words to make clear the order of the actions.

Assignment 2   Prewriting/Writing/Revising   Plan and write a narrative of at least four paragraphs about a time when you felt proud of something that you did. *Step 1:* Make notes about the characters, the setting, and the situation or problem. In your notes list the actions in chronological order and identify the high point. *Step 2:* Using your notes as a guide, write the narrative. Be sure to write an interesting beginning and a definite ending. *Step 3:* Revise your narrative.

Assignment 3   Prewriting/Writing/Revising   Using one of the topics listed below, plan and write a true or fictional narrative of four to twelve paragraphs. Then revise your narrative.

1. A family custom
2. An adventure

400

3. Learning something new
4. Finding (or losing) something
5. A funny experience

Continuing Assignment Writing/Revising   Use your notes from the Continuing Assignment on page 388 to write your narrative. It should be no shorter than four paragraphs and no longer than twelve. *Step 1:* Write a beginning that will interest your readers. Be sure to identify the situation or problem and to present the characters and the setting. In the middle of your story, tell the actions in chronological order, using transitional words. Include dialogue if possible. In the ending of your story, settle the situation or problem introduced in the beginning, and bring your story to a definite conclusion. *Step 2:* Using the Assignment Checklist, revise your narrative. *Step 3:* Make a finished copy, following the suggestions on pages 228–229.

Assignment Checklist

Check your assignments for the following points:

✓ 1. Did you identify the problem or situation and present the characters and the setting at the beginning of your story?
✓ 2. Did you write a beginning that is likely to interest your reader?
✓ 3. Did you present the actions of the story in chronological order?
✓ 4. Did you place each group of related actions in a separate paragraph?
✓ 5. Did you include dialogue where it is appropriate?
✓ 6. Did you include a high point in the action?
✓ 7. Did you settle the situation or problem by the end of the story?
✓ 8. Did you proofread your story for correct grammar, usage, spelling, and punctuation?

401

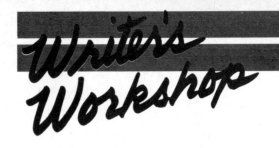

The Understudy: Narrating a Fictional Story

Situation: You are writing a fictional story for your school magazine. Because you like being in plays, you have chosen a story topic about an understudy in a school play. (An understudy is an actor who learns a role in order to be able to replace the regular performer if necessary.) You have prepared a set of prewriting notes, and you have worked on the story beginning. Now you need to write the middle of the story, which includes the high point. As you write, you will keep in mind the following information.

Writer: you as a writer for a school magazine
Audience: readers of the magazine
Topic: an understudy who has to play a leading role
Purpose: to narrate the middle section of a story

Directions: To write your narrative, follow these steps.

    Step 1. Read the prewriting notes, which appear on the facing page. Study the middle section carefully.
    Step 2. Narrate the first three actions in the middle section, using dialogue where it is appropriate. Try to create suspense as you lead to the high point.
    Step 3. As you narrate the high point and Action 5, include details that make clear how Connie feels. For example, she may be too excited and too dazzled by the lights to be able to see the audience clearly.
    Step 4. As you narrate Actions 6 through 9, make clear

(Continue on page 404.)

402

```
                        Prewriting Notes
BEGINNING

Situation    At the last minute, an understudy has to take over a
             leading role.

Characters   Connie Alvarez, the understudy. Mrs. Miles, the
             director. Bill Chu, the student stage manager. Kevin
             O'Connor, the student who plays the leading male role.
             Other cast members.

Setting      The stage of the Prairie View Junior High School on
             the opening night of the play The Tillsdale Mystery

Actions       1. Connie and other cast members are backstage being
                 made up.
              2. Mrs. Miles tells Connie that the female lead has
                 suddenly become ill and that Connie must play Lady
                 Marlowe.
              3. Connie is so startled that she can scarcely reply.

MIDDLE

Actions       1. Connie puts on Lady Marlowe's costume and make-up.
              2. She feels frightened. Her heart beats faster, and
                 her hands shake.
              3. Trying to remember Lady Marlowe's lines, Connie
                 waits in the wings.
              4. High Point: When Bill Chu beckons to her, Connie
                 walks onstage.
              5. Connie is aware of the audience, of Kevin, and of
                 the spotlight on her.
              6. Kevin addresses his first line to Connie.
              7. Connie hears herself speak Lady Marlowe's first
                 line in a low but clear voice.
              8. Kevin replies, and Connie says her next line
                 perfectly.
              9. As the scene continues, Connie feels more confident.
             10. Toward the end of the scene, Connie realizes that
                 she is enjoying her role.

ENDING

Actions       1. Connie says her last line in the scene.
              2. She walks offstage.
              3. Other members of the cast congratulate her.

             Conclusion:  Connie tells Bill, "It's really fun."
```

403

to your readers that Connie at first feels frightened but later enjoys her role. The change must be believable. The notes are only an outline. Supply descriptive details and other information to make the story vivid and real.

Step 5. As you narrate Action 10, build to a good stopping point. Make Connie's feelings very clear.

Step 6. Read what you have written. Do the sentences flow smoothly? Are the actions clear? Will readers be able to picture what happens? Revise your work as necessary.

404

Unit Assignments

Assignment 1 Write a narrative of at least four paragraphs about a time when an experience that you were not looking forward to turned out to be truly enjoyable. Give your narrative the proper form, with a beginning, a middle that includes a high point, and a definite ending.

Assignment 2 Write a narrative of at least six paragraphs about a character who gives badly needed help to another person. Make clear how both characters feel at the end.

Assignment 3 Write a fictional story in which you imagine yourself living during a particular period in American history. For example, you might imagine living in an Indian pueblo ten centuries ago or working on the first transcontinental railroad. Look up any historical information that you need, but do not let it control your story. Focus on a particular incident and use appropriate dialogue.

Assignment 4 Write a narrative about an event that occurred in connection with one of your main interests, such as a sport, a hobby, or music.

Assignment 5 Narrate a true or fictional story in which the setting is unusual. Use your imagination to create the details, the setting, and the effect that the setting has on the characters.

Revising Your Assignments

For help in revising a narrative, consult the Checklist for Revision on the last page of this book.

405

Unit Tests

Test 1

Test 1 (pages 406–407)

A.

1. True
2. False
3. True
4. False
5. True

B.

6. e
7. c
8. d
9. b
10. a

(Continue on the next page.)

A. Number your paper from 1 to 5. Next to each number, write *True* if the sentence is true or *False* if it is false.

1. You should plan a narrative around a specific problem or situation.
2. You cannot be a character in a narrative that you write.
3. When you use chronological order, you present the events in the order in which they happen.
4. You should present the high point at the beginning of your narrative.
5. In a narrative you should place each group of related actions in a separate paragraph.

B. Number your paper from 6 to 10. Next to each number, write the letter of the item that correctly completes the sentence. You will use all but one of the items.

> a. dialogue   d. setting
> b. high point   e. character
> c. fictional   f. nonfictional

6. A __?__ is one of the people in a narrative.
7. In a __?__ narrative, you may invent the characters and the actions.
8. The __?__ is the time and place of the story.
9. The __?__ is the action that creates the most suspense.
10. In __?__ you present the exact words of your characters.

C. Number your paper from 11 to 15. Next to each number, write the letter of the item that correctly answers the question.

11. In the beginning of a narrative, which of the following sentences introduces the characters in the most interesting way?

406

a. My friends Max and Paul had an interesting experience last week.
b. Something unusual happened to Max and Paul last week.
c. When Max and Paul boarded the subway, they had no idea that they would be stuck there for hours.
d. This is a story about the time that Max and Paul spent hours on a subway.

12. Which of the following sentences introduces the setting of a narrative?
    a. I showed the film to the assembly.
    b. When Thea woke up at seven on a hot July morning, she was the only one left in her tent at Green Valley Camp.
    c. When Adam entered the art contest last fall, he did not think that he had a chance to win.
    d. Juan plays trombone in the band.

13. Which of the following is *not* a good strategy for writing dialogue?
    a. Put each sentence in a separate paragraph.
    b. Use dialogue to show the feelings of your characters.
    c. Use dialogue to tell actions in the story.
    d. Include explanatory details to tell who is speaking.

14. In which part of a narrative should you place the high point?
    a. In the beginning   c. In the ending
    b. In the middle   d. Anywhere in the story

15. Which of the following should you do at the end of a narrative?
    a. Explain how the characters are involved in the story.
    b. Explain the setting
    c. Identify the problem or situation
    d. Settle the problem or situation

Test 2

Choose one of the Unit Assignments. Write the assignment as directed and hand it in to your teacher.

Test 1 *(pages 406–407),* continued

C.
11. c
12. b
13. a
14. b
15. d

Test 2 *(pages 407)*

Answers will vary.

Objectives

After studying this unit, students should be able to do the following:

- Select and limit a topic for a written report.

- Gather information for a written report, preparing source cards and taking notes.

- Organize information for a written report, including a topic statement and an outline.

- Write the first draft of a report, including a list of sources.

- Revise and finish writing a report.

- Write book reports on works of fiction and on works of nonfiction.

Teaching Suggestions

See "Classroom Insights" for Unit 15 in the front of this Teacher's Edition.

Program Resources

Resource Book, Second Course:
   Bonus Activities, Unit 15
   Composition Checklist, Unit 15
Practice Book, Second Course, Unit 15
Tests, Second Course, Unit 15
Composition Workshops, Second Course, Unit 15

Writing a Report

Unit Preview

A **report** presents facts that you learn while researching, or investigating, a specific topic. A report is based on information about your topic that comes from encyclopedias, books, magazines, and newspapers. You should not base a report on your personal experience.

The following paragraphs begin a report on alligators. It is clear from the beginning what the topic of the report is. Notice that the writer tries to capture the reader's attention by including interesting details in the first paragraph.

The Abilities of Alligators

Many people think that alligators are thick-skinned, unfeeling creatures. However, this belief is not accurate. Scientists are learning that alligators are highly sensitive to conditions around them.

Alligators seem to be able to predict weather conditions. Mother alligators build their nests of mud and sticks during the dry season, when the water level of the swamp is low. Before the eggs hatch three months later, rain will raise the level of the water. Amazingly, no matter how much rain falls and how high the water rises, the nests are always just above the water line. If the nests are built low, the season turns out to be dry. On the other hand if the nests are built high, it rains so much that the swamp floods.

408

For Analysis   On your paper, answer the following questions about the opening paragraphs that you have just read.

1. What is the topic of the report?
2. Which sentence states the topic?
3. What details does the writer include in the first paragraph to interest readers in the report?
4. What is the topic of the second paragraph?
5. How does the second paragraph develop the topic of the report?

By answering questions about the opening paragraphs of one report, you have observed important characteristics of all reports. In this unit you will learn how to plan, write, and revise a report. In addition, you will learn how to write book reports. As you prepare your reports, you will follow the three steps of the writing process: prewriting, writing, and revising.

15.1   Selecting and Limiting a Topic

The first step in preparing a report is to select a topic. Once you have chosen a topic, you must limit it to suit the length of your report.

15.1a   Selecting a Topic

If you may select your own topic, choose one about which you will enjoy reading and writing. Also, choose one that requires research. Do not select a topic that you know so well that you can write about it from your own experience. Your report should be based on factual information, not on personal experience.

The examples on the following page illustrate how topics that are based on personal experience can be revised so that they are suitable for reports.

409

Related Resources

Houghton Mifflin Microcourse:
   Language Arts, Levels 7, 8
*The American Heritage
   Dictionary of the English
   Language*
Roget's II: The New Thesaurus

For Analysis *(page 409)*

Answers may vary. Samples:

1. The topic of the report is the environmental sensitivity of the alligator.
2. Scientists are learning that alligators are highly sensitive to conditions around them.
3. The writer mentions that most people think alligators are unfeeling but that this is not true.
4. The topic of the second paragraph is the alligator's seeming ability to predict weather conditions.
5. The second paragraph gives an example of how the alligator reacts sensitively to surrounding conditions.

Exercise 1 *(page 410)*

1, 3, 5, 7, 8, 9

Exercise 2 *(page 410)*

Answers may vary. Samples:

2. My goals in life
   How Sir Edmund Hilary realized his goal—to climb Mount Everest
4. My visit to the Erie Canal
   How the Erie Canal was built
6. The last time I had a cold
   Failed attempts to find a cure for the common cold
10. My first ride in a sports car
    Recent developments in sports cars

UNSUITABLE TOPIC	My first trip to northern Michigan [cannot be researched]
REVISED TOPIC	Industry in northern Michigan
UNSUITABLE TOPIC	How I learned to read [cannot be researched]
REVISED TOPIC	Methods of teaching reading
UNSUITABLE TOPIC	My twin brothers [cannot be researched]
REVISED TOPIC	What scientists know about twins

Exercise 1 Prewriting: Report Topics Read the following list of topics. On your paper, list the numbers of the topics that are suitable for a report.

1. Franklin Roosevelt's first term as President
2. My goals in life
3. The uses of lasers in medicine
4. My visit to the Erie Canal
5. The world's tallest building
6. The last time I had a cold
7. The effects of a fever on the human body
8. Magellan's search for a passage to the Pacific
9. The invention of the camera
10. My first ride in a sports car

Exercise 2 Prewriting: Report Topics On your paper, copy the topics from Exercise 1 that are not suitable for a report. Revise each topic to make it suitable for a report.

SAMPLE	How I spent my summer at the lake
ANSWER	How lakes were formed

410

15.1b Limiting a Topic

After choosing a topic, you need to limit it, or make it specific. A limited topic can be covered thoroughly in a report. The report that you write will have a length of 250 to 500 words (two to three pages). The subject "Astronauts" is so general that it would take many pages or even a book to cover it adequately. By limiting the topic to "Requirements for becoming an astronaut," you can cover the topic completely in a brief report. In addition, having a limited topic will make finding good sources of information on your topic easier for you.

To limit your topic, ask yourself the following questions:

1. Can I limit my topic to one aspect of the general topic?
2. Can I limit my topic to one person, one group, or one example?
3. Can I limit my topic to a brief time period?
4. Can I limit my topic to one event or one place?

The following general topics have been limited so that they are suitable for reports.

GENERAL TOPIC	Thomas Jefferson
LIMITED TOPIC	Thomas Jefferson's years in France [one time period]
GENERAL TOPIC	How the human body works
LIMITED TOPIC	How your lungs work [one example]
GENERAL TOPIC	Animals
LIMITED TOPIC	Animals in the Everglades [one place]

When you have limited a topic, test its suitability. You need to check how much information is available on your topic. Begin by looking in a general encyclopedia. Next,

411

Exercise 3 *(page 412)*

1. Too general
2. Limited
3. Too general
4. Too general
5. Limited
6. Limited
7. Too general
8. Limited
9. Limited
10. Too general

check the library card catalog *(pages 539–541)* for the titles of books on your topic. A glance at the table of contents and the index in these books will quickly tell you whether they will be useful. To locate magazine articles, look in the *Readers' Guide to Periodical Literature (page 546)*, which indexes articles according to subject and author. There also are indexes for some newspapers. You may check them, too, for information on your topic.

There may be so much material on your topic that you cannot possibly discuss it fully in 250 to 500 words. In that case, you will need to limit your topic further. On the other hand, if you cannot find at least two sources that cover your topic, it may be too limited. If you find that your topic is too general or too limited, you do not have to reject it completely. The material that you found as you tested your topic may suggest related topics that are better suited to a short report.

Exercise 3 Prewriting: Limited Topics Number your paper from 1 to 10. Then rate each of the following topics by writing *Too general* or *Limited* after each number.

> **SAMPLE** How computers can be used in the home
> **ANSWER** Limited

1. Dance
2. What causes monsoons
3. Weather
4. Oceans
5. Benjamin Franklin's early life
6. Vincent van Gogh's style of painting
7. United States Presidents
8. Why oceans are salty
9. The 1936 World Series
10. Modern painters

412

Assignment **Prewriting** *Step 1:* Choose five of the subjects from the list that follows. *Step 2:* For each, write a general topic that can be researched. *Step 3:* Limit each general topic so that it is suitable for a report of two to three pages.

1. Nutrition
2. Space science
3. Careers
4. Motorized vehicles
5. Artists
6. Clothing
7. Law enforcement
8. Sports
9. Nations
10. World leaders

Continuing Assignment **Prewriting** *Step 1:* On your paper, list five topics that can be researched. *Step 2:* Choose the three topics about which you would like to learn more, and limit each topic to make it suitable for a report of two to three pages. *Step 3:* Test your limited topics by checking sources, and select one for which you have found at least three sources. Write down your topic. Save your paper.

Assignment Checklist

Check your assignments for the following points:

✔ 1. Did you select topics that are interesting to you?
✔ 2. Did you select topics that require research?
✔ 3. Did you limit your topic?

Check your Continuing Assignment for this additional point:

✔ 4. Did you find sources that contain information on the topics?

15.2 Gathering Information

After selecting and limiting a topic, you are ready to begin gathering information about it. First, you will list facts about your sources. Then you will take notes on the useful information in those sources.

413

15.2a Preparing Source Cards

As you find sources for your limited topic, make a source card for each one. List information about each source on a separate three-by-five-inch index card. The type of information that you list on a source card depends on the type of publication. You will refer to these cards later.

Encyclopedias. On your source cards, list the author's name (last name first) and then the title of the article (in quotation marks). If the name of the author is not given, begin with the title of the article. Next, list the name of the encyclopedia (underlined) and the year of the edition. The correct form and punctuation of the listing are shown in the following example.

> Hoover, J. Edgar. "Fingerprinting." The World Book Encyclopedia. 1982 ed.

Books. List the author's name (the last name first), the book title (underlined), and the city where the publisher is located. Then list the publisher and the date of publication. Note the form and punctuation of the following example.

> Wentworth, Patricia. The Fingerprint. New York: Bantam Books, Inc., 1980.

Magazines and Newspapers. List the author's name if it is given (last name first), the title of the article (in quotation marks), the name of the newspaper or magazine (underlined), the date of publication, and the pages on which the article appears. If the article runs on consecutive pages, list the first and last page numbers of the article (for example: pp. 7–9). For articles that do not run on consecutive pages, list each page on which the article appears (for example: pp. 3, 25). For newspaper articles only, list the section in which the article appears before you list the page number. Note the form and punctuation of the following examples.

MAGAZINE   "Fingerprints Revealed in the Laboratory."
         <u>Science News</u>, 18 July 1978, p. 24.

NEWSPAPER   Beck, Joan. "Eavesdropping in the Galaxy."
         <u>Chicago Tribune</u>, 23 Nov. 1982, Sec. 1,
         p. 16.

The following are sample source cards:

Source Card for a Book

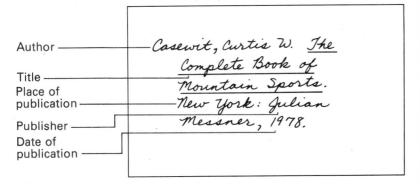

Author — Casewit, Curtis W. *The*

Title — *Complete Book of*

Place of publication — *Mountain Sports.*

Publisher — *New York: Julian*

Date of publication — *Messner, 1978.*

Source Card for a Magazine Article

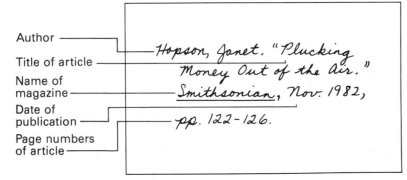

Author — Hopson, Janet. "Plucking

Title of article — Money Out of the Air."

Name of magazine — <u>Smithsonian</u>, Nov. 1982,

Date of publication —

Page numbers of article — pp. 122-126.

Use the preceding examples as a guide when you prepare your source cards.

415

Exercise 1 *(pages 416–417)*

1. White, Theodore H. In Search of History. New York: Harper & Row, 1978.

2. Oswalt, Wendell H. This Land Was Theirs: A Study of the North American Indian. New York: John Wiley & Sons, 1966.

3. "Earthquakes, Volcanoes, and Fireballs." Earth Science, Fall 1981, pp. 26–28.

4. Boraiko, Allen A. "The Chip: Electronic Mini-marvel." National Geographic, Oct. 1982, pp. 421–457.

5. "Air Quality Concerns at Cement Plant Voiced." Huron Plainsman, 18 Apr. 1982, Sec. 2, p. 26.

6. Klein, Heywood. "Trade-Show Hospitality is Changing." The Wall Street Journal, 25 Jan. 1983, Sec., 2, p. 35.

7. Critchfield, Howard J. "Jungles." The New Book of Knowledge. 1966 ed.

8. "Four Outstanding Doctors." International Library of Afro-American Life and History. 1979 ed.

Exercise 1   Prewriting: Source Cards   Use the following information to write source card listings. For this exercise write the listings on a sheet of paper. Be sure to use correct punctuation.

AUTHOR	TITLE	PUBLICATION FACTS
Books		
1. Theodore H. White	*In Search of History*	Harper & Row New York 1978
2. Wendell H. Oswalt	*This Land Was Theirs: A Study of the North American Indian*	John Wiley & Sons New York 1966
Magazines		
3. Not given	"Earthquakes, Volcanoes, and Fireballs"	*Earth Science* Fall 1981 pp. 26–28
4. Allen A. Boraiko	"The Chip: Electronic Mini-marvel"	*National Geographic* October 1982 pp. 421–457
Newspapers		
5. Not given	"Air Quality Concerns at Cement Plant Voiced"	*Huron Plainsman* 18 April 1982 Sec. 2, p. 26
6. Heywood Klein	"Trade-Show Hospitality Is Changing"	*The Wall Street Journal* 25 January 1983 Sec. 2, p. 35
Encyclopedias		
7. Howard J. Critchfield	"Jungles"	*The New Book of Knowledge* 1966 edition

| 8. Not given | "Four Outstanding Doctors" | *International Library of Afro-American Life and History* 1979 edition |

15.2b Taking Notes

The next step in preparing a report is taking notes from the sources listed on your cards. The following strategies will help you to take notes that are clear and useful. (You may also wish to refer to Unit 19, "Study Skills," for further information.)

Strategies

1. *Skim each source.* Check whether the source covers your limited topic. If the source is a book, scanning the table of contents and the index may be helpful. If the source contains material about your limited topic, read that information carefully.

2. *Write your notes on index cards.* Use either three-by-five-inch or four-by-six-inch index cards. When you are ready to make an outline, you will find it easier to arrange your notes if they are on index cards.

3. *Write notes on only one idea on each card.* Then you can rearrange your note cards easily. For example, if you are doing research for a report on the climate of a certain area, you may find a paragraph that discusses both temperature and rainfall. Even though this information is contained in a single paragraph, make one card for details about temperature and another card for details about rainfall.

417

4. *Summarize important information from each source.* In a summary you briefly state the author's point in your own words. You may write a summary in phrases rather than in complete sentences.

5. *Write a subject heading in the upper left corner of each card.* Choose a word or a phrase that identifies the central idea of the card. You can sort your cards by these headings when you organize your report.

6. *Write the author's name if it is given and an abbreviated title in the upper right corner of each card.* This information will help you to identify the source if you need to check your facts.

7. *Write the page number from which the information came on the bottom of each card.* This reference will help you if you need to check your information.

Review the following example of a note card. The notes summarize a point from an encyclopedia entry.

Note Card

Subject heading ———
Author's name ———
Abbreviated title ┘
Note ———

Page reference ———

Follow the preceding example when you prepare the note cards for your report.

418

Exercise 2   Prewriting: Note Cards   You are writing a report on animal tracks. Read the following passage. Then write a note card with the subject heading "Signs other than paw prints." The passage is from an article titled "How Wildlife Leaves Its Mark," which appeared in the October–November 1982 issue of *National Wildlife*. The article was written by Anthony Acerrano. The passage appears on page 17 of the magazine.

> There are, of course, dozens of other signs that mark an animal's presence. A felled tree may signify that a beaver has been at work; several rows of holes in a tree trunk probably display the efforts of a member of the woodpecker family. In winter, a leafy area or bare ground, surrounded by snow, may indicate where a deer has spent the night. Even insects leave a variety of tracks and other markings. Taken together, such signs form an unusual portrait of life in the wild for anyone who takes the time to look carefully.

Assignment 1   Prewriting   Choose one of the following limited topics. Using materials in your library, make at least three source cards for that topic.

1. Drilling oil wells
2. Paths of comets
3. Events in the Olympics
4. Uses of precious metals
5. Prevention of forest fires
6. Musical instruments

Assignment 2   Prewriting   Find a short article in a magazine or a newspaper. Read the article and prepare two note cards based on it. Be sure to include all the necessary information on each note card.

Continuing Assignment   Prewriting   In the Continuing Assignment on page 413, you selected and limited a topic for your report. Now prepare source cards for at least three sources on your topic. Then prepare at least fifteen note cards from these three sources. Save your source cards and your note cards.

419

Exercise 2 *(page 419)*

Answers may vary. Sample:

Signs other than paw prints	Acerrano, "Wildlife"

—Felled tree: beaver
—Rows of holes in tree trunk: woodpecker
—Leafy area or bare ground in winter: deer slept there

p. 17

Assignment Checklist

Check your assignments for the following points:

  ✓ 1. Did you make a source card for each book, magazine, newspaper, or encyclopedia that you used?

  ✓ 2. Did you take notes on each source in your own words, summarizing what you read?

  ✓ 3. Did you limit the notes on each card to one idea?

  ✓ 4. Did you write a subject heading on each note card?

  ✓ 5. Did you write the author's name (if given), an abbreviated title, and the page number from which the information came on each note card?

15.3 Organizing Your Information

Now you are ready to organize the information that you have collected about your limited topic. To organize the material, you must write a topic statement and make an outline. A **topic statement** is a single sentence that presents the main idea of a report. An **outline** is a list of ideas arranged in a logical order. Your outline will be a guide when you write your report. The following steps tell how to use your note cards to write a topic statement and to make an outline.

Procedure

1. *Separate your note cards into stacks by subject headings.* Combine stacks with headings that are closely related.

2. *Read through each stack of cards and choose the most important subject heading for each.* These subject headings will become the main headings in your outline. The following headings might be used for a report on how fingerprints identify people.

> How fingerprints are classified
> How fingerprints are made
> How fingerprints are catalogued

420

3. *Use your note cards and your main headings to write a topic statement* that presents the main idea of your report. The following is the topic statement for the report on fingerprints.

> *Topic statement:* Fingerprinting is the only sure way of identifying people.

Place your topic statement at the beginning of your complete outline.

4. *List the main headings from your stacks of note cards in logical order.* You can list these headings in chronological order, spatial order, order of importance, or whatever order seems suitable for your topic. This list is your **rough outline.** The main headings for the report on fingerprints can be arranged in chronological order to show the steps in the process.

> How fingerprints are made
> How fingerprints are classified
> How fingerprints are catalogued

5. *Assign Roman numerals to the main headings in your rough outline.* Use "Introduction" as your first main heading and "Conclusion" as your last main heading, as in the following example:

> I. Introduction
> II. How fingerprints are made
> III. How fingerprints are classified
> IV. How fingerprints are catalogued
> V. Conclusion

6. *Review each stack of note cards.* Arrange the cards within each stack so that similar details are grouped together. To complete your outline, put the grouped

421

Exercise *(pages 422–423)*

Order of subheadings may vary. Sample:

I. Introduction
II. Why camels are useful work animals
  A. Feet unhurt by sharp gravel
  B. Need little food or water
  C. Can each carry six hundred to twelve hundred pounds
III. Why the United States Army decided to invest in camels
  A. Ability of camels to travel in desert or mountainous land
  B. Inability of horses and wagons to travel safely in desert and mountains.
IV. How the use of camels declined
  A. Turning of Army's attention from the West
  B. Sale of camels to miners and circuses
V. Conclusion

cards in logical order within the stack. Make the points on these cards subheadings under each main heading in your outline. Then place a capital letter before each subheading.

The complete outline with a topic statement for the report on fingerprints follows.

Topic statement: Fingerprinting is the only sure way of identifying people.

I. Introduction
II. How fingerprints are made
  A. Ink rolled onto glass or metal plate
  B. Each finger rolled on inked plate
  C. Each finger rolled on fingerprint card
  D. All ten fingers pressed on card as a set
III. How fingerprints are classified
  A. Arch
  B. Loop
  C. Whorl
  D. Composite
IV. How fingerprints are catalogued
  A. By number of whorls—number code
  B. Ridge-counting for loops
V. Conclusion

Exercise   Prewriting: The Outline   On your paper, make an outline that develops the following topic statement. The blank outline that follows the topic statement shows how many main headings and subheadings you will need. To complete the outline, use the main headings and the subheadings that follow the outline. Arrange the main headings and the subheadings in a logical order. Save your paper.

Topic statement: For a while, it seemed as though the camel—not the horse—would become the most useful work animal in the West.

422

I.   <u>?</u>
II. <u>?</u>
    A. <u>?</u>
    B. <u>?</u>
    C. <u>?</u>
III. <u>?</u>
    A. <u>?</u>
    B. <u>?</u>
IV. <u>?</u>
    A. <u>?</u>
    B. <u>?</u>
V. <u>?</u>

Main Headings:
How the use of camels declined
Conclusion
Why the United States Army decided to invest in camels
Introduction
Why camels are useful work animals

Subheadings:
Need little food or water
Turning of the Army's attention from the West
Feet unhurt by sharp gravel
Inability of horses and wagons to travel safely in desert and mountains
Sale of camels to miners and circuses
Can each carry six hundred to twelve hundred pounds
Ability of camels to travel in desert or mountainous land

Assignment Prewriting   Choose one of the following limited topics. On your paper, write a topic statement and prepare a rough outline based on the topic statement. Include at least two main headings. You may consult reference books for information.

1. How fossil fuels were formed
2. The first steam-operated carousel
3. How bees make wax and honey
4. What causes volcanoes to erupt

423

Continuing Assignment Prewriting   *Step 1:* Using the note cards that you made for the Continuing Assignment on page 419, write a topic statement and make a rough outline for your report. *Step 2:* Make a complete outline with Roman-numeral main headings and capital-letter subheadings. Save your paper.

Assignment Checklist

Check your assignments for the following points:

✓ 1. Did you choose the most important main headings for your outline?

✓ 2. Did you use the main headings to write a topic statement?

✓ 3. Did you arrange the main headings in a logical order?

Check your Continuing Assignment for these additional points:

✓ 4. Did you use the points on your note cards as subheadings in your outline?

✓ 5. Did you make a complete outline with Roman numerals before main headings and capital letters before subheadings?

15.4 Writing Your Report

You are now ready to write your report. Your notes, your topic statement, and your outline will guide you as you write the **first draft,** or first version, of your report.

15.4a Writing the First Draft

Follow your outline as you write the first draft of your report. In a brief report, you should write one paragraph for each of the Roman numeral headings in your outline. Be sure to present all of the information in your own words.

424

The Introductory Paragraph

Your reader's first impression of your report comes from your introductory paragraph. To write an effective introductory paragraph, follow these guidelines.

1. *Capture the reader's interest.* Begin your report by making your topic seem important, unusual, or memorable in some way.
2. *Present your topic statement.* Your topic statement is usually the last sentence of the introductory paragraph.
3. *Give any necessary background information.* Include facts that will help your reader understand your topic.

The introductory paragraph that follows comes from a report on fingerprints.

> For many centuries, people have known that human fingerprints differ from person to person. However, it was not until the mid-1850s that Sir William Herschel, a British government official, used fingerprints as a way of identifying people. He reasoned that signatures can be forged, that appearances can be disguised, and that voices can be changed. *Fingerprinting is the only sure way of identifying people.*

Notice how the paragraph captures the reader's interest by giving historical information on the use of fingerprints to identify people. The topic statement, which is in italic type, brings the paragraph to a close.

The Body

The body of your report consists of the paragraphs that cover the main points of your outline. Begin the first body paragraph with a topic sentence that identifies the main idea in the second Roman-numeral heading of your outline. Then

425

follow the capital-letter subheadings of your outline as you write the rest of the paragraph. Refer to your note cards and to your outline as you work. Repeat this process for the rest of the body paragraphs in your report.

The following paragraph was written from the second Roman-numeral heading of the outline on page 422.

> Fingerprints can be recorded using printer's ink and a standard fingerprint card. First, the ink is rolled evenly across a glass or metal plate. Next, each finger is rolled once across the plate so that the part of the finger above the first joint is covered with ink. Then each finger is rolled once across the fingerprint card in the space labeled for that finger. Finally, all ten fingers are pressed on the card at once to give a complete fingerprint set.

Notice that the writer covers the points in the same order in which they appear in the outline. Notice, too, that the entire main heading and its subheadings are treated in one paragraph.

The Concluding Paragraph

Your concluding paragraph helps your reader to grasp the full meaning of your report. It should be brief. Do not bring up major ideas that should have been covered in the body paragraphs. The following suggestions will help you to write a good concluding paragraph.

Strategies

1. *Review the main points of your report.* Briefly restate the main ideas covered in the body.

2. *Rephrase your topic statement.* Use different words to repeat your topic statement.

3. *If appropriate, make one or two observations about your topic.* You might discuss why the topic is important or what might happen in the future.

426

The paragraph that concludes the report on fingerprints follows.

> The process of recording a set of fingerprints is simple, and experts have devised methods of classifying and cataloguing fingerprints. No two fingerprints have been found to be exactly alike. Fingerprints are the only easily recognizable key to a person's identity. In the future, fingerprints, rather than signatures, may be used to identify people.

Exercise 1 Prewriting: Introductory Paragraphs Read the two introductory paragraphs that follow. Choose the paragraph that would be the better introduction to a report on how ships in the northern Atlantic Ocean are protected from ice. On your paper, write one or two sentences to explain why you chose that paragraph.

1. In the northern part of the Atlantic Ocean, there is a lot of ice. Ships passing through that part of the ocean can be damaged by ice. Methods have been developed to protect the ships. Icebreakers and the ice patrol provide the most effective means of protection.

2. Northern parts of the Atlantic Ocean remain frozen for most of the year. In the spring the ice often becomes ten feet thick. In addition, icebergs that may be miles long float into the unfrozen waters of the ocean. All of this ice can damage ships that travel on the ocean. Therefore, the ships must be protected. Icebreakers and the ice patrol provide the most effective means of protection.

Exercise 2 Writing: Introductory Paragraphs Using the topic statement and the outline that you made for the Exercise on page 422, write a brief introductory paragraph for the report on camels in the Old West.

Exercise 3 Writing: Body Paragraphs Using your outline from the Exercise on page 422, write a body paragraph based on the main heading "Why camels are useful work animals."

Exercise 1 *(page 427)*

Answers may vary. Sample:

Paragraph 2 would be the better introduction. The first sentence is specific and captures the reader's attention. The sentences that follow give background information, and the last sentence states the topic.

Exercise 2 *(page 427)*

Answers may vary. Sample:

In books and movies about the Old West, the animal that we most often read about and see is the horse. Horses could not travel comfortably over desert and mountains, however. For a while, it seemed as though the camel—not the horse—would become the most useful work animal in the West.

Exercise 3 *(page 427)*

Answers may vary. Sample:

Camels are useful work animals. For one thing, their feet are not hurt by sharp gravel. Furthermore, they need little food or water, having adapted to life in the desert. Finally, they can each carry six hundred to twelve hundred pounds.

427

Exercise 4 *(page 428)*

Answers may vary. Sample:

The camel appeared to be an animal well suited for work in the Old West because of its ability to go long stretches without food or water and to travel without difficulty in the desert and mountains. With other demands for the camel's services, however, and a weakening of the Army's interest, the horse took over. Otherwise it is possible that the Lone Ranger might have ridden away on a camel called Silver.

Exercise 5 *(page 428)*

3. Inder, Stuart. "Fiji." The World Book Encyclopedia. 1981 ed.

2. Quain, Buell. Fijian Village. Chicago: University of Chicago Press, 1948.

1. Suggs, Robert. The Island Civilizations of Polynesia. New York: New American Library, 1951.

Exercise 4   Writing: Concluding Paragraphs   Using your outline from the Exercise on page 422, write a concluding paragraph for the report on camels in the Old West.

15.4b Listing Your Sources

When you write a report, you must always list the sources of information that you used. Listing your sources is necessary for two reasons. First, you must give credit to the sources from which you learned new ideas. Second, you must list your sources for readers who wish to consult them for additional information on your topic.

Your list of sources should be the last page of your report. To prepare that page, begin by alphabetizing your source cards by the author's last name. If no author is given, alphabetize a source by the first word in the title, disregarding the articles *A, An,* and *The.* If you wrote the information on your source cards in the form shown on page 415, you can simply copy it onto your list of sources. Double-space all lines on the page. Indent all lines five spaces except for the first line. You may refer to the model on page 433.

Exercise 5   Writing: List of Sources   The following sources were used for a report on the Fiji Islands. On your paper, revise the entry for each source, punctuating it correctly. Then copy the entries in alphabetical order.

1. New American Library, *The Island Civilizations of Polynesia,* New York, Robert Suggs, 1951.
2. Chicago, Buell Quain, 1948, University of Chicago Press, *Fijian Village.*
3. Stuart Inder, 1981 edition, "Fiji," *The World Book Encyclopedia.*

428

Assignment 1 Writing Write a first draft of an introductory paragraph for a report on what cities are doing to increase the use of buses. Use the following topic statement and partial outline. Save your paper.

> *Topic statement:* Many cities are trying to get more people to ride the buses to and from work.

   I. Introduction
 II. Why cities want people to ride buses
     A. To decrease traffic jams
     B. To conserve fuel
     C. To save money

Assignment 2 Writing Using the topic statement and the partial outline in Assignment 1, write a first draft of a body paragraph for a report on increasing the use of buses. Save your paper.

Continuing Assignment Writing Using the note cards, the topic statement, and the outline that you prepared for the Continuing Assignments on page 419 and page 424, write the first draft of your report. Its length should be from 250 to 500 words. Include a list of sources.

Assignment Checklist

Check your assignments for the following points:

  ✔ 1. Did you include a topic statement in your introductory paragraph?
  ✔ 2. Did you try to capture the reader's interest with your introductory paragraph?
  ✔ 3. Did you write a topic sentence for each body paragraph based on the appropriate main heading in your outline?

Check your Continuing Assignment for these additional points:

  ✔ 4. Did you develop each body paragraph with the details from your outline and from your note cards?
  ✔ 5. Did you close your report with a concluding paragraph?
  ✔ 6. Did you include a list of sources?

429

15.5 Revising and Finishing Your Report

Revising the First Draft

Revising your report involves more than simply recopying or typing your first draft. You must reread your draft several times to find ways that you can improve it. The following suggestions will help you as you revise your report.

Strategies

1. *Check your report against your outline.* Make sure that you covered all the points in your outline. If your outline does not work in certain places, however, you may depart from it. Check to see that you did not include any unnecessary information in the report.

2. *Check your sentences to see that they state your ideas clearly.* If necessary, combine short, choppy sentences *(pages 316–326)* or separate long, awkward ones. Replace unclear language with words and phrases that say exactly what you mean.

3. *Read your report for correct grammar, sentence structure, and word choice.* Correct any errors that you may find.

4. *Proofread your report.* Correct any errors in spelling, capitalization, and punctuation.

When you are satisfied with your first draft, select a title for your report that is both informative and interesting. Titles that simply name the topic may not motivate your reader to begin reading. For example, the title "Soaring" sounds more interesting than the title "Airplanes." Keep in mind, however, that your title should not be too clever or too humorous. A title that is too humorous will distract the reader's attention from the topic of your report.

Preparing the Finished Report

The last step in writing your report is to copy or type your revised draft so that it has the best possible appearance. Follow the guidelines on pages 228–229 for preparing your final copy. Then proofread your final copy to correct any mistakes that you may have made when you copied it.

The final copy of the report on fingerprints follows.

Model

Ellen Deering
Science
October 18, 19___

Fingerprints Are Always Right

For many centuries, people have known that human fingerprints differ from person to person. However, it was not until the mid–1850s that Sir William Herschel, a British government official, used fingerprints as a way of identifying people. He reasoned that signatures can be forged, that appearances can be disguised, and that voices can be changed. Fingerprinting is the only sure way of identifying people.

Fingerprints can be recorded using printer's ink and a standard fingerprint card. First, the ink is rolled evenly

431

across a glass or metal plate. Next, each finger is rolled once across the plate so that the part of the finger above the first joint is covered with ink. Then each finger is rolled once across the fingerprint card in the space labeled for that finger. Finally, all ten fingers are pressed on the card at once to give a complete fingerprint set.

Fingerprints are classified according to the pattern of ridges on each finger. There are four basic patterns that appear from the first joint to the top of the finger. These patterns are the arch, the loop, the whorl, and the composite. One person may have all or some of these patterns on his or her ten fingers.

There was a time when fingerprint cards had to be reviewed one at a time in order to identify someone. Today, however, the patterns of each set of fingerprints are given numerical codes. These codes are fed into a computer. An expert can identify someone within a few hours using these computerized files.

The process of recording a set of fingerprints is simple, and experts have devised methods of classifying and cataloguing fingerprints. No two fingerprints have been found to be exactly alike. Fingerprints are the only easily recognizable key to a person's identity. In the future, fingerprints rather than signatures may be used to identify people.

432

Sources page

```
                          Sources

Ares, Charles.  "Fingerprint."  Merit Students Encyclopedia.

     1978 ed.

Breckon, William.  Science Versus Crime.  Sussex, England:

     Wayland, 1978.

Hoover, J. Edgar.  "Fingerprinting."  The World Book

     Encyclopedia.  1982 ed.
```

Exercise *(pages 433–434)*

1. b
2. b

(Continue on the next page.)

Exercise Revising: Body Paragraphs   Number your paper from 1 to 5. Then read the following passage from the body of the first draft of a report on cattle ranching in Hawaii. Some of the numbered sentences need revision. On your paper, write the letter of the revision that will improve the sentence.

(1) Hawaiian cowhands are called *paniolos*.   (2) Their name comes from the Spanish word *español*.   (3) They were given that name because of the first paniolos. (4) Paniolos ride across black lava volcano slopes or through rain forests.   (5) Rather than over flat, grassy plains. (6) They wear chaps, just like cowhands, to protect their legs, and they skillfully rope and herd cattle.   (7) The islanders had never seen cows before.

1. Sentence 2
   a. Make no change.
   b. Rewrite the sentence: *Their name comes from the Spanish word* español, *which can mean "Spanish person."*

2. Sentence 3
   a. Remove the sentence.
   b. Rewrite the sentence for clarity: *They were given that name because the first paniolos came from Mexico.*

433

Exercise *(pages 433–434),*
continued

3. a
4. a
5. b

3. Sentence 5
    a. Combine the fragment with the preceding sentence: *Paniolos ride across black lava volcano slopes or through rain forests, rather than over flat, grassy plains.*
    b. Remove the fragment.

4. Sentence 6
    a. Rewrite the sentence: *Just like cowhands, they wear chaps to protect their legs. They also skillfully rope and herd cattle.*
    b. Rewrite the sentence: *They are just like cowhands because they wear chaps to protect their legs, and they also skillfully rope and herd cattle.*

5. Sentence 7
    a. Rewrite the sentence: *The islanders had never seen cows before because cows are not native to the island.*
    b. Remove the sentence.

Assignment Revising Revise the first draft of the paragraphs that you wrote for Assignments 1 and 2 on page 429. Then prepare a final copy of those paragraphs.

Continuing Assignment Revising *Step 1:* Revise the first draft of the report that you wrote for the Continuing Assignment on page 429. *Step 2:* Prepare the final copy of your report. Submit your first draft, your final copy, and your outline to your teacher.

Assignment Checklist

Check your assignments for the following points:

✔ 1. Did you revise and proofread your report?
✔ 2. Did you choose a title that is both informative and interesting?
✔ 3. Did you prepare a finished copy that is neat and free of errors?

434

15.6 Writing a Book Report

A **book report** shows that you understand a work and gives you the opportunity to express your reaction to it. The guidelines for writing book reports vary depending on whether the book is fiction or nonfiction. Like other reports, however, all book reports have an introductory paragraph, body paragraphs, and a concluding paragraph.

15.6a Book Reports About Fiction

Works of **fiction** include novels, short stories, and plays. The characters and the events in a fictional work are the product of the author's imagination. A book report about fiction describes the characters, the action, and the ideas from the story. The writer of a book report also states personal reactions to the book.

Before you begin to write your book report, you should take notes to make sure that you have the necessary information. Your notes should include the following:

1. Title and author
2. Type of fiction (adventure, mystery, romance, or science fiction, for example)
3. Brief description of the main characters
4. Brief summary of the action
5. Brief description of the main character's problem and how he or she deals with it
6. Your reaction to the book

Use your notes as a guide when you write your report. Write in the present tense and follow these steps as you write.

Procedure

1. *Begin your introductory paragraph with a sentence that identifies the title and the author.* This sentence

435

is the topic statement for your book report. The introduction should also tell what type of fiction the book is.

2. *Describe briefly the main characters and their relationships to one another* in your first body paragraph.

3. *Give a brief summary of the action of the story* in your second body paragraph. Include only the important events. Identify the main character's problem and tell how he or she deals with it.

4. *Discuss your reaction to the book* in the last paragraph. It is not enough to tell whether you liked the book. Try to present your reaction to its characters, its ideas, and its action. You might answer the following questions: Was the book memorable for some reason? Did you learn something new?

The following example shows that a book report can be much more than a summary.

Model

Emily Hostler

English

March 3, 19__

Playing Detective

The Westing Game by Ellen Raskin is a mystery story.

Sixteen people are surprised to learn that they will inherit

$200 million if they can just find the answer to a game

described in a will. Not only do the characters find it

nearly impossible to solve the mystery, but the reader does as well.

The characters in the book are residents of a small town outside Milwaukee, Wisconsin. Each of these heirs is tricked into renting an apartment in a new building that overlooks both Lake Michigan and the mansion of the mysterious Samuel W. Westing. The characters include a man who runs the Chinese restaurant in the penthouse of the building, his son, a foot doctor, a secretary who paints her crutches to match her clothes, a cleaning woman who runs a soup kitchen on the side, and others. The character that the reader gets to know the best is Turtle Wexler. She is thirteen years old and loves to play the stock market. Turtle eventually figures out the solution to the game but chooses to keep the answer a secret.

The game begins when the heirs are summoned to Westing House. Each heir is given four single-word clues and $10,000. They are told that Mr. Westing did not die of natural causes and that some of the heirs are not who they appear to be. Then they must find out who is responsible for Mr. Westing's death. Naturally, they all assume that there was foul play and rush around trying to find the clues. They also try to find out who the other heirs are. They don't make any progress until they finally agree to pool their clues, which turn out to be all but a few words

437

Exercise 1 *(pages 438–439)*

1. Introduction
2. Body
3. Conclusion
4. Body
5. Introduction

of the song "America." The missing words name one of the heirs, whose identity unravels the mystery. In the end, Turtle discovers that Mr. Westing is alive and is now known as J.R. Eastman. Throughout the game, Westing has been posing as various people: Sandy McSouthers, the apartment doorkeeper; the real estate agent who rented out the apartments, Barney Northrup; and J.R. Eastman. The names give him away: <u>West</u>ing, <u>East</u>man, Mc<u>Southers</u>, and <u>Northrup</u>.

I enjoyed trying to solve the mystery along with the characters, although I admit that I made the same errors that they did. Each of the characters learns something about himself or herself as the game proceeds. The players become happier, more successful, and more honest about themselves. That may be a better inheritance than a share in millions of dollars.

Notice that the writer not only provides a description of the important characters and the main actions, but also provides reactions to the book. The writer explains why the book was enjoyable and what a reader can learn from the book.

Exercise 1 Prewriting: Organizing The following notes were taken for a book report on a work of fiction. For each note, identify the part of the report in which the information belongs. On your paper, write *Introduction, Body,* or *Conclusion.*

1. The book is by Vera and Bill Cleaver
2. The main character is Fern Drawn, a fourteen-year-old girl who lives on a sheep farm in South Dakota.

3. The characters and the actions of the book seemed very real to me. I enjoyed the book because I became involved in the lessons that Fern was learning.
4. Most of the action in the book centers on the work that must be done on a sheep farm.
5. The book is a novel.

15.6b Book Reports About Nonfiction

Nonfiction presents real people, events, and things. Nonfiction can be divided into two groups: biography or autobiography and general nonfiction.

Biography and Autobiography

Biography is the story of a person's life written by another person. **Autobiography** is the story of a person's life written by that person. Both are nonfiction because they deal with events in the lives of real people. Take notes on a biography or an autobiography before you begin to write your book report. Your notes should include the following:

1. Title and author
2. Explanation of why the person is important
3. Summary of two or three important events in the person's life
4. Your reaction to the book

You can use your notes as a guide for writing your report. Follow these steps when you write your report.

Procedure

1. *Begin your introductory paragraph by identifying the book and its author.* Tell whether the book is a biography or an autobiography. Include a sentence or two about the importance of the subject of the book.

439

2. *Summarize two or three important events in the person's life.* This summary can be given in the first body paragraph. If more space is required, write one paragraph about each event. Tell why each event is important.

3. *Explain why the person is noteworthy* in your next body paragraph. Tell why the person is important in a particular field or in history.

4. *Give your reaction to the book.* Discuss why you liked or did not like the book. Indicate whether you learned a great deal about the person by reading the book.

General Nonfiction

This category includes books on science, history, the arts, government, and so on. Your notes on general nonfiction books should include the following:

1. Title and author
2. Type of book (science or history, for example)
3. Description of the subject
4. Summary of two or three major ideas in the book
5. Your evaluation of the book

Use your notes to write your book report. Follow these steps as you write.

Procedure

1. *Begin your introduction by identifying the book and the author.* Tell what type of general nonfiction the book is. Your introduction should also include a description of the subject.

2. *Explain two or three of the major ideas in the book.* Be brief; discuss only the most important ideas. You

may discuss all of the ideas in one paragraph, or you may devote a separate paragraph to each idea.

3. *Evaluate the book.* Give answers to some of the following questions: Does the author support his or her arguments with facts? Is the information presented in an interesting way? Did you learn something new about the subject?

The book report that follows is about a biography of Charles Lindbergh.

Model

Arthur Santos
English
October 10, 19__

A Twentieth-Century Hero

Brendan Gill writes about Charles A. Lindbergh's youth in <u>Lindbergh Alone</u>. Charles A. Lindbergh was a young aviator who became a hero when he made the first nonstop transatlantic flight in May of 1927. Gill's biography does not cover Lindbergh's entire life, but instead shows how he grew into a person who was able to make the flight.

The author states that there were two important influences on young Lindbergh's life. The first was his father, who taught him to face danger as a kind of adventure

441

and a thrill. Later, when Lindbergh would attempt to fly the Atlantic, he did not worry about the risk he was facing. He actually looked forward to it.

The author states that the second important influence on Lindbergh was experiencing failure. He did poorly in school. He tried farming but found that he had no talent in that area. Therefore, he began to do what had always interested him: flying. In the early 1920s, when most people considered airplanes dangerous, Lindbergh learned to fly. He became a barnstormer, a pilot who traveled about giving rides for five dollars and flying stunts in the air. Then he qualified for the Army Air Service School, where he did well. During the two years before his transatlantic flight, he helped start one of the first regular airmail services between St. Louis and Chicago.

Charles Lindbergh's transatlantic flight earned him a place in history. His knowledge of flying and his courage made it possible for him to do something that others had been unable to do. He showed that people can achieve great things in spite of past failures.

Brendan Gill's biography of Lindbergh was especially enjoyable to read because the author did not try to give a detailed account of Lindbergh's life. Instead, he tried to help the reader understand the kind of person Lindbergh was and why he deserved the admiration of his country and the world.

442

Notice that the writer of the report presents an evaluation of the book as well as a summary of the major ideas in the biography. The writer explains why it is good that the author of the book did not try to cover all of Lindbergh's life.

Exercise 2 Prewriting: Introductory Paragraph
The following notes were taken for a report about a general nonfiction book. Use the notes to write an introductory paragraph for the report.

1. Presents details of life on the frontier in the United States
2. Written in an interesting way with bits of humor
3. Focuses on the area east of the Mississippi River
4. *Frontier Living,* written by Edwin Tunis
5. Is a history book

Assignment 1 Prewriting Choose a book of fiction that you have read recently. If the details are not fresh in your mind, skim the book again. Then prepare notes for a book report on the work.

Assignment 2 Writing Using your notes from Assignment 1, write the first draft of your book report.

Assignment 3 Revising Revise the first draft of your book report from Assignment 2. *Step 1:* Make sure that your report is brief and to the point. *Step 2:* Check for errors in grammar, usage, spelling, and punctuation. *Step 3:* Prepare your final report.

Assignment 4 Prewriting Go to your library and find biographies and autobiographies of notable people. Skim several books and choose the one that interests you the most. Then read the biography or the autobiography that you chose and take notes for a book report on the work.

443

Exercise 2 *(page 443)*

Answers may vary. Sample:

Frontier Living, by Edwin Tunis, presents the details of life on the United States frontier, focusing on the area east of the Mississippi River. It is a history book that is written in an interesting way with bits of humor.

Assignment 5 **Writing / Revising**   *Step 1:* Using your notes from Assignment 4, write the first draft of your book report. *Step 2:* Revise your first draft. *Step 3:* Write your final report.

Assignment 6 **Prewriting**   Choose a topic about which you would like to learn more. Go to your library and look up your topic in the card catalog. If there are nonfiction books available on your topic, select the one that looks most interesting to you. If there are no nonfiction books available on your topic, choose another topic. Then read the book and take notes for a book report on that book.

Assignment 7 **Writing / Revising**   *Step 1:* Using your notes from Assignment 6, write the first draft of your book report. *Step 2:* Revise your first draft. *Step 3:* Write your final report.

Assignment Checklist

Check your book reports for the following points:

   ✔ 1. Did you begin your introductory paragraph with a sentence that identifies the title and the author of the book?
   ✔ 2. Did you evaluate or give your reaction to the book in your last paragraph?
   ✔ 3. Did you check your book report for correct grammar, usage, spelling, and punctuation?

Check your book reports on works of fiction for these additional points:

   ✔ 4. Did you include a brief description of the main characters and their relationship to one another?
   ✔ 5. Did you give a brief summary of the action, including the main character's problem?

Check your book reports on biographies and autobiographies for these additional points:

✔ 6. Did you discuss the two or three main events in the person's life?

✔ 7. Did you explain why the person is important in a particular field?

Check your book reports on general nonfiction for these additional points:

✔ 8. Did you describe the subject and tell how the author handles it?

✔ 9. Did you discuss the major points that were made by the author?

445

The Beginning of the Whig Party: Preparing an Outline

Situation: To increase interest in politics and voting, the director of the election board in your community has decided to put together a booklet on political parties. The booklet will be sent to all registered voters. As an assistant to the election board, you have been asked to prepare an outline for a report on the beginning of the Whig party in the United States. You have found several useful books and have written note cards from them. As you prepare your outline, keep in mind the following information.

Writer: you as an assistant to the election board
Audience: voters in your community
Topic: the beginning of the Whig party in the United States
Purpose: to make an outline

Directions: To prepare your outline, follow these steps.

    Step 1. Read the note cards on the facing page that you have prepared for your topic.

    Step 2. On your paper, list the subject headings of the note cards. Remember that more than one card may have the same subject heading, and do not list a heading more than once. Then arrange the headings in a logical order. These headings will be the main headings of your outline.

    Step 3. Using the main headings that you listed, write a topic statement for the report on the beginning of the Whig party.

(Continue on page 448.)

446

Why the party formed   McCoy,
"Whig Party"

Wanted to promote goods produced
in the United States in two ways.
1. by placing higher tax on
   imported goods
2. by building roads and canals
   to link farmers with their
   markets
p. 235

First leaders   McCoy,
of the party   "Whig Party"

Henry Clay led the party when
it was formed in 1834. He
had a plan— "the American
system"—to combat President
Andrew Jackson.

p. 235

First leaders   Smith, Banner
of the party

William Henry Harrison was
the first official Whig
Presidential candidate.
He won the election
of 1840.

p. 256

Why the party formed   Johnson,
    Brief History

— To oppose Jackson's use of the
  spoils system
— Jackson had given jobs to
  more than two thousand
  of his supporters.

p. 362

Why called Whigs   Johnson,
    Brief History

— During the Revolutionary War, those
  people opposed to the King of
  England were called Whigs.
— New Whigs disliked Jackson
  because they thought that he
  wanted the power of a king.
— The name Whig was meant
  to emphasize how much
  Jackson was like a king.
p. 365

Why party was formed   Coit,
    Westward

— To oppose Jackson's banking
  policies
— Whigs wanted the Bank of the
  United States to be strong.
— Did not want government
  money sent to the individual
  states

p. 40

Step 4. Using the note cards, choose at least two subheadings for each main heading that you listed.

Step 5. Include the main headings and their corresponding subheadings in a complete outline for a report on the beginning of the Whig party. Place your topic statement at the top of the outline.

Unit Assignments

Assignment 1 Write a report about a wild animal that is native to your state or region. Explain how that animal is unusual or important to the people of your area.

Assignment 2 Write a report about the Olympic event called the decathlon. You might include information on famous winners of the decathlon or discuss how athletes train for the event.

Assignment 3 Write a book report about a novel that takes place in your part of the country. Include information about your reactions to the book as well as information about the actions of the characters.

Assignment 4 Write a book report about a biography or an autobiography. Choose a book about someone whose career interests you or someone from your community or state.

Assignment 5 Write a book report about a nonfiction book dealing with a topic in the news, such as a scientific advance or invention. You might choose a book on computers or about a new medical discovery.

Revising Your Assignments

For help in revising a report, consult the Checklist for Revision on the last page of this book.

449

Unit Tests

Test 1

Test 1 *(pages 450–451)*

A.
1. True
2. False
3. True
4. False
5. True

B.
6. f
7. a
8. c
9. d
10. b

(Continue on the next page.)

A. Number your paper from 1 to 5. Next to each number, write *True* if the sentence is true or *False* if it is false.

1. In a report you should inform your reader about one topic.
2. The *Readers' Guide to Periodical Literature* contains information about the books in a library.
3. On each note card, you should take notes on only one idea.
4. You should include new, interesting points in the concluding paragraph of your report.
5. When preparing a list of sources, arrange the entries in alphabetical order according to the author's last name.

B. Number your paper from 6 to 10. Next to each number, write the letter of the term that correctly completes the sentence. You will use all but one of the items.

a. summary   d. evaluation
b. autobiography   e. biography
c. body   f. introductory paragraph

6. The topic statement of a report is included in the ? .
7. When you take notes, write a(n) ? to state the author's point in your own words.
8. The ? of a brief report consists of two or more paragraphs that present the points from your outline.
9. The last section of a book report should be a(n) ? of the work.
10. A(n) ? is the story of a person's life written by that person.

C. Number your paper from 11 to 15. Next to each number, write the letter of the item that correctly answers the question.

11. Which of the following is an appropriate topic for a report?
    a. Why I enjoy drawing portraits
    b. The appearance of the new sculpture in the park

450

c. Prehistoric cave paintings in France

d. How I learned to make pottery

12. Which of the following is *not* true about a source card?

    a. It should contain the title of the work.

    b. It should contain the name of the author, if it is given.

    c. You will use it when you prepare your outline.

    d. You will use it when your prepare your source list.

13. Which of the following is true about an outline?

    a. It must contain at least eight main headings.

    b. Each main heading must be preceded by a Roman numeral.

    c. It does not contain main headings for the introduction and the conclusion.

    d. Its main headings must be arranged in chronological order.

14. Which of the following should you *not* do when you revise your report?

    a. Check to make sure that you have followed your outline.

    b. Replace unclear language with words and phrases that say exactly what you mean.

    c. Evaluate your sources to see whether they are useful.

    d. Proofread the report.

15. Which of the following should you *not* include in the introductory paragraph of a book report?

    a. The title of the work

    b. The reasons that you liked the work

    c. The name of the author of the work

    d. The type of book: fiction, biography, autobiography, or general nonfiction

Test 2

Choose one of the Unit Assignments. Write the assignment as directed and hand it in to your teacher.

Test 1 *(pages 450–451)*, continued

C.

11. c
12. c
13. b
14. c
15. b

Test 2 *(page 451)*

Answers will vary.

Objectives

After studying this unit, students should be able to do the following:

- Use the appropriate form and content for social letters and write a thank-you note.

- Use the appropriate form and content for business letters and write a request letter and an order letter.

Teaching Suggestions

See "Classroom Insights" for Unit 16 in the front of this Teacher's Edition.

Program Resources

Resource Book, Second Course: Bonus Activities, Unit 16 Composition Checklist, Unit 16
Practice Book, Second Course, Unit 16
Tests, Second Course, Unit 16
Composition Workshops, Second Course, Unit 16

Related Resources

Houghton Mifflin Microcourse: Language Arts, Levels 7, 8
The American Heritage Dictionary of the English Language
Roget's II: The New Thesaurus

Writing Letters

Unit Preview

A letter is a valuable tool, whether you use it to socialize or to transact business. You can use letter-writing skills to entertain, to convey news, to express gratitude, to request information, or to place an order for merchandise.

The social letter on the next page is filled with news of interest to a friend.

For Analysis   On your paper, answer the following questions about the social letter on the next page.

1. What is the purpose of the letter?
2. How does the letter begin?
3. Where does the writer live?
4. What places and events does the writer mention?
5. Why is this called a social letter?

In this unit you will learn how to write two kinds of letters: the social letter and the business letter. You will study the forms of thank-you notes, letters to request information, and letters to order items through the mail. As you write your letters, you will follow the three steps of the writing process: prewriting, writing, and revising.

452

Heading	1513 Tintop Bridge Road Laramie, Wyoming 82070 February 28, 19—
Salutation	Dear Amanda,
Body	It seems as if we've been under three feet of snow since Thanksgiving. Aren't you the lucky one to live in New Orleans! Really, though, it's not so bad. Betsy and I spent the days we couldn't get to school redecorating our room. We made blue-denim drapes and bedspreads. The best news at school is about our basketball team. In the last game, Grover White scored twenty points, and David Volker scored sixteen. This year we're sure to make the play-offs. Yes, I did receive a letter from Peggy. I'm so glad that she got the lead in the play. I wish I could be there on opening night. Will you be there? I hope you are still planning to spend your spring vacation with us. Our team should be in the play-offs by then.
Complimentary close	With love,
Signature	Rachel

For Analysis *(page 452)*

1. The purpose of the letter is to convey news about the writer.
2. The letter begins with news about the weather.
3. The writer lives in Laramie, Wyoming.
4. The writer mentions the weather, her sister, redecorating their room, the school basketball team, Peggy, and a visit during spring vacation.
5. This is called a social letter because it is written from one friend to another and conveys friendly thoughts.

16.1 Writing Social Letters

The purpose of a social letter is to convey friendship, and sometimes thanks, to a friend, a relative, or an acquaintance. A good social letter can be as rewarding as an actual visit. In this section you will learn how to make your letters interesting and entertaining.

453

16.1a Form and Content

Parts of the Social Letter

The five parts of a social letter are named in the left margin of the model letter on page 453. Look at each part as you study its description in the following sections.

Heading.   The heading is your mailing address. It has three lines. In the first line, write your street address, with apartment number if you have one or route number, with box number. In the second line, write your city, state, and ZIP code. In the third line, write the month, day, and year.

Salutation.   The salutation is a greeting. Capitalize the first word and all names. Put a comma after the salutation.

Body.   The body of the social letter contains your message. Refer to events, people, or places that you and your reader have written or talked about in the past, and include current news. Write the body in paragraphs.

Complimentary Close.   Place the complimentary close below the body and to the right. Use a phrase that expresses your affection courteously, such as *Yours truly* or *Affectionately* or *With love,* and follow it with a comma.

Signature.   Sign your name below the complimentary close.

Use the following strategies when writing a social letter.

Strategies

1. *Use unlined, light-colored paper and an envelope to match, and write in blue or black ink.*

2. *Center your letter on the page, using margins of about one inch.*

3. *Write neatly and clearly.*

4. *Capture your reader's interest at the beginning.* Start

454

with a lively news item or a question that you would use in an actual conversation. Do not insult your reader by saying that you are writing because you have nothing else to do.

5. *Keep your reader in mind as you write.* Make sure that your letter sounds cheerful, not gloomy. Include details to help your reader visualize the events that you are writing about. Ask questions that will make it easy for your reader to reply to your letter.

Addressing the Envelope

Write the address of the person who will receive the letter just below and a little to the right of the center of the envelope. In the first line, write the receiver's name. Always include a title, such as *Mr., Mrs., Ms.,* or *Miss.* In the second line, write the exact street address. In the third line, write the city, state, and ZIP code. Use the Postal Service abbreviation (*page 204*) for the state.

In the upper-left corner of the envelope, write your return address. In the first line, write your name; in the second, your street address; in the third, your city, state, and ZIP code. Be sure that all information is complete and correct.

The addressed envelope should look like the following example.

Rachel Gibson
1513 Tintop Bridge Road
Laramie, WY 82070

Miss Amanda Rowe
1021 Sherwood Lane
New Orleans, LA 70126

455

Exercise 1 *(page 456)*

1. Complimentary close
2. Salutation
3. Heading
4. Signature
5. Body

Exercise 2 *(page 456)*

2730 Camp Bowie Boulevard
Pine Knot, Kentucky 42635
August 3, 19—

Dear Linda,
    Thursday night was the start of a surprising and fun-filled birthday weekend for me. I hope your birthday was as much fun as mine. Did you have a party?

    Yours sincerely,

    Jason

Exercise 1   Prewriting: Parts of Social Letters

Number your paper from 1 to 5. Name the part of a social letter to which each of the following items belongs.

1. Very truly yours,
2. Dear Harold,
3. 610 South Third Street
   Ann Arbor, Michigan 48103
   July 27, 19—
4. Natalie
5. I'm writing this letter while riding on a narrow-gauge railway train that goes way up into the mountains.

Exercise 2   Writing: The Social Letter

On a sheet of unlined paper, write the following information as it should appear in a social letter. You will find a beginning and an ending statement for the body of the letter.

1. Yours sincerely,
2. 2730 Camp Bowie Boulevard
3. Thursday night was the start of a surprising and fun-filled birthday weekend for me.
4. Dear Linda,
5. Pine Knot, Kentucky 42635
6. Jason
7. August 3, 19—
8. I hope your birthday was as much fun as mine. Did you have a party?

16.1b The Thank-You Note

    Whenever you receive a gift or a favor from someone, you should show courtesy and gratitude by sending that person a thank-you note. On the following page, study the example of a thank-you note.

456

1301 Locust Street
Chula Vista, California 92011
September 28, 19—

Dear Uncle Mario,

Because you like jazz yourself, I'm sure you know how much I appreciate the book you sent me. Just from glancing through _A Pictorial History of Jazz_, I know that I have many happy and informative hours in store.

Attending the Maple Leaf Jazz Festival during our family vacation in Canada has really made me more interested in jazz. The book you sent will always have a special place on my bookshelf.

Thank you so much.

Love,
Rosa

You may also have occasion to write a note to friends or relatives to thank them for their hospitality while you were visiting them. An example appears on the next page.

Use the strategies on the following page when writing a thank-you note.

457

1021 Rosebud Drive
Dayton, Ohio 45459
August 17, 19—

Dear Mr. and Mrs. Gregory,
    I am really glad that I took so many pictures of the Lazy-8 Ranch while I was visiting there. The photos bring back all those wonderful times. Hiking, fishing — even doing the chores is fun at your place. Without the pictures I would have had a hard time making my friends believe that I rode herd with real cowhands.
    Thank you so much for everything you did to make my visit special. I will always remember it.

                Yours truly,
                Edward Rye

Strategies

1. *Write your note promptly.*
2. *Mention the gift or the favor that you received.* In writing a note, refer to a specific event that occurred during your visit.

458

Exercise 3   Writing: The Thank-You Note   On a sheet of unlined paper, rewrite the following information in the form of a thank-you note. Supply punctuation where needed. Write the body of your note in three paragraphs. Be sure to place the five parts of the letter correctly.

347 Monticello Drive
Norfolk Virginia 23510
july 18, 19—

Dear Aunt Sheila

I had such a wonderful visit with you. I brought home so many souvenirs that I'm still wondering where to put them all. I think that we can say we painted the town red this trip. Thank you for all the special times sightseeing, eating the wonderful meals that you prepared, and just talking. I enjoyed every minute of my visit, especially our visit to the Transportation Museum. Have a good time on your vacation. I hope you will send me a postcard from Canada.

Your nephew

Mike

Assignment 1   Writing   *Step 1:* Suppose that you met someone once while you were away from home with the school band. Write that person a letter. Refer to your school activities, your recreational activities, and your family. Be sure to include questions for your reader. *Step 2:* On your paper, draw an envelope, and address it to your acquaintance. Make up an address, but use your own return address.

Assignment 2   Writing   The parents of a friend of yours in another city invited you to stay with them, so that you and your friend could try out for parts as extras in a

459

Exercise 3 *(page 459)*

347 Monticello Drive
Norfolk, Virginia 23510
July 18, 19—

Dear Aunt Sheila,

I had such a wonderful visit with you. I brought home so many souvenirs that I'm still wondering where to put them all.

I think that we can say we painted the town red this trip. Thank you for all the special times sightseeing, eating the wonderful meals that you prepared, and just talking. I enjoyed every minute of my visit, especially our visit to the Transportation Museum.

Have a good time on your vacation. I hope you will send me a postcard from Canada.

Your nephew,

Mike

movie. You were chosen as an extra, and you stayed with the family for several days. Write a thank-you note to your friend's parents.

Assignment Checklist

Check your assignments for the following points:

    ✔ 1. Did you include all the necessary parts of a social letter?
    ✔ 2. Did you leave uniform margins?
    ✔ 3. Did you mention specific details in your thank-you note?
    ✔ 4. Did you proofread your letter for correct grammar, usage, spelling, and punctuation?
    ✔ 5. Did you check your envelope for completeness, correct spelling, and punctuation?

16.2 Writing Business Letters

You will occasionally need to write a business letter to place an order or to make a request. Your letters should always be neat, courteous, and clearly written.

Read the business letter that appears on the facing page.

16.2a Form and Content

The appearance of your business letter makes an impression on the person who reads it. The letter that makes a good impression most likely will receive a favorable reply. Refer to the parts of the example letter as you study their descriptions.

Parts of the Business Letter

Heading. Place the three lines of the heading in the upper-right corner of your letter or in the upper-left corner, depending on which letter style you use (page 462). Write your street address or your route number in the first line. In

460

Heading	3930 Rainbow Avenue, Apartment 116 Newark, New Jersey 07108 May 19, 19__
Inside address	Preston and Little, Publishers 8200 North Western Avenue Chicago, Illinois 60648
Salutation	Dear Sir or Madam:
Body	I would like to place an order from your current catalogue, <u>Young Readers' Paperbacks</u>. Please send me <u>The Sword of the Spirits Trilogy</u>, by John Christopher, ISBN 0-02-042770-0. The books are paperback and come as a boxed set. The catalogue number is 32-1797. The price for the boxed set is $8.50. I have enclosed a money order for $10.25, which includes the cost of the books and $1.75 for postage and handling. Since the books are for a summer reading program for school, please fill my order by June 6, which is when my summer vacation begins.
Complimentary close	Sincerely,
Signature	*Gwendolyn Noles* Gwendolyn Noles Enclosure

the second line, write your city, state, and ZIP code. Write the month, day, and year in the third line.

Inside Address. The inside address usually has four lines. If you are sending your letter to a particular person, write that person's name or title in the first line. In the second line, write the name of the company. In the third line, give the

461

street address or postal box number of the company. In the last line, give the city, state, and ZIP code.

Salutation.   Use *Dear Sir or Madam* if you do not know the person who will read your letter. Always use a colon after the salutation.

Body.   The body of the letter contains the paragraphs that state your message. Whether you indent your paragraphs depends on which letter-writing style you are using.

Complimentary Close.   Put the complimentary close either at the left margin or slightly to the right of center, depending on which letter-writing style you are using. *Yours truly* or *Sincerely yours* or *Sincerely* are appropriate complimentary closes for business letters.

Signature.   Always write your full name under the complimentary close in longhand, even if you type your letter. Then type or print your name below your signature.

Forms of Business Letters

Business letters are usually written in one of two forms: the block style or the modified block style.

Block Style.   When you use the block style, write the heading, the complimentary close, and your signature at the left margin. Leave a line of space between paragraphs, but do not indent the paragraphs. Use the block style only when you are typing your letter. The letter on page 461 is written in the block style.

Modified Block Style.   When using the modified block style, place the heading, complimentary close, and signature on the right. You may indent paragraphs or begin them at the left margin. The letter on page 467 is written in modified block style.

Addressing the Envelope

Place the same address that you used for the inside address on the front of the envelope. Write or type it slightly below and a little to the right of the center.

For the correct placement of the address and your return address, see page 455.

Folding and Inserting the Letter

Follow the steps shown in the diagrams for folding letters for both long and short envelopes.

Procedure

Long Business Envelopes

1. Place the letter on your desk face up.

2. Fold the bottom of the letter slightly less than one third of the way up.

3. Fold the top of the letter down to within about ½ inch of the first crease.

4. Put the letter into the envelope, inserting the last crease first.

STEP 1	**STEP 2**	**STEP 3**

Short Business Envelopes

1. Place the letter on your desk face up.

2. Fold the bottom of the letter up to within ½ inch of the top edge.

463

3. Fold from right to left about one third of the way.

4. Fold the left side over to within ½ inch of the right side.

5. Put the letter into the envelope, inserting the last crease first.

STEP 1 STEP 2 STEP 3

STEP 4 STEP 5 STEP 6

Use the following strategies when you write a business letter.

Strategies

1. *Use unlined paper measuring 8½ inches by 11 inches.*

2. *Use dark blue or black ink.* Type the letter if it is possible.

3. *Use an appropriate salutation and follow it with a colon.*

4. *Use an appropriate complimentary close and place a comma after it.*

464

5. *Sign your name the way that you want a return letter to be addressed to you.* Print or type your name under your handwritten signature.

6. *Center your letter* so that it has even margins on all four sides.

Exercise 1 Prewriting: Parts of Business Letters
Number your paper from 1 to 4. Rewrite the following parts of a letter, correcting any errors in capitalization, punctuation, and form.

1. very truly yours:

2. dear Sirs,

3. 2835, Oakwood street
   Secaucus New Jersey 07094
   Jan., 5th, 19—

4. james m carroll

Exercise 2 Writing: The Business Letter Using the information in the following list, write a business letter in modified block style on a sheet of unlined paper. Add appropriate punctuation. Then fold your letter to fit a long envelope.

1. Heading: 2736 Asbury Avenue Evanston Illinois
             60201 May 1, 19—

2. Inside Address: Summer Program Director
                  Chicago Park District 425 East
                  McFetridge Drive Chicago,
                  Illinois 60605

3. Salutation: Dear Sir or Madam

4. Body: I heard on the radio that the Chicago Park District is
        planning a series of concerts to be performed in
        various Chicago parks this summer. They will be called
        "Music in the Air" concerts. Would you please send

465

Exercise 1 *(page 465)*

1. Very truly yours,

2. Dear Sirs:

3. 2835 Oakwood Street
   Secaucus, New Jersey 07094
   January 5, 19—

4. James M. Carroll

Exercise 2 *(pages 465–466)*

The letter should follow the style shown on page 467. The letter should be folded as shown on page 463.

2736 Asbury Avenue
Evanston, Illinois 60201
May 1, 19—

Summer Program Director
Chicago Park District
425 East McFetridge Drive
Chicago, Illinois 60605

Dear Sir or Madam:

I heard on the radio that the Chicago Park District is planning a series of concerts to be performed in various Chicago parks this summer. They will be called "Music in the Air" concerts. Would you please send me a schedule for these concerts, including dates and locations. I have enclosed a self-addressed, stamped envelope.

Thank you very much.

Sincerely yours,

Leslie Krantz

Exercise 3 *(page 466)*

The letter should follow the style shown on page 461. The letter should be folded as shown on page 464.

2736 Asbury Avenue
Evanston, Illinois 60201
May 1, 19—

Summer Program Director
Chicago Park District
425 East McFetridge Drive
Chicago, Illinois 60605

Dear Sir or Madam:

I heard on the radio that the Chicago Park District is planning a series of concerts to be performed in various Chicago parks this summer. They will be called "Music in the Air" concerts. Would you please send me a schedule for these concerts, including dates and locations. I have enclosed a self-addressed, stamped envelope.

Thank you very much.

Sincerely yours,

Leslie Krantz

me a schedule for these concerts, including dates and locations. I have enclosed a self-addressed, stamped envelope.

Thank you very much.

5. Complimentary close: Sincerely yours
6. Signature: Leslie Krantz

Exercise 3 Writing: The Block Style   Rewrite the letter that you wrote for Exercise 2, using the block style. Then fold your letter to fit a short envelope.

16.2b The Request Letter

When you need information or when you wish someone to do a favor for you, you have to write a **request letter.** Begin your letter by stating your purpose, give any necessary background information, and finish your letter with a courteous statement. Study the example on the facing page.

Use the following strategies when you are writing a request letter.

Strategies

1. *Give specific details about what you want.*

2. *Provide the necessary background information.* Mention why you are making your request of this particular person or organization.

3. *Make your request courteously.*

4. *Include a self-addressed, stamped envelope, when necessary, for the convenience of the person you are writing.*

466

Exercise 4 *(pages 467–468)*

See page 468 for sample answers.

```
                              1211 Gretna Street
                              Miami, Florida 33134
                              April 4, 19__


        Dr. Paul Adams, Curator
        Fort Marion Museum
        St. Augustine, Florida 32084

        Dear Dr. Adams:
```

Purpose and background

```
            The eighth-grade class at Rainbow Lakes
        School is studying pioneer settlements in
        Florida.  We plan to prepare a set of papers to
        be bound and placed in the local library.
```

Request with details

```
            Will you come and speak to our class about
        pioneer settlements?  We need to know which
        places to visit on field trips and how to do
        our on-site research.
```

Arrangements expressed

```
            Our class meets at 1:15 daily.  We will be
        pleased to have you come at any time that is
        convenient for you within the next three weeks.

            I have enclosed a self-addressed, stamped
        envelope for your answer.

                              Sincerely yours,

                              Mattie Heinz
                              Mattie Heinz
```

Enclosure noted

```
        Enclosure
```

Exercise 4   Revising: The Request Letter   *Step 1:* On your paper, list at least six errors in the following request letter. *Step 2:* Using your answers from Step 1 and any additional information that you may need, write a courteous request letter in block style. The address is The Milwaukee Bucks, 901 North Fourth Street, Milwaukee, Wisconsin 53203. *Step 3:* On your paper, draw a long business envelope

467

Exercise 4 *(pages 467–468)*

Answers may vary. Samples:

1. There is no street address in the heading.

2. There is no ZIP code in the heading.

3. There is no inside address.

4. The salutation is inappropriate.

5. There are no specific details as to how many students or when or why they want to visit.

6. The complimentary close is inappropriate.

The letter should follow the style shown on page 461. The letter should be folded as shown on page 463.

Edgewood Junior High School
150 Edgewood Road
Milwaukee, Wisconsin 53203
May 1, 19—

The Milwaukee Bucks
901 North Fourth Street
Milwaukee, Wisconsin 53203

Dear Sirs:

The basketball team at Edgewood Junior High has the opportunity of winning our league championship this year. One thing we feel will help us is to watch how the pros play and perhaps pick up some new strategies.

(Continue on the next page.)

and write the correct information on it. *Step 4:* Neatly fold your letter to fit a long business envelope.

Edgewood Junior High
Milwaukee, Wisconsin
May 1, 19—

Dear friend,
The students at Edgewood Junior High would like to come watch the Milwaukee Bucks at training.
We need an answer right away.

Yours,

Zeke Benson

16.2c The Order Letter

When you wish to order an item through the mail, you may sometimes have to write an **order letter.** Read the order letter that appears on the facing page.

Use the following strategies when writing an order letter.

Strategies

1. *Mention where you saw the item advertised.* If you are ordering from a catalogue, give the date and number.

2. *Include all necessary information about the item that you wish to purchase:* quantity, name, model number, and price. Often, you will need to give size, color, and weight as well.

3. *Say how you will pay for the merchandise.* Do not send cash. Use a check or a money order.

4. *Indicate whether you need to have the order filled by a certain date.*

468

```
                    Post Office Box 1809
                    Tortilla Flat, Arizona 82590
                    September 10, 19__

Williams Discount House
100 East Central Avenue
Los Angeles, California 90026

Dear Sirs:

     Please send me the following items from
your fall catalogue number 2587:

1    One Hundred-Piece Rock
     and Mineral Set      No. 71-126   $ 5.95
1    Assortment of Oregon
     Jasper               No. 41-956     3.75
1    Field Bag (Medium)   No. 31-365M    4.95
                                       $14.65
                          Handling       2.50
                          Total        $17.15

     I have enclosed a money order for $17.15.

     Because I need these items for a school
project, I would appreciate their delivery by
October 5.

     Thank you very much.

                    Sincerely yours,

                    Katrina Gibbs
                    Katrina Gibbs

Enclosure
```

5. *Write the word* Enclosure *in the bottom left corner if you have enclosed your payment.*

Exercise 5   Writing: The Order Letter   On a sheet of unlined paper, use the following information to write an order letter in modified block style.

469

Exercise 4 *(pages 467–468),* continued

Therefore, we were wondering if it would be possible for twelve students and our coach to come and watch you at training one day during the second week in May. Since we need to make appropriate plans, we would like your reply as soon as possible. I am enclosing a self-addressed, stamped envelope for your convenience.

Thank you very much.

Sincerely yours,

Ezekiel Benson
Team Captain

Envelope

Ezekiel Benson
Edgewood Junior High School
150 Edgewood Road
Milwaukee, Wisconsin 53203

   The Milwaukee Bucks
   901 North Fourth Street
   Milwaukee, Wisconsin 53203

Exercise 5 *(pages 469–470)*

See page 470 for sample answers.

Exercise 5 *(pages 469–470)*

The letter should follow the style shown on page 467. Answers may vary. Sample:

62 Center Street
Clear Spring, Maryland
                    21722
May 1, 19—

Thomson's Novelty Company
926 Menlo Street
Espanola, New Mexico 87532

Dear Sir or Madam:

I would like to order the following items that I saw in your advertisement in the November issue of <u>Your World</u> magazine:

12	yellow pencils imprinted with *Frances Harper*	$2.95
2	lined notepads (5x7 in.) imprinted with *Frances* at the top, at $1.95 each	$3.90

I am enclosing a money order for $8.35, which includes $6.85 for the pencils and notepads and $1.50 for shipping costs.

Thank you very much.

Yours truly,

Frances Harper

Enclosure

1. The letter is from Frances Harper, 62 Center Street, Clear Spring, Maryland 21722. Frances is writing the letter today.

2. Frances is writing to Thomson's Novelty Company, 926 Menlo Street, Espanola, New Mexico 87532.

3. From an advertisement in the November issue of *Your World* magazine, Frances is ordering a dozen yellow pencils imprinted with her full name, costing $2.95 a dozen; and two lined notepads measuring five-by-seven inches, with her first name printed at the top. The notepads cost $1.95 each.

4. Frances has enclosed a money order for $8.35, which includes $6.85 for the pencils and notepads and $1.50 for shipping costs.

Assignment 1   Writing   *Step 1:* Write a request letter to a local newspaper and ask for information about how you can become a newspaper carrier. Make up a name and address for the paper, but use your own return address. *Step 2:* Draw an envelope on your paper, and address it to the paper. Use your own return address.

Assignment 2   Writing   *Step 1:* Order a new pair of Western-style boots from the latest catalogue for Starr Boot Company. The boots come in black, brown, and tan. The cost is twenty-nine dollars, and the company pays the postage. Be sure to include your shoe size. The address is Starr Boot Company, 42 West Main Street, Pocatello, Idaho 83201. *Step 2:* On your paper, draw a long envelope for your letter. Address it, using your own return address.

Assignment 3   Writing   *Step 1:* Write a letter to a local television station in which you request a transcript of a recent interview with your favorite movie performer. *Step 2:* On your paper, draw an envelope, and address it to the television station. Use your own return address.

470

Assignment Checklist

Check your assignments for the following points:

✔ 1. Did you include all the necessary parts of the business letter?

✔ 2. Did you choose one style and use it throughout your letter?

✔ 3. Did you state your purpose clearly, and give appropriate background?

✔ 4. Did you write courteously?

✔ 5. Did you include all the necessary details in your order letter?

✔ 6. Did you proofread your letter for correct grammar, usage, spelling, and punctuation?

✔ 7. Did you proofread your envelope for correct spelling and punctuation?

471

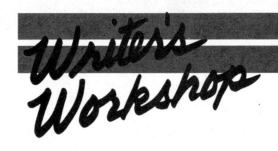

Writer's Workshop

Pen Pals: Hands Across the Ocean

Situation: You want to write a letter to a student in a foreign country. The Pen Pals Around the World Association has sent you a list of names of students your age from many countries, along with a brochure entitled *So You Want a Pen Pal*. As you write your first letter to your pen pal, keep in mind the following information.

Writer: you as an American student

Audience: a student in another country

Topic: interests and activities shared by you and your pen pal

Purpose: to write a social letter

Directions: To write your letter, follow these steps.

Step 1. Read "Pen Pal Questions" on the next page from the Pen Pals Around the World Association.

Step 2. Using the correct format for a social letter, write a letter of two paragraphs to one of the persons whose address you received. In the first paragraph, answer enough questions to give a vivid picture of yourself and your activities. In the second paragraph, ask your pen pal questions about himself or herself. Encourage your pen pal to write and to send you a picture.

Step 3. Address an envelope to your pen pal, using the address on the following page.

472

Pen Pals Around the World
Amarillo, Texas

Pen Pal Questions

Now you have a pen pal. What do you write in your first letter?
Use the following questions as a guide.

<u>Ask these questions.</u>

Where do you live? In an apartment? In a house? On a farm?

What do you look like?

What are you studying in school? What is your favorite
subject? Least favorite?

Is there anything unusual about the community in which you
live? Beautiful scenery? Historic sites?

What activities do you enjoy? Movies? Games? Athletics?

Do you have sisters and brothers?

What are your favorite foods? What is your country famous for?

Your pen pal will want to know the same information about you.

Terry Gwynne
Highgate Station #12
Edinburgh, Scotland EH 2 1EW

Gillian Newman
St. John's Road
Inglewood
Western Australia 6052

Rafael Santos
Plaza Rio de Janeiro
22-302
Mexico City, Mexico

Musa Massaquoi
Lower Buchanan
Grand Bassa County
Liberia

Hans Overath
Lessingweg 4
7400 Tubingen 1
West Germany

473

Unit Assignments

Assignment 1   You have a friend who has moved to Birmingham, Alabama. Write your friend a letter in which you describe recent events at school and in your neighborhood. Remember to ask questions as well.

Assignment 2   You recently visited your grandfather in Portland, Maine. While you were there, you saw a whale for the first time. Also you went to a museum in an old lighthouse. Write a thank-you note to your grandfather.

Assignment 3   You have been considering dentistry as a career. Recently you have been told about related careers that are beginning to emerge in the field of dental health. Write a request letter to the local dental school, asking that a representative talk to your class about dentistry and related career possibilities.

Assignment 4   An article in the November 13, 1968, issue of the *Charleston Bugle* describes the effects of coal mining on the Hundred Canyon prehistoric American ruins in West Virginia. You would like a copy of the article for a project that you are doing in school. Write to the newspaper and request a reprint of the article. The address is

> The *Charleston Bugle*
> 900 Wayne Avenue
> Charleston, West Virginia 25310

Assignment 5   You are concerned about the rising number of stray animals that you have seen wandering in the city. To discover what you can do to help, write a letter to the Society for the Prevention of Cruelty to Animals. You can look up the address of the S.P.C.A. nearest you. Indicate your particular area of concern and request information about S.P.C.A. activities in your neighborhood.

474

Assignment 6 Order these books from the Wheeling State University Press fall catalogue: *Spotted Tail's Folk,* by George E. Hyde, at $1.95; and *The Sacred Pipe,* by Joseph Brown, at $2.75. Both books are paperbacks. The shipping instructions require 63 cents for the first book and 23 cents the second book. The address is

Wheeling State University Press
1005 Ash Avenue
Norman, Oklahoma 73109

Revising Your Assignments

For help in revising a letter, consult the Checklist for Revision on the last page of this book.

Unit Tests

Test 1

Test 1 *(pages 476–477)*

A.

1. True
2. False
3. True
4. True
5. False

B.

6. c
7. a
8. b
9. d
10. f

(Continue on the next page.)

A. Number your paper from 1 to 5. Next to each number, write *True* if the sentence is true or *False* if it is false.

1. A comma always follows the salutation in a social letter.
2. The inside address of a social letter gives the sender's name.
3. The signature in a social letter is always handwritten.
4. The salutation of a social letter is the same as a greeting.
5. The social letter should begin with courteous questions about the reader's health.

B. Number your paper from 6 to 10. Next to each number, write the letter of the word or phrase that best fills in the blank.

a. thank-you note	e. modified block
b. block	f. enclosure
c. heading	g. social letter
d. inside address	

6. The writer's mailing address is the __?__ of any letter.
7. When you have been a guest in someone's home, you express your thanks to your hosts by writing a __?__.
8. All parts of the letter start at the left margin in the __?__ style of business letter.
9. The social letter has all the parts of the business letter except for the __?__.
10. Write __?__ at the bottom of your business letter when you have included a check, a money order, or a self-addressed, stamped envelope.

C. Number your paper from 11 to 15. Next to each number, write the letter of the item that correctly completes the statement.

476

476 Unit 16

11. Which of the following would you write to obtain brochures about camping areas in your state?

    a. Order letter

    b. Social letter

    c. Request letter

12. Which of the following is *not* an appropriate salutation for a business letter?

    a. Dear Sir:

    b. Dear Sir,

    c. Dear Sir or Madam:

13. Which of the following should be added to the bottom left of your order letter when you are including a payment?

    a. A money order

    b. Background details

    c. The word *Enclosure*

14. The signature of a business letter should always be which of the following?

    a. Handwritten and printed

    b. Handwritten or printed

    c. The last item on the page

15. Which of the following is *not* a strategy for writing a business letter?

    a. Make certain that the heading and the inside address are complete.

    b. Write your letter in pencil.

    c. Choose either the block style or the modified block style, and use it consistently in your letter.

Test 2

Choose one of the Unit Assignments. Write the assignment as directed and hand it in to your teacher.

Test 1 *(pages 476–477),* continued

C.

11. c

12. b

13. c

14. a

15. b

Test 2 *(page 477)*

Answers will vary.

477

Part Three

Related Skills

Unit 17   Spelling Skills   480

Unit 18   Vocabulary Skills   492

Unit 19   Study Skills   504

Unit 20   Listening Skills   514

Unit 21   Speaking Skills   524

Unit 22   Library Skills   536

Unit 23   Test-Taking Skills   548

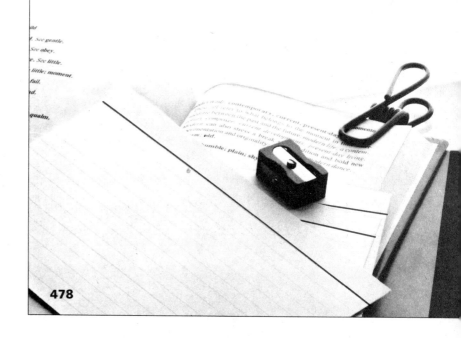

478

The information and strategies that are presented in Part Three will be useful in your school assignments and in your activities outside of school. By learning skills that are related to writing, you will be able to write more effectively, and you will discover how to apply your writing skills to a variety of tasks. Techniques for improving your spelling and enlarging your vocabulary will make all of your writing more precise and more interesting. Study skills, library skills, and test-taking skills will help you in many kinds of assignments. Listening and speaking skills will enable you to participate in group discussions, to listen critically when other people speak, and to give effective presentations yourself.

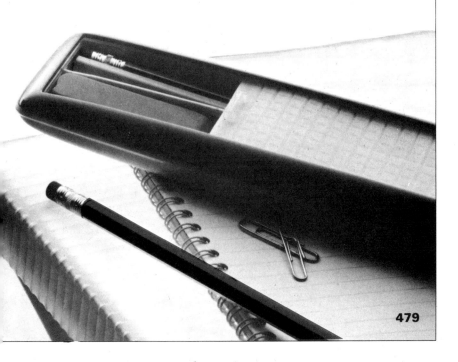

479

Unit 17

Objectives

After studying this unit, students should be able to do the following:

- Use a step-by-step procedure to study spelling words.

- Use spelling rules to make nouns plural and to add endings.

- Spell words with *ie* or *ei*.

- Avoid pronunciation errors that can lead to spelling errors.

- Avoid spelling errors associated with homophones, words that may be confused, and overlooked letters.

- Use a set of strategies to improve their spelling, use the dictionary as a spelling aid, and spell a list of twenty-five frequently misspelled words.

Teaching Suggestions

See "Classroom Insights" for Unit 17 in the front of this Teacher's Edition.

Program Resources

Resource Book, Second Course: Bonus Activities, Unit 17
Practice Book, Second Course, Unit 17

Related Resources

The American Heritage Dictionary of the English Language

Spelling Skills

Knowing how to spell is important, both as a student and as an adult. In developing the skills that will help you to spell correctly, your goal should be to master those words that you misspell frequently. The methods and rules presented in this unit will help you to achieve that goal.

17.1 How to Study Spelling Words

Use the following steps to study words that you want to learn to spell.

Procedure

1. *Look at the word carefully* and study its letters.

2. *Pronounce the word.* If it has more than one syllable, say the word slowly—syllable by syllable. Note the sound that each letter spells or helps to spell.

3. *Write the word.* Pay special attention to difficult letter combinations.

4. *Check your spelling* to see whether it is correct.

5. *Write the word once more* if your spelling is correct. If it is not correct, note the part of the word that you misspelled. Then repeat the steps of this procedure until you are confident of your ability to spell the word.

480

17.2 Spelling Rules

17.2a Making Nouns Plural

A **singular noun** names one person, place, thing, or idea. A **plural noun** names more than one person, place, thing, or idea. You can improve your spelling by learning the rules for making nouns plural.

Regular Plurals

Most nouns form their plurals by adding either *-s* or *-es* to the singular form.

Rule Form the plural of almost all nouns by adding *-s* to the singular.

coat	empire	motor
coats	empires	motors

Rule Form the plural of a noun ending in *s, x, z, ch,* or *sh* by adding *-es* to the singular.

class	wax	waltz	starch
classes	waxes	waltzes	starches

Rule Form the plural of a noun ending in *o* preceded by a vowel by adding *-s* to the singular.

igloo	patio	rodeo
igloos	patios	rodeos

Rule Form the plural of a noun ending in *ay, ey, oy,* or *uy* by adding *-s* to the singular.

tray	monkey	alloy	buy
trays	monkeys	alloys	buys

481

Rule   Form the plural of a noun ending in *y* preceded by a consonant by changing the *y* to *i* and adding *-es*.

berry	energy	courtesy
berries	energies	courtesies

Rule   Form the plural of most nouns ending in *f* or *fe* by adding *-s* to the singular.

fife	proof	waif
fifes	proofs	waifs

Rule   Form the plural of some nouns ending in *f* or *fe* by changing the *f* or *fe* to *v* before adding *-es*.

calf	knife	leaf
calves	knives	leaves

Rule   Form the plural of proper nouns by adding *-s* or *-es* to the singular.

Viking	John and Ana Lopez	the Hardy boys
the Vikings	the Lopezes	the Hardys

Irregular Plurals

The following are examples of some irregular plurals. To improve your spelling, you should memorize the correct irregular forms as you come across them. Whenever you are in doubt, however, check the spelling in your dictionary.

1. Nouns that end in *o* preceded by a consonant. For some nouns, add *-s* to the singular:

alto	photo	tango
altos	photos	tangos

For some nouns, add *-es* to the singular:

echo	torpedo	veto
echoes	torpedoes	vetoes

482

For some nouns, add either -*s* or -*es* to the singular:

halo	lasso	zero
halos	lassos	zeros
haloes	lassoes	zeroes

Assignment 1 *(pages 483–484)*

See page 484 for the answers.

The preferred spelling for this kind of noun will be the first spelling listed in your dictionary entry. (See Unit 18, Section 18.5.)

2. Nouns that do not add -*s* or -*es* to form the plural.

foot	goose	man
feet	geese	men

3. Nouns that are the same in both the singular and the plural.

Japanese	moose	trout

Compound Nouns

Rule Form the plural of a compound noun that is written as one word by changing the last word in the compound to its correct plural form.

bottleneck	grandchild	sidewalk
bottlenecks	grandchildren	sidewalks

Rule Form the plural of a compound noun that is hyphenated or written as separate words by changing the most important word to its correct plural form.

mother-in-law	rule of thumb	swimming pool
mothers-in-law	rules of thumb	swimming pools

Assignment 1 **Rules for Plurals** Write the plural form of each of the following singular nouns by applying one of the rules in Section 17.2a. Check the spelling of each plural form in your dictionary. Use each plural noun in a sentence.

483

Assignment 1 *(pages 483–484)*

Only the plural forms are given.
Sentences will vary.

1. deer
2. donkeys
3. boxes
4. wolves
5. radios
6. strategies
7. women
8. cattle
9. safes
10. tomatoes
11. chiefs
12. sisters-in-law
13. mice
14. heads of state
15. Chinese

1. deer	6. strategy	11. chief
2. donkey	7. woman	12. sister-in-law
3. box	8. cattle	13. mouse
4. wolf	9. safe	14. head of state
5. radio	10. tomato	15. Chinese

17.2b Adding Endings

You have just studied the rules for making nouns plural. The following rules will help you to add other endings to nouns and to words used as other parts of speech.

Doubling the Final Consonant

Double the final consonant of the base word only when you are adding an ending that begins with a vowel, for example, *-ing, -ed,* and *-ance.* Then follow these rules.

Rule   Double the final consonant if the word has only one syllable and ends with a single consonant preceded by a single vowel.

cap	dip	pop	set
capped	dipper	popped	setting

Rule   Double the final consonant if the word (1) has more than one syllable, (2) ends with a single consonant preceded by a single vowel, and (3) is stressed on the final syllable.

abut	begin	permit	refer
abutting	beginning	permitted	referral

Answering the following questions about the base word can help you to apply the preceding rules.

1. Is the base word a one-syllable word, or is it a multi-syllable word that is stressed on the final syllable? The words *dip* and *begin* meet this test. The word *happen* does not, for it is stressed on the first syllable.

2. Does the base word end in a single consonant? The words *dip* and *begin* meet this test. However, the words *cost* (*st*) and *sport* (*rt*) do not.
3. Is the final consonant in the base word preceded by a single vowel? The words *dip* and *begin* meet this test. However, the words *creep* (*ee*) and *reveal* (*ea*) do not.

Dropping the Final *e*

Rule If a word ends in silent *e,* drop the final *e* before adding an ending that begins with a vowel.

approve	sincere	slice
approval	sincerity	slicing

Rule If a word ends in silent *e* preceded by *c* or *g*, keep the final *e* when adding an ending that begins with *a* or *o*.

change	manage	notice	outrage
changeable	manageable	noticeable	outrageous

Rule If a word ends in silent *e*, you usually keep the final *e* when adding an ending that begins with a consonant.

	manage	care	late
	management	careless	lately
BUT	true	whole	
	truly	wholly	

Changing Final *y* to *i*

Rule If a word ends in *y* preceded by a consonant, you usually change the *y* to *i* before adding any ending except *-ing*.

	apply	friendly	cry
	applied	friendliness	crying
BUT	sly	wry	
	slyness	wryly	

485

Assignment 2 *(page 486)*

Only the words with added endings are given. Sentences will vary.

1. dropped
2. priceless
3. likable
4. controlling
5. shopping
6. referring
7. courageous
8. stayed
9. tried
10. happiness

Rule If a word ends in *y* preceded by a vowel, you usually do not change the *y* to *i* before adding an ending.

	buy	delay	enjoy
	buyer	delayed	enjoying
BUT	day		
	daily		

Assignment 2   Adding Endings On your paper, add the indicated endings to the following base words. Use the rules in Section 17.2b to help you write your words. Check the spelling of each word in your dictionary. Write a sentence for each new word.

1. drop *(-ed)*
2. price *(-less)*
3. like *(-able)*
4. control *(-ing)*
5. shop *(-ing)*
6. refer *(-ing)*
7. courage *(-ous)*
8. stay *(-ed)*
9. try *(-ed)*
10. happy *(-ness)*

17.3 The *ie/ei* Pattern

The following rules establish a pattern for spelling words that contain the vowel combinations *ie* or *ei*.

Rule When the vowel combination has the long *e* sound (as in *achieve*), you usually write *ie* except after *c*. After *c*, write *ei*.

	believe	thief	conceit
	field	shield	deceit
BUT	protein	either	

Rule When the vowel combination has the long *a* sound (as in *weigh*), always write *ei*.

freight   eighty   neighborly   weighty

486

Rule When the vowel combination does not have the long *e* sound, you usually write *ei*.

	foreign	forfeit	sleight
BUT	friendly	mischief	

Assignment *ie/ei* On your paper, write each of the following words, completing each blank with *ie* or *ei*. Check the spelling of each word in your dictionary. Use each completed word in a sentence.

1. p_?_ce
2. dec_?_t
3. w_?_gh
4. fr_?_nd
5. handkerch_?_f
6. n_?_ther
7. rec_?_ve
8. ch_?_f
9. n_?_ce
10. l_?_sure

Assignment *(page 487)*

Only the words are given. Sentences will vary.

1. piece
2. deceit
3. weigh
4. friend
5. handkerchief
6. neither
7. receive
8. chief
9. niece
10. leisure

17.4 Spelling What You Hear

How you pronounce a word can affect how you spell it. Here are some pronunciation problems that often lead to misspellings.

Extra Syllables. Do you pronounce *athlete* with two syllables or three? Do you pronounce *disastrous* with three syllables or four? Adding syllables when you pronounce a word can result in adding extra letters when you spell the word. This kind of error can occur in the following words. The number in parentheses tells how many syllables the word has. Be careful not to add extra syllables when you pronounce these words.

decathlon (3) laundry (2) grievous (2) umbrella (3)

Omitted Sounds. Do you pronounce the final *t* in *attempt*? Do you pronounce the second *i* in *privilege*? People sometimes misspell a word because they omit a sound when they pronounce the word. The words in the following list are

487

examples of words from which sounds are sometimes omitted. Be sure to include the sound or sounds for the underlined letters when you pronounce these words. If you do, you are more likely to spell the words correctly.

arctic   library   nothing   surprise

Transposed Letters.   When you pronounce *children,* do you say "chil**dren**" or "chil**dern**"? People sometimes misspell a word because when they pronounce it, they transpose certain letters. The words in the following list are examples of words in which letters are sometimes transposed. Be sure that you pronounce and spell the underlined letters in the right order.

modern   hundred   perspective   secretary

Assignment   Pronunciation and Spelling   Pronounce each of the following words. Check your pronunciation in a dictionary. Then use each word in a sentence.

1. surgery
2. something
3. perhaps
4. realize
5. bachelor
6. cavalry
7. tragedy
8. fact
9. bronchial
10. larynx

17.5 Spelling What You See

The explanations that follow describe some other common sources of misspelling.

Homophones.   Do you write "*Deer* Mary" when you mean "*Dear* Mary"? Words that have the same pronunciation but different spellings and meanings are **homophones.** You can learn the spellings of these kinds of words by fixing both the meanings and the spellings firmly in your mind. Be sure that you know the spelling and meaning of each word in the following list of homophones.

488

bare, bear	hole, whole	plain, plane
blew, blue	hour, our	right, write
board, bored	it's, its	their, there, they're
cell, sell	knew, new	to, too, two
hear, here	peace, piece	your, you're

Words Often Confused. Did you see *statues* in the museum, or did you see *statutes*? Some words are not homophones but are similar enough in sound or spelling to cause confusion. The following list includes commonly confused words.

affect, effect	later, latter	quiet, quite
choose, chose	partition, petition	weather, whether

Overlooked Letters. Do you sometimes forget about the *p* in *pneumonia* or the *n* in *column*? Sometimes people overlook letters that help another letter spell a sound. When you spell the following words, pay special attention to the underlined letters.

answer   condemn   descend   knowledge

Assignment   **Commonly Confused Words**   Use a dictionary to write simple definitions for five sets of words from the preceding list of homophones. Make sure that your definitions show the difference in the meanings of the words in each of the sets. Then write a sentence or two using the words in each set. Underline the words from the list.

SAMPLE   their, there, they're

ANSWER   Their is the possessive form of them.
               There is an adverb meaning "in that place."
               They're is a contraction of *they* and *are*.
               They're planning to drive there in their new car.

489

17.6 Other Spelling Helps

This section offers some additional strategies that will help you to improve your spelling. You will also find some guides for finding dictionary entries for words that you do not know how to spell. Also included is a list of twenty-five frequently misspelled words for you to learn to spell.

Strategies

1. *Keep a list of troublesome words.* Whenever you are unsure of the spelling of a word, write the word correctly in a special section of your notebook. This will be your personal spelling list. At least once a week, study your list by following the steps on page 480.

2. *Think carefully about how words are pronounced and written.* Pay special attention to the issues discussed in Sections 17.4 and 17.5.

3. *Make up memory aids.* There are a number of ways that you can help yourself to remember the trouble spots in a word. Here are some examples:

   A *critic* writes **criticism.**
   Can you find *them* in **mathematics**?

4. *Proofread your written work.* Be on the alert not only for misspellings but also for careless handwriting that makes the spelling unclear; for example, avoid *o*'s that look like *a*'s and uncrossed *t*'s that look like *l*'s.

The Dictionary as a Spelling Aid

Whenever you are unsure of the spelling of a word, use your dictionary (Unit 18, Section 5). Remember that most dictionaries include as part of the entry those word forms that involve a doubled final consonant, a dropped final *e*, and other irregularities.

490

To find a word that you cannot spell, you have to be familiar with the various spellings for consonant and vowel sounds. The following list shows different spellings for some of the sounds that occur at the beginning of words.

CONSONANT SOUNDS	OTHER SPELLINGS
f, as in *fence*	*ph*, as in *physics*
j, as in *jaw*	*g*, as in *gem*
k, as in *kit*	*c*, as in *cape; ch*, as in *chemical*
n, as in *not*	*gn*, as in *gnat; kn*, as in *knit*
	pn, as in *pneumonia*
r, as in *rice*	*wr*, as in *wrap*
s, as in *sit*	*c*, as in *civil; ps*, as in *psychology*

VOWEL SOUNDS	OTHER SPELLINGS
a, as in *ate*	*ei*, as in *eighty*
e, as in *echo*	*a*, as in *any*
i, as in *if*	*e*, as in *erase*
u, as in *user*	*yu*, as in *yule; you*, as in *youth*

Frequently Misspelled Words

The following list contains twenty-five words that you probably use often in your writing. Use the steps on page 480 to learn to spell these frequently misspelled words.

among	guarantee	rhythm
apparent	incidentally	ridiculous
approximately	indefinite	suspicion
control	interfere	temporarily
convenience	mathematics	Tuesday
criticism	opinion	typical
exhibition	ordinarily	until
existence	profession	
experience	pursue	

Assignment Frequently Misspelled Words On your paper, write sentences in which you use ten of the frequently misspelled words in the preceding list. Underline the words in your sentences.

491

Unit 18

After studying this unit, students should be able to do the following:

- Use a set of strategies to learn new words.
- Use context to determine the meanings of unfamiliar words.
- Use word parts to determine the meanings of unfamiliar words.
- Choose the best word for a given situation, making use of synonyms and of denotation and connotation.
- Use the dictionary.

Teaching Suggestions

See "Classroom Insights" for Unit 18 in the front of this Teacher's Edition.

Program Resources

Resource Book, Second Course: Bonus Activities, Unit 18
Practice Book, Second Course, Unit 18

Related Resources

Houghton Mifflin Microcourse: Language Arts, Levels 7, 8
The American Heritage Dictionary of the English Language
Roget's II: The New Thesaurus

Vocabulary Skills

Your **vocabulary** consists of the words that you use when you speak or write and the words that you understand when you listen or read. A good vocabulary can help you to communicate effectively.

18.1 How to Learn New Words

This unit will provide you with strategies to increase your vocabulary through the use of context clues, word parts, word choices, and the dictionary.

Strategies

1. *Keep a vocabulary notebook.* Use a special section in your notebook for listing unfamiliar words that you read or hear.

2. *Use your dictionary to find the meanings of unfamiliar words.* Write the meanings in your notebook next to the words on your list. Then write a sentence using each word in a way that conveys its meaning.

3. *Review the words in your notebook to fix their meanings in your mind.*

4. *Use the words in your notebook in your conversation and writing,* and watch for them when you read or listen.

492

5. *Add prefixes and suffixes to the words on your list and to words that you already know.* Forming new words from familiar words can help you to expand your vocabulary.

18.2 Using Context to Get Meaning

The general setting in which something appears is its **context.** When you come across an unfamiliar word, use the words that you do know in the context to figure out the meaning of the unfamiliar word.

There are three things to look for in the context that can help you to determine the meaning of an unfamiliar word: the sense of the passage, synonyms, and examples.

Sense of the Passage.   Use the general idea of the passage to look for clues to the meaning of an unfamiliar word. For example, in the following passage, notice how the idea of fighting without any thought of surrender provides a clue to the meaning of the word *flag*.

> We shall not *flag* or fail. We shall go on to the end . . . we shall fight in the seas and oceans . . . we shall fight in the fields and in the streets . . . we shall never surrender.
>
> Winston Churchill

The familiar words *fail* and *surrender*, as well as the overall meaning of the passage, tell you that in this context *flag* probably means "to weaken" or "to slacken."

Synonyms.   Sometimes the context includes a synonym *(page 498)* for an unfamiliar word. If you know the meaning of the synonym, you can usually figure out the meaning of the unfamiliar word.

A *prudent* person makes wise decisions.

In this sentence, the synonym *wise* provides a meaning for the word *prudent*.

493

Examples.   Sometimes a writer includes examples that explain the meaning of an unfamiliar word or idea. Knowing what kinds of things a word refers to can help you to figure out the meaning.

The speaker *digressed* several times from the subject of astronomy; for example, he told a story about his trip to an amusement park and several jokes about his attempts at gourmet cooking.

The examples in the preceding sentence are instances of not keeping to the subject. You can therefore figure out that to *digress* probably means "to stray from the subject."

The following words often signal that examples follow:

as	for example	like
especially	for instance	such as

Assignment   Context   *Step 1:* In a newspaper or a magazine find four paragraphs that contain at least one word that is unfamiliar to you. Write the paragraphs in your notebook and circle the unfamiliar words. *Step 2:* Use the context to figure out the meaning of each circled word. Then, write the word and its meaning in your notebook. *Step 3:* In your dictionary, find each word and compare the dictionary definition with the one that you determined from the context.

18.3 How to Learn New Words from Word Parts

Words may consist of three parts: (1) the base word, (2) a prefix, and (3) a suffix. The word *unknowing,* for example, is made up of the prefix *un-,* the base word *know,* and the suffix *-ing.* Words usually have only one prefix, but they often have more than one suffix: *un-know-ing-ly.* Knowing the meanings of prefixes and suffixes can help you to unlock the meaning of an unfamiliar word.

Prefixes. A **prefix** is a letter or a group of letters added to the beginning of a base word to make a new word. When you add a prefix, the spelling of the base word does not change.

The meaning of a base word often does change when you add a prefix. For example, the prefix *un-* means "not." When you add *un-* to a base word, the new word usually has a meaning opposite to that of the base word.

un- + knowing = unknowing (not knowing)
un- + helpful = unhelpful (not helpful)

Here are some common prefixes and their meanings:

PREFIX	MEANINGS	EXAMPLES
co-	together, mutually	copilot, coexist
in- (il-, im-, ir-)	not	insecure, illiterate immature, irregular
inter-	between, among	intersect, interact
pre-	prior, before	preheat, prehistoric
re-	back, again	replace, react

Suffixes. A **suffix** is a letter or a group of letters added at the end of a base word. A suffix sometimes changes the meaning of the word to which it is added. Most suffixes also change the part of speech of the base word. Like prefixes, suffixes have meanings that can be found in the dictionary.

Noun suffixes. Certain suffixes are used to make nouns from other words. Study the following examples.

SUFFIX	MEANINGS	EXAMPLES
-ance	action, quality, condition	acceptance, buoyance
-ee	receiver of action, condition	addressee, standee
-ist	one who does, believes in, is an expert in	artist, motorist
-ment	product, means, action, state	basement, judgment
-ness	state, quality, condition	roughness, kindness

495

Verb suffixes. Certain suffixes are used to make verbs from other words. The following examples illustrate the use of four more suffixes.

SUFFIX	MEANINGS	EXAMPLES
-ate	make, apply, do	activate, regulate
-en	cause to be, become	lighten, frighten
-fy	make, cause to be	humidify, glorify
-ize	make into, cause to be	idolize, homogenize

Adjective suffixes. Certain suffixes are used to make adjectives from other words.

SUFFIX	MEANINGS	EXAMPLES
-able, -ible	capable, worthy of, inclined to	flexible, honorable, lovable
-ful	having, full of	beautiful, careful
-ish	suggesting, like	foolish, fiendish
-ous	having, full of	courageous, vivacious
-less	without	careless, fearless

Adverb suffixes. Many adverbs are formed by adding the suffix -*ly* to an adjective.

avid	bright	honest	immediate
avidly	brightly	honestly	immediately

Suffixes and Spelling.   When you add a suffix to a base word, apply the rules for doubling or not doubling the final consonant *(pages 484–485)*, for dropping or keeping the final *e (page 485)*, and for changing *y* to *i (pages 485–486)*.

run	fame	play
runner	famous	playful
edit	hope	plenty
editor	hopeful	plentiful

When you add the suffix *-ly* to a word that ends in *l*, remember to write both *l*'s. When you add the suffix *-ness* to a word that ends in *n*, remember to write both *n*'s.

joyful   open
joyfully   openness

Assignment 1 Prefixes   On your paper, combine the base word in parentheses with one of the prefixes listed on page 495 to form a new word that will replace the blank in each of the following sentences. Use a different prefix for each new word. Write a sentence using each new word.

1. Someone who works with you is a __?__. (worker)
2. Someone who is deep in thought is __?__. (occupied)
3. When you bring unused merchandise back to the store you get a __?__. (fund)
4. A law that is mutually observed by two states is an __?__ law. (state)
5. A measurement that is not exact is __?__. (exact)
6. A garment with a defect in it is __?__. (perfect)
7. Something that is prohibited by law is __?__. (legal)
8. A remark that is not relevant is __?__. (relevant)

Assignment 2 Suffixes   On your paper, use the suffixes listed on pages 495–496 to change each of the words in italic type to the part of speech that is indicated. Use each new word in a sentence.

1. Change the verb *tour* to a noun meaning "one who tours."
2. Change the noun *height* to a verb meaning "to cause to grow or extend."
3. Change the noun *youth* to an adjective meaning "having the characteristics of being young."
4. Change the adjective *rapid* to an adverb meaning "with great speed."
5. Change the verb *transport* to an adjective meaning "able to be moved from one place to another."

497

Assignment 3   *(page 498)*

1. envious (*or* enviable)
2. emptiness
3. actually
4. impish
5. artist (*or* artful)
6. inflatable
7. encouragement
8. lengthen
9. tasteless
   (*or* tastable, tasteful)
10. merciful (*or* merciless)

Assignment 3   Suffixes and Spelling   On your paper, copy the words numbered from 1–10. Add a suffix from the following list to each word to make a new word. Do not use a suffix more than once. Check the spelling of each new word in your dictionary.

WORDS

1. envy	5. art	9. taste
2. empty	6. inflate	10. mercy
3. actual	7. encourage	
4. imp	8. length	

SUFFIXES

-able	-ist	-ment
-en	-less	-ness
-ful	-ly	-ous
-ish		

18.4 How to Choose the Best Word

When you use your vocabulary, be sure to choose the word that expresses exactly what you want to say. Choosing the best word will make what you say interesting and easy to understand.

You can learn to choose the best word by studying synonyms and their meanings and by recognizing the difference between denotations and connotations.

Synonyms

Synonyms are words that have the same or nearly the same meaning. To help you distinguish the difference, many dictionaries include paragraphs that show the various shades of meaning of synonyms. The synonym paragraph for the word *fragile* might look like this:

> **Synonyms:** *fragile, breakable, frail, delicate, brittle.* These adjectives mean "susceptible to being broken or injured." *Fragile* describes objects whose lightness or delicacy requires

498

that they be handled with great care. *Breakable* refers to what can be broken but does not imply inherent weakness. *Frail* is applicable to persons and things and implies a slightness of structure and a lack of durability. *Delicate* suggests lack of durability or a susceptibility to injury. *Brittle* refers to the hardness and inelasticity of a material that makes it especially subject to fracture.

Use the synonym paragraphs in your dictionary to help you choose the right words. You can also use a specialized book of synonyms called a **thesaurus** to help you to distinguish the different meanings of synonyms.

Denotation and Connotation

Many words have two kinds of meanings. The dictionary meaning of a word is its **denotation.** The attitudes and feelings associated with a word are its **connotation.**

The difference between denotation and connotation can often be seen in the synonyms given for a word. For example, each of the following synonyms for *tired* carries a different connotation: *weary, exhausted, fatigued.*

You can detract from what you want to say by using a word that has an inappropriate connotation. For example, to describe someone who has just finished running in a marathon as *weary* would be an understatement.

Sometimes the same word can have different connotations when used in different contexts. Notice the different connotations of the noun *idealist* in the following contexts.

Paul is such an idealist; he always has his head in the clouds.

Joanne is an idealist, and she puts her ideals into practice through her work.

Assignment 1 Synonyms Use the synonym paragraph for *fragile* to help you complete the following sentences using these words: *fragile, breakable, frail, delicate,* or *brittle.*

Assignment 1 *(pages 499–500)*

See page 500 for sample answers.

499

Assignment 1 *(pages 499–500)*

Only sample completions are given. Sentences will vary.
1. brittle
2. delicate
3. breakable
4. fragile
5. frail

Assignment 2 *(page 500)*

Answers will vary.

Use each word only once. Then use each synonym in an original sentence that clearly conveys its meaning.

1. When we grow older, our bones may become __?__.
2. Those china teacups are too __?__ for everyday use.
3. Do not load the dishwasher with items that are easily __?__.
4. The __?__ glassware was delivered in a carton packed with shredded newspaper.
5. The cottages along the beach look too __?__ to withstand the force of a hurricane.

Assignment 2   Connotation   Choose four pairs of the following eight pairs of synonyms. In your dictionary, look up the meaning of each of the words. Then write one or two sentences that clearly show the difference in the connotative meanings of the words in each of the pairs. Underline the words in your sentences.

SAMPLE	thrifty—stingy
ANSWER	Marie is quite *thrifty*. She always compares prices and checks for sales before making major purchases.
	Frances is one of the *stingiest* people I know; she hates to part with a nickel.

1. scheme—plan
2. ask—beg
3. linger—loiter
4. reason—argue

5. flatter—praise
6. shrewd—clever
7. retreat—withdraw
8. sloppy—casual

18.5   Using the Dictionary

From time to time in this unit, you have been referred to your dictionary as a source for building your vocabulary. If you wish to find the meaning, the pronunciation, or other information about a word, you need to know how to use your dictionary.

500

Locating a Word

Guide Words. Guide words are the words printed in boldface type at the top of a dictionary page. The first guide word is the first entry word on the page. The second guide word is the last entry word on the page. All the entry words that fall alphabetically between the two guide words can be found on that page. For example, the words *contravene, contribute, controller,* and *convalesce* can be found on a dictionary page with the guide words **contrast** and **conviction.**

The Entry Word and the Entry. The words listed in a dictionary are called **entry words.** The entry word and the information that follows it are called the **entry.**

Finding Information About a Word

Syllabication. A centered dot in the entry word is used to show how a word is divided into syllables.

Pronunciations. Most entries show the pronunciation immediately after the entry word. Pronunciations are usually enclosed in parentheses, brackets, or bars. Hyphens are usually used to show the syllables in a word.

In the front of most dictionaries you will find a guide to the pronunciation symbols and a complete key. A shortened key usually appears at the bottom of facing pages. Because pronunciation keys differ from one dictionary to another, you should become familiar with the key used in your dictionary.

Parts of Speech. An abbreviated part-of-speech label usually follows the pronunciation. The following abbreviations are used in most dictionaries to indicate the parts of speech:

n.—noun	*conj.*—conjunction
adj.—adjective	*prep.*—preposition
adv.—adverb	*v.*—verb
pron.—pronoun	*interj.*—interjection

501

The abbreviations *sing.* and *pl.* indicate singular and plural forms.

Changes in Form. In English there are three major changes in word form: (1) a change in the form of a noun to show the plural, (2) a change in the form of a verb to show the principal parts, and (3) a change in the form of an adjective or an adverb to show degrees of comparison. In most dictionaries these changes in form are shown after the part-of-speech label.

The entry for regular verbs usually gives the past form, the present participle, and the singular form. For irregular verbs only, the past participle form is also given. Pronunciation is given for some, but not all, verb forms.

Definitions.   Many English words have three or four separate meanings or shades of meaning. In most dictionaries, the different meanings are numbered. Letters may also be used to indicate meanings closely related to the numbered definitions. Often an example is given to show the sense of a word in a particular context.

Homographs.   Words that are spelled alike but have different origins and different meanings are **homographs.** Homographs are usually listed as separate entry words and are identified by a small raised numeral placed before or after the entry word.

Synonyms.   On pages 498–499 of this unit, you studied an example of a synonym paragraph for the entry word *fragile.* In most dictionaries a cross-reference is provided at each entry that is included in a synonym paragraph. For example, the cross-reference at the entry words *breakable, frail, delicate,* and *brittle* would read "See Synonyms at **fragile.**"

Usage Labels.   Most dictionaries use labels to restrict the use of certain words. Some commonly used usage labels are *Nonstandard, Informal,* and *Slang.* Such labels are explained

502

in detail in the introduction to the dictionary. Some dictionaries also include usage notes that explain the use of a word in a particular sense.

Assignment 1 Improving Your Vocabulary In a newspaper or a magazine, find at least two articles that interest you. From the articles choose five or more words whose meanings are unfamiliar to you. Check the meanings of these words in your dictionary. Then use each word in a sentence that clearly conveys its meaning.

Assignment 2 You and Your Dictionary Spend some time becoming familiar with the dictionary that you use for your school work. Plan to report to your class on how your dictionary gives the information described on pages 500–503. For example: How are pronunciations shown? How and where are changes in form shown? How are homographs identified? Be prepared to give specific examples.

Assignment 1 *(page 503)*

Answers will vary.

Assignment 2 *(page 503)*

Answers will vary.

503

Unit 19

Objectives

After studying this unit, students should be able to do the following:

- Improve their reading skills by becoming familiar with the parts of a book and by using the SQRRR method (survey, question, read, recite, review).

- Improve their note-taking skills.

Teaching Suggestions

See "Classroom Insights" for Unit 19 in the front of this Teacher's Edition.

Program Resources

Resource Book, Second Course: Bonus Activity, Unit 19
Practice Book, Second Course, Unit 19

Related Resources

The American Heritage Dictionary of the English Language

Study Skills

Improving your study skills can help you perform better in all your classes. In this unit, you will learn how to locate information in books, how to read effectively, and how to take good notes.

19.1 Reading Skills

19.1a Parts of a Book

You will be able to locate specific information more efficiently if you are familiar with the important parts of a book.

Table of Contents. The table of contents lists the titles of units or chapters, their subdivisions, and the pages on which they begin. You will find the table of contents at the front of a book. Study the following example.

9 A Growing America   193

   The Beginning of Industry   194

   Changes in Transportation   197

   The Rise of Cities   203

   The Growth of Nationalism   209

504

Index. The index, located at the back of a book, is an alphabetical list of persons, places, events, and ideas, with page numbers for each entry. Some indexes also contain references to maps, charts, and other illustrations.

Subentries may be listed with the main entry. In the following example, under the main entry "California," you will find several subentries, including "under Spanish," "and Mexico," and "Gold Rush in."

The *m*'s in the example indicate pages with maps.

Main Entry —— California, under Spanish, 63, 64-5, *m* 65; and Mexico, 251, *m* 250; trails to, 254-255, *m* 240;

Subentry —— Gold Rush in, 256-260; admitted, 260, 290; today, *m* 673

Some entries, using the words *See* and *See also,* refer you to related main entries. The main entry "Legislative branch," for example, may tell you to "*See also* Congress."

Use these strategies to locate specific information in a book.

Strategies

1. *Skim the table of contents* to see what subjects are covered.

2. *Read the titles of units, chapters, and subdivisions* that relate to your subject.

3. *Turn to the index* for additional information, if the table of contents contains subjects that you need.

4. *Use the index to find page numbers* for information on a particular person, place, event, or idea.

Subheadings. A subheading is a word, a phrase, or a sentence that introduces and summarizes the material that follows it. Subheadings often follow unit and chapter titles. Together, chapter titles and subheadings form an outline of the text.

505

Assignment 1 *(pages 506–507)*

See page 507 for the answers.

As you read, notice the special devices often used to separate subheadings from the text below them. Subheadings may appear in capital letters, boldface or italic type, or in color.

Illustrations. Illustrations help to explain the contents of a book. Many books include study aids such as maps, diagrams, charts, tables, graphs, and time lines.

Maps show large or small areas of the earth's surface. Some maps show countries, cities, mountains, rivers, lakes, forests, deserts, or roads. Other maps include information on population size, annual rainfall, natural resources, and other items of interest. Most maps have a key or a legend to explain the symbols that they use, such as a scale of miles to help you compute distances.

Diagrams are detailed drawings that show how a mechanism works, how it is put together, or how its different parts are related. A diagram usually includes labels and brief explanations.

Charts and **tables** use rows or columns of numbers or other data to show changes and relationships. A great deal of information can be presented in a clear, compact, and understandable form in a chart or a table.

Graphs show changes that take place over a period of time and compare one thing with another. For example, a graph might show population growth in a city over a period of time. Pie graphs, bar graphs, and line graphs are frequently used to display different kinds of numerical information.

Time lines are another kind of study aid, showing a series of events in chronological order.

Assignment 1 Parts of a Book Look at the following portion of a table of contents from a history book. On your paper, write the subheading and the number of the page where you would look to find the answer to each of the questions that follow.

506

16 THE END OF THE FRONTIER   **347**

    Crossing the Continent   **348**

    The Indians of the West   **352**

    Taming the West   **358**

    The Sod-House Frontier   **364**

1. What effects did government treaties have on the Indians?
2. What were sod houses and who lived in them?
3. How did people travel from the East to the West?
4. What did gold-mining communities do to combat lawlessness?
5. Why were railroads important?

Assignment 2 Parts of a Book Look at the following index entry. On your paper, write the subentry and the number of the page where you would look to find the answer to each of the questions that follow the entry.

> Technology, as part of culture, 27; and exploration, 42; exchange of, between Indians and Europeans, 56–57; in late 1800s, 375–382; in 1920s, 492–497 *See also* Factories, Industry, Inventions

1. How is technology related to culture?
2. How did technology change life in America between 1920 and 1930?
3. How is technology used to explore the world?
4. What other main entries have information about technology?

Assignment 3 Illustrations Find examples from your social studies, mathematics, or science textbooks of three of the types of study aids mentioned in this unit. On your paper, explain what each study aid is and how it helps you to understand the material.

Assignment 4 Subheadings Select a chapter or a unit from a textbook or a reference book. On your paper,

507

Assignment 1 *(pages 506–507)*

1. The Indians of the West, 352
2. The Sod-House Frontier, 364
3. Crossing the Continent, 348
4. Taming the West, 358
5. Crossing the Continent, 348

Assignment 2 *(page 507)*

1. as part of culture, 27
2. in 1920s, 492–497
3. and exploration, 42
4. Factories, Industry, Inventions

Assignment 3 *(page 507)*

Answers will vary.

Assignment 4 *(pages 507–508)*

Answers will vary.

make a list of the subheadings and tell what special devices are used to make the subheadings stand out from the text.

19.1b Reading Effectively

SQRRR Method

The SQRRR reading method is a way to organize and remember what you read. **SQRRR** stands for *Survey, Question, Read, Recite,* and *Review.* The following passage will be used to illustrate how the SQRRR method may be used. First, read this passage.

America's Transportation Crisis

The Cost of Cars

For every dollar that your car costs you, it costs other people thirty cents to fight air pollution, to maintain and police highways, and to handle court cases. In addition to these expenses more money is spent building highways.

However, we pay much more than money for our cars. *Pollution.* In 1970 the United States Forest Service sold a thousand acres of hundred-year-old ponderosa pines to a private lumber company. The trees were dying from air pollution that came from Los Angeles, eighty miles away. Most of the air pollution in Los Angeles is caused by cars.

Deaths and Injuries. Every year, America's cars and trucks kill more than fifty thousand people. The total number of injuries from traffic accidents each year is between three and four million.

Traffic Jams. In 1906, New York City traffic, pulled by horses, moved along at eleven or twelve miles an hour. By the 1970s, behind high-powered engines, it averaged eight and a half miles an hour. One of New York's highways, the Long Island Expressway, has been called the world's longest parking lot. Many people spend an hour or two of every workday jammed in traffic.

508

Now follow the steps of the SQRRR method to increase your understanding of the passage.

Survey. Read all section titles and subheadings, words in boldface or italic type, and all summary statements and lists. Look at any illustrations.

By surveying the preceding passage, you find the following information:

The topic is America's transportation crisis. [title]

The cost of cars is part of this crisis. [subheading]

Pollution, deaths and injuries, and traffic jams contribute to the transportation crisis. [italic type]

Question. From your survey, think of questions that can be answered by reading the selection. The following questions are examples based on the sample passage.

What is the cost of owning a car?

In what ways do cars cost more than money?

How does pollution affect cost?

What price is paid in deaths and injuries?

How do traffic jams affect the car owner?

Read. Read the entire selection to find answers to your questions. Write down the answers. Note also any important information not covered by your questions and answers.

Recite. After you have read the selection, answer each question aloud to yourself or in writing. Think of questions for any new information that you have found. Recite or write the answers to those questions.

Review. Try to review within twenty-four hours. To review, answer the questions again without looking at your notes. Then check your answers. Repeat this process until you can answer all of the questions correctly.

Assignment SQRRR Reading Method   Use the SQRRR method to read the following selection. On your

Assignment *(pages 509–512)*

See page 511 for the answers.

509

Assignment *(pages 509–512)*

See page 511 for the answers.

paper, write the letters for the correct answers to the questions that follow the selection. Each question has more than one correct answer.

The Wise Shopper

Whether buying a sweater or a loaf of bread, shopping for the best interest rate or for the best TV repair service, the wise shopper compares and contrasts products and services. **Comparison shopping,** or examining the quality and price of several items or services before choosing the best one, will help you to avoid costly mistakes.

Finding the Best Buy

The best buy is not necessarily the most expensive, top-quality product. When possible, you should look for **factory rejects.** The flaws in factory rejects are usually so slight as to be hardly noticeable. **Manufacturer's seconds** may also be a good buy. Again, the quality is only slightly less than that of the top-of-the-run or "first" quality product. Another slightly imperfect product that can save you money is a factory or manufacturer's **irregular.** The imperfections are not usually noticeable.

Unit Pricing. Faced with deciding among eight cans of fruit juice, all of different prices and weights, which are you going to buy? **Unit pricing,** basing the price on a common measurement such as ounces or grams, is a device that can help you to decide. For instance, if the unit price of Brand A is seventy cents a quart and the unit price of Brand B is seventy-nine cents a quart, Brand A is cheaper *by the quart* than Brand B. It is therefore the better buy.

It is possible that you may still prefer Brand B, merely because you have seen it and heard it referred to in commercials and other forms of advertising. Many advertisers rely on *brand-name identification* by consumers who believe that only the better-known brands are of high quality. The wise shopper is aware that lesser-known brands can be of a similarly high quality, while also being less expensive than the well-known product.

510

Reading Labels. If you are a wise shopper, you will always read the labels on products. The label on a can of fruit juice must list the contents, with their amounts. Medicine bottles list all active ingredients and provide warnings for people who might suffer ill effects from taking the medicine. Clothing labels give cleaning or care instructions. Furniture labels give details on construction and design.

Most labels are required by federal agencies such as the Federal Trade Commission or the Food and Drug Administration. They are intended not only to protect you from fraud, but also to help you make a wise and informed buying decision.

Assignment *(pages 509–512)*

1. a, c, d, e
2. b, d, e
3. a, c, e

1. On your paper, indicate which of the following statements you can make after a survey of "The Wise Shopper."

   a. Comparison shopping is an important aspect of careful shopping.
   b. It is easy to use credit.
   c. Furniture labels give design details.
   d. Unit pricing can help you to find the best buy.
   e. Lesser-known brands may be of the same quality as well-known brands.

2. On your paper, indicate which of the following questions you should think about while reading the selection.

   a. How much of a family's budget should be spent on food?
   b. What are factory rejects?
   c. When should I buy on credit?
   d. How does brand-name identification affect me as a consumer?
   e. How can I compare the prices of different products when they come in different sizes?

3. On your paper, indicate which of the following five answers would help you to remember important information in "The Wise Shopper."

   a. It is a good idea to compare and contrast products and services.
   b. You may not always have enough cash with you to buy what you want.

511

Assignment 1 *(page 513)*

Answers may vary. Sample:

The Solar System Is Like a Circus

Thousands of tiny asteroids, or very small planets, can be observed flocked together, mostly in the space between Mars and Jupiter. Once in a while, a stray asteroid passes close to Earth. Asteroids are probably iron or rocks quite similar to those on earth.

Scientists have proposed several explanations to account for the formation of asteroids:

1. Asteroids are the pieces of several small planets that broke up and no longer exist. The pieces keep colliding in space, splitting into smaller and smaller bits.

2. Asteroids are small chunks of matter that have been floating around since the formation of the solar system. The seven small outer moons of Jupiter are probably asteroids captured by the strong pull of gravitation on Jupiter.

3. A large planet broke up. Mars and possibly even the moon were formed from its larger pieces and the rest of the asteroids from its smaller ones.

c. Top quality products are not always the best buy.
d. The unit price of Brand A is seventy cents a quart.
e. Labels on products give information that can help you to make better buying decisions.

19.2 Note-Taking Skills

Taking notes will help you to remember what you read in your textbooks. Taking notes efficiently is a good study habit. Before you take notes, read an entire selection carefully. Then use the following strategies.

Strategies

1. *Write your notes in your own words.*

2. *Use words and phrases, not complete sentences.* Omit articles (*a, an, the*). Use adjectives and adverbs sparingly. Use mostly nouns and verbs.

3. *Use abbreviations and symbols when possible.*

4. *Pay close attention to titles, to subheadings, and to words in boldface and italic type, in quotation marks, or in color.* These clues will help you to find important ideas or concepts in the passage.

5. *Watch for words and phrases that signal main points.* Such signal words and phrases include *first, then, finally, in summary, in conclusion, important, more important, the reason for, the causes of, the result was, for instance,* and *for example.*

6. *Keep your notes from different classes in separate sections of your notebook or in separate notebooks.*

7. *Review your notes shortly after you write them.*

8. *Write your notes in ink.* Notes that are written in pencil will fade or blur.

512

Assignment 1 Taking Notes   On your paper, copy the following passage. Underline the important words to include in notes. Use the strategies that you have just studied to decide what is important.

The Solar System Is Like a Circus

Thousands of tiny asteroids, or very small planets, can be observed flocked together, mostly in the space between Mars and Jupiter. Once in a while, a stray asteroid passes close to Earth. Asteroids are probably iron or rocks quite similar to those on earth.

Scientists have proposed several explanations to account for the formation of asteroids:
1. Asteroids are the pieces of several small planets that broke up and no longer exist. The pieces keep colliding in space, splitting into smaller and smaller bits.
2. Asteroids are small chunks of matter that have been floating around since the formation of the solar system. The seven small outer moons of Jupiter are probably asteroids captured by the strong pull of gravitation on Jupiter.
3. A large planet broke up. Mars and possibly even the moon were formed from its larger pieces and the rest of the asteroids from its smaller ones.

Assignment 2 Taking Notes   Write notes for the passage in Assignment 1. Use the words that you underlined.

Assignment 1 *(page 513)*

See page 512 for the answers.

Assignment 2 *(page 513)*

Answers may vary. Sample:

—Solar system like a circus
—Thousands of asteroids, small planets, flock together, mostly between Mars and Jupiter
—Asteroids probably iron or rocks
—Explanations for formation:
  1. Pieces of broken-up planets; keep colliding and splitting
  2. Chunks floating since formation of solar system; Jupiter's 7 outer moons are asteroids captured by gravitation
  3. Planet broke up; Mars, moon formed from larger pieces, rest of asteroids from smaller ones

513

Unit 20

Objectives

After studying this unit, students should be able to do the following:

- Understand the importance of listening skills and the different kinds of listening.

- Get ready to listen actively.

- Understand what to listen for in a speech.

- Listen reponsively and courteously.

Teaching Suggestions

See ''Classroom Insights'' for Unit 20 in the front of this Teacher's Edition.

Program Resources

Resource Book, Second Course: Bonus Activity, Unit 20
Practice Book, Second Course: Unit 20

Related Resources

The American Heritage Dictionary of the English Language

Listening Skills

20.1 Why Learn Listening Skills?

Listening, like speaking, is a skill that you can learn and practice. When you really listen, you pay attention and think about what you are hearing. In this unit, you will learn listening skills that you can apply both when you listen to speeches and in other situations.

Occasions for Listening

During each school day, you listen to your teachers, to announcements on the public address system, to films and film strips, to oral reports and class discussions, and to your friends in the hallways and cafeteria. You may also listen to the school nurse, the school librarian, and other people who are part of your school. In fact, you spend more than half your time in school listening.

At home and elsewhere, you also spend a good part of your time listening. You listen to members of your family, to radio and television programs, to clerks in stores, to the dentist, and to many others.

Kinds of Listening

There are several kinds of listening that fit different circumstances. When you are **listening for information,** your

514

purpose is to increase your knowledge about a certain topic. When your teacher presents new material, for example, you should listen for information.

When you are listening to decide whether to accept or reject what you are being told, you are doing **critical listening.** In listening to a campaign speech, for instance, you need to decide whether the speaker should be elected. Of course, you would probably need to listen for information at the same time.

When you listen to friends on the way home from school, your purpose may be neither to gain specific information nor to make a judgment. However, you do want to understand what is being said and to respond appropriately. In this case, you are doing **conversational listening.**

Listening for information, critical listening, and conversational listening require different approaches and different kinds of effort on your part. In all three cases, though, it is important for you to be an active listener.

Active listening means paying attention and thinking about what you are hearing. Active listeners weigh and evaluate information. In contrast, **passive listening** involves little effort at understanding. Passive listeners allow their minds to wander and hear only part of what is said. An active listener is better able than a passive listener to understand information, judge how accurate it is, remember it, and act on it intelligently. Sometimes, of course, passive listening is quite suitable. If you are listening to background music, for example, you are probably listening simply for recreation.

Assignment Kinds of Listening In your notebook or on separate paper, list at least eight specific situations in which you spend time in active listening during one school day. For each one, list the speaker and the topic. Then tell the kind of listening involved: informational, critical, conversational, or a combination. Bring your list to class.

515

20.2 Getting Ready to Listen

A positive attitude is one of the keys to good listening. Plan to obtain as much information and understanding as you can from what you are about to hear. You can take certain steps to prepare yourself for active listening.

The Setting

Whether you are listening to an important speech or having a casual conversation with a friend, you can listen better when your surroundings are comfortable. The fewer distractions there are, the more you will be able to concentrate on what is being said. Use the following strategies to improve your setting for listening.

Strategies

1. *Arrive on time or a little early,* so that you will be ready to listen when the speaker begins to speak.

2. *Get your materials ready ahead of time.* Have pencils and paper ready if you plan to take notes.

3. *Choose a seat where you can see the speaker,* and sit in an alert but comfortable position.

4. *Listen quietly and politely.* Do not make noises or movements that might distract those around you.

5. *Be ready to concentrate.* Put other thoughts out of your mind and look forward in a positive way to what you are going to hear.

Questions to Ask Yourself Before Listening

You will probably listen more effectively if you have some information beforehand about the topic of the speech and about the speaker. In preparing to listen, ask yourself questions similar to these:

1. What is the speaker's topic? What do I already know about it? Where can I find out more?
2. Who is the speaker? How is the speaker qualified to talk about this subject?
3. What is the speaker's purpose—to inform, to persuade, or to entertain?
4. What is my purpose in listening?
5. Do I have an open mind? Am I ready for new ideas?

Assignment Preparing to Listen Choose a situation in which you were an active listener during the past week. *Step 1:* On your paper, write a brief description of the setting. For instance, where were you? How well could you see and hear the speaker? What distractions, if any, were there? *Step 2:* Write a brief statement telling how well you were prepared. For example, how much did you know about the topic and the speaker? In what specific ways, if any, did your preparation help you to listen effectively?

20.3 What to Listen For

You listen to a speech in order to understand certain information or to evaluate a certain point of view. A good speaker gives signals that help you to listen more effectively.

Listen for the Speaker's Purpose

Early in the speech, listen for a statement that tells the speaker's purpose. The speaker may want to give you some specific information, persuade you to hold a particular opinion or take a certain action, or entertain you. Listen for statements like those on the following page.

517

STATEMENT	PURPOSE
"Today I will explain the uses for the new computer in the math lab."	To inform you about the new computer and how it will be used
"I want to tell you why I am the best person to be class treasurer."	To persuade you to vote for the candidate
"I thought you might enjoy hearing about my adventures as a professional dog-walker."	To entertain you with a story about a personal experience

Listen for the Method of Organization

As you listen for the speaker's purpose, listen also for statements that tell you how the speech is organized. Methods of organization vary depending on the topic and purpose. Knowing what method the speaker has used will help you to know what to listen for later in the speech.

One way that a speech may be organized is by the topical method, dividing the topic into parts. The speaker might make a statement like the following:

Let us examine three basic areas of Iroquois life: the family, farming, and religion.

Another way a speech may be organized is in chronological order, or time order. Listen for a statement like this:

I will trace the career of Thomas Edison from his first patented invention to his last.

Sometimes a speaker describes a place or tells how objects are placed in relation to each other. Such a speech would be organized by the spatial method. The speaker might give a signal like the following:

Here is how a medieval village might have been laid out.

518

The problem-solution method of organization is used when a speaker outlines a problem and presents possible solutions. The speaker's purpose may be to persuade you that a particular solution is the best. This example is from a speech organized by the problem-solution method:

> Let us look at the problem of mosquito control in our region.

Listen for Signals and Transitions

Speakers often use words or phrases that alert you to what follows. Listen for such signals, which will guide you through the speech.

Words or phrases like the following give you notice that the speaker is about to state the purpose of the speech.

> My purpose is to show . . .
> Today I will tell you about . . .
> I would like to explain . . .

Other expressions tell you to listen for the method by which the speech is organized. Here are two examples:

> My topic today can be divided into . . .
> Let us trace the development of . . .

When the speaker is about to present a major point, a signal like the following may alert you.

> Let me emphasize this point.
> An important issue is . . .

Sometimes a speaker presents background. Listen for signals that this kind of information is about to follow.

> The events leading up to this situation were . . .
> Here is how the problem developed.

519

Speakers often use summaries, brief reviews of material presented in the speech. A summary usually comes at the end of the speech. Sometimes, however, a speaker may also summarize in the middle, to review one part of the speech before going on. Be alert for signals that the speaker intends to present a summary.

Before going on, let me review briefly . . .
To summarize what I have been saying . . .

A transition marks a change from one idea to another. Some transitions are marked by pauses, or by a shift in the speaker's tone. Words and phrases like *therefore, in contrast,* and *in conclusion* indicate a transition.

The transitions in a speech are often related to the method of organization. Here are some examples:

METHOD	TRANSITIONS
Topical	The second point
	Our next consideration
Chronological	After a few months; Then, in 1964
Spatial	Moving eastward; Next in line
Problem-solution	Another possible answer
	Having outlined the problem

Listen for Main Ideas

Certain ideas in a speech are basic to your understanding. Just as you look for the main ideas in your reading, you need also to listen for the main ideas in a speech.

Some of the signals and transitions in the preceding examples can also alert you that the speaker is about to state a major point.

Understanding the method by which the speech is organized can help you to listen for main ideas. If you have noted that the speaker is dividing the subject into three parts, you know that you should listen for three main ideas.

520

In a summary the speaker reviews the major points in the speech. You can then check on whether you have identified the main ideas correctly.

Listen for Supporting Material

The main ideas of a speech should be supported by facts, reasons, examples, or details. Listen for signals that the speaker is about to provide supporting material.

Depending on the topic, you may need to remember many of the supporting details. When you listen to instructions or a demonstration, you will probably want to note each step. In other cases, however, the supporting information is important to help you understand the main idea.

As an active listener, you should evaluate what you hear. Especially in a persuasive speech, it is important that you judge carefully how well the supporting details actually support the main idea. Judge also whether the material that is presented is fact (*page 289*) or opinion. When a speaker states an opinion, listen to find out whether that opinion is supported with appropriate facts or reasons.

Listen to Take Notes

You cannot expect to remember accurately everything that you hear. Good notes, however, enable you to refresh your memory. Taking notes helps you to keep your mind from wandering, for you must pay close attention and think about what you are hearing and writing.

Before you begin to take notes, listen for a moment to get an idea of how the speech will probably go. Then use the following strategies.

Strategies

1. *Jot down the speaker's purpose, the main ideas, and other important information.* If you are not sure

521

what the purpose is or what the main points are, make a note of the problem.

2. *Make notes of any questions* you have or any points with which you disagree.

3. *Keep your notes brief and specific.* You cannot write down everything that you hear. Take down key points and important details in as few words as possible. Do not write in complete sentences.

4. *Write neatly* so that you can understand your notes.

5. *Look over your notes if the speaker gives a summary*, to be sure you have included the main points.

Assignment 1   Listening for Signals   Listen to an oral report, a demonstration, or a speech on radio or television. While you listen, jot down on your paper all the signals that you hear the speaker give. Afterward, describe each signal in a sentence or two. Tell how it did or did not help you to understand the speech better.

Assignment 2   Taking Notes   *Step 1:* Listen to another oral report or speech. As you listen, take notes on your paper, using the strategies given on pages 521–522. Check over your notes to be sure that they include the speaker's purpose, the main ideas, and any questions that arose in your mind. *Step 2:* Several days later, use your notes to write a paragraph telling about the report or speech that you heard.

20.4 Being a Responsive and Courteous Listener

You respond to a speaker in several important ways. One way is by listening quietly and alertly. Active listening is

522

also courteous listening because you focus on the speaker and do not create distractions.

Often you are able to respond more directly to a speaker with applause or with questions and comments at the close of the speech. In asking questions, follow these strategies, and be sure to thank the speaker for answering.

Strategies

1. *Ask the speaker to explain or restate a point.*

    Would you please explain what you mean by . . . ?

2. *Restate briefly* what you think the speaker said. Ask whether you have understood correctly.

    I believe that you said. . . . Is that correct?

3. *Ask about a related point* that has occurred to you while listening.

    Do you think another reason might be . . . ?

4. *Ask for more information* or for suggestions for future action.

    Where can I find out more about . . . ?
    What can we do about . . . ?

5. *Keep your questions brief* and to the point.

6. *Speak up* so that you can be heard easily by everyone present. Do not hesitate to ask a question. The speaker wants you to understand the information presented in the speech.

Assignment **Responsive Listening** Listen with your class to a speech, a report, a demonstration, or some other spoken presentation. Afterward, write on your paper two questions and two comments about what you have just heard. Then, in a class discussion, compare your questions and comments with those of your classmates.

523

Unit 21

Speaking Skills

21.1 Speaking to a Group

Whenever you speak to other people, your goal is the same: to communicate some message to your listeners.

Although often you speak to just one or two people, on many occasions you speak to a group. In this unit you will learn the basic steps that will help you to give a speech or an oral report. You can also apply these techniques to other situations.

21.1a Formal and Informal Speeches

Occasions for speaking range from very casual to quite serious and formal. A speech can be either **formal** or **informal,** depending on the occasion, the purpose, and the audience. In this book the word *speech* refers to any prepared talk given before a group. Here are some examples:

FORMAL   As a candidate for club president, you address the members.

A well-known author speaks at an assembly in your school.

You speak about student government at your school's Open House.

524

INFORMAL   You explain your laboratory results in science class.

Your school's principal answers questions about the upcoming science fair.

You give your little brother's baseball team some pointers on fielding.

The types of speeches that you give include announcements, informal talks, demonstrations, and oral reports.

ANNOUNCEMENTS   The History Club president announces the winners of an essay contest.

You announce the week's volleyball scores to your gym class.

INFORMAL TALKS   Your school principal drops by your English class to compliment the students on their recent essays.

You tell other members of the Drama Club about a play that you saw recently.

DEMONSTRATIONS   The school librarian shows how to use the library's new cassette player.

You demonstrate to an art class how to make a linoleum block print.

ORAL REPORTS   You give a speech to your English class on the life of Carl Sandburg.

After research, you report to your health class on the benefits of regular exercise.

21.1b Purposes of Speaking

When you speak before a group, your purpose is to **inform,** to **persuade,** to **entertain,** or a combination of these. For example, you may want to inform your listeners about a problem and persuade them to do something about it.

As you think about your purpose, you must also think about your audience. Because your goal in speaking is to

525

Assignment *(page 526)*

Answers may vary. Samples:

1. Formal, to persuade, town school committee or parent organization
2. Formal, to inform, the Biology Club or science students
3. Informal, to entertain, cooking class
4. Informal, to inform, group of students or arts and crafts club
5. Informal, to inform, group of children or visitors to a science fair

communicate with your listeners, every decision you make in planning your speech should be made with them in mind.

When the purpose of your speech is to inform your listeners, you want to increase their knowledge about the topic.

You explain to the Science Club the difference between an alligator and a crocodile.

When the purpose of your speech is to persuade your listeners, you want them to change their minds or to take some action.

You explain to the Library Committee why you think your school should subscribe to *Horticulture* magazine.

When the purpose of your speech is to entertain your listeners, you want them simply to enjoy hearing your speech. Sometimes a speech that is designed to inform or persuade also includes some entertaining material.

You make a farewell speech for a teacher who is retiring.

Assignment Purpose and Audience For each topic listed, write on your paper (1) whether the speech would be formal or informal, (2) what the purpose would be, and (3) who would be a suitable audience.

1. The need for new band uniforms
2. Medical uses for laser beams
3. The worst way to learn to cook
4. How to make a soft sculpture
5. Keeping reptiles as pets

21.2 Planning Your Speech

When you need to give a speech, you will find the task easier if you take one step at a time. Follow these steps in preparing and giving your speech:

526

1. Selecting and limiting a topic
2. Gathering information and developing ideas
3. Organizing your speech
4. Preparing and rehearsing your speech
5. Delivering your speech

21.2a Selecting and Limiting Your Topic

A **speech topic** must be narrow enough for you to cover well. A subject such as travel, astronomy, or gardening is too broad a topic for a speech. Decide on a specific portion of the broad subject as you would for a paragraph (*pages 280–281*) or a report (*pages 411–412*).

SUBJECT	LIMITED SPEECH TOPIC
Travel	How to save money on vacations
Astronomy	The pleasures of stargazing
Gardening	A good way to grow tomatoes

In choosing an appropriate topic, think about your purpose, your audience, and your time limit. All of these will affect how you should limit your topic.

Your Purpose

Your **general purpose** is to inform, to persuade, or to entertain. In limiting your topic, you also must decide on your **specific purpose:** a statement of exactly what you want to accomplish with your speech.

GENERAL PURPOSE	SPECIFIC PURPOSE
To inform	I want my audience to understand how marching-band competitions are judged.
To persuade	I want to persuade my audience to support the marching band.
To entertain	I want my audience to be amused by hearing about my surprise performance at a marching-band competition.

527

Assignment 1 *(page 528)*

Answers will vary.

Your Audience

In selecting and limiting your topic, give careful thought to the interests and experiences of your listeners. A good topic for one audience might not be suitable for another audience. Ask yourself these questions:

1. Who are my listeners?
2. Will they be interested in my topic?
3. What do they already know about this topic?
4. What do I want my listeners to learn, to think, or to do as a result of my speech?

Use the preceding questions to guide you throughout the process of planning and delivering a speech.

Your Time Limit

Sometimes you will be given a time limit for a speech. If not, try to find out roughly how long you will have, for the length of your speech will affect how you limit your topic. The time limit will also guide you as you organize and rehearse your speech.

Assignment 1   Speech Topics   *Step 1:* On your paper, write a limited speech topic for each subject in the list that follows. *Step 2:* For each topic that you write, give a general purpose and a specific purpose. *Step 3:* Choose one of your topics, and write a brief statement telling how a speech on that topic would differ for these audiences: a third-grade class, your own English class, and an organization of adults. Save your paper.

1. An amusing experience that you have had
2. A subject that you would like to know more about
3. An issue that concerns you

528

21.2b Gathering Information and Developing Ideas

Assignment 2 *(pages 529–530)*

Answers will vary.

Gathering material for a speech is similar to preparing for a written report (*pages 413–418*). For some topics, you may be able to use your own knowledge and experiences. Often, however, you will have to use other sources. Material from the library (*Unit 22*) may help you. Films, filmstrips, and radio and television programs may also be useful. If appropriate, you might interview one or more people in person or by telephone.

The information in your speech should be clear and complete. Your audience cannot stop listening to look up the meaning of a word. Plan to define unfamiliar terms and to present only information that your audience can understand.

If your speech topic involves statements of opinion, be sure to find facts and reasons to support your opinions. Other kinds of supporting material are quotations from experts, survey results, statistics, and historical background.

The material that you include should be both appropriate to your audience and related to your topic. Look for examples and illustrations that will help you to make your point and that will interest your listeners. Be sure to think carefully about your material and to develop your own ideas about it.

Assignment 2 Gathering Information Use the speech topic and the specific purpose that you selected for Assignment 1 on page 528. You will develop it for a five-minute speech to your English class. *Step 1:* List the information that you already know or have about the topic. *Step 2:* List the kinds of information that you need to gather about the topic. List also any questions about the topic that need to be answered. *Step 3:* List all the sources you can

529

think of that might provide the needed information and answers. *Step 4:* Find the needed information. Take accurate notes and record all your sources. Save your papers.

21.3 Organizing Your Speech

Like a written report, a speech should be outlined in advance and should have an introduction, a body, and a conclusion.

After you have gathered your material, organize it by making an outline (*pages 420–422*) with main headings, subheadings, and supporting details. Your listeners will be able to follow your speech better if you present your material in a well-organized form.

The Body

The body of your speech is the main part. You should plan it first. Organize your material into groups according to your major points. These points will be the main headings in your outline. The number of main headings will depend on your specific purpose, your audience, and the length of your speech.

Under the main headings, write subheadings to include your facts, reasons, evidence, and examples. Place all your supporting details under the appropriate headings.

Depending on your topic and your specific purpose, you may organize the main headings for your speech outline in one of several ways.

Use **topical order** when your subject matter can be divided into distinct parts.

> Thomas Jefferson distinguished himself in politics, education, science, and architecture.

530

Use **chronological order,** or time order, when your topic involves a set of steps or a series of events.

> We can trace the history of our city from its founding in colonial times to the present.
> I will explain the steps for building a homemade rain gauge.

Use **spatial order** when your topic concerns locations or geographical relationships.

> Here is how the interior of a space shuttle is arranged.

Use **problem-solution order** when you want to explore with your listeners one or more solutions to a problem.

> Let us consider some solutions to problems of interference with television reception by ham radios.

The Introduction

Once you have organized the content of your speech, you can write an effective introduction. These opening sentences are very important in preparing the audience for the rest of your speech. To create an interesting and effective introduction, use the following strategies.

Strategies

1. *Make your first words strong and interesting* to capture your listeners' attention. In some cases you might use a question, a startling statement, a quotation, or a bit of humor to begin your speech.

2. *Create interest in your topic.* Make your audience care about what you are going to say by showing them how this topic relates to their own needs, interests, or experiences.

3. *State your topic clearly.* Let your listeners know exactly what you plan to talk about.

531

4. *Reveal your plan of organization.* Give signals (*page 519*) that help your listeners to follow your speech.

5. *Establish a good relationship with your audience.* Let them see that you know about your topic and that you feel confident and comfortable talking about it.

Be sure that the content and wording of the introduction are suitable for the occasion and for the audience. Your introduction should relate closely to your topic and purpose.

The Conclusion

A forceful and colorful conclusion will help your listeners remember what you said. You may conclude your speech in various ways, depending on your topic and purpose.

Be sure that your conclusion is appropriate to your topic and suitable to the audience and the occasion. In some cases you may end a speech with a summary or a review of important points. You can frequently end an informative speech this way. A persuasive speech can sometimes end with a challenge to the audience or a call to action. You may wish to end an entertaining speech with an anecdote, a quotation, or even a question.

Helping Your Audience to Listen

A good speaker helps the audience to listen and to follow the content of a speech. Unlike readers, listeners cannot go back to check on something they missed or failed to understand. You need to explain difficult points, define special terms, repeat or restate some ideas, and summarize where appropriate.

Use signals and transitions (*pages 519–520*) to help your listeners know how the speech is organized and what is coming next. Let them know what to listen for, what your main points are, and when you are presenting background or supporting information.

An idea that is expressed in a complicated way is hard for listeners to follow. Keep your sentences clear and short enough for the audience to understand. Vary your sentence structure, though, to keep your speech from sounding choppy.

Try to express your thoughts concisely. Do not use wordy expressions where simpler ones will do.

WORDY	CONCISE
at this point in time	now
due to the fact that	because
on a previous occasion	previously

Assignment Organizing Your Speech Use your statement of specific purpose and your notes from Assignments 1 and 2 on pages 528 and 529. Choose an appropriate method for organizing your speech. Then write an outline, organizing your material into main headings, subheadings, and supporting details. Write an introduction and a conclusion for your five-minute speech. Save your papers.

Assignment *(page 533)*

Answers will vary.

21.4 Delivering Your Speech

Once you have organized and outlined your speech, the next step is to prepare for delivering it. Good preparation will lead to a successful presentation and help keep you from being too nervous.

Preparing to Deliver Your Speech

You can prepare for the delivery of your speech in two important ways: by making note cards and by rehearsing.

533

You will feel much more confident about giving your speech if you take the time to prepare carefully.

Note Cards.   Using note cards to guide you in speaking has several advantages over memorizing a speech word for word or reading it from a written text. When you use note cards, you can speak more naturally and look at your audience. Neither you nor your listeners will be distracted by your turning pages or losing your place.

On your note cards, write key words and phrases that will remind you of what you want to say. Do not write complete sentences. Write no more than one main point on each card, with its subheadings and supporting details. You may want to use different colored inks to separate main points, subheadings, and details.

Write on your cards any material that you must present in exact form, such as quotations, names, numbers, or dates. Because you will need to be able to read your notes quickly and easily, write neatly and do not crowd your material. Number your note cards so that you can keep them in the right order.

Rehearsing.   Take time to practice your speech. Rehearsing will help you to become familiar with what you are going to say. It also will help you to speak well from your notes. Always rehearse aloud. Use a tape recorder if one is available, and ask friends or family members to listen and to make suggestions.

If you have difficulty or become confused while rehearsing, make changes on your note cards. Rehearse until your speech goes smoothly.

Presenting Your Speech

How you deliver your speech will affect how well your audience understands and accepts your message. Stand in a natural and comfortable way. Use gestures and facial expressions as you would in everyday conversation. Look at your listeners, letting your eyes move from one person to another. Show that you care about your message and about how well your listeners understand it.

Like your gestures and your facial expressions, your voice should reflect your feelings as you speak. Speak distinctly, slowly enough, and loudly enough for everyone in the room to understand you.

Avoiding Nervousness. If you know that you have done a thorough job of planning, organizing, and rehearsing your speech, you will feel less nervous. Almost all speakers feel somewhat nervous, but you can lessen this feeling by concentrating on what you are saying. Do not think about yourself. Think about the message you want to communicate to your listeners.

Assignment Delivering Your Speech Use your notes, outline, introduction, and conclusion from the Assignment on page 533 to prepare note cards for your speech. Rehearse your speech several times, making any needed improvements in your notes. Then deliver your five-minute speech to your English class.

535

Unit 22

After studying this unit, students should be able to do the following:

- Locate works of fiction, nonfiction, and biography in the library.

- Use the card catalog in the library.

- Use general reference books, including dictionaries, encyclopedias, almanacs and yearbooks, and atlases and gazetteers.

- Use biographical reference books.

- Use the *Readers' Guide to Periodical Literature.*

Teaching Suggestions

See "Classroom Insights" for Unit 22 in the front of this Teacher's Edition.

Program Resources

Resource Book, Second Course: Bonus Activities, Unit 22
Practice Book, Second Course, Unit 22

Related Resources

The American Heritage Dictionary of the English Language
Roget's II: The New Thesaurus

Library Skills

The library is a good place to find books to read for enjoyment and to locate information on almost any subject. In this unit, you will learn how to use the resources found in most school and public libraries.

22.1 How to Locate Books

Fiction

You will find books on the fiction shelves of the library arranged in alphabetical order by the authors' last names. When two authors have the same last name, their first names are used for alphabetizing. For example, books by Robert Arthur come before books by Ruth Arthur. Books by the same author are arranged alphabetically by title. For example, Betsy Byars's book *The Midnight Fox* would come before her book *Rama, the Gypsy Cat.* Notice that the words *The, A,* and *An* are not considered in alphabetizing when they appear as the initial word in a title.

Nonfiction

Melvil Dewey, a librarian, created a simple system in 1876 for arranging nonfiction books. Called the Dewey decimal system, this method of classification is still used by many libraries. Dewey named and numbered ten groups of subjects. The ten groups are numbered from 000 to 999.

536

The Dewey Decimal System

000–099 General Works	Includes encyclopedias, almanacs, and newspapers
100–199 Philosophy	Includes philosophy and psychology
200–299 Religion	Includes the Bible and mythology
300–399 Social Sciences	Includes government, economics, law, education, folklore
400–499 Language	Includes dictionaries, grammar, and foreign languages
500–599 Science	Includes mathematics, physical and biological sciences, and geology
600–699 Technology	Includes agriculture, business, engineering, and medicine
700–799 Fine Arts	Includes art, music, films, sports
800–899 Literature	Includes plays, essays, and poetry
900–999 History	Includes history, geography, travel, and collective biography

Every subject in each group has its own number. For example, in the science group (500–599), books about mammals are numbered 599. Decimals after the subject numbers indicate even more specific subjects. For example, books numbered 599.5 are about whales.

You do not have to memorize Dewey numbers, for they are usually posted in libraries.

Biography

Books in the biography section of a library are arranged alphabetically by the last name of the subject of the biography. For example, a biography of Robert E. Lee would come before a biography of Abraham Lincoln. All books about one person are arranged alphabetically by the authors' last names. Books containing short biographies of several people are called **collective biographies.** They are classified in the 920s under the Dewey system.

537

Assignment 1 (page 538)

4. Fahrenheit 451, by Ray Bradbury
1. The Limner's Daughter, by Mary Stetson Clarke
2. The Cave Above Delphi, by Scott Corbett
5. Cutlass Island, by Scott Corbett
6. All Creatures Great and Small, by James Herriot
3. The Hobbit, by J.R.R. Tolkien

Assignment 2 (page 538)

1. 700–799
2. 800–899
3. 000–099
4. 600–699
5. 400–499
6. 200–299

Assignment 3 (page 538)

3. Bach, by Imogen Holst
5. Angel of Appalachia: Martha Berry, by Elisabeth P. Myers
6. Langston Hughes: A Biography, by Milton Meltzer
2. Mary Lyons of Putnam's Hill, by Evelyn I. Banning
1. Edith Wharton, by Olivia Coolidge
4. Frank Lloyd Wright: America's Greatest Architect, by Herbert A. Jacobs

Assignment 1   Locating Fiction   On your paper, list the following book titles in the order in which you would find them in the fiction section of a library.

1. *The Limner's Daughter,* by Mary Stetson Clarke
2. *The Cave Above Delphi,* by Scott Corbett
3. *The Hobbit,* by J.R.R. Tolkien
4. *Fahrenheit 451,* by Ray Bradbury
5. *Cutlass Island,* by Scott Corbett
6. *All Creatures Great and Small,* by James Herriot

Assignment 2   Locating Nonfiction   On your paper, write the number of the Dewey classification in which you would find each of the following subjects or titles. Refer to the Dewey classification list on page 537.

SAMPLE   The French Revolution
ANSWER   900–999

1. Baseball
2. Shakespeare's plays
3. *The World Almanac and Book of Facts*
4. Organic gardening
5. A French dictionary
6. Greek myths

Assignment 3   Locating Biography   On your paper, list these book titles in the order in which you would find them in the biography section of a library.

1. *Edith Wharton,* by Olivia Coolidge
2. *Mary Lyons of Putnam's Hill,* by Evelyn I. Banning
3. *Bach,* by Imogen Holst
4. *Frank Lloyd Wright: America's Greatest Architect,* by Herbert A. Jacobs
5. *Angel of Appalachia: Martha Berry,* by Elisabeth P. Myers
6. *Langston Hughes: A Biography,* by Milton Meltzer

538

22.2 The Card Catalog

You can find information about all the books in the library in the card catalog. The **card catalog** is a cabinet of drawers containing cards in alphabetical order. The cards tell what books are available in that particular library and where they are located. In some libraries the card catalog actually consists of a computer display terminal. The information shown on the card is the same, whether in a drawer or on a computer display.

A card for a nonfiction book has a Dewey number, or **call number,** in the top-left corner. The shelves of the library have shelf numbers that match these call numbers. Cards for fiction have the letters *FIC* or the author's initials in the top-left corner instead of call numbers. You can find these books on the fiction shelves.

Every nonfiction book has three cards in the catalog: an author card, a title card, and a subject card. Each card tells the author's name, the complete title, the publisher, the year the book was published, the number of pages, and the call number. The card may also tell whether the book has illustrations, maps, or photographs.

Fiction books have only title and author cards.

Author Cards.   On an author card, the author's name appears beside the call number or the letters *FIC*. The cards are filed alphabetically by the author's last name. Author cards can help you find all the books in that library that were written by a certain author.

Sometimes you will see the abbreviation *comp.* (for *compiler*) after the author's name. This means that the listed author gathered or compiled the works by one or more writers. For example, a compiler may choose stories by several different authors and publish them in one book.

539

Author Card

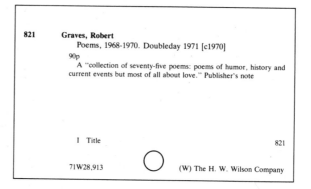

Title Cards.   A title card gives the title of the book above the author's name beside the call number or the letters *FIC.* Title cards are filed alphabetically by title. They are especially helpful when you are trying to locate a book but you do not know the author's name.

Title Card

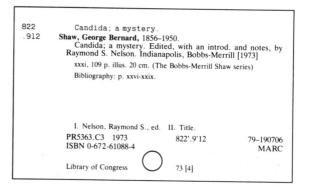

Subject Cards.   When you want to locate information about a particular topic, you will find subject cards most helpful. Each subject card lists the title of a book, the author,

540

and the call number. There may be several cards about the same subject filed alphabetically.

Subject Card

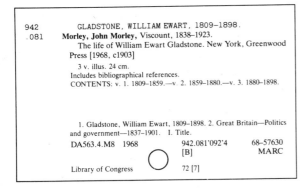

Cross-Reference Cards.   Some cards, called cross-reference cards, refer you to other subject headings in the catalog. The terms *See* and *See also* refer you to other topics. For example, the card for *Architecture, Church* might read, "See Church Architecture." The card for *Architecture* might read, "See also Buildings, Castles, Church Architecture, Libraries, Schools." You would find subject cards for those topics elsewhere in the card catalog.

Guide Cards.   Blank cards with a word or a letter at the top are used to alphabetize the card catalog. Use these guide cards to help you locate author, title, and subject cards.

Assignment 1   Card Catalog   On your paper, write *Title card, Author card,* or *Subject card* to tell which kind of card would help you to locate each of the following.

1. *The Strongest Man in the World*
2. A book by Jules Verne

Assignment 1 *(pages 541–542)*

1. Title card
2. Author card

(Continue on the next page.)

541

Assignment 1 *(pages 541–542),*
continued

3. Subject card
4. Subject card
5. Subject card

Assignment 2 *(page 542)*

Answers will vary.

Assignment 1 *(pages 542–543)*

Answers may vary. Samples:

1. A pool left by an ebbing tide,
   as in a rock basin
2. gladioli, gladioluses, gladiola
3. Twenty meanings
   On hand means "available."
   At hand means "close by,
   near, accessible."
   Hands down means "with no
   trouble, easily."
4. instrument, implement,
   utensil, appliance, gadget
5. a. southwest
   b. medical doctor
   c. junior
   d. post meridiem
   e. pound

3. Information about the Incas of Peru
4. A biography of Walt Disney
5. A book about the pyramids of Egypt

Assignment 2   Card Catalog   On your paper, list the author, title, and call number for each of the following books. Use the card catalog in your school or public library.

1. A book about gardening
2. A biography of an astronaut
3. A collection of poems by Edna St. Vincent Millay
4. A book about fishing, tennis, or baseball
5. A book about wildlife in Africa

22.3 General Reference Books

Dictionaries

Dictionaries contain a variety of useful information in addition to word meanings. There are special dictionaries of slang, foreign languages, rhyming words, sports, music, and many other subjects.

An **unabridged dictionary** contains hundreds of thousands of words. It can usually be found in the reference section of the library. An **abridged dictionary** is usually smaller, and contains fewer words than an unabridged dictionary.

A dictionary of synonyms is useful in choosing the best word for your writing. *Roget's II: The New Thesaurus, Webster's New Dictionary of Synonyms,* and *Roget's International Thesaurus* are several well-known dictionaries of synonyms.

Assignment 1   Dictionaries   On your paper, write the answers to the following questions. Use a dictionary.

542

1. What is a *tide pool?*
2. What is the plural of *gladiolus?*
3. How many meanings are given for the noun form of *hand?* What are the meanings of *on hand, at hand, hands down?*
4. What are the synonyms for *tool?*
5. What do these abbreviations mean?

   a. SW   b. M.D.   c. Jr.   d. P.M.   e. lb

Encyclopedias

Encyclopedias contain information on hundreds of topics and are illustrated with pictures, charts, maps, and diagrams. The articles are arranged in alphabetical order. An index gives the volume number and page numbers for the main entry and the subentries for each topic. An index may be included in each volume of the encyclopedia or contained in a separate volume.

The following encyclopedias are available in most public libraries:

> *Compton's Encyclopedia*
> *The Encyclopedia Americana*
> *The New Encyclopaedia Britannica*
> *The World Book Encyclopedia*

Assignment 2   Encyclopedias   On your paper, answer the following questions. Use an encyclopedia and its index.

1. What is the Great Circle?
2. Who were Sir Henry Stanley and David Livingstone?
3. Name a pioneer in the field of rocketry and space flight.
4. What is the Pine Tree Dance?
5. Where did the metric system begin?
6. What is a sand dollar and what does it look like?

543

Assignment 1 *(pages 542–543)*

See page 542 for sample answers.

Assignment 2 *(page 543)*

Answers may vary. Samples:

1. The Great Circle is the circle formed on the surface of a sphere by the intersection of a plane passing through the center of the sphere. In navigation, it is the shortest distance between two positions on the earth's surface.
2. David Livingstone was a Scottish missionary and explorer in Africa who, in 1871, was stricken with fever at Ujiji on Lake Tanganyika. Sir Henry Stanley, an English newspaper correspondent, found and rescued him.
3. Robert Goddard, who invented the first liquid-fuel rocket, was a pioneer in rocket and space flight.
4. The Pine Tree Dance is a harvest celebration of the Southwest Pueblo Indians.
5. The metric system began in France.
6. A sand dollar is an animal that lives on the ocean floor. It is circular, about four inches in diameter, and is perforated with elongated holes in a symmetrical pattern.

Assignment 3 *(page 544)*

1. The man who won the Boston Marathon in 1981 is Toshihiko Seko of Japan. The woman who won is Allison Roe of New Zealand.
2. Mexico City has the highest altitude of any North American city.
3. *Answers will vary according to date.*
4. The countries that have flags of red, white, and blue are Australia, Burma, Chile, Republic of China, Costa Rica, Cuba, Czechoslovakia, Dominican Republic, France, Iceland, North Korea, Laos, Liberia, Luxembourg, Netherlands, New Zealand, Norway, Panama, Samoa, Thailand, United Kingdom, United States
5. 637,651 *(Answer may vary.)*

Assignment 4 *(page 545)*

1. about 4150 miles long; in Egypt
2. in South America
3. Alaska

(Continue on the next page.)

Almanacs and Yearbooks

You will find current facts about world events, sports, and many other topics in almanacs and yearbooks. The following almanacs, published yearly, are in most libraries:

The World Almanac and Book of Facts
The Information Please Almanac
The Hammond Almanac of a Million Facts, Records, Forecasts
Guinness Book of World Records

Assignment 3   Almanacs   On your paper, answer the following questions. Use a current almanac.

1. What man and what woman won the 1981 Boston Marathon?
2. What North American city has the highest altitude?
3. When is the next total eclipse of the sun? of the moon?
4. What countries have flags of red, white, and blue?
5. What is the population of the District of Columbia?

Atlases and Gazetteers

An **atlas** is a book of maps and geographical information. Special maps show information about rainfall, land use, population, and so on. Charts and tables present related facts.
The following atlases are found in most libraries:

Ambassador World Atlas
The World Book Atlas
Rand McNally Cosmopolitan World Atlas
National Geographic Atlas of the World

A **gazetteer** is a dictionary of geographical names with the location, pronunciation, and brief facts for each entry. Some atlases and some dictionaries include gazetteers. *Webster's New Geographical Dictionary* is a separate gazetteer that is widely used.

544

Assignment 4 Atlases and Gazetteers On your paper, answer the following questions. Use a current atlas or gazetteer.

1. Approximately how long is the Nile River? In what country is it located?
2. Where are the Andes?
3. Which state is farther west, Alaska or Hawaii?
4. What is the largest island in Hawaii?
5. How many time zones are there around the world?
6. Where is 0° longitude? By what other name is it known?

22.4 Biographical Reference Books

You can find biographies of living persons in reference works that are published monthly or yearly. *Current Biography* is a monthly publication featuring biographies and photographs of prominent people. The issues for each year are collected in the *Current Biography Yearbook,* which includes an index listing persons by name and by profession. Yearly publications such as *Who's Who in America* present biographies of hundreds of living people. Other biographical reference books include *Who's Who in the World, Who's Who Among Black Americans, Who's Who of American Women,* and *Who's Who in Canada.*

Assignment Biographical References On your paper, write one or two sentences to identify each of the following people. Use appropriate biographical reference books to find information about the people.

1. Daniel Inouye
2. Robert Rauschenberg
3. Gwendolyn Brooks
4. Alex P. Haley
5. Maureen Stapleton
6. Twyla Tharp

545

Assignment 4 *(page 545),* continued

4. the island of Hawaii
5. twenty-four
6. the imaginary line from which longitude east and west is measured, passing through Greenwich, England; also known as the prime meridian

Assignment *(page 545)*

Answers may vary. Samples:

1. Daniel Inouye, a resident of Hawaii, was a member of the United States Senate.
2. Robert Rauschenberg was an artist from Texas whose work appears at the Museum of Modern Art in New York City and the Tate Gallery in London, among other places.
3. Gwendolyn Brooks is a poet. She won the Pulitzer Prize for Poetry in 1950 and was named poet laureate of Illinois in 1968.
4. Alex Palmer Haley is an author. In 1976 he wrote Roots, an account of his own family history, for which he received the Pulitzer Prize in 1977.
5. Maureen Stapleton is an actress who has appeared quite often on the stage and in the movies. She received a Tony Award for her performance in the Gingerbread Lady in 1970.
6. Twyla Tharp is a dancer and choreographer. She is the creator of forty works for the Joffrey Ballet and has won many creative arts awards.

Assignment 1 *(page 546)*

Answers will vary.

22.5 The *Readers' Guide to Periodical Literature*

You can find current information about topics such as government, science, and entertainment in many magazines. The *Readers' Guide to Periodical Literature* is an index of the important articles from more than 180 magazines. Articles are indexed alphabetically by subject and author.

The following excerpt from the *Readers' Guide* shows how the information is presented. Notice that the information for each article includes the following: title, author, name of magazine, volume number, pages on which the article appears, and date of the magazine.

```
                          ASTRONOMY (periodical)
                             Behind the scenes [cont] R. Berry. Astronomy
                                8:51 My '80
Subject entry ——————      ASTRONOMY, Ancient
                                   See also
                             Astronomy, Indian(American)
                             Astroarchaeology: reading our past in the
Magazine title —————            heavens. S. Loebl. Sci Digest 88:58-63 Ag '80
                          ASTRONOMY, Chinese
Article title —————          China's elegant old instruments. K. P. Tritton
                                and S. B. Tritton. il Sky & Tel 59:377-80 My
Illustration —————              '80
                          ASTRONOMY, Indian (American)
Author —————                 Astroarchaeology: reading our past in the
                                heavens. S. Loebl. Sci Digest 88:58-63 Ag '80
Volume and                   Unique solar marking construct: Fajada Butte in
page numbers —————              New Mexico. A. Sofaer and others. bibl il map
                                Science 206:283-91 O 19 '79; Discussion.
                                209:858+ Ag 22 '80
"See also"                ASTRONOMY, Spherical and practical
reference —————                 See also
                             Azimuth
Date of issue —————          How to find 'em even if you can't see 'em. E.F.
                                Dodds. il Astronomy 8:41-3 Ag '80
"See" reference —————     ASTRONOMY and religion. See Religion and science
```

Assignment 1   *Readers' Guide*   Use the *Readers' Guide* to find one magazine article about each of the following topics. On your paper, copy the complete entry for each of the four articles.

1. Astronomy
2. Education
3. Travel
4. Weather

546

Assignment 2   Reference Books   On your paper, tell which of the following references you would use to find the requested information.

Card catalog   Encyclopedia   *Current Biography*
Dictionary   Almanac or yearbook   *Readers' Guide*
                 Atlas, gazetteer

1. The meaning of *googol*
2. The gold medal winners of the 1976 Olympics
3. The author of *The Orphans of Simitra*
4. The biography of a first-term senator
5. A magazine article about ice fishing
6. The major rivers of China

Assignment 2 *(page 547)*

1. Dictionary
2. Almanac or yearbook
3. Card catalog
4. Current Biography
5. Readers' Guide
6. Atlas, gazetteer

547

Unit 23

After studying this unit, students should be able to do the following:

- Prepare for a test.
- Take a test with objective questions, short-answer questions, or paragraph questions.

Teaching Suggestions

See "Classroom Insights" for Unit 23 in the front of this Teacher's Edition.

Program Resources

Resource Book, Second Course: Bonus Activity, Unit 23
Practice Book, Second Course, Unit 23

Related Resources

The American Heritage Dictionary of the English Language

Test-Taking Skills

23.1 Preparing for a Test

To be well prepared for every test, you should develop good study habits and study skills. A regular routine for study will help you to learn better and to remember more so that you can perform better on tests.

Place and Time. You will study better if you have a special place and time for studying. Find a quiet place where you are not likely to be disturbed. You will be able to concentrate better if you do not play the radio, the stereo, or the television while you study.

Daily studying will help you to avoid the need to cram the night before a test. If a test is announced several days in advance, start studying then rather than waiting until the last night. If you have more than one test to study for, you may want to spend part of your study time preparing for one test. Then take a break and study for the next one.

Keep a portable study kit with all the tools that you are likely to need to prepare for a test: paper, pencils, pen, ruler, drawing compass, dictionary, and perhaps a clipboard. Then you will not waste your study time looking for these items.

Emphasis of Studying. Teachers often give you an idea of what you should review for a test. Reread any pages or chapters in your textbook that your teacher has indicated are

548

important. Unit or chapter summaries, definitions, rules, formulas, and all words and phrases in boldface or italic type are also important. Review them carefully.

Your teacher will usually emphasize important points in class notes and in homework assignments. Therefore, it is a good idea to study your notes and past assignments as well as your textbook.

Active Studying. To make the most of your study time, you should combine your reading with active studying. The first step in active studying is to think over what you already know about the subject. Then reread your textbook, notes, and past assignments. As you read, write down any questions that you can think of that might be on the test.

After you finish reading, ask yourself the questions. Try to answer them from memory. Then look up answers that you do not remember. Continue studying your questions until you are sure of all the answers.

Active studying will help you to prepare for a test. The following strategies will help you to do your best when you take the test.

Strategies

1. *Take with you all the equipment that you will need* for the test: paper, pens, pencils, rulers, and so forth.

2. *Be sure to get a good night's sleep and eat a good breakfast.* You will feel better and perform better.

3. *Be confident.* Because you have prepared well, you should feel less nervous about taking a test. Make up your mind that you will do your best, and then do it.

Assignment Preparing for a Test The following sentences tell some ways that a person may prepare for a test.

Assignment (pages 549–550)

See page 550 for the answers.

549

Assignment *(pages 549–550)*

1. Poor habit
2. Good habit
3. Poor habit
4. Poor habit
5. Poor habit
6. Good habit
7. Poor habit
8. Good habit
9. Good habit
10. Good habit

On your paper, write *Good habit* or *Poor habit* next to the number of each statement.

1. Eat a quick breakfast on the morning of the test if you have time.
2. Study at the same place and time every day.
3. Play your favorite kind of music while you study.
4. Study all evening without taking a break, until you get sleepy.
5. Spend all your study time reading.
6. Prepare a study kit with all the tools that you need.
7. Study late into the night on the evening before a test.
8. Review your class notes.
9. Ask yourself questions that might be on the test.
10. Reread unit or chapter summaries.

23.2 Taking a Test

If there is sufficient time, skim the entire test before you begin to answer questions. Pay close attention to any oral instructions and read all the directions. Be sure to do exactly what the directions tell you. If you are told to answer Question A *or* B, do not answer A *and* B. If you are asked to give three facts, do not give more than or fewer than three. Try to keep track of your time. Do not waste time on questions that you cannot answer. Make sure you allow time to complete each question.

Tests may include objective questions, short-answer questions, and paragraph questions. An **objective question** has only one correct answer. You may write a word or a letter, make a mark, or fill in a circle or a box to indicate your answer. Many tests of this kind are designed to be scored by machines. **Completion questions** may require you to write words in blanks or to answer in a few words or in a sentence or two. **Paragraph questions** ask you to write one or more paragraphs.

550

Objective Questions

There are three types of objective questions: **true-false,
multiple-choice,** and **matching.** You will use somewhat
different strategies to answer each type of test question.

True-False Statements.   A true-false test item makes a
statement and asks you to indicate whether it is true or false.
As the following example shows, these statements are usually
simple and direct.

> The chief crops of every Southern state are cotton and
> peanuts.

Use the following strategies for answering true-false
questions.

Strategies

1. *Read each word carefully.* A single word such as *not*
   or *some* can affect the meaning of a statement.

2. *Look for words that mean that there are no exceptions* to the statement. Such words include *no,
   never, always, none, all, only,* and *every.* A single
   exception to such a statement makes that statement
   false.

3. *Look for words that permit exceptions.* Such words
   include *generally, usually, most, some, few, may,*
   and *sometimes.*

4. *Study all key words and all parts of the statement.* If
   any part of the statement is false, then the entire
   statement is false.

Look again at the true-false statement: "The chief crops
of every Southern state are cotton and peanuts." An important word to notice is *every.* This word means that there can
be no exceptions to the statement. Other key words are *chief*

551

crops, Southern state, cotton, and *peanuts.* Since Florida is a Southern state whose chief crop is citrus fruit, the statement should be marked *False.*

Multiple-Choice Questions. A multiple-choice question provides a question with a list of possible answers and asks you to choose the answer that is correct. Read the following example.

> Which one of the following pairs of words are homonyms?
> a. slow, fast   c. imaginary, real
> b. fall, autumn   d. their, there

Use the following strategies to answer multiple-choice questions.

Strategies

1. *Read the question carefully.*

2. *Look at all of the choices* before you choose an answer.

3. *Eliminate the answers that are clearly wrong.* Pick the one that seems best from those that are left.

4. *Avoid wild guesses.*

Look again at the multiple-choice example. If you remember what homonyms are, you may be able to answer as soon as you see the choices. If you do not remember, you can use the strategies to help you figure out the answer. You may remember, for example, that words with similar meanings are called synonyms. Since choice *b* is a pair of synonyms, you can eliminate that choice.

Note that choices *a* and *c* are both pairs of words with opposite meanings. If homonyms were opposites, both answers would be correct. You can eliminate these choices, leaving only the correct answer, *d.*

552

Matching Questions. A matching question asks you to match words or phrases in one column with words or phrases in a second column. The two columns do not always contain the same number of items. Look at the following example.

Match the words in the right column with the parts of speech on the left. You will not use one of the choices.

_?_ 1. noun	a. slowly
_?_ 2. pronoun	b. them
_?_ 3. adverb	c. into
_?_ 4. adjective	d. song
_?_ 5. preposition	e. think
	f. delicious

The following strategies are helpful in answering matching questions like the one in the preceding example.

Strategies

1. *Read the directions carefully.* You may be told to use answers more than once or not to use some answers.

2. *Match first the items that you know are correct.*

3. *Look at the remaining items for clues.* You can tell that a term such as *explorer* will match a name, not a date or a place.

4. *Check answers off as soon as you use them,* if your teacher permits you to do so.

Now look again at the sample matching question. The directions tell you that you will not use one word in the second column. Looking at that column, you may discover that each of the words is an example of a different part of speech. If you know that *song* is a noun, you may match those terms. Since *delicious* is an adjective, you can match those items also. You may then remember that adverbs often end in *-ly*

553

Assignment 1 *(page 554)*

1. False
2. True
3. False
4. False
5. False

Assignment 2 *(page 554)*

Answers may vary. Samples:

1. only
2. It is necessary to know what a periodicals section is in order to know whether other reading material may be found there.
3. Yes, you can respond to the statement, for then you will know that magazines are not the only reading material in the section in which they are kept.

and decide to match *slowly* with *adverb*. You now have only two parts of speech left. If you know that *think* is a verb, you can eliminate that choice. If you can then remember what either a pronoun or a preposition is, you can match both of the remaining items with the correct answers.

Assignment 1   Objective Questions   On your paper, write *True* for each true statement and *False* for each false statement.

1. All objective questions ask you to match columns of items.
2. The word *usually* in a true-false statement means that there may be exceptions.
3. A good strategy for matching questions is to match first the items that you are not sure about.
4. A statement may be true even if part of it is false.
5. If you do not know the answer to a multiple-choice question, you should guess and hope that you get it right.

Assignment 2   Objective Questions   On your paper, write the answers to the questions that follow this true-false statement.

Magazines are the only reading material kept in the periodicals section of the library.

1. What word in the statement indicates that there are no exceptions?
2. Is it necessary to know what a periodicals section is in order to answer the question? Explain.
3. If you know that magazines and newspapers are kept in the same section at your local library, can you respond to the statement? Explain.

Short-Answer Questions

A short-answer test item makes a statement or asks a question. You have to supply a word, a phrase, a sentence, or

554

several sentences to complete the statement or to answer the question. Some short-answer items, called **fill-in-the-blank**, are sentences with one or more blanks for which you must supply the word or phrase. Study the following example.

The _?_ was built to connect the Hudson River to Lake Erie.

The strategies that follow will help you to answer fill-in-the-blank items like the preceding example.

Strategies

1. *Read the entire sentence carefully.*

2. *Find the key words* that may be clues to the answer.

3. *Write what you do know,* even if you cannot remember or are not sure of the exact answer.

4. *Write neatly* in order to make your answers easy to read.

Now look again at the example question: "The _?_ was built to connect the Hudson River to Lake Erie." If you follow the strategies, you will notice that the answer refers to a connection that was built, rather than one that exists in nature. The phrase "to connect the Hudson River to Lake Erie" is important because it refers to a definite geographic location. If you know that people build canals to connect bodies of water, that phrase may help you to recall the correct answer: the Erie Canal.

Other short-answer items are similar to completion items, except that they require an answer of one or two sentences, as in the following example.

Who wrote *Common Sense,* and what was it about?

Use the following strategies for short-answer questions that require an answer of one or two sentences.

555

Strategies

1. *Read the question carefully.*

2. *Watch for key words.*

3. *Give the best answer that you can,* even if you are not sure that it is correct or complete.

4. *Answer in complete sentences,* unless your teacher tells you not to. Include the wording of the question in your answer. For example, begin your answer to "What is the capital of Ohio?" with the words "The capital of Ohio is. . . ."

Look again at the question: "Who wrote *Common Sense,* and what was it about?" Notice that you have two questions to answer. "Thomas Paine wrote *Common Sense*" answers the question *Who?* and "It presented arguments in favor of American independence from British rule" answers *What?*

Paragraph Questions

Paragraph questions are those that require recall of specific information and general knowledge of a subject. Your answers will be one or two paragraphs in which you describe by giving details or explain by giving reasons. Study the following example.

Describe the process by which a bill becomes law.

Use the following strategies to answer paragraph questions.

Strategies

1. *Read the directions carefully before you begin your answer.*

2. *Make a list on scrap paper of dates, names, facts, or formulas* that will help you when you prepare your answer.

3. *Be specific.* Do not pad your answer with unnecessary information.

4. *Check your answer for correct grammar, usage, spelling, and punctuation.*

Assignment 3 Short-Answer Questions On your paper, write complete sentences to answer the questions about this fill-in-the-blank item.

Encyclopedias, dictionaries, almanacs, and yearbooks are all found in the __?__ section of a library.

1. What are the key words in the item?
2. Is it possible to know the answer before you read the entire item?
3. If you think that you know the answer, should you finish reading the item? Why or why not?
4. If you know the section of the library where you would find just one of the kinds of books mentioned, could you answer the item? Explain.

Assignment 4 Paragraph Questions Look at the end of chapters or units in one of your textbooks and find a question that requires an answer of more than one paragraph. On your paper, answer the question, following the strategies that you learned.

Assignment 3 *(page 557)*

Answers may vary. Samples:

1. Encyclopedias, dictionaries, almanacs, yearbooks, all, section, library
2. It is possible to know the answer before you read the entire item if you know what kind of material is contained in any of the types of books mentioned.
3. You should finish reading the item because it may conclude differently from the way you expect.
4. You could answer the item because you are told that <u>all</u> of the kinds of books mentioned are found there.

Assignment 4 *(page 557)*

Answers will vary.

557

Index

Abbreviations: capitalizing, 200, 204; period after, 207; Postal Service, 204, 207, 455

Actions, of story: in narratives, 384–386; summarizing, in book reports, 436

Action verbs: defined, 12; distinguishing from linking verbs, 13–14; objects after, 56–57

Adjective clauses: answering *Which? What kind? How many?*, 98–99; defined, 98; diagraming, 104–105, 125; relative adverbs in, 99; relative pronouns in, 10–11, 99; subordinating ideas with, 321–322

Adjective phrases: defined, 74

Adjectives: answering *Which? What kind? How many?*, 17, 27; articles, 17; comparision of, 171–173; defined, 17; demonstrative pronouns used as, 21; in descriptions, 365, 366, 373; diagraming, 62; distinguishing from adverbs, 26–27; ending in *-ly,* 26–27; indefinite pronouns used as, 21; infinitives and infinitive phrases used as, 81–83; interrogative pronouns used as, 21; after linking verbs, 18, 60; nouns used as, 20; participles and participial phrases used as, 77–79, 80; placement of, 18; possessive nouns used as, 20; possessive pronouns used as, 20–21, 166; prepositional phrases used as, 31, 74; proper, 19–20; relative pronouns used as, 21; set off by commas, 18; subordinate clauses as, 98–99

Adjective suffixes, 19–20, 496

Adverb clauses: answering *How? When? Where? To what extent or degree? Why?*, 101–102; comma after, 211; defined, 101; diagraming, 106–107, 125; subordinating conjunctions in, 102; subordinating ideas with, 323

Adverb phrases: defined, 75

Adverbs: answering *How? When? Where? How often? To what degree or extent?*, 23, 27; comparison of, 175; defined, 22; in descriptions, 365, 366, 373; diagraming, 62–63; distinguishing from adjectives, 26–27; infinitives and infinitive phrases used as, 81–83; modifying adjectives, 22, 25; modifying adverbs, 23, 26; modifying verb phrases, 23–24; modifying verbs, 22, 23–24; *not, never,* 23, 48; placement of, 24, 25, 26; prepositional phrases used as, 31, 75; clauses used as, 101–102

Agreement of pronouns and antecedents: antecedents joined by *and,* 158; antecedents joined by *or, nor,* 158–159; collective nouns as antecedents, 161; in gender, 161; indefinite pronouns as antecedents, 159–160; in number, 158–159; in person, 162–163

Agreement of subjects and verbs: auxiliary verbs, 146; collective nouns, 153–154; compound subjects connected by *and,* 149; compound subjects connected by *or, nor,* 150–151; after *Here, There,* 148; indefinite pronouns, 151–152; *I, you,* 146; names, 155; nouns ending in *s,* 154; phrase between subject and verb, 147–148; plural subjects, 146; in questions, 148; singular subjects, 145–146; subject after verb, 148; titles, 155; verb phrases, 146; words of amount and time, 155–156

Alphabetical order, 501, 536, 539, 543

Antecedent: agreement of pronouns with, 158–163; defined, 7, 158; reference of pronoun to, 169–170; of relative pronoun, 10–11

Apostrophe: in contractions, 220; to form plural of letters, numbers, etc., 220; to show possession, 20, 219–220

Articles: defined, 17; in titles, 202

Atlases, 544

Audience: defined, 249; in speaking, 528, 532–533; in writing, 250, 268

Author card, 539–540

Autobiography: book reports about, 439–440; defined, 439

Auxiliary (helping) verbs: agreement with subjects, 146; defined, 14; forms of *be* as, 15, 131, 133–134, 143, 145; forms of *do* as, 15, 145; forms of *have* as, 15, 132, 133–134, 138, 140, 141, 145; list, 15; *will, shall* as, 138

Biographical references, 546

Biography: book reports about, 439–440; defined, 439; locating in library, 537–538

Body: of business letter, 462; of report, 425–426; of social letter, 454; of speech, 530

Book reports: about fiction, 435–438; about nonfiction, 439–441

Business letters, 460–469

Call number, 539

Capitalization: of abbreviations in titles of persons, 200; of *A.D., B.C., A.M., P.M.*, 204; of compass points, 200–201; of family-relationship words, 199; of first word in direct quotation, 197; of first word in line of poetry, 198; of first word of sentence, 197; of initials, 199; of interrupted quotation, 197; of names of awards, documents, 201; of names of days, months, 201; of names of gods of mythology, 200; of names of heavenly bodies, 201; of names of historical events, periods, 201; of names of holidays, special days, special events, 201; of names of languages, 201; of names of organizations and their members, 202; of names of people, 199; of names of peoples, races, tribes, nationalities, 201; of names of school subjects, 202; of names of ships, trains, etc., 202; of personal or official titles, 199–200; of place names, 200; of Postal Service abbreviations, 204; of pronoun *I,* 204; of proper adjectives, 19, 204; of proper nouns, 4, 199–202; in social letters, 454; of titles of books, movies, etc., 201–202; of trade names, 202

Card catalog, 539–541

Case. *See* Pronoun case.

Characters: describing, in book reports, 436; in narratives, 384, 386, 390

Chronological order: defined, 294; in directions, 344–345; in explanations, 350; in narratives, 385, 386, 396–398; in paragraph development, 294–295; in reports, 421; in speeches, 531

Clauses: 94–111: adjective, 98–99, 115; adverb, 101–102, 115; defined, 95; diagraming sentences with, 104–107; independent, 95, 114, 116; kinds, 95–102; subordinate, 96–102, 116

Collective nouns: agreement of verbs with, 153–154; as antecedents, 160; defined, 6

Colon, 215, 462

Comma: with abbreviated title or degree, 212; with adjectives, 18; 211; after adverb clause, 211; to avoid confusion, 211; after complimentary close, 213, 454, 462; before coordinating conjunction, 32, 95, 114, 212; in dates and addresses, 213; with direct address, 212; with

559

independent clauses in a series, 209; after interjection, 36, 211; after introductory expressions, 210–211; with modifiers in a series, 209; with nonessential phrase, 212; after participial phrase, 210; with phrases in a series, 209; after prepositional phrase, 210; after salutation of social letter, 213, 454; to separate sentence parts, 212–213; in a series, 209; after *yes, no,* 211

Common nouns: defined, 4

Comparative degree: of adjectives, 172–173; of adverbs, 175; defined, 172

Comparison: of adjectives, 171–173; of adverbs, 175; degrees of, 171–173, 175; double, 176; with *-er, -est,* 172, 175; irregular, 173, 175; with *less, least,* 173, 175; with *more, most,* 172, 175

Complements: defined, 55; diagraming, 63–65; kinds, 55–60; objects, 56–57; subject, 58–59, 60; in verbal phrases, 80, 83

Complete predicate: defined, 51

Complete sentence: defined, 118; writing, 118–122

Complete subject: defined, 51

Complex sentence: defined, 115; diagraming, 124–125

Complimentary close, 213, 454, 462

Compound-complex sentence: defined, 116

Compound nouns: defined, 5; with hyphens, 5; spelling plurals, 483

Compound numbers, 223

Compound predicate: combining sentences by using, 317; defined, 49; diagraming, 65–66

Compound prepositions, 29

Compound sentence: combining simple sentences into, 318–319; coordinating conjunction in, 114, 212; defined, 114; diagraming, 124; punctuating, 114, 212, 214

Compound subject: agreement of

verb with, 149–150; combining sentences by using, 316; defined, 49; diagraming, 65–66; pronouns in, 165

Conciseness: defined, 327; in speeches, 533; in writing, 327–328

Concluding paragraph: in book report, 436; in a report, 526–527

Concluding sentence: defined, 277, 300; in explanations, 349, 350; writing, 300–302

Conclusion: of narrative, 399–400; of speech, 532

Conjugation, of verbs, 138–139

Conjunctions: coordinating, 32–33; correlative, 33; defined, 32; subordinating, 34–35; in titles, 202

Connotation, 499

Context, and meaning, 493–494

Contractions, apostrophe in, 220

Coordinating conjunctions: comma before, 33, 95, 114, 212; defined, 32; joining independent clauses, 33, 95, 114; joining phrases, 33; list, 32

Correlative conjunctions: defined, 33; list, 33

Cross-reference card, 541

Dash, 224

Declarative sentence: defined, 45; diagraming, 61; placement of subject and predicate in, 53; punctuating, 45, 206

Definite article: defined, 17

Definitions: in dictionary, 502; writing, 341–342

Degrees of comparison, 171–172, 502

Demonstrative pronouns: as adjectives, 21; defined, 10; list, 10

Denotation, 499

Dependent clause. *See* Subordinate clause.

Descriptions: adjectives and adverbs in, 365, 366, 373; of persons, 372–373; of places, 368–370; sensory details in,

560

361–363; spatial order in, 369, 370, 372–373; specific nouns in, 365, 366, 373; strong verbs in, 365, 366, 373

Details: in definitions, 341–342; in descriptions, 369, 372; in directions, 345; in paragraph development, 282–283, 284–285; sensory, 361–363

Dewey decimal system, 536–537

Diagraming, 61–67, 85–88, 104–107, 124–125

Dialogue: defined, 395; interjections in, 37; in narratives, 394–396; punctuating and paragraphing, 395–396

Dictionary: abridged, 542; alphabetical order in, 501; changes in word forms in, 502; definitions, 502; entry, 501; entry word, 501; guide words, 501; homographs in, 502; locating a word in, 501; part-of-speech labels in, 501; pronunciations in, 501; as spelling aid, 490–491; syllabication in, 501; synonym paragraphs in, 498–499, 502; of synonyms, 542; unabridged, 542; usage labels, 502–503

Direct address, 212

Directions: strategies for writing, 344–345

Direct objects: defined, 56; diagraming, 63

Direct quotations: capitalizing, 197; defined, 197; punctuating, 216–218. *See also* Dialogue.

Encyclopedias, 411–412, 414, 415, 543

Entry word, in dictionary, 501

Envelope address, 455, 463

Essential phrase, 212

Examples: in context, 494; in definitions, 341–342; in paragraph development, 290–291

Exclamation point: after exclamatory sentence, 46, 208; after interjection, 36, 208

Exclamatory sentence: defined, 46; placement of subject and

predicate in, 54; punctuating, 46, 208

Explanations: chronological order in, 350; defining a word, 341–342; of how to get from one place to another, 344–346; of how to make or do something, 348–350; limiting topics for, 348–349; transitional words and phrases in, 350

Facts, in paragraph development, 289

Fiction: book reports about, 435–438; locating in library, 536, 539

Future perfect tense, 141

Future tense, 141

Gender: agreement of pronouns in, 161; of personal pronouns, 8, 161

Guide cards, 541

Guide words, in dictionary, 501

Heading: of business letter, 460–461; of social letter, 454

Helping verbs. *See* Auxiliary verbs.

Homophones, 488–489

High point, in narratives, 385, 386

Hyphen, 5, 221–223

Imperative sentence: complete predicate in, 54; defined, 46; diagraming, 62; punctuating, 46; subject understood, 48, 54

Indefinite articles: defined, 17

Indefinite pronouns: as adjectives, 21; agreement of verbs with, 151–152; as antecedents, 159–160, 163; defined, 9, 151; list, 9, 152, 159; singular, 151–152, 159; singular or plural, 152, 159–160; plural, 152, 159

Independent clause: in compound sentence, 114; defined, 95; in a series, 209

Index, as study aid, 504–505

Indirect objects: defined, 57; diagraming, 64; distinguishing from objects of preposition, 57

561

Indirect quotation: defined, 217
Infinitive phrases: defined, 83; diagraming, 87–88; uses of, 83
Infinitives: defined, 81; distinguishing from prepositional phrases, 82; uses of, 81–82
Inside address, 461–462
Interjections, 36, 208, 211
Interrogative pronouns: as adjectives, 21; case of, 167–168; defined, 10
Interrogative sentence: defined, 46; diagraming, 62; placement of subject and predicate in, 53; punctuating, 46, 207
Introduction, to speech, 531–532
Introductory expressions, comma after, 210–211
Introductory paragraph: in book reports, 435–436, 439, 441; in reports, 425
Irregular comparisons, 173, 175
Irregular verbs: defined, 133; in dictionary, 502; past participles as adjectives, 78–79; principal parts of, 132–133
Italics, 224–225

Library skills, 536–547
Linking verbs: adjectives after, 18, 60; defined, 13; distinguishing from action verbs, 13–14; forms of be as, 13, 58; lists, 13, 58; nouns and pronouns after, 58–59; subject complements after, 58–59, 60
Listening, 514–523: active, 515; conversational, 515; courteous, 522–523; critical, 515; for information, 514–515; for main ideas, 520–521; for method of organization, 518; occasions for, 514; passive, 515; questions before, 516–517; responsive, 522–523; setting for, 516; for signals and transitions, 519–520; for speaker's purpose, 517–518; strategies for, 516, 523; for supporting material, 521; to take notes, 521–522
Lists, prewriting, 245

Main heading, in outline, 420, 530
Main verb: defined, 14; forms of be, have, do as, 15
Manuscript form: guidelines for, 228–229; for report, 431–432
Matching questions, 553–554
Mechanics, rules of, 197–227
Misplaced modifiers, 177–178
Modifiers: compound, 222; correct use of, 171–178; diagraming, 62–63; expanding sentence with, 265–266; placement of, 177–178; in a series, 209
Multiple-choice questions, 552

Narratives: actions in, 384–386; characters in, 384, 386, 390; choosing topic for, 383–384; chronological order in, 385, 386, 396–398; ending of, 399–400; high point in, 385, 386; planning, 383–387; prewriting notes for, 385–386; setting in, 384, 386, 390; situation in, 385, 386, 390; strategies for beginning, 389–390; strategies for using dialogue in, 395; transitional words and phrases in, 396–397, 398
Nominative case, 164, 165
Nonessential phrase, 212
Nonfiction: book reports about, 439–441; locating in library, 536–538, 539
Note cards, for reports, 417–418; for speeches, 534
Notes, prewriting, 238, 239–240: for narratives, 385–386
Note taking: for book reports, 435, 439, 440; as listening aid, 521–522; for reports, 417–418; strategies for, 512, 522; as study aid, 512
Nouns: as adjectives, 20; collective, 6, 153–154, 160; common, 4; compound, 5, 483; defined, 3; in descriptions, 365, 366, 373; ending in s, 154; infinitive and infinitive phrases used as, 81–83; kinds, 3–6; plural, 481–483; possessive, 20; proper, 4

Number: agreement of pronouns and antecedents in, 158–159; agreement of subjects and verbs in, 144–156

Numbers, in writing, 222–223, 225, 226–227

Objective case, 164–165

Objective tests, 551–553

Objects: compound, 57, 74, 165; defined, 56; direct, 56; indirect, 57; of prepositions, 30, 73–74

Order of importance: defined, 297; expressions used in, 298–299; in paragraph development, 297–299; in reports, 421

Order letter, 468–469

Organization: of paragraphs, 293–299; strategies for revising for, 314

Outlining: reports, 420–422; speeches, 530–531

Paragraph questions, 556–557

Paragraphs: chronological order in, 294–295; concluding sentence in, 300–302; defined, 277; indenting, 217, 229, 276; limiting topics for, 280–281; listing and choosing details for, 282–283; order of importance in, 297–299; organization of, 293–299; planning, 280–283; revising, 311–314; selecting topics for, 280; to show change of speaker, 217, 396; spatial order in, 295–297; supporting sentences in, 277, 288–291; topic sentence, 277, 285–287, 289, 290, 301; transitional words and phrases in, 294; unity in, 278–279

Participial phrases: comma after, 210; defined, 80; diagraming, 85–86; modifiers in, 80; placement of, 80

Participles, as adjectives: defined, 77; past, 78–79; present, 78

Parts of speech, 2–43. See also Adjectives, Adverbs, Conjunctions, Interjections, Nouns, Prepositions, Pronouns, Verbs.

Past perfect tense, 140–141

Past tense, 140

Period, 45, 46, 206–207

Personal pronouns: agreement with antecedent, 157–163; case, 163–165, 166; chart, 8; gender, 8, 161; person, 7–8, 162–163; plural, 8, 158; number, 8, 158–160; possessive, 8, 164, 166; singular, 8

Person, of pronoun: agreement with antecedent in, 162–163; chart, 8; uses of, 7, 162

Phrases, 72–93: defined, 73; infinitive, 83; kinds, 73–75, 77–79, 80, 81–82, 83; participial, 80; prepositional, 30–31, 73–75; as sentence fragment, 119; in a series, 209; verb, 14–15, 23–24, 61–62; verbal, 80, 83

Plurals, spelling, 481–483

Positive degree: of adjectives, 171; of adverbs, 175; defined, 171

Possessive case, 166–167

Possessive nouns: as adjectives, 20; spelling, 219–220

Possessive pronouns: as adjectives, 20–21, 166; replacing or referring to nouns, 166

Predicate: complete, 51–52; compound, 49; diagraming, 61–62; expressing ideas as, 261–262; in independent clause, 95; placement of, 53–54; simple, 48; in subordinate clause, 96

Predicate adjective: compound, 60; defined, 60; diagraming, 64–65

Predicate nominative: compound, 59; defined, 58; diagraming, 64

Prefixes: defined, 495; dividing words after, 222; hyphen after, 222; list of common, 495; and word meaning, 495

Prepositional phrases: as adjectives, 31, 74; as adverbs, 31, 75; comma after, 210; defined, 30, 73; diagraming, 85; modifiers in, 30, 73; objects in, 30, 73–74; revising with, 325–326

Prepositions: compound, 29; compound objects of, 74;

defined, 28; distinguishing from subordinating conjunctions, 34; lists, 28–29; objects of, 30, 73–74; placement of, 30, 74; in titles, 202

Present participle: defined, 131

Present perfect tense, 139–140

Present tense, 139

Prewriting, 238–259: defined, 238; developing ideas, 244–247; finding ideas, 239–241; focusing ideas, 249; interest inventory, 241; lists, 245; notes, 238, 239–240, 385–386

Principal parts of verbs: defined, 131; of irregular verbs, 132–133; of regular verbs, 132–133

Pronominal adjectives. *See* Possessive pronouns.

Pronoun case: chart, 164; defined, 163; of interrogative pronouns, 167–168; nominative, 164, 165; objective, 164–165; of personal pronouns, 163–165; possessive, 166–167; of relative pronouns, 168

Pronouns: agreement with antecedents, 158–163; antecedents, defined, 7; cases, 163–165, 167–168; clear reference to antecedents, 169–170; in compound construction, 165; correct use of, 157–170; defined, 7; demonstrative, 10, 21; indefinite, 9, 21, 151–152, 159–160, 163; interrogative, 10, 21, 167–168; kinds, 7–11; plural, 158; relative, 10–11, 21, 99, 167–168; singular, 158

Pronunciation: key, 491; spelling and, 487–488

Proofreading symbols, 227–228

Proper adjective: capitalization of, 19, 204; defined, 19; forming, 19–20

Proper nouns: capitalization of, 4, 199–202; defined, 4

Punctuation: apostrophe, 219–220; colon, 215; comma, 209–213; dash, 224; exclamation point, 36, 46, 208; hyphen, 221–223;

period, 45, 206–207; question mark, 46, 207–208; quotation marks, 216–218; semicolon, 214

Purpose: defined, 249; listening for speaker's, 517–518; in speaking, 525–526, 527; in writing, 249–250, 268–269

Question mark, 46, 207–208

Questions: for limiting topics, 411; before listening, 516–517; prewriting, 246–247

Quotation marks, 216–218. *See also* Dialogue, Direct quotations.

Readers' Guide to Periodical Literature, 412, 546

Reading: skills, 504–509; SQRRR method, 508–509

Regular verbs: defined, 132; in dictionary, 502; past participles as adjectives, 78; principal parts of, 132–133

Relative adverbs, 99

Relative pronouns: in adjective clauses, 99; as adjectives, 21; antecedents, 10–11; case of, 167–168; defined, 10; list, 10, 99

Reports, 408–51: body of, 425–426; book, 435–441; concluding paragraph in, 426–427; finished form of, 431–432; gathering information for, 413–418; introductory paragraph in, 425; outlining, 420–422; procedure for organizing, 420–422; selecting and limiting topics for, 409–412; source cards for, 414–415; strategies for revising, 430–431; taking notes for, 417–418; title for, 430–431; topic statement for, 420, 421, 425

Request letter, 466

Return address, 455

Revising: by coordination, 316–317; defined, 310; for paragraph organization, 313–314; paragraphs, 311–314; for paragraph unity, 312–313; with prepositional phrases, 325–326; proofreading, 333–334; a report, 430–431; for sentence conciseness, 327–328; sentences, 316–317, 318–319, 321–322, 323, 325–326, 327–328, 330–331; for sentence variety, 330–331; by subordination, 321–323

Rough outline, 421

Run-on sentence: correcting, 121–122; defined, 120

Salutation: of business letter, 462; comma after, 213, 254, 262; of social letter, 454

Semicolon, 114, 214

Sensory details, 361–363

Sentence: classified by purpose, 45–46; classified by structure, 113–117; complements, 55–60; complete, 118–122; complex, 115–116; compound, 114; compound-complex, 116–117; conciseness, 327–328; declarative, 45, 53, 61; defined, 45; diagrams, 61–67, 85–88, 104–107, 124–125; exclamatory, 46, 54; expanding with modifiers, 265–266; fragments, 118–120; imperative, 46, 54, 62; independent clause as, 95; interrogative, 46, 53, 62; revision, 316–317, 318–319, 321–322, 323, 325–326, 327–328, 330–331; run-on, 120–122; simple, 114; strategies for writing, 262; subject and predicate, 47–48, 49–50, 51–54, 61–62; suiting to audience and purpose, 268–269; supporting, 277, 288–291; topic, 277, 285–287, 344, 368–369, 372; variety, 330–331

Sentence fragment: correcting, 119–120; defined, 118

Setting: for listening, 516; in narratives, 384, 386, 390

Short-answer questions, 554–556

Signature, in letter, 454, 462

Simple predicate: defined, 48

Simple sentence: defined, 114

Simple subject: defined, 47; of imperative sentence, 48

Single quotation marks, 217

Social letters, 453–458

Source cards: for books, 414, 415; for an encyclopedia article, 414, 415; for magazine and newspaper articles, 414–415

Spatial order: defined, 295; in descriptions, 369, 370, 372–373; in paragraph development, 295–297; in reports, 421; in speeches, 531; words and phrases used in, 295–296, 369, 370

Speeches: audience for, 528, 532–533; body of, 530; conclusion of, 532; delivering, 533–535; developing ideas for, 529; formal, 524–525; gathering information for, 529; informal, 524–525; introduction to, 531–532; note cards for, 534; organizing, 530–533; outlining, 530–531; planning, 526–528; presenting, 534–535; purposes of, 525–526, 527; rehearsing, 534; selecting and limiting topic for, 527–528; time limits for, 528

Spelling skills, 480–491

SQRRR reading method, 508–509

Study skills, 504–513, 548–549

Subheadings: in outline, 421–422, 530; as study aid, 506

Subject card, 540–544

Subject complements: defined, 58; diagraming, 64–65; predicate adjectives, 60; predicate nominatives, 59

Subject, of sentence: agreement of verb with, 144–156; complete, 51; compound, 49, 149–151, 165; diagraming, 61–62; expressing ideas as, 261–262; in independent clause, 95; locating, 147–148; placement of, 53–54; relative pronoun as, 99; simple, 47–48; in subordinate clause, 96; understood, 48

Subordinate clauses: as adjectives, 98–99; as adverbs, 101–102; combined with independent clauses, 96–97; defined, 96; distinguishing from independent

565

clauses, 97; interrupting independent clauses, 115–116, 117; as sentence fragments, 119–120

Subordinating conjunctions: defined, 34; distinguishing from prepositions, 35; list, 102; relationships expressed by, 34–35; in subordinate clauses, 34, 102

Suffixes: adjective, 19–20, 496; adverb, 496; defined, 495; dividing words before, 222; lists of common, 495–496; noun, 495; and spelling, 496–497; verb, 496; and word meaning, 495–497

Superlative degree: of adjectives, 172–173; of adverbs, 175; defined, 172

Supporting sentences: defined, 277; writing, 288–291

Syllables: in dictionary, 501; dividing words between, 221

Synonym paragraph, 498–499, 502

Synonyms: in context, 493; in dictionary, 502; distinguishing shades of meaning, 498–499

Table of contents, as study aid, 504

Tense: defined, 137; future, 141; future perfect, 141; past, 140; past perfect, 140–141; present, 139; present perfect, 139–140

Tests, taking, 548–557

Thank-you note, 457

Title card, 540

Titles: agreement of verbs with, 155; correct manuscript form, 229; italics with, 224–225; quotation marks with, 217; for reports, 430–431

Topic: defined, 252; limiting, for an explanation, 348–349; for narrative, 383–384; procedure for choosing, 252–253; questions for limiting, 411; for report, 409–412; for speech, 527–528; strategies for limiting, 281

Topical order, 530

Topic sentence: defined, 277; in description, 368–369, 372; in directions, 344; writing, 285–287

Topic statement, for report, 420, 421, 425

Transitional words and phrases: in directions, 345, 346; in explanations, 350; listening for, 519–520; in narratives, 396–397, 398; in paragraph development, 294

True-false statements, 551–552

Unity: in paragraphs, 278–279; strategies for revising for, 312–313

Usage: correct, 130–178; labels in dictionary, 502–503; notes on, 179–189

Variety, in sentences, 330–331

Verbal phrases, 80, 83

Verbals: defined, 77; distinguishing from verb phrases, 79; infinitives, 81–82; participles, 77–79

Verb phrase: defined, 14; diagraming, 61–62; interrupted by another word, 15, 24; modified by adverb, 23–24; in questions, 15; and subject-verb agreement, 146; with two or more auxiliary verbs, 15

Verbs: action, 12, 13–14, 56–57; active voice, 142–143; auxiliary, 14–15, 131, 133–134, 138, 140, 141, 143, 145, 146; conjugation, 138–139; correct use of, 131–143; defined, 11; in descriptions, 365, 366, 373; irregular, 78–79, 133–135, 502; kinds, 11–15; linking, 13–14, 18, 58–59, 60; main, 14, 15; passive voice, 142–143; principal parts, 131–135; regular, 78, 132–133, 502; tense, 137–141; in verb phrases, 14–15; voice, 142–143

Vocabulary, 492–503

Voice, of verbs, 142–143

Writer's notebook, strategies for keeping a, 239–240

ZIP code, using, 204, 454, 455, 461, 462

566

Acknowledgments (continued)

From "How Wildlife Leaves Its Mark" by Anthony Acerrano in *National Wildlife.* Copyright 1982 by the National Wildlife Federation. Reprinted from the October-November issue of *National Wildlife* by permission of the National Wildlife Federation.   From *Freedom's Trail* by Richard A. Bartlett, Clair W. Keller, and Helen H. Carey. Copyright © 1979 by Houghton Mifflin Company. Reprinted by permission.   From *The Real Book About Amazing Animals* by Alec Dickinson. Copyright © 1951. Used by permission of Franklin Watts, Inc.   From *The Wind Shifting West* by Shirley Ann Grau. Copyright © 1962. Reprinted by permission of Alfred A. Knopf, Inc.   Adapted from pp. 118–119 in *Spaceship Earth, Earth Science* by Joseph H. Jackson and Edward D. Evans. Copyright © 1976 by Houghton Mifflin Company. Used by permission.   From *Fascinating Facts* by David Louis. Copyright © 1977 by the Ridge Press and Crown Publishers, Inc. Used by permission of Crown Publishers, Inc.   Adapted from pp. 295–296 and 131–133 in *Consumer Action* by John S. Morton and Ronald R. Rezny. Copyright © 1983 by Houghton Mifflin Company. Used by permission.   From *Rascal* by Sterling North. Copyright © 1963. Reprinted by permission of E.P. Dutton, Inc. and Hodder & Stoughton, Ltd.   From *My Friend Flicka* by Mary O'Hara. (J.B. Lippincott Company) Copyright 1941, 1969 by Mary O'Hara. Reprinted by permission of Harper & Row, Publishers, Inc., Laurence Pollinger Ltd., and the Estate of the late Mary O'Hara.   Adapted from *Magnets and How to Use Them* by T.S. Pine and J. Levine. Copyright © 1963. Published by Scholastic Book Services. Used by permission of McGraw-Hill, Inc.   From *Readers' Guide to Periodical Literature.* Copyright © 1981, 1982 by The H.W. Wilson Company. Material reproduced by permission of the publisher.   From *The Red Pony* by John Steinbeck. Copyright © 1939 by John Steinbeck. Copyright renewed 1967 by John Steinbeck. Reprinted by permission of Viking Penguin Inc., McIntosh and Otis, Inc., and Curtis Brown Ltd., London.   From *On Safari* by Theodore J. Waldeck. Copyright 1940 by Theodore J. Waldeck. Copyright renewed 1968 by Jobesse McElveen Waldeck. Reprinted by permission of Viking Penguin Inc.   From "Ta-Na-E-Ka" by Mary Whitebird. Copyright © 1974 by Scholastic Inc. Reprinted by permission of Scholastic Inc.

Student sample by Kathy Beall was provided by Ms. Judy Van Kirk, Walnut Ridge High School, Columbus, Ohio.

Credits

Cover concept, book design, and art production: Ligature Publishing Services, Inc.

Photos
Carl Corey: cover, viii–1, 478–479
James L. Ballard: 236–237, 257, 273, 305, 337, 355, 377, 378, 403, 447, 473
Page 337 (left): Courtesy of the General Electric Company, Schenectady, N.Y.   Page 337 (right): Courtesy of the American Meteorological Society   Page 377: Courtesy of the U.S. Forest Service   Page 447 (left): National Portrait Gallery, Smithsonian Institution, Washington D.C.; Gift of the Swedish Colonial Society through Mrs. William Hacker   Page 447 (right): National Portrait Gallery, Smithsonian Institution, Washington, D.C.; Transfer from the Library of Congress, Prints and Photographs Division

567

Checklist for Revision

As a guide in revising your writing, consider the following questions:

✔ 1. Did you cover your topic thoroughly?

✔ 2. Did you remove any information not directly related to your topic?

✔ 3. Did you include a topic sentence or a topic statement?

✔ 4. Did you present your information in a logical order?

✔ 5. Did you use transitional words and phrases to emphasize the order of your ideas?

✔ 6. Did you write an appropriate conclusion?

✔ 7. Did you use words and details that are suitable for your audience?

✔ 8. Did you achieve your purpose for writing?

✔ 9. Did you vary the length and structure of your sentences?

✔ 10. Did you use accurate and precise words?

✔ 11. Did you use the correct forms for reports and letters?

✔ 12. Did you avoid using sentence fragments, run-on sentences, and other incorrect sentence structures?

✔ 13. Did you use correct usage, spelling, punctuation, and capitalization?

✔ 14. Did you carefully proofread your finished copy?